Environmental change and
international law

Note to the Reader from the UNU

The United Nations University's programme on Human Dimensions of Global Change recognizes that environmental changes have reached new levels of global complexity and that a need exists to cope more comprehensively with the human interactions that are helping to shape these changes. The objectives of the programme are: (1) to increase awareness of the complex dynamics governing human interaction with the Earth as a whole system; (2) to strengthen efforts to anticipate social change affecting the global environment; (3) to analyse policy options for dealing with global environmental change; and (4) to identify broad social strategies to prevent or mitigate undesirable impacts of global environmental change.

As part of this programme, the UNU's project on International Law and Global Change was undertaken to help further the development and application of international law in a changing global environment. The main objectives of the project are to assess the impact of environmental changes on international law, make proposals on how existing legal norms may be adapted to the changing conditions and what new ones are needed, as well as develop and analyse different possible scenarios and their likely impact.

This book addresses issues relating to the changing role of international law and includes topics such as the emerging principles of prevention and mitigation, the implementation of environmental law and the third world, risk assessment, international organizational restructuring, state responsibilities, and quality. Particular focus is given to the need to anticipate approaches to international law for the prevention of environmental harm and the role scientific information can play in establishing cross-national agreements.

Environmental change and international law: New challenges and dimensions

Edited by Edith Brown Weiss

United Nations
University Press

United Nations University Press
The United Nations University
53–70, Jingumae 5-chome, Shibuya-ku,
Tokyo 150, Japan
Tel.: (03) 3499-2811   Fax: (03) 3499-2828
Telex: J25442   Cable: UNATUNIV TOKYO

Typeset by Asco Trade Typesetting Limited, Hong Kong
Printed by Permanent Typesetting and Printing Co., Ltd., Hong Kong
Cover design by Apex Production, Hong Kong

HDGC-1/UNUP-818
ISBN 92-808-0818-4
United Nations Sales No. E.92.III.A.5
04000 P

This book is dedicated to the memory of
Edward Ploman

Edward Ploman, known to colleagues and
friends as Eddi, served as the Vice-Rector of
the Global Learning Division of the United
Nations University from 1982 to 1986. He was
keenly interested in global environmental issues
and in the role that international law could
play. At the time of his death, he was a member of the group contributing to this book. The
draft of his contribution to the book is contained in appendix A.

Contents

Acknowledgements

This book was undertaken as a project of the United Nations University. I am extremely grateful to the United Nations University for its generous support and for its constant dedication to facilitating the scholarship of the authors.

The authors represent a broad cross-section of scholars and practitioners from various parts of the world. All of them have extensive experience with international environmental issues. They write solely in their individual capacities as scholars.

The group held two workshops to define and analyse the issues and to discuss the contents of the various chapters. Both were held at the International Court of Justice, the Hague. I am grateful to the Hague Academy of International Law for allowing us to use these facilities and for the gracious hospitality of the Academy and its staff.

During the course of preparing this book, the authors have received numerous comments on earlier drafts of the manuscripts from each other and from outside commentators. All of us express our deep gratitude to our colleagues for this valuable input.

I am especially grateful to Anna Paiewonsky, Steven Porter, Kathleen Haviland, and Robert McDade, students at the Georgetown University Law Center, for their assistance in this project, to the administrative staff of the Law Center for their excellent support, and to Ellen Schaefer, the International Law Librarian, for her untiring efforts to locate difficult references.

Finally, I must express appreciation to Roland Fuchs and Dieter Koenig of the United Nations University for making this project possible.

List of abbreviations

A.F.D.I.   Annuaire française de droit international
A.J.I.L.   American Journal of International Law
Am. U.L. Rev.   American University Law Review
Ann. de l'Inst. de droit int'l   Annuaire de l'Institut de droit international

C.F.R.   Code of Federal Regulations (United States)
Ch. Envt'l Mgmt.   Chinese Environmental Management
Ch. Leg. Sys. Nwspr.   China Legal System Newspaper
Ch. Y.B. Int'l L.   Chinese Yearbook of International Law

Den. J. Int'l L. & Pol'y   Denver Journal of International Law and Policy

Ecol. L.Q.   Ecology Law Quarterly
Env't J.   The Environment Journal
Env't Rep.   Environment Reporter (BNA)
Envt'l L.   Environmental Law
Envt'l L. & Pol'y J.   Environmental Law and Policy Journal
Envt'l Pol'y & L.   Environmental Policy and Law
Euro. J. Int'l L.   European Journal of International Law

F.2d.   Federal Reporter Second Edition (United States)

G.A. Res.   United Nations General Assembly Resolution

Gaz. St. Cnc'l Peo. Rep. Ch.   Gazette of the State Council of the People's Republic of China

Geo. Int'l Envt'l L. Rev.   Georgetown International Environmental Law Review

Harv. H.R.Y.B.   Harvard Human Rights Yearbook

Harv. Int'l L.J.   Harvard International Law Journal

Harv. L. Rev.   Harvard Law Review

Hou. J. Int'l L.   Houston Journal of International Law

H.R.L.J.   Human Rights Law Journal

H.R.Q.   Human Rights Quarterly

I.C.J.   International Court of Justice Reports

I.L.M.   International Legal Materials

I.L.R.   International Law Reports

Ind. J. Int'l L.   Indian Journal of International Law

Int'l & Compar. L.Q.   International and Comparative Law Quarterly

Int'l Env't Rep.   International Environment Reporter

Int'l Hrld. Trib.   International Herald Tribune

Int'l J.   International Journal

Int'l J. Refugee L.   International Journal of Refugee Law

Int'l L. & Politics   International Law and Politics

Int'l Prot. Env't   International Protection of the Environment

Int'l Soc. Sci. J.   International Social Science Journal

Mich. J. Int'l L.   Michigan Journal of International Law

Neth. Int'l L. Rev.   Netherlands International Law Review

N.Y. Times   New York Times

N.Y.U.J. Int'l L. & Pol'y   New York University Journal of International Law and Policy

O.J. Eur. Comm.   Official Journal of the European Communities

Österch. Ztshrft. für öffntlchs. Recht und Vlkrcht.   Österreichische Zeitschrift für öffentliches Recht und Völkerrecht

Pace Envt'l L. Rev.   Pace Environmental Law Review

Phil. & Pub. Aff.   Philosophy and Public Affairs

Prologue: J. Am. Archvs.　　Prologue: The Journal of the American Archives

R. Int'l Arb. Awards　　United Nations Reports of International Arbitral Awards

R.R.　　Renmin Ribao (People's Daily, China)

R. 3rd For. Rel. L. U.S.　　Restatement Third of the Foreign Relations Law of the United States

Rec. des cours de l'Ac. de droit int'l　　Recueil des cours de l'Academie de droit international

Rev. des droits de l'hom.　　Revue des droits de l'homme

Rev. Gen. de Droit Int. Public　　Revue Generale de Droit International Public

Rivsta. Giur. dell'Amb.　　Rivista Giuridica dell'Ambiente

Rutgers L. Rev.　　Rutgers Law Review

S.D.L. Rev.　　South Dakota Law Review

So. Afr. J. Hum. Rts.　　South African Journal of Human Rights

Soc. Theory & Prac.　　Social Theory and Practice

Stat.　　United States Statutes at Large

Tex. Int'l L. J.　　Texas International Law Journal

T.I.A.S.　　United States Treaties and Other International Acts Series

Tn. L. Rev.　　Tennessee Law Review

T.S.　　Treaty Series

U.N. GAOR　　United Nations General Assembly Official Record

U.N.Y.B.　　United Nations Year Book

U.S.C.　　United States Code

U.S.T.　　United States Treaties

U.S.T.S.　　United States Treaty Series

Va. J. Int'l L.　　Virginia Journal of International Law

Verfsg. und Rcht. in Übersee　　Verfassung und Recht in Übersee

X. Gen. Oseas. Nws. Svc.　　Xiahua General Overseas News Service

Y.B. Int'l L. Comm'n　　Yearbook of the International Law Commission

Introduction

1

Global environmental change and international law: The introductory framework

Edith Brown Weiss

International law has been based on the relationship between independent states that exercise exclusive national sovereignty over their territories. Global change is altering this vision by causing states to realize that they are locked together in sharing the use of a common global environment. While human activities have always contributed to environmental change, it is only within the last half of this century that their effects have become global and serious, and in many cases irreversible. This has led to a growing awareness that the interests of humankind must constrain the interests of individual states. Moreover, actors other than states have become essential to managing global environmental change. These developments are leading to a fundamental shift in the paradigm of international law that is evolving in the international environmental field. This book examines some of the ways in which international environmental law is responding to global environmental change and suggests new directions for the field.

I. Trends in global environmental change

Concern among primarily industrialized countries about the serious risk of environmental harm to countries around the world motivated

The author thanks Steven Porter for his assistance, particularly with the chapter summaries.

3

states to convene the 1972 Conference on the Human Environment, the first world conference on the environment.

By 1970 the world population had more than doubled since the beginning of the century (from 1.6 to 3.4 billion), industrial processes were generating unprecedented amounts of pollutants, and in some countries popular concern for the environment had sky-rocketed.[1] The United States, for example, had passed its first piece of national environmental legislation, the National Environmental Policy Act of 1969.

At the time of the Stockholm Conference countries were deeply divided over the issue of whether environmental protection and economic development were compatible. The conceptual breakthrough that provided the paradigm for joining these two important goals emerged from a meeting of experts held in Founex, Switzerland, just prior to the Stockholm Conference. Today countries recognize that sound economic development must be environmentally sustainable and are concerned about how to do this. They realize that we need to substantially increase the living standards of the poor in a manner that is environmentally sustainable. The issue in 1992 that divides countries is an equity one: how to finance environmentally sustainable economic development for present and future generations.

Today, 20 years after the Stockholm Conference, countries are concerned with global environmental problems that were either not yet identified or barely addressed. These include acid precipitation, ozone depletion, climate change, hazardous waste disposal, loss of biological diversity, and forest degradation and loss and land-based sources of marine pollution.

The trends in population, resource consumption, and environmental degradation that caused such concern in the early 1970s have continued, or accelerated, while our capacity to address them has increased at a slower rate, albeit arguably more rapidly than for some other problems.

Population growth, resource consumption, and technological development continue to be primary catalysts for global environmental change. By 1990, world population had reached 5.3 billion, more than triple that in 1900 and almost 2 billion more than in 1970. Current estimates are that world population will reach at least 8.5 billion by

1. In 1960 there were roughly 150 articles in the *New York Times* on environmental topics, whereas there were over 1,650 such articles in 1970. Significantly, the number dropped by the end of the decade to about 600 articles. United Nations Environment Programme, *The World Environment 1972–1982*, 581 (Tycooly International, 1982).

the year 2025.[2] The bulk of population growth is projected to be in the developing world.[3]

The link between population growth and environmental degradation is complex and not well understood, as reflected in the several competing schools of thought on the issues. However, a larger population generally translates into greater demands on the Earth's resources. As has been demonstrated, population size that exceeds local carrying capacity of the ecosystems can cause soil depletion, deforestation, and desertification. If we multiply projected population increases by the substantially higher standard of living that equity requires for impoverished communities today and for future populations, the potential demands on the environment in the decades ahead are dramatic.

Since 1968, the world's consumption of energy has grown. Overall, the total energy requirements of industrialized countries have increased almost 30 per cent from 1970 to 1988, although this masks two periods of decline after the oil-price shocks.[4] The rate of increase in energy consumption in the developing countries has declined, but remains high. Most of the world's energy continues to come from burning fossil fuels, whose general by-products are a primary contributor to global warming. Annual emissions of carbon dioxide from fossil fuels more than doubled from 1960 to 1988.[5]

In addition, the release of ozone-depleting chloro-fluorocarbons (e.g. CFC-11 and CFC-12), which were virtually non-existent prior to World War II, has risen from 35 million kilograms in 1950, to 506 million kilograms in 1970, and to 707 million kilograms by 1988.[6] Fortunately, countries have now agreed to phase out their production and consumption by the year 2000, and likely sooner. Human-caused emissions of trace metals have followed a similar growth pattern.

Agriculture demands and practices have also raised important environmental concerns. Irrigated crop land, which accounts for about

---

2. World Resources Institute in collaboration with the United Nations Environment Programme and the United Nations Development Programme, *World Resources 1990–91*, 50 (Oxford University Press, 1990).
3. The percentage of world population living in the less-developed regions was 67 per cent in 1950, grew to 76 per cent in 1987, and is forecast to reach 84 per cent by 2025. *World Resources 1990–91, supra* note 2 at 50.
4. OECD, *The State of the Environment*, 222–223 (OECD, 1991).
5. They increased from 2.6 billion metric tons in 1960, to 4.1 billion in 1970, and to 5.9 billion in 1988. *Environmental Quality 1991*, 317 (Executive Office of the President, CEQ, 1991).
6. *World Resources 1990–91, supra* note 2 at 319.

5

17 per cent of the world's crop land and one-third of the global harvest,[7] is being eroded by waterlogging and made less productive by salinization (the cumulative build-up of salts left by evaporation of irrigation water). Deforestation, loss of biological diversity, and soil erosion have significantly increased.[8]

Fresh water continues to be a critical resource. In addition to the well-documented water-quality problems of surface waters, new concern has emerged over groundwater resources. Contamination results from the disposal of wastes, both hazardous and non-hazardous, and from the seepage of chemicals such as pesticides and fertilizers into the aquifers. Pesticides, whose use has doubled in the US since 1961, have created groundwater contamination problems in 40 of the 50 US states.[9] Pesticides are used worldwide, with an over-$18-billion market in 1987, and their use is frequently unregulated or not well monitored. The agricultural use of chemicals has also grown dramatically, leading to increased run-off and contamination of lakes, streams, and groundwater.[10] While the open oceans remain relatively undisturbed by humankind's activities, the oceans' coastal zones, the most biologically productive areas, are under severe pressure from population growth and development activities. In addition, there is evidence that we may be reaching the limits of the seas' natural productive capacity. The average annual catch of marine fisheries (79 million metric tons for 1987) are at or near estimates of their sustainable yield (between 62 and 96 million metric tons per year).[11]

In the past, pollution and environmental degradation have operated largely on the local level and hence their effects have been isolated in impact. Given the increasingly global scale of environmental degradation and the ever-increasing volume of pollutants entering the environment, however, their effects are now being felt on regional and global levels. In addition, the scope and irreversible nature of

7. Worldwatch Institute, *State of the World 1990*, 40 (Norton, 1990).
8. While problems of deforestation and loss of biological diversity have been well publicized, the loss of soil is less well known. Estimates of soil-erosion rates in the Amazon Basin, for example, show an increase from 6–10 tons per hectare annually in 1960 to as high as 190 tons per hectare in 1985, while estimates for southern India show a corresponding increase from 10–20 to 40–100 tons per hectare. R. Lal, "Soil Degradation and Conversion of Tropical Rainforests," in *Changing the Global Environment: Perspectives on Human Involvement*, 45 (Academic Press, 1989).
9. *OECD Environmental Data, Compendium 1987*, 135 (Organization for Economic Cooperation and Development, 1987).
10. The use of nitrogen fertilizers has more than doubled, from 32 million tons in 1970 to 71 million tons in 1986, *OECD Environmental Data, Compendium 1987, supra* note 9 at 279.
11. *The World Environment 1972–1982, supra* note 1 at 340.

some global changes reach through time to affect the well-being of future generations.

II. The development of international environmental law

Modern international environmental law dates to approximately 1972, when countries gathered for the United Nations Stockholm Conference on the Human Environment and the United Nations Environment Programme was established. Many important legal developments took place in the period surrounding the Conference, including negotiation of the World Heritage Convention, the Convention on International Trade in Endangered Species, the London Ocean Dumping Convention, and, shortly after the Conference, the UNEP regional seas conventions. Since then, there has been a rapid rise in international legal instruments concerned with the environment, to the point where we are concerned today with developing new means for coordinating the negotiation and implementation of related agreements, in particular their administrative, monitoring, and financial provisions.

At the turn of the century there were relatively few multilateral or bilateral international environmental agreements. International environmental law was based on the principles of unfettered national sovereignty over natural resources and absolute freedom of the seas beyond the three-mile territorial limit. Such international agreements as existed largely addressed issues concerning boundary waters, navigation, and fishing rights along shared waterways, particularly the Rhine River and other European waters. It is worth noting, however, that Article IV of the 1909 United States–United Kingdom Boundary Waters Treaty stated that water "shall not be polluted on either side to the injury of health or property on the other."[12]

Early in the century, a few agreements were concluded to protect commercially valuable species, such as the 1902 Convention for the Protection of Birds Useful to Agriculture and the Treaty for the Preservation and Protection of Fur Seals signed in 1911.[13]

The classic adjudication during the first part of the century was the Trail Smelter Arbitration between Canada and the United States, which affirmed Canada's responsibility for the damage from copper

12. Treaty Between the United States and Great Britain Relating to Boundary Waters Between the United States and Canada, 11 Jan. 1909, 36 Stat. 2448, T.S. No. 548.
13. For complete references for these agreements and the others cited in this chapter, *see* appendix B.

smelter fumes that transgressed the border into the state of Washington.[14] The language of the Arbitral Tribunal has been widely cited as confirming the principle that a state is responsible for environmental damage to foreign countries that is caused by activities within its borders.[15] The fact that the Arbitration is a rare example of international environmental adjudication in this early period has given it an unusually important place in the legal literature.

By the 1930s and 1940s, conservation and preservation had emerged as conceptual approaches to natural-resource management, which led to agreements to protect fauna and flora. These agreements included the 1933 London Convention on Preservation of Fauna and Flora in Their Natural State (focused primarily on Africa) and the 1940 Washington Convention on Nature Protection and Wild Life Preservation (focused on the Western Hemisphere). Conventions relating to whaling practices, other ocean fisheries, and birds were also negotiated during this time.

During the 1950s and early 1960s, new environmental concerns emerged. Agreements governing international liability for nuclear damage were negotiated, as was the 1954 International Convention for the Prevention of Pollution of the Sea by Oil.

In the late 1960s, there was a significant increase in the number of multilateral international environmental agreements. Several conventions were negotiated relating to interventions in case of oil-pollution casualties, to civil liability for oil-pollution damage, and to controlling oil pollution in the North Sea. The African Convention on the Conservation of Nature and Natural Resources was concluded in 1968.

Since 1970, hundreds of international environmental instruments

---

14. Trail Smelter Arbitration (United States v. Canada), 3 R. Int'l Arb. Awards 1911 (1938), reprinted in 33 A.J.I.L. 182 (1939), 3 R. Int'l Arb. Awards 1938 (1941), reprinted in 35 A.J.I.L. 684 (1941). The Trail Smelter dispute lasted for a number of years. Damage within the United States was reported as early as 1925. In 1928 the two countries established a joint commission to examine the dispute. A report was issued, and damages were awarded to the US in 1931. Convention for Settlement of Difficulties Arising from Operation of Smelter at Trail, B.C., 15 April 1935, U.S.T.S. No. 893, reprinted in 30 A.J.I.L. (Supp.) 163. Continued pollution and disagreements led to the creation of a mixed arbital tribunal that issued opinions in 1938 and 1941, *supra. See* generally, A.K. Kuhn, Comment, "The Trail Smelter Arbitration – United States and Canada," 32 A.J.I.L. 785 (1938).
15. "Under the principles of international law, as well as the law of the United States, no State has the right to use or permit the use of its territory in such a manner as to cause injury by fumes in or to the territory of another or the properties of persons therein, when the case is of serious consequence and the injury is established by clear and convincing evidence." Trail Smelter Arbitration, 3 R. Int'l Arb. Awards. at 1965, 35 A.J.I.L. at 716.

have been concluded. If we include bilateral and multilateral instruments (binding and non-binding), there are more than 870 international legal instruments that have one or more provisions addressing environment. The relevant players on the international environmental law stage now include not only states but corporations, intergovernmental and non-governmental organizations, and individuals.

The subject-matter of international environmental agreements has expanded significantly from the focus in the first half of this century on facilitating navigation, guaranteeing fishing rights, and protecting particularly valued animal species; today there are agreements to control pollution in all media, conserve habitats, and protect global commons, such as the high-level ozone layer.

Ever since 1972, the scope of international agreements has expanded significantly: from transboundary pollution agreements to global pollution agreements; from preservation of designated species to conservation of ecosystems; from control of direct emissions into lakes to comprehensive river-basin-system regimes; from agreements that take effect only at national borders to ones that constrain activities and resource use within national borders, such as those for world heritages and wetlands. The duties have also become more comprehensive: from a focus on research and monitoring to provisions for reductions in pollutants. Most notably, there is not a single example in which the provisions of earlier conventions have been weakened; in all cases, they have been strengthened or their scope has been expanded.

There is a growing realization in the international community that the time has come not only to monitor and research environmental risks but also to reduce them. Thus we have moved from international agreements that deal largely with research, information exchange, and monitoring to agreements that require reductions in pollutant emissions and changes in control technology. The Protocol on Sulphur Dioxide to the UN ECE Convention on Long-Range Transboundary Air Pollution calls for a 30 per cent reduction in national annual sulphur emissions or their transboundary fluxes by 1993,[16] and the Montreal Protocol on Substances That Deplete the Ozone Layer, including the 1990 Adjustments and Amendments, requires that chloro-fluorocarbons and halons be phased out (except for a few

---

16. Helsinki Protocol to the 1979 Convention on Long-Range Transboundary Air Pollution on the Reduction of Sulphur Emissions or Their Transboundary Fluxes by at Least 30 Per Cent, Art. 2, 8 July 1985, UN Doc. EB.AIR/12, 27 *I.L.M.* 707 (1988).

essential uses) by the year 2000.[17] This focus on pollution prevention is likely to continue as we come to appreciate the limited capacity of our environment to absorb the by-products of our society.

The increase in international agreements concluded in just the last six years, from 1985 to 1992, illustrates the increasingly rapid rate at which international environmental law is being formed. During this period, countries have negotiated a surprisingly large number of global agreements. These include the Vienna Convention on the Protection of the Ozone Layer, which provides a framework for protecting the ozone layer but primarily calls for research, monitoring, and exchange of information; the Montreal Protocol on Substances That Deplete the Ozone Layer with the London Adjustments and Amendments; the Protocol on Environmental Protection (with annexes) to the Antarctic Treaty; the Basel Convention on the Transboundary Movements of Hazardous Wastes and Their Disposal; the London Guidelines for the Exchange of Information on Chemicals in International Trade; the two International Atomic Energy Agency conventions on Early Notification of a Nuclear Accident and on Assistance in the Case of a Nuclear Accident or Radiological Emergency; and the International Convention on Oil Pollution Preparedness, Response and Co-operation.

Negotiations for regional environmental agreements have proceeded at a similarly rapid rate. Under the auspices of the United Nations Economic Commission for Europe (ECE), countries have concluded three protocols to the UN ECE Convention on Long-Range Transboundary Air Pollution: a protocol providing for 30 per cent reductions in transborder fluxes of sulphur dioxides, a protocol freezing the emissions of nitrogen oxides, and a protocol controlling emissions of volatile organic chemicals. They have also concluded agreements on environmental-impact assessment and transboundary industrial accidents and transboundary watercourses and international lakes.

In the regional seas programme, countries have concluded the South Pacific Resource and Environmental Protection Agreement with two protocols, one on dumping and the other on emergency assistance. Under the Caribbean Regional Seas Convention, coun-

17. Montreal Protocol on Substances That Deplete the Ozone Layer, 16 Sept. 1987, Art. 2, 26 *I.L.M.* 1550 (1987); London Adjustments and Amendments to the Montreal Protocol, and Non-Compliance Procedure, 29 June 1990, Adjustments A and B, UNEP/OzL.Pro.2/3.

tries have negotiated a new protocol on protected areas, and are considering negotiation of a protocol on land-based sources of marine pollution.

For freshwater resources, countries have concluded an innovative, comprehensive agreement for the Zambezi River Basin. Canada and the United States agreed to a protocol to their 1978 Great Lakes Water Quality Agreement that addresses groundwater contamination affecting the Great Lakes and the airborne transport of toxics into the Great Lakes. Amazon Basin countries have issued the Declaration of Brasilia and provided under the auspices of the Amazon Pact for the establishment of two new commissions, one to conserve the fauna and flora and the other to protect indigenous peoples. In Asia, members of ASEAN have concluded the Convention on the Conservation of Nature, which provides ecosystem protection and controls on trade in endangered species.[18]

Within the European Community, there have been many important developments, including notably the Single European Act, which provides clear authority for the Community to act on environmental and natural-resources issues. The Community has already issued many directives and regulations designed to control pollution and protect the environment. A new European Environment Agency and European Environment Information and Observation Network are being established.

Bilateral agreements have also proliferated during this period. There are important examples within North America. The United States has signed bilateral agreements on the transport of hazardous wastes with Canada and Mexico. A recent air-pollution agreement between the United States and Mexico addresses urban air pollution problems in Mexico City. In Latin America, Brazil and Argentina concluded an agreement (contemporaneous with the two IAEA agreements) that provides for consultation in case of nuclear accidents in either country.

Many of these agreements were thought to be impossible 10 years ago; some were thought impossible as briefly as 2 years before they were concluded. The provisions in the new agreements are generally more stringent than in the previous ones; the range of subject matter is broader; and the provisions for implementation and review are more sophisticated. One encouraging observation from this experi-

18. The Agreement is not yet in effect.

ence is that the learning curve demonstrated in international environmental law is unexpectedly steep. This should give us hope that the
international community may be able, with at least some success, to
confront the immense challenges posed by global environmental
change.

Given the astonishing developments of the past 20 years, what
then awaits us in the future?

In the next decade more international agreements and other legal
instruments will be concluded. The rate of negotiating these instruments shows no sign of abating. Countries have just reached
agreement on a framework convention on climate change, forest
principles, and an agreement on biological diversity. As this book
goes to press, negotiations continue on several agreements: an agreement on the marine transport of hazardous and noxious substances,
and a liability protocol to the Basel Convention on Transboundary
Movements of Hazardous Wastes.

At the same time, however, a countervailing theme is emerging –
one that says it is time to slow the rate of negotiating international
agreements. Some countries, especially the developing ones, are becoming overtaxed by the resources needed to engage in negotiations
and to implement effectively the agreements already concluded. This
may mean that a "go slow" light will appear and caution against continuing the rapid pace of concluding new international agreements. In
turn this may presage greater reliance on international legal instruments that are not formal conventions, or what some jurists call "soft
law."

The new international conventions are likely to continue to be
ever more demanding in terms of the actions they ask of countries.
Frequently this may take the form of a framework convention, followed by protocols that provide for detailed obligations. This is the
form of the recent Antarctic Environment Protocol (with four
annexes), the Vienna Ozone Layer Convention (with the Montreal
Protocol), and the regional-seas conventions.

Further, there is likely to be increased emphasis on monitoring
compliance with the conventions and on providing means to facilitate
implementation and compliance. The role of non-governmental organizations in the negotiation and implementation of agreements has
grown and will likely continue to grow.

Finally, we will likely see new attention to the trade implications
of the agreements that are negotiated and to addressing issues of con-
sistency between environmental and trade regimes.

III. Themes

This book addresses new directions in international environmental law and, to a lesser extent, in international institutions. To accomplish this, the authors look at the challenges posed by issues of global environmental change and sustainable development and at historical experience.

Six themes, which emerged in good part from the discussions of the group, appear throughout the book. These include the growing common interest in the environment, the recognition of the scientific uncertainty about the environment, the adoption of an anticipatory approach, the relevance of human rights, the relationship between economic development and environmental protection, and the new approaches in implementing international environmental agreements.

The common interest in the global environment

Traditional international law is based on the territorial sovereignty of states, whose legal status is characterized by the three principles of sovereignty, independence, and equality.

Within states there has been an expanding recognition of a common interest among people in elaborating general environmental principles and rules that are not based on principles of appropriation – such as rules governing hunting, fishing, the use of national parks, and the disposal of wastes.

Similarly, at the international level, there has been a growing body of norms that restrict the actions of states in furtherance of general international community interests. Alexandre Kiss comments on this theme as follows:

Thus, as the concept of appropriation – territorial sovereignty – fades out, states are more and more considered – and even consider themselves – as obliged to act inside the limits of their jurisdiction on behalf of the interests of mankind. The developments during the last 40 years in the two main fields where basic needs of the planet and of its inhabitants must be met, human rights and environmental protection, very clearly show this general trend. As early as 1968, this conception appears as far as environment is concerned, in particular in the African Convention on the Conservation of Nature and Natural Resources, according to which where an animal or plant species threatened with extinction is represented only in the territory of one State, that State has a particular responsibility for its protection (art. 8).

Such a fundamental change in our conceptions of international law can be

13

compared to the Copernican revolution which proclaimed that the center of the universe was not the earth but the sun: States are less and less the center of international legal relations, the focus becoming more and more mankind and its individual representatives, human persons. The growing number of international conventions which do not provide for reciprocity in the obligations accepted by States is very significant in this regard. It is clear that international treaty rules aiming at environmental conservation are among the best examples of such provisions corresponding to general interest.

The recognition of a common interest of States in the global environment may lead to international rules which are considered *erga omnes*, applicable to all states and enforceable by all States. The International Court of Justice, in the well-known *Barcelona Traction* case, set forth this distinctive category: "(A)n essential distinction should be drawn between the obligations of a State towards the international community as a whole, and those arising vis-a-vis another State in the field of diplomatic protection. By their very nature the former are the concern of all States. In view of the importance of the rights involved, all States can be held to have a legal interest in their protection; they are obligations *erga omnes*.[19]

In international environmental law, we are redefining the concept of national interest. National interest has traditionally meant the identification of interests of one country that are distinct from or even contrary to those of another. But increasingly we recognize that the global environment has interests that are common to all countries. In the case of ozone depletion, for instance, at the most basic level the US interest is not contrary to that of England or Germany – rather there is a common interest in controlling ozone depletion. The same can be said for controlling marine pollution, the transport of hazardous waste, or the concentrations of greenhouse gases. The traditional definition of national interest, based on the underlying assumption that one state's national interest conflicted with that of other states, is increasingly irrelevant. Environmental protection is not a zero-sum game.

This is not to say that we no longer have conflicting interests on these issues within or between countries. The allocation of financial resources to control pollution or conserve natural resources or the designation of suitable places to dispose of nuclear wastes remain contentious issues. Moreover, transboundary interest groups often conflict with each other and with governments on these issues. However, there is an emerging common interest among countries that it is in their national interest to address issues of global and re-

19. A. Kiss, Commentary provided to editor (mimeo, 1990).

gional environmental change. That is reflected in the rapid developments in international environmental law.

The authors analyse in their chapters many of the elements that point to the emergence of the common interest in conserving the global environment. Kiss, in his analysis of systemic changes in international law, develops the point in depth.

Scientific uncertainty

Scientific uncertainty is as inherent in international environmental issues as it is in domestic ones. The environmental system, including the human component, is complex and incompletely understood. We are a part of that system: our actions affect the system and we are in turn affected by it. We do not have a full understanding either of the system or of our interactions with it. Since scientific uncertainty characterizes all environmental issues, a major challenge of international environmental policy-making is to identify, assess, and manage risks. This calls for early-warning systems and a system for prioritizing risks, since resources to address risks are always limited. Thacher discusses issues of risk assessment and risk management, as does Brown Weiss in the intergenerational context. The theme appears, often implicitly, in almost all of the chapters.

Diplomats must rely on scientists to identify and help assess risks and to relate policy options to effective risk management. The international community is increasingly relying on international assessments by government-appointed experts as a basis for action. On the one hand, this gives governments confidence in the outcomes, which is essential; on the other it may invite what has been termed "negotiated science," a matter about which some of the international scientific community have been particularly critical. In the negotiations for a climate-change convention, for example, the report of the Intergovernmental Panel on Climate Change (IPCC), which consists of government-appointed experts, was instrumental to the opening of the agreement negotiations. Yet the conclusions of the panel have been criticized by some non-governmental scientists as representing compromises rather than pure scientific findings.

Governments receive scientific input from sources other than appointed experts. Traditionally we have emphasized the direct link between the scientist and the governmental policy maker, with communication flowing in both directions, but primarily upward to the policy maker. In environmental matters the relationship is actually

15

triangular, with the public serving as the third vertex. Scientists communicate their findings to the public, and the public in turn influences policy makers, particularly elected representatives, on the basis of their scientific understanding and broader perceptions. Conversely, governments affect the public understanding of science, which in turn affects the public's relationship with the scientists.

While policy makers often resist acting under conditions of scientific uncertainty, the reality is that there will always be some uncertainty. It is a policy decision to decide what degree of scientific certainty is required before taking certain kinds of actions. The effort to formulate a precautionary principle, or precautionary approach, reflects the desire to develop international guidance on when and how to restrain activities that risk harming the environment in the future. This issue is specifically addressed in the chapter by Iwama.

Those who draft international legal instruments also have to be concerned increasingly with designing the instruments and implementation mechanisms with sufficient flexibility so that parties can adapt to changes in scientific understanding.

In negotiations for the Montreal Protocol on Substances That Deplete the Ozone Layer, policy makers knew that there would be subsequent advances in our scientific understanding of the ozone-depletion problem, and hence drafted the text of the Montreal Protocol accordingly. Thus, parties meet on a regular basis, so that they can respond to new scientific findings. The agreement also provides for regular technical assessments that are made available to parties before a meeting. The procedures in the Montreal Protocol for agreeing to reduce further the consumption of chemicals already on the list of controlled substances are easier than the procedures for adding new chemicals to the control list, and they do not require that parties formally amend the agreement.[20]

Other devices in international agreements to enable parties to respond to changing scientific knowledge include appendices or lists attached to the agreement that can be easily updated, scientific advisory councils or panels to monitor, assess, and/or report on environmental problems, and regular meetings of the parties.

Szasz focuses on the need for flexibility in his first chapter and identifies the various means used in treaties and the international legislative process to provide the flexibility in meeting obligations to

---

20. *See* R. Benedick, *Ozone Diplomacy* (Harvard Press, 1991) for a detailed analysis of the role of science in the Montreal Protocol negotiations.

adapt to changes in scientific knowledge. Thacher discusses this need in the context of designing information systems, and Kiss explores its implications for the international legal system.

Systems as the focus

The third characteristic of international environmental law is an increasing focus on ecological systems rather than only on measures to control trade in species or emissions of specific pollutants. This reflects the growing awareness that ecological problems are problems of whole systems. For example, the ASEAN Convention on the Conservation of Resources addresses the conservation of ecosystems and habitats. The 1978 Great Lakes Water Quality Agreement contained language not found in the 1972 agreement to include reference to basin-wide ecosystems in the Great Lakes. This change reflects the recognition that what feeds into lakes through groundwater or by air deposition is as relevant to protecting the Great Lakes as what feeds directly into the fresh water. The 1987 Protocol explicitly includes annexes that address groundwater pollution and atmospheric transport of pollutants as sources of contamination of the Great Lakes. Similarly, in marine pollution, the focus is no longer only on specific commodities that are dumped into the marine environment, but rather on maintaining the marine ecosystem. This means a new emphasis on the importance of controlling land-based sources of marine pollution and on understanding all the sources of contamination of a marine environment.

The preventive approach

The fourth important theme states that it is much more effective to prevent pollution than to remedy its effects or to assign liability for damage. Economically it is usually much less costly to prevent the damage than to clean it up. Within the United States, the "Super Fund" legislation designed to clean up hazardous waste sites exemplifies the staggering costs of remedial measures. Unless the focus is on pollution prevention, it could happen that many of the costs of pollution will be shifted to other states or to future generations because they have no ability to bring the polluting state to account for its actions. Many of the damages are long-term. They may involve important synergisms in the environment or be effectively irreversible.

17

As a consequence, if international agreements are to be effective in protecting the environment, they must focus foremost on pollution prevention and on the sustainable use of renewable resources. There are a number of ways international environmental legal instruments are beginning to accomplish this. Many instruments are adopting an anticipatory approach. Early-warning systems, risk assessment, and stronger monitoring provisions are being developed. Principles are emerging that would strengthen procedural requirements such as notification, consultation, access to information or environmental impact assessment that would have to be fulfilled before states could engage in activities that could significantly harm the environment outside their jurisdiction.

Another approach often mentioned as a way to discourage international environmental damage is the "polluter pays" principle. It derives from the OECD principle formulated to capture the concept that goods and services should reflect the full costs of production, including pollution externalities. However, it was not intended as a principle of international legal liability, and indeed the attempt to transform it into a principle of international liability has been questioned.

It is difficult to find instances where one country has succeeded in holding another liable for pollution damage. Moreover, in some instances of transfrontier pollution, the state suffering from the pollution may pay the polluting state to abate or control it, because it is less expensive to cover the cost of installing pollution-control equipment than to continue to suffer the damage. For example, the Netherlands and other countries bordering the Rhine agreed to pay part of the cost of controlling the pollution from French potash mines. Similarly, Germany reportedly offered to bear the cost of installing air filters in a Czech industrial plant near the border, rather than continue to suffer pollution damage.

There is ample evidence to suggest that in most instances it is more effective to prevent pollution and natural-resource degradation, such as eroded watersheds, than to compensate for damages caused. Often the damages are irreversible, or if reversible only at unacceptable costs. Moreover, there is frequently no way to calculate damages accurately, particularly in regard to the natural environment, to provide adequate compensation, nor to apportion liability if many sources contribute. From both an equitable and cost-effective approach, the emphasis should be on pollution prevention. This theme runs through many of the chapters. Iwama focuses on the procedures for pollution prevention, and Orrego Vicuña notes the difficulties with implementing liability for environmental damage. Brown Weiss raises the intergenerational dimensions, and Timoshenko uses the theme as the premise for his arguments on ecological security. Prevention is also noted in most of the other chapters.

Human rights

There is a growing link between human rights and global environmental change. First, many of the human rights conventions and principles are relevant to issues of environmental change. Rights of participation, access to information, freedom of speech, among others, are important for the effective management of global environmental change. Secondly, problems created by global environmental change raise new issues for those rights already articulated, such as by the creation of environmental refugees and by the potential loss of a way of life by indigenous peoples of the Amazon or of the Arctic. Thirdly, there has been considerable discussion of a right to environment, either as implicitly found in existing human rights instruments or as part of a new articulation of rights. Finally, there is discussion of the rights of future generations in the global environment. While intergenerational rights are not linked explicitly to human rights law, they can be viewed as an extension of it and may carry important implications for the so-called group rights. The chapters by Thacher, Pathak, Cançado Trindade, Kiss, and Brown Weiss address various of these issues in detail.

Economic development and environmental protection

Sustainable economic development requires development that is environmentally sound. It is inherently an intergenerational issue. The World Commission on Environment and Development defined sustainable development as "meet[ing] the needs of the present without compromising the ability of future generations to meet their own needs."[21]

It is well known that poverty is a primary form of ecological degradation. Thus, meeting the basic needs of peoples is essential to environmental conservation. We are only beginning to chart the pathways for globally sustainable development by all countries. An essen-

21. WCED, *Our Common Future* (Oxford, 1987) at 8.

tial part of this process will be the reconciliation and integration of environmental protection with economic growth, including environmental measures and trading practices.

Several of the chapters, particularly those by Lai and Thacher, address the link between environmental protection and economic development. Lai stresses the conflicts between development goals and environmental protection, and notes that poverty is a primary force for environmental degradation. Thacher points to pathways of achieving environmentally sustainable development. The link between economic development and environmental protection is referenced in most of the other chapters as well, including the chapters on intergenerational equity and ecological security.

Implementation

If we look into the future, we can anticipate increased emphasis on the implementation of and compliance with international environmental instruments. Several new directions deserve highlighting: the information revolution and the transparency of information; public participation in developing and implementing international environmental instruments; the emergence of economic incentives and market mechanisms as a tool of implementation; and the treatment of third parties within the agreements.

We are now in the midst of an information revolution that will have fundamental implications for international environmental law and institutions. We can now gather and disseminate information at speeds and in quantities that far surpass the capabilities of 20 years ago. This makes possible monitoring on such a vast scale and in such detail that the implications are only now beginning to be recognized. The corollary to the information explosion is the growing transparency of environmental information; information is increasingly available to governments, non-governmental organizations, and the public. This means an unprecedented empowerment of non-governmental organizations and individuals with respect to the decision-making processes and the implementation of international legal instruments. Thacher in particular develops these themes, and Cançado Trindade addresses them in the context of human rights and the environment.

The more recent international environmental instruments have recognized the importance of including all the relevant parties in the agreement. Otherwise, the agreements could create environmental

20

degradation havens or, alternatively, "free-rider" problems. The latter problems result because remedial or preventive environmental actions taken by some countries (often at great expense) automatically benefit other countries, which bear no share of the costs. Thus, the question in addressing both pollution havens and free-rider problems is how to include all relevant actors in the agreement. One method is to offer economic incentives, such as technical assistance and financial support, and differentiated implementation schemes for developing countries. In the Montreal Protocol, for example, parties created a fund to provide assistance to the developing countries that join, and established a 10-year delay in compliance for developing countries that fall below a certain level of chloro-fluorocarbon consumption.

The other way of encouraging participation is to ban trade with non-parties to the agreement. The concept was incorporated into the Convention on International Trade in Endangered Species, but has seldom been used since then. It has been incorporated, however, into two recent agreements: the Montreal Protocol on Substances That Deplete the Ozone Layer and the Basel Convention on the Transboundary Movements of Hazardous Wastes. Both the Environmental Working Group of the General Agreement on Tariffs and Trade and the OECD Trade and Environment Working Groups are now considering whether such provisions are consistent with the GATT, which prohibits restrictions on trade except under certain conditions.

Finally, market mechanisms offer a way to increase the efficiency of implementing international environmental agreements, and they have been gaining new attention. In Europe, this has taken the form of proposed taxes on specific resources (such as energy) or particular "pollutants" (such as carbon dioxide). In the United States, it has taken the form of a trading scheme involving marketable permits to emit limited amounts of air pollutants. This is reflected in the implementation of the Montreal Protocol and in the proposed implementation of the provisions of the 1991 Clean Air Act addressing the precursor pollutants to acid rain. Market mechanisms have also been discussed in connection with implementing the Canada–United States Air Quality Accord and with a global regime for controlling greenhouse gas emissions.

IV. Important future themes

There are several important themes that are not widely treated in the book but that deserve such attention in future works. The first con-

21

cerns how to increase compliance with those international legal instruments that have already been negotiated. We need better data on the extent to which states are complying with these agreements and on whether the agreements as drafted are accomplishing their purposes. The analysis of these issues is often complex, and the data difficult to obtain.[22] In addressing these issues, we need to understand not only whether implementing legislation or directives satisfies the requirements of the agreement, but also the extent of compliance with such legislation. Moreover, it is important to understand the role of the international secretariats in assisting with compliance, the methods of compliance that are most successful, and the factors that influence national compliance with international environmental instruments.

A second issue of growing importance is the linkage between environment and trade. Global change can be expected to generate more rules of environmental protection, some of which may be challenged as barriers to trade. Conversely, trade rules have important implications for the ability of countries to protect the environment.

The trade issues raised by environmentally oriented actions take several forms: environmental restraints on imports are viewed as disguised trade barriers; differential environmental standards are seen as preventing a level playing-field and affecting competitiveness; and trade prohibitions and trade sanctions contained in international environmental agreements are perceived as a violation of the non-discriminatory provisions of GATT. The recent report of a GATT dispute panel stating that US legislation banning imports of tuna from Mexico if harvested in a manner harmful to the sustainability of dolphins violates the GATT raises important issues of the application of GATT to production processes and to the unilateral right of a country to take measures to protect the environment beyond national jurisdiction. The United States Congress has also been considering legislation that would limit imports of other products, such as tropical woods, if harvested in an environmentally unsustainable manner.

There is an increasingly important host of issues involving the

---

22. Two recent studies have examined the effectiveness of international agreements. The UNCED Secretariat has prepared a review of existing international agreements in conjunction with the UN Conference on Environment and Development, to be held in Rio de Janeiro, Brazil, in June 1992. The United States General Accounting Office recently released a study focused on compliance with selected agreements entitled "International Environment: International Agreements Are Not Well Monitored" (January 1992) GAO/RCED-92-43.

nexus between environment and trade. Both the environment and the trade communities recognize this linkage now, albeit somewhat reluctantly. The OECD, for the first time, held in 1991 joint meetings of its environment and trade committees and has engaged countries in serious consultations on the issues. The GATT Environment Working Group has also started to meet. The environment and trade issues deserve careful treatment in future work on global environmental change.

V. Organization of the book

The book is divided into three parts: the rules and processes of international environmental law; special issues related to the further development of human rights law; and institutional and systemic issues.

In "International Norm-making," Paul Szasz summarizes the international legislative process. He emphasizes that the process, although imperfect, has responded well to burgeoning environmental problems by producing an unprecedented volume of international legal norms. He suggests that what are commonly perceived as flaws in the process (e.g. delays, the need for compromises and finding a reasonably high common denominator, or the fact that international agreements are generally binding only on the ratifying parties) are the very features that have contributed to the prolific output of international legislation by creating the flexibility to generate new approaches to new problems.

Szasz argues, however, that a major impediment to the effective implementation of these norms is their often uneven applicability. Unevenness may stem from countries approving international agreements with reservations that exempt them from certain provisions or, alternatively, from the fact that many countries (particularly developing countries) fail to ratify agreements simply because they are unable to handle the administrative burdens of the domestic ratification process.

One way to prevent the patchwork effect of uneven applicability is the simplification of treaty adoption and amendment procedures to assure that all parties subscribe to the same version of an agreement. Intergovernmental organization (IGO) secretariats should also have a greater role in assisting countries struggling with the domestic administrative burdens of ever increasing numbers of international agreements.

Szasz examines conventional and, to a lesser extent, customary

23

sources of law in order to shed light on how international norms are created. With respect to the conventional law, he traces the steps and the parties involved at each stage in the treaty-making process, including the initiation of the process, and the formulation, adoption, and bringing into force of multilateral treaties. He then includes a section on the necessity of and mechanisms for keeping international legislation up to date in a world where the pace of change is rapid. With respect to customary law, Szasz argues that it, too, is subject to deliberate legislative activities, albeit more subtly than in the treaty-making arena. International resolutions (such as those issued by the United Nations General Assembly) may, depending upon the circumstances, help to form and guide customary international law. The effect of UNGA resolutions, particularly as they relate to the evolution of human rights law, is discussed in the chapters by Pathak and Cançado Trindade.

"Changing Requirements for International Information," by Peter Thacher, explores the evolving role of information in the global response to environmental problems. While progress in gathering and sharing of environmental information has been made since the 1972 Stockholm Conference, Thacher points out that it has been largely limited to the field of pollution control and has served primarily "assessment" purposes. The current challenge is to infuse information into the decision-making process and to move to a deeper level of inquiry – that of gathering data on the effects of economic activity on global environmental systems. Thacher argues that to be effective in moving the planet toward the goal of sustainable development, information gathering and exchange efforts must be "transparent" and accessible to all.

This chapter touches on many of the themes mentioned earlier. The crucial role of information in international responses to global change forces consideration of issues of scientific uncertainty and credibility, intrudes into matters traditionally cloaked by state sovereignty, throws stark light on the disparity among countries in their ability to produce or make use of more information, and suggests a systemic or ecosystem approach to global environmental problems.

Thacher echoes the thrust of Lai's chapter by noting that global environmental problems cannot be resolved without a concomitant effort to reduce poverty and wasteful consumption patterns. Thacher parts company with Lai in advocating the use of conditional aid to promote compliance with international information needs.

Thacher discusses recent trends in the role of environmental information in assessment efforts, environmental impact minimization efforts, and international agreements. He highlights the need for unfettered, independent scientific judgements to guide policy, the challenge that sovereignty issues present to the free exchange of information (even though such issues are less important for environmental than other types of information), and the requirement that international regimes be flexible enough to account for the inevitable and often rapid change in environmental, economic, and social data.

Thacher then turns to the information-exchange effects of proposed or experimental regimes designed to foster a global transition to sustainable development. He discusses the proposals contained in the WCED report, *Our Common Future*, including the creation of a UN Commission for Environmental Protection and Sustainable Development that could serve *"inter alia"* as a collection and dissemination centre for environmental data. He also considers the Global Environmental Facility, which aims to aid developing countries respond to global environmental risks, the International Geophysical Biological Program, whose purpose is to identify and refine the precise information necessary to manage global change, and the precautionary principle that speaks to hedging our global bets in the face of an uncertain future by ensuring that the available information is effectively used.

Thacher concludes that these proposals and pilot programmes may very well form part of new international arrangements regarding the generation and use of information that are likely to emerge from the UNCED in 1992.

In "Emerging Principles and Rules for the Prevention and Mitigation of Environmental Harm," Toru Iwama identifies newly developing norms, principles, and rules for the prevention and mitigation of environmental harm: these principles and rules are emerging in light of global change and the growing recognition that anticipatory action is necessary to protect mankind's common interest in a healthy environment.

Iwama distinguishes between legal and economic approaches to environmental protection. Both are designed to modify behaviour, the former through customary and conventional law, the latter through economic incentives created by taxation or pollution charges. Iwama also distinguishes between prevention and mitigation responses on the one hand and *ex post facto* liability and reparation re-

25

sponses on the other. In both of these comparisons Iwama prefers the former.

Iwama discusses both the substantive and procedural aspects of traditional principles and rules that stem from notions of limits on sovereignty in customary law and that underlie Principle 21 of the 1972 Stockholm Declaration. While he acknowledges that traditional international law has effectively addressed some transfrontier pollution problems, he notes that these traditional principles and rules are inadequate to meet the challenges of the new global environmental threats.

Iwama then turns to a brief review of global environmental change, touching on problems of scientific uncertainty, intergenerational equity, interconnectedness of natural systems, divergence of North and South perspectives, time-lag effects, and the global scale of change.

He then analyses environmental law principles that are emerging in response to these unprecedented changes. Seven emerging principles are identified. First, mankind has a common interest in global environmental change. Second, a "double-track" approach has emerged to allow anticipatory action to be taken in light of scientific uncertainty. This approach typically features a general framework convention and is later supplemented by annexes or protocols. Third, cooperation in matters of scientific research and systematic observation is becoming standard procedure. Fourth, the exchange of scientific and other information is becoming increasingly commonplace. Fifth, new requirements for prior notice, environmental impact assessments, and consultation are emerging – all of these are reflective of the emphasis on preventive measures. Sixth, risk assessment, warning, and emergency assistance are also becoming more widely accepted. Finally, the use of trust funds to support prevention and mitigation efforts has gained wider acceptance.

Iwama concludes that these emerging principles constitute a move towards a form of "international governance," typified by the Vienna Convention and its Montreal Protocol, which might serve as a prototype for agreements on global climate change.

In "State Responsibility, Liability, and Remedial Measures under International Law: New Criteria for Environmental Protection," Francisco Orrego Vicuña moves from these rules of international law that prevent and mitigate environmental harm to focus on those rules that are designed to redress the harm once it has occurred. Orrego Vicuña begins with the same basic principle of international law cited by Iwama, namely that states are responsible for environmental damage caused by activities within their jurisdiction or control. He devotes considerable time to an analysis of how this basic principle has evolved in response to the exigencies of environmental problems.

The concept of state responsibility has expanded to include transnational and global consequences and in doing so has created entirely new obligations for states. These new obligations, coupled with other emerging developments, combine to greatly expand liability for international environmental degradation. Orrego Vicuña identifies the following developments in the international law of state responsibility: (1) a trend toward stricter forms of international responsibility that may assign liability for environmental damage in the absence of fault or even in cases where a lawful activity caused the harm; (2) a looser definition of damage that begins to recognize environmental harm as damage in itself sufficient to invoke liability; (3) a movement towards the idea that any state may bring an action to enforce an *erga omnes* obligation owed to the international community at large; and (4) relaxed procedural arrangements that allow foreign access to domestic court systems.

Orrego Vicuña insists that while the theoretical aspects of state responsibility can be quite complicated, the concept is more straightforward and less abstract in practice. He cites numerous examples of developments in treaty and domestic law to illustrate this point. He also includes an in-depth discussion of the international regimes for the protection of the seas and of the Antarctic as case-studies of how new developments in the law of state responsibility have already been incorporated into international environmental law.

Orrego Vicuña thus argues that the essential building blocks of an effective international law response to global environmental problems are already in existence and therefore the challenge is not to develop entirely new mechanisms but rather to implement more widely existing concepts and principles. He suggests, among others, the following steps: assigning liability directly to the private actor responsible for the harm or using "product liability" concepts to extend responsibility to the ultimate source of the harm; invoking subsidiary state liability when a private operator cannot meet the obligation; using financial guarantees such as environmental bond posting; establishing an International Claims Commission; establishing liability for wrongful enforcement measures; developing procedural rules to ease barriers to effective enforcement; and expanding definitions of environmental damage to include large ecosystems. Orrego Vicuña also mentions proposals to create international licensing mechanisms and to expand the use of trust funds by adopting levies on consumption of certain raw materials or emissions of certain pollutants. However, he cautions that such schemes may be overly intrusive on traditional notions of state sovereignty and may impede the operation of free markets.

Orrego Vicuña concludes that although environmental change is driving a process of new thinking and conceptual development in international environmental law, the harmonization process that underlies the creation of international law will ensure that the opposing extremes of either environmental degradation or creating a "world ecological government" are avoided.

In chapter 6, "Law and Global Environmental Management: Some Open Issues," Peider Könz provides a fresh perspective on how national and international legal systems together address international environmental issues. He describes the historical reliance on principles of tort law in the common law and civil law traditions and the need for alternative doctrines. In Könz's view, the soft-law instruments that have proliferated at the international level are a welcome feature, for they ensure the formation of a consensus that can in turn lead to the development of binding international agreements imposing significant obligations and commitments.

Könz devotes considerable attention to the methods available to resolve international environmental disputes, analysing in particular the use of national courts and fora for raising claims of damages to individuals (as in the *Bhopal* or *Amoco Cadiz* cases). He points to a "jurisdictional ballet" surrounding environmental damage claims in national courts and suggests that in the long run, treaty provisions may be important for ensuring uniformity of treatment.

Könz admirably addresses the often overlooked issues of compliance and enforcement and points to the need to ensure that legal instruments are enforced. He argues that it may be worse to have laws that are never enforced than to have no laws, since existing but unenforced laws may give the illusion that problems have already been addressed. Könz suggests several ways to increase compliance and enforcement, including economic and fiscal incentives compatible with market mechanisms. He also highlights the role of nongovernmental organizations in enforcing environmental norms at both the local and international levels.

In "Legislation and Implementation of International Environmental Law and the Third World," Lai Peng Cheng develops the theme that progress with the international environment and with third-world economic development must proceed on parallel tracks. Lai believes that for progress to be made on the former, the third world must participate fully in the process of legislating and implementing international environmental law. He concludes that the developing countries will be unable to participate fully in global environmental efforts until they are able to build sound economies based on agricultural and industrial progress.

Lai places the bulk of the blame (and consequently the responsibility) for global environmental problems on the developed world. He points out that the developed world is responsible for most of the industrial emissions believed to cause acid rain, ozone destruction, and global warming. However, he stresses that the third world, which represents the majority of the world's countries and the vast majority of its people, has a shared interest in and a responsibility for the global environment.

Although Lai blames underdevelopment caused by "colonial plunder" as the primary source of third-world environmental problems, he also recognizes that "governmental and cultural negligence" have played a role. He cites weak economies, high debt burdens, and rapid population growth as further impediments to third-world environmental efforts.

Lai suggests a number of steps to enhance third-world participation in international environmental efforts. He emphasizes the importance of development assistance, arguing that if third-world countries are forced to choose between economic development and environmental protection, environmental protection will always lose. He suggests that international and regional development banks make low-interest, long-term financing available for environmental programmes and that international trust funds earmarked for third-world environmental efforts be expanded to address this problem. He also suggests that international regimes allow for creative participation by third-world countries, an example being the two-tiered approach adopted by the Montreal Protocol. He exhorts the developed countries to co-sponsor environmental studies, monitoring, and educational efforts in the developing countries. Finally, Lai insists that technology transfer and other incentives (such as tax breaks or low-interest loans) be offered free of strings attached in order to encourage third-world participation in global environmental efforts without infringing on the sovereignty of independent states.

Lai concludes his chapter with a brief examination of the People's

Republic of China's efforts to protect the environment and to participate in international environmental efforts. He cites numerous laws
and regulations designed to protect the environment and points to
China's participation in a number of international fora and bilateral
and multilateral collaborations as evidence of China's positive attitude towards environmental protection.

In "The Human Rights System as a Conceptual Framework for
Environmental Law," R.S. Pathak explores the emergence of the right
to a healthful environment as a new human right. He suggests that
international human rights law may provide a conceptual framework
for environmental rights, and he re-examines the relation between
environmental protection and development within the human
rights context.

Pathak concludes with a brief survey of the evolution of man's relationship to nature and observes that, for the first time in history,
the human mind has turned to recognizing, preventing, and repairing
environmental damage. He traces this new development to an emerging global consensus (framing a more optimistic view of North/South
relations than expressed by Lai) on the necessity of preserving our
natural and cultural heritage in order to assure both the continued
existence of human life and the quality of that life.

Pathak begins his analysis by examining the philosophical roots of
the right to a healthful environment. He concludes that the human
need for a healthful environment in order to preserve and enhance
the quality of life and the moral imperative of preserving cultural
evolution establishes the philosophical underpinnings of the right to a
healthful environment. He then considers whether this right is a mere
right or a more fundamental human right. Observing that the right to
a healthful environment satisfies the four qualities of a human right
(i.e. that it be general, important or fundamental, essential and enduring, and inalienable), that the right is an inherent feature of
societal value structures, and that it serves as a source of other rights
and laws, he concludes that philosophically, the right to a healthful
environment is clearly a basic human right.

While philosophical concepts of human rights have existed for cen-
turies, Pathak traces their emergence from doctrines of international
law to the United Nations Charter and subsequent declarations and
conventions. Pathak divides existing human rights law into two "generations." The first generation established primary liberties and freedoms and intruded on state sovereignty by recognizing individual

rights and proscribing certain state activities. The second generation further limited notions of sovereignty by assigning proactive duties to states to provide for the basic economic and social needs of individuals.

Turning again to environmental rights, Pathak points to clear evidence of those rights in international regimes, but notes that there is no distinct integrated system of international law for the environment. He then makes the case for merging environmental law into the value structure of human rights, thereby ensuring its juridical status as a source of international law. He cites the similarities between environmental law and human rights law: both "pierce the veil of sovereignty" to protect individual and global rights; both stem from broad global principles that exist despite multicultural perspectives, and both are considered humanitarian.

While the right to a healthful environment may be considered either as a corollary to the most basic of human rights, the right to life, or as a separate, specific legal norm implied by the Universal Declaration on Human Rights and subsequent covenants, declarations, and treaties, Pathak suggests that the right may form part of a third generation of human rights. This third step in the evolution of international human rights represents the development of collective rights that reflect global concerns and that can only be enforced through the cooperation of all the actors on the global stage, including individuals, states, public and private organizations, and international organizations.

Pathak concludes that regardless as to how it is categorized, the right to a healthful environment already enjoys significant status in international law, as witnessed by its incorporation into numerous municipal law systems and international treaties.

The final section of the chapter seeks to clarify the relationship between the right to a healthful environment and the right to development. In contrast to Professor Lai's approach, Pathak suggests that the two rights are not in tension but rather that they are compatible because a healthful environment is essential to sustained development. Pathak goes on to suggest that because individual humans need both a healthful environment and the benefits of development in order to realize their full dignity and worth, the two rights are part of the same interdependent system of human rights that continues to evolve within international law.

In "The Contribution of International Human Rights Law to Environmental Protection," Antônio Cançado Trindade examines the interrelationship between human rights protection and environmental protection.

Cançado Trindade traces the similarities and affinities between human rights law and international environmental law. He notes that in both areas the trend has been first towards internationalization (i.e., a recognition of human rights and environmental problems that require limits on state sovereignty) and then towards globalization (i.e., a reflection of the indivisibility of fundamental human rights and of the global nature of environmental threats). Both domains of international protection reflect the decline of reciprocity as the basis for international obligations. Cançado Trindade analyses the emergence of absolute or objective obligations based on the "common good of mankind," framing the discussion in terms of the most fundamental of human rights, the right to life, being added to the right to health.

Cançado Trindade points to a shared temporal dimension in human rights and environmental law that reflects an orientation towards the prevention of harm. He points to the theme that is developed more fully in Orrego Vicuña's chapter, namely that actual direct or indirect damage is no longer a prerequisite to international action. Rather, in both cases, the issue may turn on an assessment of the *risk* that harm (either in terms of environmental degradation or human suffering or persecution) will ensue from a given activity. Thus, both bodies of law reflect a concern with the effects of present actions on the future.

In addition, there is a shared *ratio legis* of human rights and environmental law: the right to life. The right to life implies both positive and negative obligations and further implies individual as well as social or group rights. These characteristics are shared by both human rights law and environmental law.

As in Pathak's chapter, Cançado Trindade traces the right to a healthy environment to the right to health, which in turn follows from the right to life, with each of those fundamental rights serving to define more fully the broader right, the right to a healthy environment.

Cançado Trindade gives special consideration to the case of vulnerable groups such as children, handicapped, minorities, and indigenous populations by stressing the social aspect of human and environmental rights, which provides an opportunity to empower these vulnerable groups. The protection of these groups lies at the confluence of human rights law and environmental law.

He further illustrates the interrelatedness of human rights and environmental law by examining recent developments in international human rights law, international humanitarian law, and international refugee law, which encompass environmental concerns and thus provide support for the concern for human rights protection found in the realm of international environmental law.

Cançado Trindade then suggests several lessons to be drawn from the development of human rights law that may be applicable to the implementation of environmental rights. First he points to traditional notions of "justiciability and enforceability" and suggests that environmental law may benefit from the less formal approach that has developed in human rights law, namely that of "implementation and supervision." Here the human rights mechanisms of petitioning, fact-finding, and reporting may also prove to be effective in enforcing environmental obligations. Second, he examines the German concept of *Drittwirkung,* the applicability of human rights and environmental obligations to third parties. Because of their "collective dimension," everyone enjoys the benefits of enforcement of these rights; however, this also implies an attendant duty to respect and promote these rights upon individuals, groups, states, and humankind as a whole. He indicates that the issue of protection *erga omnes* has a direct bearing on the question of the *mise en oeuvre* of the right to a healthy environment.

Cançado Trindade closes by addressing the argument advanced by some authors that the existence of environmental rights restricts other human rights (e.g., the right to development as limited by conservation of the environment). He argues that such criticisms are short-sighted, concluding that over the long-term, emerging environmental rights serve only to preserve, expand, and strengthen other basic human rights. In his argument, the recognition of the right to a healthy environment entails the enhancement rather than the restriction of pre-existing human rights.

In "The Implications of Global Change for the International Legal System," Alexandre Kiss examines the effect of global change on the functions and institutions of international law. Focusing first on the former, Kiss considers the law-making and implementation functions of international environmental law.

Kiss sees a trend in law-making towards an international legal system that is more flexible, open to change, and adaptable to the "intricate web of foreign relations." He catalogues a number of new approaches in the making of international law that illustrate this point. Soft-law provisions that create no immediately legally binding obligations have emerged as tools to formulate societal values and express consensus. Such provisions may later be ratified in binding form, become adopted as part of domestic law systems, become part of a framework for cooperation or more precise rule-making, or enter customary law. Similarly, "cooperation treaties," programmes for action, and "umbrella treaties" also serve as important intermediate steps towards more comprehensive regimes. Kiss also points to the adoption of more flexible standards, such as percentage reductions that result in either different obligations for different but similarly situated countries or the adoption of different standards for developed and developing countries. Kiss additionally cites the use of multiple regional conventions that apply generally agreed-upon principles to the specific conditions of a region and the use of simplified updating mechanisms. Many of these developments are also discussed in more detail by Szasz in the first chapter.

Kiss then turns to the implementation function. Global change has in some areas forced states to act as organs of implementation of international law by virtue of their domestic legal systems; while in other areas, international bodies have emerged to oversee implementation. As an example, Kiss cites human rights law and the institutional mechanisms designed to oversee its implementation (these are also discussed in detail by Cançado Trindade). Although no complete international framework exists to oversee the environment, Kiss, like Szasz in chapter 11, sees progress towards such a framework in the rise of "reporting systems," the expanding role of UNEP, and the increasing participation of non-governmental organizations.

There are also related important changes in the law of liability. Despite persistent civil-law notions of liability that require the existence of actual damage to identifiable individuals, Kiss sees an emerging public-law concept of liability that allows enforcement where there is merely a threat or risk of harm or, alternatively, for the protection of global commons on the basis of harm to humankind as a whole. Orrego Vicuña discusses this evolving law of liability in greater detail in chapter 5.

In the second part of the chapter, Kiss examines the impacts of global change on international structures. First, he sees growing limitations on the actions of individual states as the focus of international law starts to shift from relations among states to humankind. Second, he examines a number of new factors influencing the international system. The injection of public opinion via non-governmental organizations, the emergence of "peoples" and humankind as entities with legal rights, and the incorporation of a temporal dimension through concern for the future combine to create what Kiss views as dynamic and flexible elements within a normally static legal system. Third, in contrast to the view expressed by Orrego Vicuña, Kiss believes the implication of global change is the emergence of a "real system" of international institutions to address the global concerns of humankind. He predicts the continuing trend toward global cooperation, negotiation, and international regulation as conservation and resource-management efforts increase.

"Restructuring the International Organizational Framework," by Paul Szasz, asserts that global change and the evolving legal doctrines discussed throughout this book highlight the need for a restructuring of the international organizations that oversee environmental protection. To that end, Szasz surveys the many different models for change that are possible.

Szasz begins with a review of the "modest" current structure and discusses the problems with it. First he points to the insufficient clout of UNEP, which is constrained by a limited budget and by its location in Nairobi, far from the headquarters of the programmes that it is supposed to coordinate. Szasz then attributes the low priority and amount of debate of environmental issues within the General Assembly and the Economic and Security Council to their status as relative newcomers on the international scene. Finally, Szasz cites the lack of a high-level advocate for the environment (such as the UNEP Executive Director) at UN headquarters in New York or as part of the Secretary-General's cabinet.

Szasz recognizes that any change will be a function of the objective of such change, but nevertheless he stresses several important limitations on international institutional change. One limitation is the trade-off between a single large organization that may reduce duplicative efforts but become increasingly unmanageable and many smaller organizations that have the opposite effects. Another limitation is "getting there from here," or how difficult it is politically to achieve a transition to the new structure.

Szasz then examines potential changes both within and without the United Nations system. First he considers creating new responsibilities and powers for the principal United Nations organs, such as the General Assembly and the Security Council, or possibly creating a new principal organ for the environment. Most substantial changes to the structure or roles of the principal UN organs would require amending the UN Charter, a difficult and rarely used process; however, having environmental issues decided within the core UN organs would greatly enhance the visibility and potentially binding nature of those decisions. Second, Szasz considers extending and upgrading subsidiary UN organs, particularly UNEP, and established coordinating bodies. Third, he examines the use of organs created through the treaty process, pointing out that while such organs are very flexible and can readily adapt to changing conditions, the difficulty is coordinating these many organs for an organized global response to environmental change. Finally, he explores the use of specialized or related UN agencies that, while falling under the UN umbrella, are less bound by the formal strictures of the UN. Szasz concludes that most of the models for change to the international organizational structure of environmental protection have precedents in existing structures and are thus achievable if it is what the world community wants. He includes a brief annex on the learning capacity of international institutions.

In "Intergenerational Equity: A Legal Framework for Global Environmental Change," I argue that the need for intergenerational equity is inherent in sustainable economic development and must guide our approach to managing global environmental change.

I point out that the human species has two important relationships: the first is the relationship between generations of the human species and the second is the integral relationship of the human species to the natural system. As the most sentient of species, we have a special responsibility to care for that system.

International law has traditionally focused on relationships between states in the present generation, with intertemporal rules linking the present to the past. But there has also been a growing recognition of the link to the future, as reflected particularly in the environmental and human rights fields.

The theory of intergenerational equity posits that all generations are part of a human partnership extended over time with rights to use the planet for their own benefit and obligations to care for it for future generations. Every generation has a right to receive the planet in at least as good a condition as previous generations received it. This leads to a set of intergenerational rights and obligations, defined as comparable options, comparable quality, and comparable access.

These rights are distinct from individual human rights because they are rights that generations hold as a group and do not depend on

36

knowing the number or kind of individuals in the group, and that can be defined by objective criteria.

I argue that the concept that future generations have rights in the condition of the natural system has fundamental implications for our institutions. I perceive it to mean that future generations must be represented in the market-place and in decision-making processes in ways that reflect the fact that they have an equal right to the resources of the planet.

I conclude with an analysis of steps that might be taken to implement norms of intergenerational equity. I analyse the relationship between intergenerational equity and equity among communities today and show that implementing *intra*-generational equity is an important component of achieving intergenerational fairness.

In "Ecological Security: Response to Global Challenges," Alexandre Timoshenko explores other new approaches to international environmental issues, namely expanding traditional notions of security to encompass environmental threats and focusing on global as well as the more traditional national concerns. Citing continued environmental degradation in the face of "mushrooming" activity designed to control such deterioration, Timoshenko argues that a new conceptual approach to ecological problems is necessary. While other new concepts such as primacy of international law, common interest, intergenerational equity, and common heritage of mankind are important elements of any new legal regime to protect the environment, Timoshenko asserts that only an ecological security conceptual framework will provide the basis for ordinary people (i.e., not just academics and politicians) to understand environmental problems and the basis for the personal involvement necessary to redress them.

Timoshenko sees three different levels of ecological security: first, environmental problems may threaten economic and political stability; second, environmental disagreements may erupt into military conflicts; and third and most important, from the global perspective, ecological imbalances may become so severe that they will disrupt the life-sustaining processes of the Earth.

Timoshenko then traces the movement of ecological security from the realm of political debate to juridical thinking. He documents the linkage between environment and security in a multitude of works by international legal scholars, in United Nations resolutions and documents, and in the works of numerous international commissions and expert study groups. According to Timoshenko, the benefits of such a linkage are: (1) higher priority for ecological issues; (2) shifting the

37

burden onto the international community; (3) linking the environment to other important international concerns; and (4) integrating the world's peoples into a unified whole with a common purpose.

As a start towards a more useful conceptual approach, Timoshenko suggests 11 principles that would underlie a system of ecological security. The principle of equal ecological security would require that no state achieve well-being at the expense of another. Although it needs further elaboration, the principle to ban ecological aggression would discourage wartime exploitation of the environment. The principles to control and monitor compliance with rules of ecological security and to exchange information on national and regional ecological situations would combine to reduce tensions surrounding suspected non-compliance. The principle of prevention of transboundary harm would mark the shift from "react and correct" to "foresee and prevent" that Iwama discusses in chapter 4. The principle of cooperation in ecological emergencies exists in several treaty regimes but is not yet universal. Further cooperation is envisaged in the principle of the obligation to share scientific knowledge and environmental technologies. The principle of peaceful settlement of environmental disputes would seek to prevent bloodshed, and the principle of international responsibility for ecological harm would provide the teeth for ecological security. The principle of sustainable development would harmonize development and environmental concerns. Finally, the principle of a human right to a favourable environment (fully explored in part 3) would define individuals' benefits and obligations under an ecological security framework and thus lead to increased public participation in decision-making.

The chapters provide a framework for addressing many of the issues raised by global environmental change. They were drafted before both the Gulf War and the United Nations Conference on Environment and Development in Rio in June 1992, although they were informed by the debates for the latter. They reflect the perspectives of a culturally diverse group of authors. The book is not a final pronouncement on any of the issues, nor does it address all the issues. Rather, the authors hope that it will serve to stimulate further discussion and analysis.

Issues in international
environmental law

2

International norm-making

Paul C. Szasz

A. The international legislative process

Fatalists may attribute it to serendipity and mystics to the Gaia hypothesis, but when the world community, due to its increasing interdependence, required an ever greater number of important international norms, the international legislative process, i.e. the process for creating these norms, accelerated its output enormously – indeed to the point where both those who are charged with implementing these norms and those who merely must keep track of them threaten to be overwhelmed. However, a glance around the international legal landscape into other areas, such as the settlement of disputes and the enforcement of rules and decisions, indicates that in those areas the demonstrated need has not translated itself into corresponding solutions, suggesting that there may be structural reasons why one process – and that the least-known one – is more fruitful than the others.

Further reflection will suggest that, peculiarly, the international legislative process is as productive as it is – depending on how one counts, there are well over 1,000 multilateral treaty instruments, to which several score are being added each year[1] – precisely because it is by its very nature an imperfect process. That is, not only does it

1. *See* the treaties listed in Bowman & Harris, *Multilateral Treaties: Index and Current Status* (1984) and in the annual Supplements thereto.

41

share the well-known multiple weaknesses of most municipal law-making: it is often slow and delay-prone; politically necessary or convenient compromises may reduce the final product to a low common denominator; other distortions are introduced by special interests or the vagaries of unduly influential participants, and there are damaging cross-connections to other, irrelevant issues – in addition, the products of the international legislative process are generally speaking not binding *per se*, but only in respect of those states that specifically accept them, and then only if a sufficient number of states do so, a requirement that may take more time to fulfil than the formulation and adoption of the instrument. But it is this very possibility, of not accepting subjectively unacceptable international legislation, that makes the process itself acceptable to governments. That is, they know they can only be bound if they decide they wish to be bound, and even though they themselves participate in the collective law-formulating and -adopting process, they do not have to decide whether to subject themselves to the product until *after* they have seen the precise wording of the treaty in question – while in agreeing to a judicial or arbitral settlement of a dispute they must make an advance commitment to abide by an as yet unformulated decision to be made by a third party.

In spite of its considerable productivity, the international legislative or norm-making process has so far been insufficiently studied, though a relatively recently concluded General Assembly exercise gathered a great deal of useful background material and considered a number of (but endorsed only a few) interesting suggestions for proposed improvements of the multilateral treaty-making process.[2] For the purpose of the present exercise it will be useful to draw on that earlier study, though here the focus will be more sharply on the creation of environment-related norms.

There are of course several sources of international law, of which the most important for the modern environmentalist are multilateral international agreements, so-called law-making treaties, which may be concluded on a universal, on other worldwide, on regional, or on subregional or local bases. Not to be entirely disregarded, however,

---

2. For the General Assembly's decisions, *see* A/C.6/39/8 and A/RES/39/90 of 13 Dec. 1984. For the data gathered, *see Review of the Multilateral Treaty-Making Process*, 21 *UN Legislative Series* (ST/LEG/SER.B/21, 1985) (hereinafter: *Review of Treaty-Making*). For a description of the review exercise, *see* P.C. Szasz, "Reforming the Multilateral Treaty-Making Process: An Opportunity Missed?", *International Law at a Time of Perplexity: Essays in Honour of Shabtai Rosenne*, 409–441 (Y. Dirnstein, ed., Martinus Nijhoff, 1988).

is customary law, which though not as easily and unambiguously manufactured as conventional law, is still to some extent subject to consciously directed adjustment and thus will also be examined briefly here. Finally, of particular importance for the international environmental regimes is so-called soft law, i.e. norms that are not strictly binding but are still generally likely to be observed.

The forge or forum in which new international law is created, whether the conventional or customary "hard" law or the quite extensive "soft" kind, has since the Second World War, and especially in the closing decades of the twentieth century, almost exclusively become the international intergovernmental organizations (IGOs). Indeed, the development of the process (described in some detail in the following sections) and the great increase in its output have been due largely to these IGOs, many of which are dedicated entirely to the formulation of new international norms or have established specialized organs for that purpose.

B. Steps in the treaty-making process

Although the international legislative process is by no means as standardized and centralized as the corresponding municipal ones, nevertheless, at least for purposes of analysis, it is possible to distinguish a number of successive steps.

1. Precursors to the treaty-making process

In certain instances an international organ, faced with a newly emerged or recognized problem as to which international action appears desirable and urgent and as to the general tenor of which a wide consensus appears to exist, will in the first instance adopt a declaration expressing that consensus, making certain recommendations (that in the parlance of international lawyers may be considered as "soft," or non-binding, law) and perhaps taking the initial steps (described below) towards the formulation of a law-making treaty.[3]

---

3. The best-known examples of such declarations are those of the UN General Assembly in the human rights field, starting with the *Universal Declaration of Human Rights* (A/RES/ 217A[III]) and followed by others relating to racial and gender discrimination, torture, the rights of children, etc.; in other areas one might mention the declarations on outer space and on the seabed – all of which were later followed by detailed conventions. In the environmental field there are fewer examples, of which the most important is the 1972 Stockholm Declaration; one might, however, also mention the General Assembly's first resolu-

Though in some instances the adoption of such a decision occurs as soon as the organ is seized of the subject (i.e. at the same session), in others there is a lengthier process of consideration, including by subsidiary organs, which itself constitutes an abbreviated version of the treaty-making process.[4] Indeed, in some instances the organ may in effect embark on the quest for a treaty, only to discover that that may be a difficult goal to attain and that at the current stage only the adoption of a non-binding resolution can be achieved.

2. Initiating the treaty-making process

Evidently an idea that eventually becomes an international convention originates somewhere in the brain of some person, though in retrospect it may be impossible to identify the author and indeed the creative process may from the very beginning have been a substantially collective one. However, for official purposes a proposal generally enters the consciousness of the international community when it is first advanced, usually in some IGO organ, by the representatives of one or more member states – or possibly by those of a nongovernmental organization (NGO).

Assuming that IGO organ to be a formally competent one (or, if not, that it forwards it, as part of a resolution or report, to one that is)[5] to decide on whether or not to initiate a process for formulating a

---

tion on "Protection of Global Climate for Present and Future Generations of Mankind" (A/RES/43/53 of 6 Dec. 1988), which, though not designated as a solemn declaration, did contain both substantive recommendations and procedural arrangements for starting the treaty-making process.

4. Both the 1972 Stockholm Declaration and the 1982 World Charter for Nature took several years to develop in specialized organs, respectively the Preparatory Commission for the United Nations Conference on the Human Environment and the Ad Hoc Group of Experts on the draft World Charter for Nature.

5. Within the UN system, it is clear that UNEP has become the predominant sponsor of international environmental treaties, both on a worldwide and on regional and local levels (e.g., in connection with its Regional Seas Programme). It is therefore interesting to note that nothing in its charter (A/RES/2997[XXVII] of 15 Dec. 1972) specifically authorizes it, or its Governing Council or its Environment Secretariat, to undertake that function. Nevertheless, the only time when the General Assembly has interfered with UNEP's initiation of work on a multilateral treaty negotiation was in connection with the proposed agreement for protecting the global climate, for which the Assembly established the ad hoc Intergovernmental Negotiating Committee for a Framework Convention on Climate Change (A/RES/45/209 of 21 Dec. 1990) after UNEP and WMO had in effect initiated the process through their joint Intergovernmental Panel on Climate Change (IPCC).

treaty in the proposed sense, that organ must then consider whether it should do so. In effect it must decide if the perceived need for and the anticipated value of the proposed instrument, and the likelihood of achieving it, justify the commitment of the resources expected to be required to formulate, adopt, and bring the instrument into force. For this, each of the following points must appropriately be taken into account:

(a) The need that the new instrument is to meet
(b) The existing legal regime, including the extent of its applicability to the perceived problem
(c) Any relevant legislative efforts in other fora
(d) The likelihood of success in developing an instrument, i.e. is it foreseeable that the required measure of agreement can be reached on the solution aimed for?
(e) The optimal form for the proposed instrument: treaty, solemn declaration, model law or rule, etc.
(f) The likelihood that the proposed instrument will be accepted by a sufficient number of significant states
(g) An anticipated time-schedule for the project
(h) The expected costs of formulating and adopting the proposed instrument, both to the IGO concerned and to the states participating in the process
(i) Particularly in formulating instruments in relation to technical or scientific problems (such as outer space or the environment) it may be necessary to carry out extensive scientific studies or research to determine the parameters of the problem and the lines of potential solutions[6]

To develop answers to these several questions, various devices may be used, ranging from secretariat research carried out in a library, to surveys of member states and of interested IGOs and NGOs, to meetings of experts. Sometimes the initiator of the proposal will have anticipated some or all of these issues and presents a report addressing them.

6. Thus, at an early stage of the ozone negotiations, UNEP convened an Ad Hoc Working Group of Legal and Technical Experts for the Preparation of a Global Framework Convention for the Protection of the Ozone Layer, which worked from 1982 to 1985. *See* R.E. Benedick, *Ozone Diplomacy,* 42–44 (Harvard University, 1991). The negotiations on a climate-protection convention were preceded by several years of work by the Intergovernmental Panel on Climate Change (IPCC), established jointly by UNEP and WMO in November 1988, which presented its final report in 1990. *See* the Annex to this Chapter, *infra.*

In any event, in due course a decision must be taken as to whether to proceed with a full-scale effort to formulate the instrument in question. In taking such a decision, the organ concerned should be conscious (but often apparently is not, at least sufficiently) that by the nature of institutional inertia a project of this type, once undertaken, is not likely to be abandoned, even if the prospects of success should fade, due to either a later, better understanding of the problem or actual changes in circumstances, and even if time and cost projections are wildly exceeded.

Other types of unsatisfactory outcomes must also be anticipated. One is the eventual production of an emasculated instrument, reflecting an inability to agree on actually useful rules, and that in particularly unfortunate circumstances actually constitutes a retreat from a higher level of international obligation previously existing or in the course of development. Alternatively, an instrument may be formulated and adopted that contains such a high level of obligations that many states, or at least certain crucial ones, refuse to participate. In either event, an ill-planned project may then constitute, at least for a time and in a particular forum, a bar to further productive work.

For these reasons, the question of whether any limits should be placed on the initiation of the multilateral treaty-making process was one of those most intensively explored by the General Assembly in its above-mentioned review exercise. In the end the Assembly refrained from establishing or even endorsing any explicit restraints, as allegedly incompatible with the sovereign right of any state to introduce proposals in any international organ in which it participates. Nevertheless, the General Assembly in effect appealed to states to show self-restraint in initiating proposals of this type, and by indicating the criteria by which IGO organs should study such proposals it at least implied that those that do not measure up should be rejected.[7] In addition, the studies that were carried out as part of the review exercise brought to light several examples, particularly in IGOs that are systematically engaged in the legislative process, such as the International Labour Organisation (ILO) or the Council of Europe (C/E),[8] of elaborate safeguards against formally starting up the treaty-making machinery without establishing in advance the prospect of success within a reasonable time.

---

7. A/C.6/39/8, Section I, para. 1, and A/RES/39/90, para. 3.
8. *See* the description of these processes in *Review of Treaty-Making, supra* note 2 at Part Four.II.D, III.B.

In this connection it should be pointed out that one distinctive feature of the international legislative process, compared to municipal ones, is its highly decentralized and consequently at best poorly coordinated nature. Competence to deal with particular questions, such as environmental ones, may exist simultaneously in political organizations such as, on the worldwide level, the United Nations, and, on regional ones, the Organization of American States (OAS) or the Organization of African Unity (OAU), in certain technically oriented specialized agencies on the worldwide or the regional level, in specialized worldwide (e.g., UNEP) or regional organs, in regional organs of worldwide organizations (such as the Regional Commissions of the United Nations), or even in some treaty organizations or organs (such as the Meeting of Parties to the Vienna Ozone Convention). Which of these chooses to initiate a particular project may thus depend on chance, on the aggressiveness of an executive head, or on obscure political considerations that lead interested states to approach a particular institution. Though the UN General Assembly can of course issue directives to its own subsidiary organs and those of the Economic and Social Council (ECOSOC), in respect of specialized agencies it can only issue recommendations, which the latter are obliged to duly consider, while independent regional organizations are not even under such a gentle restraint. Though within the UN system there are coordinating organs, such as the Administrative Committee on Co-ordination (ACC), these operate primarily on the inter-secretariat level and therefore can influence the political organs only indirectly by facilitating the flow of information about what activities are underway or planned in the various organizations participating in the system.[9] Ultimately, it may therefore be left to states, acting through their representatives in the various IGOs, to prevent or discourage overlaps and duplications, and selectively to eliminate lacuna.

3. Formulating multilateral treaties

Once a competent IGO organ decides formally to initiate the process of formulating a multilateral law-making treaty – or, for that matter,

---

9. In the environmental field, the General Assembly originally assigned the coordinating function to UNEP's Environment Co-ordination Board (A/RES/2997 [XXVII]) of 15 Dec. 1972, part III), which was later superseded by an ACC committee called the Inter-Agency Board of Designated Officials (DOEM). *See* chapter 11 *infra*.

some other type of norm-establishing instrument – the second major stage in the international legislative process commences. This stage, in turn, consists of a number of steps, which, however, do not necessarily follow each other in a neat sequence but may overlap, iterate, in part be omitted, and in any event be structured in many different ways. All that is possible is to give a general description of the purpose and preferred means of executing each of these steps, on the understanding that the actual process may differ in respect of any given exercise, driven either ad hoc by the internal dynamics of the particular process or by certain more or less rigid schedules that may be characteristic of a particular organ (such as the International Law Commission, the ILC) or organization (such as ILO).

(a) Preliminary studies

Depending on what studies were carried out before the project was first proposed or in any event as part of the decision to initiate it, it may or may not be necessary to carry out further investigations before beginning to formulate the instrument. Such studies may deal, especially in respect of proposed environmental instruments, with scientific or technical matters, or with the current state of national and international activities and laws in the area.

As to how any necessary studies are carried out, this depends in part on their nature and in part on the usages of the IGO concerned. Often this task is assigned to the organization's secretariat, which can either perform it with its own resources, with specially engaged staff (especially if the exercise is a large-scale one – such as the Third UN Conference on the Law of the Sea, UNCLOS III), or with consultants. Another favoured approach is to convene expert groups, the members of which are either appointed by the executive head of the IGO (who is likely to do so on the basis of governmental recommendations and will in any event take into account various political balances) or by particular states interested in and able to participate in the project. Finally, the task may be carried out by a particular subsidiary organ of the sponsoring IGO, especially if such organ has itself an expert character (such as ILC).

(b) Preparing an initial draft

Perhaps no other step can be carried out in so many different ways as the preparation of the initial draft of a proposed norm-creating instrument. Sometimes a draft is submitted by the initiating state as part of its first proposal of the project – though, unless such submission is preceded by careful albeit informal consultations, it is likely to create suspicions and even a backlash. Sometimes the preparation of such a draft is assigned to the organ charged with preparing the above-mentioned initial studies and constitutes part of its report. Sometimes a draft is prepared entirely outside the sponsoring IGO, for example by an interested NGO. Lastly, the draft may be prepared in the negotiating forum (see next subheading) by a specially assigned rapporteur, a working group, or the secretariat, or simply evolve gradually out of the consideration of the subject.

Rather than starting with a complete draft text, with each of at least the substantive provisions spelled out completely, even if only tentatively, it is sometimes found preferable to start with only "heads of agreement," i.e. with just indications of the principal issues and how it is proposed to resolve them. In any event, the so-called "formal" or "final clauses" are often omitted entirely at this stage, unless some aspect of them (e.g., the number or type of parties; the arrangements for entry into force) impinge directly on the substance.

(c) Negotiation
The most difficult and generally the longest substage in formulating a new instrument is that required to negotiate its terms and text. It is this part of the process that is most clearly political, in that it involves the mediation of the various interests concerned: those that favour a strong and those that favour a weak instrument; those that desire a wide and those that prefer a narrow one: those that prefer different approaches based on differing scientific perceptions or legal habits; and especially those that may wish to obtain resources from the proposed new regime and those that might have to contribute resources in order to make such a regime feasible and acceptable.

The need for such negotiations naturally informs the entire legislative process – indeed, it is one of the reasons why that term is appropriate, for the negotiations required to formulate international laws may differ in scope but not in any other essential respect from those required for national or even local laws. Often negotiation starts before the treaty-formulating process has been formally initiated, in that the initiator may consult with leading states before ever introducing a proposal. The considerations involved in whether to initiate the process may also already involve advance decisions as to substance and form, which may be reflected in the terms of the IGO resolution approving the start of the process[10] and also in the choice of or in the composition of any ad hoc organs (whether expert or representative) mandated to carry out or to assist in the formulating process. Though in principle the negotiations culminate in the decision on the adoption of the proposed instrument, in practice they may continue (as they have in respect of UNCLOS and especially the protection of the ozone layer[11]) even into the post-adoption period.

Naturally, the preferred organ for carrying out negotiations is a representative one, that is an organ consisting of the instructed representatives of states. If the sponsoring IGO is a worldwide or large regional one, then most often the designated organ is a restricted one, that is not a plenary one in which all IGO members are represented. A standing restricted organ (such as the 58-member UNEP Council or the governing organ of a specialized agency) always has a balanced composition considered appropriate for the general business of the IGO[12]; if the task is assigned to an ad hoc organ, then the agreement about its composition may constitute, as pointed out above, one of the initial manoeuvres in the negotiating process.[13]

However, it should be understood that even if certain steps in formulating an instrument are assigned to an expert organ, the latter is likely to function, in effect, as a negotiating forum. This is so because

10. Thus the General Assembly directed the Intergovernmental Negotiating Committee it established by resolution 45/212 of 21 Dec. 1990 to prepare "an effective framework convention on climate change."

11. As pointed out by Benedick in *Ozone Diplomacy, supra* note 6, the negotiation of the 1985 Vienna Convention merged essentially seamlessly into that of the 1987 Montreal Protocol, and these in turn into the 1989 and 1990 Meetings of the Parties in Helsinki and London, at which crucial amendments to the Protocol were adopted. Even thereafter negotiations have continued, now in fora established by the Convention and the amended Protocol, such as the Executive Committee for the Multilateral Fund.

12. The Governing Council of UNEP, whose geographic composition is defined by para. I.1 of the establishing resolution (A/RES/2297[XXVII] of 15 Dec. 1972), consists of 16 African, 13 Asian, 6 eastern European, 10 Latin American, and 13 western European and other states. Though by gentlemen's agreements the members from each geographic region are selected by the region itself (i.e. by the meetings of the regional group representatives that take place continuously at UN Headquarters in New York), it is understood that the weightiest states (e.g. the permanent members of the Security Council) will always be included.

13. For example, in establishing the Intergovernmental Negotiating Committee for a Framework Convention on Climate Change, the General Assembly decided that it should be "open to all States Members of the United Nations or members of the specialized agencies" (i.e., in effect all states) (A/RES/45/212 of 21 Dec. 1990, para. 2), to remove it from the more restricted ambit of the Intergovernmental Panel on Climate Change (IPCC) that UNEP and WMO had previously established for this purpose.

practically always such a body is established with a politically/ geographically balanced composition, and because many of the experts, whether nominally appointed *ad personam* or directly by governments, will in effect speak for, and only after consultations with, their national authorities; thus it is most unlikely that even an expert committee report will be entirely apolitical.

Although the negotiations are normally carried out by persons formally designated as state representatives, such as the members of IGO organs, it has become more and more customary to permit a certain participation to the representatives of non-official organizations, in particular of NGOs.[14] Although such representatives cannot participate in any formal decision-making, whether by voting or in formulating consensi, they can often attend many of the meetings of representative and even some expert organs, they can sometimes address these organs orally, and often may submit written observations and sometimes even proposals. It is this device that increasingly permits the interested public, i.e. that which supports the NGOs that have standing to intervene, to participate in the international legislative process, in somewhat the same way as the public can participate in the work of certain national legislative organs. This is a most significant and relatively recent development, which is particularly important in the environmental field, where a number of well-financed and knowledgeable NGOs (including, of course, those established by interested business and industrial councils) operate and consider their participation in international norm-making to be a major aspect of their work.

(d) Consultations with governments

The international legislative process is, in spite of the increasingly frequent but still peripheral involvement of *ad personam* experts and of NGOs, primarily a dialogue among governments, carried out by their designated representatives for the most part in IGO organs.

14. *See*, for example, the many references to the role of NGOs, such as Friends of the Earth International, Greenpeace International, and the National Resources Defense Council (NRDC) in Benedick's *Ozone Diplomacy, supra* note 6. In setting into motion the formal negotiations for a framework climate convention, the General Assembly specifically called for "the organization of a broad-based preparatory process at the national level involving, as appropriate, the scientific community, industry, trade unions, non-governmental organizations and other interested groups" (A/RES/45/212 of 21 Dec. 1990, para. 3), and also called for the participation of observers in the work of the Intergovernmental Negotiating Committee established by the same resolution. *Id.* at para. 2.

Thus, in a sense, governments, at least the principal ones, are technically always up to date with the state of progress of any given legislative project.

Nevertheless, especially since the bulk of this work is normally carried out in low-profile IGO organs with restricted membership, it is useful for many governments, and especially for the majority not represented on such organs, to receive periodic progress reports and in particular to be given an opportunity to make a direct input. This may be accomplished in several ways, but two are the most usual.

Organs with restricted membership, whether or not these are constitutional principal organs (i.e. established directly by the treaty creating the IGO) or subsidiary ones, normally report periodically to a plenary organ, either on their work in general or by request on particular projects. In reporting on a legislative project, they may, depending on the custom of the organization, report in greater or lesser detail, ranging from a mere statement that work is continuing, to transmission of the texts of the latest draft, perhaps indicating areas of disagreement (often by the use of square brackets to designate disputed or alternative texts), or even the submission of summary or verbatim records of the relevant debates.[15] These may then be discussed in the plenary organ, again at greater or lesser length as is the house custom, thus giving all the members of the organization a chance to indicate their views. The culmination of such a discussion may be a specific resolution asking that the legislative exercise proceed in a certain way or take into account certain points, or it may merely result in the relevant records of the plenary organ being transmitted to the junior organ for its information as reflecting the reaction of a larger circle of governments.

An alternative method is to inform the governments of member states directly about the progress of the legislative project, usually through communications addressed to them individually by the executive head of the IGO. Such communications may be required by the mandate of the formulating organ to be made at certain stages of

15. In this connection it might be noted that the UNEP Governing Council, in reporting to the General Assembly on its annual session, rarely mentions any details of its multifaceted norm-making activities and certainly includes no texts-in-progress (*see*, e.g., the Report of the Governing Council on the work of its sixteenth session, A/46/25), while the International Law Commission (ILC) annually reports on every sentence of text it has considered, including the details of its debates (*see*, e.g., the Report of the International Law Commission on the work of its forty-third session, A/46/10).

the work (e.g., when a complete draft has been prepared)[16] or may be required on an ad hoc basis by the plenary organ. In many instances the communication will request that reactions to the report, and sometimes answers to specific questions, be communicated within specified deadlines to the executive head for transmission to the organ concerned. This process, which is not likely to be undertaken routinely or frequently, gives an opportunity to all potential parties to the instrument under consideration, and especially to those not otherwise represented, to communicate their considered and detailed views as to all questions at issue.

(e) Consultations with the public

Although, as just pointed out, provision is frequently made in the international legislative process for formal consultations with governments, the same is rarely if ever true in respect of consultations with other entities, i.e. such as might be considered as representing the public in a different way from governments. Nevertheless, as multilateral treaty-making is generally carried out in the open, i.e. in meetings at least in principle open to the media and to interested NGOs, and at least the reports made from one organ to another or from one session of an organ to another are rarely subject to classification, the public usually has sufficient access so as to be able to exert such influence as it can – which usually means through the normal process in democratic societies by which popular views may be translated into legislative recommendations addressed to the executive, which in turn instructs the negotiators.

This process is, of course, at best unsystematic and often ineffective, in particular in respect of the views of those who do not happen to be citizens of an advanced democratic country. And even in those, certain categories of persons are traditionally politically powerless. Nor are the interests of future generations systematically protected, but only insofar as certain articulate and sensitive individuals or groups take account of them.

4. Adopting multilateral treaties

When it is judged by the competent organ (which may be the one charged with the formulation of the proposed treaty instrument or

16. *See*, e.g., Article 16(g) – (h) of the Statute of the International Law Commission.

the plenary organ to which it reports) that the process of treaty formulation is complete or at least that it has progressed as far as it can
at that stage, a decision as to its adoption must be taken. One possible decision of course is that the instrument under consideration
should not be adopted, either at all or at the current time. If it seems
otiose to return it to the formulating organ, the project may be put
into indefinite abeyance or may be terminated entirely, for example if
a change in circumstances, such as the formulation of a similar instrument in some other forum, makes it pointless to proceed. If, however, as is usually the case, the prospects of a carefully elaborated
treaty do not appear to be entirely unpromising, a number of further
decisions must be taken.

(a) Choice of forum

If it is decided to move to adoption, the forum in which this should
occur must be designated. In some instances that decision is predetermined by the constitution or practices of the IGO, which may dictate
a particular procedure.[17] If the decision is open, the choice is normally between a standing organ and an ad hoc conference and will be
based on several considerations, of which the following are the most
important:

(a) The adopting organ should, as closely as possible, consist just of
all the potential parties to the instrument – it being equally undesirable to have decisions as to the provisions of a treaty made
by governments that may not or will not become parties as it is
to exclude governments that are expected to participate. Thus, if
there is no standing organ that fulfils that specification (e.g., in
respect of a regional-seas agreement), then it is preferable to
convene a specially composed conference.

(b) If all that remains to be done is to agree on the formality of the
adoption, then this can usually be handled as part of the routine
business of the competent standing organ; however, if extensive
work still has to be done, it may be difficult to accomplish this
within the crowded work programme of a standing organ, and for
that reason a specially convened conference with no other business may be preferable.

(c) Depending on the nature and importance of the subject-matter,
it may be thought preferable to arrange for adoption in a high-

---

17. This, for example, is true of the International Labour Organisation, whose conventions,
under its Constitution, must be adopted by the International Labour Conference.

profile senior IGO organ, such as the UN General Assembly; alternatively, in certain circumstances a special conference, even if convened for only a few days, may be considered as the better launching platform.[18]

(b) Tasks of the adopting forum

The adopting forum must, at the end of its work, be able to approve the texts of one or more instruments to be then submitted for formal action by states. In effect, therefore, it must complete whatever the formulating organ has not, since the work of the two organs is complementary – indeed, in certain situations one organ can perform both sets of tasks. These include:

(i) Completion of the substantive negotiations – usually only on a few especially difficult points that the primary negotiating forum was not able to resolve;[19]

(ii) Perfection of the text, which may require the addition, at this stage, of further languages, and the use of a Drafting Committee;

(iii) Formulation of the final clauses, which determine *inter alia* what international entities can become parties to the proposed instrument and on what terms – requiring political decisions for which a technical formulating organ may not have been competent;

(iv) Consideration of potential reservations, to be regulated either by a clause in the instrument itself or in a Final Act (see section 5(b) below);

(v) The making of a formal record to enable all potential parties to announce and have preserved their interpretations of the instrument and politically important statements and reservations.

The final product of the adopting forum will, particularly if it is an

---

18. For example, every effort is being made to hurry to completion the negotiation of several environmental agreements, such as the framework convention on climate protection and that on biodiversity, before the 1992 UN Conference on Environment and Development (UNCED), so that these instruments may be opened for signature at that auspicious occasion.

19. As to the ozone negotiations, Benedick describes in chapters 6 and 7 of *Ozone Diplomacy, supra* note 6, the many important issues that remained to be resolved in Montreal, after three separate negotiating sessions had already taken place after the adoption of the 1985 Vienna Convention. Although every negotiation has its own dynamics, it is not unusual for the most important issues to remain open until the bitter end (and sometimes a little bit past it) as many participants are unwilling to make their final concessions (or to squeeze from their governments the authorization for still further ones) until faced with the prospect that they or their governments may be blamed for the collapse of a long-lasting high-profile negotiation.

ad hoc conference, consist of one or more instruments meant for action by states (which instruments may include several coordinated treaties or a principal treaty and subordinated protocols), of resolutions presenting the collective views of the adopting forum, and of a Final Act that pulls all of these together and supplies or refers to a sufficient record to put the entire exercise into context and to permit differing views to be formally preserved, whether for political or for eventual legal reasons.[20]

(c) Decision-taking

All the fora so far referred to, but particularly the adopting one, must take a series of decisions in advancing the legislative process and especially in completing each stage thereof. In principle all these decisions can be taken by votes, but in practice increasingly more of them are taken without that formality – which again is a feature in which the international differs from the municipal legislative process.

The gradual decrease in the amount of voting in international organs is by no means a casual phenomenon. The one-nation-one-vote rule is increasingly recognized as being entirely unrealistic, by pretending to equate in this single respect the influence of individual states that differ drastically in all others: population, size, military or economic power, and contribution to the international community. However, since on the one hand there was no immediate possibility of changing this rule (which has been incorporated into most international constitutional instruments and is even considered by many as constituting one of the basic principles of international organization law) while on the other the more powerful states are steadily more reluctant to subject themselves to this artificial type of "majority rule," it has become necessary in order to ensure the continued participation of these states in important political processes to avoid voting as much as possible. This avoidance is most frequently expressed as an attempt to attain "consensus" or "general agreement."

In the first instance it would appear that this development represents a giant step backwards, in effect to the League of Nations,

20. For example, the Kuwait Regional Conference of Plenipotentiaries on the Protection and Development of the Marine Environment and the Coastal Areas (Kuwait, 15–23 Aug. 1978) adopted: (i) a Final Act of the Conference; (ii) an Action Plan; (iii) the Kuwait Regional Convention for Co-operation on the Protection of the Marine Environment from Pollution; (iv) the Protocol concerning Regional Co-operation in Combating Pollution by Oil and Other Harmful Substances in Cases of Emergency; and (v) five Resolutions on matters such as the Interim Secretariat, Financial Arrangements, Establishment of the Marine Emergency Mutual Aid Centre, etc.

whose principal organs operated on the unanimity principle and thus were rarely able to take effective action. Indeed, the need to obtain consensus is likely on the one hand to be time-consuming, for progress can be held up almost indefinitely by any participant, and on the other to tend to reduce the content of substantive decisions to no more than just the low highest common denominator[21] on which general agreement can be reached.

There are, however, some mitigating factors. One is that the extended consideration that the search for consensus almost always entails frequently results in an improvement in the text under consideration, as ingenuity is applied to ways of overcoming real and perceived obstacles to particular solutions. The other is that in most instances the consensus requirement is not an absolute one; while an absolute requirement in effect allows any participant, great or small, to prevent a decision for any reason, whether important or trivial or merely capricious, the usual consensus requirement merely constitutes a political overlay on the fundamental decision-taking rules of the IGO concerned. This means that if a representative is generally perceived as acting unreasonably in preventing the taking of decisions and cannot be moved by other appeals, then a resort to voting under the standard rules can always be threatened and, if necessary, carried out.[22]

If resort is had to voting, then it is in effect useful to have in mind a dual count: one relating to the formal majority requirements, which in most IGO organs and IGO-convened conferences requires that substantive matters be approved by two-thirds of those casting yes or no votes – i.e. absentees and abstainers are disregarded; the other relates to the importance, for the issue at hand, of the dissenters or non-participants. Thus, even if adoption in a formal sense can be attained, but it is clear that implementation will be fatally crippled by the non-participation of important states, it is often regarded as sensible to suspend the process until a more generally satisfactory

21. It is often said that decisions reached by extensive negotiations, such as are usually required in order to reach consensus, represent the "lowest common denominator" (LCD) of the views of the participants. This terminology is mathematically incorrect, for the LCD of any set of numbers is one. In any negotiation one strives to reach the "highest common denominator" (HCD), but that HCD may be very low if the parties are many and their positions far apart.

22. The first important negotiation for which such a procedure was formalized was the Third UN Conference on the Law of the Sea – *see* the very elaborate Rule 37 of the Rules of Procedure of the Conference (A/CONF.62/30 or the several revisions thereof). For much simpler, more recent versions of such a rule, see Article 9(3) of the Vienna Ozone Convention and Article 10(9) of its Montreal Protocol as amended in 1990 in London.

solution can be secured through continued negotiations – or, and this is particularly important in respect of environmental matters, until international or domestic pressures bring dissenting governments around.[23]

5. Bringing multilateral treaties into force

(a) General considerations

As already mentioned, the international legislative process differs from the municipal one in one important feature: once a municipal law is adopted by the legislature and, if necessary, approved by the executive and perhaps even vetted by the judiciary, then it automatically binds all who are subject to the government in question; in contrast, the adoption of an international treaty by an IGO or a conference normally has no immediate legal effect at all. What is required is that individual states take action in respect of the instrument – normally by having an authorized representative sign it and then having that signature ratified by appropriate governmental action, which may involve parliamentary approval – and also that enough states do so, sometimes within a specified time limit. Even then the treaty only enters into force for the states that have ratified, and subsequently for those that do so later.

Consequently, some approved treaties do not enter into force for many years, and even some that do may only be in force for a few states, thus rendering them ineffective. Indeed, the international legal landscape is littered with treaties not yet in force but still capable of becoming so,[24] others as to which all hope has been abandoned,[25]

23. Though formal "weighted voting" is anathema in most of the UN system IGOs and treaties (except of course for the Bretton Woods institutions), it cannot be entirely eliminated. Thus, for example, Article 16 of the Montreal Ozone Protocol provides that for entry into force at least 11 ratifications are required, but these must include those of states (or regional economic integration organizations) "representing at least two-thirds of 1986 estimated global consumption of the controlled substances." This means that states whose collective consumption equals just over a third of that of the world as a whole (i.e. just two or three) can block entry into force, regardless of how many other states are prepared to enter into the Protocol.
24. One such treaty, with important environmental provisions, is the 1982 UN Convention on the Law of the Sea, 21 *I.L.M.* 1261 (1982), which in spite of 161 signatures has now been waiting nearly 10 years for the necessary ratifications.
25. For example, the 1988 Wellington Convention on the Regulation of Antarctic Mineral Resource Activities, 27 *I.L.M.* 868 (1988) (6 signatories) and the 1977 Convention on Civil Liability for Oil Pollution Damage Resulting from Exploration for and Exploitation of Seabed Mineral Resources, 16 *I.L.M.* 1451 (1977) (unchanged since 1978: 6 signatures, no ratifications or accessions).

while still others lead a shadow existence for want of sufficient participation.[26]

Evidently an important determinant of the fate of any treaty is its specific provision concerning its entry into force. There is no general rule about what such a provision should be, though naturally it must reflect the special nature of the instrument concerned. If the substantive provisions are such that they can sensibly and beneficially apply if only a few states are parties, then this can be provided.[27] In other situations, however, there is no point in bringing a particular regime into force without the participation of all or substantially all the states concerned, or of particular states, and in that event it should be so provided.[28] There are also situations in which a regime might function even with uneven participation, but certain states consider themselves disadvantaged if they are bound if their neighbours or rivals are not.[29] Finally, some treaties foresee large potential expenditures, for example for establishing an IGO, and until sufficient contributors agree to participate others will hesitate to enter lest they be required to finance the entire operation.[30]

In principle it should not be difficult to specify entry-into-force conditions to take into account the appropriate factors of the type listed above. In practice, however, not only may there be disagreement about the weights to be assigned to each factor, but certain ways of expressing conditions may be politically precluded. For example, even if it is generally understood that a number of potentially large contributors must become parties to a proposed treaty in order to make it effective, it is likely to be unacceptable to specify these by name or even to provide that entry into force requires that contributors responsible for a certain percentage of the potential contributions of all eligible states join; to articulate such conditions would in

26. For example, the several nuclear liability treaties, such as the 1963 Vienna Convention on Civil Liability for Nuclear Damage (10 geographically scattered parties, only 2 of which have significant nuclear programmes.)

27. For example, both the 1986 IAEA conventions on Early Notification of a Nuclear Accident and on Assistance in the Case of a Nuclear Accident or Radiological Emergency, 25 *I.L.M.* 1370, 1377, could enter into force with just three parties, and their commitment could even be provisional.

28. *See* the entry-into-force provision for the Montreal Protocol, *supra* note 23.

29. This, for example, is true of the 1968 Nuclear Non-Proliferation Treaty (NPT), which explains why Pakistan will not join unless India does so, and Israel unless all the Arab states do.

30. This is evidently one of the reasons for the reluctance of many states to ratify the UN Convention on the Law of the Sea, *see supra* note 23, as it is known that at present certain financially important states, such as Germany and the United states, are not prepared to join.

effect give a veto or an unduly large "vote" to certain states as to entry into force, which may be unpalatable to the large majority of states dedicated to the principle of equal voting powers. The actual formulae adopted may, in trying to achieve indirectly what may not be said directly, therefore create controversy or be difficult to implement.[31]

(b) Reservations and options

Domestic legislation generally applies uniformly throughout the jurisdiction in question, for any exceptions or variations have to be expressed in the legislative instrument itself. International treaties are different, because usually states can accept them with reservations that modify the obligations as between the reserving state and the other parties, in part depending on how the latter react to the reservation. Furthermore, reservations may create problems as to whether the reserving state is a party at all, if there is a question about the compatibility of a reservation with express or implied conditions of the treaty. Some treaties also include optional provisions (typically as to disputes settlement) offering choices to potential parties. The result is that there may be considerable variations in the respective obligations of the parties, and a most complicated network of non-uniform bilateral relations among them.

To a considerable extent these problems of uncertainty and inhomogeneity may be resolved through the careful drafting of the reservation provisions of the proposed treaty, which may range from absolutely prohibiting any reservations to permitting almost all. But even more important than careful drafting is the policy decision meant to be implemented through these provisions. In general, liberal reservation and option provisions will on the one hand facilitate the participation of states that have different views as to some sub-

---

31. An example of such a provision is Article 25(1) of the 1979 Constitution of the United Nations Industrial Development Organization (UNIDO), which provided for entry into force when 80 states that had ratified had, after consultations, agreed thereon; even then, the Constitution would enter into force only for the states that had so agreed. The object of this baroque clause was to permit the states concerned to make certain that enough of the large contributors were on board, without having to specify them (as Article 110[3] of the UN Charter or Article XXI.E of the IAEA Statute had done many years earlier) or even specifying a minimum contributions quota for the initial members. The result was that the Soviet Union was able to hold up entry into force for a period of some years, while attempting to negotiate conditions it had failed to have included in the Constitution. A much more common-sensical approach was used in respect of the 1987 Montreal Protocol, *see supra* note 23, though it left the depositary (the UN Secretary-General) with the technical difficulty of determining when the specified condition had been fulfilled.

stantive provisions of the treaty; at the same time they may permit variations in obligations that are damaging and possibly even fatal to the instrument. A restrictive provision on the other hand will help preserve the unity of the instrument but may reduce, again perhaps fatally, the number of participants. The optimal balance must be determined carefully for each instrument, in a highly political decision, that in a nuanced way takes into account both the substantive contents of the treaty and the attitudes of the potential parties.

(c) The domestic aspects of ratification

Although ratification itself is an international act, what precedes it is carried out subject to domestic law and domestic political and administrative considerations. While the representatives who participated on the international plane may have been impatient to achieve the formulation and adoption of a treaty, the domestic actors who must approve ratification (who in any event include executive officials, but may also involve those of the legislature) may have at best different priorities and at worst different substantive objectives. In particular, in democratic states a whole series of steps may have to be taken to ensure that the proposed treaty is both politically and legally acceptable, each such step constituting an obstacle to speedy or even to any action.

That this constitutes a real problem is confirmed by any examination of the spotty record of ratifications of practically all multilateral treaties, very few of which can boast even one-half of the potential participation. If one tries to establish the reasons for this widespread abstention,[32] one will generally find few objective reasons but rather the sheer administrative difficulty that most states have in coping with the decisions concerning the desirability of ratifying, possibly with reservations, hundreds of treaties that may be of interest to them or to their neighbours – with perhaps two to three dozen increasingly complex multilateral instruments added each year. This is true of states ranging from the developing, with perhaps simple procedures but minimal trained manpower, to the developed, with potentially adequate staffs but extremely complex devices for securing and coordinating the reactions of all potentially interested domestic organs and entities.

It has indeed been recognized that the volume of international leg-

---

32. For the leading study on this subject, *see* O. Schachter, *Wider Acceptance of Multilateral Treaties* (UNITAR/ST/2) (1969).

islation has become such that states are practically unable to keep up with the backlog and with new instruments.[33]

However, except for defeatist suggestions that the flow should be reduced – which would mean that international norms that are needed and as to which agreement can be reached would have to be delayed – little effective action has been taken or planned to assist states in coping. Only a few treaty-sponsoring IGOs provide technical assistance in translating treaty instruments into local languages, in preparing presentations to parliamentary and other bodies, and in drafting domestic legislation and regulations to facilitate implementation of treaty obligations. Instead, IGOs sometimes unintentionally add to the burden of domestic administrations by well-meaning demands for periodic progress reports on treaty actions and implementation – which may be designed to stimulate ratification but may also reduce the time of those available to take such action.

There is no doubt that in many fields, and this is particularly true of the environment, numerous states need assistance to enable them to participate in the international legislative process so that their interests be adequately represented, but in particular at the stage where the new international norms must be accepted and then be implemented by domestic legal processes.

One persistent problem that should be easy to solve – particularly in the age of automated information systems – is the making of up-to-date information about the status of multilateral treaties (e.g., list of signatories, ratifications and other corresponding actions, withdrawals, reservations and objections thereto) readily and currently available. While good annual reports are available on those treaties of which the UN Secretary-General is the depositary,[34] this is less true of treaties deposited with other entities, and in particular with states – such as all the regional-seas conventions and their protocols.[35]

---

33. *See* the discussion in Part Three.IX of the *Review of Treaty-Making, supra* note 2.
34. For example, *Multilateral Treaties Deposited with the Secretary-General: Status as of 31 December 1991* (ST/LEG/SER.E/10), chapter 27 of which reports on environmental treaties. As of that date, just three instruments and their related protocols were listed under that heading, because most UNEP-sponsored treaties (such as those for the Regional Seas Programme) are unfortunately not deposited with the UN Secretary-General but with the host state of the adopting conference, which makes it more difficult to secure regular, up-to-date information about them.
35. Information about these can be found in the not so readily available UNEP *Register of International Treaties and Other Agreements in the Field of the Environment,* of which the latest version is: UNEP/GC.16/Inf.4, Nairobi, May 1991.

6. The process of keeping international legislation up to date

In today's fast-moving world, international law, just as its domestic counterpart, must be kept up to date – and that sometimes at almost breakneck speed, as witness the developments concerning the ozone-protection regime. The following are certain devices for accomplishing this in an effective manner.

(a) Simplified treaty-adopting and -amending practices

Traditionally, treaty law has been adjusted from time to time by additional treaty actions, either by amending existing instruments, by creating others to complement older texts, or by entirely superseding those that cannot easily be adapted to serve modern purposes. Generally, all these measures technically require full-scale treaty-initiating, -formulating, -adopting, and entry-into-force procedures, with all the work and complications described above. Furthermore, because each such amendment or new treaty is subject to the same domestic treaty-acceptance procedures as the original instrument, and these procedures are accomplished with uneven speed and efficiency by different states, the pattern of ratifications becomes yet more complicated, creating an entirely uneven and ultimately unintelligible pattern of obligations among states that are parties to the same agreement but with different amendments, or that participate in different supplementary or superseding agreements.[36] Instead of progressing towards a generally applicable international regime, the volume of international law may be growing at the cost of uniformity of coverage.

It is for this reason that a number of devices have been developed for simplifying the process of updating treaties, devices that concern one or both of the major phases of the legislative process described above. These devices include: the use of framework or umbrella conventions that merely state general obligations and establish the machinery for the further norm-formulating devices described under this heading;[37] the supplementation of such conventions and by indi-

---

36. In general these questions are governed by Articles 39–41 and 58–59 of the 1969 Vienna Convention on the Law of Treaties.
37. Framework conventions have proven to be particularly useful in the field of international environmental regulation. They include the 1979 Geneva Convention on Long-Range Transboundary Air Pollution, the 1985 Vienna Convention for the Protection of the Ozone Layer, as well as the basic agreement of each of the regional seas regimes, such as the 1976 Barcelona Convention for the Protection of the Mediterranean Sea against Pollution. It is

vidual protocols establishing particular substantive obligations in implementation of the general objectives of the convention;[38] the use of easily amendable technical annexes.[39]

In respect of all these devices, the international phase of the treaty-making process – initiation, formulation, and adoption – can be simplified and accelerated by assigning them to specially designated, dedicated expert or representative organs that either meet periodically or that are easy to convene as the need for further legislative action arises, and that are serviced by a specialized secretariat thoroughly familiar with the regime in question as well as with other related regimes that must be taken into account.[40] Thus the usual start-up time for these phases of the international legislative process can be largely eliminated, as well as much routine reporting and the repeated transfer of proposed texts among expert, restricted representative and plenary organs. Consequently texts ready for adoption by the states participating in the regime can be prepared in substantially shorter times – subject, of course, to the need to negotiate generally acceptable terms.

Another important saving in time and effort can, however, be achieved in respect of the second, domestic, phase of the process. This may be done by providing in the basic convention that all or certain of these new instruments do not require ratification but enter into force in some simplified way:

(a) It may be provided that supplementary instruments require only signatures in order to bind states.[41] While of course the constitutional requirements of certain of these parties will require that such signatures only be affixed after the completion of domestic procedures that correspond to those required for ratification, many other states will be able to take advantage of such provisions to achieve instant participation.

(b) It may be provided that once an amendment enters into force for

---

therefore not surprising that the General Assembly decided that the protection of the climate could best be initiated by a framework convention (A/RES/44/207 of 22 Dec. 1989, para. 10).

38. *See*, e.g., Articles 2 and 8 of the 1985 Vienna Convention for the Protection of the Ozone Layer.

39. *See*, e.g., *id.* at Article 10(2) (a).

40. *See*, e.g., *id.* at Article 6 (establishing a Conference of the Parties [to the 1985 Vienna Convention for the Protection of the Ozone Layer]); *id.* at Article 7 (establishing a Secretariat).

41. This is specifically foreseen in Article 12 of the 1969 Vienna Convention on the Law of Treaties.

a sufficient number of states, it automatically enters into force for all;[42] this short-circuiting of the ratification process by those states that do not act early may, however, have to be purchased at the cost of providing in the basic treaty that a state on which an amendment is thus imposed can denounce the treaty in some simplified manner.[43]

(c) It may be provided that certain amendments, especially to technical annexes, do not require any signatures and ratifications at all, but automatically enter into force for all parties to the basic treaty unless a sufficient number of them object within a stated time limit from the adoption of the amendment, or that such amendment enters into force for all treaty parties except those that object within a specified time period.[44]

Evidently, all such devices for somehow taking out of the hand of states the need for each of them to act positively on any treaty instrument before it enters into force for it will be accepted only most reluctantly by many of them and generally only if restricted to basically subordinated and technical matters; as already pointed out, it is usually necessary to preserve some method for the state to opt out simply, either from the new legislative feature or, perhaps, from the entire regime.[45] Although in a sense these are instances of an IGO organ "legislating" directly for states, the legal obligation of each state ultimately derives from its consent to the underlying treaty in which the particular empowerment of the IGO is set out, and consequently one might refer to a "derivative treaty obligation."

42. Such provisions frequently appear in the constitutional instruments of IGOs, since it would not be feasible for such an instrument to have different provisions with respect to different members of the organization, nor is it usually considered satisfactory to wait for every member to act on an amendment – which would, in effect, give a veto to every member. *See*, e.g., Article 108 of the UN Charter; Article XVIII.C of the IAEA Statute.

43. *See*, e.g., Article XVIII.D of the IAEA Statute.

44. *See*, e.g., Article 10(2)(c) of the 1985 Vienna Ozone Convention.

45. There are, however, some instances in which no arrangement was made for States Parties to exclude themselves from the effect of certain dispositions made by an IGO organ pursuant to a provision of a treaty. One minor but relatively early example is the power of the Board of Governors of the International Atomic Energy Agency to determine, under Article XX.3 of the 1956 IAEA Statute, whether certain nuclear materials are "source material" within the meaning of the Statute (with all the consequences that flow from such a determination). The IAEA Board was later given the power, by Article I(2) of the 1963 Vienna Convention for Nuclear Damage, to determine the maximum limits within which small quantities of nuclear material can be excluded by States Parties from the application of the Convention (a power that it exercised by a resolution adopted on 11 Sept. 1964) (the texts of the Convention and the resolution are set out in IAEA Legal Series No. 4, Vienna, 1976).

(b) The establishment of new intergovernmental organizations and organs

It has already been pointed out that the international legislative process is one that takes place largely, indeed more and more almost exclusively, under the auspices of competent IGOs. It is also true that more and more, the new international agreements that are formulated and adopted either provide new tasks for existing organizations (usually the one sponsoring the agreement) or they provide for the creation of new organizations through which the states' parties can collectively carry out some of the objectives of the new instrument or be assisted in doing so individually, but most particularly to help develop the new law even further.

Under the previous heading various devices were discussed for accelerating the process of formulating and adopting supplementary or amending treaty provisions in respect of a basic treaty, which may indeed be merely a framework convention. Since these devices for the most part function optimally if implemented by specialized and dedicated expert, representative and secretariat organs, this can best be accomplished by creating a special international organization for that purpose – but naturally only if such a step can also be justified by the other tasks to be assigned to the new IGO.

In the event that there is no call for creating a full-blown new IGO, another device is merely to establish the necessary expert and representative organs, leaving these to be serviced by the secretariat of some existing, willing, and competent IGO – which will usually be the one under whose auspices the treaty in question was formulated.[46]

C. The creation of customary law

So far this chapter has dealt almost exclusively with international legislation through the multilateral treaty-making process, which indeed is the principal method of manufacturing new international law.

---

46. For example, the 1979 Geneva LRTAP Convention provides in Article 11 for the Executive Secretary of the Economic Commission for Europe (ECE), under whose auspices the Convention was negotiated, to assume the secretariat functions to be performed under the new instrument. On the other hand, Article 7(2) of the 1985 Vienna Convention for the Protection of the Ozone Layer provides that UNEP, the sponsor of that instrument, is to assume the secretariat functions only on an interim basis, and that at the first meeting of the parties to the Convention a permanent choice be made among the secretariats of existing and interested IGOs. The parties to the Vienna Convention decided at their first meeting (Helsinki, 1989) to retain the secretariat within UNEP.

However, as already mentioned in the introduction, customary law is the other main source of rights and obligations under international law and therefore cannot be entirely neglected in the present context. This is especially so because customary, unlike conventional, law generally applies to all states (except those that have always and consistently excluded themselves from the practice in question) and not only to the parties to a particular instrument.

At first sight, it seems oxymoronic to suggest that customary law – which is derived inductively from the practice of states insofar as such practice is motivated by a sense of legal obligation – can be "legislated" in the usual sense of that term. And, of course there is no straightforward way of doing so, comparable to the treaty route, which though long and tortuous, can be seen as proceeding step by step from the proposal to initiate to the entry into force of a multilateral law-making treaty.

Nevertheless, customary law can be somewhat shaped and directed, because the practices of states can be consciously affected by various international actions, particularly by significant IGOs. Many of the hundreds of resolutions that are adopted each year by international organs are addressed to states and recommend that they act in particular ways and may even suggest that they are legally obliged to do so – obviously in the hope, if not the firm expectation, that some or many will conform their conduct as a result of these importunings.

Although most such recommendations are expressed in ordinary resolutions and deal with issues of lesser or transitory moment, some are deliberately framed as solemn or universal declarations and adopted with ceremony by a senior organ, such as the United Nations General Assembly. The expectation that states will make a real effort to conform their conduct to such texts appears from their preambles or from the adopting resolutions, and sometimes also from later inquiries, usually solicited by the adopting organ and addressed to the executive head of the IGO, as to how states have actually responded to the declaration.

The formulation of such a declaration is often subject to essentially the same procedures as described in respect of multilateral treaties, involving consideration by expert and representative organs, consultations with governments and with NGOs, and adoption in a plenary organ by a high majority or by consensus.[47] Indeed sometimes

47. *See supra* note 4.

when this process is started it may not be clear whether the final product will be a declaration or a treaty, and the choice between these
two may only be made at a relatively advanced stage of the process –
that is, when it can be determined if at that stage a sufficient number
of states is prepared to enter into a binding treaty. But, whether or
not a declaration is originally adopted only as a second-best solution,
it may then serve as the forerunner of a later treaty, in that the
groundwork is laid and the general legal principle is established by
the former instrument, while the later treaty covers the same lines,
though in greater detail and with more precision.

Solemn legislative declarations[48] can thus contribute to the international legislative process in two entirely separate ways. They may
be precursive to and guide a later treaty-making process, in which reference is often made to the general legal principle already stated in
the declaration.[49] And they are also and perhaps primarily designed
to influence the conduct of states directly – and to the extent that
they are successful in doing so international customary law may be
created. In effect they may catalyse the creation of customary law by
expressing in normative terms certain principles whose general
acceptance is already in the air (for otherwise their adoption by an
IGO organ would not receive the necessary support) and thereby
making it easier and more likely for states to conform their conduct
to them.

There is yet another and in a sense more circuitous way in which
the creation of new customary law can be furthered through deliberate international action: i.e. through the adoption of multilateral law-
making treaties. Though of course these instruments primarily create
rights and obligations only for their parties and thereby influence
their conduct, to the extent that such conduct then becomes the international standard, even states that for some reason have not become
parties to the treaty may feel obliged to conform their conduct to
some or all of the treaty provisions.[50] Thus the process of creating

---

48. In the environmental field, the two principal general declarations are of course the 1972
   Stockholm Declaration (proclaimed by the UN Conference on the Human Environment
   and endorsed by the General Assembly) and the 1982 World Charter for Nature (adopted
   by the General Assembly); the 1982 Nairobi Declaration is of lesser import because it was
   only issued by the UNEP Governing Council (albeit at a special session in which 105 states
   participated).

49. Thus Principle 21 of the Stockholm Declaration is quoted in the preambles of both the 1979
   Geneva Convention on Long-Range Transboundary Air Pollution and the 1985 Vienna
   Convention on the Protection of the Ozone Layer.

50. It is basically on such grounds that the International Court of Justice held in *Military and*

new law-making treaties may, as a by-product, also facilitate the creation of new customary law.

This having been said, it must also be admitted that so far there are few clear instances of customary environmental legal principles. This is largely so because environmental law itself is of relatively recent vintage, and thus there has been little time for consistent state practice to develop, either in response to solemn declarations by IGOs or through the general acceptance of norms set out in multilateral treaties.[51] However, the processes described above have in other areas, and in particular that of human rights, been notably productive in the creation of customary law, and there is therefore every reason to expect that the same will apply in respect of environmental principles.

D. The creation of soft law

Both conventional and customary rules are binding, or "hard" law – in a sense, the only type of international law that properly deserves that designation.[52] However, in recent times another type of international law has more and more come to be recognized, that is non-

---

Paramilitary Activities in and against Nicaragua (Nicaragua v. United States of America), Merits, Judgment (I.C.J. Reports 1986, p. 14) that the United States was bound by certain fundamental customary international legal principles also expressed in the UN and OAS charters, even though in the suit by Nicaragua these instruments could not be relied on directly because of the Vandenberg reservation to the US acceptance of the optional clause.

51. One area in which this may have occurred is in respect of the protection of the environment in warfare. As a consequence of the environmental outrages committed by Iraq in the course and especially at the conclusion of the Gulf War (spilling oil into the Persian Gulf and especially the torching of the Kuwaiti oil wells), several enquiries were undertaken to determine whether such conduct violated a number of relatively recently proclaimed rules designed to protect the environment in warfare, and in particular the 1976 Convention on the Prohibition of Military and Other Hostile Uses of Environmental Modification Techniques (ENMOD), 1108 UNTS 151, 16 *I.L.M.* 88 (1977); Articles 35(3) and 55 of the 1977 Protocol I to the 1949 Geneva Conventions on Humanitarian Warfare, 1125 UNTS Reg. No. 17512, 16 *I.L.M.* 1391 (1977); Principles 2, 5, 6, and 7 of the Stockholm Declaration and paragraphs 5 and 20 of the World Charter for Nature; although it appeared that Iraq was not a party to the two treaties and of course could assert that the Declaration and Charter were merely hortatory, the Chairman of a Canadian/UN Conference of Experts on the Use of the Environment as a Tool of Conventional Warfare (Ottawa, 10–12 July 1991) concluded (in a not uncontroverted statement) at the end of the session that "the customary laws of war, in reflecting the dictates of public conscience, now include a requirement to avoid unnecessary damage to the environment."

52. These are the main forms of international law referred to in Article 38(1) of the Statute of the International Court of Justice.

binding, or "soft," law. What that term describes are numerous norms that are in effect observed by states even though, strictly speaking, they are not obliged to do so; however, the fact that they are generally observed, and are expected to be so, gives them a predictive value similar to those norms expressed in hard law – which of course is also not always observed.

Generally a norm may be "soft" when it either does not constitute part of a binding regime, whether of conventional or customary law, or because, even though it is contained in a binding instrument, it is not expressed in obligatory language. In environmental regimes, examples of both types of soft law abound, and most are ones created by IGOs.

As already pointed out, many important environmental principles are merely set out in resolutions or other decisions of IGO organs that, with few exceptions, are not binding *per se*. This is true, for example, of the Principles set out in the Stockholm Declaration and of the paragraphs of the World Charter for Nature, except insofar as these may either merely restate pre-existing rules of customary international law[53] or may have become such by the mechanisms discussed in the previous section.[54] Possibly even more significant because more numerous and practical are the many "guidelines," "principles," or recommended practices adopted by or under the authority of IGO organs, such as the UNEP Governing Council[55] or other corresponding bodies, and largely followed by states.

With respect to the second type of soft law described above, many multilateral treaties negotiated under the aegis of IGOs contain clauses that are not intended to create firm obligations – evidently because the prospective parties were not, at least at the time, willing to bind themselves as to these points. This is particularly true of the

53. For example, the oft-cited Principle 21 of the Stockholm Declaration is largely a restatement of the classic *sic utere* rule.
54. For example, paragraphs 5 and 20 of the World Charter for Nature dealing with the protection of the environment in wartime may have become principles of customary international law. *See supra* note 50.
55. *See*, e.g., the 1978 UNEP Principles of Conduct in the Field of the Environment for Guidance of States in the Conservation and Harmonious Utilization of Natural Resources Shared by Two or More States (UNEP Environmental Law Guidelines and Principles [ELGP] #2); 1985 Montreal Guidelines for the Protection of the Marine Environment against Pollution from Land-Based Sources (ELPG #7); 1987 London Guidelines for the Exchange of Information on Chemicals in International Trade (ELPG #10); 1988 Environmental Guidelines for Coastal Protection Measures (Environmental Management Guidelines [EMG] #17).

70

framework or umbrella agreements, the substantive provisions of which tend to be merely hortatory or programmatic,[56] while the ultimately effective dispositions are the procedural ones pursuant to which subsidiary instruments with binding substantive obligations are formulated and adopted.

Why, if soft law norms are not binding, are they in fact observed? There are indeed several reasons. One is that if a particular norm is negotiated within an IGO and then included either in a non-binding declaration or in a non-obligatory form in a treaty, the states concerned are generally desirous or at least content to observe it – for otherwise they would not have adopted it at all; thus the very fact that the norm has been articulated, usually by consensus, suggests that even if at that stage governments were not willing to bind themselves (perhaps because they first wished to observe the consequences of actual implementation), in practice they would normally follow it. Another reason for observance might be that the IGO concerned through some mechanism or other follows up on implementation of the norms it has promulgated; such follow-up may consist of no more than periodic reminders of the importance of faithful observance,[57] to arrangements for receiving reports on compliance, which the IGO may then discuss in an expert or a representative organ – i.e. the "mobilization of shame." Finally, in some instances certain states particularly interested in the observance of a non-binding norm may unilaterally exert effective pressure for compliance by other states.[58]

In evaluating the importance of soft law, account must also be taken of the various ways in which it may, often quite rapidly, be hardened. One way of course is the incorporation of an initially non-binding norm into a binding treaty – which, for example, is the normal and expected course when a general framework convention

56. *See*, for example, Article 2 of the 1979 Geneva Convention on Long-Range Transboundary Air Pollution, by which the parties undertake that they "shall *endeavour* to limit and, *as far as possible, gradually* reduce and prevent air pollution. . . . " (emphasis added).
57. Thus the General Assembly has given many reminders of the importance of observing the Stockholm Declaration. *See*, e.g., A/Res/37/219 of 20 Dec. 1982, Final Preambular Paragraph.
58. For example, the practically universal compliance with the several moratoria on the killing of whales pronounced by the International Whaling Commission is largely due to United States pressures, which has threatened a number of recalcitrant states with miscellaneous trade sanctions (denial of fishing rights in American waters or prohibition of exports of marine products to the United States). Through similar devices a large measure of compliance or promises of future compliance have been secured for the General Assembly's successive appeals to ban large-scale pelagic drift-net fishing (resolutions A/44/225, A/45/197, and A/46/215).

is supplemented by binding protocols. Another is the creation of customary law when states adopt as their practice, acting out of a combination of a sense of legal obligation and in response to some of the pressures described above, rules that originally were merely expressed in solemn (but nevertheless non-binding) declarations.

All in all, in considering how IGOs actually influence the action of states in the environmental field, it is important to take account of the large number of at least initially non-binding norms that are formulated and promulgated in various forms by these organizations.

E. Concluding remarks

The international legislative process is productive and capable of expressing as international law whatever rules and regimes the world or the appropriate special or regional community can agree on. Such law is most conveniently set out in the form of multilateral treaties applicable to the states that become parties, but may also take the form of less precise but generally applicable customary law stimulated and crystallized by the systematic adoption of formal declarations and even as the by-product of widely accepted conventional rules: finally, certain norms may, at least initially, take the form of non-binding but still generally observed soft law.

The quality of the international environmental rules thus established depends in the first instance on the expertise of the specialized representative, expert, and secretariat organs charged with carrying out or assisting these legislative tasks, which for the most part are likely to be the organs of a number of existing IGOs active in this field. Such organs are already quite numerous in the UN system and in some of the major regional agencies, though it may be useful to establish some even more technically specialized organizations and organs, for example such as might be required to deal with the threats of global climatic changes or to protect certain international commons from pollution. The establishment of such organizations and organs of course itself requires and is also part of the international legislative process.

The great weakness of that process, i.e. the considerable unevenness in the applicability of even carefully formulated conventional law, due in part to reservations and options but largely to the quantitative and technical incapability of many states to deal with the increasing flow of international legislation, should be recognized and countered by effective measures to assist states, particularly the developing ones, in becoming parties to and in absorbing into their domestic legal systems the considerable body of existing conventional environmental law, and then to perform the same service in respect of later additions to the canon.

Because of the great expertise, energy, and sometimes the material resources of national and international environmental NGOs, these should be encouraged and permitted to participate as far as possible in all aspects of the relevant international legislative process: the studies required to decide whether to initiate the process in respect of a particular problem; the formulation of instruments designed to deal with that problem; the adoption of such instruments by competent international bodies; and finally the rapid ratification of such instruments by as many as possible of the potential parties thereto. Such encouragement will also make the process more responsive than most international actions to the aspirations and concerns of the world's people.

It has been pointed out that the international legislative process is anything but too rigid; indeed, its formlessness and flexibility may be disturbing to some who, used to well-established but narrowly constrained municipal procedures, consider anything so variegated as multilateral treaty-making to constitute not really a "process" but at best unstructured diplomatic interactions that may fortuitously result in some useful codification or progressive development of international law but cannot really be relied on to do so. Actually, however, while an overall survey of the process may, at least at first sight, be confusing because of its manifold manifestations, certain specialized law-making units have over the years evolved rather precise and predictable legislative methodologies, which those who are experienced can rely on and use. However, and generally speaking this should be deemed an advantage, with the possible exception of a few organizations and fora, the multilateral treaty-making process remains flexible enough so that it can be adapted to the needs of particular situations and proposed instruments. Moreover, being flexible, it can more easily adapt as improvements are suggested, either by the imagination of some of the participants or arising out of institutional experience or news of the experience of other similar bodies. In short, international institutions are basically young and can and do learn,[59] and that learning generally – unless occasionally false lessons are absorbed – results in improving the operations of these organizations.

---

59. *See* the annex to chapter 11, *infra*.

There is another, perhaps more surprising, observation to make about international law-making. One might believe that in a process largely carried out by the instructed and to a considerable extent free-ly replaceable governmental representatives, there would not be much room for individual initiative or merit, or cause to assign indi-vidual credit – or blame – for the success or failure of a particular leg-islative enterprise. Such a conclusion, however, would be quite wrong. The international legislature ultimately consists of people who interact, often for many years, sometimes in respect of many political enterprises and sometimes predominantly in respect of one. This in-teraction breeds loyalties both to persons and more often to causes that may transcend a particular representative's instructions and espe-cially the vaguely expressed directives that emanate from most gov-ernments in respect of international political enterprises far from home.[60] There are therefore any number of examples of how a par-ticular individual, or sometimes several, will decisively and essentially personally influence the formulation of a particular treaty. These per-sons more often than not are representatives of minor states (the ma-jor ones tending to control their delegates more closely) who through their merits (usually including a dose of longevity) capture key posi-tions in developing some instrument: chair of an influential expert group, of a drafting committee, or of a more prominent body such as the formulating organ; indeed, often they work their way up, tending to a particular draft instrument in different and sometimes ever-more prominent roles over the years. Alternatively such persons may occupy leading positions (e.g. executive head) in the competent sec-retariat or unit. In other instances, strong support has come from rank outsiders, who are persistent and skilful in lobbying or pressur-ing governments or their representatives in some self-adopted cause on behalf of a public-spirited body. In any event, an instrument or project that attracts the support of one or more talented and dedi-cated legislative heroes, preferably from nominally opposite camps, is much more likely to succeed than can be predicted by a sober polit-ical analysis of the supposed interests of power blocks.

---

60. Social scientists have characterized these as "epistemic communities"; *see*, e.g., J. Ruggie, 29 *International Organization*, 557 (1975); P. Haas, 43 *International Organization*, 377 (1989).

Annex

Chronology of principal development in international legislation concerning the atmosphere

A. *Protection against transboundary air pollution*[1]

1969	*Eric Oden, studies on acidification of Scandinavian lakes by long-range air pollution*
Jun. 1972	*Swedish case-study on "Air Pollution Across National Boundaries: Impact on the Environment of Sulfur in Air and Precipitation" (submitted to the Stockholm Conference)*
18 Jun. 1974	**OECD Council Recommendation on Guidelines for Action to Reduce Emissions of Sulphur Oxides and Particulate Matters from Fuel Combustion in Stationary Sources**
14 Nov. 1974	**OECD Council Recommendation on Measures Required for Further Air Pollution Control**
1 Aug. 1975	**Helsinki Final Act of the Conference on Security and Co-operation in Europe (calling, *inter alia*, for promoting international law in respect of long-range air pollution)**
1977	*OECD study on lang-range transboundary air pollution in Europe*
1978	Establishment of the Co-operative Programme for Monitoring and Evaluation of the Long-Range Transmission of Air Pollutants in Europe (EMEP), by ECE in co-operation with WMO and UNEP
1978	Negotiation of a long-range transboundary air pollution convention within the framework of

1. Code:
   Scientific Developments and Meetings Not Part of International Legislative Process

   Legal and Political Meetings and Statements Not Part of Non-Regional International Legislative Process

   Meetings Relating to the International Legislative Process

   LEGAL INSTRUMENTS ADOPTED

	the Senior Advisers to ECE Governments on Environmental Problems
13 Nov. 1979	CONVENTION ON LONG-RANGE TRANSBOUNDARY AIR POLLUTION, GENEVA
Jul. 1982	Ministerial Conference on Acidification, Stockholm
28 Sep. 1984	PROTOCOL ON LONG-TERM FINANCING OF THE CO-OPERATIVE PROGRAMME FOR MONITORING AND EVALUATION OF THE LONG-RANGE TRANSMISSION OF AIR POLLUTANTS IN EUROPE, GENEVA
21 Mar. 1984	Ministerial Conference on Acid Rain, Ottawa
27 Jun. 1984	Multilateral Conference on Environment, Munich
8 Jul. 1985	PROTOCOL ON THE REDUCTION OF SULPHUR EMISSIONS OR THEIR TRANSBOUNDARY FLUXES BY AT LEAST 30 PER CENT, HELSINKI
Oct. 1985–Aug. 1988	Negotiation of a Protocol on Nitrogen Oxides
31 Oct. 1988	PROTOCOL CONCERNING THE CONTROL OF EMISSIONS OF NITROGEN OXIDES OR THEIR TRANSBOUNDARY FLUXES, SOFIA
31 Oct. 1988	Declaration on 30 Per Cent Reduction of Nitrogen Oxide Emissions, Sofia
24 Nov. 1988	**EEC Directive on the Limitation of Emissions of Certain Pollutants in the Air from Large Combustion Plants**
Feb. 1989–Aug. 1991	Negotiation of a Protocol on Volatile Organic Compounds
18 Nov. 1991	PROTOCOL CONCERNING THE CONTROL OF EMISSIONS OF VOLATILE ORGANIC COMPOUNDS OR THEIR TRANSBOUNDARY FLUXES, GENEVA

B. *Protection of the ozone layer*

| 1973–1974 | *Richard Stolarski and Ralph Cicerone, studies of release of chlorine in the atmosphere* |

1974	*Mario Molina and Sherwood Rowland, studies of CFCs in the atmosphere and stratosphere*
8 Mar. 1977	**UNEP's World Plan of Action on the Ozone Layer, Washington**
Apr. 1980	**UNEP Governing Council resolution on restriction of CFC usage**
May 1981	UNEP Governing Council resolution initiating negotiations towards an ozone agreement
1981	Meeting of legal experts convened by UNEP, Montevideo
Jan. 1982	First session of Ad Hoc Working Group of Legal and Technical Experts for the Preparation of a Global Framework Convention for the Protection of the Ozone Layer, convened by UNEP, Stockholm (NB: There were seven sessions, until 1985)
1983	**Establishment of the "Toronto Group"**
22 Mar. 1985	VIENNA CONVENTION ON THE PROTECTION OF THE OZONE LAYER
1986	*WMO/UNEP Report on Atmospheric Ozone*
May 1986	*Workshop on CFC production and consumption trends, convened by EEC and UNEP, Rome*
Sep. 1986	*Workshop on alternative regulatory strategies on protection of ozone, convened by USA and UNEP, Leesburg (USA)*
Dec. 1986	First negotiating session on a protocol to the Vienna Convention, convened by UNEP, Geneva
Feb. 1987	Second negotiating session on a protocol to the Vienna Convention, convened by UNEP, Vienna
Apr. 1987	Third negotiating session on a protocol to the Vienna Convention, convened by UNEP, Geneva

Jun. 1987	Meeting of heads of key delegations, convened by UNEP, Brussels
8–13 Sep. 1987	Preliminary meetings preceding the Montreal Conference, convened by UNEP, Montreal
16 Sep. 1987	MONTREAL PROTOCOL ON SUBSTANCES THAT DEPLETE THE OZONE LAYER
Apr.– May 1989	First Meeting of the Parties to the Vienna Convention and the Montreal Protocol, Helsinki
27–29 Jun. 1990	Second Meeting of the Parties to the Vienna Convention and the Montreal Protocol, London (adoption of ADJUSTMENTS AND AMENDMENTS TO MONTREAL PROTOCOL)
Jun. 1991	Third Meeting of the Parties to the Vienna Convention and the Montreal Protocol, Nairobi (also Executive Committee of Interim Multilateral Fund)
Oct. 1992	Fourth Meeting of the Parties to the Vienna Convention and the Montreal Protocol, Copenhagen

C. *Protection of the climate*

12–23 Feb. 1979	**First World Climate Conference, convened by WMO**
9–15 Oct. 1985	**International Conference on the Assessment of the Role of Carbon Dioxide and Other Greenhouse Gases in Climate Variations and Associated Impacts, Villach (Austria), sponsored by UNEP, WMO, and ICSU**
28 Sep.– 2 Oct. 1986	**Conference on Developing Policies for Responding to Future Climatic Change, Villach (Austria)**
1986	**Establishment of the UN system inter-agency Advisory Group on Greenhouse Gases (AGGE)**
Nov. 1987	**Policies Issues Workshop on Developing Policies for Responding to Climatic Change, Bellagio (Italy)**

27–30 Jun. 1988	**Conference on the Changing Atmosphere: Implications for Global Security, convened by the Canadian Department of External Affairs, Toronto**
Nov. 1988	First session of the Intergovernmental Panel on Climate Change (IPCC), Geneva, established by UNEP and WMO
6 Dec. 1988	**UNGA Resolution: Protection of Global Climate for Present and Future Generations of Mankind (A/RES/43/53)**
20–22 Feb. 1989	**Meeting of Legal and Policy Experts on the Changing Atmosphere, convened by the Canadian Department of External Affairs, Ottawa**
11 Mar. 1989	**Declaration of the Hague**
28–30 Jun. 1989	Second session of IPCC, Nairobi
7 Nov. 1989	**Noordwijk Declaration of the Ministerial Conference on Atmospheric Pollution and Climate Change**
1990	Third session of IPCC
27–31 Aug. 1990	Fourth session of IPCC, Sundsvall (Sweden)
29 Oct.– 7 Nov. 1990	**Second World Climate Conference, convened by WMO, Geneva, and Ministerial Declaration**
21 Dec. 1990	Establishment of Intergovernmental Negotiating Committee for a Framework Convention on Climate Change (A/RES/45/212)
4–14 Feb. 1991	First session of the Intergovernmental Negotiating Committee for a Framework Convention on Climate Change, Washington
13–15 Mar. 1991	Fifth session of IPCC, Geneva
19–28 Jun. 1991	Second session of the Intergovernmental Negotiating Committee for a Framework Convention on Climate Change

9–20 Sep. 1991	Third session of the Intergovernmental Negotiating Committee for a Framework Convention on Climate Change
29–31 Oct. 1991	Sixth session of IPCC
9–20 Dec. 1991	Fourth session of the Intergovernmental Negotiating Committee for a Framework Convention on Climate Change
10–12 Feb. 1992	Seventh session of IPCC, Geneva
18–28 Feb. 1992	Fifth session of the Intergovernmental Negotiating Committee for a Framework Convention on Climate Change, New York
Apr. 1992	Informal consultations among principal delegations, Paris
30 Apr.– 8 May 1992	Sixth session of the Intergovernmental Negotiating Committee for a Framework Convention on Climate Change

3

Changing requirements for international information

Peter S. Thacher

In essence, sustainable development is a process of change in which the exploitation of resources, the direction of investments, the orientation of technological development, and institutional change are all in harmony and enhance both current and future potential to meet human needs and aspirations.[1]

Introduction

This chapter addresses the evolving role of information in a regime to deal with international environmental issues that must now be adjusted to reduce global risk and achieve sustainable development. The goal set by governments at the 1972 UN Conference on Human Environment was not merely to be better informed about changing environmental conditions but also to "protect and enhance the quality of the human environment for present and future generations."[2]

1. World Commission on Environment and Development, *Our Common Future,* 46 (Oxford University, 1987) (hereinafter *Our Common Future*).
2. "Man . . . bears a solemn responsibility to protect and improve the environment for present and future generations." Stockholm Declaration on the Human Environment of the United Nations Conference on the Human Environment, 16 June 1972, 11 *I.L.M.* 1416 (1972) (hereinafter Stockholm Declaration), at Principle 1. "Convinced of the need for prompt and effective implementation by governments and the international community of measures designed to safeguard and enhance the environment for the benefit of present and future generations of man." G.A. Res. 2997 (1972).

Thus, information is sought both *for better understanding* of environmental conditions and trends and *to serve as a basis for planning and managing* human activities to protect and enhance environmental conditions. In the framework governments approved for the 1972 Stockholm Action Plan these were identified as "assessment" and "management" functions.

Parallel with great technical and social advances in recent years that improve access and free exchange of environmental information, there have been several developments that pose new difficulties in promoting the free flow of pertinent information at the international level:

1. As the 1972 environmental agenda has broadened the initial focus on pollution has given way to international concern about natural resources and, now, poverty, population, and a host of *environment-and-development* issues; all these touch more directly on domestic matters than does pollution.

2. Improved assessment results since 1972 have highlighted the need to take action to counter deterioration, to slow accumulation of pollutant levels and high rates of loss of soils, forests, etc., i.e., to move from "assessment" to "management" actions, some of which carry economic and other difficult implications.

3. "Global change" is now recognized as driven by local action or lack of it, and therefore the place where corrective steps are needed is closer to home than far away places like Antarctica and the high seas.

Conditions favouring "transparency," "glasnost," and public access to information have greatly improved since 1972, both nationally and internationally, and the end of the Cold War removes social constraints from broad application of new technologies that can improve availability of information useful for reducing global risk and putting development on a sustainable basis. However, the kinds of information sought for the goals to be set in 1992 will be challenging, especially since the parallel issues of *environment and development* are now formally joined for the first time, and we are forced to recognize links between *local development* action and *global environmental change*; even national or local actions taken in the name of "development" – to improve the quality of life for present generations or to satisfy consumption demands of the affluent[3] – can pose risks of *global* as well as *local* impacts.

3. "Development" is not restricted to so-called "developing countries"; it embraces economic

As always, the future will not be like the past. And now, as the Brundtland Commission alerts us, the rate and scale of global change is itself changing:

Our human world must make room in a finite environment for another human world. The population could stabilize at between 8 billion and 14 billion sometime next century. . . . More than 90 percent of the increase will occur in the poorest countries, and 90 percent of that growth in already bursting cities. Economic activity has multiplied to create a $13 trillion world economy, and this could grow five- or tenfold in the coming half-century. Industrial production has grown more than fiftyfold over the past century, four-fifths of this growth since 1950. Such figures reflect and presage profound impacts upon the biosphere, as the world invests in houses, transport, farms, and industries. Much of the economic growth pulls raw material from forests, soils, seas, and waterways.[4]

As attention turns to the new agenda at the 1992 UN Conference on Environment and Development in Rio, a major challenge will be to take advantage of new openness and freedom of access to information under conditions of transparency and glasnost in ways that encourage international cooperation and avoid stimulating resistance by those who feel at a disadvantage. New requirements for information to understand and reduce global risk, while putting economic and social development on a sustainable basis, may appear threateningly intrusive to information-poor states, especially when outsiders are better informed than domestic officials and experts. This suggests the desirability of a major international effort to strengthen human and institutional capabilities in relation to gathering and analysing information for domestic as well as international use so that all states can participate on a more equal basis without feeling threatened by freely available information about subjects they consider sensitive in terms of national interests.

In any case, since sound information is a necessary basis for negotiation, it follows that information competence must be strengthened internationally if wide participation is sought for international agreements to cope with global change.[5]

---

and social growth in all countries, including *over*development in some, where destructive lifestyles can have more severe global environmental consequences than poverty.

4. *Our Common Future, supra* note 1.

5. Current calculations suggest that even if all industrialized countries curtailed their CO_2 emissions, sheer demographic growth elsewhere – with no change in per-capita energy consumption – would only delay global heating commitments by a few decades.

This chapter outlines changing information requirements since 1972, some of which evolved out of improved understanding and assessments launched at the Stockholm Conference, which, in turn, laid the basis for the new environment-and-development agenda and the goals of "sustainable development" and coping with "global change." Principles have been proposed that could guide future work in this area, but, as a practical matter, and given the nature of information that will be needed, it will probably be necessary first to use existing mechanisms to improve human and institutional skills in the field of information.

Changing environmental information requirements

The kinds of information needed to support the 1972 goal have been identified and considerable progress made since then on cooperative programmes to produce credible information about environmental conditions and trends, assessments of their significance for present and future generations, and ways to present it in forms that can influence planning and decision-making.

The most successful example concerns pollutants whose *global* significance has been highlighted by research and monitoring programmes initiated in 1972 to cope with risks to stratospheric ozone that were then seen in terms of high-flying, second-generation supersonic aircraft.[6] A study of such "outer limits" as the ozone content of the stratosphere was proposed in 1973 by UNEP's first Executive Director, Maurice Strong, and as speculation developed over the possible role of CFCs, UNEP and a number of specialized agencies (including WMO, WHO, FAO, Unesco) and others (like ICSU and the International Chamber of Commerce) drew up a "World Plan of Action on the Ozone Layer" that was approved by governments in 1977. Cooperative investigations under this plan led to the discovery of the Antarctic Hole phenomenon and negotiation of the 1985 Vienna Convention and the 1987 Montreal Protocol; continuing information flows support its ongoing revision.

Although CO_2 was recognized over 100 years ago as a potential greenhouse gas, comparable levels of understanding have not yet

---

6. The Stockholm Conference "Pollutants" paper called for research on "stratospheric transport and distribution of ozone . . . as a result of high flying aircraft" to understand "the influence of human activities on the global climate." United Nations Conference on the Human Environment, Identification and Control of Pollutants of Broad International Significance. U.N. Doc. A/Conf. 48/8 at p.71 (7 Jan. 1972).

been achieved with regard to climate change, but negotiations on a possible convention are under way as part of the preparations for UNCED.

Pollutants of international significance at the *regional* scale have also been investigated under cooperative programmes initiated since Stockholm, such as "acid rain," for which region-wide monitoring programmes in Europe led to the 1979 Long-Range Transboundary Air Pollution Convention and subsequent protocols.

Many pollutants, such as those commonly found in the workplace or in urban concentrations, have purely local effects and are therefore not often dealt with by international agreements but nonetheless benefit from international cooperation because many countries share similar problems. Considerable progress has been made in improving knowledge and making it available in forms that aid those trying to cope with these problems at the national and local levels.

But whereas concern over pollutants dominated the environmental agenda at Stockholm, since then attention has turned increasingly to natural-resource problems such as desertification, deforestation, and the loss of biological diversity. These problems often result from deliberate domestic practices to exploit natural resources that are clearly within national jurisdiction, and since the practices are directly relevant to national development goals and their external effects are less visible than in the case of pollutants, there are more obstacles to the free flow of information about them than about pollutants, whether the information is needed for assessment or for management purposes.

International cooperation to produce and exchange scientific information for the purpose of better understanding started long before the Stockholm Conference and in many important ways shaped what followed in the UN Environment Programme (UNEP). This experience will undoubtedly be taken into account when, 20 years later, far more difficult issues are tackled at the 1992 "Earth Summit" in Rio. What started out as a 20-year review of progress since the Stockholm Conference has been given a more demanding task by the UN General Assembly; namely, to "elaborate strategies and measures to halt and reverse the effects of environmental degradation in the context of strengthened national and international efforts to promote sustainable and environmentally sound development in all countries."[7]

7. G.A. Res. 44/228 (December 1989).

Better understanding of environmental conditions and trends

Many international assessment activities launched under UNEP's "Earthwatch" programme since 1972 drew on well-established procedures; international scientific activities in Antarctica started in the last century, and cooperative investigations in the fields of meteorology and health were well advanced long before the UN came into being.

Antarctica shows how cooperative scientific research contributed to an international regime of the sort that may now be developing for "sustainable development" and "global change."

Under the first International Polar Year of 1882–1883, 12 nations studied meteorology, geomagnetism, and the Aurora Borealis and Australis. The clear advantages of cooperative research and observations led, in 1932–1933, to the Second International Polar Year, in which 44 countries joined forces for scientific work in the polar regions. Then, in 1957, the proposed Third Polar Year was converted into the International Geophysical Year (IGY), during which 12 countries established 48 new stations in Antarctica, while man's first artificial satellite – Sputnik – demonstrated the feasibility of synoptic observation of Earth phenomena on a global scale. Only two years later, in 1959, the US convened the 11 other states that had collaborated in Antarctica for negotiation of what became the 1959 Antarctica Treaty.[8] This treaty paved the way for much that was to follow, including the 1967 Outer Space Treaty,[9] and laid the basis for the concept that commons areas beyond national jurisdiction deserved protection under international legal regimes.

IGY successes in 1957–1958 also inspired similar programmes in related fields, notably the International Biological Programme that was subsequently converted into Unesco's Man and the Biosphere (MAB) programme, and highlighted the need to protect natural resources such as biological diversity; this information laid the basis for a convention now being negotiated to protect biological diversity.

With this background it was not surprising that when governments

8. For a recent review of background and prospects, *see* L. Kimball, *Southern Exposure: Deciding Antarctica's Future* (World Resources Institute, 1990).
9. Treaty on Principles Governing the Activities of States in the Exploration and Use of Outer Space, Including the Moon and Other Celestial Bodies, 27 Jan. 1967, 610 U.N.T.S. 205, 18 U.S.T. 2410, T.I.A.S. 6347.

set up a new Environment Fund in 1972, they defined its use primarily in terms of supporting *assessment* functions with a rich information component, while giving less-specific attention to other purposes – such as improved management and public awareness. The new fund was to support

regional and global monitoring, assessment and data-collecting systems, including, as appropriate, costs for national counterparts; the improvement of environmental quality management; environmental research; information exchange and dissemination; public education and training; assistance for national, regional and global environmental institutions; the promotion of environmental research and studies for the development of industrial and other technologies best suited to a policy of economic growth compatible with adequate environmental safeguards; and such other programmes as the Governing Council may decide upon.[10]

In carrying out these "programmes of general interest," the Assembly directed that "due account should be taken of the special needs of the developing countries," and a major portion of UNEP's "catalytic" funding ever since has been for this purpose, as in supporting research and monitoring stations in developing-country regions under UNEP's Global Environmental Monitoring System (GEMS).[11]

UNEP's "Earthwatch" programmes have proven their worth by developing reliable data on global environmental conditions and trends ranging from pesticide levels in human tissue and methyl mercury levels in regional fisheries, to rates of loss of arable soil and changes in the mass balance of glaciers as an indicator of climate change. These activities are now ready for expansion and there is widespread agreement on the need for major reinforcement of UNEP's capacity to take the lead in providing "early warning" of major environmental risks, assessing these risks and helping states to develop cooperative measures required to reduce them or mitigate the consequences – such as through contingency planning.

10. These examples are specified in the enabling General Assembly Resolution for UNEP and the Environment Fund, G.A. Res. 2997 (December 1972).
11. Although the bulk of UNEP's "catalytic" funding stimulates action in developing countries, it also supports activities in industrialized countries. An example was the assistance provided to laboratories in western Europe under the 1977 Cooperative Programme for Monitoring and Evaluation of the Long-Range Transmission of Air Pollutants in Europe (EMEP) as a joint ECE/WMO/UNEP venture that prepared the way for the 1979 Convention on Long-Range Transboundary Air Pollution, which was followed by protocols on EMEP (in 1984) as well as on specific atmospheric pollutants.

But to serve these purposes information must be assessed and converted into credible statements about conditions and trends and their significance for human well-being. To cope with scientific uncertainty about likely changes and basic cause-and-effect relationships – that often cross over sectoral lines – assessment processes have relied on international groups of experts to assemble the best scientific capabilities.

A major problem is the large number of countries that lack human and institutional capabilities to gather information and assess its significance in terms of local planning and decision-making. UNDP's "Sustainable Development Network" is intended to address this problem and will undoubtedly figure prominently at UNCED, as will the new Global Environment Facility, discussed below.

The growing influence of *international* experts working with international civil servants in the UN system reflects the fact that even highly developed countries gain by pooling their expertise and setting up international groups of experts for this purpose.

An early such group was the UN Scientific Group of Experts on the Effects of Atomic Radiation – UNSCEAR – set up by the General Assembly some 30 years ago.[12] Their work contributed to negotiation of one of the few international agreements that measurably lowered global risk; the Partial Test Ban Treaty of 1963 reduced man-made radiation from about 7 per cent of natural background radiation in the early 1960s to less than 1 per cent in 1980.[13]

Another group well-known in environmental circles is GESAMP – the Group of Experts on Scientific Effects of Marine Pollution, whose third decadal review was recently published.[14] Experts in GESAMP are selected and appointed by international organizations to provide advice and assessments they need to improve the effectiveness of the UN system in dealing with related matters. GESAMP assessments have gained increasing credibility, in part because its expert members – many of whom come from government institutions – are expressly working in an expert, non-instructed status.

---

12. In 1988 the UN General Assembly commended UNSCEAR for its three-decade contribution to "wider knowledge and understanding of the levels, effects and risks of atomic radiation and for fulfilling its original mandate with scientific authority and independence of judgement." G.A. Res. 43/55 (1988).
13. *Radiation: Doses, Effects, Risks*, tables 4.1, 4.7 (UNEP, 1985).
14. Group of Experts on Scientific Effects of Marine Pollution, *The State of the Marine Environment* (UNEP, 1990). This document was drawn on extensively in *World Resources 1990–91* (World Resources Institute, 1991).

More recently, the Intergovernmental Panel on Climate Change (IPCC) was set up by the governing bodies of WMO and UNEP in order to harness scientific and other expertise in preparing the 1990 Second World Climate Conference. Three working groups were established – on research, on climate impacts, and on possible response strategies. In effect, IPCC supplanted the work of an earlier interagency group – the Advisory Group on Greenhouse Gases (AGGG) – in which experts chosen by WMO, UNEP, and ICSU provided scientific advice and issued a consensus warning in 1985 about the likelihood of climate change and the need to study the implications.[15] An important difference between the AGGG and IPCC is that IPCC experts are under government instruction, whereas those in AGGG – whose message was clearly unpalatable to some governments – were not.[16]

"Impartiality" of international organizations and civil servants has been demanded and contested ever since the League of Nations, but here the issue is whether scientific judgement should be in the hands of *instructed* or *uninstructed* experts. Clearly it is useful to engage government experts whether or not under instructions in the study of policy matters, especially when the economic consequences may be severe, as in the case of policy responses to climate warming. But problems of credibility arise when international expert groups on scientific assessments are dominated by experts from developed countries or by "instructed" experts – whether from government, industry, or various "pressure" or "special-interest" groups. In the production of assessments of environmental conditions and trends the presence of such experts is bound to raise questions as to the reliability and credibility of the final product and thereby reduce its ability to help decision makers.[17]

15. *An Assessment of the Role of Carbon Dioxide and of Other Greenhouse Gases in Climate Variations and Associated Impacts* (statement issued at the Villach Conference) (WMO, October 1985).
16. Consensus on "current basic scientific understanding" was reached at Villach on estimated rates of global warming and its consequences. Also included were recommendations that governments "should take into account the results of this assessment in their policies on social and economic development" and that "support for the analysis of policy and economic options should be increased," including the "widest possible range of social responses aimed at preventing or adapting to climate change should be identified, analyzed, and evaluated. . . . "*Id.*
17. The UN system and associated scientific institutions can draw on more extensive experience than most governments in fields such as epidemiology and toxicity studies, yet their experts

As the scope of required information expands from scientific to include economic and social data, it will be increasingly desirable to broaden participation in international assessments and strengthen strict peer-review proceedings that are fully "transparent." This is merely an extension of the increasing role of international non-governmental organizations (INGOs) in partnership with the UN system – like ICSU's role with WMO and UNEP in climate assessment, and IUCN's role alongside UNEP and FAO in drawing up action plans to protect tropical forests and biological diversity. But national NGOs also are playing roles of greater significance, and their participation may be critical when it comes to trying to apply international findings locally, where decisions are made that determine whether or not sustainable development can be achieved.

International environmental impact assessments?

For over two decades the conventional approach to reducing harmful risks has been first to improve "assessment" processes of monitoring, research, and information exchange so that current environmental conditions and trends can be measured and their significance for human well-being weighed, and then to find ways to incorporate this information into "management" decisions to make them less harmful.[18]

Accordingly, attention has focused on the need to develop environmental information and integrate it in development planning processes so as, in the words of the World Commission on Environment and Development (WCED), "to make development sustainable – to ensure that it meets the needs of the present without compromising the ability of future generations to meet their own needs."[19]

---

are constantly pressured by "instructed" experts on such topics as safe levels of pesticides, and information that might be politically or economically distasteful is sometimes withheld by states, just as is information about communicable diseases that can affect tourist revenues. This can lead to tension between international civil servants and the governments they serve, as well as with experts representing special-interest groups.

18. For an early review *see* ICSU/SCOPE, *Environmental Impact Assessment: Principles and Procedures* (SCOPE, Report No. 5, 2nd ed. 1979).

19. *Our Common Future, supra* note 1 at 8 (Overview: "From One Earth to One World"). *See also* the earlier definition of "conservation" in International Union for the Conservation of Nature and Natural Resources (IUCN), United Nations Environment Programme (UNEP), World Wildlife Fund (WWF), *World Conservation Strategy: Living Resource Conservation for Sustainable Development* (1980) (hereinafter *World Conservation Strategy*).

Considerable progress has been made in refining this approach and applying it nationally at the project level in what are called "Environmental Impact Assessment" (EIA) procedures.[20] Growing awareness of international risks arising from local acts suggests that EIA procedures should now be strengthened and applied internationally, at least where international financial assistance is being provided. This leads to contentious issues about interference in domestic affairs and "conditionality" in assistance.

The obligation to avoid harmful external impacts has been evolving since Stockholm. It has long been recognized that *local* actions can have environmental effects far beyond the place (and time) of origin, and nations were able to agree at the 1972 Environment Conference on the principle of responsibility not to cause external damage:

States have, in accordance with the Charter of the United Nations and the principles of international law, the sovereign right to exploit their own resources pursuant to their own environmental policies, and the responsibility to ensure that activities within their jurisdiction or control do not cause damage to the environment of other States or of areas beyond the limits of national jurisdiction.[21]

But state sensitivities on this issue were highlighted at Stockholm when an "information" principle was approved calling for promotion of scientific research and support for "the free flow of up-to-date scientific information . . . to facilitate the solution of environmental problems. . . ."[22] It was noteworthy that this principle could only be adopted after deletion of a disputed portion:

Relevant information must be supplied by States on activities or developments within their jurisdiction or under their control whenever they believe, or have reason to believe, that such information is needed to avoid the risk of significant adverse effects on the environment in areas beyond their national jurisdictions.[23]

---

20. Note that comparable procedures, and the information to support them, have not yet been developed to apply at the *policy* level.
21. Stockholm Declaration, *supra* note 2 at Principle 21.
22. *Id.* at Principle 20.
23. Report of the Stockholm Conference, UN Doc. A/CONF.48/14/Rev.1, paragraph 331. Note also unresolved amendments by Brazil and by 18 other developing countries. Earlier negotiation of General Assembly resolution language having to do with "freedom of scientific research" had shown growing awareness by developing countries that they were not benefiting as much from equal access to such information as were better-organized corporations interested, for example, in negotiating for mineral-exploration rights.

Despite the reluctance of many states as a matter of principle to release information on possible external environmental impacts, when the issue arose in specific terms at a regional level agreement was possible; a provision was incorporated into the 1978 Kuwait Convention under UNEP's Regional Seas Programme to the effect that,

each Contracting State shall endeavor to include an assessment of the potential environmental effects in any planning activity entailing projects within its territory, particularly in the coastal areas, which may cause significant risks of pollution in the Sea Area.[24]

A further provision encouraged the development of procedures for disseminating this information with an undertaking to develop technical guidelines "to assist the planning of development projects in such a way as to minimize their harmful impact on the marine environment."[25]

A similar obligation was agreed upon in the Abidjan Convention of 1981, according to which parties "shall develop technical and other guidelines to assist the planning of their development projects in such a way as to minimize their harmful impact on the Convention area," and to include an assessment of potential environmental effects in the area and develop procedures for dissemination of such information.[26]

To encourage the incorporation of assessment information in planning and decision-making for activities that risk environmental impacts, UNEP's Governing Council in 1982 requested that appropriate "guidelines, standards and model legislation" be drawn up in the field of "Environmental Impact Assessment."[27] The resulting 13 principles were approved by UNEP's Governing Council "for use as a basis for preparing appropriate national measures, including legislation, and for international cooperation. . . ."[28]

To ensure that environmental effects are taken fully into account *before* decisions are taken by "the competent authority or authorities," and to encourage reciprocal procedures for information ex-

24. Kuwait Regional Convention for Co-operation on the Protection of the Marine Environment from Pollution, 24 April 1978, 17 *I.L.M.* 511 (1978), at Article XI.
25. *Id.*
26. Abidjan Convention for Co-operation in the Protection and Development of the Marine and Coastal Environment of the West and Central African Region, 23 March 1981, 20 *I.L.M.* 746 (1981), at Article 13.
27. This request was based on recommendations of a meeting of Senior Government Officials Expert in Environmental Law in Montevideo in November 1981.
28. UNEP G.C. Decision 14/25 (June 1987).

change, notification, and consultation between states when proposed activities are likely to have significant transboundary effects, these principles recommend that government agencies, members of the public, experts in relevant disciplines, and interested groups should have an opportunity and time to comment on EIA information before any decision is made; that any such decision should be in writing, state the reasons therefor, and include the provisions, if any, to prevent, reduce, or mitigate damage to the environment, and that:

when information provided as part of an EIA indicates that the environment within another State is likely to be significantly affected by a proposed activity, the State in which the activity is being planned should, to the extent possible: (a) notify the potentially affected State of the proposed activity; (b) transmit to the potentially affected State any relevant information from the EIA, the transmission of which is not prohibited by national laws or regulations; and (c) when it is agreed between the States concerned, enter into timely consultations.[29]

However, a recent hint of continuing sensitivity on this issue is found in a 1989 definition of the term "sustainable development" that was adopted in UNEP's Governing Council and has since been cited in other fora, including the 1990 Climate Conference: "Sustainable development is development that meets the needs of the present without compromising the ability of future generations to meet their own needs *and does not imply in any way encroachment upon national sovereignty.*"[30]

Whereas free exchange of environmental information among technicians is, fortunately, far less difficult in practice than in principle, an examination of the treatment of information exchange in the Law of the Sea Treaty suggests that while state sensitivity about research information is less pronounced for environmental information than for non-environmental information, coastal state sensitivity increases as information gathering approaches land, especially within the exclusive economic zone (EEZ).

For example, under Part XII of the Law of the Sea Treaty on

29. *Id.* at Principles 6, 7, 8, 9, 12; "Environmental Impact Assessment" (UNEP Report No. 9, 1987).
30. UNEP G.C. Decision 15/2, Annex II (May 1989). Note that the Ministerial Declaration adopted at the Second World Climate Conference, Geneva, November 1990, could not refer to the desirability of "sustainable development" as part of the approved global strategy without a footnoted reference to this definition. U.N. Doc. A/45/696/Add 1, para 5.

"Protection and Preservation of the Marine Environment," states are encouraged without qualification to cooperate in scientific research and exchange of information and data about marine pollution (Art. 200) and, "to observe, measure, evaluate and analyse . . . risks or effects of pollution of the marine environment" (Art. 204), and "publish reports of the results obtained" (Art 205).

But under Part XIII on the broader topic of "Marine Scientific Research," international cooperation is to be promoted "in accordance with the principle of respect for sovereignty and jurisdiction and on the basis of mutual benefit" (Art. 242), and much stricter requirements are applied to near-shore activities where coastal states have "the exclusive right to regulate, authorize and conduct marine scientific research in the territorial sea" (Art. 245) and, in their EEZ and continental shelf, have full authority to withhold consent for scientific research when it is "of direct significance for the exploration and exploitation of natural resources, whether living or non-living," among other characteristics (Arts. 245 and 246).[31]

Information to strengthen international agreements

Information – scientific or otherwise – is not static in a changing world and the need for flexibility in international agreements is now well accepted. During negotiation of the London Ocean Dumping Convention in 1971–1972, it became clear that flexibility was needed in selecting substances that require strict international control and in adjusting them to take account of evolving information about their toxicity or other characteristics. This led to the use of "black" and "grey" annexes attached to the formal agreement, with eased provisions for revision of these annexes as new knowledge came to light. This device has been used since then in a number of other treaties, notably in those regulating dumping in regional seas and, most recently, in the 1987 Montreal Protocol[32] and the 1989 Basel Conven-

---

31. The issue of coastal-state sensitivity arises particularly in relation to land-based sources of marine pollution. For a detailed review of early experience, and the way in which information was generated to support negotiations, see S. Kuwabara, *The Legal Regime of the Protection of the Mediterranean against Pollution from Land-Based Sources* (Tycooly International, 1984).
32. Montreal Protocol on Substances that Deplete the Ozone Layer, 16 Sept. 1987, 26 *I.L.M.* 1550 (1987) (hereinafter Montreal Protocol). Annex A lists "Controlled Substances" and their "Ozone Depleting Potential," which are "estimates based on existing knowledge and will be reviewed and revised periodically."

tion on the Control of Transboundary Movements of Hazardous Wastes and Their Disposal.[33]

A recent example of the changing nature and greater intrusiveness of information needed to improve and measure performance under an environmental agreement is found in the 1987 Montreal Protocol on Stratospheric Ozone. Here information is called for on production and consumption levels of controlled substances (including import and export figures), as well as the transfer of such production as permitted under "industrial rationalization" provisions (Articles 1 and 2). Parties are required to provide initial statistical data on production, imports, and exports or "best possible estimates of such data where actual data are not available," and thereafter to

provide statistical data to the secretariat on its annual production (with separate data on amounts destroyed by technologies to be approved by the Parties), imports, and exports to Parties and non-Parties, respectively, of such substances for the year during which it becomes a Party and for each year thereafter. It shall forward the data no later than nine months after the end of the year to which the data relate.[34]

Additional information is called for on "Research, Development, Public Awareness and Exchange of Information":

1. The Parties shall cooperate, consistent with their national laws, regulations and practices and taking into account in particular the needs of developing countries, in promoting, directly or through competent international bodies, research, development and exchange of information on:
(a) best technologies for improving the containment, recovery, recycling or destruction of controlled substances or otherwise reducing their emissions;
(b) possible alternatives to controlled substances, to products containing such substances, and to products manufactured with them;
(c) costs and benefits of relevant control strategies.
2. The Parties, individually, jointly or through competent international bodies, shall cooperate in promoting public awareness of the environmental

---

33. Basel Convention on the Control of Transboundary Movements of Hazardous Wastes and Their Disposal, 22 Mar. 1989, 28 *I.L.M.* 657 (1989) (hereinafter Basel Convention). Article 18 sets up the procedure for additional annexes or amendments that "shall take due account, *inter alia*, of relevant scientific and technical considerations." Such annexes are, by definition, "restricted to scientific, technical and administrative matters." Article 17 spells out the voting procedures for amendments to the Convention, and under Article 18, amendments to them become effective six months from the date of circulation of communication by the Depositary for all Parties that have not submitted a notification of inability to accept them.
34. Montreal Protocol, *supra* note 32 at Article 7.

effects of the emissions of controlled substances and other substances that deplete the ozone layer.

3. Within two years of the entry into force of the Protocol and every two years thereafter, each Party shall submit to the secretariat a summary of the activities it has conducted pursuant to this Article.[35]

There is a corresponding obligation on the secretariat of the Montreal Protocol to "receive and make available, upon request by a Party, data provided pursuant to Article 7, to prepare and distribute regularly to the Parties reports based on information received pursuant to Articles 7 and 9, and to provide, as appropriate, the information and requests referred to (above) to such non-party observers."

The Basel Convention provides another example of new kinds of information parties are obliged to provide:

– to share information with a view to promoting environmentally sound management of hazardous wastes, including "harmonization of technical standards and practices" for their management;
– to cooperate in "monitoring the effects" of waste management on human health and the environment;
– to cooperate in the development of "new environmentally sound low-waste technologies" with a view to "eliminating, as far as practical, the generation of hazardous wastes . . . ";
– to cooperate in the "transfer of technology and management systems" including in "developing the technical capacity among Parties, especially those which may need and request technical assistance in this field";
– to cooperate in developing "appropriate technical guidelines and/or codes of practice."[36]

At a time when some governments are finding it difficult to keep up with reporting requirements under international agreements, the expansion of information sought is adding a burden that will require assistance if all states are to comply.

Ecosystem and resource information with policy implications

Pollutants per se are a significant part of the problem but far from the whole environmental dimension of "global change," especially as food and other shortages reflect population pressures as well as the

35. *Id.* at Article 9
36. Basel Convention, *supra* note 33 at Article 10.

degradation of natural resources and the capacity of natural systems to perform functions vital for human well-being. Now that anthropogenic contributions are seen to be driving global change, non-pollutant environmental impacts are gaining more attention; especially the impact on natural systems of larger numbers of consumers. Information needed to cope with these problems tends to focus on national resources important to a country's economy and is frequently "ecosystem" specific, i.e., it may require aggregation of data across frontiers that can raise concerns about national sovereignty.

This new direction was signalled in 1980 when the General Assembly approved the World Conservation Strategy, in which "conservation" was defined in terms that foreshadowed "sustainable development": "the management of human use of the biosphere so that it may yield the greatest sustainable benefit to present generations while maintaining its potential to meet the needs of future generations."[37]

The strategy raised additional issues that some countries find difficult in that it also encouraged a strong role for local NGOs in collecting and analysing resource information, as well as increased access to planning and decision-making on the part of people who may be affected. This approach was warmly endorsed in the 1987 Brundtland Report.

Over time, monitoring and other assessment functions have significantly improved human *understanding* of processes and trends of change, and attention has focused on providing the kinds of data that should be useful for economic planning and decision-making in the "development" context.[38]

The precautionary principle

The obvious need for caution when proceeding rapidly in the face of uncertainty led ministers from countries of the ECE region meeting in May 1990 to adopt the "Bergen Ministerial Declaration on Sustainable Development in the ECE Region," containing what has since become known as the "precautionary principle":

In order to achieve sustainable development, policies must be based on the precautionary principle. Environmental measures must anticipate, prevent

---

37. World Conservation Strategy, *supra* note 19 at Section 1, Introduction, para 4.
38. A current ICSU/SCOPE project addresses the need to shape information in terms useful for development planning; "Scientific Information for Sustainable Development."

97

and attack the causes of environmental degradation. Where there are threats of serious or irreversible damage, lack of full scientific certainty should not be used as a reason for postponing measures to prevent environmental degradation.[39]

Acknowledging that "environmental problems require greater and more systematic use of science and scientific knowledge," ECE ministers agreed to "invite the international science community to contribute towards the advancement of sustainable development policies and programmes. Scientific analyses and forecasts are especially needed to help identify longer term policy options."

The "symbiotic nature of economy and the environment" was reflected in a call in the Bergen Declaration for development of "sound national indicators for sustainable development to be taken account of in economic policy making" by means of supplementary national accounting systems to reflect as fully as possible the importance of natural resources as depletable or renewable economic assets.[40]

As a measure of sustainability, or the ability of a society to protect the interests and equity of future generations, better indicators than are now available will be needed; for example, a measure of changing ratios between food production and population growth, or of arable soil per capita in those countries unable to afford high-energy food-production techniques.

Education and public awareness were also recognized in the Stockholm Declaration as

. . . essential in order to broaden the basis for an enlightened opinion and responsible conduct by individuals, enterprises and communities in protecting and improving environment in its full human dimensions. It is also essential that mass media of communication . . . disseminate information of an educational nature, on the need to protect and improve the environment in order to enable man to develop in every respect.[41]

In a section of the Bergen Declaration on Awareness Raising and Public Participation, a number of more specific steps for "optimizing

---

39. Bergen Ministerial Declaration on Sustainable Development in the ECE Region, in *Action for a Common Future,* Report on the Regional Conference at Ministerial Level on the Follow-up to the Report of the World Commission on Environment and Development in the ECE Region (Norway Ministry of Environment, 1990), reprinted in 20 *Envt'l Pol'y & L.* 100 (1990), at para. 7.
40. *Id.* at Section II, para. (b) (The Economics of Sustainability).
41. Stockholm Declaration, *supra* note 2 at Principle 19.

democratic decision making related to environment and development issues" are proposed, among them:

- to integrate and use environmental knowledge in all sectors of society;
- to stimulate national and international exchanges of environmental information and foster scientific and technological cooperation in order to achieve sustainable development;
- to encourage . . . schemes for informing the consumer of the environmental qualities and of the risks of industrial products from "cradle to grave";
- to develop further national and international systems of periodic reports of the state of the environment;
- to undertake the prior assessment and public reporting of the environmental impact of projects;
- to reaffirm and build on the CSCE conclusions regarding the rights of individuals, groups and organizations concerned . . . to have access to all relevant information and to be consulted . . . ;
- to develop rules for free and open access to information on the environment; and
- to ensure that members of the public are kept informed and that every effort is extended to consult them and to facilitate their participation in the decision-making process on plans to prevent industrial and technological hazards in areas where they live or work.[42]

Because the Bergen meeting was a regional contribution to the preparations for UNCED, it is likely that these new approaches will be reflected in decisions in 1992, but not all countries are likely to find these new information requirements convenient.[43]

Another current example of expanding information requirements is found in the EEC Council Regulation on the establishment of the European Environment Agency and the European environment information and observation network intended to provide "objective, reliable and comparable information" to enable these governments "to take the requisite measures to protect the environment, to assess

42. Bergen Declaration, *supra* note 39 at Section V (Awareness Raising and Public Participation).
43. A similar conclusion was reached at about the same time by international jurists meeting in Italy who agreed that gaps in international conventions can often be explained as a consequence of inadequate knowledge, and that "the 'react and correct' model should be complemented by a 'forecast and prevent' approach; this would enhance security in global environmental matters." Report of the Siena Forum on International Law of the Environment, 17–21 April 1990.

the results of such measures and to ensure that the public is properly informed about the state of the environment."[44]

In furnishing

information which can be directly used in the implementation of Community environmental policy, . . . priority will be given to the following areas of work: air quality and atmospheric emissions, water quality, pollutants and water resources, the state of the soil, of the fauna and flora, and of biotopes, land use and natural resources, waste management, noise emissions, chemical substances which are hazardous for the environment, and coastal protection.[45]

While an approach along these lines might be highly desirable to reduce global risk, in many regions of the world it would be difficult to find human and institutional capabilities up to the task of providing the required information.

A new regime for sustainable development

Looking back at the 1972 Stockholm Declaration of Principles, the Brundtland Commission suggested in 1987 the need to "consolidate and extend relevant legal principles in a new charter to guide state behaviour in the transition to sustainable development."

Towards this end they suggested that 22 principles should be negotiated, first in a declaration, then in a Convention on Environmental Protection and Sustainable Development. Five of these applied specifically to information:
– cooperation in the exchange of information;
– prior notice of planned activities;
– consultations;
– cooperative arrangements for environmental assessment and protection; and
– cooperation in emergency situations.[46]

Other suggested principles would assert the fundamental human right to an environment adequate for health and well-being; require states to conserve natural resources for the benefit of present and future generations and maintain ecosystems and related ecological

44. EEC Council Regulation: Establishment of the European Environment Agency and the European Environment Information and Observation Network, 7 May 1990, EEC Reg. No. 1210/90 at Article 1, para. 2.
45. *Id.* at Article 3.
46. *Our Common Future, supra* note 1 at Annex 1, Principles 15–19.

100

processes so that benefits are available indefinitely; promote optimum sustainability; establish specific environmental standards and both collect and disseminate data and carry out prior environmental impact assessments and inform all persons in a timely manner who may be affected and grant those persons access to and due process in judicial proceedings.

States also would ensure that natural resources and the environment are an integral part of development planning and would cooperate with other states or through international organizations in fulfilling their obligations. With regard to transboundary aspects, shared natural resources should be used in a reasonable and equitable manner, and serious risks of substantial harm should be prevented or abated and compensated for under special procedures for negotiations between states without discrimination between external and internal detrimental effects. Finally, states should be held responsible under these principles and resolve any disputes peacefully through a step-by-step approach including, as a last resort, a binding process of dispute settlement.

The World Commission was assisted in this work by an Experts Group on Environmental Law that drew up specific recommendations to strengthen the international legal framework in support of sustainable development. In his Foreword to this report, former President of the World Court of Justice, Nagendra Singh, observed that the general principles recommended do not merely apply in areas beyond the limits of national jurisdiction, or in the transboundary context; they are also intended to apply in the entirely domestic domain, and thus purport to break open traditional international law on the use of natural resources or environmental interferences and follow the practice that has developed since the 1948 adoption of the Human Rights Declaration.[47]

Looking to the future this group called for a new UN Commission for Environmental Protection and Sustainable Development based on a membership of "competent individuals serving in a personal capacity...elected preferably by secret ballot by States Parties to the Convention."

The proposed functions of the Commission would be to review regular reports from states and the UN system and other internation-

---

47. Experts Group on Environmental Law of the World Commission on Environment and Development, *Environmental Protection and Sustainable Development – Legal Principles and Recommendations* (Graham & Trotman/Martinus Nijhoff, 1987).

al governmental and non-governmental organizations on actions taken in support of the Convention. The Commission would be empowered to issue periodic public reports, assess and report on alleged violations, and review recommendations for proposed improvements to the Convention and other relevant international agreements.

They also recommended the appointment by the Commission of a UN High Commissioner for Environmental Protection and Sustainable Development with functions similar to an "ombudsman" and "trustee" for the environment, who would assess communications from private entities on compliance or violations of the Convention (and related agreements) and who could submit such cases for consideration by the UN Commission or other appropriate organizations. The High Commissioner would have special responsibilities for areas beyond national jurisdiction, as well as for representing the interests of future generations.

Unfortunately, in the absence of any follow-up to the Commission recommendations, there is no basis on which to judge the feasibility of these far-reaching proposals. Perhaps their feasibility can only be tested after improvements have been made in information-handling capabilities of states now weak in them.

Recent developments

Possible future directions with regard to information are suggested by two other recent developments: a new facility at the World Bank, and the International Geophysical Biological Program. Both developments offer the prospect of mobilizing financial and human resources to strengthen information-handling capabilities in developing countries without which it is difficult to see how a "precautionary" approach could be widely applied.

The Global Environmental Facility (GEF)

In 1989 France proposed at the World Bank that a new special facility be set up alongside, but separate from, the Bank's "soft-loan" affiliate, the International Development Association, with a target of $1–$1.5 billion for concessional aid devoted to preservation of natural resources, protection of atmosphere, energy efficiency, and other activities aimed at reducing global risk and supportive of sustainable development. As agreed in late 1990 by 25 developed and developing countries with the World Bank, UNDP, and UNEP, GEF is a "pilot program to obtain practical experience in promoting and adopting environmentally sound technologies and in strengthening country-specific policy and institutional frameworks to support prudent environmental management."[48] It will also provide operational information relevant in formulating other global conventions and in advancing the agenda that governments will be addressing at UNCED in June 1992. GEF has four objectives:

1. to support energy conservation, the use of energy sources that will not contribute to global warming, forestry management, and reforestation to absorb carbon dioxide in order to limit the increase in greenhouse gas emissions;
2. to preserve areas of rich ecological diversity;
3. to protect international waters where transboundary pollution has had damaging effects on water purity and the marine environment; and
4. to arrest the destruction of the ozone layer by helping countries make the transition from the production and use of CFCs, halons, and other gases to less damaging substitutes.[49]

GEF shows that new concern over "global" risks has led governments to set up new funds to cover the extra costs of specific actions that countries in need of assistance could take in a common effort to reduce global risks. According to this new approach, when such actions should also be taken to reduce *local* risks or impacts, these costs should be covered by normal development funds; only when the costs of these actions can*not* be internalized domestically are they eligible for coverage by GEF funds.

The case is clear that many countries need additional help as an incentive to join a common effort to reduce global risk. The incentive, under both the Montreal Protocol and GEF, is the provision of financial support to cover such aspects as the difference between a fair commercial price for technology to reduce global risk and what the intended user can afford. Hopefully, this approach will reduce abstract arguments about the sanctity of intellectual property to a more practical basis on which progress can be made.

The current appreciation of actions needed at *local* levels to reduce *global* risks – notably concerning depletion of stratospheric ozone by CFCs, and actions to slow the less-certain threat of climate

---

48. *See* World Bank/UNDP/UNEP Press Release issued at the conclusion of the 27–28 Nov. 1990 meeting.
49. *Id.* and working papers for the Paris meeting; *see also* World Bank, *The World Bank and the Environment: First Annual Report* (World Bank, 1990).

change – has led to the identification of technical-assistance costs and capital investments that must be provided if all countries are to join in an agreed attack on the problem. Under present conditions of indebtedness and lack of capital flows into developing countries, the need for greater international financing is clear if *preventive* action is to be taken to reduce risks from future actions in the developing world.

International Geophysical Biological Program (IGBP)

Traditionally, precise data and information requirements for "assessment" purposes have been identified by the relevant scientific community, such as the work of ICSU/SCOPE in helping the design in 1971 of what since became UNEP's Global Environment Monitoring System (GEMS), and current work under ICSU in relation to the forthcoming International Geophysical Biological Program (IGBP), better known as "Global Change," to:

describe and understand the interactive physical, chemical, and biological processes that regulate the total Earth system, the unique environment that it provides for life, the changes that are occurring in this system, and the manner in which they are influenced by human activities.[50]

Along with the World Climate Research Program (WCRP) and other international research efforts, IGBP will address critical unknowns related to global environmental change that can provide insights necessary if future development is to be put on a sustainable basis. Increasingly the needs of non-scientific users are recognized as vital if human impacts on natural systems are to be made less destructive, especially "policy and decision-makers" at the national and local levels, where key decisions are made daily.

An important proposal late in 1990 was "START" – the Global Change System for Analysis, Research, and Training. It calls for major strengthening of regional networks and national capabilities, both to contribute information needed for global assessments and to strengthen local capabilities to employ it for planning.[51] The concept is a world-encompassing system of Regional Research Networks,

---

50. This objective is described in greater detail in *A Study of Global Change* (ICSU Secretariat). *See also Global Change Report No. 12* (1990) for descriptions of the initial core projects, including remote-sensing data requirements for the 1990s and beyond. *Id.* at chapter 10.

51. *Global Change System for Analysis, Research and Training (START),* Report of a Meeting at Bellagio, 3–7 Dec. 1990, IGBP Report No. 15 (Boulder, 1991).

each of which would have a Regional Research Centre to serve as the information centre for the regional network. Each regional centre would engage in five functions supporting national institutes within the region:
- research, including documentation of environmental change
- training
- data management
- synthesis and modelling
- communications between scientists and private and public-sector decision makers.

Looking ahead

Great progress has been made during the past two decades in collecting and sharing information about environmental conditions and trends worldwide. Experience gained with pollution problems is now being applied to natural-resource issues and new accounting methods are being explored to capture values that escape normal economic analysis. With greater insights now available about anthropogenic inputs to "global change," it is clear that environment and development issues are linked and that global environmental issues cannot be resolved in the long run without major reductions of poverty and wasteful consumption.

As was foreseen by the Brundtland Commission, the breadth of information being sought will be difficult as we move from current experience, in which

human activities and their effects were neatly compartmentalized within nations, within sectors (energy, agriculture, trade), and within broad areas of concern (environmental, economic, social). These compartments have begun to dissolve. This applies in particular to the various global "crises" that have seized public concern, particularly over the past decade. These are not separate crises: an environmental crisis, a development crisis, an energy crisis. They are all one.

Further progress in communications and other technical breakthroughs will make the world increasingly "open" to information flows of potentially great value during the transition to sustainable development. And much of this information can reach people at all levels whose day-to-day decisions contribute to global environmental change.

But, despite the unavoidable openness of an "interdependent

world," expanding demands for information may prompt resistance by those who are unable themselves to take full advantage of it and are determined to protect state sovereignty in such matters. To the degree that international finance is required for national development, it is normal that the provision of supporting information will be a condition. Here too, great sensitivity is called for, as well as the provision of additional support to enable countries to strengthen internal capabilities to collect and analyse information pertinent to their own development, as well as to global security. While mechanisms are in place that lay down the rules for private finance, whether in the form of loans or investments, the fact that all countries have a voice in multilateral organizations of the UN system gives them the opportunity to use that system to encourage greater transparency and access to information being shared for the common good, and to negotiate the conditions under which this will flourish.

Clearly, a regime encouraging transparency and free movement of information to support sustainable development can be promoted – if governments wish it – by investing in traditional "technical assistance" programmes in which the UN system has extensive experience to strengthen human and institutional capabilities to handle information useful for sustainable development and global-risk reduction. Partnership in this exercise with the non-governmental scientific and other groups is offered, and financial support might be garnered through GEF.

UNCED provides a unique opportunity to agree on steps to strengthen human and institutional capacities to generate information useful for promoting global security and sustainable development.

4

Emerging principles and rules for the prevention and mitigation of environmental harm

Toru Iwama

Introduction

Traditional norms, principles, and rules of international environmental law, as typically shown in the transfrontier pollution context, centre mainly on how to reconcile the conflicting interests of the concerned states in order to reach an equitable solution. Presumptions inherent in traditional international environmental law are that the concerned states are identifiable and geographically adjacent (i.e., "acting" and "affected" states, upstream and downstream states, etc.); that the effect of pollution is of limited geographical expansion; that it is relatively easy to identify causation between polluting states and victim states; and that damage can be calculated and compensated.

It may be correct to say that in the case of transfrontier pollution, traditional norms, principles, and rules have functioned in an effective way to prevent or mitigate environmental harm and to provide relief through damages. However, traditional norms, principles, and rules will prove to be ineffective in responding to global environmental change. Global environmental change entails a transformation and new formulation of the norms, principles, and rules of international environmental law. In this chapter, an attempt is made to review the traditional principles and rules of prevention and mitigation of pollution or environmental harm, to identify the major characteristics of global environmental change, and to analyse the principles and rules newly emerging in response to such change.

1. Significance and role of principles and rules of prevention and mitigation

Prevention and mitigation are two tools used for the protection of the environment. The principle of prevention purports to prevent specific harms from arising, e.g., alteration of the environment, damage to people or the environment, interference with legitimate and legal uses of the environment, and overload of the assimilative capacity of the environment.[1] The principle of mitigation, on the other hand, purports to minimize the occurrence of such specific harms. Principles of prevention and mitigation work together in the international regulation of pollution or environmental harm.

Prevention is less costly than reparation both in economic and social terms because of the intrinsic nature of pollution or environmental harm – i.e., their long-lasting and irreversible detrimental effects upon people and the environment. Consequently, more importance has been given in international environmental law to the principles of prevention and mitigation than to reparation. While the principle of liability does have a deterrent effect on environmental harm, preventive and mitigative measures have an even more direct and effective deterrent effect.

2. Traditional norms, principles, and rules

The fundamental norms and principles of international environmental law are embodied in customary law regarding the use of a state's territory. The principle of limited territorial sovereignty as expressed in the Roman law "maxim sic utere tuo ut alienum non laedas" means that states cannot use or permit the use of their territories to the detriment of the rights and legitimate interests of other states. This principle is intrinsically related to that of state responsibility: states are responsible for the damage that they cause to other states. The principle of limited territorial sovereignty has been invoked in the

---

1. *See* the definition of pollution, e.g., A.L. Springer, *The International Law of Pollution: Protecting the Global Environment in a World of Sovereign States*, 65–78 (Quorum Books, 1983). Organization for Economic Cooperation and Development, Recommendation (77)28.

transfrontier pollution context by international tribunals, e.g., the Trail Smelter arbitration.[2] It was also incorporated in Principle 21 of the Stockholm Declaration on Human Environment:

States have, in accordance with the Charter of the United Nations and the principle of international law, the sovereign right to exploit their own resources pursuant to their own environmental policies, and the responsibility to ensure that activities within their jurisdiction or control do not cause damage to the environment of other States or of areas beyond the limits of national jurisdiction.[3]

The principle has also been codified into positive principles and rules in various treaty-making processes.

(A) Substantive principles and rules

Substantive principles and rules have been developed in the process of treaty-making on marine pollution, pollution of international rivers and lakes, atmospheric pollution, and the protection and conservation of fauna and flora. The international regulation of these problems has placed emphasis upon prevention rather than upon *ex post facto* remedies. Common legal techniques that are used include the identification of regulated activities and pollutants, the demarcation of the extent of jurisdiction, and the establishment of a regulating method, e.g., total prohibitions or restrictions on the production, trade, consumption, disposal, or emission of certain substances or pollutants, and standard-setting for those purposes.[4]

In contrast, principles and rules of state responsibility have not emerged in environmental treaty law. They are thought to be one of the problems that can be dealt with within the framework of general international law. However, certain treaties on marine pollution and nuclear hazards have established strict civil liability for the ship owner or the operator.[5]

---

2. 3 U.N.R. Intl. Arb. Awards, 1911 (1941).
3. Declaration of the United Nations Conference on the Human Environment, 16 June 1972, 11 *I.L.M.* 1416, 1420.
4. A.C. Kiss, *Survey of Current Developments in International Environmental Law,* 141 (published with the assistance of the Fund for Environmental Studies [by the] IUCN, 1976); A.C. Kiss, *Droit International de L'Environnement,* 349 (A. Pedone, 1989); A.L. Levin, *Protecting the Human Environment: Procedures and Principles for Preventing and Resolving International Controversies,* 131 (UN Institute for Training and Research, 1977).
5. *See,* e.g., Paris Convention on Third Party Liability in the Field of Nuclear Energy, 29 July 1960, 55 A.J.I.L. 1082; Convention on the Liability of Operators of Nuclear Ships and

(B) Procedural principles and rules

Procedural principles and rules have emerged simultaneous to the development of the substantive principles and rules. These procedural principles and rules, both customary and conventional, clarify and/or elaborate upon the procedural duties of due care or diligence of the states to protect the environment. They also supplement the implementation of the objectives of the substantive principles and rules. Examples include the principle of information exchange, the principle of environmental impact assessment, the principle of prior notification, the principle of warning, and the principle of consultation.[6]

3. Characteristics of global environmental change

1. Global environmental change, e.g., rain-forest deforestation, desertification, long-range transfrontier air pollution, including acid rain, marine pollution, destruction of the ozone layer, global climate change, and the endangerment of species, is a common concern of humankind[7] because it will imperil the sustainable basis for human life by threatening the security of the biosphere. Global environmental change is a common concern of present and future generations.[8]

2. Global environmental changes are complex and intrinsically related to each other. For example, global climate change is related to rain-forest deforestation, desertification, ozone-layer depletion, and the extinction of certain species of fauna and flora upon which human survival depends. It is therefore necessary to take a systemic and comprehensive approach to the problems of global environmental change.[9]

Optional Protocol, 25 May 1962, 57 A.J.I.L. 268; the Convention on Civil Liability for Nuclear Damage, 21 May 1963, 2 *I.L.M.* 727; Convention on the Civil Liability for Oil Pollution Damage, 29 Nov. 1969, 9 *I.L.M.* 25.

6. For specific treaties and conventions embodying these principles, see *supra* note 4.

7. The forty-third session of the UN General Assembly recognized in Resolution 43/53 that climate change is a common concern of humankind, since climate is an essential condition that sustains life on earth.

8. E. Brown Weiss, *In Fairness to Future Generations: International Law, Common Patrimony, and Intergenerational Equity* 385 (Transnational/United Nations University, 1989).

9. D.M. Johnston, "Systemic Environmental Damage: The Challenge to International Law and Organization," 12 *Syracuse Journal of International Law and Commerce,* 257 (1985): P.S. Thacher, "International Agreements and Cooperation in Environmental Conservation and Resource Management" (a paper prepared for the Workshop on Managing the Global

3. One aspect of global environmental change, global climate change, is particularly closely related to human activities, i.e., energy consumption and industrial and agricultural production. Hence, it becomes extremely difficult to postulate a trade-off between economic development and environmental protection.

4. Global environmental change is a good example of the fallacy of composition. For example, while rain-forest deforestation is beneficial to the economy of a certain sector of people or to a certain country, its overall effect is a threat to the entire earth and to humankind because it leads to global warming and it endangers ecosystems.

5. Because of complex interactional processes among natural environmental factors, there is a prolonged time-lapse between causes and their effects, e.g., between CFC emissions and the destruction of the ozone layer; between reduction of CFC emissions and its positive effect; between emission of greenhouse gases and global warming; and between reduction of greenhouse gases and its positive effect. Therefore, problems of global environmental change are also matters of intergenerational equity (see, e.g., Brown Weiss's chapter in part IV).

6. The effects of global environmental change are irreversible. It is virtually impossible to remedy injuries to the environment, e.g., extinction of species, destruction of the ozone layer, and climate change. Even if successful remediation is possible, it takes time and can entail staggering costs.

7. The effects of global environmental change, e.g., ozone-layer destruction and climate change, extend worldwide. All people and all states are polluters and victims simultaneously. It is therefore impossible to apply traditional principles of state liability. More importance needs to be given to the principles of prevention and mitigation.

8. The effects of global environmental change threaten to widen the gap between wealthy industrialized states and developing states. While the former may afford to adapt to the changes with their technical and economic capacities, the latter cannot rely on such resources. Thus a need arises for giving both technical and economic assistance to developing countries.

Commons: Decision Making and Conflict Resolution in Response to Climate Change, 1 Aug. 1989), p. 5.

9. Scientific uncertainty is a significant factor in global environmental change. For example, in the case of climate change, the actual degree of contribution by greenhouse gases to the increase of atmospheric temperature and the extent and impacts of the greenhouse effect are not yet precisely known. Yet we cannot wait until a perceived environmental threat becomes an actual harm.

10. In view of the effects of global environmental change, it is necessary to take an anticipatory approach to solving these problems. An emphasis must be placed upon the need for carefully designed and sufficiently organized techniques of prevention and mitigation.[10]

4. Double-track approach as a treaty-making technique

Because of underlying scientific uncertainty regarding the problems of global environmental change, and because there is an urgency to take anticipatory actions to prevent or abate a future environmental harm or risk, it becomes imperative for the Contracting Parties to take all possible preventative actions. To wait for the threat to become an actual problem would be to wait until it is too late.[11]

One treaty-making device commonly used to cope with this situation is called a "double-track" approach. This approach utilizes a framework convention and annexes and/or protocols. The framework convention sets out the general obligations of the Contracting Parties; annexes and protocols are then formulated to the general obligations set by the framework convention. New multilateral treaties on global environmental change follow this approach.

The 1985 Vienna Convention for the Protection of the Ozone Layer provides in Article 2 that:

The Contracting Parties are, in accordance with the means at their disposal and their capabilities, under obligations to:
(a) cooperate by means of systematic observations, research and information exchange in order to better understand and assess the effects of human activities on the ozone layer and human health and the environment from modification of the ozone layer;
(b) adopt appropriate legislative or administrative measures and cooperate in harmonizing appropriate policies to control, limit, reduce or prevent human activities under their jurisdiction or control should it be found that these activities have or are likely to have adverse effects resulting from modification or likely modification of the ozone layer;

10. Johnston, *supra* note 9 at 269.
11. *Id.* at 271.

(c) cooperate in the formulation of agreed measures, procedures and standards for the implementation of this Convention, with a view to the adoption of protocols and annexes;

(d) cooperate with competent international bodies to implement effectively this Convention and protocols to which they are party.

Scientific knowledge on the physical and chemical processes that may modify the ozone layer and affect human health and other biological systems were not evident during the adoption of the Vienna Convention. The Contracting Parties therefore agreed to cooperate under the general terms as stated *supra*. In contrast, the 1987 Montreal Protocol on Substances that Deplete the Ozone Layer set out concrete control measures by which the Parties agreed to reduce the calculated amount of consumption of the controlled substances.

Another example is the 1979 ECE Convention on Long-Range Transfrontier Air Pollution. In Articles 2–5, the Contracting Parties agreed in general terms to protect humans and their environment and to cooperate in information exchange, consultation, research, and monitoring. Article 9 in particular stresses the need for the implementation of the existing "Cooperative Programme for the Monitoring and Evaluation of the Long-Range Transmission of Air Pollutants in Europe" (EMEP). In 1984, the Protocol was adopted for the long-term financing of EMEP. And in 1985 and 1989, protocols were adopted respectively for the reduction of sulphur emissions or their transboundary fluxes by at least 30 per cent, and for the control of emissions of nitrogen oxides or their transboundary fluxes. Many support the argument that the Vienna Convention and the Montreal Protocol are a paradigm for international cooperation to challenge global climate change.[12]

5. Emerging principles and rules of prevention and mitigation

Norms, principles, and rules of international environmental law have evolved, particularly since the 1972 Stockholm Declaration on Human Environment, to address problems of global environmental change. In the following paragraphs, an attempt is made to clarify the newly emerging principles and rules of prevention and mitigation.[13]

---

12. *See,* e.g., R.E. Benedick, "Lessons from the Ozone Hole," 16 *EPA Journal,* 43 (1990).

13. For an overall discussion on international legal response to global environmental change,

(A) The principle of a common interest of humankind

As discussed in section 3 *supra,* global environmental change is not only a matter of concern among discrete states, i.e., "acting" states and "affected" states, but is a matter of concern to the entire international community. Indeed it can be said to be a common concern of humankind. There is a general recognition that humankind has common interests in protecting and managing the climate system, the ozone layer, the rain forests, and biological diversity for both present and future generations. It is also recognized that these common interests are superior to those of the individual states and total more than merely their sum (*see*, e.g., Professor Kiss, *infra*).

International instruments incorporate this recognition in specific fields of environmental protection. For instance, Resolution 43/53 of the UN General Assembly recognizes that climate change is a common concern of mankind.[14] The 1972 Convention for the Protection of the World Cultural and Natural Heritage considers in the preamble that "deterioration or disappearance of any item of the cultural and natural heritage constitutes a harmful impoverishment of the heritage of all the nations of the world" and that "parts of the cultural and natural heritage . . . need to be preserved as part of the world heritage of mankind as a whole" and that "it is incumbent on the international community as a whole to participate in the protection of the cultural and natural heritage of outstanding universal value." It then recognizes in Article 4 the duty of the Contracting Parties to ensure "the identifications, protection, conservation, presentation, and transmission to future generations of the cultural and natural heritage." The 1973 Convention on International Trade in Endangered Species of Wild Fauna and Flora recognizes in the preamble that "wild fauna and flora in their many beautiful and varied forms are an irreplaceable part of the natural systems of the earth which must be protected for this and the generations to come." A Draft Convention on the Conservation and Sustainable Use of Biological Diversity,[15] prepared by FAO on 11 June 1990, stipulates that the states are guardians to conserve biological diversity. It provides in Article 2 that

---

see E. Brown Weiss, "Legal Dimensions of Global Change: A Proposed Research Agenda," *International Social Science Journal* (August 1989).

14. *See supra* note 7.

15. This draft was prepared at the working level by members of the FAO Legal Office and the FAO Working Group on Biological Diversity.

"[T]he Parties accept as fundamental principle that biological diversity is a heritage of humankind and, where located within the limits of national jurisdiction, is under the sovereignty of the states where it is located. States have the duty of guardianship of biological diversity, in time and space."

It is noteworthy that, although the protection of the atmosphere and climate, cultural and natural heritage, and endangered species are under the jurisdiction of the sovereign states where they are located, the states are additionally under international obligations to protect and conserve these resources for the benefit of present and future generations. These natural or cultural resources are regarded as international or global commons[16] whose uses are limited by a common interest of mankind. The states are regarded as guardians or custodians of the international community.[17] It should also be noted that some newly emerging pollution-control rules, such as those concerning CFC and halon phase-out measures and potentially carbon dioxide reduction measures and conservation rules of global natural or cultural heritage are and will be based upon this general recognition of a common interest of humankind.

The high seas, the deep seabed, the moon, and their respective resources are located beyond the boundaries of natural jurisdictions. Their uses are open to every nation of the world and they are regarded as international or global commons; the deep seabed, the moon, and their resources are especially regarded as the common heritage of humankind.[18] The common heritage of humankind is under the stewardship of the international community as a whole and must be managed by existing and future international regimes.

Implementation of the principles and rules of prevention and mitigation under the auspices of international institutions and agencies is one of the characteristics of international environmental law. It is common that multilateral treaties that stipulate newly emerging principles and rules of prevention and mitigation provide for an institutional framework – such as an Executive Body, a Conference or

---

16. *See* discussion in O. Schacter, *Sharing the World's Resources,* 172 (Columbia University, 1977).
17. E. Brown Weiss, "The Planetary Trust: Conservation and Intergenerational Equity," 11 *Ecology Law Quarterly,* 495 (1984).
18. The UN Convention on the Law of the Sea, 10 Dec. 1982, Art. 136, 21 *I.L.M.* 1261, 1293; the Agreement Governing the Activities of States on the Moon and Other Celestial Bodies, 5 Dec. 1979, Article 11, 18 *I.L.M.* 1434, 1438–1439.

115

Meeting of the Parties, and a Secretariat – to implement the objectives of the treaties on the basis of a general obligation to cooperate. Such principles and rules are discussed *infra* in more detail.

(B) The principle of cooperation in scientific research, systematic observations, and assistance

Because of scientific uncertainty regarding environmental change, the Contracting Parties usually promise as a first step in agreements to cooperate in scientific research to identify the nature and the extent of problems. The principle of cooperation in scientific research and in systematic observations is widely used in international instruments for confronting global environmental change. Cooperation helps the Contracting Parties determine future specific control measures in any particular situation by helping to provide them with increasing scientific knowledge and expertise. It is often much easier for the Contracting Parties to agree upon cooperation in scientific research than to take specific control measures.

One of the recent developments in the principle of cooperation is the role played by international institutions and agencies through which the Contracting Parties cooperate for scientific research and systematic observations, environmental monitoring, and the collection, validation, and transmission of scientific data. International institutions and agencies also assist developing states with scientific research and systematic observations through financial arrangements. These developments facilitate scientific research, help generate comparable or standardized observational and monitoring instrumentation and methods, and foster worldwide reliable scientific data that are the prerequisites for international action to cope with global environmental change.

The 1982 UN Convention on the Law of the sea is a good example. Part XII of the Convention contains provisions on protection and preservation of the marine environment. Article 200 provides that states cooperate, directly or through competent international organizations, to promote studies and undertake programmes of scientific research. Article 204 provides that the parties endeavour, directly or indirectly or through competent international organizations, to observe, measure, evaluate, and analyse, by recognized scientific methods, the risks or effects of pollution of the marine environment. States also agreed in Article 202 to promote, directly or through competent international organizations, programmes of scientific, educational, technical, and other assistance to developing states for the protection and preservation of the marine environment, and the prevention, reduction, and control of marine pollution.

The Vienna Convention for the Protection of the Ozone Layer is another example. The Contracting Parties agreed in Article 3 to initiate and cooperate in, directly or through competent international bodies, the conduct of research and scientific assessments on such issues as the physical and chemical processes that affect the ozone layer and on alternative substances and technologies. They also agreed to promote or establish, directly or through competent international bodies, joint or complementary programmes for systematic observations of the state of the ozone layer and other relevant parameters. Furthermore, they agreed to cooperate, directly or through competent international bodies, in ensuring the collection, validation, and transmission of research and observational data through appropriate world-data centres in a regular and timely fashion. Article 4(2) provides that the Parties cooperate to promote, directly or through competent international bodies, the transfer of technology and knowledge to the developing countries, and Annex I of the Convention provides that the Parties cooperate to promote, directly or through competent international bodies, appropriate scientific and technical training, taking into account their particular needs.

In addition to funds directed towards compensating states damaged by pollution or environmental disasters, there are some funds used for conserving natural and cultural heritage, and for protecting the marine environment and the atmosphere. Funds function as a supporting mechanism for the principles of prevention and mitigation.

The 1972 Convention for the Protection of the World Cultural and Natural Heritage established the World Heritage Fund; it is financed by the Parties. The Fund is used for assisting the Parties, upon their request, in conserving properties listed on the World Heritage List.

UNEP administers two types of trust funds, general trust funds and technical cooperation trust funds,[19] both funded by member states. The main purpose of the funds is to provide member states with financial support for the protection of the marine environment of six regional seas and other specified technical cooperations.

The Second Meeting of the Parties to the Montreal Protocol in

19. Management of Trust Funds: Report of the Executive Director, UNEP/GC.14/23, 18 May 1987.

117

London in June 1990 set up a Multilateral Fund financed by contributions from developed Parties (i.e., Parties not operating under Paragraph 1 of Article 5), the contributions being calculated on the basis of the United Nations scale of assessments.[20] The Fund covers all agreed-upon incremental costs, including the transfer of technology, of the developing Parties (i.e., Parties operating under Paragraph 1 of Article 5) to enable their compliance with the control measures of the Protocol. According to Article 5 of the Protocol, developing Parties are entitled to delay their compliance with the control measures by 10 years.[21] The Multilateral Fund may well be an important paradigm for the prevention and mediation of climate change.

(C) The principle of exchange of information

Pertinent scientific, technical, socio-economic, business, commercial, and legal information are prerequisites for the implementation of international concerted actions to prevent or mitigate environmental harm arising from global environmental change. The Parties to international instruments cooperate both individually and jointly to exchange such information through international institutions; in fact, information can be more easily exchanged and disseminated to all the Parties if they are supplied to international bodies. There are two types of information exchange: information exchange upon request of the states and periodic information dissemination by international bodies (the latter being the other side of the coin of periodical information supplied *to* international bodies).

The Vienna Convention is a noteworthy example of the latter. In accordance with Article 4, the Parties should provide scientific, technical, socio-economic, commercial, and legal information as further elaborated in Annex II to (international) bodies agreed upon by the Parties. The bodies then disseminate such information to any requesting Parties. Articles 200 and 204 of the UN Convention on the Law of the Sea adhere to the same principle.

Information exchange raises questions of confidentiality – which information is regarded as confidential and by whom? Most international instruments provide that any information regarded as confiden-

---

20. UNEP/OzL. Pro. 2. 2/L/4 Rev. 1; UNEP/OzL. Pro. 2/L/5/ Rev.1; UNEP/OzL. Pro. 2/L/6.
21. Such provision can be legally justified by the theory of the compensation of potential opportunity costs incurred by developing countries. *See* G. Handl, "International Efforts to Protect the Global Atmosphere: A Case of Too Little, Too Late?", 1 *European Journal of International Law,* 256 (1990).

tial by the supplying state should not be disclosed by the receiving body. The principle of information exchange is governed by national laws and regulations and practices regarding patents, trade secrets, and the protection of confidential and proprietary information.[22] However, it is important that more information be made open to foster international concerted actions to cope with future global environmental change common to the international community – some international standards need to be formulated to clarify confidentiality issues in this regard.

(D) Principles of prior notice, environmental impact assessment, and consultation

These principles help to prevent disputes from arising in the transfrontier pollution context between the "acting" state(s) and the "affected" state(s) by providing the "affected" state with pertinent information of the planned activities of the "acting" state and with chances to reach an amicable solution to the potential problem between them. The so-called Montreal Rules of International Law Applicable to Transfrontier Pollution adopted by the International Law Association at the sixtieth conference[23] include these principles in Articles 7 and 8:

Article 7 (Prior Notice)

1. States planning to carry out activities which might entail a significant risk of transfrontier pollution shall give early notice to States likely to be affected. In particular, they shall on their own initiative or upon request of the potentially affected States, communicate such pertinent information as will permit the recipient to make an assessment of the probable effects of the planned activities.

2. In order to appraise whether a planned activity implies a significant risk of transfrontier pollution, States should make environmental assessments before carrying out such activities.

Article 8 (Consultations)

1. Upon request of a potentially affected State, the State furnishing the information should enter into consultations on transfrontier pollution prob-

---

22. *See*, e.g., Vienna Convention for the Protection of the Ozone Layer, 22 Mar. 1985, Art. 4, 26 *I.L.M.* 1529, 1530–1531.
23. International Law Association, "Rules of International Law Applicable to Transfrontier Pollution," *Report of the 60th Conference,* 171–176 (International Law Association, 1982).

lems connected with the planned activities and pursue such consultations in good faith and over a reasonable period of time.

2. States are under an obligation to enter into consultations whenever transfrontier pollution problems arise in connection with the equitable utilization of a shared natural resource as envisaged in Art. 5.

The Montreal Rules link procedures of prior notice, environmental assessment, and consultations in a systematic way.

As indicated in Principle 11 of the Principles of Environmental Impact Assessment adopted by the 14th Governing Council of UNEP in July 1987,[24] it will become necessary for states to conclude bilateral, regional, or multilateral arrangements by providing for notification, exchange of information, and agreed-upon consultation on the potential environmental effect of planned activities under their jurisdiction or control that are likely to significantly affect other states or areas beyond their national jurisdiction.

Some brief comments are in order regarding environmental assessment and consultations. The environmental assessment can be used to decide whether planned activities will or will not lead to a breach of substantive legal obligations incumbent upon states to prevent unlawful transfrontier pollution, and if they are to be specified in legal instruments.[25] In comparison, consultation means something more than notification, but less than consent.[26] Consultation does not require agreement with the "affected" state(s) but it does take into account that state's(s') views or recommendations. Consultation is thus a preliminary stage to negotiation; however, negotiation implies a more sustained effort to reach an agreement than does consultation.[27]

The Montreal Rules will not alone suffice to prepare for and remedy global environmental change. It is necessary for a competent international body to intervene on behalf of the international community as a whole in the decision-making processes of planned activities that may significantly affect the global environment.

The Meeting Statement adopted in February 1989 by legal and policy experts from every continent of the world includes elements to be addressed in any framework "umbrella" convention on protection

---

24. *See* documents in 17 *Environmental Policy and Law,* 36–37 (February 1987).
25. World Commission on Environment and Development, *Environmental Protection and Sustainable Development: Legal Principles and Recommendations,* 103 (Graham & Trotman, 1987).
26. F.L. Kirgis, Jr., *Prior Consultation in International Law,* 11 (Univ. Press of Va., 1983).
27. *Supra* note 23 at 11.

of the atmosphere[28] and provides for an innovative approach. According to the principles of prior notice and environmental impact assessment adopted in the Meeting Statement, when a state has reasonable grounds to believe that planned activities under its jurisdiction or control may cause an atmospheric interference[29] outside its jurisdiction, it shall give timely notice of such planned activities to the competent international organization (and to the other states concerned), make an assessment of the potential effects of such activities, and on its own initiative or upon request of the competent international organization (or of the other states concerned), provide such relevant information as will permit the competent international organization (or the other states concerned) to make an assessment of the probable effects of the planned activities. The Meeting Statement made a clear distinction between the protection of the atmosphere and protection of the climate, and advised to delete texts between brackets for the purposes of an instrument on climate protection.

The Meeting Statement also included the principle of consultation, according to which consultations shall be held upon request at an early stage between both the competent international organization and states concerned and between the international organization and the states under whose jurisdiction or control activities that require prior notice are planned.

These principles embodied in the Meeting Statement are newly emerging and are applicable to global environmental change, a threat that entails extended effects upon the majority of members of the international community. It is necessary for international institutions, with full expertise, to participate in consensus-making processes.

(E) The principle of risk assessment, warning, and emergency assistance

In coping with environmental disasters, such as nuclear accidents and oil spills, it is necessary to have made a prior risk assessment to the

28. Meeting Statement of International Meeting of Legal and Policy Experts on the Protection of the Atmosphere, 20–22 Feb. 1989, Ottawa, Canada. This conference was a follow-up conference of The Changing Atmosphere: Implications for Global Security, held in Toronto in 1988.
29. According to the Meeting Statement, "atmospheric interference" means any change in the physical or chemical condition of the atmosphere resulting directly or indirectly from human activities and producing effects of such a nature as to appreciably endanger human health, harm living resources, ecosystems, and material property, impair amenities or interfere with other legitimate uses of the environment.

121

states concerned and to competent international organization(s) and to provide emergency assistance to the affected states.[30] A plausible approach to emergency situations was proposed in the 1989 Ottawa Meeting Statement. According to the Statement:

When a State becomes aware of an emergency situation or other change of circumstances arising from incidents or activities under its jurisdiction or control and suddenly giving rise to an atmospheric interference or significant risk thereof causing or likely to cause harm in an area under the jurisdiction of another State or in an area beyond the limits of national jurisdiction, it shall immediately take appropriate measure, to control the cause of the emergency situation and immediately notify other States affected or likely to be affected by such an atmospheric interference, as well as the competent international organization.

Other approaches are included in the two 1986 IAEA Conventions, the Convention on Early Notification of a Nuclear Accident and the Convention on Assistance in the Case of a Nuclear Accident or Radiological Emergency. The former says that in the event of nuclear accident the state Party shall notify, directly or through IAEA, affected states or states likely to be affected by the accident and provide them, directly or through IAEA, with relevant information specified in Article 5. In contrast, the latter provides that when a state Party is in need of assistance in the event of such an accident, it can call for such assistance from any other state Party, directly or through IAEA, and from IAEA or other IGO – such accident need not originate within the territory, jurisdiction, or control of the requesting state.

6. Toward an international management of global environmental change

The Vienna Convention, the Montreal Protocol, and recent amendments to the Protocol provide a prototype of international environmental management of the atmosphere that may be called "international governance."[31]

Regarding the protection of the ozone layer, international institu-

---

30. For the international legal framework for coping with emergency disasters, see Bruha, "Internationale Regelungen zum Schutz vor technisch-industriellen Umweltnotfallen," 44 *Zeitschrift für ausländisches öffentliches Recht und Völkerrecht*, 1–63 (1984).
31. N. Myers, "Environmental Challenges: More Government or Better Governance?", 17 *AMBIO*, 411–414 (1988).

tions established by international instruments perform three functions – standard-setting, licensing, and auditing. Once an initial standard of consumption reduction of a controlled substance is established by the Contracting Parties to the Protocol, the Conference of the Parties (a kind of international institution affiliated with the Secretariat) makes a review of the control measures. A licence or permit to emit the controlled substances may be granted. Treaty compliance is then audited by the same body. The Second Meeting of the Parties to the Montreal Protocol adopted, on an interim basis, procedures for determining non-compliance with the provisions of the Protocol and the institutional mechanism for the treatment of Parties held to be in non-compliance.[32] According to the decision, the Implementation Committee is established to receive, consider, and report on any submission made by Parties who have reservations regarding another Party's implementation of its obligations under the Protocol.

"International governance" also applies in the climate-change context. The Contracting Parties to a framework Convention on Climate Change and associated Protocols will agree on an international ambient standard for greenhouse gases such as carbon dioxide and will allocate emission limitations among the Contracting Parties to meet the ambient standard.[33] Such allocation is to be calculated on the basis of such factors as the population or gross national product of the states. Each Contracting Party will implement its allocated standard at the national level. At present, developing countries are exempt from complying with limitations on emissions because of the time-lag in their development. An international institution, such as the Conference of the Parties, will later review an international ambient standard and consequent emission limitations.

Monitoring is essential for this type of international management of the atmosphere. An international system can be devised to annually monitor the production of and the export and import of fossil fuels. However, monitoring of greenhouse gases other than carbon dioxide seems extremely difficult. Perhaps non-compliance mechanisms can be modeled after the ozone-layer precedents.

---

32. UNEP/OzL. Pro. 2/L.1; UNEP/OzL. Pro. 2/L.5/Rev.1.
33. E. Brown Weiss, "A Resource Management Approach to Carbon Dioxide during the Century of Transition," in *World Climate Change: The Role of International Law and Institutions* 181 (V. Nanda, ed., Westview Press, 1983).

5

State responsibility, liability, and remedial measures under international law: New criteria for environmental protection

Francisco Orrego Vicuña

1. The evolving law of state responsibility

The Law of State Responsibility[1] emerged in the international legal order as a concept basically meant to operate in an *ex post facto* manner and has generally followed the characteristics of the law of torts in domestic legal systems. The very idea of injury on which this aspect of the law was based assumed that an unhappy event had already taken place before the operation of responsibility. The restrictive nature of this body of law was further revealed by the requirement of a causal link between the injury and an official act or omission attributable to the state in question. In addition, the doctrine only applied when such an act or omission was wrongful, that is, contrary to a precise obligation under international conventional or customary law. This was not always easy to establish, particularly in view of the vagueness that has occasionally accompanied the consolidation of a rule of law in the international order.

Rationae materiae, the Law of State Responsibility was conceived

---

1. I. Brownlie, *System of the Law of Nations: State Responsibility* (Part I) (Clarendon; Oxford, 1983). F.V. García-Amador, *The Changing Law of International Claims* (Oceana, 1984). *See also* generally, with particular reference to the work of the International Law Commission, Centre for Studies and Research of the Hague Academy of International Law, *International State Liability* (1982), Selective Bibliography prepared by the Library of the Peace Palace.

in a limited manner. It initially protected personal rights and later evolved to protect economic rights of nationals of other states. Given the limited scope of international relations at the time of these legal developments, it was quite natural that the law would cover only those aspects in which contacts among nations were more frequent, and hence where conflicts were most likely to arise.

In this context it is hardly surprising that the remedies attached to the operation of responsibility were equally of a limited value. In essence, remedies purported to lead to *restitutio in integrum* where at all possible through compensation or other forms of reparation. Unilateral or anticipatory remedial action has never been favoured in international law in view of the risk of abuse involved, which has meant an even more limited availability of remedies. Needless to say, procedural arrangements have in general been slow and drawn out.

None of the above detracts from the useful role of State Responsibility under international law and the manner in which it has helped to solve many disputes among states and redress the rights of individuals that may have been affected by unlawful acts or omissions. In spite of its many shortcomings, the law specifically applicable to international claims, including those related to property and other economic rights, bears witness to the important developments and improvements that have taken place in this field.

The primary problem affecting the operation of the Law of State Responsibility is that since this body of law became consolidated in the early part of the century, the nature and extent of international relations have dramatically changed. Occasional international interactions among individuals have given way to a global economy. Rights that might have been considered as appertaining to foreign nationals are today a part of the law of human rights applicable to all without distinction. Distant events that previously escaped attention because they did not fall within the domain of exclusive national jurisdiction are today the concern of humankind as a whole. Industrialization, resource exploitation, and development have prompted environmental effects of a global nature that were unknown in the past.

Most of these changes have had an impact on the Law of State Responsibility, both in terms of its material content and its procedural arrangements. The law has not been static and has not remained frozen in time; it has evolved significantly, albeit not in every respect. Many of the responses to the violation of economic rights of individuals, or more broadly, the protection of human rights, are the result of the evolution of the Law of State Responsibility. This evolution has led to new conceptual insights, introduced a greater degree of flexibility in its operation, and allowed for new and more effective remedial measures.

This chapter examines specifically the changing conditions arising from the need to ensure adequate environmental protection in the international domain, and the impact this has had on the Law of State Responsibility. It is through this perspective that one can best realize to what extent there has been an evolution in this body of law and to what extent some of its prevailing shortcomings still remain.

2. New environmental realities and their impact upon the law

The experience gathered in environmental studies and the design of action plans and other means for the protection of the global environment show that things have generally worsened rather than improved. Since the 1972 Stockholm Conference,[2] which served of course as a landmark in the growing awareness of the international community on the matter, the environmental impacts flowing from major disasters or simply from the magnitude of industrial operations have grown considerably. In this regard, the many plans and organizations that have emerged since then cannot generally be viewed as an example of success.

Three conclusions are particularly worth retaining from this experience because they represent a broad consensus of opinion among most authors: (1) the problems of the global environment are becoming more serious as their risks and consequences become better understood, while at the same time it is increasingly difficult to pinpoint a single source of such problems and attach a causative link to a given agent, private or public, national or transnational; (2) growing lead times are usually needed to take preventive or corrective action; and (3) some of these impacts may become irreversible if left unchecked.[3]

These three basic premises have had a profound impact on the na-

2. Stockholm Declaration on the Human Environment of the United Nations Conference on the Human Environment, 16 June 1972, 11 *I.L.M.* 1416 (1972) (hereinafter Stockholm Declaration).
3. *See* generally *The Human Dimensions of Global Change: An International Programme on Human Interactions with the Earth,* Report of the Tokyo International Symposium on the Human Response to Global Change, Tokyo, Japan, 19–22 Sept. 1988.

ture and extent of the Law of State Responsibility and the corresponding developments in the specific field of liability, both domestic and international. Because they are based on a broad consensus in the international community, these conclusions are becoming reflected in the body of international law through gradual responses to the new needs. There are of course other aspects that have not attained that same degree of consensus and that on occasion have been objected to. These other aspects are presently mere policy suggestions that cannot form the basis for consolidation as a rule of law.

While the scientific conclusions mentioned above pertain to the consensual category, a number of ideological issues prompted by the debate on the environment do not. This dichotomy explains both the opportunities and the limits facing the development of the Law of State Responsibility and related matters as applied to the environment. In particular, it highlights the differing views about the scope of the basic principles, rules, and institutions necessary to address global environmental change.

3. Conceptual developments and the new basic principle of international law

The work of the International Law Commission, learned societies, and distinguished writers of international law have greatly clarified the conceptual framework governing this particular area of the law. First, a useful distinction has emerged that separates international "responsibility" from international "liability," the former arises from unlawful acts while the latter has come to encompass both lawful and unlawful activities. The idea of state liability for acts not prohibited by international law has also emerged in this context.[4]

This distinction has not passed unchallenged. Brownlie has made the argument that the normal principles of state responsibility can well sustain liability, particularly as it concerns extra-hazardous operations.[5] In this context the critical issue is the content of the rules and not the distinction between lawful and unlawful activities, especially since either way leads to reparation and compensation. In prac-

4. For a discussion of the work of the International Law Commission and the conceptual issues raised by the topic of "International Liability for Injurious Consequences Arising out of Acts Not Prohibited by International Law," *see* generally Daniel Barstow Magraw, "Transboundary Harm: The International Law Commission's Study of 'International Liability,'" 80 A.J.I.L. 305 (1986).
5. Brownlie, *supra* note 1 at 50.

127

tice, however, this distinction is gaining ground in several treaty regimes, although it is also true that a number of legal consequences are attached to given activities resulting in damage irrespective of their lawful or unlawful character.

A second conceptual development serves as a useful analytical tool: the distinction between "primary" and "secondary" rules. The former relate to obligations, the breach of which may lead to responsibility, while the latter relate to the legal consequences of failure to comply with the obligations arising from the primary rules. Secondary rules are those specifically dealing with the issue of responsibility and liability, although these issues cannot always actually be separated from the operation of the primary rules.

The important document prepared by the Italian government on the international law of the environment[6] indicates that in practice one can observe significant developments in the treaty rules dealing with the environment (the primary rules), but not a parallel evolution in the rules on responsibility, which are either non-existent or overly general in those regimes. The result is that the secondary rules lag behind those developed in the primary level.

In spite of these shortcomings, practice shows the acceptance of a general principle of responsibility for environmental damage caused by activities within state jurisdiction or control.[7] While this principle is generally accepted, it would not seem that the International Law Commission approach of regarding its violation as an international crime meets with general approval. The existence of a principle of international law embodying the obligation not to degrade the environment is further reinforced by the new conceptual approaches influencing the development of the law in this field, namely the concepts of intergenerational equity, human rights, and environmental security.

4. The expanding scope of the law: Global reach and international cooperation

These conceptual developments have not taken place in a vacuum, as they correspond to the actual evolution of the law and state practice.

---

6. *Introductory Document Prepared by the Italian Government for the Forum on International Law of the Environment, Siena, 17–21 April 1990,* 53 (Rome, January 1990), hereinafter cited as *Siena Forum.*
7. *Siena Forum, supra* note 6 at 53.

A number of fundamental developments characterize the contemporary evolution of this body of law, and they have in turn contributed to the clarification of the extent and scope of the basic principle referred to above.

One development to note is that environmental law applies today not only to activities that cause transboundary effects between neighbouring states – as was very much the case at the time of the *Trail Smelter*,[8] the *Lake Lanoux*,[9] or the *Gut Dam*,[10] but also to those that have effects at a long distance or, still more important, that have an effect upon areas beyond territorial jurisdiction. Thus the law has evolved from a purely national level in its origins to a transnational dimension and then to a properly international or global role. This geographical extension of the law, quietly developing during this century, has set the stage so that the current problems affecting the environment can be addressed.

The most significant breakthrough in this process of innovation came with the *Trail Smelter* decision in 1941.[11] Relying on principles and decisions of US courts and on the basis of identifying a general principle of international law, the arbitral tribunal concluded that "no state has the right to use or permit the use of its territory in such a manner as to cause injury by fumes in or to the territory of another or the properties or persons therein. . . . "[12] Such a principle meant in fact that international law had entered the field of transboundary environmental protection, albeit still limited to the territories of states. A somewhat similar conclusion was reached by the International Court of Justice in the *Corfu Channel Case*[13] in relation to acts contrary to international law or the rights of other states. It should be noted, however, that in the specific domain of the utilization of rivers, a similar principle had been identified since the early part of the century.[14]

---

8. Trail Smelter Arbitration (U.S. v. Can.) 1941, 11 Mar. 1941, 3 R.I.A.A. 1905 (1949).
9. Lake Lanoux Arbitration (Spain v. France) 1957 – I.L.R. 101 (1957).
10. Gut Dam Arbitration (U.S. v. Can.) 22 Sept. 1968, Report of the Agent of the United States before the Lake Ontario Claims Tribunal, 8 *I.L.M.* 118 (1969). The compromise of 25 May 1965 establishing the tribunal is found at T.I.A.S. No. 6114 (1965). *See also* the Agreement on the Settlement of Claims Relating to Gut Dam, 18 Nov. 1968, 6 U.S.T. 7863 (1968), T.I.A.S. No. 6624 (1968).
11. *Restatement (Third), The Foreign Relations Law of the United States* (1987), at 109–110 (hereinafter *Restatement*).
12. Trail Smelter Arbitration, *supra* note 8 at 1965.
13. *Corfu Channel Case* (U.K. v. Alb.) 1949, I.C.J. 4 (Judgment of 9 April 1949).
14. *Restatement, supra* note 11 at 100–101.

The *Trail Smelter* decision had other interesting impacts on the development of the law. First, the tribunal ordered the smelter to "refrain" from causing further damage, which involves a preventive measure to forestall harmful activities in the future. The tribunal then established a regime for the control of emissions, including technical improvements to the industry and the institutional mechanism of an ad-hoc commission of three scientists that had the power to adopt binding decisions.[15]

After these first steps were given specific applications, the basic principles could be found in different situations before national courts or international tribunals. Thus it was no surprise when the 1972 Stockholm Declaration included the often quoted Principle 21, which links states' sovereign rights relating to the exploitation of resources and national environmental policies to the "responsibility to ensure that activities within their jurisdiction or control do not cause damage to the environment of other States or of areas beyond the limits of national jurisdiction."[16] The link had already been established under international law, which explains why there was general agreement to express it in this Principle.

Various international documents and treaties have since reaffirmed the essence of Principle 21 or further expanded it in order to cope with new situations affecting the environment. The case of the *Cosmos 954*,[17] the EEC environmental policy adopted in 1973,[18] the 1979 Convention on Long-Range Transboundary Air Pollution[19] with its 1985 Protocol setting in place precise obligations for the reduction of sulphur emissions,[20] and the IAEA Conventions on Notification and

---

15. *Id.* at 109–110.
16. *Report of the United Nations Conference on the Human Environment,* U.N. Doc. A/ CONF. 48/14, Rev. 1, 3, 5 (1973). *See also* Stockholm Declaration, *supra* note 2.
17. Canada, Claim against the USSR for Damage Caused by Soviet Cosmos 954, Notes of 23 Jan. 1979 and 15 Mar. 1979, 18 *I.L.M.* 899 (1979). Canada-USSR, Protocol on Settlement of Canada's Claim for Damages Caused by Cosmos 954, 20 *I.L.M.* 689 (1981). The Canadian Claim was based on the convention on International Liability for Damage Caused by Space Objects, 29 Mar. 1972, 24 U.S.T. 2389, T.I.A.S. No. 7762, and on general principles of international law.
18. European Economic Community, Declaration on the Environmental Action Programme, 22 Nov. 1973, 13 *I.L.M.* 164 (1974).
19. Convention on Long-Range Transboundary Air Pollution, 13 Nov. 1979, 18 *I.L.M.* 1442 (1979), T.I.A.S. No. 10541 (1979).
20. 1985 Protocol to the 1979 Convention on Long-Range Transboundary Air Pollution, on the Reduction of Sulphur Emissions or Their Transboundary Fluxes by at Least 30 Per Cent, 8 July 1985, 27 *I.L.M.* 707 (1985).

Assistance in the case of Nuclear Accidents[21] are all cited as examples of the outreaching scope of environmental law today.[22]

Principle 21 was a further step of the utmost importance because it extended the transboundary reach of the law to include areas beyond the limits of national jurisdiction, thereby improving upon the reach of the *Trail Smelter* decision and providing the global scale referred to above. This development has been particularly apparent in relation to the marine environment and the atmosphere. The regime established under the 1982 Convention on the Law of the Sea for the marine environment,[23] like the Convention on the Prohibition of Military or Any Other Hostile Use of Environmental Modification Techniques,[24] the Vienna Convention for the Protection of the Ozone Layer of 1985,[25] and its Montreal Protocol on Substances That Deplete the Ozone Layer of 1987[26] have all established broad international regimes based on the principle of responsibility. The special case of Antarctica will be discussed further below.

However, as commented upon by the Italian document referred to above, many of these developments lack precise rules on responsibility, primarily because of the difficulty in identifying a single source or establishing the causal link between conduct and damage. The traditional requirements of international law were not always well suited to meet the changing conditions of industrial activity that are at the heart of current environmental problems. However, international law has begun to respond to the new challenges, and recent international regimes have included a more elaborate set of secondary rules governing responsibility. In addition, as suggested by the Italian document, it is always possible to complement the existing treaties with protocols dealing with responsibility.[27]

---

21. IAEA Convention on Early Notification of a Nuclear Accident, 26 Sept. 1986, 25 *I.L.M.* 1370 (1986); IAEA Convention on Assistance in Case of a Nuclear Accident or Radiological Emergency, 26 Sept. 1986, 25 *I.L.M.* 1377 (1986).
22. *Siena Forum, supra* note 6 at 54.
23. United Nations Convention on the Law of the Sea, 10 Dec. 1982, 21 *I.L.M.* 1261 (1982) (hereinafter Law of the Sea Convention).
24. Convention on the Prohibition of Military or Any Other Hostile Use of Environmental Modification Techniques, 18 May 1977, 16 *I.L.M.* 88, 31 U.S.T. 333, T.I.A.S. No. 9614 (1977) (hereinafter Enmod Convention).
25. Vienna Convention for the Protection of the Ozone Layer, 22 Mar. 1985, 26 *I.L.M.* 1529 (1987).
26. Montreal Protocol on Substances That Deplete the Ozone Layer, 16 Sept. 1987, 26 *I.L.M.* 1550 (1987).
27. *Siena Forum, supra* note 6 at 54–55.

A second major development was prompted by the changing international reality. As the *Restatement of the Law (Third)* states, "it soon became obvious that unilateral action by states to control pollution was not sufficient, and that international cooperation and regulation to protect the environment were necessary."[28] Here again the legal measures evolved from the national to the binational level, then to the regional ambit, and most recently to the global level, thereby setting the appropriate stage for dealing with current issues.

As a consequence of increased international cooperation to protect the environment, new obligations have devolved upon states in the environmental field. Some examples of how these obligations have broadened the scope of the basic principle of responsibility for environmental damage are: (1) the responsibility to control activities taking place beyond the state territory – like the jurisdictional outreach provided for under IMO[29] and the Law of the Sea Conventions;[30] (2) the responsibility engaging the state for activities of private entities; (3) the need to obtain the consent of other states for given activities, as provided for under the Convention on the Control of Transboundary Movements of Hazardous Waste and Their Disposal;[31] and (4) the more general obligation to notify and consult in environmental matters.[32]

In the light of the present debate about whether treaties are an adequate source of rules of international law as to ensure the protection of the global environment, or whether more flexible procedures should be sought, it is worth remembering that treaties are not the only source of law to consider. Some of the major developments in the Law of State Responsibility in an environmental context have emerged from the operation of customary law and general principles of law as understood by international tribunals and the writings of eminent authors. In addition, the fundamental principle embodied in the maxim *sic utere tuo ut alienum non laedas* (use your own property

---

28. *Restatement, supra* note 11 at 99.
29. *See* IMO Convention on the Prevention of Marine Pollution by Dumping of Wastes and Other Matter, 29 Dec. 1972, 2 U.S.T. 2403, T.I.A.S. No. 8165 (1972) (hereinafter Dumping Convention); London International Convention for the Prevention of Pollution from Ships, MARPOL, 2 Nov. 1973, 12 *I.L.M.* 1319 (1973).
30. Law of the Sea Convention, *supra* note 23 at Part XII.
31. Basel Convention on the Control of Transboundary Movements of Hazardous Wastes and Their Disposal, 22 Mar. 1989, 28 *I.L.M.* 657 (1989) (hereinafter Basel Convention).
32. *Restatement, supra* note 11 at 107.

so as not to injure the property of another)[33] has repeatedly been applied to the settlement of environmental disputes, on both national and international levels, and has formed the basis of the rationale inspiring the *Trail Smelter* decision, the work of the International Law Commission, and most of the international regimes in force for the protection of the environment. In fact, the very principle of international responsibility for environmental damage is an expression of this older general principle of law. Because the flexible use of the sources of international law has not historically been a problem, it should not really be a contemporary one either.

5. Material changes in the law of state responsibility

Three levels of state responsibility have been identified in relation to the environment: the mildest and most traditional one is that related to responsibility on the basis of fault or lack of due diligence; an intermediate level, called objective or strict responsibility, is related to an obligation of result, which is the obligation not to damage the environment and the violation of which will engage responsibility regardless of fault; the most stringent level, referred to as absolute responsibility, concerns liability for acts not prohibited by international law irrespective of fault or of the lawfulness of the activity in question.[34]

Examples of all these types of responsibility can be found in contemporary international environmental law. The Law of the Sea Convention regime is mostly based on the due diligence test,[35] an obligation of result involving objective or strict liability is found in the Convention on Environmental Modification Techniques,[36] and finally, absolute international liability is found in the Convention on International Liability for Damage Caused by Space Objects.[37] Most treaties rely on general obligations of cooperation or the commitment to take appropriate measures to prevent pollution, and thus involve only a

---

33. *Id.* at 100, citing the opinion of Judge Lauterpacht in Oppenheim, *International Law*, 346–47 (8th ed., 1955).
34. *Siena Forum, supra* note 6 at 57.
35. *Id.*, citing Law of the Sea, *supra* note 23 at Articles 235(1), 263(3), 304(139).
36. Enmod Convention, *supra* note 24 at Article I.
37. Convention on International Liability for Damage Caused by Space Objects, 29 Mar. 1972, 24 U.S.T. 2389, T.I.A.S. No. 7762, 66 A.J.I.L. 702 (1972), Article II. *See also Siena Forum, supra* note 6 at 57.

due diligence obligation to prevent pollution, the mildest of the three standards.

However, the fact that international law has been exploring more stringent forms of responsibility is, in and of itself, indicative of the sense of change that is taking place.[38] The most significant of these changes is the introduction of the concept of absolute and strict liability. Delinking the adverse effects of a given hazardous or dangerous activity from the element of *culpa* of the state or operator incorporates the test of "objective" responsibility as opposed to the "subjective" criteria of traditional international law.[39] Still more stringent criteria have been emerging lately, particularly as concerns the idea of holding a state responsible for damage ensuing from given activities irrespective of whether it took all necessary measures to prevent injury. The result is that responsibility will attach in spite of due diligence having been observed. Liability for acts not prohibited by international law is another major development that will be examined in more detail below.

The issue of environmental damage has also given rise to interesting developments in the international law of responsibility. First, in addition to traditional notions of economic damage, international law is beginning to recognize environmental damage as such for the purpose of invoking the responsibility of states.[40] In this context the environment becomes a value on its own merits and is protected by the law, as evidenced by *Cosmos 954*,[41] the recent *Patmos Case*,[42] and, above all, by the Antarctic arrangements.[43]

Second, the International Law Commission has made the point that material damage would not be an essential element in the case of responsibility for wrongful acts. The attribution of the conduct to the state and the breach of an international obligation would suffice to invoke responsibility.[44] Under traditional international law, however, the violation of the obligation would be sufficient to engage responsibility, which means that the old rules are very helpful indeed to

38. It should be noted that in some cases due diligence has been separated from fault, thus amounting in itself to the breach of a primary obligation regardless of fault; this means that the first level of responsibility has become more stringent as well.
39. *Siena Forum, supra* note 6 at 57.
40. *Restatement, supra* note 11 at 113.
41. *See supra* note 17.
42. *Patmos* case, Messina Court of Appeals, 1989 (cited in *Siena Forum, supra* note 6 at 60).
43. Wellington Convention on the Regulation of Antarctic Mineral Resource Activities, 2 June 1988, 27 *I.L.M.* 868 (1988) (hereinafter CRAMRA).
44. *Siena Forum, supra* note 6 at 60–61.

broaden the scope of the law at present. On the other hand, when the international liability is for acts not prohibited by international law, material damage would be the essential basis of compensation,[45] resulting in the paradox that, on this point, the new rules are more restrictive than the old.

Although the seriousness of the damage is another issue where the practice is not entirely uniform, certain gravity is, without a doubt, required. This requirement, however, is qualified by two considerations that relate to the evolving state of international law. First, given the emphasis on preventive measures characterizing present environmental law, the adoption of all necessary preventive and remedial measures even where no injury has occurred is beginning to emerge as a new type of obligation. Second, as mentioned in the *Restatement of the Law (Third),* when pollution is caused by substances that are highly dangerous to human life and health, there is no need to prove a significant impact or injury, thereby altering rather dramatically the traditional standards of international law.[46] Examples of this trend are blacklisting of hazardous products and abnormally dangerous activities like the launching of space objects.[47]

6. Expanding the protection of the affected interests

In many instances environmental damage will affect the territory of a given state and thus provide the legal basis for the exercise of claims. Increasingly, however, damage extends to areas beyond national jurisdiction and thus becomes global in nature. This situation prompts the question of who shall be entitled to a claim, demand the termination of the activities in question, and eventually receive compensation. Because of the need to avoid competing claims and the lack of institutions representing the interest of the international community, international law has so far been reluctant to recognize an *actio popularis*, requiring instead a direct legal interest on the part of states.

As the Italian document correctly points out, this situation could lead to the unacceptable result of leaving a case of serious damage

---

45. International Law Commission, *Third Report on International Liability for Injurious Consequences Arising out of Acts Not Prohibited by International Law,* U.N. Doc. A/CN. 4/360 and Corr. 1 (1982); *Schematic Outline,* sect. 1, Art. 1, in conjunction with "Fourth Report," U.N. Doc. A/CN. 4/373 and Corr. 1 (1983), at 29.
46. *Restatement, supra* note 11 at 113.
47. *Id.*

without any remedy.[48] International law has begun to react to this new challenge in several ways. Firstly the public interests of the world community are gradually being recognized since the *Barcelona Traction* case.[49] The violation of obligations *erga omnes* would provide legal standing to all states to react. Secondly, the concept of *jus cogens* also provides a legal ground for the action of states not directly damaged. And finally, the rules of the Law of Treaties on the breach of a multilateral treaty equally allow for the action of all states concerned.[50] In addition, the work of the International Law Commission on the codification of the Law of State Responsibility follows a similar orientation.[51]

While lacking judicial or arbitral precedents, the view has been expounded to the effect that any state may bring a claim to redress the violation of an obligation owed to the international community as a whole and request that the threat of environmental damage be terminated.[52] If this approach were adopted, a number of problems would still remain, but most of them could be handled by developing technical legal rules. Concurrent claims can eventually be harmonized by means of a balancing of interests, as seen to an extent in the field of antitrust laws and concurrent jurisdictions. International institutions could eventually be empowered to proceed on behalf of the international community, thus avoiding numerous individual claims. The beneficiary of compensation could also be determined as the process of institutionalization progresses in the environmental field. Precedents for solutions along these lines already exist in the regimes created for the marine environment and the Antarctic.

The apportionment of responsibility also reflects the evolution of the law. When two or more states are involved in an activity giving rise to responsibility, the ensuing liability will be apportioned among them.[53] This principle also justifies the apportionment of responsibility between a state and private operators under its control, or the operation of subsidiary liability in given instances. This limited extension of responsibility is the initial reaction of the international legal system to the fact that every passing day, it is more difficult to iden-

48. *Siena Forum, supra* note 6 at 63.
49. Barcelona Traction, Light and Power Co., Ltd., 1970, I.C.J. 4.
50. *Siena Forum, supra* note 6 at 65.
51. *Id.* at 66.
52. *Restatement, supra* note 11 at 104, 121.
53. *Id.* at 113.

tify a single source of given forms of pollution. What international law has not yet done, but could very well do in the near future, is to extend responsibility beyond the state undertaking an activity to reach the entity ultimately responsible for pollution (for instance, the manufacturer of defective equipment).[54] This corresponds to what is known in domestic law as "product liability."

Given that international law has been broadening the definition of pollution and environmental processes in order to include large ecosystems and that the emphasis has clearly been put on the development of preventive measures, the consolidation of the obligation to notify and consult has been, as noted above, another major development.[55] While consensus on this point could not be attained at the Stockholm Conference,[56] principally because of the concern of delaying development projects in an excessive manner, gradually such obligations have become accepted. These obligations were finally consolidated in the aftermath of the Chernobyl accident in the Convention on Early Notification of a Nuclear Accident and the Convention on Assistance in the Case of a Nuclear Accident or Radiological Emergency (1986).[57] The policy of major lending institutions evaluating the environmental effects of projects applying for financing has also helped to reduce the concern about excessive delays referred to above.[58]

Most of these developments have arisen out of specific areas of environmental interest and concern, such as the marine environment, Antarctica, outer space, nuclear-test bans, weather modification, and others. Some of these areas will be examined individually below, focusing on their historical development and on their potential to evolve into the *corpus juris gentium,* including treaties, customary law, and general principles of law. It is this broader *corpus* that is now beginning to be applied to large-scale climatic changes in the world.

Domestic law has also had a major input into this process of material change. From United States domestic law come the procedural arrangements for the participation of foreign states in the domestic-

---

54. *Id.* at 106. For a comment on the Bhopal accident and related views on the export of dangerous industries, see Magraw, *supra* note 4 at 325.
55. *See supra* note 32 and accompanying text.
56. *Restatement, supra* note 11 at 114–115.
57. *Supra* note 21.
58. *The World Bank and the Environment,* First Annual Report, 1990.

137

planning process or the presentation of claims.[59] In fact, under both the Clean Water Act[60] and the Clean Air Act,[61] a foreign state can participate, on conditions of reciprocity, in hearings for the revision of a state implementation plan in order to eliminate adverse consequences for that foreign state. Also under the Comprehensive Environmental Response, Compensation, and Liability Act of 1980,[62] a foreign claimant may assert a claim in given circumstances as if it were a United States claimant. Some of these arrangements are of evident interest for international law.

Another development of interest under domestic law is the requirement of an environmental-impact statement for major actions, including occasionally the effects on the global commons. Actions of this kind are envisaged, for example, in the United States National Environmental Policy Act (1969),[63] the Executive Order on Environmental Effects Abroad of Major Federal Actions of 1979,[64] and the policy of the Nuclear Regulatory Commission.[65]

7. Liability for acts not prohibited by international law: The ongoing debate

International liability for acts not prohibited by international law involves a rather stringent form of responsibility-liability, which in turn has a strong impact on the nature and extent of remedial measures in the field. It follows that the debate about the present state of international law on this point has been most lively.

First, it should be noted that the much discussed decision of the International Law Commission in 1976,[66] referred to above (which lists among international crimes those relating to the breach of an international obligation of essential importance for the safeguarding and pres-

---

59. *Restatement, supra* note 11 at 118–119.
60. Clean Water Act, 33 U.S.C. §§1251–1376.
61. Clean Air Act, 42 U.S.C. §§7401–7642.
62. Comprehensive Environmental Response, Compensation, and Liability Act of 1980, 42 U.S. §9601.
63. U.S. National Environmental Policy Act of 1969, 42 U.S.C. §§4321, 4332.
64. Executive Order 12114 on Environmental Effects Abroad of Major Federal Actions, 4 Jan. 1979, 44 F.F. 1957, 3C.F.R., 1979 Comp. 356.
65. *See* Natural Resources Defense Council, Inc. v. Nuclear Regulatory Commission, 647 F. 2d 1345 , 1348, 1377 (D.C.Cir. 1981); *Restatement, supra* note 11 at 120.
66. 31 U.N. GAOR Supp. (No. 10) Report of the Int'l. L. Comm. Art. 19(3)(d) at 226, U.N. Doc. A/31/10 (1976).

ervation of the human environment), has to be understood more as an expression of concern in line with the Stockholm Conference than as a radical departure in terms of the consequences attached to the breach of such an obligation.

The work of the International Law Commission on "International Liability"[67] reveals a cautious approach to the state of international law on the matter. On the one hand the separation of liability for acts not prohibited by international law from State Responsibility is indicative of the policy of attaching a legal consequence – liability – even to international lawful activities, yet on the other hand State Responsibility could well apply to extra-hazardous operations,[68] thus also attaching a legal consequence to activities that are not, *per se,* unlawful. In this regard the remedial aspect of the law would not be different under either approach. What is of importance is that international law is accepting legal consequences for a variety of activities that may result in an adverse impact upon the environment.

The "compound 'primary' obligation" identified by the International Law Commission in its schematic outline on "international liability" refers to four basic duties: prevent, inform, negotiate, and repair.[69] The emphasis is on preventive measures as well as the new obligation to notify and consult. However, it is surprising that the failure to comply with the first three duties mentioned is not regarded as wrongful and, consequently, no action can be brought against such failure; only the failure to make reparations is ultimately identified with a wrongful act and, hence, engages the State's responsibility.[70]

It follows that from the perspective of the International Law Commission, there is really not much difference between international liability and state responsibility, since the ultimate test of wrongfulness in both lies in the failure to make a reparation. While it is true that under international liability the initial activity can be lawful and under state responsibility normally it will be unlawful (although neither excludes both lawful and unlawful activities), the two are equated in terms of the end result.

It has been rightly observed that one consequence of the International Law Commission approach could "allow a state to persist in an

---

67. *See supra* note 44 and accompanying text.
68. *See* Brownlie, *supra* note 1 at 50.
69. "Fourth Report," *supra* note 45 at 29.
70. "Third Report," *supra* note 45 at 16.

unlawful act even without the consent of the injured state, as long as the acting state pays monetary reparations to the injured state."[71] In the field of environmental protection this result would be utterly unacceptable and self-defeating, which is why there has been an emphasis on both preventive measures and new developments that require that pollution be terminated and allow all states to bring actions to this effect.

Although there has also been debate about whether the *Trail Smelter* decision involved, in addition to its pioneering invocation of international liability, an element of international responsibility given that a wrongful act had been committed, it is quite clear that the effect of the decision never would have allowed the harmful activity to persist. As noted above it ordered the smelter to "refrain" from such activity and put in place a regime for the control of emissions.[72] This result is in line with the emerging consensus that international law ought to provide adequate protection of the environment.

Another element of the debate prompted by the International Law Commission's work is the method of determining reparation. The schematic outline favours the method of reparation determined by a "balance-of-interests" test, which takes into account the shared expectations of the states involved, a number of principles and factors, and the extent to which the duties to prevent, inform, and negotiate have been complied with.[73] This approach offers the advantage of introducing an element of flexibility that allows the weighing of the different circumstances of the case, but, on the other hand, it involves greater subjectivity. The alternative test of strict liability is in a sense more objective, because the harmful result will be separated from the intention of the state and even from the fact of having discharged the relevant duties. Again this last approach is more in line with the needs of environmental protection.

8. The expanding role of practice: Substantive and procedural developments

However articulate most of these arguments are, in practice the solutions sought are more straightforward and less abstract, particularly in the field of international environmental law. Furthermore, interna-

---

71. Magraw, *supra* note 4 at 330.
72. *See supra* note 15 and accompanying text.
73. *Schematic Outline, supra* note 45 at Art. 3.

tional liability can hardly be separated from liability in general, since the essential issue is how to make available rules of substance and procedure that will ensure adequate compensation to those affected by environmental damage. An innovative approach to the traditional state of the law is developing in treaty and domestic practice as evidenced by the following:

1. Based on principles of "federal common law," which to an extent resemble the principles of international law, it has been concluded that a state can present a claim for injury to its environment independently from any injury to its nationals or property.[74] The environment, as noted above, thus becomes a value protected on its own merits. The concept of remedy under international law is thereby significantly broadened. In addition, preventive and remedial measures will be highlighted even in the case where there has been no injury. Treaty practice is beginning to reflect this innovative approach.[75]

2. Liability for pollution injuries is becoming increasingly recognized by means of treaties, which provide a number of uniform principles in matters such as strict liability, identification of the competent forum, limitations of liability, insurance and financial guarantees, subsidiary state liability, and international funds, to name a few.[76]

Proposals have been introduced for extending state liability not only to directly caused damage but also to indirect state action that has ultimately led to an environmental harm. As explained above, states may be liable for private actions of entities and individuals under their jurisdiction, or they may have a form of subsidiary liability. International joint commissions are becoming a common mechanism for dealing with the matter of transboundary environmental problems. Nor is self-help ruled out in given circumstances as a preventive or remedial measure.[77]

The most elaborate rules in the matter of civil liability are those of (1) the 1969 Convention on Civil Liability for Oil Pollution Damage,[78] the related International Convention on the Establishment of an International Fund for Compensation for Oil Pollution

---

74. *Restatement, supra* note 11 at 122–123 (with particular reference to the U.S. case-law).
75. *See, e.g.,* CRAMRA, *supra* note 43.
76. *Restatement, supra* note 11 at 121–123.
77. *Id.* at 121.
78. Brussels International Convention on Civil Liability for Oil Pollution Damage, 29 Nov. 1969, 9 *I.L.M.* 45 (1969).

Damage,[79] and their respective supplementary agreements,[80] and (2) the Conventions on Third Party Liability in the Field of Nuclear Energy,[81] including the Convention on Civil Liability for Nuclear Damage[82] and related agreements. Agreements of private operators in the case of oil pollution, such as TOVALOP,[83] OPOL,[84] and CRISTAL[85] are also important elements in the development of the law in the field of liability.

3. In spite of the developments evidenced by some instances of treaty practice, such practice is generally limited to only a few sectors of activity.[86] Some efforts are being made to broaden this practice, as evidenced by the 1988 Joint Protocol on the Conventions on Nuclear Liability,[87] but they are still far from becoming comprehensive. Discrepancies between domestic legislation and treaty practice are sometimes a bar to the adoption of appropriate solutions. Limitations on liability have also become an obstacle for adequate remedial action.[88] This has prompted a number of national legislatures to establish unlimited liability or the alternative approach followed by the Antarctic arrangements, which will be discussed below. Civil liability provisions are now at the heart of many international negotiations, recent examples of which include the 1989 Basel Convention on Transboundary Movements of Hazardous Wastes[89] and the 1989 Geneva Convention on Civil Liability for Damage Caused during Carriage of Dangerous Goods by Road, Rail, and Inland Navigation Vessels.[90]

---

79. Brussels International Convention on the Establishment of an International Fund for Compensation for Oil Pollution Damage, 18 Dec. 1971, 11 *I.L.M.* 284 (1972).
80. *See* the Protocols to the Conventions cit., *supra* notes 78, 79, 19 Nov. 1976 16 *I.L.M.* 617, 621 (1976).
81. Paris Convention on Third Party Liability in the Field of Nuclear Energy, 29 Jul. 1960, 55 A.J.I.L. 1082 (1960), Brussels Supplementary Convention, 31 Jan. 1963, 2 *I.L.M.* 685 (1963).
82. Vienna Convention on Civil Liability for Nuclear Damage, 21 May 1963, 2 *I.L.M.* 727 (1963).
83. Tanker Owners Voluntary Agreement Concerning Liability for Oil Pollution (TOVALOP), 7 Jan. 1969, 8 *I.L.M.* 497 (1969).
84. Oil Companies Offshore Pollution Liability Agreement (OPOL), 4 Sept. 1974, 13 *I.L.M.* 1409 (1974).
85. Oil Companies: Contract Regarding an Interim Supplement to Tanker Liability for Oil Pollution (CRISTAL), 14 Jan. 1971, 10 *I.L.M.* 137 (1971).
86. *Siena Forum, supra* note 6 at 77.
87. *Id.* at 78, 79.
88. *Id.* at 78.
89. *See* Basel Convention, *supra* note 31.
90. *Siena Forum, supra* note 6 at 79.

4. As a consequence of the limitations just discussed, more comprehensive and integrated arrangements concerning liability are being sought, with particular reference to the payment of full compensation to those affected. Here subsidiary state liability plays a fundamental role. "Product liability" would also be a helpful development, a first hint of which may be discerned in the negotiations leading to a protocol on liability for damages relating to transboundary movements of hazardous wastes that would involve the liability of the exporting state.[91] Procedural aspects are also relevant for this discussion of more comprehensive arrangements. The elimination of the requirement of exhausting local remedies before a claim is presented, the presentation of a "consolidated claim" on behalf of all those affected, and the establishment of international claims commissions for certain priority matters are all suggestions that aim at a more flexible and timely procedure.[92]

5. None of the above precludes recourse to domestic remedies, as evidenced by the *Bhopal*[93] and *Amoco Cadiz*[94] cases and many other transboundary incidents involving smoke and coal-dust damage, chemical insecticides, salinization, or noise pollution.[95] Domestic case-law has given rise to other developments of interest.

6. Given the difficulty of identifying a single source of pollution, some domestic legal systems have introduced the general remedial measure of having the various enterprises involved in an activity pay a tax or forms of compensation. Proposals to this effect have also been made at the international level, but international law has not yet introduced such measures, except in very specific fields, notably nuclear energy.[96]

7. Particularly in the United States courts, jurisdictional choice of law difficulties arising in cases of interstate damages have gradually led to a clarification of the pertinent rules.[97] It has been suggested that in transboundary cases, the governing law should be

91. *Id.* at 81–82.
92. *Id.* at 82.
93. In Re Union Carbide Corp. Gas Plant Disaster 809 F 2d 195 (2nd Cir., 1987).
94. In Re Oil Spill of "Amoco Cadiz" 699 F 2d 909 (17th Cir. 1983).
95. For recent developments relating to transboundary pollution cases, *see* A.C. Kiss, "La réparation pour atteinte à l'environnement," *23e Colloque de la Société Française pour le Droit International, "La Responsabilité dans le système international", Le Mans, 31 Mai–2 Juin 1990.*
96. *Restatement, supra* note 11 at 124.
97. *Id.* at 124–126.

that of the state where the suit is brought, or that the wrongful act should be considered to have been committed in both states so that either one of them will have jurisdiction, or alternatively, that the law where the damage has occurred should apply.[98] Although these questions are particularly relevant for private remedies under domestic legal systems, they also have an important bearing upon international law solutions. As mentioned above, some of the treaty regimes have provided rules as to the competent forum and applicable law. Special arrangements for transboundary activities have also been made, particularly in terms of the posting of bonds for guaranteeing compensation for potential damage and requiring subsidiary state liability.[99]

8. Equal access to remedies and courts by nationals and foreigners alike on a non-discriminatory basis is also a trend that should be noted since the 1977 OECD recommendations to this effect.[100]

Although the developments of state practice in relation to remedial measures are not quite systematic, they clearly reveal a trend toward the broadening of claims and liability and their legal consequences, both in terms of the material content of the law and the introduction of more flexible procedural rules. This can be further confirmed by the following discussion of some specific areas of concern.

9. The protection of the marine environment: A leading case of innovation

The 1982 Convention on the Law of the Sea and related treaties have significantly developed the rules of international law applicable to the preservation of the marine environment and illustrate the evolution of state responsibility. In point of fact, states are under the obligation to ensure that activities under their jurisdiction or control "are so

---

98. *Id.*
99. A Canadian corporation involved in drilling for oil in the Beaufort Sea, on the Canadian side of the boundary, was required to post a $20 million bond to secure compensation to potential U.S. pollution victims, in addition to the Canadian government subsidiary liability, as provided for in a special arrangement with the United States. *See* generally *Restatement, supra* note 11 at 125; Handl, "State Liability for Accidental Transnational Environmental Damage by Private Persons," 74 A.J.I.L. 525 (1980), at 547–548.
100. Organization for Economic Cooperation and Development (OECD), Recommendation of the Council for the Implementation of a Regime of Equal Right of Access and Non-Discrimination in Relation to Transfrontier Pollution, 17 May 1977, 16 *I.L.M.* 977 (1977).

conducted as not to cause damage by pollution to other States and their environment" and that any pollution arising from such activities "does not spread beyond the areas where they exercise sovereign rights."[101] The activities included in this obligation are those undertaken both by the state and by entities of a private nature under state jurisdiction and control. It is also quite apparent that this provision covers not only transboundary effects of pollution but also harm to areas beyond national jurisdiction. In other words, the global scale of environmental effects is incorporated into this particular regime.

This regime encompasses all sources of pollution, a further indication of the broadening concern and scope of international law. In addition, a broad definition of pollution of the marine environment is included in this and other treaty regimes as an expression of the very same concern.[102] Important IMO and related conventions have developed a well-structured normative regime dealing with specific questions of marine pollution particularly in terms of oil pollution, discharge and dumping of waste, and safety at sea.[103]

In light of this more advanced regime, it follows quite naturally that international law has accepted holding a state responsible for pollution injuries resulting from a violation of its obligations in this field. Although the primary obligation to enforce the law is bestowed upon the flag state of the ships concerned, other states are not prevented from taking the necessary preventive or remedial actions. In addition to the powers allocated to the coastal state and the port state in given instances, there is the most important right of intervention on the high seas, which is ultimately related to a measure of self-help under international law.[104] The obligation to notify is also prominent in this field. These developments of course do not prejudice the rules dealing specifically with issues such as the environmental consequences of seabed-mining operations, cooperation in emergencies, or the protection of fragile ecosystems.[105]

Remedial measures have also evolved significantly in the area of the law of the sea. In addition to recourse to the general remedies provided for under international law, coastal and port states can participate actively by detaining and investigating ships and by instituting

101. Law of the Sea Convention, *supra* note 23 at Art. 194(2).
102. *Id.* at Art. 1(1)(4).
103. *See supra* note 29 and accompanying text.
104. Law of the Sea Convention, *supra* note 23 at Art. 221.
105. *Restatement, supra* note 11 at 130–131.

proceedings.[106] The following trends are important in light of their innovative character:

1. It has been concluded that obligations of states in relation to the common environment are *erga omnes* and that any state can pursue remedies for violations resulting in significant injury to the environment.[107] This is an important expression of the global extent of the issues involved.

2. A number of special conventions have developed the rules on civil liability of persons violating environmental obligations, notably in regard to the operation of nuclear ships[108] and to oil-pollution damage.[109] Under the first regime, immunity from legal process under national or international law is to be waived, and claims may be brought before the courts of either the licensing state or of the state where the injury occurred.[110] Under the second regime, only the latter courts are competent, but decisions are enforceable in any state party to the Convention.[111] Supplementary compensation systems have also been established in the case of oil-pollution damage.[112]

3. Shared liability schemes have been provided for under the various non-governmental agreements referred to above (TOVALOP, OPOL, and CRISTAL).[113]

4. Liability has also been established for the adoption of wrongful enforcement measures, described in one regime as measures that "exceed those reasonably necessary."[114]

5. Domestic remedies ought to be available to the injured person to obtain compensation, it being a duty of the state to ensure the availability of and to enforce the payment of compensation. The limitations on liability provided for under some regimes have been occasionally interpreted by the courts in a restrictive manner, thus

---

106. Law of the Sea Convention, *supra* note 23 at Part XII, Section 6.

107. *Restatement, supra* note 11 at 137.

108. Brussels Convention on the Liability of Operators of Nuclear Ships, 25 May 1962, 57 A.J.I.L. 268 (1963).

109. International Convention on Civil Liability for Oil Pollution Damage, 29 Nov. 1969, 9 *I.L.M.* 45 (1970).

110. *Restatement, supra* note 11 at 141.

111. *Id. See also* the 1976 and 1984 Protocols to the 1969 Convention; 16 *I.L.M.* 617 (1977), 13 *Envt'l Pol'y & L.*, 66 (1984).

112. *See supra* note 78, and 1976 and 1984 Protocols: 16 *I.L.M.* 621 (1977), 13 *Envt'l Pol'y & L.*, 61 (1984).

113. *See supra* notes 83, 85.

114. Brussels International Convention Relating to Intervention on the High Seas in Cases of Oil Pollution Casualties, 26 U.S.T. 765, T.I.A.S. No. 8068, Art. 6.

allowing other possible forms of compensation to the injured person.[115]

10. The Antarctic environment: Developing a comprehensive regime for responsibility and liability

Concern for the protection of the Antarctic environment has resulted in major developments of the Law of State Responsibility, especially the specific issue of liability. These developments are particularly evident in the Convention on the Regulation of Antarctic Mineral Resource Activities.[116] This Convention is based on very stringent principles and requirements for the protection of the environment, which is a noteworthy development in itself, however the more important development is that no mineral resource activity shall take place until it is judged that it is environmentally safe under those stringent standards.[117] The emphasis on prevention thus becomes quite evident.

Observance of the Convention is to be enforced by States Parties and the regulatory committees through a combination of measures that include monetary penalties. Enforcement can lead to the modification, suspension, and cancellation of the pertinent management scheme, which in essence embodies the terms of the contract and provides authorization to engage in mineral activities.

Beyond the general measures, however, there are very specific rules dealing with responsibility and liability, some of which are highly innovative. The salient features of these rules are summarized as follows:

1. An operator involved in mineral resource activity, including prospecting, exploration, and development, has the obligation to take necessary and timely response action, with particular reference to prevention, containment, clean-up, and removal measures, if the activity results or threatens to result in damage to the Antarctic environment or dependent and associated ecosystems.[118] The geographical scope and the definition of damage included in this Convention are very broad. The emphasis on preventive measures

---

115. *Restatement, supra* note 11 at 137, 142.
116. CRAMRA, *supra* note 43. *See* generally Laura Pineschi, "The Antarctic Treaty System and General Rules of International Environmental Law," *International Law for Antarctica,* 187 (Francioni, Scovazzi, eds., 1987).
117. CRAMRA, *supra* note 43 at Art. 4.
118. CRAMRA, *supra* note 43 at Art. 8(1).

is again apparent. It should also be noted that here the responsibility is an unconditional type, not subject to limitations and other defensive factors.

2. If damage ensues in spite of the above measures, the operator is subject to a system of strict liability. The operator is liable for damage to the Antarctic environment and related ecosystems, loss or impairment of an established use, loss or damage to property of a third party, loss of life or personal injury of a third party, and reimbursement of reasonable costs to whomever has undertaken the response action.[119] The operator may also be liable for damages and other consequences not arising directly from these activities, in which case liability shall be governed by the applicable national or international law and procedures. It is interesting to note that these rules protect the Antarctic environment as such, irrespective of damage to property or life.

3. The regime relating to strict liability, unlike that which governs the responsibility of the operator, is subject to some conditions of relief for the operator, such as a natural disaster of an exceptional character, armed conflict and terrorism, or an intentional or grossly negligent act or omission by the party seeking redress.[120]

4. The sponsoring state has subsidiary liability in conjunction with that of the operator if the damage would not have occurred or continued if such state had carried out its obligations under the Convention.[121] These obligations are different for prospecting and for exploration and development, but in either event they may engage subsidiary liability to the extent the harm is not satisfied by the operator or otherwise. This is without prejudice to the application of international law to other types of damage engaging state liability. Thus we have an interesting case in which the activity of an operator may indirectly engage state responsibility and liability, in addition to the obligations that the Convention bestows upon the state directly.

5. Some specific aspects of this regime have been left open for additional negotiation by means of a Protocol to the Convention.[122] These open issues refer only to the liability provisions and not to those on responsibility explained under (1) above. One such issue

119. *Id.* at Art. 8(2).
120. *Id.* at Art. 8(4), (6)
121. *Id.* at Art. 8(3).
122. *Id.* at Art. 8(7).

concerns limits on liability: such limits do not refer to a curtailment of the obligation to pay full compensation, but only to the establishment of a ceiling on the portion to be paid by the operator in order to facilitate insurance; the balance would be paid by other mechanisms or by the state. Another mechanism to satisfy liability is the establishment of a compensation fund similar to that relating to oil-pollution damage. In addition, other means to assist with immediate-response action will have to be decided in the pending negotiations. Procedures and mechanisms for the adjudication of claims will also have to be worked out and will likely be of an international character.

6. Pending the entry into force of the Protocol referred to above, prospecting, unlike exploration and development, can be undertaken but each Party shall ensure the availability of recourse in its national courts for the adjudication of liability claims against the sponsored operator.[123] There is no provision here for actions against the state itself. The Commission established by the Convention shall be able to appear as a party in such procedures. These provisions coincide with the trend to provide access to national courts for remedial measures arising under international activities.

This set of important principles and mechanisms have been incorporated into the discussions of a comprehensive regime for environmental protection in Antarctica, in addition to their operation specifically in relation to mineral activities.[124] The comprehensive regime has also favourably considered an environmental-impact-assessment procedure and an early-warning notification obligation.

11. The new law of state responsibility: Improvement and caution

The present discussion about the global environment does not proceed in a vacuum, rather it is closely related to the evolution of environmental concerns throughout the century and consequently to the

123. *Id.* at Art. 8(10).
124. "Antarctic Treaty, Recommendation XV-1 on Comprehensive Measures for the Protection of the Antarctic Environment and Dependent and Associated Ecosystems," *Handbook of the Antarctic Treaty System,* October 1990, at 2103. The preparation of a draft Convention on the matter was undertaken by the XIth Antarctic Treaty Special Consultative Meeting, the first session of which was held in Viña del Mar, Chile, 19 Nov.–6 Dec. 1990.

state of international environmental law. The question that remains to be answered is whether the evolution that has been described meets the requirements of global environmental problems, and if not, then to what extent further developments should be introduced in the applicable international law.

From the discussion so far it is clear that international law is not as obsolete as has been supposed by some authors since it has shown a remarkable capacity to adapt in response to new situations and concerns. Furthermore, a number of its approaches and rules – even among the most traditional – are of interest for the solutions required in the new dimension of environmental concerns. But there are of course also important shortcomings. The major issues in this context will be discussed next.

Sovereignty and international cooperation

It is obvious that solutions for global environmental questions require increased international cooperation, both regionally and globally. International law has long subjugated national sovereignty to this end, particularly in the environmental field. In this regard there are no major conceptual difficulties. A different proposition altogether is that which advocates the virtual elimination of national sovereignty in this field;[125] however, neither international law nor the political will of states is quite ready for this radical step. The expanding scope of international environmental law is the best evidence of the progress made by international cooperation.

Sources of global environmental law

Concern has been repeatedly expressed that as a source of environmental law, treaties are inadequate in view of the time lags between signature and entry into force, the occasional need to adopt national implementing legislation, and above all that consensus or unanimity in their negotiation often results in the lowest common denominator substantively.[126] While this criticism is valid to a large extent, it overlooks the important fact that most of the basic principles of modern environmental law have emerged not so much from treaties but from

125. For a discussion on recent proposals for the international governance of the environment, *see* generally Peter S. Thacher, "Institutional Options for Management of the Global Environment and Commons," *United Nations Associations Project on Global Security and Risk Management*, 1989.
126. Peter H. Sand, "Institutions for Global Change: Whither Environmental Governance?", Fifth Talloires Seminar on International Environmental Issues, 14–18 May 1989.

case-law, general principles of law, declarations of principles, and customary law.

Thus there is great flexibility as to the sources of the law that may be used to fashion new approaches, such as the development of general principles, adoption of declarations, preparation of a framework convention to be supplemented by means of protocols and other agreements, or the recourse to regulatory instruments adopted by international institutions that might be established. The limit to this flexibility is not related to the form of the various legal instruments but to their substantive policy content, which must be generally acceptable to states, economic agents, and public opinion, in both the developed and the developing world.

A new basic legal principle
As a result of the evolution of international law a new basic legal principle can today be identified: the acceptance in state practice of responsibility for environmental damage. This means in fact that there is a legal obligation not to degrade the environment. However difficult it might be to put this principle into operation, the fact is that it has already been established under international law and a number of domestic legal systems.

A number of new corollary obligations have gradually been attached to this principle: the duty to notify and consult, the need to obtain prior consent of other states for given activities, state responsibility for given activities of private operators, and development of early-warning mechanisms and environmental-impact assessments.[127] Most of these obligations are preventive, thus responding to the new emphasis of international law on this point. The fact that many of these obligations operate only in the context of specific treaties or subject matters does not alter the trend toward a more generalized application. In the course of this evolution it is quite probable that additional obligations will emerge, such as information sharing, forecasting, and monitoring.

These are the bases on which the primary rules have been developing at a rapid pace. It is unlikely, however, that a comprehensive agreement dealing with all aspects of the environment will be achieved in the short or medium term, unless it were of a very general nature and built on successive compromises, which could well de-

---

127. Laura Pineschi, "La valutazione di impatto ambientale e il diritto internazionale del mare," 3 *Rivista Giuridica dell'Ambiente,* 505 (1988).

feat its original purpose.[128] It is more likely that the law will continue to develop piecemeal within the context of specific areas or issues; however, the cumulative effect of such developments represents significant progress across the board.

Developing the law of state responsibility

In addition to the role played by traditional rules of state responsibility, new conceptual and normative approaches have been developed, a number of which attend specifically to the needs of environmental protection. A first major development is that due diligence is no longer equated with fault, such that now failure to observe due diligence will amount to a violation of the substantive obligation under primary rules and hence engage responsibility regardless of fault. An important consequence of this development is that it will often provide the basis of responsibility for the activity of private operators.

A second fundamental development is related to the effect of strict liability: in addition to delinking responsibility from fault, it goes one step further in that it may also engage responsibility in spite of due diligence having been observed. Precisely because of this very innovative characteristic, strict liability is only found today in specific conventional regimes, but it could well become generalized in the future.

A third major area of development relates to state liability for acts not prohibited by international law, which is the natural outgrowth of the developments just described. Here responsibility is delinked from the traditional requirement of international law that the act be unlawful in nature. It is not difficult to foresee that this approach will be gradually and increasingly applied to environmental questions.

A fourth area of important development concerns the question of damage. As mentioned above, one point of view holds that damage is no longer a constitutive element of responsibility, there being damage implicit in the violation of the primary obligation. Certainly damage need not be of an economic nature. The environment thus becomes a protected value on its own merits and eventually damage will not need to be proved. The net result is that the operation of responsibility or liability becomes very efficient as compared to traditional standards.

---

128. *See* generally United Nations General Assembly, "Report of the Preparatory Committee for the United Nations Conference on Environment and Development," A/45/46, 17 Oct. 1990.

Extending the protection of the affected interest

Obligations *erga omnes* are beginning to emerge in the environmental field and might even become the basis of a rule of *jus cogens*. This latter development, however, will take some time to materialize. Similarly, the effort to typify an international crime does not meet with general approval today.[129] There have been proposals for declaring environmental harm a *delicta juris gentium*, like piracy, and even to establish some form of international criminal court to deal with the matter,[130] but this is not quite a realistic or feasible approach.

The concept of *actio popularis* as such will also take time and it is not currently favoured by international law. However, a number of steps are being taken to facilitate claims, particularly in terms of equal access to domestic courts and related issues. Problems such as concurrent claims, the intervention of international institutions, the distribution of compensation, and others will be solved without much difficulty on the basis of precedents or technical rules.

The following additional developments could be encouraged to make the operation of responsibility and liability more timely and effective:

- Assign responsibility and liability directly to the operator in given activities, as is evident in the Antarctic minerals regime.
- Require subsidiary state liability when the private operator cannot meet its obligations.
- Establish unlimited liability for given activities, while allowing for limited liability in relation to each basic component or segment: for example, the operator, the insurance company, special funds, and the state.
- Enlarge limits of liability presently affecting international funds or other potential sources of compensation.
- Introduce "product liability" to extend responsibility to the ultimate source of harm.
- Require environmental assessment in project financing or other major actions.

129. *See* generally the discussion of this point in P.M. Dupuy, "Action publique et crime international de l'Etat, à propos de l'Article 19 du projet de la Commission du Droit International sur la responsabilité des Etats," A.F.D.I. 539 (1979).
130. For a discussion of these proposals, *see* Paul C. Szasz, "The Role of International Law: Formulating International Legal Instruments and Creating International Institutions," Research Workshop on Managing the Global Commons, Knoxville, Tennessee, 1–4 Aug. 1989, at 14.

- Develop insurance and financial guarantees such as environmental bond posting.
- Develop appropriate rules on jurisdiction so as to easily identify and have recourse to the competent forum, with particular emphasis on the establishment of international claims commissions.
- Eliminate the requirement of exhausting local remedies in given situations or emergencies.
- Abolish immunity from legal process.
- Develop shared liability schemes among private operators.
- Establish liability for wrongful enforcement measures.
- Expand the definitions of pollution and environmental damage to include large ecosystems.
- Develop alternative methods of compensation for when the entity involved in environmental damage obtains relief on the ground of natural disaster or other exceptional circumstances.

New directions of the law

In one way or the other, examples of all of the above can be found in contemporary international law and the related domestic legal developments. Thus the critical step is not to design new concepts or mechanisms, but rather to ensure a more generalized application of such rules beyond the conventional regimes that have established them. This may be accomplished either by enacting additional or more comprehensive regimes or by developing general principles of law and customary international law.

There are, however, new conceptual developments and specific measures that are only beginning to enter the domain of international law or have only limited precedent in the law related to environmental protection.[131] The three most important new concepts in international environmental law are those related to intergenerational equity, the relationship with human rights, and the security dimension of environmental protection. All three are at the very heart of the preventive emphasis that international law has assumed.

The broader conceptual framework that has evolved is leading to the discussion of new types of measures or approaches:

- Inspection, verification, and enforcement are becoming the keys to successful compliance with the law, more so than the *ex post facto*

---

131. Edith Brown Weiss, "Our Rights and Obligations to Future Generations for the Environment," 84 A.J.I.L. (1990)

sanction of responsibility and liability. In all these matters international law is most experienced.

– Early-warning systems are being increasingly recognized as an effective mechanism for prevention and minimizing damage to the environment.

– Monitoring of the environment is also an increasingly accepted approach since it provides appropriate information for triggering the warning steps and, eventually, emergency responses.[132] However, monitoring involves the danger of encroaching upon legitimate decisions or actions appertaining to national sovereignty and thus requires very balanced implementation. To this end international cooperation can be harmonized with national monitoring. In addition, cooperative arrangements and plans can easily be developed for monitoring common spaces and extended to planetary monitoring systems.

– Assistance in the field of environmental protection is beginning to develop as a new type of measure. In part this approach relates to technical assistance and emergency assistance, including the establishment of appropriate international centres. However, assistance also relates in part to the major problem of industrial reconversion and its enormous costs. In this last dimension it is basically a problem of financial assistance.

– The role of scientific advisory bodies is being enhanced in the context of these new developments and is particularly relevant as to warning, monitoring, and delivering assistance.[133] Since this approach was used in the *Trail Smelter* case, it has been repeatedly applied to numerous conservation and environmental regimes. Beyond any doubt this role will continue to develop. In addition, useful suggestions have been made for the establishment of similar expert bodies in international environmental law.[134]

– Recourse to scientific bodies also relates to the concern that environmental regimes be adapted and updated in light of new scientific knowledge and experience. Adaptation by means of protocols,

132. Szasz, *supra* note 130 at 9–11.
133. Edith Brown Weiss, "Legal Dimensions of Global Change: A Proposed Research Agenda," 121 *International Social Science Journal,* 399 (1989), at 403–404.
134. The establishment of an International Environmental Law Commission under Article 13 of the United Nations Charter was suggested at the United Nations University Workshop on International Law and Global Change, the Hague, 8–10 Nov. 1989, for which see the Report of the Co-ordinator, Edith Brown Weiss, at 4.

annexes, and other procedures is also an expression of this concern.

– Licensing in accordance with environmental criteria has been applied in a few regimes, such as endangered species[135] and dumping of wastes.[136] Suggestions are being advanced to establish an international licensing system much broader in nature and extent.[137] Controlling individual private corporations by means of this environmental regulatory mechanism has also been suggested.[138] While justified in very specific circumstances, this approach should be used with the greatest of caution since it could well lead to some "world environmental governance" scheme that would not only run counter to national sovereignty concerns but also impinge on the freedom of private enterprise and market economies that characterize the world today.

– International auditing procedures based on reporting by states has also been suggested as a kind of preventive measure, following the model of the International Labour Organisation and human rights regimes.[139] Failure to comply with the agreed standards could trigger a process of economic or legal sanctions, including the request of an injunction from a judicial organ. It should be noted, however, that sanctions of this type have never been successful in international law. Thus it may be more effective to rely either on the preventive mechanisms outlined above, including compliance and enforcement, or on the traditional sanction of international law requiring payment of compensation.

– Establishing international funds for the payment of compensation is another of the major trends of the law in this field. This approach can also help meet the new requirements of intergenerational equity. The limited experience with existing funds shows that there is a trend to relax the limits of compensation and other restrictions originally envisaged. In addition to an oil-pollution fund,[140] the World Heritage Fund,[141] and the trust funds estab-

---

135. Washington Convention on International Trade in Endangered Species of Wild Fauna and Flora 1973, reprinted in S. Lyster, *International Wildlife Law,* 239 (1985).
136. *See* the Dumping Convention, *supra* note 29; Basel Convention, *supra* note 31.
137. Sand, *supra* note 126 at 17–18.
138. Szasz, *supra* note 130 at 8–9.
139. Sand, *supra* note 126 at 18–22.
140. *See supra* note 79.
141. UNESCO Convention Concerning the Protection of the World Cultural and Natural Heritage, 16 Nov. 1972, 11 *I.L.M.* 1358 (1972), art. 15.

lished by UNEP for the marine environment,[142] there are a number of proposals for extending the practice to other areas: the Antarctic minerals regime,[143] the World Atmosphere Fund proposed by the 1988 Toronto Conference,[144] the control of carbon-dioxide emissions, and the maritime carriage of certain substances.[145]

Existing international funds are normally financed by means of contributions. By contrast, a number of national funds are being financed by levies on the pertinent activities: 36 states in the United States have established funds for contingencies related to hazardous wastes financed by those generating the waste or storing it,[146] and France applies an air-pollution charge for certain emissions of sulphur dioxide.[147] Other funds rely on severance taxes on coal, oil and gas, minerals, and timber.[148] Relying on this experience, some have proposed that the World Atmosphere Fund be partly financed by a levy on fossil-fuel consumption and that other funds should apply levies on emissions of greenhouse gases, movement of tropical timber, and other related activities.[149] Here again the greatest caution should be used for the same reasons explained above.

12. Avoiding environmental degradation and opposing the world ecological government: A conclusion

The conclusion that emerges from all of the foregoing is that the law of state responsibility, including its aspects relating specifically to liability, is not at all inefficient or ineffective in the environmental field. The state of international law has evolved rapidly. As a result, the basic conceptual instruments and rules necessary to deal with the new requirements of environmental protection are available. These include both the traditional restoration and compensation mechanisms for when harm has ensued and the new emphasis on preventive

142. Brown Weiss, *supra* note 133 at 405.
143. CRAMRA, *supra* note 43 at Art. 8(7).
144. "The Changing Atmosphere: Implications for Global Security," Conference Statement, Toronto, 30 June 1988, proposing the "World Atmosphere Fund" and other Trust Funds; *see* generally Thacher, *supra* note 125 at 57.
145. Brown Weiss, *supra* note 133 at 405.
146. *Id.*
147. Sand, *supra* note 126 at 19, n. 36.
148. Brown Weiss, *supra* note 133 at 406.
149. Thacher, *supra* note 125 at 57–60.

measures. The state's conduct is governed by a large number of primary rules, while secondary rules are being perfected and extended to induce compliance and safeguard the environment.

A number of new approaches are being suggested in order to meet the needs of global environmental change. Conceptual innovation is rapidly influencing the new thinking of international law on the matter. Among the specific mechanisms that have been proposed, some are useful and reasonable and some are not. The former will no doubt lead in the short and medium term to the development of new rules of international law, a number of which are already in the process of formation; the latter will probably lack the necessary consensus.

In this, like in any other matter, international law responds with a difficult process of harmonization of interests. Concern for the environment is one interest in which the interests of states and humankind as a whole coincide. This is not true, however, with respect to the specific policies and rules that could be enacted and enforced. While for a number of industrialized countries environmental considerations are a top priority, for many developing countries the priority lies in production and economic performance. Very strict environmental standards in the former often contrast with ideas such as "debt-for-nature" swaps that are prevalent in the latter. Convergence of views will take time and effort.

Because international law relies on the harmonization of interests it tends to avoid extreme solutions. In this regard it can be expected that international law will not allow environmental degradation and will develop the necessary rules and institutions to ensure this fundamental obligation. But it can also be expected that it will not favour a kind of world ecological government that might subject states, individuals, and corporations to a highly regulated discipline contrary to sovereignty, freedom, or economic efficiency. To the extent that such a vision underlies some of the proposals being advanced, they are unlikely to be adopted.

6

Law and global environmental management: Some open issues

Peider Könz

The point of departure

The considerations presented in this chapter have had the benefit of two trial runs. One, in 1989 and 1990, was a post-graduate seminar offered in the International Law Department of the University of São Paulo. The second was a paper contributed to a reflection and publication on development economics and the environment, involving and addressed primarily to a group of distinguished economists.[1] In either case the subject included not only the natural environment – geosphere and biosphere, tangible and intangible values, and rational resource management – but also the well-being of society as such, and consequently its protection against future *Bhopals* and *Sevesos,* as well as against ecological disasters of the *Amoco Cadiz* or *Exxon Valdez* type. And in both instances "law" was seen as encompassing a complex, interactive system of substantive, procedural, and institutional norms, ranging from domestic law – private and public, civil and penal – to international law governing relations among states. The non-severability of national and international law has various reasons; in the first place, of course, the fact that many or most environmental phenomena transcend national boundaries; secondly,

1. Project UNU/WIDER (World Institute for Development Economics Research), Helsinki, 1990–1991.

159

both national and international law in that area are conditioned by the same concepts and pressures; thirdly, however, and as will be discussed below, it must be kept in mind that the application and enforcement of international law depends to a large extent on national implementation measures, i.e. on domestic legislation.

The message that emerged from the São Paulo seminar was that while law was an essential policy tool, efficiency, efficacy, and equity of environmental management could not be achieved simply by legislation and by recourse to traditional legal concepts – certainly not the Manicheistic "right" and "wrong" norms customary in civil and criminal law. It called instead for a balancing of many different interests intersecting in space and in time – economic interests, but also aesthetic and moral ones, and the interests of future generations – that had thus to be given a value, weighed against each other, and ultimately reconciled with some semblance of equity in the context of a system in which processes and institutions were as important, and perhaps more so, than absolute norms. The message to the economists, on the other hand, was that while economic considerations were essential for the design and operation of such a system, economists should not let themselves be carried away by econometric constructs based on data so soft, and so unreliable, that they would at best justify simple, common-sense working hypotheses to guide policy formulation and management.

In fact, the uncertainties and lack of knowledge – with regard to environmental phenomena – causal links other than in terms of probabilities; nature and extent of effects remote in time and space, direct or indirect, and so on – constitute the major problem confronting lawyers as well as economists. Certainty and predictability are fundamental prerequisites for the operation of tort and penal law – the two main instruments used in the past to deal with environmental harm and the interference with community interests. Related to the problem of uncertainty is the fact that while up to the middle of this century environmental problems were (or were at least perceived as being) essentially local, and confined to the private sphere of individuals or, where states were involved, to contiguous border zones and international water bodies, the spacial reach of many new environmental risks has become global, or "planetary," just as their time-frame is now clearly transgenerational, involving more often than not the probability of irreversible, irreparable harm.

The emergence of these new environmental risks had profound implications for the legal system in the sphere of both public and private law. It entailed new demands on the state, its administrative apparatus and civil society, and a new set of duties and rights governing relations between states. Most importantly, it called for a fundamental reassessment of tort law and, ultimately, the shift of emphasis from traditional compensatory remedies to a system of preventive norms coupled with more purposeful enforcement measures.

At a national level statutory changes occurred quite rapidly, essentially in the course of the past four decades:[2] public opinion and pressures from a structured civil society obviously accelerated the legislative process. At the international level, positive law developed more slowly, but the same pressures of public opinion generated an impressive body of "soft law" that may not be executory *per se*, but clearly points the way to the new norms and processes expected to govern the international community and, in some instances, were recognized as customary law[3] or translated into binding bilateral or multilateral compacts in a process much more dynamic and purposeful than the traditional meandering from doctrine to ad hoc conflict resolution to commissions of learned jurists and eventually treaty law. Indeed, the importance of "soft law" – Stockholm, Brundtland, OECD declarations and resolutions, and directives such as those of the European Economic Community – cannot be underrated in the genesis of a new international law of the environment.

The changes in domestic tort law and its compensatory remedies did, in fact, reach back to the last century, when traditional concepts had to be adjusted as the risks of harmful interference increased with the industrial revolution and subsequent technological progress. Most notably, the standards of care underlying tort liability (or liability for abuse of rights) were thus more sharply and strictly defined, to the point of generalizing the concept of "no-fault" or objective liability

---

2. The advent of the nuclear age, and the awareness of new, man-made risks of a magnitude never before experienced had a determinant effect on the speed with which this change occurred.
3. For example, although completed in 1982 after eight years of negotiations and signed by over 150 states, the United Nations Convention on the Law of the Sea has not yet entered into force. However, "by express or tacit agreement accompanied by consistent practice, the United States, and States generally, have accepted the substantive provisions of the Convention, other than those addressing deep sea-bed mining, as statements of customary international law binding upon them apart from the Convention." Introductory Note to Part V: The Law of the Sea, 2 Restatement Third of the Foreign Relations Law of the United States, 5 (1987).

for activities considered inherently hazardous, or at least creating a presumption of fault or negligence whenever damage occurred, and expanding the concept of "product liability." Except for the latter, this trend is clearly confirmed in the post–World War II legislation and conventions on liability for nuclear damage,[4] which generally provide for objective, though limited, liability channelled to one responsible entity and backed by insurance and/or the subsidiary responsibility of the state.

A similar hardening has occurred in the course of this century in the law related to the responsibility of states. This was derived mainly from the concept of abuse of rights, or from the precept of good neighbourhood, as articulated in a series of jurisprudential pronouncements starting with the *Trail Smelter* arbitration,[5] as well as in treaties generally concerning transboundary environmental harm in narrowly defined border areas or international water bodies.[6]

In today's perspective, however, it is generally recognized that this is not enough. Even if reinforced by the concept of objective liability, tort law (or its equivalent in inter-state relations) no longer constitutes an adequate bulwark against the environmental risks to which mankind, including future generations, is now exposed. There are several basic reasons for this.

In the first place, tort remedies are designed to operate where a clearly definable damage to property, patrimonial rights, or the personal integrity of identifiable victims can be traced to a clearly defined external source; the element of fault or negligence has, as noted earlier, lost its importance where inherently hazardous activities are involved. On the other hand, much of today's environmental harm – or potential environmental harm – is diffuse in time and in space, involving cumulative sources. It can affect a multiplicity of victims – often across national boundaries – and tends to touch not, or not only, on the property or physical-integrity sphere of individuals but

---

4. *See* Paris Convention on Third Party Liability in the Field of Nuclear Energy, 29 July 1960, as amended in 1964 and 1982, *International Conventions on Civil Liability for Nuclear Damage*, 43–51 (IAEA Legal Series No. 4, rev. ed. 1970); Vienna Convention on Civil Liability for Nuclear Damage, 21 May 1963, 1063 U.N.T.S. 265, 2 *I.L.M.* 727 (1963).
5. The Trail Smelter Arbitration, 3 U.N. R. Int'l Arb. Awards 1905 (1941). *See also* A. Kuhn, "The Trail Smelter Arbitration between the United States and Canada," 35 A.J.I.L. 665 (1941).
6. *See*, e.g., Canada-United States of America: Great Lakes Water Quality Agreement, Ottawa, 22 Nov. 1978, 30 U.S.T. 1383, T.I.A.S. 9257.

on community interests, i.e. on what is called the "commons" – global or local. In many instances, damage may manifest itself decades or generations after the event. This means, of course, that it will often be difficult to determine the damage, to identify the victims and potential victims, and to establish – and prove – the causal link upon which tort remedies are by necessity predicated. Lastly, it must be expected that where large-scale environmental damage is involved, the persons (or entities) responsible for it may not have the resources to compensate the victims.

Some legislative improvements are of course possible to overcome these shortcomings. Beyond the introduction of no-fault liability, periods of prescription can be extended, insurance coverage or other guarantees can be required for hazardous activities, procedural mechanisms can be adjusted to facilitate collective actions and to make the courts accessible to foreign claimants in the event of trans-boundary damage; funds can be established for future victims and latent damage, and risks – or excess risks – can be socialized by the intervention of the state as a guarantor. As already noted, nuclear liability legislation and treaty law have innovated in many of these areas, demonstrating how far traditional legal concepts and mechanisms can be stretched to meet large-scale environmental hazards. So has recent jurisprudence concerning coastal pollution by major accidental oil spills and, with some limitations, in the Bhopal and other large-scale industrial accidents.

The fact remains, however, that legal norms designed essentially to provide compensation are, by themselves, a rather inept tool where the damage is potentially irreversible and irreparable and surrounded by uncertainties with regard to causes and effects, as is the case for many of today's environmental risks. Compensatory liability may be a deterrent, of course, and thus an effective disincentive, and it may provide some immediate relief – a pecuniary liniment – to victims of many environmental accidents. But no more than that.

Recognizing the limits inherent in the tort law approach, the emphasis of the legislator – national as well as international – has shifted from compensation after the event to prevention, i.e., from civil liability to the imposition and enforcement of positive duties intended to prevent the occurrence of harm. At the national level, this takes the form of licensing or approval mechanisms, generic prohibitions, and a variety of regulations linked to specific technical norms and standards applicable to dangerous substances or activities. Recent legislative schemes tend to include a specific obligation to assess potential risks (risk assessment) and to notify the persons concerned.

Similar preventive schemes involving positive duties, prohibitions, technical norms, and supervisory mechanisms are emerging also at the international level – bilateral, regional, or global: it is significant that even *Trail Smelter,* generally remembered as the main precedent for the obligation of states to provide compensation for environmental damage caused beyond its boundaries, placed even greater emphasis on the preventive norms and control mechanisms under the bilateral US-Canadian treaty relating to the Great Lakes.[7]

Today the pressure for such international preventive schemes based on the application of technical safety norms has outgrown the bilateral stage and calls for action at the global or at least regional level. This reflects a growing awareness that environmental risks transcend geographic contiguities and often affect humanity as a whole. However, the pressure for global schemes and global compliance derives also from considerations of economic self-interest, in the sense that countries applying strict environmental standards would be at a disadvantage in international trade when competing with countries that did not observe such norms. This motivation was and remains evident in the EEC efforts toward a common environmental policy and environmental standards.

International preventive norms and mechanisms

While the preventive schemes emerging at multilateral levels – whether regional, subregional, or global – are still to a large extent in the nature of "soft" law, their basic concept follows the approach of national legislation: generically formulated obligations ("framework" norms); absolute or conditional prohibitions; requirement of prior authorization and creation of the corresponding regulatory and supervisory mechanisms, as well as technical norms setting qualitative and quantitative standards; special organs charged with environmental policy formulation or coordination, monitoring, and control; statutory provisions calling for the prior assessment of environmental impact, the notification of risks, as well as emergency plans and damage-containment schemes for high-risk activities; direct commun-

7. Washington Treaty Relating to Boundary Waters and Questions Arising Along the Boundary between the United States and Canada, 11 Jan. 1909, T.S. 548

ity involvement in policy formulation and environmental management, information of the public, etc.

The difference between national and multilateral schemes is, of course, that the international community and its organs have no power of coercion other than through public opinion, boycotts, or retaliation and the very limited scope of compulsory international jurisdiction; nor are there at that level – except in limited regional contexts – any standing legislative bodies, budget authorities, and, consequently, budgetary allocations sufficient to implement and enforce serious environmental policy. It follows from this that unlike their counterparts in domestic law (or in EEC *decisions*), preventive treaty-norms cannot be executory, but take the form of explicit duties of the contracting states to regulate, supervise, monitor, legislate on matters such as liability for damage, provide access to courts, etc. Implementation and enforcement remain the responsibility of each state concerned.

There are nevertheless some basic issues common to both national and international law. One of them has become particularly visible in the current global-warming debate – as it was, in the 1960s, with regard to nuclear hazards, and in particular the disposal of radioactive waste: should the legislator, when facing substantial uncertainties with regard to the potential hazard of particular activities, assume the worst and prohibit an activity (or regulate it, setting rigorous safety standards for it) unless its harmlessness has been proved, or should prohibitions and strict standards be adopted only when the hazard has been clearly demonstrated, at least in terms of probabilities? While the standards of care implicit in strict tort liability, and, in international law, the Ozone Layer Convention and Montreal Protocol[8] denote a cautious, pessimistic approach, there continue to be strong pressures in the opposite direction in current international negotiations.

A second perplexity, also reflecting the wide area of uncertainty characteristic of environmental phenomena, concerns the formulation of technical norms, and in particular the qualitative and quantitative criteria underlying safety standards. At the national level, these are often left to schedules or ad hoc determinations by regulatory agen-

8. Vienna Convention for the Protection of the Ozone Layer, 22 Mar. 1985, 26 *I.L.M.* 1529 (1987); Montreal Protocol on Substances That Deplete the Ozone Layer, 16 Sept. 1987, 26 *I.L.M.* 1550 (1987).

cies. With the exception of regional bodies such as the European Economic Commission, such a delegation of regulatory powers seems at present rather utopian in an international setting. Instead, treaty law tends to relegate technical norms, schedules, or standards to annexes or protocols with a limited duration, or provision for their revision – periodically or not – under procedures less cumbersome than the negotiation of the treaties themselves.

In connection with international technical norms, the question has been raised as to whether more lenient standards (or more gradual timetables for their adoption) should apply to developing countries. While such double standards may be an attractive political expedient, one wonders whether it would not be preferable for the international community to provide direct financial support for the introduction of environment-friendly technologies in such countries, the more so as the adoption of double standards might, in the long run, condemn developing countries to chronic technological obsolescence.

There are a few other issues specific to international preventive schemes relating to the environment and the corresponding duties of states that deserve special comment.

One set of issues concerns the duty of states to provide for adequate compensation and a forum for environmental-damage claims, without discrimination based on the nationality or residence of the claimants. The Paris and Vienna nuclear liability conventions[9] stipulate specific norms on this subject, as does the convention on damage caused by objects in space (which, unlike the Paris and Vienna conventions, provides for the direct responsibility of the state) and, indirectly, the convention on the establishment of an indemnity fund for pollution damage. Most other treaties, however, like the UN Convention on the Law of the Sea, have opted for a generic clause calling upon member states to legislate, ensuring adequate compensation and a forum, but without specifying the nature of the remedies and guarantees involved. Significantly, efforts of the European Economic Commission to touch upon this subject in the context of its post-Seveso directive have so far met with considerable resistance – no doubt because a rethinking of liability rules with a view to their harmonization and modernization would – and should – affect diverging doctrinal conceptions of tort law, and perhaps also powerful economic interests.

A second issue concerns the settlement of disputes. Most interna-

9. *See supra* note 4.

tional compacts relating to environmental subjects contain traditional conciliation and arbitration clauses; the UN Convention on the Law of the Sea, however, provides for a special tribunal competent also for issues relating to pollution.[10] In the perspective of a global compact on the environment, the question has been raised as to whether there should be a special international court for environmental disputes, or whether the International Court of Justice – perhaps sitting in special chambers – could not be given jurisdiction – preferably compulsory jurisdiction – over them. There is no doubt that this would constitute an important step toward enforceable international environmental law; on the other hand, experience shows that it is not easy to negotiate compulsory jurisdictional schemes in an international community still obsessed with the concept of sovereignty. It might be more realistic, as a first step – and would correspond to a priority need given the uncertainties that surround environmental phenomena – to settle for an international body of experts charged with the elucidation of issues of fact underlying environmental disputes, without entering into the legal consequences that might ensue.

Thirdly, many treaties and draft treaties dealing with the environment stipulate a general obligation of states to collaborate (whether or not in the context of a particular intergovernmental organization or programme) with regard to research, monitoring, supervision, and the development of international law. In some instances, this is reflected in the "plans of action" appended to hortatory instruments such as the Stockholm Declaration and its subsequent endorsement by the UN General Assembly.[11] These clauses or plans of action do not, by themselves, entail very concrete obligations, but would evidently gain in significance in the perspective of a future strengthening of intergovernmental institutions – sectoral or general – charged with environmental matters.

A further clause postulated in environmental treaty law concerns the commitment to allow the free flow of information on environment-friendly technologies, particularly for the benefit of developing countries. It must be expected, however, that before becoming positive law, this concept – possibly in the form of compulsory licensing with no (or only nominal) royalties – will involve tough negotiations,

---

10. Convention on the Law of the Sea, 10 Dec. 1982, Arts. 279–299, U.N. A/CONF. 62/122, 21 *I.L.M.* 1261 (1982).
11. Action Plan for the Human Environment of the UN Conference on the Environment, 16 June 1972, U.N. Doc. A/CONF.48/14/Rev.1, Ch.II.

167

insofar as environment-friendly (or depolluting) technological innovations are generally the subject of proprietary rights (patents; industrial secrets) of powerful industrial groups in developed countries.

Compensatory remedies: Gaps and trends in international law

In spite of the shift of emphasis to preventive norms and operational schemes, and in spite of the fundamental shortcomings pointed out earlier, compensatory remedies retain their importance, both as a deterrent – especially where states or transnational enterprises notoriously sensitive to public opinion are concerned – as well as to repair harm once it has occurred. It has also been noted that progress has been made to tighten tort law as it applies to environmental and other major risks, as well as in private and public international law. There nevertheless remain some critical areas in which international law needs further adjustment.

Conflict of laws

Major instances of environmental harm, whether or not accidental, are likely to have transfrontier connotations. The sources of the damage, or the persons responsible for it, may be in countries other than those where the damage occurs: there may be victims or defendants from several countries, and so on. Among the accidents that occurred in recent decades, many, if not most, gave rise to litigation before civil courts, involved private plaintiffs and defendants, and were governed by private law. *Chernobyl, Seveso,* and the more recent *Rhine* pollution cases never came before the courts and were not resolved by reference to any legal norms and processes, but the *Torrey Canyon, Amoco Cadiz, Exxon Valdez,* and *Bhopal* disasters did, as well as earlier Rhine pollution cases. In fact, private litigation has been, and may be expected to remain, the first and principal resort for victims of environmental harm.

As regards the choice of courts, the tendency has been to bring jurisdiction closer to the victims. Problems nevertheless remain where damage is caused (or manifests itself) in several countries or – as on the high seas – outside the jurisdiction of any country. Also, victims will evidently seek the forum that applies the law most favourable to them. The "forum shopping" that surrounded the

Bhopal litigation[12] is a case in point: The Indian victims wanted to proceed before American, and the American co-defendant before Indian courts. A similar situation occurred in the *Amoco Cadiz* litigation, where the American courts, unlike the tendency of the courts manifested in the *Bhopal* case, accepted jurisdiction. Since the current tendency is to apply the substantive law most favourable to claimants,[13] the choice of forum might, in the long run, be expected to lose some of its importance. The fact remains, however, that a number of critical issues – e.g., the availability of collective remedies; type and measure of damages; statute of limitations; distribution of a limited fund (e.g., covered by insurance, or in bankruptcy proceedings), etc. – are seen as procedural questions governed by the law of the court. A solution may be found, in the long run, by treaty provisions or – in a more utopian perspective – the day an international tribunal will be created to hear also claims by and against private parties. Until then, however, the jurisdictional ballet surrounding claims for environmental damage is likely to continue.

Piercing the corporate veil

A second important issue, dramatically exposed in the *Bhopal* case, concerns the responsibility of parent companies for the civil liability of subsidiaries – whether based on fault or derived from a no-fault rule. The tendency, at least in American law, is to "pierce the corporate veil" and recognize the responsibility of the parent. This occurred in the *Bhopal* case, although it appeared that the parent company itself had also been negligent. At any rate, the issue re-

---

12. In December 1984 a toxic gas leak killed over 2,000 people and injured tens of thousands more in Bhopal, India. The leak occurred at a plant owned and operated by a subsidiary of Union Carbide, a US corporation. The Government of India acted to assume responsibility for all the victims and filed suits in US courts against Union Carbide seeking compensatory and punitive damages. The consolidated claims were dismissed on the grounds of *forum non conveniens*, thereby sending the litigation back to Indian courts. V. Nanda, "For Whom the Bell Tolls in the Aftermath of the Bhopal Tragedy: Reflections on Forum non Conveniens and Alternative Methods of Resolving the Bhopal Dispute," 15 *Denver Journal of International Law and Policy*, 235, 236–240 (1987). *See*, Indian Law Institute, *Inconvenient Forum and Convenient Catastrophe: The Bhopal Case* (1986) (for a critical look at the US Court's decision not to hear the case and many of the documents relevant to the litigation).
13. *See*, R. Weintraub, *Commentary on the Conflict of Laws*, 284–291 (3rd ed., 1986) (which highlights the "pervasive trend" in the law of torts toward a rebuttable presumption that law favourable to the plaintiff will apply).

mains open in many jurisdictions, inhibiting the effectiveness of civil-law remedies for large-scale environmental damage in situations where potential defendants, whether or not qualifiable as multinational enterprises, seek to insulate themselves from liability by "one-ship corporations" or by hiding behind a web of subsidiaries and holding companies.

Collective remedies

A third major area in which the law must be expected to grow concerns the availability of collective remedies – e.g. class actions, or actions by communities rather than by private claimants – as well as the representation of the interests of future generations. Meanwhile, if no workable solutions are found under domestic or treaty law, there will always remain – as a last resort for foreign collective claims – state responsibility under public international law.

State responsibility

The responsibility of states under public international law – not only for environmental damage attributable to their own acts or omissions but also for damage that can be led back to private sources on their territory or subject to their control – is recognized by legal doctrine and jurisprudence of relatively recent date (derived from the *Trail Smelter* arbitration, the *Lake Lenoux* and *Corfu Channel* and subsequent cases),[14] as well as by some treaties dealing with potentially hazardous activities. State responsibility is obviously also a corollary of the new norms, soft or hard, that impose on states specific and explicit obligations to prevent environmental damage. In fact, it must be assumed that the breach or non-observance of an agreed safety norm or preventive obligation constitutes fault (and an abuse of sovereignty rights) from which there flows a direct responsibility of the state concerned as long as damage and a causal link are demonstrated. Some doubts have been raised as to whether this responsibility is objective or based on fault; where a prohibition has been violated, however, or a specific treaty obligation accepted by the

---

14. The Trail Smelter Arbitration, 3 U.N. R. Int'l Arb. Awards 1905 (1941); Lake Lanoux Arbitration (France v. Spain), 16 Nov. 1957, 24 *I.L.R.* 101 (1957), digested in 53 A.J.I.L. 156 (1959); Corfu Channel Case (U.K. v. Albania), 1949 I.C.J. 4 (Judgement of 9 April 1949).

state concerned was breached, the question would appear to be academic, provided of course that the treaty obligation was clear and unambiguous.

It should be remembered, in this context, that the responsibility of the state is in principle direct and primary, although the claimant state may represent injuries to persons (nationals or residents) and property within its jurisdiction, as long as these claimants have exhausted local remedies. There is also another type of state responsibility, however – subsidiary and not primary – assumed under particular treaty norms, e.g. in the nuclear liability conventions and, presumably, where under general or treaty law, a state has the obligation to ensure prompt, equitable, and non-discriminatory compensation but the victims are not, in fact, able to recover.

Beyond this, one major issue relating to environmental harm continues unresolved: it concerns the responsibility of states for allowing the export (often by or through subsidiaries of powerful transnational enterprises) of polluting or dangerous technology, substances, and equipment that result in environmental harm. Relatively little attention has been paid to this issue by legal doctrine. The US Restatement of Foreign Relations Law simply takes the position that product liability does not extend to international law.[15] Yet the question is by no means moot – *Seveso*, *Bhopal*, and the export to or disposal of toxic waste in developing countries of Africa or the Caribbean are cases in point. To the extent that the country of origin could in fact regulate such exports, or is actually encouraging them, equity clearly calls for an affirmative duty and consequent responsibility.

This issue – even if couched only in terms of an obligation to regulate, while the problem of liability for compensation is limited to a generic obligation to "cooperate" – is squarely raised by the 1989 Basel Convention on the Control of Transboundary Movements of Hazardous Wastes and Their Disposal, and by an earlier EEC directive on the same subject[16] that requires authorization by the exporting country and a formal notification of and authorization by the country of destination, even when it is not a member of the European Community. Quite apart from the fact that the Basel Convention has not yet entered into force, and that the EEC directive is not

15. Restatement (Third) Foreign Relations Law of the United States, Part VI (Law of the Environment), *see* 601, comment D (1987).
16. Basel Convention on the Control of Transboundary Movements of Hazardous Wastes and Their Disposal, 22 Mar. 1989, 28 *I.L.M.* 657 (1989); EEC Council Directive: Transboundary Shipment of Hazardous Waste, 6 Dec. 1984, EEC Dir. No. 84/231.

171

applied with great diligence, both recognize that the exporting country has an affirmative duty of care not only to other member countries but to the international community at large. Should such an affirmative duty of supervision and control, and responsibility of the state where it is remiss in living up to it, extend also to the export of inherently dangerous equipment or technology, especially when encouraged by official export credits, and when the exports are directed to developing countries notoriously unable to apply adequate safety norms? And what about turnkey contracts for environmentally substandard plants, or the export of pharmaceuticals, insecticides, and herbicides that do not meet the safety standards in the exporting country? No doubt a norm involving the responsibility of the exporting state may seem utopian at the present stage – and would be opposed by powerful economic lobbies. It does, however, touch on a reality that cannot be ignored in the perspective of global environmental management.

Responsibility for harm to the global commons

Lastly, there remains the problem of responsibility for damage to the *global commons*. Specifically: what indemnities are due, and who may claim them, for damage to environmental values that cannot be related to the sphere of sovereignty of any state (or to the interest of its citizens) but that are recognized as the objects of protection under customary international law or – more often – under treaty law? Antarctica, the high seas, the atmosphere, and outer space are examples. The endangered fauna and flora are others – as may conceivably be the preservation of genetic diversity seen as a distinct object of environmental concern.

Treaties generally include settlement-of-disputes clauses that allow the parties – i.e., member states – to submit claims for their violation to an impartial procedure of conciliation and arbitration. The Convention on the Law of the Sea – which has not yet entered into force – goes much further, by establishing a tribunal open not only to states, but also to private claimants and even to non-governmental organizations. Beyond this, the International Court of Justice has recognized, in its *obiter dictum* in the *Barcelona Traction* case[17] that there exist basic obligations to the international community as a

---

17. Case Concerning Barcelona Traction, Light and Power Company, Ltd. (Belgium v. Spain) 1970 I.C.J. 4 (New Application, 1962, Second Phase).

whole (*erga omnes*) that can consequently be asserted by any state. It may be assumed that this would apply also to serious harm to the global commons. And in the future, the legitimation to present such claims may be extended to intergovernmental organizations concerned with the environment.

Indemnities for damage to the global commons (as distinguished from the *local* commons, with respect to which claims by community organizations are increasingly – though not always fully – recognized by the courts) may conceivably be claimed by non-governmental bodies or by the state – including foreign states – also in tort proceedings before ordinary courts. If, as may often still be the case, their legitimation to present such claims is denied, the only avenue remains state-to-state litigation under public international law.

As regards the nature and amount of the compensation that might be claimed for harm to the global commons, it must be assumed that it would cover only the actual cost of reparation, reposition, and containment of the environmental damage (e.g., the cost of depollution and salvage of the affected fauna and flora and the cost of reasonable preventive measures). Beyond this, of course, there remain injunctive remedies, and penal sanctions under internal and perhaps – in the future – under international law; it has thus been suggested that international sanctions might include special fines or contributions channelled to a global environment fund.

Enforcement: Deterrence: Incentives and disincentives

Domestic law

National legal systems have a variety of ways to ensure compliance with safety norms and affirmative obligations. In addition to the threat of civil liability, there exist injunctive tools addressed to individuals, writs to compel action by public officials and public entities, and finally criminal law with its panoply of preventive and punitive instruments.

The concept of environmental crime, for instance, and the application of penal sanctions for environmental misdeeds, has grown considerably in the past decades. Where its enforcement has been consistent, e.g., in much of northern Europe, including the United Kingdom – it is proving an effective instrument of control. Significantly, the tendency is to extend penal sanctions for environmental crimes also to corporate officials and to bodies corporate. However, and quite apart from the fact that levels of enforcement are generally low for non-violent, "white-collar" offences, and even more so for crimes that do not involve individual victims, penal law as an instrument of control suffers from the same basic weakness as civil law: it generally operates only after the event. On the other hand, it is of course easier to mobilize official means of coercion (as well as public opinion) to prevent the commission of a crime than that of a civil tort, or the non-observance of an administrative regulation.

The question may nevertheless be asked as to whether persuasion and deliberate forms of inducement would not, in many instances, be more effective than (or an important complement to) coercion or the threat of civil or criminal responsibility. It should not be assumed that the public, and in particular also industry and utilities responsible for most of today's environmental hazards, are impervious to such an approach. The insurance industry should obviously play a lead role in that connection.

In fact, experience with voluntary restraints on the part of industry has been mixed. Corporate stockholders have, in recent times, become conscious of environmental issues – as of issues in the area of human rights – and may in the long run contribute to environment-friendly corporate policy. In Latin America, one of the largest mining and transport companies – a public-sector enterprise – has been responsible for some of the most successful environmental research and conservation programmes in Amazonia. Major oil companies have introduced "self-regulation" programmes and established a compensation fund for environmental damage; after the *Torrey Canyon* disaster, however, they had resisted all attempts to establish official norms on shipping lanes. Unfortunately, neither self-imposed restraints nor official regulations on shipping were sufficient to avoid the *Amoco Cadiz* and *Exxon Valdez* disasters.

It is in that perspective that a combination of economic and in particular fiscal incentives and disincentives may have a major role to play, at least in a national context, reinforcing the pressure of public opinion and the threat of penal or civil liability by inducing voluntary compliance with safety norms and standards.

There are, in fact, numerous instances in which fiscal incentives and disincentives have been successfully used to reinforce public policy: energy-saving programmes during the recent oil crises are cases in point. While it would go beyond the scope of the present paper to consider in detail the fiscal and other economic measures – pricing policy, surtaxes, rebates, investment credits, etc. – designed to induce compliance with environmental norms and policies, it is evident that this area – concerning both lawyers and economists – is central to effective environmental management schemes.

Related to it is the concept of a special environmental levy or levies on the use or production of polluting substances or, generally, on environmentally harmful activities; such a tax (or pollution charge) can also – to the joy of those who like to rely on market mechanisms – be combined with a system of allowable quotas and negotiable "credits." While the principle of an environmental (or pollution) levy still meets considerable industry resistance, its design and implementation would pose no major technical problems and is already being considered in various countries, and even at the level of the European Economic Community. It is in fact a logical consequence of the postulate that "the polluter pays," especially where it is proposed to use its proceeds to finance preventive and reparatory measures, and perhaps finance or at least stimulate the massive technological changes (e.g., in energy policy) that will be required to contain the further deterioration of the environment.

Coercion and inducement at the international level

If it may be assumed that effective enforcement schemes will be adopted in most countries – and in regional groupings such as the EEC – in the foreseeable future, the same cannot be said for international schemes that, to be effective, should by necessity be global. Inducements, disincentives, environmental levies, and even fines or criminal sanctions are in principle conceivable also at that level. The problem, as has already been noted, is the lack of enforcement power and the low managerial capacity (actual or perceived) of intergovernmental organizations. Perhaps the most that can be expected from them at this stage, pending a fundamental restructuring of international mechanisms, would be more purposeful research and information programmes, technical assistance, and, possibly, the management by multilateral lending agencies of special credit facilities[18] to finance environment-friendly infrastructure, technol-

18. E.g., the Global Environmental Facility (IBRD/UNEP/UNDP) concerning protecting the ozone layer, limiting emissions of greenhouse gases, protecting biodiversity, and protecting international waters. For the documents establishing GEF, *see* 30 *I.L.M.* 1739 (1991).

ogy, and policies. The main problem to be faced in that connection may not be the mobilization of funds – voluntary, assessed, or levied – but their effective utilization through viable projects.

It might indeed be concluded that, in the short term, transparency and the flow of information on environmental risks and environmental damage that have already occurred constitute both the central function of international organisms and the most effective tool to induce compliance with international postulates and norms, in the sense that information mobilizes public opinion in support of environmental policy. In terms of responsibility, the obligation to inform and notify the international community of existing hazards was confirmed by the International Court of Justice in the *Corfu Channel*[19] case. It is explicit in a variety of clauses on notification, monitoring, the exchange of information, and reporting contained in recent treaties – bilateral, regional, or global – dealing with particular environmental risks. Related to them are obligations – hard or soft – to collaborate in research on environmental phenomena and the containment of environmental harm, as well as obligations concerning prior risk assessments and joint measures after the occurrence of major accidents.

Future outlook

There can be no doubt that in the long run environmental management, and indeed the very concept of sustainable development, presupposes an effective normative and institutional system accepted by the international community as a whole. The question is therefore not whether, but only how, and how soon the shortcomings and hurdles discussed in this paper can be overcome. In that perspective, it must be remembered that unlike domestic law, which flows from a continuing legislative process, treaty law grows by leaps and bounds – most notably as a result of large global events such as the Stockholm Conference. At least in terms of soft law, Stockholm represented an important landmark, and it may be hoped that, 20 years later, the UN Conference in Rio de Janeiro will play a similar role, even if the negotiation of hard, positive law may take longer. Meanwhile, it might be possible – and has in fact been proposed both by NGOs and by the UNCED Secretariat – that the Rio Conference adopt a global covenant or "Earth Charter" – i.e., a conceptual (and political)

19. *See supra* note 14.

framework for what is still, and may remain for some time, a fragmented non-system composed of a variety of international compacts, each with its different membership, focus, and time-frame.

Among the new approaches likely to develop within such a global framework is the suggestion that rights and obligations relating to the environment be activated as parts of a negotiated development contract or contracts.[20] This concept, which might for instance be applied to the preservation and management of tropical forests or of particular river basins, is related to the concept of balancing of conflicting interests in the allocation of natural resources and in the assignment of responsibility for environmental harm. Both stand in contrast to the vision of environmental law as a construct of absolute, Manicheistic commandments and are reflected both in treaty law and jurisprudence related, for instance, to international water rights and rights to the resources of the continental shelf.[21]

Ultimately, however, international environmental law will have to go beyond the concept of a development contract. Improved compensatory remedies will be part of it, although it will be important to avoid the excesses that characterize the practice of tort law in the United States.[22] Gradually, international environmental law should become an operational system in its own right, no longer dependent upon the good will of individual states for its implementation. To that end, international adjudicatory mechanisms, endowed with compulsory jurisdiction and accessible also to individual claimants or communities seeking compensatory or injunctive relief, are also an essential ingredient of a future system of international law relating to the environment. And so will be truly international, permanent policy mechanisms, as well as an institutional infrastructure endowed with executive, supervisory, and monitoring powers, and with sufficient resources – perhaps even in the form of a substantial environment fund! – to stimulate or induce compliance with environmental policy imperatives.

Admittedly all this represents an ambitious legislative agenda – and the very magnitude of the challenge implies some danger that an

---

20. *See* L. Jayawardene, *A Global Environmental Compact for Sustainable Development* (UNU/WIDER, 1991).
21. North Sea Continental Shelf Cases (F.R.G. v. Denmark, F.R.G. v. Netherlands) 1969 I.C.J. 48.
22. It cannot in fact be assumed that tort litigation will play the same role in countries with a legal structure different from that of the United States, with its 750,000 lawyers versed in the nuances of adversarial procedures, fueled by contingent fees and helped by civil juries.

overly enthusiastic legislator will forget the importance of implementation. In fact, law that is not applied and thus constitutes a screen to conceal reality is hardly any better, and often worse, than no law at all. This danger is apparent in many national legal systems, where environmental norms and standards exist but are not enforced. At the international level, the history of overly ambitious treaty schemes is also revealing. Either they have to be watered down in order to meet the lowest common denominator among prospective member countries, thus losing their significance, or they run the risk that some key country may defect when the chips are down, as was the case for the United States in the end stretch of the negotiations on a UN Convention on the Law of the Sea. Careful and realistic (if determined) strategy planning – often building upon a first phase in which agreement is limited to soft law – will thus remain of the essence. When the time is ripe to enter into hard-law commitments, however, the international community should not content itself with non-binding, hortatory declarations.

7

The legislation and implementation of international environmental law and the third world: The example of China

Lai Peng Cheng

On the spectrum of third-world ecosystems, colonial plunder is the primary cause of environmental degradation, which is the historical reason, and cultural and governmental negligence of the green peace mission caused by failing economic strength, excessive indebtedness, stretching of ecosystem capacity to sustain the pressure of population growth underlie the process of environmental erosion. In spite of these handicaps, third-world countries should take an active part in global environmental protection and maintain a sustainably healthy environmental order.

Leaving the above aside, the legislation and implementation of international environmental law have a tendency to neglect the social factors and the differing economic development status of states; but the objective reality is that any global issue is an inseparable and organic whole. This suggests that in respect of global environment control we should consider the objective conditions of those states that are undeveloped economically and technologically.

Consideration should be given to how to encourage all states, especially the vast number of third-world states, to protect our global environment, particularly in order to distribute fairly the burden of legislating and implementing international environmental law.

The third world refers to those countries developing economically that are newly independent and not aligned politically. These are mainly found in Asia (except Japan), Africa, and Latin America.

179

An overview of international environmental legislation and its implementation

As viewed from the historical development of international environmental law, especially the convening of the United Nations Conference on the Human Environment in 1972,[1] two fundamental aspects should not be overlooked: rapid development of international environmental law and the grim environmental landscape of our globe.

(1) Rapid development

International environmental law is the body of rules that regulate the relations between states in respect of the exploitation or improvement of the environment. That law evolved and developed at the same time as the problems between development and environment became a global issue. Although the earliest international environmental rules can be traced back 100 years, when the 1856 Vienna Congress established some regulations concerning shipping on international rivers applicable to the Danube,[2] or even earlier, global environmental legislation was not considered until after the 1970s. Before that time, environmental protection was treated mainly as a technical problem of pollution control. Generally speaking, with some notable exceptions, the aims of environmental policy or legislation before the 1970s did not address the economy or the degradation of the ecosystem.[3] Even shortly after World War II, pollution problems were addressed by simply enacting separate restrictive agreements. Viewing the fundamental principles of international environmental law from a global perspective was not considered until the 1970s.

The rationale that the legislation and implementation of international environmental law should be viewed from a global ecology perspective was applied at the United Nations Conference on the Human Environment.[4] At this conference in Stockholm, the Declaration

1. Stockholm Declaration of the United Nations Conference on the Human Environment, 16 June 1972, 11 *I.L.M.* 1416 (1972).
2. General peace treaty between Austria, France, Great Britain, Russia, Sardinia, Prussia, and Turkey, Paris, 30 Mar. 1856. 6 *International Protection of the Environment*, 5388.
3. Convention on Nature Protection and Wildlife Preservation in the Western Hemisphere, 12 Oct. 1940, 161 U.N.T.S. 228, 38 A.J.I.L. Supp. 193 (1940); Convention on the Conservation of Migratory Species of Wild Animals, 23 June 1979, reprinted in 19 *I.L.M.* (1980).
4. United Nations Conference on the Human Environment, *supra* note 1.

on Human Environment was issued and the Action Program for the Human Environment was adopted. During the following years, international environmental law has developed and expanded rapidly in its systematization, standardization, and sphere of application. Consecutive international conventions were reached concerning international rivers, lakes, the sea, the air, outer space, natural resources, and the social, as well as the cultural environment. The following are examples: the International Convention for the Prevention of Pollution from Ships in 1973;[5] the Convention on International Trade in Endangered Species of Wild Fauna and Flora in 1973;[6] the Convention for the Prevention of Marine Pollution from Land-Based Sources in 1974;[7] the Convention Concerning the Protection of the Rhine Against Pollution by Chlorides in 1976;[8] the Convention on Conservation of Nature in the South Pacific in 1976;[9] Recommendations IX-2 and IX-6 Adopted at the Ninth Consultative Meeting under Article IX of the Antarctic Treaty in 1977;[10] the Convention on the Conservation of Migratory Species of Wild Animals in 1979;[11] and the Agreement Governing the Activities of States on the Moon and Other Celestial Bodies in 1979.[12] These agreements established legal rules for pollution control, environmental improvement, rational use and protection of natural resources, and liability for environmental damages. Furthermore, environmental administrative agencies in many countries and states have established several important principles in order to implement these international agreements; for example the "Water Charter"[13] of the Council of Europe and FAO's

5. Convention for the Prevention of Pollution from Ships, 2 Nov. 1973, *supra* note 2, II, 552.
6. Convention on International Trade in Endangered Species of Wild Fauna and Flora, Washington, 3 Mar. 1973. *Id.* V, 2228.
7. Convention for the Prevention of Marine Pollution from Land-Based Sources, Paris, 4 June 1974. *Id.* II, 748.
8. Convention Concerning the Protection of the Rhine against Pollution by Chlorides, 3 Dec. 1976. *Id.* XXV, 440
9. Convention on Conservation of Nature in the South Pacific, Apia, 12 June 1976. *Id.* XX, 10.359.
10. Recommendations IX-2 and IX-6 Adopted at the Ninth Consultative Meeting under Article IX of the Antarctic Treaty, London, 19 Sept.–7 Oct. 1977. *Id.* XXIV, 119.
11. Convention on the Conservation of Migratory Species of Wild Animals, with Final Act of the conference, Bonn, 23 June 1979. *Id.* XXIII, 1.
12. Agreement Governing the Activities of States on the Moon and Other Celestial Bodies, New York, 18 Dec. 1979. *Id.* XXIX, 267.
13. European Water Charter, Strasbourg, 1967, proclaimed 6 May 1968.

"World Soil Charter"[14] suggested by the European Council. In addition, the concepts of international liability for marine damage and the 200-mile coastal "exclusive economic zone" (EEZ) were developed at the urging of the Latin American countries for the purpose of protecting their natural resources.[15] African countries also put forward many important principles concerning protection of their natural environment and resources.[16] All of these programmes were designed to help implement the international environmental agreements and they have contributed greatly to a better global environment.

Ever since the 1980s, many third-world states have taken an active part in developing international environmental legislation. They were motivated by their common aspirations to protect the international environment and natural resources. This involvement has made the legislation and implementation of international environmental law move forward with greater force. Now international environmental law has become an important discipline and an integral part of contemporary international law. International environmental law is in a state of constant and continuous development.

(2) The grim situation

While we observed that international environmental law has developed by leaps and bounds, there is no need to conceal the fact that the legislation and implementation of international environmental law is still facing a grim situation and that there are many problems requiring prompt solutions.

Modern man's global ecosystem is in a more desperate situation than ever before and new sources of pollution have aggravated the situation. There has been a sharp increase in the quantity of solid waste degrading the human environment. Acid-rain impact on larger territories and its virulence are increasing; the marketing of ever greater quantities of synthetic chemical products threatens human health; in addition the worldwide greenhouse effect, caused largely by excessive production of CO_2, and nuclear pollution have, in quick succession, brought disastrous consequences. A recent report from the Fourth International Conference on the Conservation and Man-

14. World Soil Charter, Principle 2, 1981, FAO Doc. C/81/27 (1981).
15. United Nations Convention on the Law of the Sea, 10 Dec. 1982, 21 *I.L.M.* 1261 (1982).
16. African Convention on the Conservation of Nature and Natural Resources, 15 Sept. 1968, 1001 U.N.T.S. 3 (1968). Zaire proposed the World Charter for Nature, which was adopted by the United Nations General Assembly, *infra* note 17.

agement of Lakes confirmed the warnings of an overwhelming majority of scientists all over the world that the globe is warming up; it predicted that the average temperature of the globe will be 3°C warmer by the end of the next century. It also pointed out that global warming will cause world sea levels to rise and also change the pattern of rainfall throughout the world. In areas of drought or semi-drought, the decrease of rainfall due to global warming will cause a loss of surface water by 40 to 70 per cent. This will significantly affect the supply of drinking water, the management of lakes, and agricultural irrigation.[17] All of these pollution sources, new as well as old, interact to make more difficult tasks of implementing and complying with international environmental protection plans and legislation. In addition, these pollution sources burden us with inescapable responsibilities, which we cannot ignore. The following measures need immediate attention:

1. It's more urgent now than ever before that people throughout the world cooperate in order to solve effectively the problems of environmental pollution and ecological degradation.

2. Great efforts should be made to strengthen the way in which the legal system is utilized to enforce international environmental law. We should proceed from the existing international environmental rules to formulating a series of conventions, through global consultation, that should in any event include conventions on the human environment; preserving natural resources and global ecology; controlling global atmospheric pollution and acid rain; the control of marine pollution; improving international environmental surveillance and monitoring; the obligation to pay damages for international environmental pollution and the method of establishing these; researching, utilizing, and protecting outer space; and punishing as crimes acts that endanger the global environment.

3. We should create favourable conditions to encourage all nations, especially third-world countries, to take an active part in environment-related cooperative activities. We should consider the social and economic capacities of the third-world countries, fully respect their environmental sovereignty, consider their special difficulties, address their needs, as well as protect their material interests from harm. Each third-world country should draw up

17. *People's Daily* (overseas edition) Sect. 6, 7 Sept. 1990.

its own strategy and guidelines to keep social developments in balance with the ecological.

It should be pointed out that the key to realizing these urgent tasks lies in mobilizing all nations, including third-world states, to participate in the legislative and enforcement process of international environmental law, and particularly to respect the binding force of treaties. The differing economic and political situations of states may have an impact on the implementations of international environmental law in different countries. Without involving a majority of the world's population in this global endeavour, international environmental protection and the legislation and implementation of international environmental law will fall short of success. There must be global collaboration if we are to meet this global challenge.

The status of third-world states in international environmental legislation and its implementation

It can be asserted that nowadays no country can effectively protect its environment and solve its various environmental problems on its own. No matter how advanced its science and technology are or how perfect the means of legislation and implementation of environmental law are, an independent effort to resolve global problems is not enough. Global problems require a global effort. To name a few, the problems include pollution of the atmosphere, of marine life, of coastal and inland waters, and of all areas reached by acid rain.

We can also say with certainty that no country on its own is able to pay the cost of environmental damage, including the ever-increasing cost of the new technologies developed to remedy the damages caused by pollution. Since we have only one earth and given that the international community is an organic whole, it could also be asserted that man's endeavour to solve global environmental problems will not be accomplished and will be of no avail if we fail to bring into play every positive factor and unite all available forces.

Given this situation, contemporary international jurists have clearly realized that the settlement of environmental issues, the drafting of legislation, and the implementation of international environmental law must take into account the contributions and the needs of third-world countries. The participation of third-world countries in international environmental protection, legislation, and implementation of international environmental law is very relevant.

As a matter of fact, although limited by insufficient resources and by unbalanced economies, the third-world countries deserve the following observations regarding the arena of international environmental protection:

1. The rise of the third world has indeed been the greatest event of our times. Ninety newly independent states (including Namibia, which proclaimed its independence recently) were established after the Second World War. Thirty states already threw off the yoke of colonialism before the Second World War.[18] These states constitute a majority, since the total number of states in the world is about 167. Third-world countries all share the same historical experience of material and cultural gains under colonialism that are the reason for their current economic underdevelopment and scientific backwardness. They stand for the common historical goals of eliminating North-South disparities, developing their national economies, and consolidating their economic and political independence. Even though these countries are in the category of third world, they are a highly productive force that must not be underestimated if implementation of international environmental law is going to succeed. Fortunately, in the world community, they not only enjoy rights and undertake duties under international law, but they also enjoy the same sovereign rights as the more developed countries. The third world joins with the others in formulating international rules and participating in international legal processes.

   It is imperative that the third world make a more appropriate contribution to the formulation of international environmental law. The adoption of the Declaration on the Human Environment in 1972,[19] the enactment of the United Nations Convention on the Law of the Sea in 1982,[20] the adoption of Resolution 1803 (XVII) by the United Nations General Assembly in 1962,[21] and the enactment and the adoption of the United Nations Declaration on the Right to Development in 1986[22] could not have transpired without

---

18. Wang TieYak, "The Third World and International Law," *Chinese Yearbook of International Law,* 9–36 (1982).
19. United Nations Convention on the Human Environment, *supra* note 1.
20. Law of the Sea, *supra* note 7.
21. Resolution on "Permanent Sovereignty over Natural Resources," G.A. Res. 317, 28 U.N. GAOR Supp. 30, at 52, U.N. Doc. A/9030 (1974).
22. U.N.G.A. res 41/128 of Dec. 1986. General Assembly Official Records: Forty-first Session Supplement No. 53 (A/41/53) at 186.

the great support and efforts by third-world countries.

2. The present economic situation of third-world nations is in part the result of low levels of development, their backward industry, and outdated agricultural methods. It is understandable why their economies have vestiges of colonialism. The third-world nations, with 70 per cent of the world's population, subsist on only 30 per cent of the world's GNP. Their per capita income is only one-twelfth of that of the other countries, and the discrepancy is still rising. At the recent UN conference of the least-developed states, in Paris, the Secretary-General of the United Nations, Javier Pérez de Cuéllar, said: "in the past decade, the social and economic situations in the most undeveloped nations worsened, GNP per capita decreased and the amount of foreign trade was only one percent of that of world trade."[23] In addition, although these countries contain and produce the main portion of the world's energy and raw materials, three-fourths of the oil supply, one-third to one-half of the world's most important non-ferrous metals and many other minerals, they only utilize a small portion of their wealth for themselves, most of these materials satisfying the needs of the developed countries for energy and raw materials.

It would be very one-sided and would not conform with the actual situation, if we argued that the main difficulties in the legislation and implementation of international environmental law should be attributed to the weak economic bases and low productive levels of third-world states. Even if it were true, developed countries cannot shift all the responsibility and blame to the third-world countries. On the contrary, the developed countries must give more support and cooperation in this joint undertaking of international environmental protection in light of the limited economic and social capacity of third-world nations as well as their inadequate scientific and technological levels. Nevertheless third-world countries should rely on their own resources to overcome the obstacles to environmental improvements.

3. Generally speaking, the environmental problems facing developed countries are caused by their excessive discharge of hazardous substances, which affect not only themselves but also their neighbours, and ultimately threaten other areas of the world. In third-world states, the predominant cause of environmental problems is underdevelopment. The objective facts show that developed coun-

23. *People's Daily* (overseas edition) 5 Sept. 1990.

tries should bear major responsibility for global environmental degradation: misguided industrial development and overconsumption by developed countries are the main causes of the greenhouse effect, the excessive release of chloro-fluorocarbons (CFCs), causing the ozone depletion, and the excessive diffusion of SO_2, causing acid rain.

Although developed countries and third-world nations are both responsible for global environmental degradation, there are profound differences between the way each has contributed to that degradation. Underdevelopment and lack of environmental sensitivity are the main explanations for third-world contribution to environmental problems. The underdevelopment results from the prolonged colonial plunder, control, exploitation, and oppression to which they have been subjected. As a result, their natural resources and environments were seriously harmed and wasted. Today, because of the combined effects of a weak economic base, irrational economic structures, a low level of science and technology, overpopulation with no sign of improvement, as well as heavy domestic and foreign indebtedness, these countries are unable to sustain the financial and technological burdens necessary to substantially improve the environment. Although they have attained independence, in order to survive, some of these countries have no alternatives but to interact with the environment in a destructive manner. This result is inevitable because in balancing the economic viability of a country against the need to protect the environment, the former will invariably win.

Furthermore, as the international environment continues to deteriorate, the third-world states will be less and less able to clean up their own environments. This is further complicated by the indifference of the developed countries toward the developmental problems of third-world countries. For example, several delegations at the ninth session of the Governing Council of the United Nations Environment Programme, in May 1981, called attention to the problem of "hazardous chemicals being exported to developing countries" and "to the need for co-operation with relevant international programmes, particularly the International Programme on Chemical Safety."[24]

It can be concluded from the above that third-world states are not

24. United Nations Environment Programme, Report of the Governing Council on the work of its ninth session, 13–26 May 1981, General Assembly Official Records, page 45. Thirty-sixth Session Supplement No. 25 (A/36/25).

only the owners of tremendous natural and environmental resources, but they also are the principal victims of environmental pollution. The third-world nations contain the majority of the world's population; they are an indispensable force in the legislation and implementation of international environmental law. They have become promoters and drafters of legislation affecting the international environment.

Some personal views and suggestions to encourage a more positive role of the third world in the legislation and implementation of international environmental law

Firstly, it should be pointed out that, in spite of their low economic and technological levels, the third-world nations have not taken a passive attitude nor have they been indifferent toward international environmental protection. On the contrary, many of them exerted their utmost efforts by taking an active part in international environmental legislation and implementation. Especially since the 1980s, they have made active appeals for the strengthening of international cooperation; the provision of assistance to expand coastal jurisdiction; protection against sea-coast pollution; the control of the export and transport of hazardous products; the control of the processing of solid wastes; and the protection of the soil. Owing to their active initiative, participation, and support, such instruments as the World Soil Charter,[25] the World Charter for Nature,[26] and the United Nations Convention on the Law of the Sea[27] were enacted. Here, it is appropriate to mention that the third-world countries united to ensure the adoption of the United Nations Declaration on the Right to Development (1986),[28] whereby the bases and contents of international environmental laws were further expanded.

Secondly, there is no doubt that what the third-world nations urgently need is to develop their national economies, establish their own modernized industries, improve their agricultural methods, obtain their economic independence, as well as to maintain and con-

25. World Soil Charter, *supra* note 6.
26. World Charter for Nature, adopted by the United Nations General Assembly, 9 Nov. 1982, G.A. Res. 37/7, 37 U.N. GAOR Supp. (no. 51) at 17, U.N. Doc. A/37/51 (1982).
27. Law of the Sea, *supra* note 7.
28. The United Nations Declaration on the Right to Development was adopted by 146 votes to 1 (US) with 8 abstentions (Denmark, FRG, Finland, Iceland, Israel, Japan, Sweden, and the UK). U.N.G.A. Res. 41/128 of 4 Dec. 1986, *supra* note 23.

solidate their political independance and sovereignty. Then and only then will third-world countries be able to exert their utmost efforts towards improving the environment. Such improvement must come gradually, according to their financial and social capacities. The environmental plight in third-world nations cannot be mentioned in the same breath with that of developed countries. There is a great difference in the damage caused by the latter countries. Even though environmental pollution in some developing states is very serious and affects other states, as well as the world's ecosystem, the attitudes toward such pollution are different. In the United Nations Declaration on the Human Environment of 1972 it was said that " . . . in developing countries most of the environmental problems are caused by underdevelopment. . . developing countries should devote themselves to development."[29] Experience also shows that only on the basis of self-reliance, after their national economies have been developed, modern industries have been established, and agricultural methods have been improved, can third-world nations gradually achieve effectiveness in maintaining and improving their own environments. Then and only then can they effectively throw themselves into the struggle for international environmental protection. Needless to say, while engaging in domestic production and construction, third-world nations should interact appropriately with the environment and constantly balance parochial and global interests, thereby taking the necessary measures to protect the environment and to control pollution.

Thirdly, it should also be mentioned that developed countries should continue to keep a high profile on pollution control, especially since they are the main contributors of environmental pollution. The earth is a single entity and global environmental protection is a matter of life and death for all of humanity. As a result, all of its members are jointly liable. Developed countries must utilize their economic and technological advantages to create an international environment favourable to economic development and to improve that which the third-world states are unable to do because of their poverty. Developed countries should also do more to help third-world nations financially and technologically, in addition to encouraging them to become involved in efforts to control the global environment.

Lastly, considering the economic and political features of third-

29. United Nations Conference on the Human Environment, *supra* note 1.

world states as well as the cause and nature of their environmental pollution, the incentives adopted to attract them to active participation in the drafting and implementing of international environmental legislation should be based on the principles that all nations, big or small, are equally important and that full consultation in any international cooperation or action is imperative. No country is allowed to encroach on another's sovereignty, interfere with another's internal affairs, or impair another's interests under the pretext of environmental protection. Coercion, sanctions, and conditional investments or technical transfers are all unworkable.

Hence I would like to put forward the following propositions:

1. The increased participation by third-world nations in legislating and implementing international environmental law should proceed from the principles listed in the Declaration on the Human Environment of 1972.[30] Among those principles the following are especially important: the international cooperation principle; the state equality principle; as well as the principle of special assistance to developing countries in financing and transferring technology. The establishment of a new international economic order as a global means to reverse the course of environmental degradation was put forward in the Nairobi Declaration on the Global Environment of 1982.[31] This declaration should also be implemented, in its entirety, as a way of encouraging participation by third-world nations.

2. It is necessary to take into full consideration the conditions and needs of the developing countries and to envisage creative participation of the third-world countries in environment-related cooperative activities.

3. The environmental funds raised by the Governing Council for the United Nations Environment Programme should benefit the third-world states in order to help them protect and improve their environment, as well as to develop their environmental technology, as they see fit.

4. Development banks, which are either global or regional, should provide third-world nations with long-term favourable loans at low interest rates to meet their financial and technological needs as they begin to implement environmental protection programmes.

30. *Id.* at Recital 7, Principle 24, 1420.
31. *Id.* at Recital 7, Principles 12, 20–22, and 24, 1419, 1420.

5. Financial and technological assistance provided by developed countries to third-world nations should be chosen by the recipient countries according to their economic conditions. Moreover, third-world nations should be assured of a good command of the technology, so as to prevent developed countries from manipulating or exploiting third-world countries in order to test their environmental technology.

6. In order to encourage third-world nations to participate in the drafting and implementation of environmental legislation, such incentives as tax exemptions, interest-free or low-interest loans, transfers of environmental technology and information should be adopted. However, these incentives must be provided without strings or discriminatory terms. Furthermore, lessons might be drawn from the UNEP Montreal Protocol to Protect the Ozone Layer, which provided for different standards for controlling CFC use for developed and for developing countries according to their differing situations. This model could help in reaching agreements on the control and use of other pollutants, and finally could improve the management and conservation of the global environment.[32]

7. In order to advance the development of third-world nations on environmental protection, which is also to the advantage of the world community, developed countries should co-sponsor studies or symposia on environmental protection, cooperate with third-world nations, become involved as environmental monitors, conduct scientific investigations, implement personnel training programmes, and conduct feasibility studies and other pollution-control projects.

In conclusion, the formulation of any international environmental legislation by the world community should be based on the principles of the permanent sovereignty over natural resources of states, in addition to the five principles of peaceful coexistence.[33] The economic and social capacity of the third world, as well as its special problems and needs, must be considered at all times. We must also respect the sovereignty of third-world states and protect their mate-

32. J. Tripp, "The UNEP Montreal Protocol: Industrialized and Developing Countries Sharing the Responsibility for Protecting the Stratospheric Ozone Layer," 20 *N.Y.U. J. Int'l L. & Pol'y,* 733 (1988).

33. B.A. Ramundo, *Peaceful Coexistence, International Law in the Building of Communism,* 14–15 (Johns Hopkins, 1967).

rial interests. Sanctioning third-world nations is undesirable and ineffective. International treaties have been negotiated on the basis of equality and they have established international commitments that must be abided by and implemented at the municipal level. I am convinced that a vast number of third-world nations will play an influential role in the creation of international environmental legislation and its implementation, thereby making an even greater contribution to the protection of the earth.

Appendix: A case-study: China's positive attitude toward the adoption and implementation of international environmental legislation

China is a third-world country, a vast territory with a large population. In the process of economic growth, pollution has posed a major threat to the human environment. We need more consensual arrangements and a more specialized legal domain on the planning of environmental behaviour to bring about a positive environmental culture. That is why we have insisted that maintaining and improving the human environment has a role in humanity's well-being and economic development, not to mention the aspirations of the world's people. As a long-standing practice, the Chinese government has regarded environmental protection and improvement as a national policy and one of the necessary ingredients in the formulation and implementation of a national economic plan. The Constitution of the People's Republic of China states that "the state must protect and improve the environment in which people live. It must prevent and control pollution and other public hazards."[1]

Apart from the Constitution, dozens of laws and regulations to protect the environment have been enacted. Such legislation includes, for example, the Environmental Protection Law of the PRC (for trial implementation) (1979),[2] the law of the PRC on the Prevention and Control of Water Pollution (1984),[3] the law of the PRC on the Prevention and Control of Atmospheric Pollution (1987),[4] and the Marine Environment Protection Law of the PRC (1982).[5] The important laws and regulations on the preservation of natural resources and the environment are: the Forestry Law (1984),[6] the

1. People's Republic of China Const., Art. 26.
2. Environment Protection Laws of the People's Republic of China, 17 Sept. 1979, *Renmin Ribao* (People's Daily), 2 (1979).
3. The Water Pollution Prevention and Control Law of the People's Republic of China, 13 May 1984, *Renmin Ribao*, 3; *Xinhua Yuebao (Wenxian Ban)*, No. 5, 63; *Zhonghua Renmin Gongheguo Yuan Gongbao* (Gazette of the State Council of the People's Republic of China), No. 10, 307 (1984).
4. The Law of the People's Republic of China on the Prevention and Control of Atmospheric Pollution was passed by the Standing Committee of the National People's Congress on 5 Sept. 1987 (1987).
5. Marine Environment Protection Law of the People's Republic of China, 23 Aug. 1982, *Renmin Ribao*, 3 (1982).
6. Forestry Law of the People's Republic of China (amended), 23 Sept. 1984, *Renmin Ribao* (1984).

Grassland Law (1985),[7] the Fisheries Law (1986),[8] and the Water Law (1988).[9] The Regulation on Environmental Protection of Construction Projects (1986),[10] the Interim Regulation on the Control of Environment of the Economic Open Area (1986),[11] and the Interim Procedure on the Collection of Drainage Dues (1982)[12] are the major laws concerning environmental management. In addition, China has also promulgated more than 100 normative environmental standards, including an environment quality standard,[13] a pollutant-discharge standard,[14] and an environmental base standard.[15] All these make up the framework of Chinese environmental law.

Knowing the seriousness of the deterioration of the human environment and awaking to planetary obligations, China persistently holds a positive attitude about the implementation of international environment protection. As a member of the Governing Council of UNEP, China has attended Council meetings every year since 1973 in order to consult with other countries about global environmental protection. China has also been a member of the International Union for Conservation of Nature and Natural Resources (IUCN) since the Twelfth Council session held in Sweden in 1982. In addition, China joined the World Wildlife Fund, signed the agreements on the Protection of Wildlife Resources[16] and the Establishment of a Research Centre for Panda Protection.[17] Furthermore, China has acceded to 10 international conventions and treaties relating to environment protection, such as the Antarctic Treaty,[18] the provisions of the Internation-

7. Grasslands Law of the People's Republic of China, 18 June 1985, *Renmin Ribao*, 2 (1985).
8. Fisheries Law of the People's Republic of China, 20 Jan. 1986, *Zhongguo Fazhi Bao* (China Legal System Newspaper), 22 Jan. 1986, 2 (1986).
9. Water Law of the People's Republic of China (1988), 21 Jan. 1988, *Renmin Ribao*.
10. Regulation on Environmental Protection of Construction Projects (1986), 26 Mar. 1986, *Renmin Ribao*.
11. Interim Regulation on the Control of the Environment of the Economic Open Area (1986), 4 Mar. 1986, *Renmin Ribao*.
12. Interim Procedure on the Collection of Drainage Dues (1982), 4 *Zhonghua Renmin Gongheguo Yuan Gongbao*, 121.
13. Notes 12, 13, and 14 refer to the administrative regulations and norms promulgated by the State Council prior to Sept. 1986: environmental quality standard, pollution discharge standard, and environmental base standard, respectively.
14. *See supra* note 12.
15. *See supra* note 12.
16. World Wildlife Fund Agreement on the Protection of Wildlife Resources. Xiahua General Overseas News Service, 1 July 1980.
17. World Wildlife Fund Agreement on the Establishment of a Research Centre for Panda Protection. Geneva, 30 June 1980. Item No. 070103.
18. The Antarctic Treaty, 1 Dec. 1959, 12 U.S.T. 794 T.I.A.S. No. 4780, 402 U.N.T.S. 71 (1959).

al Convention on Civil Liability for Oil Pollution Damages,[19] the Treaty on the Prohibition of the Emplacement of Nuclear Weapons and Other Weapons of Mass Destruction on the Seabed and the Ocean Floor,[20] and the United Nations Convention on the Law of the Sea.[21]

In recent years, cooperation by China, international organizations, and foreign governments has been successful in its efforts to protect the Chinese environment. China has not only established sound co-operative relations with UNDP, FAO, Unesco, and WHO, but it has also held a series of meaningful symposia.

Sino-American environmental protection is an example of co-operation with foreign governments. To illustrate, in 1984, the two countries signed a protocol on Scientific and Technological Cooperation.[22] In 1981, a co-sponsored symposium on environmental science was held in Beijing, at which research reports on land use, comprehensive planning of the regional environment, atmospheric environmental quality, as well as underground water were presented by both parties. The Institute of Environmental Hygienic Engineering of the Chinese Academy of Preventive Medical Science, in cooperation with the Institute of Health Impact of the American Environmental Protection Agency, made a pathogenic research of lung cancer in Yunnan Province of China; the initial results have already been attained. Meanwhile, the State Environmental Protection Bureau of China established a long-term cooperation with the American Center for East-West Cultural Exchange, and the two parties decided to conduct a joint research project focused on environmental management, environmental impact evaluation, human ecology, and agricultural ecology, etc. Of course, exchanges with other foreign countries and non-governmental organizations are also quite frequent. For instance, China attended a series of international conferences on environmental protection, which included the World Environmental Tribunal Conference of 1984 held in San Francisco, the Energy En-

19. International Convention on Civil Liability for Oil Pollution Damage, 29 Nov. 1969, U.N. Jurid. Y.B. 174, 9 *I.L.M.* 45, 973 U.N.T.S. 3 (1969).
20. Treaty on the Prohibition of the Emplacement of Nuclear Weapons and Other Weapons of Mass Destruction on the Sea-bed and the Ocean Floor, and in the Subsoil Thereof, 11 Feb. 1971, 23 U.S.T. 701, T.I.A.S. No. 7337, 2 Ruster 498 (1971).
21. Law of the Sea, *supra* note 7.
22. People's Republic of China–United States Agreement on Scientific and Technological Cooperation T.I.A.S. No. 10921, 12 Jan. 1984. The Agreement covers environmental protection.

vironment Conference of 1984, and the Asian-Pacific Conference on Urban Environmental Pollution.

According to incomplete statistics, China, in recent years, has sent hundreds of experts, scholars, and students to dozens of countries for advanced research and additional study. Meanwhile, more than 380 foreign environmental experts have visited China. Furthermore, Chinese research institutes have initiated more than 10 projects to research, monitor, investigate, train, and evaluate regarding the adequacy of environmental protection, in cooperation with various international organizations and foreign governments. It should be mentioned that Vice-Premier Li Peng and Qu Ge-ping, the head of the State Environmental Protection Bureau, were awarded gold medals and certificates of merit issued by UNEP because Chinese environmental policy and its achievements were recognized and admired by the international community. Both *Chinese Environment News* and the San-Bei Shelter Forest Office were listed in the UNEP "Global 500" honour roll of 1986.[23]

In short, despite problems mentioned at the beginning of this chapter, China's achievements in environmental protection, especially in the legislation and implementation of international environmental law, not only demonstrates China's positive function in international environmental endeavours, but also shows other third-world nations that they too can contribute to the drafting and implementation of international environmental legislation.

23. (The Magazine) 5 Chinese Environmental Management, 29 (1988).

International human
rights law and
environmental problems

An introductory note on a human right to environment

Alexandre Kiss

It has been stressed that environmental law derives from the common interest of mankind. So does international recognition of human rights and freedoms. It is thus normal that a link was established between the two as early as 1972, by the Stockholm Declaration itself:

Man has the fundamental right to freedom, equality, and adequate conditions of life, in an environment of a quality that permits a life of dignity and well-being, and he bears a solemn responsibility to protect and improve the environment for present and future generations (Principle 1).

Thus, the "right to environment" was proclaimed at the beginning of the "environmental era" at a worldwide level. In addition, as it is formulated, this principle includes all the essential elements of both new fields of international law. It is very clearly linked with human rights, both civil and political (freedom, equality, dignity), and economic, social, and cultural rights (adequate conditions of life, well-being). It also warns that everybody has a responsibility for the protection and the improvement of the environment. Finally – and this is new in the human rights language – it also opens a time perspective by speaking of future generations.

Of course, the Stockholm Declaration, whatever its impact could have been, is legally only a non-mandatory document. So is the World Charter of Nature, solemnly proclaimed by the UN General Assembly on 28 October 1982, which elaborates further on the rights and duties resulting from the necessity to protect the environment.[1] Legal provisions with a mandatory character have appeared in a very significant way in regional conventions aiming at the protection of human rights. The 1981 African Charter of Human and Peoples' Rights expressly recognizes the rights of "all peoples" to a "generally satisfactory environment favorable to their development."[2] Inside another human rights protection system, the American Convention, an Additional Protocol to the Convention on Human Rights in the Area of Economic, Social, and Cultural Rights (Protocol of San Salvador), provides in its Article II: "1. Everyone shall have the right to live in a healthy environment and to have access to basic public services. 2. The States Parties shall promote the protection, preservation and improvement of the environment."[3] Thus the "right to environment" has been recognized in positive international law. It has also been proclaimed in national legislation: at present, clauses related to environmental protection – either as a duty of the state or as an individual right or both – figure in 44 national constitutions, in that of a dozen state members of federal states, and in general laws of several countries.[4]

Although the formulations are different, in all these cases one may speak of a right to environment. Indeed, the drafting of most environmental conventions guaranteeing fundamental rights and freedoms shows that very often such rights and freedoms are proclaimed not only in an abstract form, but also by declaring that it is the duty of the state to protect them. As an example one may quote the formulation of the most fundamental of all human rights, the right to life, as it figures in the UN Covenant on Civil and Political Rights, Article 6: "Every human being has the inherent right to life. This right shall be protected by law. No one shall be arbitrarily deprived of his life."

Quite a few other provisions using the same drafting technique for proclaiming individual rights could be quoted, especially in the realm of economic, social, and cultural rights. It may thus be considered

1. UN General Assembly, Resolution 37/7.
2. Article 24, African Charter of Human and People's Rights (Banjul, 20 June 1981), 21 *I.L.M.* 58 (1982).
3. Protocol adopted at San Salvador on 18 Nov. 1988. 28, *I.L.M.* 698 (1989).
4. Extracts of these provisions are reproduced in E. Brown Weiss, *In Fairness to Future Generations*, 297 (Transnational/United Nations University). *See also* Unesco, Environnement et droits de l'homme, 152 (P. Kromrek, ed., Unesco, 1987).

that whatever the formulation of the principle is, an individual right to the protection of the environment can be deduced from it.

The comparison of this new human right with formerly recognized ones helps to determine its contents. Indeed, it has been objected that the terms "right to environment" are too vague to allow the utilization of judicial means of redress: the very word "environment" can hardly be defined, even if it is generally qualified ("adequate," "satisfactory," "healthy," "ecologically balanced," etc.). However, such a situation is not exceptional in the field of human rights, where concepts such as *"ordre public,"* "national security," "morality" are to be given an exact interpretation. Moreover, one should not forget that an essential aspect of protecting human rights is the creation of procedures that permit ensuring respect for these rights. The example of one of the most fundamental rights, that of liberty and security of the person, as formulated in different conventions,[5] shows that this right, an abstract concept that is not easy to translate into substance by other means, establishes itself in procedural guarantees. That which the law assures is the existence and proper functioning of certain procedures that constitute protection against arbitrary action, preventing the organs of the state from infringing upon the liberty and security of its citizens. The right to environment similarly can be interpreted, not as the right to an ideal environment, difficult if not impossible to define in the abstract, but as the right to have the present environment conserved – protected from any significant deterioration – and improved in some cases. Thus, it signifies in reality *the right to the conservation of the environment*, conservation including protection and improvement.

So conceived, the right to environment is as concrete in its implications as any other right guaranteed to individuals and groups. It includes procedures assuring that every individual is informed on time of major changes that could harm his or her environment; he or she is enabled to participate in the decision-making process and has access to adequate means of redress, either for the violation of these rights or in order to obtain satisfaction if his or her environment has already suffered damage.

One of the aspects of this new right, the right to participate, also

---

5. Article 9 of the UN Covenant on Civil and Political Rights, Article 5 of the European Convention on Human Rights, Article 7 of the American Convention on Human Rights, Article 6 of the African Charter of Human and People's Rights.

presumes an active attitude on behalf of the citizens, and even more, a citizen's duty to protect the environment. Each person has the right to have his or her environment protected, but is also obliged to contribute to the common effort. Of course, speaking of individuals includes also groups of individuals, such as associations or interest groups. This obligation is even more far-reaching than the general obligation that results from the conventions recognizing human rights, i.e., the duty to respect the fundamental rights and freedoms of other individuals, since it emphasizes that citizens are not passive beneficiaries, but partake of responsibilities on the formation of all community interests.

Another similarity between human rights in general and environmental protection is the role played by associations, both inside states and at the international level. However, as far as the latter is concerned, their action is different. Indeed, while human rights groups, which have taken an active part in the surveillance of the application of human rights rules, are more numerous and represent different points of view or even different interests, international environmental associations seem to be less numerous and better coordinated. Still more important is that there exist in this field two particularly important non-governmental organizations: the World Conservation Union (IUCN, from its former name, International Union for the Conservation of Nature and Natural Resources), in which also participate about 120 countries either by official organs or otherwise, and the Worldwide Fund for Nature (WWF). While the second is mainly active in fund-raising for different actions in order to protect the environment, the first actively participates in the elaboration of international legislation and in the drafting and disseminating of programmes of action.

Because of global change, the role of such bodies should be reinforced. Increasingly, representatives of international organizations are included in national delegations to official international meetings. Inside states such organizations also play an important role in the surveillance of the implementation of international rules protecting the environment. A step further should be made in introducing them officially in the international procedure of dispute settlement.

International dispute settlement is a favourite subject of the doctrine of international law. A ritual clause in studies and even in some international treaties related to environmental protection is the reproduction of the list of Article 33 of the UN Charter: disputes arising in this field should be resolved by negotiations, enquiry, mediation, conciliation, arbitration, judicial settlement, resort to regional agencies or arrangements, or any other peaceful means. In spite of its exhaustive character, such lists do not seem to be very useful, since the means that they suggest are not used in practice. Instead, specific techniques of surveillance on the implementation of treaty obligations, mostly provided for in the respective treaties themselves, are utilized. Now, real progress in this field would be to create mechanisms of surveillance of state obligations that the governments can really accept. In other words, "soft" means of settlement should be combined with a larger place given to individuals and non-governmental organizations, following the pattern of existing international mechanisms in the realm of human rights. One should recall here the proposals for strengthening the legal and institutional framework formulated by an international legal-expert group of the World Commission on Environment and Development.[6]

The mechanism that could be set up on the basis of these proposals would consist in a High Commissioner for Environmental Protection, appointed by the UN General Assembly, with some functions similar to an "ombudsman" and "trustee" for environment. He could receive and assess communications from states, but also from private organizations and individuals, concerning compliance with or violation of international legal rules related to environmental protection. After a first assessment, when appropriate, he could submit any of such cases for consideration to a special UN Commission. The latter would be another independent institution, composed of experts, elected by the UN General Assembly. It should examine the communications that the High Commissioner transmits to it and should decide whether a state has violated any international obligation related to environmental protection. Its findings would be transmitted to the concerned state and to the author of the communication and, if no compliance with the violated rules was assured by the concerned state, a report including the decision would be made public and transmitted to the UN General Assembly or any other competent body.

Such organs could also be invested with other functions. Also, the High Commissioner could have special responsibilities regarding the protection and use of areas beyond national jurisdiction, and for representing and protecting the interest of future generations. The Com-

---

6. Experts Group on Environmental Law of the World Commission on Environment and Development, *Environmental Protection and Sustainable Development, Legal Principles and Recommendations,* 14 (Martinus Nijhoff, 1988).

mission should receive and review regular reports from states and from relevant international organizations, both governmental and non-governmental. Together with the High Commissioner, it should also formulate recommendations and proposals for improved implementation of existing international rules, or even for the drafting of new rules and norms.

Of course, another step, becoming more and more necessary, is the drafting of a general convention on environmental protection, following the example of the two Covenants on Human Rights. Some proposals tend to the establishment of an international court specialized in environmental protection. In the present state of international law, one may ask what legal rules such an international jurisdiction could apply. But a general international convention on the protection of the global environment would also definitively designate the place of environment in our value system, as high as human rights have been placed by the successive international instruments. This could be one of the positive consequences of global change.

8

The human rights system as a conceptual framework for environmental law

R.S. Pathak

The increasing emphasis on environmental protection and ecological preservation makes it eminently desirable to analyse the conceptual values in which environmental law is based. The mounting interest evidenced in scientific, legal, political, and governmental circles in the various dimensions of environmental law constitutes sufficient justification for this exercise.

Nature has always exercised a mysterious fascination for man. Primitive man regarded the elemental forces of Nature with awe and respect, and identified them as deities to be feared and propitiated. With time man began to acquire a more intelligent understanding of the relationship between him and the natural order. In some early civilizations and ancient cultures, religious piety, philosophical princi- ples, and moral standards drew their values from that relationship. Some others focused on man as the reason for all creation. The earlier Greco-Christian attitude was that "since everything is for man's use, he is at liberty to modify it as he will."[1] This belief be- trayed man into a false assumption of paramountcy over the natural order. He misconceived his stewardship of the planet for an absolute proprietorship.[2] In the dynamics of daily existence, human life has

1. J.A. Passmore, *Man's Responsibility for Nature,* 17 (Scribner, 1976), cited in A.D. Tarlock, "Earth and Other Ethics: The Institutional Issues," 56 *Tennessee Law Review,* 45 (1988).
2. Dale and Carter, "Topsoil and Civilization" (quoted in E.F. Schumacher, *Small is Beauti- ful,* 84 [Blond and Briggs, 1973]), say: "Civilized man was nearly always able to become master of his environment temporarily. His chief troubles came from his delusion that his

been lived since in the dimensions of an anthropocentric perception that treats the rest of Creation as bonded in subservience to it. In harsh paradox, civilized man has continued in a state of alienation from Nature, abusing and degrading the planet's ecological system. We realize now that the resources of the planet have been ruthlessly yoked to human needs, and exploited with thoughtless extravagance and uneconomic waste, through methods that are altering irrevocably our existing natural heritage. The reckless speed with which this destruction proceeds issues from socio-economic pressures compounded by a rapacity for short-sighted gains. It has reached the point when the quality and condition of human life is threatened and has put into question the very survival of the human race.

During the latter half of this century, the enormous power provided by the advanced sciences and high technology has given an impetus and a momentum to environmental problems that enable them to influence living conditions in distantly separated territories. Environmental issues now call for global policies and global action. Solutions that once found adequate expression in state law now demand a wider frame of reference. For the first time, the human mind is engaged with the task of identifying areas of environmental deterioration on a global scale, of determining the nature and consequences of the damage apprehended or suffered, and of considering measures to prevent or repair it.

A single unified global approach is quite often not possible in a pluralistic world community, and there are bound to be several areas where individual evaluation on the basis of the same criteria in differently constituted economic, social, and cultural societies produces remarkably different results.[3] Environmental concerns and policies will vary, for example, with the degree of development attained by the particular society, developed countries finding it easier to emphasize environmental protection over development, while developing countries ordinarily prefer to stress development over environmental concerns. Changing circumstances with passing time have often led to a reorientation of perspectives within the same country. With insights obtained during the Stockholm Conference of 1972, the less-developed countries began to favour environmental protection, con-

---

temporary mastership was permanent. He thought of himself as 'master of the world,' while failing to understand fully the laws of nature."

3. *See* "Developments in the Law: International Environmental Law," 104 *Harvard Law Review*, 1484, 1492 (1991).

vinced that it could be incorporated into their economic development programmes. Contrariwise, the developed countries began to lose their enthusiasm for environmental projects as the intractability of some environmental problems became clearer.[4]

The fundamental significance of environmental protection in shaping the quality of life of a people was reflected, from the commencement of the second half of this century, in the enacted constitutional law of a large number of countries, which include both developed and developing nations.[5] There is a growing volume of environmental legislation and an increasing number of environmental protection agencies.

And as the gap closes between the developed and the developing countries in regard to the significance of the environmental philosophy, an enlarging consensus has become possible in the adoption of global policies and programmes providing for environmental protection.

Environmental law is concerned with our natural heritage and our cultural heritage. The natural heritage includes the atmosphere, the oceans, plant and animal life, water, soils, and other natural resources, both renewable and exhaustible. Our cultural heritage includes the intellectual, artistic, social, and historical record of mankind.[6] Natural heritage is linked with cultural heritage, the survival, protection, and progress of both being interdependent. Man is the bridge between the two. Cultural heritage is the product and record of human perceptions of the natural order through visual, ethical, or mystical perspectives. It issues from man's vision of his natural heritage. In turn, the protection and preservation of man's natural heritage depends on human attitudes emanating from cultural, ethical, and religious beliefs.

Environmental issues

Environmental issues arise out of the actual or apprehended deterioration and degradation of the environment traceable to activities by human beings. In each such case, there is an activity that causes,

---

4. D.A. Kay and H.K. Jacobson, *Environmental Protection: The International Dimension*, 7,8 (Allanheld, Osmun and Co., 1983).
5. E. Brown Weiss, *In Fairness to Future Generations: International Law, Common Patrimony, and Intergenerational Equity*, 297–327 (Transnational/United Nations University, 1989).
6. E. Brown Weiss, "The Planetary Trust: Conservation and Intergenerational Equity," 11 *Ecology Law Quarterly*, 495 (1984).

or is expected to cause, environmental damage, a person or group of persons responsible as the authors of the activity, and a person or group of persons who suffer, or expect to suffer, from the damage. There is a web of legal rights and obligations emerging out of the activity and its consequences, varying in incidence with the character of the environmental issue. The entire corpus of environmental law has evolved around environmental issues, located in municipal law where the gamut of rights and obligations is confined within a state, extending to regional treaty arrangements where two or more states in a region are affected, and expanding to global status where generally large regions over the planet are involved. The nature and character of environmental issues play a decisive role in determining the scope and content of environmental law, and indeed, the substance and direction of environmental policy. Environmental policy may be shaped by the requirements of environmental problems as they operate interspatially to affect the present generation, and in an intertemporal dimension to affect future generations through consequences extending into the future.

Environmental policy determines, among other things, the order of priority in which environmental issues need to be considered. The order of priority will vary with the perspective applied to them, and different perspectives can be expected according to the nature of the interest involved. The scientist may take a view different from the government. And emphasis on development may have an impact in the choice of priorities. Besides, a national perspective may conceivably vary from the global. However, with the growing awareness of the need to pool knowledge, information, and experience, lawmakers and men of public affairs are today paying greater respect to scientific studies, and governments are finding it necessary to consult international trends when formulating national policies. As a result, a greater approximation seems possible in the preparation of environmental issue inventories. In the final analysis, it is the seriousness and immediacy of the impact of an environmental problem on the life of human beings, as individuals or as members of a collectivity, and on planetary life in relation to man generally, that must determine the degree of gravity and, therefore, of priority. The involvement of environmental issues in human life should be measured by their consequences, and one way to determine this would be to see how they are regarded in point of critical gravity. One analysis[7] lists genetic

7. L.K. Caldwell, *International Environmental Policy,* 16 (Duke University, 1984).

loss, ecosystem disruption and destruction, deforestation, desertification, contamination of the environment (air, water, soil, and biota),
and the degrading and depletion of fresh water as critical issues on
which immediate action is necessary. Issues such as overpopulation
by humans, deterioration and erosion of topsoil, the changing che-
mistry and quality of the atmosphere, the sources and issues of energy, and the disruption of biogeochemical cycles are also acquiring an
urgency that brings them into the front rank for emergent attention.

Human rights as a conceptual philosophy of the environmental law system

It is evident from what has gone before that the protection and improvement of man's environment arise directly out of a vital need to
protect human life to assure its quality and condition, to ensure the
prerequisites indispensable to safeguarding human dignity and human
worth and the development of the human personality, and to create
an ethos promoting individual and collective welfare in all the dimensions of human existence. Centred on those goals, it needs to be examined whether the conceptual framework most appropriate to the
structuring of the environmental law system lies in the philosophy of
human rights.[8]

The right to environment defined

While environmental law has revolved around a broad understanding
of human needs, it is not easy to define the right to environment
with sufficient precision and clarity. Different views have been voiced
by different jurists. One standard adopted is that of a decent
environment.[9] Another writer speaks of a "decent and healthy environment." Principle I of the Stockholm Declaration refers to "a life
of dignity and well-being." Of all the universal or regional documents

8. M. Cranston, *What are Human Rights?* (Basic Books, 1963), quoted in P. Alston, "Conjuring Up New Human Rights: A Proposal for Quality Control," 78 A.J.I.L. 607, 615, n. 30
   (1986): "A human right by definition is a universal moral right, something which all (people) everywhere at all times ought to have, something of which no one may be deprived
   without a grave affront to justice, something which is owing to every human being simply
   because he is human."
9. W.P. Gormley, "The Right of Individuals to Be Guaranteed a Pure, Clean and Decent Environment: Future Programs of the Council of Europe," 38 *1975 Legal Issues in European
   Integration*.

relating to human rights, the most specific provision for environmental protection is contained in the African Charter of Human and Peoples' Rights, which provides that all peoples should have the right to a generally satisfactory environment favourable to their development. The World Commission on Environment and Development has proposed that, as a fundamental legal principle, "all human beings have the fundamental right to an environment adequate to their health and well-being."[10] Perhaps the most acceptable definition would be the right to a healthful environment, for that would be synonymous with an ecologically balanced environment, an environment that may be described as "healthful" in terms of both our natural heritage as well as our cultural heritage.[11] The expression is sufficiently comprehensive to cover all those objectives that environmental rights are intended to serve. Moreover, in identifying it with an ecologically balanced environment, the value base takes into account not only moral and philosophic perceptions but also indications from scientific data. Nonetheless, the scope of the definition of the right to environment will remain uncertain. The precise area cannot be defined as it will vary with local social, economic, and cultural values.

The environmental right examined in terms of the human rights jurisprudence

The right to a healthful environment points to the satisfaction of a vital need. What a vital need is in philosophical terms has been considered by several writers. In an interesting discussion on human needs and human rights, Winslade[12] discusses the concept, and describes vital needs as needs "whose satisfaction would be in the interest of, and would be wanted and desired by, nearly all intelligent and rational persons under ordinary circumstances. . . . Alternatively, one might say that vital needs are those needs which are at least necessary conditions for reaching and maintaining a decent standard

10. World Commission on Environment and Development, *Our Common Future*, 348 (Oxford University, 1987).
11. The National Environmental Policy Act of 1969 (enacted by the United States Congress) Pub. L. No. 91-190, Section 101(a), 83 Stat. 852 (1970), speaks of the need to restore and to maintain environmental quality to aid in the "overall welfare and development of man," and Section 101(c), where Congress recognized that "each person should enjoy a healthful environment."
12. W.J. Winslade, "Human Needs and Human Rights," included in *Human Rights – Amintaphil I*, 29, 35 (1971).

of living." Passing on to the relation between human needs and human rights, he considers it necessary to add the further ingredient of fundamental moral principles in order that needs may mature into human rights. He points out:

. . . the rights are based not only on the existence of unfulfilled vital needs, but also upon an appeal to fundamental moral principles such as equality and human worth. That is, unless these moral principles have operative moral and political force, the growth of rights from needs will be frustrated. For principles like equality and human worth to have moral and political force, they must be taken seriously not merely as lofty ideals but as guides for social reform.

The need for a healthful environment is, as we have seen, vital to the protection of life and to the preservation and enhancement of its quality and condition. Desirable standards of health and welfare will be impossible to sustain in an atmosphere depleted of life-giving and life-sustaining elements. Interference with man's ecological relationship with nature could destabilize his human personality that is the evolutionized product of several millennia. The destruction of his cultural heritage could set him back in time, grievously depriving him of that intellectual, artistic, and social milieu deemed essential to the sustenance of civilized man. As a moral, intellectual, and physical being, developing amidst the dynamics of the process of evolution, man needs the constant environment of a healthful natural order. That need is now increasingly finding expression in the political society in which man lives. In several democratic cultures today the political process, acting through the principal organs of the state, is busy evolving and promoting conditions for improving human dignity and human worth. There can be little doubt that upon that approach the need for healthful environment must be viewed in the maturity of a human right.

There are other conceptual criteria that should be considered. They distinguish human rights from other rights in the general family of rights. Edel[13] classifies them by their properties, status, and function. If the right to a healthful environment satisfies certain criteria, it is entitled in the view of modern jurists to be regarded as a human right and not a mere right.

Among the properties of a human right that set it apart from other

13. A. Edel, "Some Reflections on the Concept of Human Rights," included in *Human Rights – Amintaphil I,* 2 (1971).

rights is its greater generality, its importance (human rights are also referred to as fundamental rights),[14] that it is essential and enduring, and that it is inalienable.

Human rights are general rights in that they pertain to all human beings as such, and while the understanding of them may vary from region to region and from culture to culture, the concept of human rights remains universal. The right to a healthful environment is a right that belongs to every individual or group of individuals. When a group claims that right, it is not the group that possesses the human right but the individuals cooperating together in the membership of that group. The right cannot be withheld from an individual by reference to his race, citizenship, religion, sex, place of birth, or any such limiting class qualification. The right to a healthful environment belongs to all across the globe. The right satisfies the human right test of generality.

The second test of a human right lies in its importance. Human rights are more basic or fundamental than other rights. They are basic and fundamental because in the scale of values, they enjoy a transcendental position over other rights. They are, in fact, the source of other rights, which are derived or flow from them. This test, applied to the right to a healthful environment, is easily satisfied when we remember that a healthful environment is a fundamental requirement for the protection and enhancement of the quality of life and, in certain circumstances, proceeds beyond the issue of human survival on the planet. The categories of environmental issues demonstrates clearly that a degradation of the natural environment poses a grave, and sometimes an immediate, threat to planetary life. The greenhouse effect and the depletion of the ozone layer are only two kinds of the environmental damage threatening catastrophic consequences to human existence. Reference has been made earlier also to the threatened destruction of man's cultural heritage. The greater significance of that cultural heritage must not be overlooked. It occupies a central role in giving to man a conception of his essential values, besides providing an indispensable perspective in planning for the future.

On the third characteristic of human rights, whether they are essential and enduring and unvarying in identity or change with the context of time and circumstance, it seems that the preferred position is that among the several lists of human rights there will be some hu-

14. Constitution of India, Part III.

man rights that hold a pre-eminent position in comparison with other human rights. The right to life, the right to equality, and the right to freedom of expression are some of the human rights that are of primary significance to the human personality and therefore hold a superior place in the human rights hierarchy. They continue to maintain their sacred niche in the catalogue of human rights, whatever the chronology of time or the geography of place.

They represent the immutability of human values and the essential spirit of human civilization. This central niche is not complete, but will continue to accommodate fresh members. As the quality and condition of human society in its evolutionary progress moves on to occupy new fields of experience, the rising challenges facing the human spirit and human survival will call for accretionary powers of expression and control, and values that were overlooked, or considered insignificant or peripheral, will demand their inclusion in the centre of human rights. So imperative are these that the contemporary observer will find it difficult to believe that they could ever have been overlooked. The right to a healthful environment is one such right. Its importance and great significance to human life merits it a place in the central core of human rights. Viewed as a human right in itself, it is entitled to that status.

The right to a healthful environment may be regarded also as a vital aspect of the right to life, for without a sound environment it would not be possible to sustain an acceptable quality of life or even life itself. The right to life lies in the central core of human rights. It may be observed that the values incorporated in these central core rights are not stated or finally expressed, but their dimensions will continue to expand as the levels of human liberty and freedom keep on ascending and a new consciousness of their potential is realized. It is not unusual that changes of perspective induced by an enlarged or more enlightened awareness should open up new vistas of social, economic, and cultural outlook, often producing fundamental changes in the orientation of human society.

The fourth characteristic of basic human rights is said to lie in their inalienability. The American Declaration of Independence includes life, liberty, and the pursuit of happiness as inalienable rights. They constitute the central core of human rights indispensable to the nature of the human personality. There will always be a minimum of human rights that cannot be alienated if the human personality is to retain its essential character. It can be unhesitatingly concluded that the right to a healthful environment is not a right that can be waived or surrendered, having regard to its fundamental relationship with the basic life process of a human being. It is not possible to conceive of life or an acceptable quality of life without a sound environment to sustain it.

There are two further Edelian heads to be considered, namely, status and function, which distinguish human rights from other rights. Concerning "status," human rights are those grounded in reality and not in mere convention. It is apparent from what has been said earlier that human rights, in virtue of their true character, must be an inherent feature of the fundamental values of the society to which the individual belongs. They do not exist by convention but because they inhere in individuals as the owners of a human personality. The right to a healthful environment is rooted in the reality of man's inherent condition and its indispensability to his personality as a human being; it cannot be regarded as the offspring of convention. The right to a healthful environment qualifies as a human right in that context.

And now the last head. A human right is identified from other rights by its status as a conceptual source of bodies of rights constituting the general corpus of the law. Its normative values flow through and control the relations between a political society and its members. The right to a healthful environment fulfils this role. From such a right proceeds an entire bundle of environmental rights, the right to clean water and pure air, the right to the protection of the soil against degradation and of marine resources against pollution, the right to the preservation of man's cultural heritage, and a host of other rights centred in the right to a healthful environment.

Viewed in the context of all these criteria, it appears that in jurisprudential terms the right to a healthful environment qualifies as a human right.

The environmental right considered for a place in the international law system

It remains to be determined whether the right to a healthful environment can be located in an international legal system. If so, then it can be regarded as a source of international law.

The philosophy of human rights owes its origin to "the marriage of positivist and natural law doctrines."[15] That philosophy had engaged

---

15. L.B. Sohn, "The New International Law: Protection of the Rights of Individuals Rather than States," 32:1 *American University Law Review*, 9, 19 (1982).

some of the most brilliant minds on both sides of the Atlantic, but principally in a national context. In 1776, however, the American Declaration of Independence spoke of the inalienable rights of man, and in 1789 the French Declaration of the Rights of Man and the Citizen defined the concept of universal human rights as "the natural and imprescriptible rights of man." With the adoption of the United Nations Charter in 1945, the philosophy of human rights passed into the jurisprudence of international law. As Louis Sohn summarizes the position that followed,[16] individuals gained rights under international law and, to some degree, the means for vindicating those rights in the international plane in four successive law-building stages: the assertion of international concern about human rights in the United Nations Charter; the listing of those rights in the Universal Declaration of Human Rights; the elaboration of those rights in the International Covenant on Civil and Political Rights and in the International Covenant on Economic, Social, and Cultural Rights; and the adoption of an increasing number of additional declarations and conventions concerning issues of special importance, such as discrimination against women, racial discrimination, and religious intolerance.

The binding nature of those documents is no longer open to question. The United Nations Charter is a constitutional document of the highest status in the international system. As for the Universal Declaration of Human Rights, it is now considered to be an authoritative interpretation of the United Nations Charter, and along with the United Nations Charter is regarded as part of the constitutional structure of the world community.[17] The two International Covenants are treaties binding on the States-Parties thereto. Along with the Universal Declaration, they are also part of the international customary law, and as such are binding on all states.

The International Covenant on Civil and Political Rights represents the culmination of a revolution during which men struggled for primary liberties and freedoms, such as the right to liberty and security of person and the right to freedom of thought, opinion, conscience, and religion. These rights are often referred to as human rights of the "first generation."

The revolution for civil and political rights was followed by another revolution. The working class rebelled against conditions that it considered exploitative. And states emerging from colonial

16. *Id.* at 11, 12.
17. *Id.* at 16, 17.

215

domination into a new-found freedom were insistent on conditions that guaranteed the fruits of that freedom. The accent was on state action to promote economic and social well-being and to create a welfare state. The International Covenant on Economic, Social, and Cultural Rights was adopted to satisfy those aspirations, and the human rights declared by it are referred to as human rights of the "second generation." When human rights are identified as rights of the "first generation" or of the "second generation," it is not implied that "first-generation" rights have been superseded by the "second-generation" rights. The expression "generation" is used to indicate a further distinct development in the domain of human rights, that while the earlier generation of rights continues to exist, a new generation has also now come into existence. Both generations not only coexist, they also interact with each other.

A new generation of international human rights, the "third generation," has evolved for filling a significantly important gap in the international law system of human rights. They are collective rights "exercised jointly by individuals grouped into larger communities, including peoples and nations."[18] "Third-generation" human rights are occupied with planetary or global concerns such as peace, development, communication, common heritage, and humanitarian assistance. Karel Vasak, who conceived of the notion of different generations of human rights, observed, in speaking of the new human rights of the "third generation" in his Inaugural Lecture to the Tenth Study Session of the International Institute of Human Rights in July 1979, that they

are new in the aspirations they express, are new from the point of view of human rights in that they seek to infuse the human dimension into areas where it has all too often been missing, having been left to the State, or States. . . . [They] are new in that they may both be *invoked against* the State and *demanded of it*; but above all (and herein lies their essential characteristic), they can be realized only through the concerted efforts of all the actors on the social scene: the individual, the State, public and private bodies and the international community.[19]

The "third-generation" human rights have been variously described as "rights of solidarity" (by Vasak),

18. *Id.* at 48.
19. As quoted by S.P. Marks, "Emerging Human Rights: A New Generation for the 1980's?" (Stoffer Lectures), 33 *Rutgers Law Review*, 397, 441 (1981).

collective rights, or rights of every human being and of all human beings taken collectively, synthetic rights, consolidated rights, communal rights, rights of the peoples, or populist or popular rights, joint rights of individuals and other groups, or rights exercised by individuals separately and jointly, and new rights or new dimensions of existing rights.[20]

In an interesting and illuminating comparison, Vasak points out that the three generations of human rights were intended to realize the corresponding three guiding principles of the French Revolution: *liberté, égalité, fraternité*.[21]

There has been considerable debate on the point whether a "third generation" of human rights should be, or can be, conceived of. In regard to the right of development there was a divergence of opinion. Keba Mbaye, then Chief Justice of Senegal and later Vice-President of the International Court of Justice, sought to discover the right to development in the existing instruments of international law. Vasak, on the other hand, is emphatic that a new generation of human rights must be admitted, reflecting the need to recognize rights of solidarity. The different views demonstrate what is becoming increasingly apparent: that a clear demarcation is not always possible between human rights of the different generations. The comprehensive terms in which a human right may be defined often enable a fair degree of overlapping across two or three generations of rights.

Where does the right to a healthful environment find a place? It will be evident that having regard to the wide sweep connoted by the right to a healthful environment, it can find a place as a "first-generation" right, as a "second-generation" right, and also as a "third-generation" right.

The right to a healthful environment is rooted in the right to an acceptable quality of life, which, in certain circumstances, extends to the right to life itself. The Preamble to the United Nations Charter specifically refers to fundamental human rights, the dignity and worth of the human person as well as to better standards of life. In Article 1(3) of the Charter, there is a reference to promoting and encouraging respect for human rights and fundamental freedoms. If the right

---

20. L.B. Sohn, *supra* note 15 at 61, quoting from *Unesco Symposium on the Study of New Human Rights: The Rights of Solidarity,* 30 (Unesco, 1980).
21. L.B. Sohn, *supra* note 15 at 61. They have also been chromatically classified as "blue," "red," and "green" rights. Jan Glazewski, "The Environment, Human Rights and a New South African Constitution," 171 *South Africa Journal on Human Rights,* 2 (1991).

to a healthful environment is treated as an aspect of the right to life, it can be founded in Article 3 of the Universal Declaration of Human Rights and in Article 6(1) of the International Covenant on Civil and Political Rights. The right to life in those provisions will need to be construed liberally, because in its narrow, strict sense, in the context in which the right appears, it would seem confined to the protection of the individual against physical death. In the Preamble to the Stockholm Declaration of 1972,[22] the enjoyment of a healthful environment has been linked with the right to life. The growing emphasis on environmental protection and the need to find a legal basis for it in the right to life illustrate how a new human right may emerge as the manifestation of a primary human right.[23] While the right to a healthful environment is expressly mentioned in the International Covenant on Civil and Political Rights, specific mention is made in Article 12(2)(b) of the International Covenant on Economic, Social, and Cultural Rights of the obligation on the state to provide for "the improvement of all aspects of environmental . . . hygiene." If the right to a healthful environment can be construed as implied in the provisions of the Universal Declaration and its two Covenants and the several international treaties and conventions that flow from them, it may be said that the right to a healthful environment can be exercised not only against other states, that is to say, for transnational environmental injury, but also against one's own state, for local environmental damage.[24] And if the right to a healthful environment can be traced to both the International Covenants, of Civil and Political Rights and of Economic, Social, and Cultural Rights, it can be exercised not only as a right against the state to ensure against environmentally harmful acts but also as a right to call upon the state to provide the conditions for a healthful environment. It is both a negative right and a positive right.

There is, however, another aspect to environmental rights. They are generally rights that belong to a group of individuals. In certain cases, they may have a regional and even a global dimension. A nuclear fallout or acid rain may affect an entire region. The depletion of

22. Report of the United Nations Conference on the Human Environment, Stockholm, 1–16 June 1972 (U.N. Publ. Sales No. B.73.II.A.14. 1973).
23. The Supreme Court of India has developed a respectable volume of jurisprudence in this respect with reference to Part II, Article 21, Constitution of India.
24. Dr. H.J. Uibopuu, "The Internationally Guaranteed Right of an Individual to a Clean Environment," 1 *Comparative Law Year Book,* 107 (1977).

the ozone layer and the greenhouse effect could have consequences affecting the entire planet.

Clearly, the regional or global dimension implied in the consequences would bring the right to a healthful environment into the list of "third-generation" human rights.

The right to a healthful environment includes a large number of different facets and therefore traverses and overlaps the first, second, and third-generation groups of human rights. Because of the nature of environmental rights, the several facets are members of a single environmental system. It is a system that is indivisible; it is not capable of dissection and separation into individual, independently operating parts of the whole. The intimate interaction and interdependence between its different parts requires us to view the environmental system from a holistic approach as a single, indivisible, and closely integrated operating system.

The right to a healthful environment constitutes a jurisprudential reality. It has matured from an abstract concept to operating law. Because of its character, it is found embodied in other existing systems of international law; for example, in the law of the sea, international economic law, and international labour law. Indisputably it has found a place in the existing international law.

The need is to put it together, identified as a definitive area of international law, self-constituted by its particular nature and its distinctive character, its conceptual underpinnings and its several facets, its operation as a system of law in constant interaction with other systems of law identified by their own conceptual character. What is needed is an integrated system of environmental law, centred on environmental concepts and values, that will address itself with particularity, and explore all possible approaches, to the task of finding solutions to various environmental issues. Bearing in mind the several areas of overlap between environmental law and other systems of law, the task will not be easy.[25] It will be less so when the concept of environment is treated as extending to man's cultural environment.

There is undoubtedly great merit in providing, as Richard Falk suggests,[26] for "a new centralized structure that can manage the

---

25. W.P. Gormley, *Human Rights and Environment: The Need for International Co-operation*, 34 (Sijthoff, 1976).
26. R.A. Falk, "The Logic of State Sovereignty Versus the Requirements of World Order," 27 *Year Book of World Affairs*, 7, 23 (1973).

affairs of a planet on a unified basis" in order to produce an "ecological model of equilibrium." But Gormley comments:

The numerous elements contained within the motion of protecting individuals and the preservation of the environment become involved with almost every phase of man's activity. Likewise, the majority of legal problems encompass environmental (and ecological) aspects; therefore, any international or regional organization must, necessarily, select specific areas for intensive effort.[27]

The problem has its own difficulties, and in the first instance it may be, perhaps, more appropriate to proceed in a phased manner in the context of an overall plan.

Having reached this stage in our journey, it is possible now to conclude that the international law of human rights can provide an appropriate value structure for environmental rights. It will be found that certain material incidents peculiar to both the human rights system and environmental law follow a common pattern. Human rights as well as environmental law have to deal with an area where the doctrine of national sovereignty has to give way to external concern in relation to a national activity. The veil of sovereignty cannot be employed to shut out the operation of the international law of human rights nor the application of environmental law principles. Moreover the international law of human rights, unlike traditional international law, which is designed "to serve common or reciprocal national interests," proceeds from a different motivation – "it is essentially ideological, idealistic, humanitarian; its true and deep purpose is to improve the lot of individual men and women everywhere, particularly where national institutions and non-legal international forces are not adequate. . . ."[28] This makes the international law of human rights especially relevant to the cause of environmental law, which in several areas tends to beneficially affect not only national, but also transnational and even global life, that is, the life of people everywhere. It is also pertinent that the international law of human rights as well as environmental law depend for their implementation on national, regional, and international institutions, operating for a common purpose, in mutual interdependence and with jurisprudential sympathy. It will be noted further that the universality of human

27. W.P. Gormley, *supra* note 25 at 1.
28. *Introduction to the Covenant on Civil and Political Rights* 7 (L. Henkin, ed., Columbia University, 1981).

rights law, despite the plurality of national cultures and economies, makes it fit as a medium of values for the operation of an environmental law system in which multiple perspectives and flexibility of procedures may be a significant feature. In a recent meeting at Malta in December 1990, the UNEP Group of Legal Experts to Examine the Implications of the "Common Concern of Mankind" Concept on Global Environmental Issues saw in the human framework the proper place for environmental protection. It was considered that the framework of human rights, with its emphasis on the social dimension and participation, was more appropriate than the framework of international ecological security. Besides, the preventive dimension was present in both environmental protection and human rights protection. The evolutions of environmental protection and human rights protection, it was observed, disclosed many affinities, and both were undergoing a process of globalization. A bridge between the two lay in the fundamental rights to life and health in their extended dimension, comprising negative as well as positive measures. The Group noted further that the protection of valuable groups, such as indigenous populations, "lay at the confluence of environmental protection and human rights protection, suggesting the need for bringing together human and environmental considerations.[29]

These several aspects point to the admirable suitability of human rights values for providing a conceptual framework for environmental law.

Philip Alston[30] cautions the international community against rushing in to conjure up new human rights without compliance with the usual procedure adopted in law-making. In an admirable article, he analyses the manner in which, according to him, pressures operate to proclaim more new rights. He concedes, however, that laudable success in a number of areas has been achieved by the enunciation of new human rights, and acknowledges that the right to a healthful environment has already been recognized by the African Charter on Human and Peoples Rights of 1981. Stephen Marks[31] points out that all the features necessary for identifying the right to a healthful environment as a new generation right are present: the elaboration of a

29. T. Iwama, *Policies and Laws on Global Warming: International and Comparative Analysis*, 11, 12 (T. Iwama, ed., Environmental Research Center, 1991).
30. P. Alston, "Conjuring Up New Human Rights: A Proposal for Quality Control," 78 A.J.I.L. 607 (1984).
31. S.P. Marks, *supra* note 19 at 442.

221

specialized body of law, an easily identifiable legislative process, the incorporation of the right as a human right within municipal legal systems, and the need for concerted efforts of all social actors.

The right to a healthful environment is an emerging human right, and having regard to the considerable legislation that has already been enacted in municipal law systems and the manner in which the right has been recognized or aspectually applied in international treaties and in the practice of states, it is perhaps difficult to deny now that the right to a healthful environment has a significant status in international law. On the considerations adverted to earlier, the right may be traced to the right to life or treated as a new right altogether.

Environmental rights in the context of the natural order

In the consideration of the human rights philosophy as a conceptual structure for environmental law, it is desirable to survey the position of man in relation to the natural order. The quality and degree of the human right is conditioned by man's relationship to his surrounding ecology. The ancient religions tended to see all organic existence in a single framework united in harmonious interaction. More than 3,000 years ago, the Upanishads in India expressed the Vedantic viewpoint that the Supreme Reality was the undivided whole, the Brahman, which incorporated all manifestations of matter and energy together in a primordial transcendent, all-pervasive, and all-binding harmony.[32] In American Indian culture, before the European settlers

---

32. Dwivedi and Tiwari, "Environmental Protection in the Hindu Religion," in *World Religions and the Environment* (O.P. Dwivedi, ed.). "[T]he Hindu Rishis of the Vedic and the Upanishadic era perceived the value of maintaining a harmonious relationship between the needs of man and the spectacular diversity of the universe. To them, nature was not only the mother that sustained their life, it was the abode of divinity. They did not believe that man's role on earth was to exploit nature to his own selfish purpose. Nor did they subscribe to the prevailing western world-view that the true end of man was essentially to dominate and control nature by all possible means. On the contrary, sanctity of life to them included not only the effort to seek salvation, but to seek it by developing a sacred attitude towards the spiritual significance of nature. Man, in Hindu culture, was instructed to maintain harmony with nature and to show reverence for the presence of divinity in nature. Consequently, a Hindu has not been at war with nature. *Id.* at 182.

Hindu culture, in ancient and medieval times, provided a system of moral guidelines towards environmental preservation and conservation. Environmental ethics, as propounded by ancient Hindu scriptures and the seers, was practiced not only by common man, but even by rulers and kings. They observed these fundamentals sometimes as religious duties, often as rules of administration or obligation for law and order, but either way, these prin-

came to the American continent, the concept of an ultimate whole-
ness of all existence was implied when the individual sought related-
ness to all manifestations of the Great Spirit: rocks, trees, animals, or
people. The Chinese philosophers believed that man must invariably
be seen as inseparable from nature and in oneness with the
universe.[33] In the opinion of this writer, perhaps the most accurate
summation of the ecological model is embodied in the statement that
"the universe must be seen as a systematic hierarchy of organized
complexity – a myriad number of wholes within the wholes, all of
which are interconnected and interacting. Within this perspective, an
individual system cannot be properly understood apart from its relationship with the environment of which it is an integral part."[34] The
relationship between man and the several non-human components of
the planetary environment is one of constant interaction, although
not all the dimensions of that interaction may be visible or immediately and directly apparent. This truth is supported by widely
accepted scientific conclusions, including those derived from suba-
tomic physics.[35] Legal jurisprudence today must take into account
the influences that affect social structures, including those based on
data emerging from operating scientific verities.

When in formulating a human right to a healthful environment, we
conceive of values pertaining to individual man, we should view him
as a unit in the ecological system. When we focus on his position as
the bearer of the human right to a healthful environment, we should
proceed on the basis that his environmental rights are qualified by the
rights and interests of other affected sectors of the ecology. This
creed rests on the fundamental principle that man does not enjoy a
superior status over the rest of nature entitling him to exploit, for his
own ends, the ecological biosystem to its irretrievable detriment and
destruction, but that he is, indeed, merely a component equal with
the other components of the ecological biosystem. Man, it is true,
holds a higher position in the tree of evolution, but that only invests

---

ciples were properly knitted with the Hindu way of life. In Hindu culture, a human being is
authorized to use natural resources, but has no divine power of control and dominion over
nature and its elements. Hence, from the perspective of Hindu culture, abuse and exploitation of nature for selfish gain is unjust and sacrilegious. *Id.* at 184.

33. For fuller treatment of the subject, *see* the Introduction by A.M. Taylor and D.M. Taylor
in *World Religions and the Environment, supra* note 32. *See also* J. Campbell, *The Flight of
the Wild Gander* (Viking Press, 1969).

34. A.M. Taylor and D.M. Taylor, *supra* note 33 at 24.

35. *See* F. Capra, *The Tao of Physics* (Shambhala, 1983).

him with greater responsibility to the non-human components of the ecological family.[36] As their moral agent, he has the duty to articulate and defend the rights of other occupants of the planet.[37] In adopting this approach, one does not seek to view the environment in a homocentric dimension. Man is seen as a part of the environment, which consists of several interdependent patterns of existence that, operating within their own value systems and tonal emphasis, constitute the totality of the environmental system. These several patterns of existence constitute, in their interdependence, an organic whole represented by Nature, which, thus, may be seen as a vast empire of interacting and, therefore, of interwoven destinies.

In the enjoyment of the human right to a healthful environment, we must remember that the human right is generally expressed as an assertion of a claim by the individual against state authority. There can be no assertion of a human right against the non-human components of the ecological system. His right is an expression of a politico-legal reality and can only be asserted against a politico-legal entity. The relevance of non-human components of the ecological system is taken into account for determining the inherent worth and quality of the human right to a healthful environment. One manner of taking it into account is expressed in the obligation of man to exercise self-restraint when dealing with them, remembering at all times that he is their protector and defender by virtue of his superior evolution, and has a duty to maintain the integrity of the planet.

A question that has engaged considerable debate is the basis of recognizing an obligation in man towards the non-human elements of the planet. The principle of orthodox jurisprudence that an obligation arises only upon a correlative right cannot serve here inasmuch as non-human elements cannot be regarded as right-bearing. Therefore, a perspective proceeding from an entirely different approach needs to be adopted. Professor Christopher D. Stone has made an impressive contribution to the search for a solution. While stressing the need for a non-homocentric foundation for morals, "which would be more in

36. To the Burmese "men are men, and animals are animals, and men are far the higher. But he does not deduce from this that man's superiority gives him permission to ill-treat or kill animals. It is just the reverse. It is because man is so much higher than the animal that he can and must observe towards animals the very greatest care, feel for them the very greatest compassion, be good to them in every way he can. The Burmese's motto should be *noblesse oblige.*" H.F. Hall, "The Soul of a People," quoted by E.F. Schumacher in *Small is Beautiful,* 89 (Rupa and Co., 1990).

37. R.F. Nash, *The Rights of Nature: A History of Environmental Ethics,* 10 (University of Wisconsin, 1989).

line with our growing understanding of the grandness of the interrelationships of the natural world," he suggests that even if non-human,
whether animate or inanimate, objects cannot be regarded as "possessors" of rights, they must be treated as "morally considerable."
Moral considerableness, he says, creates duties in man to non-human
animate and inanimate objects. The mere circumstance that non-
human things possess an intrinsic goodness, that is, good in and of
themselves, should be sufficient to attract duties towards them.[38] He
is critical of the range given to moral monism when several dimensions of standing are involved and suggests that we "conceive moral
activities as partitioned into several distinct frameworks, each governed by distinct principles and logical textures. . . . Under moral
pluralism frameworks vary in regard to the fabric of their basic
concepts."[39] This proposition is supported by Stephen Toulmin,[40]
who regards the cosmocentric or egocentric standpoint as non-
homocentric,[41] and considers the common law jurisprudence
appropriate for analysing situations arising in consequence of the new
approach.[42]

It appears that a true understanding of environmental philosophy
can be achieved only if legal principle is defined in the context of
moral pluralism. It may indicate an extension of jurisprudence
beyond the orthodox concept of a right-duty relationship, but it
should not occasion surprise for the philosophy of law [that] has been
generally understood in the context of a moral order. In different
constitutional systems, constitutional principles and conventions test
the validity of individual and state action on the anvil of social morality, for social morality constitutes the basis of the pattern of relationships within a society. In an ecological society the needs, interests, and "moral considerableness" of all its affected components
must be taken into account. There is merit in the view that the human right to a healthful environment should not be comprehended
from a homocentric standpoint, but in the totality of an egocentric
value system. Positioning environmentalism in a human focus to the

38. C.D. Stone, "The Environment in Moral Thought," 56 *Tennessee Law Review*, 3, 5, 6
(1988).
39. *Id.* at 11.
40. S. Toulmin, "The Case for Cosmic Prudence," 56 *Tennessee Law Review*, 29 (1988).
41. *Id.* at 35. The two expressions are preferred to "non-homocentric" as more accurate in
defining the natural order and man's position therein than homocentric perspective.
42. *See* Tarlock, *supra* note 1, for critical comments respecting the views of Professor Stone
and Stephen Toulmin.

exclusion of non-human elements restricts it from the wider sweep to which it properly belongs.

Inasmuch as this approach proceeds upon a holistic perception of man positioned in the natural order, it provides a value structure most harmonious and beneficial to his development, and therefore, of fundamental significance to an understanding of the right to a healthful environment.

Duty to future generations

The human right to a healthful environment should be viewed in the context of a duty to future generations.[43] The duty to preserve and protect the environment is a duty that is owed not merely to all other human beings, non-human beings, and inanimate objects in present time but extends also to future generations. The duty is expressed in the theory of "intergenerational equity," which articulates that "all members of each generation of human beings, as a species, inherit a natural and cultural patrimony from past generations, both as beneficiaries and as custodians under the duty to pass on this heritage to future generations," and that this right to benefit from and develop this natural and cultural heritage is inseparably coupled with the obligation to use this heritage in such a manner that it can be passed on to future generations in no worse condition than it was received from past generations.[44] This theory of intergenerational equity finds support from religious and ethical norms and from numerous international instruments commencing, in modern times, from the Charter of the United Nations, the Universal Declaration of Human Rights and its two International Covenants, to a host of conventions and declarations that are concerned with the dignity, worth, and progress of mankind. When we speak of mankind, we speak of the human race as it exists today and also as it will in the future. And, therefore, an intergenerational dimension must be necessarily inferred in these international instruments extending to all future generations as an obligation *erga omnes* that derives some support from customary international law[45] and is regarded as an emerging norm of customary international law. Another view is that the universal and unequivocal recognition of the duty to protect the interests of future generations,

43. For a detailed and fully reasoned treatment of the subject, *see* E. Brown Weiss, *supra* note 5.
44. *Id.* at 293.
45. E. Brown Weiss, *supra* note 6 at 540–544.

as well as of the principles necessary to implement that duty, should be achieved on the basis of treaty rather than be left to the development of customary law.[46]

As in the case of non-human beings and inanimate objects, a question arises whether this duty to future generations is correlative to a right inhering in future generations. If rights cannot be attributed to an unborn child, can they be attributed to unborn generations? Unless life on this planet becomes extinct altogether, in which case no occasion for enjoying the benefit of planetary resources or cultural heritage will arise, future generations may be regarded as of certain and definite existence, although lying in the future. We can conceive of a time continuum in which human generations are positioned at successive points of time. They will have definite and certain positions, depending on the number of years when one generation can be said to follow another. A continuous relationship links the generations, and they succeed each other with definite certainty and constant regularity. The existing concept of a right-duty relationship will, in this context, have to be developed further to accommodate the case of rights of future generations. These rights, as Professor E. Brown Weiss[47] observes, are not rights possessed by individuals but are generational rights, conceived of in the temporal context of generations. They will be governed by considerations different from those applicable to the case of an unborn child, the incidents in each case being different from the other. Professor Brown Weiss points out that "while rights are always connected to obligations, the reverse is not always true,"[48] and she refers to Hans Kelsen[49] and John Austin[50] in support.

The concept of "the common concern of mankind"

Another dimension of man's relationship to the natural order is implied in the concept "the common concern of mankind." This concept was the subject of reference in United Nations General Assembly Resolution No. 43–53 of December 1988, and while covering climate

46. L. Gündling, "Agora: What Obligation Does Our Generation Owe to the Next? An Approach to Global Environmental Responsibility? Do We Owe a Duty to Future Generations to Preserve the Global Environment?" 84 A.J.I.L. 190, 212 (1990).
47. A.D. Tarlock, *supra* note 1 at 96; D.A. Kay and H.K. Jacobson, *supra* note 4 at 205.
48. D.A. Kay and H.K. Jacobson, *supra* note 4 at 203.
49. H. Kelsen, *Pure Theory of Law*, 62 (University of California, 1967).
50. J. Austin, *Austin's Jurisprudence, Lectures on Jurisprudence*, 413–415 (1973).

227

change directly, it focuses on issues that are generally basic to mankind. The concept possesses a social dimension as well as a temporal dimension and is considered relevant to other sectors of international environmental law, including the conservation of biological diversity. The UNEP Group of Legal Experts, which was constituted to examine the implications of that concept, at its meeting in December 1990 in Malta, expressed the view that the concept of "common concern of mankind" is a more suitable and neutral concept in dealing with planetary resources than the earlier concept of "common heritage of mankind," in that proprietary considerations were excluded. The element of reciprocity, moreover, was avoided by choosing a concept based in considerations of *ordre public*. The ingredients constituting the concept of "common concern of mankind" lay in "involvement of all countries, all societies, and all classes of people within countries and societies, long-term temporal dimension, encompassing present as well as future generations, and some sort of sharing of burdens of environmental protection."

As will be apparent from this, the concept has been considered to possess several advantages, in that the word "mankind" implies a link with the human rights framework and with the long-term temporal dimension, including the inclusion of future generations; the word "concern" emphasizes the preventive character of environmental protection as well as the consequential effects or responses called for; the word "common" implies in international law the same sense as "public order" in municipal law, all of them making the notion of "common concern" akin to the related concepts of "obligations *erga omnes*," "*jus cogens*," "common heritage," and "global commons."[51]

This emerging concept provides greater flexibility than earlier notions in describing comprehensively the true nature and measure of man's obligations to elements of a global concern and avoid many of the pitfalls implied in those earlier notions.

The right to development

The emphasis on the right to development has, at every stage, constituted a challenge to the philosophy of environmental rights. It has been, in fact, the reason for a division between the developed countries and the developing countries concerning the operation of environmental rights. Developing countries have declined to adopt fully

51. *Policies and Laws on Global Warming, supra* note 29 at 8, 9.

the perspective preferred by developed countries that environmental claims are superior to the right to development. While developed countries, already at the peak of industrialization, see dangers to the ecology from the current use of certain industrial processes and the combustion of fossil fuels, developing countries find it difficult to accept entirely the abandoning of such processes and use. Developing countries urge that they are in the early stages of development, and their economies do not permit alternative systems of energy. The position taken by them is that the developed countries should transfer appropriate technology to them to relieve them of the need to rely on present industrial processes and fossil-fuel energy. Developing countries contend that there is a moral duty owed by industrialized nations to the developing world.[52] They rely also on the Declaration on the Establishment of a New International Economic Order, which implies that colonial powers have an obligation to assist the development of their former colonies.[53] While this rationale is not readily accepted by developed countries, it seems to be conceded that underdevelopment is the by-product of the development of the Western countries, in that the growth of the colonial territories "was blocked by the destruction of the natural balance in place before colonialism, coupled with structural disadvantages built into the present international economic system."[54] Whatever view be taken, the fact of colonialism certainly is a relevant factor, and justice and equity, well accepted as concepts incorporated into international law jurisprudence[55] and fundamental international instruments,[56] support that claim.

The controversy has compelled an examination of the question of whether the claim to a healthful environment and the right to development are mutually hostile and implacable enemies. The hostility was perceived as long ago as the United Nations Conference on the Human Environment at Stockholm in 1972, but by the adoption of the concept of "sustainable development," which found favour with the World Commission on the Environment and Development in the

52. K. M'Baye, "Le droit au développement comme un droit de l'homme," 5 *Revue des droits de l'homme,* 503, 522 (1972).
53. G.A. Res. 3201, 29 U.N. GAOR, Sixth Special Sess. Suppl. No. 1, at 3, U.N. Doc. A/9559 (1974).
54. *See* R.Y. Rich, "The Right to Development as an Emerging Human Right," 23 *Virginia Journal of International Law,* 292 (1983).
55. North Sea Continental Shelf Cases, 1969 *I.C.J.* 47.
56. United Nations Charter, Preamble and Article 1.

Brundtland Report, "Our Common Future" (1987). Sustainable development is a concept that implies development that meets the needs of the present generation without compromising the ability of future generations to meet theirs.

In this context the insistence by the developing nations on the transfer of technology to them by the developed countries acquires pointed importance. Developing countries do not possess as yet the level of technological expertise that could equip them with industrial strategies from which offending industrial processes are excluded. Moreover, in the presence of high poverty levels they are unable to substitute environmentally protecting energy-production methods in place of fossil fuels. The creation of an international environmental fund has been suggested as a solution for enabling the transfer of technology from the developed countries to the developing nations. The consideration of such solutions continues to engage the international community, and the developed nations find it difficult to avoid facing the issue in view of the urgency of the threat of grave environmental danger disclosed by recent scientific data. The developed nations have now expressed a readiness to assist developing countries. The Declaration of the Hague provides for such assistance.[57] So does the Communiqué from the Paris Summit, which encourages economic incentives "to help developing countries deal with past damage and to encourage them to take environmentally desirable action."[58]

The Vienna Convention and its Montreal Protocol bear witness to the international anxiety following discovery of the damage to the ozone layer. Beside the hole in the ozone layer over Antarctica, another hole in the ozone layer has been discovered over Europe, the United States, and Canada. The Montreal Protocol, while insisting on the termination of industrial processes, such as the use of chlorofluorocarbons in air-conditioning, refrigerants, and certain other industrial products, has limited the time for, and the quantum of, use of offending industrial processes. Considerations relating to the developing nations have been given allowance by prescribing time-lags for compliance with the minimum standards. The United States has also agreed now to support a special international fund to provide financial and technological assistance to developing nations. This fund will enable these countries to shift to chemicals that are safer for

57. Declaration of the Hague, 11 Mar. 1989, 28 *I.L.M.* 1308–10.
58. Joint Committee by Industrialized Nations at Paris Economic Summit, 16 July 1989, Sections 33–50, 28 *I.L.M.* 1296–98.

the atmosphere. The fund is planned to total from US$150 to US$250 million.[59] Recent technological developments have made alternative chemicals available. A new market for hydrofluorocarbons (HFC 134a) can be developed replacing many uses for chloro-fluoro-carbons. Other ozone-friendly chemicals include terpenes, which are natural solvents. Industry continues to explore replacements for CFCs. Relevant products include hairsprays, windshield-wash fluids, and paints, but the most difficult to replace appear to be antifreeze and refrigeration compounds.

One aspect of the rival claims between environmental rights and the right to development is that while both rights can be described as emerging human rights, with both tracing their roots in the Universal Declaration of Human Rights and its two International Covenants, and the several human rights instruments following them, a relative positioning of the two rights in the hierarchy of human rights appears unavoidable. It is now settled that while human rights constitute a superior class over ordinary rights, there will be, within the categories of human rights, an observable hierarchy structured according to the relative importance of particular human rights. As between the right to a healthful environment and the right to development, one mode of preference is suggested by the existence or non-existence of alternatives. In the case of the ozone layer, it is impossible to conceive of a feasible substitute. The depletion of the ozone layer removes the protection from the sun's ultraviolet radiation that the ozone layer affords, resulting in diseases such as skin cancer, eye cataract, and other health problems of mankind. On the contrary, as has been shown, it is possible to find alternatives to the use of chloro-fluorocarbons so that chlorine atoms are not released and the ozone layer is not affected thereby. There will be other areas that call for the balancing of the dimension of environmental protection against the claims of the right to development. A balancing operation, taking into account relative needs, access to alternative procedures, the cost-benefit ratio, and related factors, will determine the fine point of balance between the two rival claims. Much will turn on local conditions such as social values, economic standards, and the like.

The apparent rivalry between environmental rights and the right to development has been occasioned by the circumstance that ecology

59. R. Dohse, Comment, "Global Air Pollution and the Greenhouse Effect: Can International Legal Structures Meet the Challenge?", 13 *Houston Journal of International Law,* 179, 204 (1990).

and economics have been regarded from the outset as two different and distinct disciplines. The eminent development economist Amartya Sen, in his book on "ethics and economics," is critical of economists who have neglected the influence of ethical considerations in the characterization of actual human behaviour. According to him, economists have adopted a very narrow view of ethics as a result of "their preference for treating economics as a task akin to engineering."[60] The Brundtland Report, in suggesting the concept of "sustainable development," has attempted to bring about a marriage of economics and ecology. The concept of sustainable development introduced some related concepts, thus incorporating the demands of intra-generational equity and intergenerational equity into a development framework – concepts such as the impact of regional and global ramifications, including spillovers; trade and cooperation; ensuring the maintenance of ecological systems and the protection of biodiversity; cautious and conservative attitudes, if there is significant risk, uncertainty, or irreversibility involved in the development project; and ensuring that the development proposed increases material and non-material well-being.[61] The concept of "sustainable development," together with these related concepts, constitute the meeting point where environment and development stand reconciled, with both constituting balanced components within the environmental mosaic.

The protection of the environment and the reduction of poverty are treated as related aspects. The transfer of technology from the developed to the developing nations is a need whose imperative nature cannot be denied. The need becomes more comprehensive when it is realized that phenomena such as the depletion of the ozone layer and the greenhouse effect are problems concerning the entire planet, and therefore there is a collective global responsibility for taking and participating in all measures necessary to keep the planet in good health. It is now broadly accepted that the countries on the two continents of North America and Europe are responsible for almost three-quarters of the carbon-dioxide emissions that contribute to global warming, while peopled by a mere eight per cent of the world's population. The developing world can be held responsible for

---

60. P. Alston as Member of the Panel on "Environment, Economic Development and Human Rights: A Triangular Relationship," *Proceedings of the 82nd Annual Meeting,* 51 (American Society of International Law, 1988).
61. P. Ellyard, "Creating an Ecologically and Economically Sustainable 21st Century," address at Australian Legal Convention, Adelaide, 9 Sept. 1991.

only seven per cent of the industrialized emission of carbon dioxide, although holding about eighty per cent of the world's population. Similarly, the environmental damage caused by CFCs must be attributed primarily to Western industrialized countries.[62]

The protection of indigenous peoples

The adverse impact of environmental degradation poses consequences for all sections of human society within its circumference. But while the more developed and economically affluent are capable of creating conditions for meeting or withstanding those consequences, or at least their full effect, there are vulnerable minorities whose very survival is threatened. In their extinction mankind loses a valuable cultural content. Indigenous communities in developing countries are most susceptible to that risk because of their intricate and fragile dependence on their natural habitat. Their survival depends upon it inasmuch as it provides, simultaneously, their shelter, their sustenance, and their fundamental culture. The nature of their dependence on their habitat is so total that any interference with it would constitute an assault on their existence. The Sub-Committee on the Prevention of Discrimination and Protection of Minorities has described their relationship with the land as comprising their "whole range of emotional, cultural, spiritual and religious considerations."[63] A thoughtless and aggressive policy that destroys their habitat, be it in pursuance of a developmental programme or in consequence of military operations, produces a traumatic end to the indigenous community. In the vast mosaic of environmental protection, indigenous peoples are entitled to particular protection by reason of their sensitive relationship to their habitat. The World Commission on Environment and Development has referred to the danger of indigenous peoples being threatened with virtual extinction unless their traditional rights are recognized. It recommends that they should be given a decisive voice in the shaping of policies and programmes for the development of their areas.[64]

---

62. Address by Barber B. Conable, President, World Bank, on 11 Sept. 1989 in Tokyo, Japan, at the Tokyo Conference on the Global Environment and Human Response towards Sustainable Development.
63. United Nations Sub-Commission on Prevention of Discrimination and Protection of Minorities, *Study of the Problem of Discrimination Against Indigenous Population*, 28, U.N. Doc. E/CN.4/Sub.2/1986/7 and Adds. 1–4 (1986).
64. *Our Common Future, supra* note 10 at 12.

Economic considerations responsible for deforestation and use of land for agricultural and industrial purposes can do violent injury to the survival of an indigenous people and the preservation of their culture. The right to a healthful environment is as much a right to the minority community as it is of the majority, and in a conflict between the two claims the operating principle would incline in favour of preserving that which will be irretrievably lost. The right to development in action possesses the capacity of doing irremedial injury to an indigenous culture. The arrogance of developmental economics, which seeks to pursue with missionary zeal the introduction of modern values into the lives of an indigenous people, can destroy that which it intends to promote.

Where an indigenous community inhabits an island, such island culture depends for its sustenance upon the marine environment. The sea provides food and brings tourism and commerce. A disruption of that ethos by whatever means could easily deprive the people of their only source of subsistence, leading ultimately to their extinction. Global warming produces consequences of immeasurable danger to an island existence, with fatal consequences for the indigenous community and its indigenous culture.

An indigenous people is entitled to the preservation of its culture. The Universal Declaration of Human Rights, by Article 22, directs the protection of individual social, economic, and cultural rights. The various facets of the right to participate freely in cultural life presupposes the maintenance by an indigenous community of its identity and its protection against assimilation by the state. It also guarantees the right to cultural participation or minimal self-determination by the minority community. Ethnocide is as significant a form of destruction as any other. Involved in the protection of cultural values is the right to life and the right to security of person construed in terms of the quality and condition of life. Protected by the doctrine of *jus cogens,* they are non-derogable. While some municipal constitutions have specifically provided for the protection of such minorities,[65] the international law regime needs to be strengthened and reinforced in its protection of indigenous peoples.

The conflict between environmental rights and the right to development, which has been treated previously, raises the same issues in the case of indigenous peoples. The notion of sustainable development applies to their context also. Informed by social justice, it is a

---

65. *See* Constitution of India, Part IV, Article 46 and the Fifth Schedule.

promise to protect their right to life and their way of life against the threat of environmental degradation.

Environmental rights and international refugee law

At various times in history individuals and groups have been compelled to abandon the home state because of the fear of persecution occasioned by policies based on religion, race, nationality, social, or political programmes and the like. The mass emigration of Russians and Armenians provoked by the installation of a Communist regime in Russia and similarly the emigration of Jews and other communities when Germany and its neighbouring territories came under East rule are historic examples of refugee movements. Natural disasters, destitute economies, and general political turmoil have also prompted large groups of people to seek refuge in more stable societies. Migrations of this character have generally taken place from less-developed countries. Environmental disasters may now be added to the list.

The international instruments incorporating the refugee law today are the Convention Relating to the Status of Refugees[66] and the related Protocol.[67] Besides there are international institutions, the primary refugee relief organization of the United Nations being the United Nations High Commissioner for Refugees (UNHCR), aided by Unesco, UNICEF, and UNDP. In the drafting and adoption of the Convention an attempt to embody a comprehensive humanitarian protection was defeated. The generality of human rights values was compelled to give way to a much narrower focus, that of persecution for reasons of race, religion, nationality, or membership of a particular social group or political opinion. Persons who feared persecution by the denial of basic civil and political rights alone fell within the Convention.[68] The grant of refugee status was broadly intended for the benefit of European refugees from Eastern Europe. Non-

---

66. Convention Relating to the Status of Refugees, 28 July 1951, 189 *U.N.T.S.* 150.
67. Convention Relating to the Status of Refugees, 31 Jan. 1967, 606 *U.N.T.S.* 267.
68. The definition of "refugee" in the Convention as adopted was: "For the purposes of the present Convention the term 'refugee' shall apply to any person who . . . as a result of events occurring before 1 January 1951 and owing to well-founded fear of being persecuted for reasons of race, religion, nationality, membership of a particular social group or political opinion, is outside the country of his nationality and is unable or, owing to such fear, unwilling to avail himself of the protection of that country. . . . " The temporal limitation of the Convention was removed by the Protocol, so that the restrictive condition that the event that gave rise to fear of persecution should have occurred before 1 January 1951 was deleted.

European states together with Belgium and the United Kingdom argued against a regional bias being given to the Convention. But the situation remained unaltered, except that subsequently by the Protocol the temporal restriction enacted in the definition of "refugee" was removed. The limitation implied by the grounds on which refuge could be sought continued as before. A narrow door was opened. The broad concept of humanitarianism was abandoned. This resulted in a two-tiered scheme for refugees, European refugees alone being granted legal protection in the context of residence abroad. UNHCR's competence enabled relief to be given to large groups of persons in Africa, Asia, and Latin America, but the assistance is not of the same quality as that provided to refugees under the Convention, being confined to an emphasis on return, local resettlement, or confinement in camps of refugees into Western countries. This dichotomy in international refugee law has been sought to be explained by the anxiety of the developed states to avoid difficulties of adjustment within their societies on account of cultural, ethnic, political, and economic differences.[69]

Differential treatment under the international refugee law proceeding essentially on considerations of territorial origin, ethnic distinctions, and cultural differences testifies to refuge being granted for reasons convenient to the state of refuge rather than considerations flowing from the broad concept of humanitarianism. The title to consideration for the grant of refuge should be determined by the nature of the forces compelling the seeking of refuge. This is reflected in the Preamble to the Convention, which, in its first two recitals, refers to the principle affirmed in the Charter of the United Nations and the Universal Declaration of Human Rights that human beings will enjoy fundamental rights and freedoms without discrimination, and that the United Nations is seized of a profound concern for refugees to whom it assures the widest possible exercise of those fundamental rights and freedoms. Having regard to the present state of the international refugee law, the criticism that "the rhetoric of human concern lingers, but the modern apparatus of international refugee law is more closely tied to the safeguarding of developed States than to the vindication of claims to protection"[70] appears to possess some merit.

---

69. For an analysis of the present state of international refugee law, *see* J.C. Hathaway, "A Reconsideration of the Underlying Premise of Refugee Law," 31 *Harvard International Law Journal*, 129 (1990).
70. *Id.* at 175.

From what has been observed, it would seem that the context of the human rights culture as a value base for environmental law is not served by the present state of international refugee law. Mankind, both in its spatial as well in its intertemporal dimensions, is entitled to an environment of equality and freedom from discrimination. Natural disasters, destitute economies, and general political turmoil constitute environmental conditions as distressing as the fear of persecution on the grounds set forth in the definition clause of the Convention. When mass distress because of environmental disasters is added to man's misfortunes, the case for a broad-based humanitarianism acquires an even greater significance.

A more rational perspective characterizes the regional arrangements obtaining today in Africa and Latin America. The Organization of African Unity's Convention Governing the Specific Aspects of Refugee Problems in Africa grants protection not only to persons covered by the United Nations Convention, but also to persons who, "owing to external aggression, occupation, foreign domination or events seriously disturbing public order in either part or the whole of his country of origin or nationality, is compelled to leave his place of habitual residence in order to seek refuge in another place outside his country of origin or nationality."[71] There is a specific obligation to receive refugees and to secure settlement of those refugees. The Organization of American States adopted the Cartagena Declaration, which also extends protection, in addition to the persons described in the definition clause of the United Nations Convention, to persons "who have fled their country because their lives, safety or freedom have been threatened by generalized violence, foreign aggression, internal conflicts, massive violations of human rights or other circumstances which have seriously disturbed public order."[72]

Insufficient provision in the present international refugee law for the protection of refugees can itself provide the conditions for environmental degradation. When masses of people are uprooted from their homes and have to seek refuge in another country, the want of proper facilities brings in problems of health, want, and demoralization. An environmental hazard begins to take shape, whose dimensions can affect not only the refugees but may extend to the resident population itself. Tensions are bred and escalate with easy provocation and an atmosphere surcharged with violence invariably adds to

71. Cited in J.C. Hathaway, *id*. at 176, n.271.
72. Cited in J.C. Hathaway, *id*. at 176, n.275.

the problem of maintaining sound environmental conditions. The right to a healthful environment is put into jeopardy, with consequences that could have been avoided by a wiser, more equitable, and more generous international refugee law.

Substantive norm-making and enforcement procedures

1. Soft law

The developing international environmental law owes its origin to "soft law," which, it is now widely accepted, has a significant status in the process of norm-making. New norms conceived in response to the felt needs of international realities for filling a vacuum in the international law system or introducing provisos to existing law because of its rigidity are often evolved through constant renegotiation in the international arena. The Stockholm Declaration of 1972, regarded as a non-binding resolution, is of that nature. Principle 21 and other "principles" of the Declaration have been relied upon by governments, and their norms are to be found in state practice. And from its frequent citation in UN documents, Principle 21 may be said to have achieved the status of customary international law. UNEP, created pursuant to the Declaration, has made an important contribution in developing the corpus of international law. Periodic endorsement by the United Nations General Assembly of the priorities set by UNEP constitute an example of soft law.[73] So have non-governmental organizations such as the International Law Association, which formulated the Montreal Rules of International Law Applicable to Transfrontier Pollution, and the Institute of International Law, which adopted resolutions on the Utilization of Non-Maritime International Waters, on the Pollution of Rivers and Lakes and International Law, and on Transboundary Air Pollution. Repeated observance of the suggested principles and rules, regarded as indicators of contemporary trends in the environmental law area, has prepared the way for the evolution, and subsequent adoption, of "hard law." In this, soft law acts as a catalyst. Meanwhile, the behaviour and conduct of states tend to follow the principles and rules embodied in soft law. National legislation and national courts, dealing with the responsibility of environmental protection, have often drawn inspiration and

---

73. *U.N. Environment Program: Report of the Governing Council,* 42 U.N. GAOR Supp. (No. 25), U.N. Doc. A/44/25 (1989).

guidance from such soft law.[74] Whereas in environmental protection hard law is not always readily possible in view of varying responses from state governments because of particular local economic conditions, societal attitudes, and the like, soft law plays an important role in providing direction and standards.

2. The World Bank

The principles and norms emerging from soft law relating to environmental protection have strongly influenced programmes of action everywhere, in international life and within national systems. Environmental values, for example, have now a definite and operational influence in banking systems. Nowhere has this been more evident than in the reorientation introduced in the activities of the International Bank for Reconstruction and Development. In the address delivered by Barber B. Conable, President of the Bank, he mentioned that lending for environmental, population, and forestry projects was increased; resources devoted to the environment were increased by more than 100 staff years; and environmental issues were fully integrated into the Bank's approach to development. A US$5 million Environmental Technical Assistance Program to accelerate the preparation of environmental projects was inaugurated. Environmental Assessment Guidelines were designed to strengthen the capacity of developing countries to deal with environmental problems and to ensure that the World Bank took environmental concerns into account at the earliest stage of designing development projects. The Bank decided to assist developing countries in reducing the emissions of greenhouse gases without adversely affecting development. An Energy Efficiency and Strategy Unit was created to deal with financial and policy issues. A Household Energy Unit was created for determining the most suitable means of delivering traditional and other more modern forms of renewable energy to the homes of the poor and to rural industry. A Gas Development Unit promoting the economic production, consumption, and export of natural gas was also envisaged.[75]

The World Bank has laid great emphasis on success for family planning programmes in developing countries and has also under-

---

74. P.M. Dupuy, "Soft Law and the International Law of the Environment," 12 *Michigan Journal of International Law*, 420 (1991).
75. B. Conable, *supra* note 62 at 245, 246.

taken studies for determining the legal status of women in the context of resource-management problems and also in relation to family-planning programmes.[76] The norm of "sustainable development" has been consistently in the forefront of the World Bank's consideration of development projects, and it has focused upon incorporating environmental considerations into each stage of the project cycle of development funding. In acting as a leader in adopting and establishing sound environmental practices, the World Bank has set an example for other lending institutions.

3. The United Nations

Violations of the right to a healthful environment, like violations of some other human rights, will not easily gain consideration in the international plane having regard to the present constitution of international institutions. A member state of the United Nations may have the issue debated in the General Assembly, but there is considerable controversy on whether resolutions of the General Assembly have binding force[77] or are merely recommendations.[78]

The United Nations Commission on Human Rights is empowered to consider violations of human rights by governments. The Commission assigns the matter to working groups or sub-rapporteurs, whose reports are debated and considered for adoption. Discussion in those proceedings of a violation of human rights committed by a government publicizes its conduct. The procedure is based on the expectation that there are few governments that are insensitive to condemnation by the international community. Besides, such public discussion results in the prescription of standards of conduct expected of governments and provides rules of guidance for future action. The resulting information is employed by individuals or groups within their own countries for the formulation of norms and their compliance by domestic administrative and judicial agencies, and for the purpose of securing reforms by law-making agencies. That information also enables non-governmental organizations to play a significant role in their contribution to the investigation and reporting of human rights

76. D. Joannides, "Restructuring the World Bank: The Environmental Light Shines on the Funding of Development Projects," 2 *Georgetown International Environmental Law Review,* 161 (1989).
77. W.P. Gormley, *supra* note 9 at 56.
78. G.P. Smith, "The United Nations and the Environment: Sometimes a Great Notion," 19 *Texas International Law Journal,* 335, 339 (1984).

violations. While violations of environmental rights by governments may effectively be the subject of complaint before the United Nations Commission on Human Rights, the problem enters a more difficult dimension when the complaint is addressed by an individual. The Sub-Commission of the Human Rights Commission has been empowered to permit individuals to petition it against violations of human rights. In the case of environmental rights violations, it is appropriate, in view of their individual and collective character, that standing be recognized in individuals as well as groups.

The International Court of Justice, as presently constituted by its Statute, is competent to entertain disputes between states only, and cannot take cognizance of a petition addressed by an individual to it.[79] This inhibition may be removed by an appropriate amendment of its Statute. In the event of the competence of the Court being enlarged, an appreciable volume of environmental rights litigation can be expected to enter its doors. To cope with it, it may be necessary to consider the constitution of specialized chambers for environmental cases.[80]

In recent years, with the increasing prospect of international environmental law disputes, profound interest has been shown in suggesting other procedures and dispute-settlement fora. The Report and Final Recommendations of the International Congress on a More Efficient International Law on the Environment and Setting Up an International Court for the Environment within the United Nations[81] has recommended the drafting of a Universal International Convention proclaiming the duty of all states to conserve and protect the environment; the creation of an international body within the United Nations system to guarantee the supervision, planning, and management of the world environment; the appointment of a United Nations High Commissioner for the Environment with adequate support facilities; and the creation of an International Court for the Environment, which should be accessible to states, United Nations organs, and private citizens.

Other recommendations include one mentioned in the Report of the Legal Experts Group of the World Commission on Environment in the form of a draft convention as well as General Principles on En-

---

79. *Statute of the International Court of Justice,* Article 34(1).
80. *Statute of the International Court of Justice,* Article 26.
81. A. Postiglione, "A More Efficient International Law on the Environment and Setting Up an International Court for the Environment within the United Nations," 20 *Environmental Law,* 321 (1990).

vironmental Protection and Sustainable Development. These recommendations envisage also the appointment of a United Nations High Commissioner for the Environment, who would hear individual complaints and issue reports, and a Commission for the Environment that would hear complaints from states and issue reports.

Another recommendation was made in the Hague Declaration[82] on the Environment, which calls upon the United Nations to establish a new institutional authority "to monitor and enforce measures to reverse global warming and climate change." The proposal, however, does not go into a detailed consideration of the recommendation. Instead of a new centralized authority within the United Nations, one writer[83] suggests the strengthening of the existing organs of the United Nations, such as the Security Council, the Trusteeship Council, and the Economic and Social Council, and an enlargement of the powers of the Secretary-General with a view to more effectively dealing with environmental problems and disputes.

4. Treaties

Bilateral or multilateral treaties may provide for remedies for violations of environmental rights. A time-honoured mode of providing relief, they will be binding as between the states parties thereto.

Conclusion

There is clear evidence that the approach adopted by the international community to environmental rights corresponds to that applied to human rights generally. That is to be expected since the right to a healthful environment proceeds out of the international law of human rights itself. The international law system took a major turn when the human rights philosophy was made part of international jurisprudence. The sanctity attached to the doctrine of state sovereignty was diluted and human rights were accorded a super-eminent status in the international system. The right of an individual to conditions conducive to his development was recognized generally, and significant areas of the human rights law became accessible to intervention by foreign states.

The development of environmental law provides the second major

---

82. Declaration of the Hague, *supra* note 57 at 1309.
83. C. Tinker, "Environmental Planet Management by the United Nations: An Idea Whose Time Has Not Yet Come?", 22 *International Law and Politics*, 793, 821 (1989).

turning point in the progress of international law. The international community has reached a stage where the individual is held entitled specifically to a natural and cultural environment ensuring the development of the different dimensions of his personality. Indeed, environmental law proceeds beyond the individual to the local or national community and even beyond, to the global community, having regard to the nature and character of the environmental phenomenon. The world has entered an era in which the fundamental relationship of man to the natural order is also beginning to dawn on him. Moreover, while the achievements of science and technology have been great and their influence far-reaching, man is becoming increasingly aware that the choice in employing that unprecedented power turns ultimately on his sense of moral responsibility towards his fellow men and to the planet itself. The significance of moral values has never been so important. In this ethos of morality and power there is something both of the West and the East, and one may conclude with what the Nobel Laureate Ilya Prigogine said:

We believe that we are heading toward a new synthesis, a new naturalism. Perhaps we will eventually be able to combine the Western tradition, with its emphasis upon experimentation and quantitative formulations, with a tradition such as the Chinese one, with its view of a spontaneous, self-organizing world. . . . Each great period of science has led to some model of nature. For classical science it was the clock; for nineteenth century science, the period of the Industrial Revolution, it was an engine running down. What will be the symbol for us? What we have in mind may perhaps be expressed best by a reference to sculpture, from Indian or pre-Columbian art to our time. In some of the most beautiful manifestations of sculpture, be it in the dancing Shiva or in the miniature temples of Guerrero, there appears very clearly the search for a junction between stillness and motion, time arrested and time passing. We believe that this confrontation will give our period its uniqueness.[84]

84. I. Prigogine and I. Stengers, *Order Out of Chaos: Man's New Dialogue with Nature,* 22, 23 (Bantam Books, 1984).

9

The contribution of international human rights law to environmental protection, with special reference to global environmental change

A.A. Cançado Trindade

Summary

  I. The Growth of Human Rights Protection and Environmental Protection: From Internationalization to Globalization.
 II. The Incidence of the Temporal Dimension in Environmental Protection and in Human Rights Protection.
III. The Fundamental Right to Life at the Basis of the *Ratio Legis* of International Human Rights Law and Environmental Law.
 IV. The Right to Health as the Starting-Point towards the Right to a Healthy Environment.
  V. The Right to a Healthy Environment as an Extension of the Right to Health.
 VI. The Protection of Vulnerable Groups at the Confluence of International Human Rights Law and International Environmental Law.
VII. The Recognition of the Right to a Healthy Environment: The Concern for Environmental Protection in International Human Rights Instruments.
VIII. Concern for the Protection of Human Rights in the Realm of International Environmental Law.
 IX. Concern for the Protection of the Environment in the Realm of International Humanitarian Law.
  X. Protection of the Environment and International Refugee Law.

I. The growth of human rights protection and environmental protection: From internationalization to globalization

1. The internationalization of human rights protection and of environmental protection

The parallel evolutions of human rights protection and environmental protection disclose some affinities that should not pass unnoticed. They both witness, and precipitate, the gradual erosion of so-called domestic jurisdiction. The treatment by the state of its own nationals becomes a matter of international concern. Conservation of the environment and control of pollution become likewise a matter of international concern. There occurs a process of *internationalization* of both human rights protection and environmental protection, the former as from the 1948 Universal Declaration on Human Rights, the latter – years later – as from the 1972 Stockholm Declaration on the Human Environment.

With regard to human rights protection, 18 years after the adoption of the 1948 Universal Declaration, the International Bill of Human Rights was completed with the adoption of the two UN Covenants, on Civil and Political Rights (and Optional Protocol), and on Economic, Social, and Cultural Rights (1966), respectively. The normative corpus of international human rights law is today a vast one, comprising a multiplicity of treaties and instruments, at both global and regional levels, with varying ambits of application and covering the protection of human rights of various kinds and in distinct domains of human activity.

As for environmental protection, the years following the Stockholm Declaration likewise witnessed a multiplicity of international instruments on the matter, equally at both global and regional levels. It is estimated that nowadays there are more than 300 multilateral treaties and around 900 bilateral treaties providing for the protection and conservation of the biosphere, to which over 200 texts from international organizations can be added.[1] This considerable growth of

---

1. Reference can further be made to domestic legislation on the matter in virtually all states:

international regulation in the present domain has, by and large, followed a "sectorial" approach, leading to the celebration of conventions turned to certain sectors or areas, or concrete situations (e.g., oceans, continental waters, atmosphere, wildlife). In sum, international regulation in the domain of environmental protection has taken place in the form of *responses* to specific challenges.

The same appears to have taken place in the field of human rights protection, where we witness a multiplicity of international instruments: parallel to general human rights treaties (such as the two UN covenants of human rights and the three regional – European, American, and African – conventions), there are conventions turned to concrete situations (e.g., prevention of discrimination, prevention and punishment of torture and ill-treatment), to specific human conditions (e.g., refugee status, nationality and statelessness), and to certain groups in special need of protection (e.g., workers' rights, women's rights, protection of the child, protection of the elderly, protection of the disadvantaged). In sum, human rights instruments have grown, at normative and procedural levels, likewise as *responses* to violations of human rights of various kinds.

This being so, it is not surprising that certain gaps may appear, as awareness grows as to the increasing needs of protection. An example of such gaps, in the field of human rights protection, can be found in our days, e.g., in the protection to be extended to certain vulnerable groups, in particular indigenous populations. Another example, in the area of environmental protection, can nowadays be found, e.g., in the needed enhancement of international regulation on climate change and protection of the atmosphere.

A significant task for the near future – if not for the present – will precisely consist in ensuring the proper *coordination* of multiple instruments that have grown in the last decades, at global and regional levels, pursuant to the "sectorial" approach (*supra*), in the domains of human rights protection[2] as well as environmental protection. Beyond the internationalization of human rights protection and of environmental protection in the pattern referred to above, it was soon realized that, in each of the two domains of protection, there existed

---

It is estimated that domestic legislative instruments reach today a total of 30,000. A.C. Kiss, *Droit international de l'environnement,* 46 (Pedone, 1989).

2. Ct. A.A. Cançado Trindade, "Co-existence and Co-ordination of Mechanisms of International Protection of Human Rights (At Global and Regional Levels)," 202 *Recueil des cours de l'Académie de droit international,* 21–435 (1987).

an interrelatedness among the distinct sectors that were the object of regulation.

2. The globalization of human rights protection and of environmental protection

The awareness of this interrelatedness has decisively contributed to the evolution, in recent years, from the internationalization to the globalization of human rights protection as well as of environmental protection. As far as human rights protection is concerned, two decades after the adoption of the 1948 Universal Declaration of Human Rights, the 1968 Teheran Conference on Human Rights, in a global reassessment of the matter, proclaimed the *indivisibility* of all human rights (civil and political, as well as economic, social, and cultural rights). This was followed by the landmark resolution 32/130, adopted by the UN General Assembly in 1977, where it stated that human rights questions were to be examined globally.

That resolution endorsed the assertion of the 1968 Teheran Proclamation of the indivisibility and interdependence of all human rights, from a globalist perspective, and drew attention to the priority to be accorded to the search for solutions to massive and flagrant violations of human rights.[3] Three decades after the adoption of the 1948 Universal Declaration, the UN General Assembly, bearing in mind the fundamental changes undergone by so-called international society – decolonization, capacity of massive destruction, population growth, environmental conditions, energy consumption, amongst others – by its resolution 32/130 endeavoured to overcome the old categorizations of rights and to proceed to a needed global analysis of existing problems in the field of human rights.

Such a new global outlook and conception of the indivisibility of human rights, rendered possible by the UN Charter itself, and externalized in GA resolution 32/130 of 1977, contributed to drawing closer attention in particular to the rights pertaining to human collectivities and the measures of their implementation. The matter was retaken by GA resolution 39/145, of 1984, and 41/117, of 1986, which reiterated the interrelatedness of all human rights, whereby the pro-

---

3. Th. C. Van Boven, "United Nations Policies and Strategies: Global Perspectives?", *Human Rights: Thirty Years after the Universal Declaration*, 88–89 (B.G. Ramcharan, ed., Martinus Nijhoff, 1979); *see id.* at 89–91.

tection of one category of rights should not exempt states from safe-guarding the other rights. Thus, human rights instruments turned to the protection of certain categories of rights, or of certain rights in given situations, or of rights of certain groups in special need of protection, are to be properly approached on the understanding that they are complementary to general human rights treaties. Multiple human rights instruments reinforce each other, enhance the degree of the protection due, and disclose an overwhelming identity of purpose.

In the domain of environmental protection, the presence – despite the "sector-by-sector" regulation – of "transversal" issues and rules contributed to the globalist approach. It was reckoned, e.g., that more and more often certain activities and products may cause harmful effects in any environment (e.g., toxic or dangerous substances, toxic or dangerous wastes, ionizing radiations, and radioactive wastes); in fact, the problem of dangerous substances is present in the whole of "sectorial" regulation, thus pointing to globalization and generating a "réglementation se superposant aux differents secteurs."[4]

Already in 1974, two years after the adoption of the Stockholm Declaration, the UN Charter on Economic Rights and Duties of States warned that the protection and preservation of the environment for present and future generations were the responsibility of *all* states (Article 30). And in 1980 the UN General Assembly proclaimed the historical responsibility of states for the preservation of nature on behalf of present and future generations.[5] While in the past states tended to regard the regulation of pollution by sectors as a national or local issue, more recently they have realized that some environmental problems and concerns are essentially global in scope.[6] In its resolution 44/228, of 22 December 1989, whereby it decided to convene a UN Conference on Environment and Development in 1992, the UN General Assembly recognized that the global character of environmental problems required action at all levels (global, regional, and national), involving the commitment and participation of all countries; the resolution further affirmed that the pro-

4. A.C. Kiss, *supra* note 1 at 275–276, 46; *see id.* at 93, 106, 204.
5. *Id.* at 38–39.
6. "Formal and informal linkages" across nations and states have contributed to this new perception; R.W. Hahn and K.R. Richards, "The Internationalization of Environmental Regulations," 30 *Harvard International Law Journal*, 421, 423, 444–445 (1989).

tection and enhancement of environment were major issues that affected the well-being of peoples, and singled out, as one of the environmental issues of major concern, the "protection of human health conditions and improvement of the quality of life" (§12 (i)).

The global character of environmental issues is reflected in the question, e.g., of conservation of biological diversity; it is further illustrated, in particular, by the problems linked to atmospheric pollution (such as depletion of the ozone layer and global-climate change). Those problems, initially thought of as being essentially local or even transboundary, were to disclose "une portée pratiquement illimitée dans l'espace."[7] The threat of damage to many nations resulting from global warming, for example, is a major problem, the cause of which would hardly be traceable to a single state or group of states, thus calling for a new approach on the basis of strategies of prevention and adaptation and considerable international cooperation.[8] Thus, the UN General Assembly, by resolution 43/53, of 6 December 1988, recognized that climate change is a common concern of mankind, and determined that action should be promptly taken to deal with it within a global framework.

Likewise, the Intergovernmental Panel on Climate Change (IPCC), set up by WMO and UNEP, has indicated, as one of the possible elements for inclusion in a future framework convention on climate change,[9] the recognition that climate change is a common concern of mankind, affecting humanity as a whole, and to be thus approached within a global framework.[10] The 1989 Hague Declaration on the Atmosphere insists on the search for urgent and global solutions to the problems of the warming of the atmosphere and the deterioration of the ozone layer. In the same line, the 1989 International Meeting of Legal and Policy Experts, held in Ottawa, in its report stated *inter alia* that the atmosphere constitutes a "common resource of vital interest to mankind."[11]

And still in 1989 (November), the Ministerial Conference on Atmospheric Pollution and Climatic Change, held in Noordwijk,

---

7. A.C. Kiss, *supra* note 1 at 212.
8. V.P. Nanda, "Global Warming and International Environmental Law – A Preliminary Inquiry," 30 *Harvard International Law Journal,* 380–385 (1989).
9. *See* UNEP Governing Council decision 15/36, of 25 May 1989.
10. WMO/UNEP, *IPCC Working Group III (Response Strategies) – Legal Measures; Report of Topic Co-ordinators,* III (1989) (mimeographed, internal circulation).
11. *See Statement of the International Meeting of Legal and Policy Experts,* 2 (1989).

Netherlands, with the participation of 67 countries, considered the elements of a future framework climate-change convention (to be further elaborated by the IPCC) and reasserted the principle of shared responsibility of all states. The 1989 Noordwijk Declaration on Climate Change pursued a globalist approach (see §§8–9) and expressly stated that "climate change is a common concern of mankind" (§7).[12] In sum, recent trends in environmental protection as well as in human rights protection (*supra*) disclose a clear and progressive tendency from internationalization towards globalization.

3. The globalization of protection and *erga omnes* obligations

The globalization of human rights protection and of environmental protection can also be attested from a distinct approach, namely, that of emergence of *erga omnes* obligations and the consequent decline and end of reciprocity. In the field of human rights protection, reciprocity is overcome and overwhelmed by the notion of collective guarantee and considerations of *ordre public*. This operates a revolution in the postulates of traditional international law. Human rights treaties incorporate obligations of an objective character, turned to the safeguard of the rights of human beings and not of states, on the basis of a superior general public interest (or *ordre public*). Hence the specificity of human rights treaties.

Traces of this new philosophy are found in international humanitarian law: pursuant to common Article 1 of the 1949 Geneva Conventions, Contracting Parties are bound "to respect and to ensure respect" to the four Conventions "in all circumstances," i.e., irrespective of considerations of reciprocity. Provisions with analogous effects can be found in human rights treaties (e.g., UN Covenant on Civil and Political Rights, Article 2; European Convention on Human Rights, Article 1; American Convention on Human Rights, Article 1). Those humanitarian instruments have transcended the purely inter-state level in search of a higher degree of protection of the human person, so as to ensure the safeguard of common superior interests protected by them. Hence the universal character of the system of protection of international humanitarian law, which creates for states obligations *erga omnes*.

---

12. *See* Ministerial Conference on Pollution and Climatic Change, *The Noordwijk Declaration on Climate Change,* 4 (Nov. 1989) (mimeographed, restricted circulation); *see, id.* at 1–13.

The evolution of environmental protection likewise bears witness of the emergence of obligations of an objective character without reciprocal advantages for states. The 1972 Stockholm Declaration on the Human Environment refers expressly to the "common good of mankind" (Principle 18). Rules on the protection of the environment are adopted, and obligations to that effect are undertaken, in the common superior interest of mankind. This has been expressly acknowledged in some treaties in the field of the environment (e.g., preambles of the 1971 Treaty on the Prohibition of the Emplacement of Nuclear Weapons and Other Weapons of Mass Destruction on the Sea-bed and the Ocean Floor and in the Subsoil Thereof; the 1972 Convention on the Prohibition of the Development, Production, and Stockpiling of Bacteriological (Biological) and Toxin Weapons and on Their Destruction; the 1977 Convention on the Prohibition of Military or Any Other Hostile Use of Environmental Modification Techniques; the 1972 Convention on the Prevention of Marine Pollution by Dumping of Wastes and Other Matter; the 1974 Convention for the Prevention of Marine Pollution from Land-Based Sources; the 1972 Convention for the Prevention of Marine Pollution by Dumping from Ships and Aircraft; the 1972 Unesco Convention for the Protection of the World Cultural and Natural Heritage); it is further implicit in references to "human health" in some environmental law treaties (e.g., the 1985 Vienna Convention for the Protection of the Ozone Layer, preamble and Article 2; the 1987 Montreal Protocol on Substances That Deplete the Ozone Layer, preamble; Article 1 of the three marine pollution conventions quoted above).

The evolution, from internationalization to globalization, of environmental protection can also be detected in its spatial dimension. In the beginnings of international environmental regulation, attention was turned to environmental protection in zones under the competence of states of the territorial type. One thus spoke of control of *transboundary* or *transfrontier* pollution (a terminology reminiscent of that employed in the OECD), with an underlying emphasis on the relations between neighbouring countries or on contacts or conflicts between state sovereignties. Soon it became evident that, to face wider threats to the environment – as in, e.g., marine pollution and atmospheric pollution (acid rain, depletion of the ozone layer, global warming) – it was necessary to consider also principles applicable, *"urbi et orbi,"* on a global scale, not only in zones where state interests were immediately affected (transboundary pollution) but also in other areas where state interests appeared not so visibly affected (e.g., protection of the atmosphere and of the marine environment). In this common international law of the environment, principles of a global character are to apply on the territory of states irrespective of any transboundary or transfrontier effect, and are to govern zones that are not under any national territorial competence.[13]

In this connection, the Brundtland Commission, reporting to the UN General Assembly in 1987, dedicated a whole chapter to the management, in the "common interest," of the so-called "global commons," i.e., those zones falling outside or beyond national jurisdictions.[14] Likewise, the Centre for Studies and Research in International Law and Relations of the Hague Academy of International Law, dwelling upon the issue of transfrontier pollution and international law in its 1985 session, singled out the gradual evolution from a transboundary or "transterritorial" to a global perspective of the preservation of the environment (and action in favour of resources of the common heritage of mankind).[15]

That international law is no longer exclusively state-oriented can be seen from reiterated references to "mankind," not only in doctrinal writings,[16] but also and significantly in various international instruments, possibly pointing towards an international law of mankind, pursuing preservation of the environment and sustainable development on behalf of present and future generations. Thus, the notion of cultural heritage of mankind can be found, e.g., in the Unesco conventions for the Protection of Cultural Property in the Event of Armed Conflict (1954) and for the Protection of the World Cultural and Natural Heritage (1974). The legal principle of the common heritage of mankind has found expression in the realms of the law of the sea (1982 UN Convention on the Law of the Sea, Part XI, especially Articles 136-145 and 311 (6); 1970 UN Declaration of Principles Governing the Sea-bed and the Ocean Floor, and the Subsoil There-

---

13. A.C. Kiss, *supra* note 1 at 93, 67–68, 70–72, 8; L.A. Teclaff, "The Impact of Environmental Concern on the Development of International Law," *International Environmental Law*, 251 (L.A. Teclaff and A.E. Utton, eds., Praeger, 1974); *see* Ian Brownlie, "A Survey of International Customary Rules of Environmental Protection," in *id.* at 5.

14. World Commission on Environment and Development, *Our Common Future*, 261–289 (Oxford University, 1987).

15. P.M. Dupuy, "Bilan de recherches de la section de langue française du Centre d'Etude et de Recherche de l'Académie," *La pollution transfrontière et le droit international – 1985*, 65–66, 68–70, 81 (Sijthoff/Académie de droit international, 1986).

16. *See* C.W. Jenks, *The Common Law of Mankind*, 1–442 (Stevens, 1958); R.J. Dupuy, *La communauté internationale entre le mythe et l'histoire*, 11–182 (Economica/Unesco, 1986).

of, Beyond the Limits of National Jurisdiction) and of the law of outer space (1979 Treaty Governing the Activities of the States on the Moon and Other Celestial Bodies, Article 11; and see the 1967 Treaty on Principles Governing the Activities of States in the Exploration and Use of Outer Space, Including the Moon and Other Celestial Bodies, Article I).[17] The reconsideration of the basic postulates of international law bearing in mind the superior common interests of mankind has been the object of attention of general works on the subject at doctrinal level (e.g., Jenks, Dupuy).[18]

Despite semantic variations in international instruments on environmental protection when referring to mankind, a common denominator underlying them all appears to be the common interest of mankind. There seems to be occurring lately an evolution from the notion of common heritage of mankind (as emerged in the contexts of the law of the sea and space law) to that of common concern of mankind. The latter has been the object of consideration by the UNEP Group of Legal Experts, which convened in Malta on 13–15 December 1990, in order to examine the implications of the concept of "common concern of mankind" on global environmental issues. In fact, it is not at all casual that the UN General Assembly resolution 43/53, of 6 December 1988, introduced the recognition that climate change was a "common concern" of mankind, since, in the wording of its first operative paragraph, climate was "an essential condition which sustains life on earth."

Such an essential or fundamental condition is inextricably linked to the new idea of "commonness." The newly proposed notion is inspired in considerations of international *ordre public*. It appears as a derivative of the earlier "common heritage" approach, meant to shift emphasis from the sharing of benefits from exploitation of environmental wealths to fair or equitable sharing of burdens in environmental protection, and the needed concerted actions to that effect with a social and temporal dimensions.[19] It could hardly be doubted, as

17. N.J. Schrijver, "Permanent Sovereignty over Natural Resources versus the Common Heritage of Mankind: Complementary or Contradictory Principles of International Economic Law?", *International Law and Development*, 95–96, 98, 101 (P. De Waart, P. Peters, and E. Denters, eds., Nijhoff/Kluwer, 1988).
18. *See supra* note 16.
19. On this last point, *see* UNEP/Executive Director and Secretariat, *Note to the Group of Legal Experts to Examine the Implications of the "Common Concern of Mankind" Concept on Global Environmental Issues*, Malta Meeting, 13–15 Dec. 1990, document UNEP/ELIU/WG. 1/1/2, pp. 1–2, §4 (mimeographed, internal circulation); *see id.* at 4–5, §§8–9.

UNEP itself has acknowledged, that environmental protection is "decisively linked" to the "human rights issue,"[20] to the very fulfillment of the fundamental right to life in its wide dimension (right to live – see section III, *infra*).

Resort to the very notion of mankind, humankind, immediately brings into the fore, or places the whole discussion within, the human rights framework – and this should be properly emphasized; it should not be left implicit or neglected as allegedly redundant. Just as law, or the rule of law itself, does not operate in a vacuum, mankind, humankind, is neither a social nor a legal abstraction: it is composed of human collectives, of all human beings of flesh and bone, living in human societies.

If it is conceded that, if and once the concept of common concern of mankind becomes widely and unequivocally accepted, rights and obligations are bound to flow from it, then one is led to consider as its manifestation or even materialization the right to a healthy environment: within the ambit of the *droit de l'humanité*, the common concern of humankind finds expression in the exercise of the recognized right to a healthy environment, in all its dimensions (individual, group, social, or collective, and intergenerational – see section XI – *infra*), precisely as mankind is not a social or legal abstraction and is formed by a multitude of human beings living in societies and extended in time. The human rights framework is ineluctably present in the consideration of the regime of protection of the human environment in all its aspects; we are here ultimately confronted with the crucial question of *survival* of humankind, with the assertion – in the face of the threats to the human environment – of the fundamental human right to live.

Just as a couple of decades ago there were questions that were "withdrawn" from the domestic jurisdiction of states to become matters of *international* concern (essentially, in cases pertaining to human rights protection and self-determination of peoples),[21] there are nowadays global issues such as climate change that are being erected as a *common* concern of mankind. Here, again, the contribution of human rights protection in piercing the so-called reserved domain of

20. *Id.* at 14 §22.
21. A.A. Cançado Trindade, "The Domestic Jurisdiction of States in the Practice of the United Nations and Regional Organizations," 25 *International and Comparative Law Quarterly* 723, 731, 737, 742, 761–762, 765 (1976).

states can be perceived in historical perspective. The globalization of the regimes of human rights protection and environmental protection heralds the end of reciprocity and the emergence of *erga omnes* obligations.

The prohibition of the invocation of reciprocity as an excuse for non-compliance of *erga omnes* obligations is confirmed in unequivocal terms by the 1969 Vienna Convention on the Law of Treaties: in providing for the conditions in which a breach of a treaty may bring about its suspension or termination, the Vienna Convention (Article 60 [5]) expressly excepts "provisions relating to the protection of the human person contained in treaties of a humanitarian character." This provision pierces a domain of international law – the law of treaties – traditionally so markedly infiltrated by the voluntarism of states, and constitutes a clause of safeguard or defence of human beings. Thus, the contemporary law of treaties itself, as attested by Article 60 (5) of the Vienna Convention, discards the principle of reciprocity in the implementation of treaties of a humanitarian character. The obligations enshrined therein generate effects *erga omnes*. The overcoming of reciprocity in human rights protection and in environmental protection has taken place in the constant search for an expansion of the ambit of protection (for the safeguard of an increasingly wider circle of beneficiaries, human beings and ultimately mankind), for a higher degree of the protection due, and for the gradual strengthening of the mechanisms of supervision, in the defence of common superior interests. Yet another affinity in the recent developments of human rights protection and environmental protection that has not been sufficiently examined so far, and to which we shall now turn, lies in the incidence of the temporal dimension in both domains of protection.

II. The incidence of the temporal dimension in environmental protection and in human rights protection

1. The temporal dimension in general international law

Time and time again one has stressed the predominantly *preventive* character of the normative corpus on environmental protection. The temporal dimension, so noticeable in the present domain, is likewise present in general international law. In fact, the element of foreseeability inheres in legal science as such, and is of the essence of law-making activity. That it permeates distinct fields or chapters of international law is undeniable, as a couple of examples may help to illustrate. The notion of time underlies, e.g., almost all basic elements of the law of treaties: the temporal dimension permeates not only the general scope of the treaty-making process, but also the very terms or conditions established for their implementation (e.g., when this latter is to take place by stages, gradually and progressively). Likewise, in the realm of the peaceful settlement of international disputes, distinct methods of settlement have been devised envisaging disputes that may occur in the future; in the settlement of economic disputes in particular, procedures of settlement have been employed even if the damage has not occurred yet, and one has thus spoken of threats of imminent injuries or potential or likely future harm.[22]

With regard to environmental protection and in the context of the distribution and sharing of resources, it may be recalled that the 1974 UN Charter of Economic Rights and Duties of States contains express references to the inter-temporal dimension.[23] In the field of the regulation of spaces, similarly, the intertemporal dimension makes its appearance: the notions of future beneficiaries and future interests (or interests of present and future generations) underlie the basic concept of "common heritage of mankind," which has definitively found its way into the law of the sea (1982 UN Convention on the Law of the Sea, Article 136) and the law of outer space (e.g., 1979 Treaty Governing the Activities of States on the Moon and Other Celestial Bodies, Articles 11 and 4; 1967 Treaty on Principles Governing the Activities of States in the Exploration and Use of Outer Space, Including the Moon and Other Celestial Bodies, Article 1).[24]

2. The temporal dimension in environmental protection

In classic international law, considerable attention was given to the interspatial dimension, evidenced by the coexistence of territorial sovereign units. In our day, growing attention is being accorded to the temporal dimension in the whole of international law (*supra*). The aspect that comes most readily to the fore is that of *prevention,*

22. *See* A.A. Cançado Trindade, *supra* note 2 at 286–290.
23. *See* Article 20 (on "Common Heritage of Mankind") and Article 30 (which refers to "Present and Future Generations" and to "The Potential of Present and Future Development of Developing Countries"); *id.* at 290 n. 932.
24. *See id.* at 288–289.

increasingly associated with regimes of protection (e.g., of human rights, of the environment). Prevention is resorted to, at first, to avoid unnecessary harm or suffering. But, more than that, prevention seems to impose itself in relation to harm that appears irreversible or that cannot be repaired.

The incidence of the temporal factor in the realm of environmental protection is well-known and widely acknowledged. In that ambit one has spoken of *potential* victims and drawn attention to the possibility of harm that may arise *in the future* (out of an activity or an incident, and well after the occurrence), in what may be taken as a warning that the study of the protection of potential or prospective victims is nowadays a real necessity and not a theoretical-academic speculation.[25] Endeavours in recent years to develop the study of the configuration of international liability in the present domain have taken into account injuries or harmful consequences that may be either actual or prospective and have considered norms for implementation; one has here spoken of potential victims, and of the general principle of the duty of states to avoid or prevent, or minimize and repair, actual or potential or prospective adverse effects or physical consequences (of acts not prohibited by international law).[26]

Furthermore, from the Stockholm Declaration until now, the notion of protection of interests of present and future generations has gained considerable ground, stressing the predominance of the underlying temporal dimension. The 1972 Stockholm Declaration on the Human Environment expressly refers to the safeguard of the interests of present and future generations in Principles 1 and 2 (and see Principles 11 and 18). The preamble of the 1982 World Charter for Nature contains a similar reference. The principles proposed in 1987 by the World Commission on Environment and Development (the Brundtland Commission) include that of intergenerational equity (Principle 2), whereby "States shall conserve and use the environ-

25. A.A. Cançado Trindade, *supra* note 2 at 286–287.
26. *See id.* at 286–288 (in particular the reports of the International Law Commission cited therein). It is not surprising that one has focused on a guarantee of reparation for possible injuries resulting from ecologically dangerous (even though not prohibited) activities; J. Juste Ruíz, "Derecho Internacional Público y Medio Ambiente," *VIII Jornadas de la Asociación Española de Profesores de Derecho Internacional y Relaciones Internacionales*, 38, 40–41 (Barcelona, 1984). For general studies, *see* P.M. Dupuy, *La responsabilité internationale des Etats pour les dommages d'origine technologique et industrielle*, 7–290 (Pedone, 1976); K. Zemanek, "La responsabilité des Etats pour faits internationalement illicites, ainsi que pour faits internationalement licites," *Responsabilité internationale*, 1–88 (P. Weil, ed., Pedone, 1987).

ment and natural resources for the benefit of present and future generations."

In the same line, the 1974 Charter on Economic Rights and Duties of States provides that the protection, preservation, and improvement of the environment for the benefit of present and future generations is the responsibility of all states (Article 30). Concern for the interests of present and future generations has entered the realm of conventional international law: the 1977 Convention on the Prohibition of Military or Any Other Hostile Use of Environmental Modification Techniques envisages in its preamble the improvement of the interrelationship between man and nature and the contribution to the preservation and improvement of the environment for the benefit of present and future generations.

The temporal dimension in environmental protection became prominent in the work of the recent Second World Climate Conference, held in Geneva, 6–7 November 1990. The incidence of the temporal dimension in that domain was acknowledged in unequivocal terms in the Ministerial Declaration of the Conference (paragraph 7), adopted on 7 November 1990, namely:

In order to achieve sustainable development in all countries and to meet the needs of present and future generations, precautionary measures to meet the climate challenge must anticipate, prevent, attack, or minimize the causes of, and mitigate the adverse consequences of, environmental degradation that might result from climate change. Where there are threats of serious or irreversible damage, lack of full scientific certainty should not be used as a reason for postponing cost-effective measures to prevent such environmental degradation. The measures adopted should take into account different socio-economic contexts.[27]

The matter at issue has lately been attracting growing attention at the doctrinal level as well. The starting point has been the premiss that each generation is both a user and a custodian of our common natural and cultural heritage and should thus leave it for future generations in no worse condition than it has received it (encouragement of equality among generations). Hence the principle of intergenerational equity (conservation of options, of quality, and of access), lucidly developed by E. Brown Weiss, as well as the need to sustain life-support systems, ecological processes, environmental conditions,

---

27. *Ministerial Declaration of the II World Climate Conference*, 3, §7 (Geneva, 7 Nov. 1990) (mimeographed, internal circulation).

and cultural resources necessary for the survival of the human species, and the need to sustain a healthy human environment.[28]

So-called generational rights – accompanied by the corresponding obligations of use[29] – are by definition group or collective rights, held by one generation in relation to other generations and defined ultimately by the position of each generation *in time*. Hence their marked temporal dimension. Moreover, the notion of common interest (*bien commun*) of mankind, acknowledged in some environmental law treaties (see *supra*), appears at the basis of the concept of "common heritage of mankind," as propounded in space law and in the law of the sea; the concept of common heritage of mankind enlarges the circle of beneficiaries so as to encompass future generations.[30] Kiss perspicaciously identifies in this "transtemporal" concept the fundamental idea whereby

ceux qui vivent aujourd'hui ne sont qu'un élément d'une chaîne qui ne doit pas être interrompue. Il existe donc une solidarité mondiale non seulement dans l'espace entre les peuples du monde, mais aussi dans le temps, entre les générations qui se succèdent.[31]

As from the adoption in 1945 of the UN Charter, which already in its preamble refers to succeeding generations, the temporal factor has become increasingly present in international law, e.g., in the gradual implementation of treaties; with the emergence and crystallization of the concept of common heritage of mankind, Kiss adds, "le temps devient un élément de finalité. Ce n'est plus un temps limité, mais un temps indéterminé, celui des générations futures qui devront se succéder."[32]

Environmental protection has contributed significantly to reveal and clarify this new perspective. Perhaps it can benefit further from the experience accumulated in a longer period of operation of experiments of international supervision in human rights protection, insofar

---

28. *See* E. Brown Weiss, *In Fairness to Future Generations: International Law, Common Patrimony, and Intergenerational Equity*, 1–291 (Transnational/United Nations University, 1989).
29. Namely, to conserve resources, to ensure equitable use, to avoid adverse impacts, to prevent disasters and minimize damage and provide emergency assistance, to compensate for environmental harm. *See id.*
30. A.C. Kiss, "La notion de patrimoine commun de l'humanité," 175 *Recueil des cours de l'Académie de droit international*, 229, 231, 240 (1982); *see id.* at 241, 130.
31. *Id.* at 113; *see id.* at 240.
32. *Id.* at 243.

as the incidence of the intertemporal dimension is concerned. To this we shall now turn.

3. The temporal dimension in human rights protection

The temporal dimension, so preponderant in international environmental law, marks its presence also in the realm of international human rights law. Awareness of the temporal dimension can be detected in the legislative phase (*travaux preparatoires* and resulting texts) as well as the implementation phase (interpretation and application) of international instruments of human rights protection, even though the matter has not attracted enough attention and has not been sufficiently explored so far. Thus, already in the preparatory work of such instruments as the UN Covenant on Civil and Political Rights (and Optional Protocol), amongst others, there were traces of an awareness of their intertemporal dimension, i.e., of the fact that those instruments were intended for the use and benefit of future generations, who were to transform them into social reality and further develop them.[33]

The underlying intertemporal dimension can in fact be perceived in the very conception of several of those human rights instruments, and ensues from some of their provisions. A few examples can here be pointed out. The 1968 Convention on the Non-applicability of Statutory Limitations to War Crimes and Crimes against Humanity, e.g., refers in its preamble also to the *prevention* of crimes against humanity – a provision that was reiterated by the UN General Assembly resolution 3074 (XXVIII) of 1973 (§3). The 1948 Convention on the Prevention and Punishment of the Crime of Genocide *inter alia* deals, in its Article VIII, with the *prevention* of that crime, referring to that effect to possible preventive action by UN organs called upon by States Parties to the Convention. Likewise, the 1973 International Convention on the Suppression and Punishment of the Crime of Apartheid contains a similar provision (Article VIII) whereby States Parties to the Convention may call upon UN organs to take action under the UN Charter for the *prevention* of the crime of apartheid.

The *Compilation of International Instruments* on human rights, undertaken by the UN Centre for Human Rights, in fact lists not less than 13 international instruments turned to *prevention* of discrimina-

---

33. *See* A.A. Cançado Trindade, *supra* note 2 at 284–285.

tion of distinct kinds.[34] Recently the UN Commission on Human Rights proceeded to a reassessment of the question of the prevention and punishment of the crime of genocide, and a study (following previous reports) was undertaken on the matter, with the assistance of the UN Sub-Commission on Prevention of Discrimination and Protection of Minorities. This revised and updated study set as its purpose "to deter future violence by strengthening collective international responsibility and remedies,"[35] and stressed from the start the primacy of the right to life. It pointed out that, in the present context, one had in mind, rather than one (individual) victim, human groups or collectivities, victim groups, that could also be potential victims (in case of threats to life).[36]

The study recalled the Sub-Commission debates as to the possibility of expanding the definition of genocide so as to encompass "ethnocide" or cultural genocide (e.g., in case of destruction of surviving indigenous communities or cultures) and also "ecocide" (e.g., in case of irreparable alterations to the environment threatening the existence of entire populations); in those debates opinion was also advanced that cultural ethnocide and ecocide constituted crimes against humanity, rather than genocide.[37] As to the enforcement of the 1948 Convention against Genocide, the above-mentioned 1985 study further recalled the argument advanced by some experts in the Sub-Commission discussions in favour of the urgent establishment of international early-warning and fact-finding systems, and the constructive role that a UN High Commissioner for Human Rights could contribute to preventing and investigating allegations of genocide.[38]

The three recent Conventions against Torture disclose an essentially *preventive* nature. This is revealed from the start by the titles of the 1985 Inter-American Convention to Prevent and Punish Torture (see in particular Articles 1 and 6) and the 1987 European Convention for the Prevention of Torture and Inhuman or Degrading Treatment or Punishment (see particularly Article 1). Likewise, the 1984 UN Convention against Torture and Other Cruel, Inhuman, or Degrading Treatment or Punishment discloses, especially in Articles 2

34. *See* U.N. doc. ST/HR/1/Rev. 3, 52–142 (1982).
35. UN doc. E/CN.4/Sub. 2/1985/6, 5 (2 July 1985) (report prepared by Mr. B. Whitaker).
36. *Id.* at 16, 6.
37. *Id.* at 17, 7. The study stressed "the element of intent to destroy a designated group wholly or partially," which raised "crimes of mass murder and against humanity to qualify as the special crime of genocide," *id.* at 19.
38. *Id.* at 29; *see id.* at 41–44.

(1) and 16, its essentially *preventive* character (see also articles 10 and 11).

Besides the harmonization and coordination among those instruments, and of those with other human rights instruments, attention has been drawn also to the need to go further, in devising other complementary means of *prevention* of torture.[39] The 1987 European Convention, in particular, institutes a non-judicial system of a preventive character, consisting of continuous monitoring and *ex officio* visits at any time by the Committee set up by the Convention.[40] This advanced technique of inspection – which, prior to the adoption of the European Convention for the Prevention of Torture, had application in the field of peaceful uses of nuclear energy – presents the advantage of not only effectively checking but also "forestalling violations, at least before they occur on any significant scale."[41] By means of its technique of supervisory and preventive inspection (of prisons, detention centres, and other places where persons are deprived of their liberty), the Committee is enabled to assist and bring relief to "otherwise helpless victims and potential victims of torture and other forms of ill-treatment."[42]

Another illustration of the temporal dimension is provided by the elements for the very definition of "refugee" under the 1951 Convention Relating to the Status of Refugees (Article 1[A][2]) and the 1967 Protocol Relating to the Status of Refugees (Article 1[2]): the key factor of that definition lies in the element of "well-founded fear of being persecuted," disclosing the deliberately subjective nature of the determination of the quality of refugee, rendering it sufficient that there exists threats or *risks* of persecution, and a well-founded fear of the individuals concerned of becoming victims of persecutions.

The temporal dimension being present in the very conception of various human rights instruments and in the philosophy of some of their key provisions (*supra*), it is not surprising to detect its ineluctable incidence in the process of *interpretation* and *application* of those

---

39. H. Gros Espiell, "Las Convenciones sobre Tortura de las Naciones Unidas y de la Organización de los Estados Americanos," *XIV Curso de Derecho Internacional organizado por el Comité Jurídico Interamericano*, 233, 240 (Secretaría General de la OEA, 1988).

40. On its preventive character, *see* Council of Europe, *Explanatory Report of the European Convention for the Prevention of Torture and Inhuman or Degrading Treatment or Punishment*, 10–11, 21 (C.E./Directorate of Human Rights, 1989).

41. A. Cassese, "A New Approach to Human Rights: The European Convention for the Prevention of Torture," 83 A.J.I.L. 151 (1989).

42. *Id.* at 152.

instruments. The development of international human rights law through interpretation is nowadays widely acknowledged. Human rights treaties embody "evolutionary" concepts that have called for an essentially dynamic interpretation, so that human rights treaties are always properly taken as living instruments. The meaning of provisions of human rights treaties has evolved in response to changed social conditions; account has been, and ought to continue to be, taken of the path of general social change, in an essentially dynamic process of evolution of international human rights law through interpretation.[43]

As for application, the practice of international supervisory organs affords illustrations of the temporal dimension in human rights protection. At the global level, the Human Rights Committee, operating under the UN Covenant on Civil and Political Rights and its Optional Protocol, in its views in the *S. Aumeeruddy-Cziffra and 19 Other Mauritian Women versus Mauritius* case (1981), accepted that the author of a communication under the Optional Protocol to the Covenant could challenge a law or practice as being contrary to the Covenant in the event of its being applicable in such a way that the alleged victim's *risk* of being affected was "more than a theoretical possibility."[44] At the regional level, the Inter-American Court of Human Rights, in its Advisory Opinion in the case of the *Proposed Amendment to the Naturalization Provisions of the Constitution of Costa Rica* (1984), held the view that if it were to decline to hear a government's request for an advisory opinion because it concerned "proposed laws" and not laws duly promulgated and already in force, that would "unduly limit" the advisory function of the Court.[45]

Particularly rich on this point is the jurisprudence of supervisory organs under the European Convention on Human Rights. After an initial period of some uncertainty and hesitation (see, e.g., the *Belgian Linguistics* cases, 1964), concentrating first on *direct* victims and later also on *indirect* victims of violations of the Convention,[46] the European Commission and Court of Human Rights came more recently to uphold the notion of "*potential* victims," or victims claiming a valid potential personal interest under the Convention. Thus, in a significant decision, in the *Kjeldsen versus Denmark* case (1972), the Commission allowed the two applicants, *prospective* or *future* victims,

43. A.A. Cançado Trindade, *supra* note 2 at 98–100.
44. Cit. in A.A. Cançado Trindade, *supra* note 2 at 285, 253.
45. Cit. in *id.* at 284.
46. *See id.* at 263–270, 280.

to raise the issue of the compatibility with the Convention (and the First Protocol) of the introduction (by an Act of Parliament of 1970) of compulsory sex education in public schools in Denmark.[47] Shortly afterwards, in the *Donnelly and Others versus United Kingdom* case (1973), the Commission allowed the applicants – who were seeking not only a decision to the effect that their rights under the Convention had been violated but also protection from *future abuses* of their rights – to raise the issue of the compatibility with the Convention of an administrative practice (of ill-treatment by security forces in Northern Ireland in 1972) in breach of the Convention.[48]

In subsequent cases the Commission dwelt further upon the matter. In the *H. Becker versus Denmark* case (1975), the applicant complained on behalf of Vietnamese orphans who were running the *risk* of being returned to Vietnam in view of the Danish Government's policy of repatriation; the Commission found that in the case the orphans were "alleged *potential victims*" and the applicant was an "indirect victim" in that he had a "valid personal interest in the welfare of the children."[49] Here the interrelationship between "indirect" and "potential" victims became apparent. One has thus gone beyond the immediate requests and interests of the individual applicants themselves. The way was thereby paved for the Commission to be concerned with the protection not only of victims of *past violations* of the Convention, but also of those who may *in the future* – in circumstances like those of the cases above – suffer likely violations of their rights (material or moral prejudice). Respondent states would thus be placed under the duty to forbid legislative or administrative acts that might result in likely violations of human rights.

In a landmark judgment in the *G. Klass and Others versus Federal Republic of Germany* case (1978), the European Court, in its turn, significantly found that a law might by itself violate the rights of an individual if the individual concerned was directly affected by the law "in the absence of any specific measure of implementation." Thus, in the Court's ruling, under certain conditions an individual might claim to be the victim of a violation "occasioned by the mere existence of secret measures or of legislation permitting secret measures, without having to allege that such measures were in fact applied to him."[50] The Court admitted the right of recourse to the Commission "for per-

47. *Id.* at 271–273.
48. *Id.* at 272–274.
49. Cit. in *id.* at 274.
50. Cit. in *id.* at 274–276.

sons *potentially* affected by secret surveillance," and concluded that each of the applicants was entitled to claim to be the victim of a violation of the Convention even though he was "not able" to allege in support of his application that he had been subjected to a concrete measure of surveillance.[51] Shortly afterwards, in the *Marckx versus Belgium* case (1979), the Court confirmed that Article 25 of the Convention entitled individuals to contend that a law (in the case, several articles of the Belgian Civil Code) violated their rights "by itself, in the absence of an individual measure of implementation, if they run the risk of being directly affected by it."[52] From then onwards, the Court's position became *jurisprudence constante* in successive cases in recent years (see *infra*).

In the same jurisprudential line of other recent decisions (see *supra*), the European Court of Human Rights, in its judgement in the *Dudgeon versus United Kingdom* case (1981), found that in the circumstances of the case the "very existence" of the legislation complained of "continuously and directly" affected the applicant's private life. To the Court, the maintenance in force of the impugned legislation constituted a "continuing interference" with the applicant's right to respect for his private life (which included his sexual life); "the threat hanging over him was real," pondered the Court, before concluding that the applicant had suffered and continued to suffer "an unjustified interference with his right to respect for his private life" in breach of Article 8 of the Convention.[53] In fact, the *threats* of modern scientific and technological developments to the protection of the right to privacy help to disclose the seemingly temporal dimension of this latter.[54]

In subsequent cases (*Adolf versus Austria*, 1982, and *Eckle versus Federal Republic of Germany*, 1982–1983), the Court insisted that the existence of a violation was conceivable even in the absence of

51. *Id.* at 276.
52. In *id.* at 276–277.
53. Cit. in A.A. Cançado Trindade, *supra* note 2 at 277. In the *Campbell and Cosans versus United Kingdom* (1982) case, even though the Court found that no violation of Article 3 of the Convention was established in the case, in the proceedings before the Court (and previously before the Commission) the issue was raised by the applicants that the "imminent *risk*" of punishment of their children at school entitled them to claim that their children were [potential] "victims" under Article 25 of the Convention; *see id.* at 277–278 n. 888.
54. This particular point was the object of attention as early as in 1970, in the III International Colloquy on the European Convention on Human Rights, organized by the Council of Europe and held in Brussels; *see Privacy and Human Rights*, 129–181 (A.H. Robertson, ed., Manchester University, 1973).

prejudice.[55] Again, in its judgement in the *De Jong, Baljet, and van den Brink versus the Netherlands* case (1984), the Court referred to its own *"well-established case-law"* to the effect that the existence of a violation of the Convention was "conceivable even in the absence of detriment."[56] This was further confirmed by the Court in its judgement in the case of *Johnston and Others versus Ireland* case (1986), where it maintained that Article 25 of the Convention entitled individuals "to contend that a law violates their rights by itself, in the absence of an individual measure of implementation, if they run the risk of being directly affected by it."[57] In the present case the applicants had raised "objections to the effects of the law on their own lives" (inability to divorce and remarry and question of respect for family life), and the Court found that in the circumstances they were entitled to claim to be victims of the breaches of the Convention that they alleged.[58]

More recently, the notion of *potential* victim was again, and under new circumstances, dwelt upon by the European Commission and Court in the *J. Soering versus United Kingdom* case. The applicant, a national of the Federal Republic of Gemany, complained that if he was extradited from the United Kingdom to the United States (to face trial in Virginia on a charge of capital murder) he would run the *risk* of being sentenced to death and spending a protracted period in prison awaiting execution, in violation of the European Convention (Article 3, prohibition of torture or inhuman or degrading treatment or punishment). The Commission, recalling its findings in the *Kirkwood versus United Kingdom* case (1984), in its 1989 report on the *Soering* case pondered that the serious *risk* run by the applicant raised the direct responsibility of the respondent state under Article 3 of the Convention; thus, to the Commission, an applicant who was faced with "an *imminent* act of the Executive" that might expose him to inhuman treatment could claim to be a victim of an alleged violation of Article 3 of the Convention.[59]

The commission drew attention to the *"anticipatory* nature of the present proceedings" and to the need to proceed to an *"assessment of*

55. *See* A.A. Cançado Trindade, *supra* note 2.
56. Cit. in *id.* at 278.
57. Cit. in *id.* at 278.
58. *Id.* at 278.
59. European Commission of Human Rights, *J. Soering versus United Kingdom* (application no. 14038/88) – *Report of the Commission*, 15–18, §§91, 96, 106 (Council of Europe, January 1989).

the risk" run by the applicant on the basis of an objective evaluation of conditions in the country concerned.[60] The Commission added that Article 13 of the Convention – on the right to an effective remedy – also applied "in respect of 'arguable' claims under Article 3 of the Convention which are prospective or anticipatory in nature"; in the ponderation of the Commission, "the examination of such a complaint after extradition has taken place would hardly be consonant with an effective system of individual application."[61] The Commission found that the applicant had no effective remedy under the law of the United Kingdom in respect of his complaint under Article 3, and concluded that there had in the case been a violation of Article 13 (but in the circumstances not of Article 3) of the Convention.[62]

In its turn, in its judgement of 1989 in the same *Soering* case, the Court admitted that in the present case, where the applicant claimed that a decision to extradite him would, if implemented, "be contrary to Article 3 by reason of its foreseeable consequences in the requesting country," it had to pronounce on the existence or otherwise of a *potential* violation of the Convention, in view of "the serious and irreparable nature of the alleged suffering risked," in order to ensure the effectiveness of the safeguard provided by Article 3 of the Convention.[63] The Court, after considering the applicant's "real risk" of treatment contrary to Article 3 (if extradited), the "likelihood of the death penalty being imposed," and the "anticipatory nature" of the alleged violation of the Convention – i.e., after an inquiry on whether the applicant ran a "real risk" of being sentenced to death in the United States[64] – held that, in the event of the UK Secretary of State's decision to extradite the applicant to the United States being implemented, "there would be a violation of Article 3" of the Convention.[65] Thus, in the unique circumstances of the present *Soering* case, the Court's decision upheld the state's duty to assess the risk run by the applicant and the likelihood of harm in another state, and to measure that against its further duty to protect human rights and to prevent the occurrence of the irreparable harm at issue. In short,

60. *Id.* at 18–19, 21, 26, §§106–108, 110, 120, 149.
61. *Id.* at 29–30, §163.
62. *See id.* at 30–31, §§165–170.
63. European Court of Human Rights, *Soering* case (no. 1/1989/161/217), Judgment of 7 July 1989, Strasbourg, Council of Europe, 1989, p. 27, §90.
64. *Id.* at 27, 34–35, 37–38; §§91–92, 110–111, 122, 117.
65. *Id.* at 40, §128; the Court further held that there had been no violation of Article 13 of the Convention.

and in a language reminiscent of that proper to environmental protection, the state was to assess the applicant's risks (abroad) and thus to exert its *duty of due diligence,* in the discharge of its basic function of protection of human rights.

The above *jurisprudence constante* of the supervisory organs under the European Convention today leaves no room for doubt that the notion of *potential* or *prospective victims* – i.e., victims claiming (under Article 25[1]) a valid potential personal interest – has become crystallized in the case-law under the Convention, thus enhancing the condition of individual applicants. This is in keeping with the marked and significant tendency under coexisting human rights instruments to *enlarge* the circle of persons entitled to submit complaints of alleged human rights violations, thus ultimately benefiting far more people than the complainants themselves. An influential doctrinal trend has argued that, by lodging an application under Article 25 of the European Convention, the individual concerned is not only pursuing a *droit subjectif* but also initiating an *action publique* under the European Convention: and this latter works out not only as a means to obtain *reparation* for particular injuries, but also – in cases of legislative measures and administrative practices – as a *preventive measure of protection,* in an *identification between the individual and the general interest.* The supervisory organs' task is then no longer confined to that of redressing a tort, but of ensuring the observance of the engagements undertaken by the parties to the Convention. The same applies in other human rights experiments, where, in addition to concrete results achieved in numerous individual cases, an important *preventive* function has been performed by supervisory organs (e.g., the Inter-American Commission on Human Rights), in obtaining, for example, the derogation or modification of legislation affecting negatively the effective exercise of human rights and the establishment and strengthening of mechanisms of protection at the level of domestic law.[66]

It may be added that the temporal dimension is clearly present,

---

66. *See* A.A. Cançado Trindade, *supra* note 1 at 279, 281–283, 298–299. For other aspects of the incidence of the temporal factor in the jurisprudence under the European Convention (e.g., case-law pertaining to a "continuing situation," subsequent events not affecting the applicant's claim of being a victim under the Convention, subsequent adequate redress affecting the applicant's original claim of being a victim under the Convention), *see id.* at 291–296; on yet other aspects (e.g., adequate redress affecting subsequent complaints of the same human rights violation under distinct instruments), *see id.* at 296–298.

and emphatically so, in the recent judgements, of 1988, of the Inter-American Court of Human Rights, in two of the three *Honduran* cases where it found that there had been a breach of the obligation to ensure the right to life set forth in Article 4 (read in conjunction with Article 1 [1]0 of the American Convention on Human Rights) (the *Velasquez Rodriguez* and *Godinez Cruz* cases).[67] After stating that "the forced disappearance of human beings is a multiple and *continuous* violation" of rights guaranteed under the Convention,[68] the Inter-American Court recalled and stressed the States Parties' duty to *prevent,* investigate, and punish any violation of the rights recognized by the Convention.[69] In a language reminiscent of that employed in the realm of international environmental law, the Inter-American Court, in those two judgments of 1988, repeatedly insisted on the states' *duty of due diligence to prevent* violations of protected human rights, in particular their duty of reasonable *prevention* of situations that could lead to suppression of the inviolability of the right to life[70] foreseen in Article 4 of the American Convention.

The Court went on to explain that the duty of prevention, in the context of the *Velasquez Rodriguez* and *Godinez Cruz* cases, was an *obligation de comportement,* which comprised "all those means of a legal, political, administrative and cultural nature that promote the protection of human rights and ensure that any violations are considered and treated as illegal acts."[71] The court added that the duty of investigation, which, like that of prevention, is also an *obligation de comportement,* is to be "assumed by the State as its own legal duty, not as a step taken by private interests that depends upon the initia-

---

67. In the third of the *Honduran* cases – the *Fairen Garbi and Solís Corrales* case – it may be recalled, the Court, unlike in the two other Honduran cases, found that it had not been proven that Honduras was responsible for the disappearances of the persons concerned. It repeated, though, its view that the phenomenon of involuntary disappearances amounted to a "multiple and *continuing* violation" of rights guaranteed under the Convention. *See* Inter-American Court of Human Rights (IACHR), *Fairen Garbi and Solís Corrales* case, Series C, no. 6, Judgment of 15 Mar. 1989, p. 128, §147.
68. Inter-American Court of Human Rights (IACHR), *Velasquez Rodriguez* case, Series C, no. 4, Judgment of 29 July 1988, p. 147, §155; Inter-American Court of Human Rights (IACHR), *Godinez Cruz* case, Series C, no. 5, Judgment of 20 Jan. 1989, p. 145, §163.
69. IACHR, *Velasquez Rodriguez* case, *supra* note 68 at 152, §166; IACHR, *Godinez Cruz* case, *supra* note 68 at 150, §175.
70. IACHR, *Velasquez Rodriguez* case, *supra* note 68 at 154–156, 158, 160, §§172, 174–175, 177, 182, 187–188; IACHR, *Godinez Cruz* case, *supra* note 68 at 152–154, 157–158, §§182, 184–186, 188, 197–198.
71. IACHR, *Velasquez Rodriguez* case, cit. *supra* n. (68), p. 155, §175; IACHR, *Godinez Cruz* case, cit. *supra* n. (68), p. 153, §185.

tive of the victim or his family or upon their offer of proof, without an effective search for the truth by the government."[72]

The incidence of the temporal dimension can be detected not only in the interpretation and application of norms pertaining to guaranteed rights but also in the conditions of their exercise. An example is afforded by the reference to public emergencies *"threatening* the life of the nation" in Article 15 (on derogation) of the European Convention on Human Rights. The point has been raised in a few cases under the European Convention (*Lawless versus Ireland,* 1957; *First Greek* case, 1969; *Ireland versus United Kingdom,* 1978; *France/ Norway/Denmark/Sweden/Netherlands versus Turkey,* 1983); according to the European Commission on Human Rights, the element of imminent public danger envisaged by Article 15 of the Convention comprises four characteristics, namely, the exceptional character of such danger, its repercussions on the whole of the nation, the requisite that the danger be present or *imminent,* and that it constitutes a *threat* to the organized life of the nation.[73] Here the temporal factor is manifest; it also underlies such ground for permissible derogations, under the European Convention, to the exercise of guaranteed rights.

The incidence of the temporal dimension can be detected in the protecting not only of civil and political rights (as under, e.g., the European and the American conventions on human rights) but also of economic, social, and cultural rights. It has in fact recently been suggested that rights pertaining not only to individuals but in particular to groups or communities, such as economic, social, and cultural rights (e.g., right to education, right to cultural integrity – or else the right to development and the right to a healthful environment) may find a "unifying basis" precisely in their temporal dimension, since such groups or communities inherently extend over time.[74] It is probable that the temporal dimension, identifiable in the implementation of civil and political rights (see *supra*), becomes even more pronounced in the implementation of economic, social, and cultural rights, or, in short, of group rights.

Manifestations of the intertemporal dimension in distinct fields of international law (*supra*) constitute a phenomenon no longer to be

72. IACHR, *Velasquez Rodriguez* case, cit. *supra* n. (68), p. 156, §177; IACHR, *Godinez Cruz* case, cit. *supra* n. (68), p. 154, §188.
73. G. Cohen-Jonathan, *La Convention européenne des droits de l'homme,* 557–559 (Univ. d'Aix-Marseille/Economica, 1989).
74. E. Brown Weiss, *supra* note 28 at 114–115; *see id.* at 117, 28–32.

minimized. Those manifestations become quite concrete especially in the field of the international protection of human rights, where they do not appear as soft law. Probably more clearly than in other chapters or fields of international law, the evolving jurisprudence, e.g., on the notion of "victim" under the European Convention on Human Rights, added to the recent judgements of the Inter-American Court of Human Rights in the *Honduran* cases, seems to afford safe and solid ground for the study of the intertemporal dimension in human rights protection in particular, which may serve as inspiration also for environmental protection, and be of interest for international law in general.

III. The fundamental right to life at the basis of the *ratio legis* of international human rights law and environmental law

The right to life is nowadays universally acknowledged as a basic or fundamental human right. It is basic or fundamental because "the enjoyment of the right to life is a necessary condition of the enjoyment of all other human rights."[75] As indicated by the Inter-American Court of Human Rights in its Advisory Opinion on *Restrictions to the Death Penalty* (1983), the human right to life encompasses a "substantive principle" whereby every human being has an inalienable right to have his life respected, and a "procedural principle" whereby no human being shall be arbitrarily deprived of his life.[76]

The Human Rights Committee, operating under the UN Covenant on Civil and Political Rights (and Optional Protocol), qualifying the human right to life as the "supreme right of the human being," has warned that the fundamental human right "ne peut pas être entendu de façon restrictive" and its protection "exige que les Etats adoptent des mesures positives."[77] The Inter-American Commission on Human Rights, likewise, has drawn attention to the binding character of the right to life.[78] In its recent resolution no. 3/87, on case no. 9647, concerning the United States, the Inter-American Commission, after identifying a norm of *jus cogens* that "prohibits the State execution of children," warned against "the arbitrary deprivation of life" on the

---

75. F. Przetacznik, "The Right to Life as a Basic Human Right," 9 *Revue des droits de l'homme/Human Rights Journal,* 589, 603 (1976).
76. IACHR, Advisory Opinion OC-3/83, of 8 Sept. 1983, Series A, no. 3, p. 59, §53.
77. Cit. in J.G.C. Van Aggelen, *Le rôle des organisations internationales dans la protection du droit à la vie,* 23 (Story-Scientia, 1986).
78. Cit. in *id.* at 38.

basis of a patchwork scheme of legislation that subjects the severity of the punishment (of the offender) to the "fortuitous element of where the crime took place."[79]

Under international human rights instruments, the assertion of the inherent right to life of every human being is accompanied by an assertion of the legal protection of that basic human right and of the *negative* obligation not to deprive arbitrarily of one's life (e.g., UN Covenant on Civil and Political Rights, Article 6 [1]; European Convention on Human Rights, Article 2; American Convention on Human Rights, Article 4 [1]; African Charter on Human and Peoples' Rights, Article 4).[80] But this negative obligation is accompanied by the *positive* obligation to take all appropriate measures to protect and preserve human life. This has been acknowledged by the European Commission of Human Rights, whose case-law has evolved to the point of holding (*Association X versus United Kingdom* case, 1978) that Article 2 of the European Convention on Human Rights imposed on states also a wider and positive obligation "de prendre des mesures adéquates pour protéger la vie."[81]

Taken in its wide and proper dimension, the fundamental right to life comprises the right of every human being not to be deprived of his life (*right to life*) and the right of every human being to have the appropriate means of subsistence and a decent standard of life (preservation of life, *right of living*). As well pointed out by Przetacznik, "the former belongs to the area of civil and political rights, the latter to that of economic, social and cultural rights."[82] The fundamental right to life, thus properly understood, affords an eloquent illustration of the indivisibility and interrelatedness of all human rights.[83]

In fact, some members of the Human Rights Committee have expressed the view that Article 6 of the UN Covenant on Civil and Political Rights requires the state "to take *positive measures* to ensure the right to life, including steps to reduce the infant mortality rate, pre-

---

79. OAS, *Annual Report of the Inter-American Commission on Human Rights – 1986–1987*, 170, 172–173.
80. Th. Desch, "The Concept and Dimension of the Right to Life (As Defined in International Standards and in International and Comparative Jurisprudence)," 36 *Österreichische Zeitschrift für öffentliches Recht und Völkerrecht*, 86, 99 (1985).
81. Cit. in J.G.C. Van Aggelen, *supra* note 77 at 32.
82. F. Przetacznik *supra* note 75 at 603; *see id.* at 586.
83. On the right to life bearing witness of the indivisibility of all human rights, *see* W.P. Gormley, "The Right to a Safe and Decent Environment," 20 *Indian Journal of International Law*, 23–24 (1988).

vent industrial accidents, and protect the environment. . . ."[84] Taking the essential requirements of the right of living (*supra*) as a corollary of the right to life, Desch argued that inequitable distribution of food or medicaments by public authorities, or even the toleration of malnutrition or failure to reduce infant mortality would constitute violations of Article 6 of the Covenant if there results an arbitrary deprivation of life.[85]

During the drafting of the 1948 Universal Declaration of Human Rights, attempts were made to make its Article 3, which proclaims the right to life, more precise.[86] A number of issues were the object of discussion in the drafting of corresponding provisions on the right to life of human rights treaties,[87] but it was the views and decisions more recently rendered by international supervisory organs that have gradually given more precision to the right to life as enshrined in the respective human rights treaties (see *supra*). Even those who insist on regarding the right to life strictly as a civil right[88] cannot fail to admit that, ultimately, without an adequate standard of living (as recognized, e.g., in Articles 11–12 of the UN Covenant on Economic, Social, and Cultural Rights, following Article 25 [1] of the 1948 Universal Declaration), the right to life could not possibly be realized in its full sense[89] (e.g., in its close relationships with the right to health and medical care; the right to food, and the right to housing).[90] Thus, both the UN General Assembly (resolution 37/189A, of 1982) and

84. Cit. in Th. Desch, *supra* note 80 at 101.
85. *Id.* at 101.
86. *See* H. Kanger, *Human Rights in the U.N. Declaration,* 81–82 (Almqvist & Wiksell, 1984).
87. On the legislative history of Article 6 of the UN Covenant on Civil and Political Rights, *see* B.G. Ramcharan, "The Drafting History of Article 6 of the International Covenant on Civil and Political Rights," in *The Right to Life in International Law* 42–56 (B.G. Ramcharan, ed., Nijhoff/Kluwer, 1985). On the legislative history of Article 2 of the European Convention on Human Rights, *see* B.G. Ramcharan, "The Drafting History of Article 2 of the European Convention on Human Rights," in *id.* at 57–61. On the legislative history of Article 4 (and antecedents) of the American Convention on Human Rights, *see* J. Colón-Collazo, "A Legislative History of the Right to Life in the Inter-American Legal System," in *id.* at 33–41.
88. *See* to this effect the analysis by Y. Dinstein, "The Right to Life, Physical Integrity, and Liberty," *The International Bill of Rights,* 114–137 (L. Henkin, ed., Columbia University, 1981).
89. Th. Van Boven, *People Matter – Views on International Human Rights Policy,* 77 (Meulenhoff, 1982).
90. On this matter, *see* S. Leckie, "The U.N. Committee on Economic, Social and Cultural Rights and the Right to Adequate Housing: Towards an Appropriate Approach," 11 *Human Rights Quarterly,* 522–560 (1989).

the UN Commission on Human Rights (resolutions 1982/7, of 1982, and 1983/43, see 1983) have unequivocally taken the firm view that *all individuals and all peoples* have an *inherent* right to life, and that the safeguarding of this *foremost right* is an essential condition for the enjoyment of the entire range of civil and political, as well as economic, social, and cultural rights.[91]

Two points are deserving of particular emphasis here. First, it has not passed unnoticed that the provision of the UN Covenant on Civil and Political Rights on the fundamental and inherent right to life (Article 6 [1]) is "the only Article of the Covenant where the inherency of a right is expressly referred to."[92] Secondly, the United Nations has formed its conviction that not only all individuals but also all *peoples* have an inherent right to life (*supra*). This brings to the fore the safeguard of the right to life of all persons as well as of human collectivities, with special attention to the requirements of the survival (as a component of the right to life) of vulnerable groups (e.g., the dispossessed and deprived, disabled or handicapped persons, children and the elderly, ethnic minorities, indigenous populations, migrant workers – see section VI, *infra*).[93]

From this perspective, the right to a healthy environment and the right to peace appear as extensions or corollaries of the right to life.[94] The fundamental character of the right to life renders inadequate narrow approaches to it in our day; under the right to life, in its modern and proper sense, not only is protection against any arbitrary deprivation of life upheld, but furthermore states are under the duty "to pursue policies which are designed to ensure access to the means of survival"[95] for all individuals and all peoples. To this effect, states are under the obligation to avoid serious environmental hazards or risks to life, and to set into motion "monitoring and early-warning systems" to detect such serious environmental hazards or risks and "urgent-action systems" to deal with such threats.[96]

In the same line, in the First European Conference on the Environment and Human Rights (Strasbourg, 1979), the point was made

---

91. Cit. in B.G. Ramcharan, "The Right to Life," 30 *Netherlands International Law Review,* 301 (1983).
92. *Id.* at 316.
93. *See id.* at 305, 306; Th. Van Boven, *supra* note 89 at 179, 181–183.
94. B.G. Ramcharan, *supra* note 91 at 303, 308–310.
95. *Id.* at 302.
96. *Id.* at 304, 329. Views reproduced in B.G. Ramcharan, "The Concept and Dimensions of the Right to Life," in *The Right to Life in International Law, supra* note 87 at 1–32.

that mankind needed to protect itself against its own threats to the environment, in particular when those threats had negative repercussions on the conditions of existence – life itself, physical and mental health, the well-being of present and future generations.[97] In a way, it was the right to life itself, in its wide dimension, that entailed the needed recognition of the right to a healthy environment; this latter appears as "le droit à des *conditions de vie* qui assurent la santé physique, morale, et sociale, la vie elle-même, ainsi que le bien-être des générations présentes et futures."[98] In other words, the right to a healthy environment safeguards human life itself under two aspects, namely, the physical existence and health of human beings and the dignity of that existence, the quality of life that renders it worth living.[99] The right to a healthy environment thus encompasses and enlarges the right to health and the right to an adequate or sufficient standard of living, and has furthermore a wide *temporal* dimension: as, "en matière d'environnement, certaines atteintes à l'environnement ne produisent d'effets sur la vie et la santé de l'homme qu'a long terme, . . . la reconnaissance d'un droit a l'environnement . . . devrait donc admettre une notion large des atteintes."[100]

Thus, the wide dimension of the right to life and the right to a healthy environment entails the consequent wider characterization of attempts or threats against those rights, what in turn calls for a higher degree of their protection. An example of those threats is provided by, e.g., the effects of global warming on human health: skin cancer, retinal eye damage, cataracts and eventual blindness, neurological damage, lowered resistance to infection, alteration of the immunological system (through damaged immune cells); in sum, depletion of the ozone layer may result in substantial injury to human health as well as to the environment (harm to terrestrial plants, destruction of the zooplankton, a key link in the food chain),[101] thus disclosing the

97. P. Kromarek, "Le droit à un environnement équilibré et sain, considéré comme un droit de l'homme: sa mise-en-oeuvre nationale, européenne et internationale," *I Conférence européenne sur l'environnement et les droits de l'homme,* 2–3, 31 (Institute for European Environmental Policy, 1979) (mimeographed, restricted circulation).
98. *Id.* at 13, 5 (emphasis added).
99. *Id.* at 12.
100. *Id.* at 43, 21.
101. J.T.B. Tripp, "The UNEP Montreal Protocol: Industrialized and Developing Countries Sharing the Responsibility for Protecting the Stratospheric Ozone Layer," 20 *New York University Journal of International Law and Politics,* 734 (1988); Ch. B. Davidson, "The Montreal Protocol: The First Step toward Protecting the Global Ozone Layer," in *id.* at 807–809.

275

needed convergence of human health protection and environmental protection.

In the realm of international environmental law, the 1989 Hague Declaration on the Atmosphere, for example, states that "the right *to live* is the right from which all other rights stem" (§1), and adds that "the right *to live* in dignity in a viable global environment" entails the duty of the "community of nations" *vis-à-vis* "present and future generations" to do "all that can be done to preserve the quality of the atmosphere" (§5). The use of the expression the right *to live* (rather than the right *to life*) seems well in keeping with the understanding that the right to life entails negative as well as positive obligations as to preservation of human life (see *supra*). The Institut de Droit International, while drafting its Resolution on Transboundary Air Pollution (Session of Cairo, 1987), was attentive to include therein provisions referring to the protection of life and human health.[102]

One has propounded as a criterion for the characterization of "severe violations" of human rights occurrences when "large numbers of people are harmed."[103] In his suggested typology of those occurrences, Falk includes "ecocide" among "severe violations" of human rights, stressing the "human dependence on environmental quality," which renders this latter a "dimension of human rights."[104] He argues that, despite the fact that "offences" to the environment (such as, e.g., the carrying on of nuclear atmospheric tests, the depletion of the global ozone layer, the disposal of toxic wastes into the oceans) have not traditionally been dealt with regularly in human rights instruments, they, however,

involve official conduct that seriously endangers the life, health, and serenity of current and future generations. The notion of human rights is incomplete to the extent that it fails to encompass those forms of deliberate behaviour that produce serious environmental damage.

. . . Environmental quality is a critical dimension of human dignity that may have a significant impact on development, and even survival, of mankind.[105]

---

102. *See* Preamble and Articles 10(2) and 11; text in 62 *Annuaire de l'Institut de droit international,* II, 204, 207–208, 211 (1987).
103. R. Falk, *Human Rights and State Sovereignty,* 158 (Holmes & Meier, 1981).
104. *Id.* at 167; *see id.* at 159.
105. *Id.* at 167. The author, comparing "ecocidal behaviour" to gross and massive violations of human rights, stresses the need to safeguard "ecological well-being," calls for "coercive measures to prevent additional nuclear weapons tests" and for "a new Covenant on Environmental and Ecological Rights"; *id.* at 177, 183. In 1973 proposals were advanced by

Together with the right to a healthy environment, the right to peace appears also as a necessary prolongation or corollary of the right to life. In fact, the Inter-American Commission on Human Rights has been attentive to address the requirements of *survival* as a component of the right to life: to the Inter-American Commission, the right to life comprises or requires not only protection in the form of preventive measures against all forms of ill-treatment and threats to life and health,[106] but also the realization of "the economic and social aspirations" of all peoples by pursuing policies that assign priority to "the basic needs of health, nutrition, and education"; in the words of the Commission, "the priority of the 'right of survival' and 'basic needs' is a natural consequence of the right to personal security."[107] The Commission has furthermore dwelt upon the requirement of cultural survival of indigenous populations as a component of the right to life.[108] At the global level, one has likewise proceeded to the last consequences of the requirements of survival: the UN General Assembly, e.g., has taken the right to life as encompassing "protection against the use of weapons of mass destruction, such as nuclear weapons"; this entails the "duty to negotiate in good faith to achieve disarmament and procedural safeguards upon the use of weapons of mass destruction."[109]

In this connection, in its general comment 14(23), of 1985, on Article 6 (on the right to life) of the UN Covenant on Civil and Political Rights, the Human Rights Committee, after recalling its earlier general comment 6(16), of 1982, on Article 6(1) of the Covenant – to the effect that the right to life, as enunciated therein, is "the supreme right from which no derogation is permitted even in time of public emergency" – went on to relate the current proliferation of weapons of mass destruction to "the supreme duty of States to prevent wars." The Committee associated itself with the growing concern, expressed during successive sessions of the UN General Assembly by representatives from all geographical regions, at what represented one of the "greatest threats to the right to life which confronts mankind to-

---

Falk for the adoption of a Draft Convention on the Crime of Ecocide, but states did not seem then willing to adopt it; cit. in W.P. Gormley, *Human Rights and Environment: The Need for International Cooperation,* 14–15, 29 (Sijthoff, 1976).

106. *See* Comisión Interamericana de Derechos Humanos, *Diez Años de Actividades – 1971–1981,* 338–339 (Secretaría General de la OEA, 1982).

107. *Id.* at 321.

108. *See id.* at 329–330.

109. B.G. Ramcharan, *supra* note 91 at 303.

day." In the words of the Committee, "the very existence and gravity of this threat generate a climate of suspicion and fear between States, which is in itself antagonistic to the promotion of universal respect for and observance of human rights" in accordance with the UN Charter and the UN Covenants on Human Rights.[110] The Committee, accordingly, "in the interest of mankind," called upon "all States, whether Parties to the Covenant or not, to take urgent steps, unilaterally and by agreement, to rid the world of this menace."[111]

The maintenance of peace is an imperative for the preservation of human life that has found expression in the UN Charter (preamble and Articles 1 and 2) and the Unesco Constitution (preamble and Article I). The Unesco Constitution, moreover, refers to the need of assuring the conservation and protection of the "world's inheritance" of knowledge, so that this latter is increased and diffused for the realization of the purpose of the Organization to contribute to peace (Article I[2] [c]). The Final Act of the 1968 Teheran Conference on Human Rights contains likewise several references to the relationship of the observance of human rights and the maintenance of peace.[112] In this connection, reference can further be made to the preambles of the two 1966 UN Covenants on Human Rights. More recently the "right to peace" has formed the object of a number of UN resolutions that relate it to disarmament and *détente*, thus disclosing the temporal dimension of the underlying duty of *prevention* of conflicts[113] (e.g., *inter alia,* GA resolutions 33/73, of 1978, and 34/88, of 1979). The states' duty to coexist in peace and to achieve disarmament is acknowledged in the 1974 Charter on Economic Rights and Duties of States (Articles 26 and 15, respectively).

The right to peace entails as a corollary the "right to disarmament";[114] attention has in this regard been drawn to the fact that limitations or violations of human rights are often associated with the outbreak of conflicts, the process of militarization, and the expenditure on arms,[115] especially nuclear weapons and other

---

110. *Report of the Human Rights Committee,* U.N. G.A.O.R. 40th Sess., Supp. No. 40 at 162 (A/40/40).
111. *Id.* at 162.
112. *See Final Act of the International Conference on Human Rights,* 4, 6, 9, 14, 36, U.N. Doc. A/CONF.32/41 (1968).
113. *See* J.M. Becet and D. Colard, *Les droits de l'homme,* 128–131 (Economica, 1982).
114. To this effect, *see id.* at 129–131; Ph. Alston, "Peace, Disarmament and Human Rights," *Armement, Développement, Droits de l'homme, Désarmement,* 324–325, 329–330 (G. Fischer, ed., Colloque à l'Unesco, 1982).
115. Ph. Alston, *id.* at 325–330.

weapons of mass destruction,[116] which have led and may unfortunately still lead to arbitrary deprivation of human life. The conception of "sustainable development," as propounded by the Brundtland Commission, points to the ineluctable relationship between the rights to a healthy environment, to peace, and to development.[117] On this specific point, it should not pass unnoticed that Costa Rica has lately submitted to the 1989 session of the UN General Assembly a Draft Declaration on Human Responsibilities for Peace and Sustainable Development.[118] References to the right to peace and disarmament can further be found in the 1982 World Charter for Nature (preamble, §4[c], and Principles 5 and 20).

Last but not least, the relationship between the right to life and the right to development as a human right becomes clearer as one moves from the traditional, narrow approach to the right to life (as strictly a civil right) into the wider and modern approach to it, as encompassing also the minimum conditions for an adequate and dignified standard of living (see *supra*). Then the interrelatedness of the right to life and the right to development as a human right becomes self-evident, as this latter purports to demand all possible endeavours to overcome obstacles (of destitution and underdevelopment) preventing the fulfilment of basic human needs.[119] Not surprisingly, the UN Working Group of Governmental Experts on the Right to Development recommended in 1984 *inter alia* that particular attention should be paid to the basic needs and aspirations of vulnerable or disadvantaged and discriminated groups.[120]

In sum, the basic right to life, encompassing the right of living, entails negative as well as positive obligations in favour of preservation of human life. Its enjoyment is a precondition of the enjoyment of other human rights. It belongs at a time to the realm of civil and political rights, and to that of economic, social, and cultural rights, thus illustrating the indivisibility of all human rights. It establishes a "link"

116. *See* discussion *in* A.A. Tikhonov, "The Inter-relationship between the Right to Life and the Right to Peace; Nuclear Weapons and Other Weapons of Mass-Destruction and the Right to Life," in *The Right to Life in International Law, supra* note 87 at 97–113.

117. *See* World Commission on Environment and Development, *supra* note 14 at 19, 290–307; *see id.* at 294–300 on conflicts as a "cause of unsustainable development."

118. Text reproduced in 19/6 *Envt'l Pol'y & L.* 230, 233 (1989); *see Supporting memorandum* by C. Vargas Pizarro, Ministerio de Relaciones Exteriores y Culto, 1st Draft 1–24 (Costa Rica, 1989) (internal circulation only).

119. P.J.I.M. De Waart, "The Inter-Relationship between the Right to Life and the Right to Development," in *The Right to Life in International Law, supra* note 87 at 89, 91–92.

120. Cit. in *id.* at 91.

between the domains of international human rights law and environmental law. It inheres in all individuals and all peoples, with special attention to the requirements of survival. It has as existensions or corollaries the right to a healthy environment and the right to peace (and disarmament). It is closely related, in its wide dimension, to the right to development as a human right (right to live with fulfilment of basic human needs). And it lies at the basis of the ultimate *ratio legis* of the domains of international human rights law and environmental law, turned to the protection and survival of the human person and mankind.

IV. The right to health as the starting-point towards the right to a healthy environment

Like the right to life (right of living, *supra*), the right to health entails *negative* as well as *positive* obligations. In fact, the right to health is inextricably interwoven with the right to life itself, and is a precondition for the exercise of freedom. The right to life implies the *negative* obligation not to practice any act that can endanger one's health, thus linking this basic right to the right to physical and mental integrity and to the prohibition of torture and of cruel, inhuman, or degrading treatment (as recognized and provided for in the UN Covenant on Civil and Political Rights, Article 7; the European Convention on Human Rights, Article 3; the American Convention on Human Rights, Articles 4 and 5). But this duty of abstention (so crucial, e.g., in the treatment of detainees and prisoners) is accompanied by the *positive* obligation to take all appropriate measures to protect and preserve human health (including measures of prevention of diseases).

Such positive obligation (as recognized and provided for in, e.g., the UN Covenant on Economic, Social, and Cultural Rights, Article 12, and the European Social Charter, Article 11, besides WHO and ILO resolutions on specific aspects), linking the right to life to the right to an adequate standard of life,[121] discloses the fact that the

---

121. As proclaimed by the 1948 Universal Declaration of Human Rights, Article 25(1). On the "negative" and "positive" aspects of the right to health, *see* M. Bothe, "Les concepts fondamentaux du droit à la santé: le point de vue juridique," *Le droit à la santé en tant que droit de l'homme – Colloque 1978,* 14–29 (Académie de droit international de la Haye, Sijthoff, 1979); Scalabrino-Spadea, "Le droit à la santé – Inventaire de normes et principes de droit international, in *Le medecin face aux droits de l'homme,* 97–98 (Pedova, Cedam, 1990).

right to health, in its proper and wide dimension, partakes the nature of at a time an individual and social right. Belonging, like the right to life, to the realm of basic or fundamental rights, the right to health is an individual right in that it requires the protection of the physical and mental integrity of the individual and his dignity; and it is also a social right in that it imposes on the state and society the collective responsibility for the protection of the health of the citizenry and the prevention and treatment of diseases.[122] The right to health, thus properly understood, affords, like the right to life, a vivid illustration of the indivisibility and interrelatedness of all human rights.

V. The right to a healthy environment as an extension of the right to health

The right to life in its positive aspect (*supra*) found expression, at the global level, in Article 12 of the UN Covenant on Economic, Social, and Cultural Rights; that provision, in laying down the guidelines for the implementation of the right to health, singled out, *inter alia* ("b"), "the improvement of all aspects of environmental and industrial hygiene." The way seemed thereby paved for the future recognition of the right to a healthy environment (*infra*).

This point was the object of attention at the 1978 Colloquy of the Hague Academy of International Law on "the Right to Health as a Human Right," where the issue of the human right to environmental salubrity was raised. On the occasion, after warning that the degradation of the environment constituted nowadays a "menace *collective* à la santé des hommes,"[123] P.M. Dupuy pertinently advocated the needed assertion or proclamation of the human right to environmental salubrity as the "supreme guarantee of the right to health."[124] Pondering that the environment ought to be protected "en fonction de l'ensemble des intérêts de la collectivité," he justified:

Il nous paraît que la chance fournie par l'affirmation d'un droit à la salubrité du milieu est justement de donner l'occasion à l'"environnement" de cesser d'être d'abord perçu en termes économiques, ainsi qu'un bien susceptible d'exploitation, afin d'apparaître au moins autant comme un patrimoine de

---

122. R. Roemer, "El Derecho a la Atención de la Salud," in OMS, *El Derecho a la Salud en las Américas* 16 (H. L. Fuenzalida-Puelma and S.S. Connor, eds., OPAS, publ. no 509).
123. P.M. Dupuy, "Le droit à la santé et la protection de l'environnement," in *Le droit à la santé, supra* note 121 at 406; *see id.* at 351.
124. *Id.* at 412; *see id.* at 409.

l'individu, nécessaire à l'épanouissement de son droit fondamental à la vie, et donc à la santé.[125]

The protection of the whole of the biosphere as such entails "indirectly but necessarily" the protection of human beings, insofar as the object of environmental law and hence of the right to a healthy environment is "protéger les humains en leur assurant un milieu de vie adéquate."[126] The right to a healthy environment, in the perspicacious observation by Kiss, "completes" other recognized human rights also from another point of view, namely,

il contribue à établir une égalité entre citoyens ou, du moins, à atténuer les inégalités dans leurs conditions matérielles. On sait que les inégalités entre humains de conditions sociales différentes sont accentuées par la dégradation de l'environnement: les moyens matériels dont disposent les mieux nantis leur permettent d'échapper à l'air pollué, aux milieux dégradés et de se créer un cadre de vie sain et équilibré, alors que les plus démunis n'ont guère de telles possibilités et doivent accepter de vivre dans des agglomérations devenues inhumaines, voire des bidonvilles, et de supporter les pollutions.

L'exigence d'un environnement sain et équilibré devient ainsi en même temps un moyen de mettre en oeuvre d'autres droits reconnus à la personne humaine.

Mais, par ses objectifs mêmes, le droit à l'environnement apporte aussi une dimension supplémentaire aux droits de l'homme dans leur ensemble.[127]

The interrelatedness between environmental protection and the safeguard of the right to health is clearly evidenced in the implementation of Article 11 (on the right to protection of health) of the 1961 European Social Charter. The Committee of Independent Experts, operating under the Charter, has in recent years been attentive, in the consideration of national reports, to measures taken at the domestic level, pursuant to Article 11 of the Charter, to prevent, limit, or control pollution.[128] With regard to the removal of causes of ill-health (Article 1[1]), the Committee has concentrated on measures taken to prevent or reduce pollution of the atmosphere.[129] Thus, in

125. P.M. Dupuy, *supra* note 123 at 410.
126. A. Kiss, "Le droit à la qualité de l'environnement: un droit de l'homme?", in *Le droit à la qualité de l'environnement: un droit en devenir, un droit à définir*, 69–70 (N. Duple, ed., Quebec/Amérique, 1988).
127. *Id.* at 71.
128. *See* Council of Europe/European Social Charter, *Committee of Independent Experts,* Conclusions IX–2, 71 (C.E., 1986) (Austrian and Cypriot reports); *Id.*, Conclusions XI–1, 110 (Swedish and British reports).
129. *See*, e.g., German and Italian reports in *id.*, Conclusions IX–2, 71–72.

the consideration of a French report, the Committee took note of "the intention of the public authorities to achieve a 50 per cent reduction in sulphur dioxide emissions into the atmosphere during the period 1980–90";[130] and in the consideration of the latest Danish report, the Committee noted the measures taken to reduce air pollution, in particular that "emissions of nitrogen oxide into the atmosphere was to be reduced by 50 per cent before 2005 and of sulphur dioxide by 40 per cent before 1995."[131]

The collection *Case Law on the European Social Charter* contains other pertinent indications. The Committee of Independent Experts has manifested its wish to find in forthcoming national reports information, under Article 11 of the Charter, on "the measures taken to reduce the release of sulphur dioxide and other acid pollutants in the atmosphere."[132] The Committee has called for amplified measures for control of environmental pollution.[133] The Committee has further expressed the opinion that states bound by Article 11 of the Charter should be considered as fulfilling their obligations in that respect if they provide evidence of the existence of a medical and health system comprising *inter alia* "general measures aimed in particular at the prevention of air and water pollution, protection from radio-active substances, noise abatement, the food control environmental hygiene, and the control of alcoholism and drugs."[134]

An attempt has in fact been made, in the European continent, to extend the protection of the rights to life and health so as to include well-being, under the realm of the European Convention on Human Rights itself: prior to the convening of the 1973 European Ministerial Conference on the Environment, a Draft Protocol to the European Convention on Human Rights to that effect was prepared by H. Steiger. The Draft Protocol, containing two articles, provides for the protection of life and health as encompassing well-being (Article 1[1])

130. In *id.* at 71–72.
131. In *id.*, Conclusions XI–1, 118.
132. Council of Europe/European Social Charter, *Case Law on the European Social Charter – Supplement,* 37 (1982).
133. Council of Europe/European Social Charter, *Case Law on the European Social Charter,* 105 (1982).
134. *Id.* at 104. On the protection of health *vis-à-vis* the environment under Article 11 of the European Social Charter, *see* Council of Europe doc. 6030, of 22.03.1989, p. 9; C.E., *Comité Gouvernemental de la Charte Sociale Européenne – 10e rapport,* 28 (1989) (control of atmospheric pollution), Conseil de l'Europe/Charte Sociale Européenne, *Comité d'Experts Indépendants – Conclusions X–2,* 111–112 (1988) (reduction of atmospheric pollution); Council of Europe/European Social Charter, *Committee of Independent Experts – Conclusions X–1,* 108 (1987) (reduction of atmospheric pollution, air and water pollution control).

and admits limitations on the right to a healthy environment (Article 1[2]); it further provides for the protection of individuals against the acts of other private persons (Article 2[1] and [2]). This point (*Dritt-wirkung*), though giving rise to much debate and controversy, has been touched upon by the European Commission of Human Rights, which, in its 1979 report in the *Young, James, and Webster* cases, admitted that the European Convention contained provisions that "non seulement protègent l'individu contre l'Etat, mais aussi obligent l'Etat a protéger l'individu contre les agissements d'autrui."[135] Although Steiger's proposed Draft Protocol, purporting to place under the machinery of implementation of the European Convention the provisions above referred to (Articles 1 and 2), was not accepted at the time by member states, it remains the sole existing proposal on the matter (insofar as the European Convention system is concerned) and its underlying ideas deserve today further and deeper considera-tion (see *infra*).[136] Though the question remains an open one, there has, however, been express recognition of the right to a healthy en-vironment in more recent human rights instruments, to which we shall turn later (see section VII, *infra*).

VI. The protection of vulnerable groups at the confluence of international human rights law and international environmental law

Means of protection may envisage the guarantee of human rights that inhere in all human beings by virtue of their very existence and of hu-man rights that pertain to the social conditions – and their improve-ment – in which they find themselves.[137] Just as there are rights that are essentially "individual," i.e., that can be protected only in the in-dividual himself, there are also rights that can "best be protected

---

135. Cit. in J.P. Jacque, "La protection du droit à l'environnement au niveau européen ou régional," *Environnement et droits de l'homme,* 74–75 (P. Kromarek, ed., Unesco, 1987); *see id.* at 72–73. And, on Steiger's proposed Draft Protocol, see W.P. Gormley, *Human Rights and Environment: The Need for International Co-operation,* 90–95 (Sijthoff, 1976); P.M. Dupuy, *supra* note 123 at 408–413.

136. W.P. Gormley, *supra* note 135 at 112–113; J.P. Jacque, *supra* note 135 at 73, 75–76; P.M. Dupuy, *supra* note 123 at 412–413. For the complete text of Steiger's 1973 proposed Draft Protocol, see Working Group for Environmental Law, "The Right to a Humane Environment/Das Recht auf eine menschenwürdige Umwelt," in *Beiträge zur Umweltge-staltung* (Heft A 13), 27–54 (Erich Schmidt, 1973) (*Rapporteur,* H. Steiger).

137. A. Berenstein, "Les droits économiques et sociaux garantis par la Charte Sociale Euro-péenne," *Perspectives canadiennes et européennes des droits de la personne,* 414 (D. Turp and G.A. Beaudoin, eds., 1986); *see id.* at 433.

through a group," particularly in case of "group victimization." There are in fact groups that appear properly qualified for group treatment and protection, and international law has devised means of protection for certain categories of groups in distress (e.g., workers, minorities, refugees, stateless persons, prisoners of war). It is essentially a matter of organization and gradual institutionalization of protection[138] (as envisaged in our day, e.g., on behalf of indigenous populations). The temporal dimension is marked in the protection of human groups, that may, along with states, "pretend to perpetuity"; after all, "group organization can assure continuity over generations."[139]

The necessity of group protection appears clearly in the cultural and linguistic fields. It can hardly be doubted that some key elements of social life can be enjoyed only through "individual integration in a group," through education, exchange of ideas or custom; "while one may individually enjoy culture in whatever language, one can take part in the creation of culture only in one's own linguistic and cultural community."[140] Hence the need of protection of group rights, in particular of rights of "specially vulnerable and disadvantaged groups" (e.g., mentally and physically handicapped persons, the vulnerability of children, the situation of women in many countries, ethnic and religious and linguistic minorities, indigenous populations); attention has lately been drawn to the need to establish an "inventory" of the protection and assistance needed by those groups and to develop "early warning systems to cushion the shocks on specially vulnerable groups because of changes in development policies."[141]

Children, the handicapped, and the elderly rank in fact among the particularly vulnerable, and stand in special need of protection. The 1988 Additional Protocol to the American Convention on Human Rights in the Area of Economic, Social, and Cultural Rights, for example, singles out precisely the rights of children (Article 16), the protection of the handicapped as a (social) "group" (Article 18), and the protection of the elderly (Article 17). The 1961 European Social Charter, in its turn, singles out the rights of women and children (Articles 7, 8, and 17), of disabled persons (Article 15), and of migrant workers (Article 19). The temporal dimension is here present,

138. J.J. Lador-Lederer, *International Group Protection*, 13, 15–17, 23–24, 30 (Sijthoff, 1968).
139. *Id.* at 27, 29, 22–23.
140. *Id.* at 19; *see id.* at 25.
141. D. Lack, "Human Rights and the Disadvantaged," 10 *Human Rights Law Journal*, 56–59 (1989).

as evidenced, e.g., by the proper training and education of children. The 1948 Universal Declaration of Human Rights itself provides that "education shall be directed to the full *development* of the human personality" (Article 26[2]). The 1989 UN Convention on the Rights of the Child warns, in its preamble, that children, precisely because of their vulnerability, stand in need of special care and protection. The Convention, thus, provides also for *preventive* measures regarding the protection of children from abuse and neglect (Article 19[2]); it recognizes *inter alia* the child's right to education (Article 28) and the right of children to benefit from an adequate standard of living, necessary for their personal development (Article 27). The 1989 Convention further provides for the right of children of minority communities and indigenous populations to enjoy their own culture and to practice their own religion and language (Article 30).

The question of indigenous rights has become an issue of international concern, as reflected in the work of the ILO on the matter (e.g. its Convention no. 107 on the Protection and Integration of Indigenous and Other Tribal and Semi-Tribal Populations in Independent Countries, of 1957) and in the establishment (in 1982) by the UN Sub-Commission on Prevention of Discrimination and Protection of Minorities of the UN Working Group on Indigenous Populations, and its subsequent work.[142] Indigenous issues have, moreover, in recent years been dwelt upon by distinct human rights supervisory organs (e.g., CERD, Human Rights Committee).[143] A Draft Universal Declaration on Indigenous Rights, submitted in 1988 (by E.I. Daes) to the UN Working Group on Indigenous Populations, conceptualizes the "collective right" to protection against genocide and ethnocide (survival and cultural survival), at a time a right of peoples and of individuals, encompassing the right "to preserve their cultural identity and traditions and to pursue their own cultural development" (§§3–6).[144]

The Draft Declaration provides *inter alia* for the preservation of areas of settlement, ways of life and economic activities of indigenous populations (§18), their right to autonomy in matters relating to their own way of life (§23), their right to participation (in the life of their state – §§21–22), and health, housing, and other socio-economic programmes to their benefit (§20). In a significant clause (§16), the 1988 Draft Declaration further provides for

142. *See* D. Sanders, "The U.N. Working Group on Indigenous Populations," 11 *Human Rights Quarterly,* 406–433 (1989).
143. *See id.* at 421–422, 428.
144. Text in *id.*, Appendix, at 431.

the rights to protection against any action or course of conduct which may result in the destruction, deterioration or pollution of their land, air, water, sea, ice, wildlife or other resources without free and informed consent of the indigenous peoples affected. The right to just and fair compensation for any such action or course of conduct.[145]

Concern for the protection of vulnerable groups can nowadays be found not only in the domain of international human rights law, but likewise in the realm of international environmental law. In fact, the protection of vulnerable groups appears today at the confluence of human rights protection and environmental protection. Thus, the World Commission on Environment and Development (the "Brundt-land Commission"), reporting to the UN General Assembly in 1987, expressly addressed the need of "empowering vulnerable groups." The Brundtland Commission began by recalling that the process of development generally led to the gradual integration into a larger socio-economic framework of most local communities, but not all: "indigenous or tribal peoples," e.g., remained isolated, preserving their traditional way of life "in close harmony with the natural environment," but becoming increasingly vulnerable in their contacts with the larger world, as they were left out of the processes of economic development. Marginalization and dispossession, social discrimination and cultural barriers, have rendered those groups "victims of what could be described as cultural extinction."[146]

The Brundtland Commission approached the issue on the basis of both *human and environmental* considerations. It pondered:

These communities are the repositories of vast accumulations of traditional knowledge and experience that links humanity with its ancient origins. Their disappearance is a loss for the larger society, which could learn a great deal from their traditional skills in sustainably managing very complex ecological systems. . . .

The starting point for a just and humane policy for such groups is the recognition and protection of their traditional rights to land and the other resources that sustain their way of life – rights they may define in terms that do not fit into standard legal systems. These groups' own institutions to regulate rights and obligations are crucial for maintaining the harmony with na-

---

145. The Draft Declaration adds another element (§17) to the benefit of indigenous populations, namely: "The duty of States to seek and obtain their consent, through appropriate mechanisms, before undertaking or permitting any programmes for the exploration or exploitation of mineral and other subsoil resources pertaining to their traditional territories. Just and fair compensation should be provided for any such activities undertaken." Text in *id.* at 432–433.

146. World Commission on Environment and Development, *supra* note 14 at 114.

ture and the environmental awareness characteristic of the traditional way of life. . . .

Protection of traditional rights should be accompanied by positive measures to enhance the well-being of the community in ways appropriate to the group's life-style. . . .

In terms of sheer numbers, these isolated, vulnerable groups are small. But their marginalization is a symptom of a style of development that tends to neglect both human and environmental considerations. Hence a more careful and sensitive consideration of their interests is a touchstone of a sustainable development policy.[147]

Protection of vulnerable groups is an issue that can be raised as a result of changing environmental conditions. Global warming, for example, could destroy the traditional way of life of native peoples (e.g., those inhabiting countries bordering the Arctic), thus raising human rights issues in the light of provisions of, e.g., the UN Covenants (on Economic, Social, and Cultural Rights, Articles 1[1], 2, and 3; and on Civil and Political Rights, Articles 1[2] and 27).[148] This is just one example; as recently warned by Brown Weiss, "in the scenario projected under global warming, it is unlikely that we can salvage the environmental conditions necessary for these people to maintain their way of life. But, the international community may have a legal obligation to ensure the protection of the human rights of native peoples in the Arctic to the extent possible. This may require special assistance to give them opportunities for sustainable economic development, to ensure the protection of their culture insofar as possible, and to ease their transition into a different society."[149] The present example, taken from the projection of global warming, suffices again to illustrate the interrelatedness of human rights and environmental factors. This invites us to an inquiry into the proper meaning of "collective" rights (see section XI, *infra*).

VII. The recognition of the right to a healthy environment: The concern for environmental protection in international human rights instruments

A point of contact between human rights protection and environmental protection can in our day be detected in the concern for environ-

147. *Id.* at 114–116.
148. E. Brown Weiss, "Global Warming: Legal Implications for the Arctic," 2 *Georgetown International Environmental Law Review*, 95–96 (1989).
149. *Id.* at 96.

mental protection in international human rights instruments and, reversely, in the concern for human rights protection in international environmental law instruments. The former can be discerned in human rights instruments at both regional and global levels. The recognition of the right to a healthy or satisfactory environment in two instruments recently adopted in the American and African continents, respectively, provides a pertinent illustration in that regard. Let us turn to one and the other, before passing on to the global level.

In the American continent, the 1988 Additional Protocol to the American Convention on Human Rights in the Area of Economic, Social, and Cultural Rights, besides providing *inter alia* for the right to health (Article 10), the right to food (Article 12), and the right to just, equitable, and satisfactory conditions of work (so as, e.g., not to prejudice health – Article 7), expressly states (Article 11) that

1. Everyone shall have the right to live in a healthy environment and to have access to basic public services.
2. The States Parties shall promote the protection, preservation, and improvement of the environment.

We have here the express recognition, in a human rights instrument – the 1988 Protocol to the American Convention – of the human right to a healthy environment.

In the *travaux préparatoires* of the Protocol,[150] it was considered that the "concept of environment" had a sufficiently established meaning, with precedents in international instruments, so as to render it appropriate to retain and assert the norms (of Article 11) on the right to a healthy environment, strengthened by the provision whereby it was incumbent upon the States Parties to promote the protection, preservation, and improvement of the environment.[151] Hence the norm of Article 11 of the Protocol, as adopted in 1988. But the Protocol is not the only modern human rights instrument to contain a provision of the kind.

In the African continent, the 1981 African Charter on Human and Peoples' Rights, likewise, provides (Article 24) that "all peoples shall

150. *See* A.A. Cançado Trindade, "La question de la protection internationale des droits économiques, sociaux et culturels: évolution et tendances actuelles," 94 *Revue générale de droit international public* (1990) no. 3 (in print).
151. *See* OAS, doc. OEA/Ser. G-CP/CAJP-694/87, of 21 Oct. 1987, p. 14, and *see* p. 13. On the comments on the draft Article on the right to health by the Pan-American Health Organization, see OAS, doc. OEA/Ser. G-CP/CAJP-622/86 Add. 5, of 15 July 1986, pp. 83–85.

have the right to a general satisfactory environment favourable to their development." The acknowledgement, by the African Charter, of the right to a "general satisfactory environment," as peoples' right, takes place in view of the recognized duty of states to ensure the exercise of the right of development. Furthermore, the Charter's assertion of the individual's right "to enjoy the best attainable state of physical and mental health" as well as of the states' duty "to protect the health of their people" (Article 16) serves as a reminder to States Parties "to extend the benefits of their resources to the generality of their citizenry rather than to a minority."[152]

At the global level, the 1966 UN Covenant on Economic, Social, and Cultural Rights recognizes *inter alia* "the right of everyone to the enjoyment of the highest attainable standard of physical and mental health" (Article 12). It further recognizes "the right of everyone to an adequate standard of living for himself and his family, including adequate food, clothing and housing, and to the continuous improvement of living conditions" (Article 11). In 1989 the UN Sub-Commission on Prevention of Discrimination and Protection of Minorities adopted a decision (n. 1989/108) to have a note prepared on the methods whereby a study on the problems of the environment and its relation to human rights could be made.

The matter has been before the UN Commission on Human Rights, at its current XLVI session (1990). The Commission has just considered a draft resolution co-sponsored by 17 states on "Human Rights and the Environment"; the document relates the realization of the right to health recognized in Article 12 of the Covenant on Economic, Social, and Cultural Rights (*supra*) to the necessity "to take the steps necessary for the improvement of all aspects of environmental and industrial health."[153] Furthermore, the document expresses the belief that "the preservation of life-sustaining ecosystems under conditions of rapid scientific and technological development is of vital importance for the protection of the human species and the promotion of human rights."[154]

There are signs that the relationship between environmental protection and human rights protection will soon be attracting considerably more attention than it has until now, in the ambits of the United

---

152. U.O. Umozurike, "The African Charter on Human and Peoples' Rights," 77 A.J.I.L. 906 (1983); *see* E.G. Bello, "The African Charter on Human and Peoples' Rights – A Legal Analysis," 194 *Recueil des cours de l'Académie de droit international*, 147–148 (1985).
153. *See* U.N. doc. E/CN. 4/1990/L. 63/Rev. 1, of 5 Mar. 1990, p. 2
154. *Id.* at 2.

Nations and of regional fori. In this respect, the attention once drawn, in the European continent, by Steiger's project, to the protection of individuals also against the acts of private persons (*Drittwirkung,* see section XI, *infra*) seems deserving of attention for future consideration of a more perfected formulation, the articulation and implications of the right to a healthy environment.

This seems so given the complexity of the legal relations involved herein. The right to a healthy environment requires the protection against harmful acts of states as well as of private persons, and imposes duties on states, groups, or collectivities and individuals.[155] Not only the states but also groups and individuals are called upon to intervene in the implementation of that right. It has been commented that the right to a healthy environment "sort les citoyens d'un statut passif de bénéficiaires et leur fait partager des responsabilités dans la gestion des intérêts de la collectivité tout entière."[156]

Environmental questions, by their very nature, are, in their complexity, surrounded by interests and conflicts that are often "diffuse and fragmented." It is not surprising that they demand environmental decisions that "involve a complex web of actors: legislators, the administration, judges, the polluter, the victims, interest groups, and those that are economically dependent on the polluters."[157] This may pose difficulties for the implementation of the right to a healthy environment; yet we need to count on enforcement procedures proper to human rights protection, possibly adapted and extended or perfected.

VIII. Concern for the protection of human rights in the realm of international environmental law

Just as there is concern for environmental protection in international human rights law (*supra*), there is likewise concern for human rights protection in the realm of international environmental law. In a way, concern for human rights protection underlies environmental law instruments to the extent that these latter aim at the protection of the environment, which will ultimately benefit human beings and man-

---

155. A. Kiss, "Définition et nature juridique d'un droit de l'homme à l'environnement," *Environnement et droits de l'homme,* 25–26 (P. Kromarek, ed., Unesco, 1987); J.P. Jacque, "La protection du droit à l'environnement au niveau européen ou régional," in *id.* at 74.

156. A. Kiss, *supra* note 155 at 26.

157. A. Cassese, A. Clapham, and J. Weiler, *1992 – What Are Our Rights? – An Agenda for a Human Rights Action Plan,* 25 (European University Institute, 1989).

kind. Besides that, explicit references with a direct bearing on human rights protection can be found in the domain of international environmental law. The 1972 Stockholm Declaration on the Human Environment, for example, opens its preamble with the acknowledgement that man is both "creature and moulder of his environment," and that the natural and the man-made aspects of man's environment are "essential to his well-being and to the enjoyment of basic human rights – even the right to life itself" (§1).[158] Environmental protection is also linked to the "well-being of peoples" (§2). Thus, environmental protection and human rights protection are to be brought together. Principle 1 of the Stockholm Declaration provides an emphatic illustration of concern for human rights protection, in determining that "man has the fundamental right to freedom, equality and adequate conditions of life, in an environment of a quality that permits a life of dignity and well-being. . . ."[159]

The 1982 World Charter for Nature warns in its preamble that, as mankind is "part of nature" and "life depends on the uninterrupted functioning of natural systems" (§2 [a]), the preservation of the species and ecosystems is to be ensured for the benefit of present and future generations" (§5).[160] In its dispositive part, the Charter further warns that "man's needs can be met only by ensuring the proper functioning of natural systems" and by respecting the principles it sets forth (Principle 6); the Charter then provides for the human right to participate in the formulation of decisions of direct concern to the human environment and for the human right of access to means of redress when the human environment has suffered damage or degradation (i.e., rights of participation and to an effective remedy, Principle 23).[161]

The World Commission on Environment and Development, which reported to the UN General Assembly in 1987, proposed a set of legal principles for environmental protection and "sustainable development" (this latter defined as "development that meets the needs of the present without compromising the ability of future generations to meet their own needs").[162] The proposed legal principles, to serve as a basis for a future global convention on environmental protection and sustainable development under UN auspices, start with the asser-

158. Text in United Nations, *Report of the United Nations Conference on the Human Environment,* 3 (UN, 1973).
159. Text in *id.* at 4.
160. Text in *The World Charter for Nature,* 136, 140 (2nd rev. ed., E. Schmidt, 1986).
161. Text in *id.* at 186.
162. World Commission on Environment and Development, *supra* note 14 at 43.

tion of the following "fundamental human right" (Principle 1): "All human beings have the fundamental right to an environment adequate for their health and well-being."[163]

The Brundtland Commission also considered the recognition of "the right of individuals to know and have access to current information on the state of the environment and natural resources, the right to be consulted and to participate in decision-making on activities likely to have a significant effect on the environment."[164] Of the 22 Principles proposed by the Commission and prepared by its Group of Experts on Environmental Law, mention should here be made also of the recognition of the right to legal remedies and redress for those "whose health or environment has been or may be seriously affected";[165] all such persons are to be granted by states "equal access, due process and equal treatment in administrative and judicial proceedings" (Principle 20).[166]

While "in primitive law harmony between man and nature was to be achieved through rules protecting man from nature and securing him nature's benefits," in modern times the growing awareness of the exhaustibility of resources has led to developments in environmental protection "designed to protect nature from man."[167] However, these latter have taken place, it may be added, for the benefit ultimately of human beings in their environment, for the survival of mankind, of the human species. It is thus a question of protecting man from man himself, given his alarming capacity of destruction. From the perspective of the interrelationships between human rights protection and environmental protection, the "anthropocentric" outlook thus could hardly be minimized or discarded.

IX. Concern for the protection of the environment in the realm of international humanitarian law

It was not until recently that concern for the protection of the environment was manifested also in the realm of international humanitarian law. Two key provisions were inserted to that effect into the

163. Text in *id.* at 348; *see id.* at 330–333.
164. *Id.* at 330.
165. *Id.* at 330.
166. *See Report of the WCED Experts Group on Environmental Law* 11 (Document WCED/86/23/Add. 1, September 1986).
167. L.A. Teclaff, "The Impact of Environmental Concern on the Development of International Law," *International Environmental Law,* 260 (L.A. Teclaff and A.E. Utton, eds., Praeger, 1974); *see id.* at 259–262 for the argument of the reduction of the "anthropocentric systems."

1977 Additional Protocol I to the 1949 Geneva Conventions, namely, Article 35(3) and Article 55. Article 35(3) provides that "It is prohibited to employ methods or means of warfare which are intended, or may be expected, to cause widespread, long-term and severe damage to the natural environment." And Article 55 states:

1. Care shall be taken in warfare to protect the natural environment against widespread, long-term and severe damage. This protection includes a prohibition of the use of methods or means of warfare which are intended or may be expected to cause such damage to the natural environment and thereby to prejudice the health or survival of the population.
2. Attacks against the natural environment by way of reprisals are prohibited.

As aptly pointed out by A. Kiss, while Article 35(3) appears under the "Basic Rules" of Part III (methods and means of warfare, combatant and prisoner-of-war status) of the Protocol, thus having a wide scope, "applicable to all the situations envisaged by the Protocol," Article 55 does not appear under the "Basic Rules" of Part IV (civilian population) and is concerned with the protection in particular of the civilian population and objects. It has thus a more circumscribed scope, and not surprisingly, it follows a rather "anthropocentric" method.[168] One and another have in mind the damages that may threaten the health and survival of the population, thus not taking the environment as "une valeur intrinsèque" in itself, but rather "en fonction de la protection des humains."[169]

In fact, it could hardly be otherwise, if one is to approach the protection of the environment from the angle of its relationship with a branch of law deeply marked by the sentiment of *humanity* and turned to the respect and protection of victims of war (in enemy hands), the permissible methods and means of combat, and the international protection of human rights in armed conflicts. The temporal dimension is also present here, as inherent in this humanitarian goal is the ultimate and predominant objective of the very *prevention* of armed conflicts, to the benefit of mankind and the advances of civilization.[170]

168. A. Kiss, "Les Protocoles additionnels aux Conventions de Genève de 1977 et la protection de biens de l'environnement," *Etudes et essais sur le droit international humanitaire et sur les principes de la Croix-Rouge en l'honneur de Jean Pictet*, 184–186, 190 (Ch. Swinarski, ed., CICR/Martinus Nijhoff, 1984).
169. *Id.* at 190–192.
170. A.A. Cançado Trindade, "A Evolução do Direito Internacional Humanitário e as Posições do Brasil," 39–41 *Boletim da Sociedade Brasileira de Direito Internacional*, 76–107 (1987–1989).

What in sum one purports to protect here is ultimately mankind itself, and, in a sense, a sort of common heritage of mankind. Meyrowitz well identified in the concept of "conservation de l'humanité" the foundation of international humanitarian law;[171] the same, it may be added, holds true of environmental law, at least from an "anthropocentric" (rather than a "cosmic") approach, ineluctable here. The *ultima ratio legis,* as it stands, is common to one and the other: survival of mankind (or, more precisely: in international human rights law and refugee law, of man – the human person – and mankind; in international humanitarian law, of mankind as such; in international environmental law, of mankind in its environment). If the safeguard of human rights – in times of peace as well as here in times of armed conflicts – requires environmental protection, and a clean and healthful environment, there is then an identification of the conceptual *ultima ratio legis* of one and the other (human rights protection *lato sensu* and environmental protection), which thus appear interrelated.

Turning back to the Additional Protocol I of 1977, a parallel has been drawn, with respect to the prohibition of methods or means of warfare having widespread, long-term, and severe damage to the environment, between its Article 35(3) and the 1977 UN Convention on the Prohibition of Military or Any Other Hostile Use of Environmental Modification Techniques.[172] The concept of "environmental modification techniques" is found in Article 2; attention should also be paid to the 1980 Convention on Prohibitions or Restrictions of the Use of Certain Conventional Weapons (especially its Protocol III on Prohibitions or Restrictions on the Use of Incendiary Weapons).

The concept of the natural environment enshrined in Article 55 of the Additional Protocol I of 1977 is to be understood in its "widest sense," so as to cover "the biological environment in which a population is living"; Article 55 stresses the securing of the survival of the population when addressing itself to damages to the environment, and even expressly refers to "health," bearing in mind acts that could seriously prejudice health.[173] One could venture to say that the *right to life,* the *right to health,* and to some extent the *right to physical in-*

171. H. Meyrowitz, "Réflexions sur le fondement du droit de la guerre," *Etudes et essais sur le droit international humanitaire et sur les principes de la Croix-Rouge en l'honneur de Jean Pictet,* 430–431 (Ch. Swinarski, ed., CICR/Martinus Nijhoff, 1984).

172. Jean de Preux, Comment, "Protocol I, Article 35 – Basic Rules," *Commentary on the Additional Protocols of 8 June 1977 to the Geneva Conventions of 12 August 1949,* 411–418 (Y. Sandoz, Ch. Swinarski, and B. Zimmermann, eds., ICRC/Martinus Nijhoff, 1987).

173. Claude Pilloud and Jean Pictet, Comment, "Protocol I, Article 55 – Protection of the Natural Environment," in *Commentary on the Additional Protocols, supra* note 172 at 662–664.

tegrity appear as "bridges" between the domains of international human rights law, humanitarian law, refugee law, and environmental law. The right to life, in particular, appears as a fundamental right that is at the basis of the ultimate *ratio legis* of the above-mentioned domains of international law turned to the protection and survival of the human person and of mankind.

Two other provisions of Protocol I of 1977 have an indirect bearing on the purposes of the present study, namely, Articles 56 and 36. Article 56 provides for the protection of works and installations containing "dangerous forces" (e.g., dams, dykes, nuclear electrical generating stations).[174] And Article 36 provides for the obligation of the High Contracting Parties to determine the possibly unlawful character of certain new weapons (existing and future weapons that may cause unnecessary suffering or have indiscriminate effects); in the preparatory work of this provision the experts were concerned (as to future weapons) with "geophysical, ecological, electronic and radiological warfare as well as with devices generating radiation, microwaves, infrasonic waves, light flashes and laser beams."[175] Concerned with the problem of the technological development of armaments and the indiscriminate character of combat, the obligation enshrined in Article 36 purported to ensure that (new) methods or means of combat would not be adopted without the issue of legality being carefully considered: hence the obligation of the Parties to determine the legality or illegality of the use of "any new weapon introduced into their armed forces," which implied "the obligation to establish internal procedures with a view to elucidating the problem of illegality."[176]

Unlike Protocol I, the Additional Protocol II of 1977 does not contain provisions directly concerning the protection of the environment, but it does contain provisions that have an indirect bearing on the purposes of the present study, namely, Articles 14 and 15. Article 14, which prohibits the starvation of civilians as a method of combat, further prohibits therefore the destruction to that end of "objects indispensable to the survival of the civilian population, such as food-

---

174. *See* Claude Pilloud and Jean Pictet, Comment, "Protocol I, Article 56 – Protection of Works and Installations Containing Dangerous Forces," in *Commentary on the Additional Protocols, supra* note 172 at 667–669; *see id.* at 669–675.

175. Jean de Preux, Comment, "Protocol I, Article 36 – New Weapons," *Commentary on the Additional Protocols, supra* note 172 at 427.

176. Thus, other Contracting Parties could "ask for information on this point"; *id.* at 424, 428; *see id.* at 421–428.

stuffs, agricultural areas for the production of foodstuffs, crops, livestock, drinking water installations and supplies and irrigation works." And Article 15 prohibits attacks on works or installations containing "dangerous forces" (e.g., dams, dykes, nuclear electrical generating stations) if such attacks could release dangerous forces thereby causing "severe losses among the civilian population."[177]

Last but not least, it should be added that the World Charter for Nature, adopted by the UN General Assembly in 1982, states that "nature shall be secured against degradation caused by warfare or other hostile activities" (§5), and that "military activities damaging to nature shall be avoided" (§20).[178] From all the above-mentioned provisions it can hardly be doubted that the protection of the environment has become a matter of concern also in the realm of international humanitarian law.

X. Protection of the environment and international refugee law

1. Protection of victims of environmental disasters under refugee law

Some recent developments in international refugee law at the regional level, in particular with regard to the current Central American crisis, are worthy of attention. In order to tackle the problem of massive flows of refugees in the Central American area, the UN High Commissioner for Refugees (UNHCR) deemed it "necessary to consider enlarging the concept of a refugee." To that effect it adopted criteria on the basis of the precedent of the 1969 OAU Convention Governing the Specific Aspects of Refugee Problems in Africa, Article 1(2) – adopted precisely to face a similar problem in Africa – and of the doctrine upheld in reports of the Inter-American Commission of Human Rights.[179] A resulting concept was reached at the UNHCR Colloquy of Cartagena de Indias of 1984,[180] embodied in the docu-

---

177. For comments, *see Commentary on the Additional Protocols, supra* note 172 at 1455–1464.
178. Cit. in A. Kiss, *supra* note 168 at 192. For the preparatory work of those provisions, *see* W.E. Burhenne and W.A. Irwin, *The World Charter for Nature*, 54–55, 79–82 (2nd rev. ed., E. Schmidt, 1986).
179. ACNUR/UNHCR, *Declaración de Cartagena/Cartagena Declaration*, 34 (ACNUR/ Universidad de Cartagena, 1984).
180. Attended by a group of experts, as well as governmental delegates from Belize, Colombia, Costa Rica, El Salvador, Guatemala, Honduras, Mexico, Nicaragua, Panama, and Venezuela; *see id.* at 3–8.

ment that came to be known as the "Cartagena Declaration on Refugees."

Therein the definition or concept of a refugee recommended for use in the Central American region is one that

in addition to containing the elements of the 1951 Convention [Relating to the Status of Refugees] and the 1967 Protocol [Relating to the Status of Refugees], includes among refugees persons who have fled their country because their lives, safety or freedom have been threatened by generalized violence, foreign aggression, internal conflicts, massive violation of human rights or other circumstances which have seriously disturbed public order.[181]

The situations referred to above, it can be assumed, are caused by man, or would in principle have to be caused by man, so as to be encompassed by the new, amplified concept of a refugee recommended by the Cartagena Declaration. It can promptly be asked, What does the expression "other circumstances" cover? Would, or could, it also comprise, e.g., victims of (man-made) environmental changes or accidents? Before turning to this point, it should be added that the Cartagena Declaration was followed, and dwelt upon, by two other documents. The first one is the 1987 Report of a Group of Experts that met at UNHCR headquarters in Geneva to examine possible solutions to the problems of Central American refugees.

The 1987 Report, after referring to the 1984 Cartagena Declaration as a regional expression of refugee law (which reflected international practice on the matter and could thus lead to the crystallization of a "regional custom"), warned that the refugee problem in Central America was inserted into a "wider context of *desplazamiento poblacional*."[182] The Report *inter alia* referred to measures aiming at the *prevention* of causes that originated current massive flows of Central American refugees; those measures concerned the settlement of the conflicts and crisis in the region on the basis of the application of the principles of international law proclaimed in the UN Charter, the consolidation of the processes of democratization in the region, the respect for the observance of human rights (in particular those recognized in the 1969 American Convention on Human Rights), and the promotion of economic and social development in the region.[183]

The second and more recent document is the one submitted by a Committee of Legal Experts to the International Conference on Cen-

---

181. *Id.* at 14, 34.
182. ACNUR/UNHCR, *Grupo de Consulta sobre Posibles Soluciones a los Problemas de los Refugiados Centroamericanos – Informe*, 2–3 (UNHCR, 1987).
183. *Id.* at 7–8.

tral American Refugees (CIREFCA) in 1989,[184] titled "Principles and Criteria for the Protection of and Assistance to Central American Refugees, Returnees and Displaced Persons in Latin America." The document was advanced as a general framework for assistance to the states concerned in their treatment of refugees, returnees, and displaced persons in the Central American region.

The 1989 document, after recalling the "fundamental importance" of the Cartagena Declaration despite its not being technically a legally binding instrument,[185] then provides an interpretation of the expanded concept of a refugee – passage quoted above – advanced by the 1984 Cartagena Declaration (*supra*). According to the 1989 document, the expression "other circumstances which have seriously disturbed public order" ought to cover "the result of human actions and not of natural disasters." Moreover, "economic migrants" should not be confused with "victims of natural disasters"; these latter – the 1989 document adds – do not qualify as refugees, unless there occur "special circumstances" closely linking them to the refugee definition.[186]

Might it here not be added that a distinction should be borne in mind between natural disasters and environmental disasters? The victims of "pure" natural disasters (e.g., volcanoes, lightning, earthquakes, hurricanes, tidal waves, etc.) would remain outside the scope of the 1984 Cartagena definition. But the victims of environmental disasters (caused by human error or negligence, e.g., nuclear disasters, international water-pollution accidents, oil spills, forest fires, droughts as a consequence of climatic change, etc.) could fall under the "other circumstances" provided for by the 1984 Cartagena definition (*supra*), and thus benefit from refugee-law protection. It could in this connection be argued that climatic change is not only a "natural disaster," or not purely one, as it presents human intervention;[187] the victims of climatic changes (e.g., affecting the

184. The Conference was held in Guatemala City 29–31 May 1989. The document, prepared in January 1989, counted on comments submitted by the governments concerned. *See* UNHCR, document CIREFCA/89/9, 1989, p. 1 (English revised version).
185. *Id.* at 3.
186. *Id.* at 7–8.
187. To environmental disasters there thus apply, besides the general duty of preventing them, the general duty of minimizing damage and providing emergency assistance – comprising the obligations to notify promptly and to provide information, to develop contingency plans, and to cooperate in minimizing damage – and the general duty of compensating for injuries from them. *See* E. Brown Weiss, "Environmental Disasters in International Law," *Anuario Jurídico Interamericano,* 141–169 (1986); A. Kiss, "L'accident de Tchernobyl et ses conséquences au point de vue du Droit international," 32 *Annuaire français de droit international,* 139–152 (1986).

production of food) could thus arguably count on the protection envisaged herein.

Displaced persons in different circumstances constitute a category that requires careful attention and not seldom they are in greater need of protection than the refugees who have left the country – as admitted by the 1989 document itself.[188] There is, furthermore, a close link between the flows of refugees and human rights protection, as gross violations of human rights bring about flows – at times on a massive scale – of refugees,[189] raising difficulties for the mechanisms of protection. The protection of refugees and displaced persons is thus to be properly coordinated with the mechanisms of human rights protection (at global and regional levels).[190] And the emergence of human collectivities in need of special attention and protection – internationally displaced persons, internal displaced persons, returnees, so-called "economic migrants," etc. – give a new and wider dimension to international refugee law.

2. The intertemporal dimension of international refugee law

For the purposes of the present study, besides the possible assimilation of victims of environmental disasters to protected persons under refugee law, there is another point deserving of attention, and likewise unexplored to date: that of the intertemporal dimension of international refugee law. This dimension is always present, at distinct levels; for example, environmental disasters, though appearing as "immediate"-term phenomena, may affect people also in the long-term. There may be victims of phenomena or accidents caused by man with long-term effects. Such long-term victims may well appear as displaced persons for the purpose of protection under international refugee law.

The temporal dimension is further manifest in the endeavours of *prevention* or *forecasting* of refugee flows. It is precisely the *threat* of violence that leads to movements of refugees; the time element is underlying the very notion of forced migrants, who leave home on perceiving a *threat* or probability of violence.[191] In this connection, the expression *"early warning,"* coined in the realm of environmental

---

188. *See id.* at 14.
189. *See id.* at 15.
190. *See id.* at 15.
191. L. Gordenker, *Refugees in International Politics*, 170, 179 (Croom Helm, 1987); *see id.* at 168–173, 176–180.

law, has lately been utilized also in the ambit of refugee law and human rights protection.

Thus, the UN Secretary-General himself has had occasion to stress the importance of providing early warning of developing situations concerning possible refugee outflows. The special rapporteur of the UN Commission on Human Rights on the question of massive exoduses recommended in 1981 the establishment of an early-warning system on the basis of impartial information-gathering so as to forewarn of potential exoduses and to consider preventive action before the start of a mass movement. In UN debates on the matter, the possibility was raised of elaborating guidelines, of a preventive nature, to avert new flows of refugees and to cope with problems raised by mass flows of refugees.[192] In that same year, the UN General Assembly established a Group of Governmental Experts on International Cooperation to Avert New Flows of Refugees, which reported on the matter in 1986. The need has been stressed of rendering the UN system "more effective in anticipating major humanitarian problems, particularly those which could lead to mass movements of populations,"[193] using the UN Centre for Human Rights as the focal point in developing UN mechanisms to that end.

Endeavours to prevent floods of refugees were in fact undertaken, on the basis of an agreement signed in 1979, by Vietnam and UNHCR.[194] In another case, in a resolution adopted in 1985, the UN Sub-Commission on Prevention of Discrimination and Protection of Minorities alerted the UN Commission on Human Rights that the *human rights situation in Pakistan* was one with "great potential to cause a mass exodus, especially of members of the Ahmadi community."[195]

Early warning, to cope with the problems raised by forced migrants – especially when in large numbers and in conditions of distress – comprises the gathering of information and projections from that information, so as to enable "a prediction of future disaster."[196] That information can further be used for "the framing of policies and pro-

192. B.G. Ramcharan, *Humanitarian Good Offices in International Law,* 141–149 (Martinus Nijhoff, 1983).
193. B.G. Ramcharan, "Early-Warning at the United Nations: The First Experiment," 1 *International Journal of Refugee Law,* 382 (1989): *see id.* at 379–382.
194. For a criticism of the "preventive programmes" of the so-called "orderly departure system" and the "moratorium on departures" in the Vietnam case (1979–1984), *see* L. Gordenker, *supra* note 191 at 181–183.
195. Cit in B.G. Ramcharan, *supra* note 193 at 384.
196. L. Gordenker, *supra* note 191 at 174–175.

grammes to cope with forced migration"; the employment of early warning can be directed largely to two main situations, namely, to "the prevention or containment of an outflow of people" or, when that is no longer possible (when migration has already begun), to the amelioration of the situation.[197] In either case, early warning would be directed at intergovernmental organizations and relevant voluntary groups concerned so as to take the necessary (preventive) measures and to prepare assistance.[198]

In 1984 the UN Centre for Human Rights suggested that the following criteria be used as a basis for the assessment of the gathered information, so as to identify situations that could lead to massive movements of people: "(a) a large number of people are affected; (b) a serious likelihood exists that a mass movement of people might take place; and (c) the movement taking place might extend across international borders."[199] Situations of the kind, affecting human collectivities, call for compliance with obligations similar to those propounded for treating victims, or potential victims, of environmental disasters (e.g., prevention, prompt information, minimization of distress, contingency plans, emergency assistance, and compensation).[200]

XI. The question of the implementation (*mise en oeuvre*) of the right to a healthy environment

1. The issue of justiciability

It can hardly be doubted that the appropriate formulation of a right may facilitate its implementation. But given that certain concepts escape any scientific definition, it becomes necessary to relate them to a given context for the sake of normative precision and effective implementation (*mise en oeuvre*); thus, e.g., the term "environment" may be taken to cover from the immediate physical *milieu* surrounding the individual concerned to the whole of the biosphere, and it may thus be necessary to add qualifications to the term.[201] In the im-

197. *Id.* at 174.
198. *Id.* at 174.
199. Cit. in B.G. Ramcharan, *supra* note 193 at 383.
200. *See supra* note 187. *See* the two 1986 IAEA Conventions on Nuclear Accidents (Early Notification and Assistance), 25 *I.L.M.* 1369–86 (1986).
201. A. Kiss, "La mise-en-oeuvre du droit à l'environnement: problématique et moyens," *II Conférence européenne sur l'environnement et les droits de l'homme,* 4 (Institute for European Environmental Policy, 1980) (mimeographed, restricted circulation).

plementation of any right one can hardly make abstraction of the context in which it is invoked and applies: relating it to the context becomes necessary for its vindication in the *cas d'espèce*.[202]

This applies not only to the right to a healthy environment, but also to any other "category" of rights. But such "new" rights as the right to a healthy environment and the right to development present admittedly a greater challenge when one comes to implementation: while many of the previously crystallized civil and political, and economic, social, and cultural rights had at a much earlier stage found expression also in domestic law and had been formally recognized in national constitutions and other legislation, the above-mentioned "new" rights, in their turn, were still "maturing" in their process of transformation into law, were "conceived directly in international forums" (such as the United Nations system), and had "not had the benefit of careful prior scrutiny at the national level."[203] Many rights, whether classified as civil and political, or else as economic, social, and cultural rights, "can only be defined with specificity when located in a given context."[204]

While the element of *formal justiciability* is taken as an "indispensable attribute" of a right in positivist thinking,[205] international human rights law has distinctly considered that "an international system for the 'supervision' of States' compliance with international human rights obligations is sufficient to satisfy the requirement of 'enforceability'."[206] In short, international human rights law has "clearly adopted the notions of 'implementation' and 'supervision' as its touchstones, rather than those of justiciability or enforceability."[207] International human rights law counts largely on means of implementation other than the purely judicial one;[208] besides recourse to such judicial organs as the European and the Inter-American Courts of Human Rights, there occurs most often resort to

---

202. *Id.* at 5.
203. Ph. Alston, "Conjuring up New Human Rights: A Proposal for Quality Control," 78 A.J.I.L. 614 (1984).
204. For example, "it would not seem inherently more difficult for a particular society to define a 'right to primary education' (an economic right) than a 'right to take part in the conduct of public affairs' (a political right)." Ph. Alston, "Making Space for New Human Rights: The Case of the Right to Development," *Harvard Human Rights Yearbook,* 35 (1988).
205. *Id.* at 33.
206. *Id.* at 38.
207. *Id.* at 35.
208. K. Vasak, "Pour les droits de l'homme de la troisième génération: les droits de solidarité," *Résumés des cours de l'Institut International des droits de l'homme* (X Session d'Enseignement, 1979), 6 (IIDH, 1979) (mimeographed).

various other means – non-judicial means – of implementation of guaranteed human rights (e.g., friendly settlement, conciliation, fact-finding).[209]

Formal justiciability or enforceability is by no means a definitive criterion to ascertain the existence of a right under international human rights law. The fact that many recognized human rights have not yet achieved a level of elaboration so as to render them justiciable does not mean that those rights simply do not exist: enforceability is not to be confounded with the existence itself of a right.[210] Attention is to be focused on the *nature* of obligations; it is certain that, for example, obligations under the UN Covenant on Economic, Social, and Cultural Rights were elaborated in such a way (e.g., the basic provisions of Articles 2 and 11) that they "cannot easily be made justiciable (manageable by third-party judicial settlement). Nevertheless, the obligations exist and can in no way be neglected."[211]

One is to reckon, in sum, as far as the issue of justiciability is concerned, that there are rights that simply cannot be properly vindicated before a tribunal by their active subjects ("titulaires"). In the case specifically of the right to a healthy environment, however, if, as pertinently pointed out by Kiss, this latter is interpreted not as the – virtually impossible – right to an ideal environment but rather as the right to the conservation – i.e., protection and improvement – of the environment, it can then be implemented like any other *individual* right. It is then taken as a "procedural" right, the right to a due process before a competent organ, and thus assimilated to any other right guaranteed to individuals and groups of individuals. This right entails, as corollaries, the right of the individual concerned *to be informed* of projects and decisions that could threaten the environment (the protection of which counts on preventive measures) and the right of the individual concerned *to participate* in the taking of decisions that may affect the environment (active sharing of responsibilities in the management of the interests of the whole collectivity).[212] To such

209. For a recent study of the operation of international mechanisms of human rights protection, *see* A.A. Cançado Trindade, *supra* note 2 at 21–435.
210. A. Eide, "Realization of Social and Economic Rights and the Minimum Threshold Approach," 10 *Human Rights Law Journal,* 36, 38 (1989).
211. *Id.* at 41.
212. A. Kiss, *supra* note 126 at 69–87. As the environment is a common good ("le bien de tous"), "l'ensemble du corps social aussi bien que les groupes ou que les individus qui le composent sont appelés à participer à sa gestion et à sa protection"; P. Kromarek, "Le droit à un environnement équilibré et sain, considéré comme un droit de l'homme: sa mise-en-oeuvre nationale, européenne et internationale," *I Conférence européenne sur*

rights to information and to participation one can add the *right to available and effective domestic remedies*. And it should not in this connection be overlooked that some economic and social rights were made enforceable in domestic law once their component parts were "formulated in a sufficiently precise and detailed manner."[213]

Focusing on the *subjects* of the right to a healthy environment, we see first that it has an individual dimension, as it can be implemented, as just indicated, like other human rights. But the beneficiaries of the right to a healthy environment are not only individuals, but also groups, associations, human collectivities, and, indeed, the whole of mankind. Hence its collective dimension as well. The right to a healthy environment, like the right to development, discloses both individual and collective dimensions at a time. If the subject is an individual or a private group, the legal relationship is exhausted in the relation between the individual (or group of individuals) and the state; but if we have in mind mankind as a whole, the legal relationship is not exhausted in that relation. This is probably why the distinction between individual and collective dimensions is often resorted to.

If we focus on *implementation,* it is conceded that all rights, whether "individual" or "collective," are exercised in a societal context, all having a "social" dimension in that sense, since their vindication requires the intervention – in varying degrees – of public authority for them to be exercised. There is, however, yet another approach that can shed some light on the problem at issue: to focus on the *object* of protection. Taking as such an object a common good, a *bien commun* such as the human environment, not only are we thereby provided with objective criteria to approach the subject, but also we can better grasp the proper meaning of "collective" rights.

---

l'environnement et les droits de l'homme 15 (Institute for European Environmental Policy, 1979) (mimeographed, restricted circulation). On the remedies (in domestic comparative law) for the exercise of the right to information and the right of participation, *see* L.P. Suetens, "La protection du droit à l'information et du droit de participation: les recours," *II Conférence européenne sur l'environnement et les droits de l'homme,* 1–13 (Institute for European Environmental Policy, 1980) (mimeographed, restricted circulation); and, on private recourses for environmental harm (in domestic comparative law), *see Environmental Pollution and Individual Rights: An International Symposium,* xvii–xxiii, 3–162 (S.C. McCaffrey and R.E. Lutz, eds., Deventer, Kluwer, 1978). On the "procedural" conception of the right to the conservation of the environment, *see* A. Kiss, "Peut-on parler d'un droit à l'environnement?", *Le droit et l'environnement – Actes des Journées de l'Environnement du C.N.R.S.,* 309–317 (1988).

213. A. Eide, *supra* note 210 at 36.

Such rights pertain at a time to each member as well as to all members of a given human collectivity, the object of protection being the same, a common good (*bien commun*) such as the human environment, so that the observance of such rights benefits at a time each member and all members of the human collectivity, and the violation of such rights affects or harms at a time each member and all members of the human collectivity at issue. This reflects the essence of "collective" rights, such as the right to a healthy environment insofar as the *object* of protection is concerned.

The multifaceted nature of the right to a healthy environment becomes thus clearer: the right to a healthy environment has both individual and collective dimensions – being at a time an "individual" and a "collective" right – insofar as its *subjects or beneficiaries* are concerned. Its "social" dimension becomes manifest insofar as its *implementation* is concerned (given the complexity of the legal relations involved). And it clearly appears in its "collective" dimension insofar as the *object* of protection is concerned (a *bien commun,* the human environment).

The matter has not been sufficiently studied to date, and considerable in-depth reflection and research are required to clarify the issues surrounding the implementation of the right to a healthy environment and the very conceptual universe in which it rests. Insofar as the subjects of the relationships involved are concerned, one has moved from the individuals and groups to the whole of mankind, and in this wide range of *titulaires* one has also spoken of *generational* rights (rights of future generations – see *supra*). Insofar as the methods of protection are concerned, it still has to be carefully explored to what extent the mechanisms of protection evolved under international human rights law (essentially, the petitioning, the reporting, and the fact-finding systems)[214] can be utilized also in the realm of environmental protection.

It seems that the experience accumulated in this respect in the last decades in human rights protection can, if properly assessed, be of assistance to the development of methods of environmental protection. Some inspiration can indeed be derived from the experience of the application of mechanisms of international implementation of human rights, for the improvement of international implementation of instruments on environmental protection. It is, in this connection,

---

214. On their functioning and coordination, *see* A.A. Cançado Trindade, *supra* note 2 at 13–435.

reassuring to note that the conclusions of the recent Forum on International Law of the Environment, held in Siena, Italy, in April 1990, recognize *inter alia* that "certain procedures used for the protection of human rights could serve as models in the field of the protection of the environment."[215] Likewise, expert writing on international environmental law has suggested that UN international environmental organs could be given "powers similar to those" of the UN Committee on Economic, Social, and Cultural Rights "to study and comment on reports submitted by States since the right to a good environment is similar to and partakes of all the difficulties and drawbacks of social and economic rights."[216] Such acknowledgements are quite understanding and beneficial to environmental protection, given the fact that human rights protection antedates it in time, and experience with the implementation of the latter can be of use and value to the implementation of the former.

2. The issue of protection *erga omnes: "Drittwirkung"*

In the fields of both human rights protection and environmental protection there occur variations in the obligations: some norms are susceptible of direct applicability, others are rather programmatic in nature. Attention ought thus to be turned to the *nature* of the obligations. An important issue, in this connection, is that of the *erga omnes* protection of certain guaranteed rights, which raises the issue of third-party applicability of conventional provisions. This issue, called *"Drittwirkung"* in German legal literature, can be examined in the domains of both human rights protection and environmental protection.

In the former, *Drittwirkung* is still evolving in, e.g., the case-law under the European Convention on Human Rights[217] *(infra)*. Bearing in mind the considerable variety of rights guaranteed under human rights treaties, there are provisions in these latter that seem to indicate that at least some of the rights are susceptible of third-party applicability *(Drittwirkung)*. Thus, Article 2(1)(d) of the UN Conven-

---

215. *Conclusions of the Siena Forum on International Law of the Environment*, 8, §23 (April 1990) (mimeographed, restricted circulation).
216. L.A. Teclaff, *supra* note 167 at 252.
217. *See* A.Z. Drzemczewski, *European Human Rights Convention in Domestic Law – A Comparative Study*, 199–228 (Oxford University Press, 1983); J. Rivero, "La protection des droits de l'homme dans les rapports entre personnes privées," *René Cassin Amicorum Discipulorumque Liber*, 311 (vol. III, Pedone, 1971).

tion on the Elimination of All Forms of Racial Discrimination prohibits racial discrimination "by any persons, group or organization."
By Article 2(1) of the UN Covenant on Civil and Political Rights
States Parties undertake not only "to respect" but also "to ensure" to
all individuals subject to their jurisdictions the rights guaranteed
under the Covenant – what may be interpreted as at least the States
Parties' duty of due diligence to prevent deprivation or violation of
the rights of one individual by others. And it has been argued that
Article 17 of the Covenant (right to privacy) would cover protection
of the individual against interference by public authorities as well as
private organizations or individuals.[218] In addition, Article 29 of the
Universal Declaration of Human Rights refers to "everyone's duties
to the community."

The European Convention on Human Rights, in its turn, states in
Article 17 that nothing in the Convention may be interpreted as im-
plying "for any State, group or person," any right to engage in any
activity or perform any act aimed at the destruction of the guaranteed
rights. Articles 8–11 indicate that account is to be taken of the protection of other people's rights; and from Article 2, whereby "everyone's right to life is protected by law," it may be inferred the state's
duty of due diligence of prevention and of making its violation a
punishable offence.[219] It can in fact be forcefully added that the supreme values underlying fundamental human rights are such that
they deserve and require protection *erga omnes,* against any encroachment, by public or private bodies or by any individual.[220]

Even though the issue of *Drittwirkung* was not considered when
the European Convention was drafted, the subject-matter of the
Convention lends itself to *Drittwirkung,* in the sense that some of the
recognized rights deserve protection against public authorities as well
as private individuals, and states have to secure everyone – in the relations between individuals – against violations of guaranteed rights
by other individuals.[221] Thus, e.g., with regard to the right to privacy

---

218. Y. Dinstein, "The Right to Life, Physical Integrity, and Liberty," in *The International Bill
of Rights,* 119 (L. Henkin, ed., Columbia University, 1981); Jan De Meyer, "The Right to
Respect for Private and Family Life, Home and Communications in Relations between Individuals, and the Resulting Obligations for States Parties to the Convention," in A.H.
Robertson (ed.), *Privacy and Human Rights,* 263 (Manchester University, 1973).
219. E.A. Alkema, "The Third-Party Applicability of *'Drittwirkung'* of the European Convention on Human Rights," in *Protecting Human Rights: The European Dimension – Studies
in Honour of G.J. Wiarda,* 35–37 (F. Matscher and H. Petzold, eds., C. Heymanns,
1988).
220. *Id.* at 33–34.
221. This has led one to speak of a sort of "indirect *Drittwirkung,"* since "it is realized *via* an

(Article 8 of the Convention, on respect for private life), there is need to protect this right also in the relations *between* individuals (persons, groups, institutions, besides states). Situations have in fact occurred in practice where the state may be involved in the relations *between* individuals (e.g., custody of a child, clandestine recording of a conversation by a private individual with the help of the police).[222] Certain human rights have validity *erga omnes,* in that they are recognized in relation to the state but also and necessarily "in relation to other persons, groups or institutions which might prevent the exercise thereof."[223]

Thus, a human rights violation by individuals or private groups can be sanctioned indirectly, when the state fails, in "its duty to provide due protection," to take the necessary steps to prevent or punish the offence.[224] Article 8 of the European Convention pertinently illustrates the "absolute effect" of that right to privacy, the need for its protection *erga omnes* against frequent interferences or violations not only by public authorities but also by private persons or the mass media.[225]

In the same line, it has been forcefully argued that the right to a healthy environment ought to be "opposable aux tiers, avoir un effet direct à leur égard," ought to be "opposable directement aux particuliers de façon à assurer la protection des intérêts des individus et des groupes en matière d'environnement."[226] *Drittwirkung* amounts to the situation whereby everyone is beneficiary of that right and everyone has duties *vis-à-vis* the other citizens and *vis-à-vis* the whole community; "tout le monde est bénéficiaire de ce droit, mais en même temps tout le monde assume aussi des obligations de son fait: Etat, collectivités, individus."[227]

---

obligation of the State." P. van Dijk and G.J.H. van Hoof, *Theory and Practice of the European Convention on Human Rights,* 14–18 (Deventer, Kluwer, 1984).

222. Jan De Meyer, *supra* note 218 at 267–269.
223. *Id.* at 271; *see id.* at 272.
224. *Id.* at 273.
225. *Id.* at 274–275.
226. P. Kromarek, "Le droit a un environnement équilibré et sain, considéré comme un droit de l'homme: sa mise-en-oeuvre nationale, européenne et internationale," in *I Conférence européenne sur l'environnement et les droits de l'homme,* 38 (Institute for European Environmental Policy, 1979) (mimeographed, restricted circulation).
227. A. Kiss, *supra* note 126 at 80; *see id.* at 83. "En ce qui concerne le droit à l'environnement, tout le monde est 'créancier' et 'débiteur' en même temps: Etat, collectivités, individus." A. Kiss, "La mise en oeuvre du droit à l'environnement: problématique et moyens," in *II Conférence européenne sur "Environnement et droits de l'homme,"* 8 (Institut pour une Politique Européenne de l'Environnement, 1980) (mimeographed, restricted circulation); *see id.* at 6–9.

XII. The right to a healthy environment and the absence of restrictions in the expansion of human rights protection and environmental protection

1. No restrictions ensuing from the coexistence of international instruments on human rights protection

In the field of the international protection of human rights, restrictions are not to be inferred from the possible effects of multiple coexisting instruments of human rights protection upon each other: on the contrary, in the present context, international law has been made use of in order to improve and strengthen the degree of protection of recognized rights. In fact, the interpretation and application of certain provisions of one human rights instrument have at times been resorted to as orientation for the interpretation of corresponding provisions of other – usually newer – human rights instruments.[228]

Normative advances in one human rights treaty may indeed have a direct impact upon the application of other human rights treaties, to the effect of enlarging or strengthening the States Parties' obligations of protection and restricting the possible invocation or application of restrictions to the exercise of recognized rights. Multiple human rights instruments appear complementary to each other; and their complementarity reflects the specificity of the international protection of human rights, a domain of international law characterized as being essentially a *droit de protection*. Where states have undertaken obligations under multiple coexisting instruments of human rights protection, it may be taken to have been the intention to accord individuals a more extended and effective protection. In sum, there is here a clear trend towards the expansion and enhancement of the degree and extent of protection of rights recognized under coexisting human rights instruments.[229]

2. No restrictions ensuing from the coexistence of international instruments on environmental protection

Likewise, in the field of international environmental law, restrictions are not to be implied from the possible effects upon each other of multiple coexisting instruments on environmental protection. To this

228. A.A. Cançado Trindade, *supra* note 2 at 401, 101; *see id.* at 104.
229. *Id.* at 110, 121–122, 125.

310

effect, in its well-known 1987 report, the World Commission on Environment and Development, in propounding the elaboration of a
Universal Declaration and a Convention on Environmental Protection and Sustainable Development, stressed the need "to consolidate
and extend relevant legal principles" on the matter in order "to guide
State behaviour in the transition to sustainable development," and
warned that multiple coexisting as well as new international conventions and agreements in the area were to *strengthen and extend* environmental protection.[230] As in human rights protection (*supra*),
there is no room for (implied) restrictions in the present domain of
environmental protection either.

Having thus considered the point at issue from the perspective, on
the one hand, of the effects of human rights instruments upon each
other, and, on the other hand, of the effects of environmental protection instruments upon each other, we have found no room for the incidence of restrictions, as those instruments, in one and the other domain, were meant to reinforce each other and strengthen the degree
of protection due. It now remains to examine the point at issue from
the perspective of the effects of norms or instruments of human rights
protection and of environmental protection *inter se,* or more precisely, of the effects of the recognition of the right to a healthy environment upon the *corpus* of human rights already recognized.

3. No restrictions ensuing from the expansion of systems of protection (as evidenced by the recognition of the right to a healthy environment) in their effects upon each other

A fairly recent trend of thought has visualized in the emergence of
environmental policies of states the incidence of *restrictions* upon the
exercise of certain recognized human rights. It has further justified
these latter to the effect of protecting the environment. I have suggested that, while some of the more classical civil and political rights
are not apparently affected, certain economic and social rights are
susceptible of suffering restrictions. As examples, reference has been
made to the rights of free circulation, of choice of residence, and to
property, in face of protected areas or zones; the rights to work, in
face of antipollution measures; the right to equality, in face of disparities in administrative measures as to the environment; the freedom of association, in face of measures against noise pollution; the

---

230. World Commission on Environment and Development, *supra* note 14 at 332–333.

311

right to family, in face of birth-control measures; the right to development and to leisure, in face of measures for conservation of nature.[231]

This approach, it is submitted, is inadequate and short-sighted, even though it cannot fail to admit that the right to a healthy environment comes ultimately to guarantee and reinforce such basic rights as the right to life and the right to health.[232]

231. *See* F. Dore, "Conséquences des exigences d'un environnement équilibré et sain sur la définition, la portée et les limitations des differents droits de l'homme – Rapport introductif," *I Conférence européenne sur l'environnement et les droits de l'homme,* 3–5, 7–12, 14 (Institute for European Environmental Policy, 1979) (mimeographed, restricted circulation); *see* F. Dore, in *id.* at 25–27, 37–38 (mimeographed, restricted circulation).
232. *See* F. Dore, "Conséquences des exigences," in *I Conférence européenne sur l'environnement et les droits de l'homme, supra* note 231 at 16–19; F. Dore, *supra* note 231 at 27.

Future directions in international regimes

10

The implications of global change for the international legal system

Alexandre Kiss

Different theories explain in different ways the origin and the creation of legal norms.[1] As far as international law is concerned, its development during the last 50 years seems to have been guided by the need to face situations created by political events or by scientific or technical evolution. The creation of international human rights law between 1948 and 1969, although intellectually prepared during the first half of the century, was a direct reaction to the massacres and atrocities of the Second World War, while international space law and the new Law of the Sea were responses to the conquest of outer space by man and to the evolution of the sea's uses.

Of course, in most cases, political or scientific factors do not act directly upon the orientations of a legal system. Their impact is made by the intermediary knowledge that we have of their nature and potential implications. Such knowledge must enhance awareness of the need to react to a given situation. The importance of these elements must be stressed since they motivate and explain action.

Thus, we must understand global change as the awareness of a situation threatening our whole biosphere. The word "change" means in fact "challenge": It reminds us of the antic fable of the Sphinx: If we do not solve its enigma, we will perish.

Still, our knowledge, which is at the very base of action, is limited.

---

1. *See, Controversies autour de l'ontologie de droit,* 11, 27, 53 (P. Amselek, ed., Presses universitaire de France, 1989).

Science necessarily includes a part of uncertainty: we never know the whole truth and, in addition, at every moment new factors can appear, so that scientists must always be prepared to revise their position. However, such considerations must not prevent the adoption of legal rules. If we had waited for unanimous approval by all the scientists in the world before adopting safety regulations for nuclear activities, today there would by practically no such rules in this field. At a certain moment decision makers must make up their mind: their action will be strongly influenced by the awareness that the public may have of the problem. Thus, the process is a complex one composed of different sequences: facts – scientific findings – knowledge – awareness – decision-making, and the formulation of legal rules.

Taking into account these considerations, we may speak of a global challenge for international law. In the process that has been represented, we arrive now at the last stages, at least as far as certain aspects of global change are concerned: In some cases some legal rules already exist[2] and must be further developed; in others, decisions still must be taken and translated into international legal rules.[3] Anyway, even by now it can be useful to ask the question, what are the implications of global change on the international legal system, and what developments may be expected for the coming decades?

It is submitted that global change modifies the functions of the international legal system. Legal rules must be drafted in new fields, using new methods; existing rules must be implemented, sometimes by unusual means. Thus, new developments in the exercise of these functions are to be examined. However, such changes may also have an impact on the very structures of the international system. Reflections on the different aspects of such implications will form the second part of the present study.

The impact of global change on different functions in international law

In all legal systems different functions have to be fulfilled: legislation, execution, and control over the interpretation and the implementa-

---

2. Vienna Convention for the Protection of the Ozone Layer, 22 Mar. 1985, 26 *I.L.M.* 1529 (1987) (hereinafter Vienna Convention), completed by the Montreal Protocol to the Vienna Convention for the Protection of the Ozone Layer, on Substances That Deplete the Ozone Layer, Final Act. 16 Sept. 1987 (Reference File) Int'l Env't Rep. (BNA) 21:3151, 26 *I.L.M.* 1550 (1987) (hereinafter Montreal Protocol).
3. This is especially the case of the "greenhouse effect" resulting from the global warming of

tion of rules. One of the main characteristics – and one of the causes of the shortcomings – of international law is that although these functions exist, there are no corresponding organs that would ensure them on a generally obligatory basis. Law-making is still an occasional operation, based on the will of states; there is no executive power in the international field and international jurisdiction can only function with the consent of the concerned governments. Thus, modifications in the functions of international law may have a different scope than in the national legal systems.

Two aspects of such modifications due to global change seem to be of particular significance: the modifications in the law-making process on one side, and those in the implementation of rules on the other.

A. Implications of global change for the law-making process

The most dramatic change that occurred in international relations in the second half of the century was the expansion of the realm of international legal rules. These now cover large fields that formerly either fell into the exclusive jurisdiction of states, or did not exist at all as a matter for legal regulation. Examples are numerous in both categories. One may mention for the first field the protection of human rights, the improvement of labour conditions, health care, in addition to a number of economic activities; while for the second field one immediately thinks of the development of poor countries, the control of the production, trade, and use of drugs, the fight against terrorism and, of course, the protection of the environment.

It must be noted that in all these fields bilateral cooperation, which has been the general rule for international law, now only plays a secondary role: most actions need a multilateral approach. It seems that this fact is not sufficiently well understood. Environmental protection is a good example. At the end of the 1960s and the beginning of the 1970s, when growing environmental awareness had made it necessary to envisage the problem of international protection of the environment, the first approach of most international lawyers was to consider the problem as a conflict between two sovereignties caused by transfrontier pollution. Although, in order to face the more and more numerous environmental problems, multilateral conventions

the earth's climate. *See,* U.N.G.A. Res. Protection of Global Climate for Present and Future Generations of Mankind, U.N. GAOR A/Res/43/53 (1989).

were multiplied in the 1970s and 1980s, even now there is a general trend among international lawyers to limit their approach to a rather archaic bilateral one. The evolution and broadening of the minds in this field should certainly be one of the consequences of global change.

As far as international legislation is concerned, the most obvious consequence of global change is the rapidly growing number of multi-lateral treaties, often covering fields and problems that either did not exist or have not formerly been discovered.

The complexity of such problems leads to a second consequence, which was hardly understood at the beginning. At a certain stage of the law-making process, problem areas cannot be treated separately. The first approaches to environmental protection were essentially sectorial: separate norms and rules were adopted for continental waters, the sea, atmospheric pollution, and wildlife conservation. An important step forward was the terminology used in the UN Convention on the Law of the Sea,[4] which speaks of the protection and preservation of the marine environment. Apparently, this means more than only the water of the sea. Moreover, Article 195 of the Convention imposes upon states the duty "not to transfer, directly or indirectly, damage or hazards from one area to another or transform one type of pollution into another."[5] Thus the *interconnection* between different components of the environment has been recognized.

The following stage in this evolution was the understanding that, although sectorial approaches to environmental problems – handling separately water pollution,[6] sea pollution,[7] air pollution,[8] and wildlife conservation[9] – are still important, more attention should be paid to the substances that create pollution and that may be found in all

---

4. United Nations Convention on the Law of the Sea, 10 Dec. 1982, 21 *I.L.M.* 1261 (1982) (hereinafter Law of the Sea Convention), Art. 175, 1297.
5. *Id.* at Art. 145, 1308.
6. *See,* e.g., Great Lakes Water Quality Agreement, 22 Nov. 1978, U.S. – Canada, Annex 9, 30 U.S.T. 1383, T.I.A.S. 9257; Bonn Convention on the Protection of the Rhine Against Chemical Pollution, 3 Dec. 1976, 16 *I.L.M.* 242 (1977); Convention Concerning Accidental Pollution of Lake Geneva, 5 May 1977, XXV *Int'l Protections of the Environment,* 285 (Ruester, Simma, and Bock, eds., Oceana, 1981).
7. Law of the Sea Convention, *supra* note 4. *See also,* London Convention on the Prevention of Marine Pollution by Dumping of Wastes and Other Matter, 29 Dec. 1972, 26 U.S.T. 2403, T.I.A.S. No. 8165; Barcelona Convention for the Protection of the Mediterranean Sea Against Pollution, 16 Feb. 1976, 15 *I.L.M.* 290 (1976).
8. Geneva Convention on Long-Range Transboundary Air Pollution, 13 Nov. 1979, 18 *I.L.M.* 1442, T.I.A.S. 10541 (1979) (hereinafter L.R.T.A.P. Convention).
9. Bern Convention on the Conservation of European Wildlife and Natural Habitats, 19 Sept.

the different areas. The latest approach to the protection of the biosphere consists thus in the international control of potentially harmful substances at the different stages of their existence: production, transport, trade, use, and elimination of chemicals and of radioactive material.[10]

This evolution already implies a strong tendency toward globalization: the international transportation of toxic or dangerous chemical substances or waste, the "exportation" of harmful activities to other – mainly developing – countries cannot be controlled without worldwide cooperation. The situation is the same in other fields, such as the trade of drugs or the struggle against certain diseases such as AIDS. In addition, during the last decade we became aware of the existence of problems that cannot be approached without planetary cooperation and thus legislation: for example, the depletion of the ozone layer, the modification of the global climate, and the threats against the world's genetic heritage. Different factors inherent in such problems need new approaches in the legal techniques used by the international community for law-making.

a.

One of the most striking features of the international legislation since 1945 is the enormous importance of "soft-law" instruments, for example, the texts that were adopted by states without being legally binding. Of course, the first and most evident cause for this is the expansion of the number of international bodies that have not been endowed with the power to adopt mandatory texts, but only recommendations. As a consequence, this is the only way to address their member states. However, one should not forget that originally such resolutions could only correspond to the current work and management of the concerned international body, while in reality resolutions of certain international organs, such as the UN General Assembly, play an important role in the international legislative process. This is not the place to discuss the legal nature of such resolutions and especially their binding force. At a minimum it can be asserted that they participate in the creation of new international law rules, formulating

---

1979, E.T.S. 107 (1979). *See also,* A. Kiss, "La protection internationale de la vie sauvage," 1980 *Annuaire français de droit international,* 661–686.

10. *See,* e.g., South Pacific Nuclear Free Zone Treaty, 6 Aug. 1985, 24 *I.L.M.* 1440 (1985); Basel Convention on the Control of Transboundary Movements of Hazardous Waste and Their Disposal, 22 Mar. 1989, UNEP/IG-80/3 (1989) (hereinafter Basel Convention).

for the first time emerging social values that later on may be formally confirmed by international conventions. This was the way international law was developed in new fields such as the international protection of human rights, or the status of outer space. For environmental protection, the evolution is less lineal, but texts such as the 1972 Stockholm Declaration[11] or the World Charter for Nature, adopted and solemnly proclaimed by the UN General Assembly on 28 October 1982,[12] certainly have paved the way for formal legislative activities.

b.

Soft-law instruments can also play a more technical role. "Resolutions," "conclusions," and "guidelines," may include technical details that are to be evaluated by states and may be included, at the end of the day, either in a formal international treaty[13] or introduced in national legislation.[14] This can be explained by the newness of the solutions suggested by the international bodies – understanding that such newness is mostly imposed by a new situation that has to be coped with.

c.

Soft-law rules can also be included in formally binding international instruments, i.e. treaty provisions. As a matter of fact, quite often such provisions contain nothing more than strong recommendations for the contracting parties. Without speaking of clauses such as "each State Party to this convention shall endeavor, in so far as possible, and as appropriate for each country. . . ."[15] which can hardly be con-

---

11. Stockholm Declaration on the Human Environment of the United Nations Conference on the Human Environment, 16 June 1972, 11 *I.L.M.* 1716 (1972) (hereinafter Stockholm Declaration).

12. U.N.G.A. Res. 37/7, 37 U.N. GAOR Supp. (No. 51); The World Charter for Nature at 17, U.N. Doc A/37/51 (1982).

13. This was the case of the Universal Declaration of Human Rights followed by the two UN Covenants on Human Rights.

14. Although it is difficult to know how far national legislation has been influenced by non-mandatory international instruments, it seems that principles such as those stated by the Council of Europe's Declaration on Air Pollution Control, 8 March 1968, Resolution (68)4, or the guidelines established by the UNEP Working Group of Experts on Environmental Law on Aspects Concerning the Environment Related to Offshore Drilling and Mining within the Limits of National Jurisdiction, February 1981, 7 *Environmental Policy and Law,* 50, February 1981, have inspired national legislators.

15. Unesco Convention Concerning the Protection of the World Cultural and Natural Heritage, 16 Nov. 1972, 27 U.S.T. 37, T.I.A.S. 8226, 11 *I.L.M.* 1358 (1972), Art. 5.

sidered as imposing strict obligations upon states, the content of the treaty itself may be, in reality, nothing more than a declaration of intention. A good example for this is the 1979 Convention on Long-Range Transboundary Air Pollution.[16] The contracting parties "are determined to protect man and his environment against air pollution and shall endeavor to limit and, as far as possible, gradually reduce and prevent air pollution. . . ."[17] They also will "develop without undue delay, policies and strategies which shall serve as a means of combating the discharge of air pollutants."[18]

They also shall undertake "to develop the best policies and strategies" in order to combat air pollution.[19] As a matter of fact, in spite of its appearances, this convention is an operative one and has created a useful framework for everyday cooperation as well as for the development of further international rules that are more stringent.[20]

d.

A growing number of treaties do not include immediate obligations for the contracting states, instead they develop programmes of action. One of the first was the Paris Convention for the Prevention of Marine Pollution from Land-Based Sources, adopted on 4 June 1974, which provides that, for carrying out the undertakings resulting from that Convention, "the Contracting Parties, jointly or individually as appropriate, shall implement programmes and measures. . . ."[21] It may be considered that such provisions are between "soft" and "hard" treaty obligations, since the content of the duties resulting from the treaty are not defined. As a result, it could hardly be enforced by an international jurisdiction.

e.

Not very different from this method is that of the "pactum contrahendi," i.e. the conclusion of a treaty that mainly provides for cooperation between the contracting parties, hoping that this may result in the adoption of more precise obligations. One of the earliest

16. L.R.T.A.P. Convention, *supra* note 8.
17. *Id.* at Art. 2, 1443.
18. *Id.* at Art. 3, 1443.
19. *Id.* at Art. 6, 1444.
20. A. Kiss, *Droit international de l'environnement,* 206 (1989).
21. Paris Convention for the Prevention of Marine Pollution from Land Based Sources, 4 June 1974, 13 *I.L.M.* 352, 355 (1974).

models in this field was the Convention on the Conservation of Migratory Species of Wild Animals, adopted in Bonn on 23 June 1979, according to which the parties shall endeavour to abide by agreements covering the conservation and management of certain migratory species.[22] The most important application of this method, so far, seems to be the 1985 Vienna Convention for the Protection of the Ozone Layer, according to which the parties shall in accordance with the means at their disposal and their capabilities:[23] "Co-operate in the formulation of agreed measures, procedures and standards for the implementation of this Convention, with a view to the adoption of protocols and annexes."[24]

As a matter of fact, the Montreal Protocol of September 1987 had determined the emission levels that different contracting parties should respect and that constitute a directly enforceable legal obligation.[25]

f.

The Montreal Protocol[26] and the two Protocols implementing the 1979 Geneva Convention on Long-Range Transboundary Air Pollution initiated a new method in the development of international regulations that may be called the method of relative standards. According to the Helsinki Protocol of the 1979 Geneva Convention, which provides for the reduction of sulphur emissions: "the Parties shall reduce their national annual sulphur emission or their transboundary fluxes by at least 30 per cent as soon as possible and, at the latest by 1993, using 1980 levels as the basis for calculation of reductions."[27]

Thus, the obligations accepted by this treaty necessarily vary from one contracting party to the other, since their sulphur emissions in 1980 were not the same. This method seems to be an important innovation in international treaty law.

22. Bonn Convention on the Conservation of Migratory Species of Wild Animals, 23 June 1979, 19 *I.L.M.* 15 (1980).
23. Vienna Convention, *supra* note 2.
24. *Id.*
25. Montreal Protocol, *supra* note 2.
26. *Id.*
27. Helsinki Protocol (to the 1979 Convention on Long-Range Transboundary Air Pollution) on the Reduction of Sulphur Emissions or Their Transboundary Fluxes by at Least 30 Per Cent, 8 July 1985 (Reference File) Int'l Env't Rep. (BNA) 21:3021, U.N. Doc. ECE/EB AIR/12, 27 *I.L.M.* 707 (1988); *see* Sofia Protocol to the 1979 Convention on Long-Range Transboundary Air Pollution, Concerning the Control of Emissions of Nitrogen Oxides or Their Transboundary Fluxes, 31 Oct. 1988, 18 Envt'l L. & Pol'y J. 228 (1988).

g.

Difference between the obligations of contracting states may also result from the recognition of the difference between their level of development. The best example of this is Article 5 of the Montreal Protocol on Substances That Deplete the Ozone Layer.[28] This provision
sets different standards for developing countries than those for industrialized states, but this principle has already been proclaimed in the
1972 Stockholm Declaration.[29]

h.

The use of umbrella conventions is very frequent in all the new fields
where global change has modified international legislative techniques: for example, the international protection of human rights,[30]
the legal regime of outer space,[31] the new Law of the Sea,[32] and, of
course, environmental protections.[33] This means that, a first agreement had to be reached on the principles of common action, while
the setting of more precise rules and standards was the aim of the
cooperation in the framework that has been created. The fact that international organizations, such as UNEP, play a growing role in the

28. Montreal Protocol, *supra* note 2 (Reference File) Int'l Env't Rep. (BNA) 21:3156, 26
    I.L.M. 1555.
29. Stockholm Declaration, *supra* note 11.
30. *See,* e.g., U.N. Convention Against Torture and Other Cruel, Inhuman or Degrading
    Treatment or Punishment, 10 Dec. 1984, U.N.G.A. Res. 39/46, Doc. A/39/51, which de-
    velops Article 7 of the UN Covenant on Civil and Political Rights, 19 Dec. 1966. The Euro-
    pean Convention for the Protection of Human Rights and Fundamental Freedoms, adopted
    in Rome on 4 Nov. 1950, had been completed by eight protocols, four out of which (Pro-
    tocols nos. 1, 20 Mar. 1952; 4, 16 Sept. 1963; 6, 28 April 1983; and 7, 22 Sept. 1984) extend
    the scope of the Convention.
31. The Treaty on Principles Governing the Activities of States in the Exploration and Use of
    Outer Space, Including the Moon and Other Celestial Bodies, 27 Jan. 1967, 18 U.S.T.
    2410, T.I.A.S. No. 6347, 610 U.N.T.S. 205 (1967), has been completed by four other inter-
    national treaties regarding the assistance to and rescue of astronauts (11 April 1968), liabil-
    ity for damages caused by space objects (29 Mar. 1972), and activities on the Moon and
    other celestial bodies (18 Dec. 1979).
32. Law of the Sea Convention, *supra* note 4.
33. The best examples of the utilization of this method are the "regional seas" treaties drafted
    under the aegis of the United Nations Environment Programme. We note here only the
    first and most developed of them, the Barcelona Convention for the Protection of the
    Mediterranean Sea Against Pollution, 16 Feb. 1976, *supra* note 7, which is an umbrella
    treaty completed by four protocols concerning: cooperation in combating Pollution of the
    Mediterranean Sea by Oil and Other Harmful Substances in Cases of Emergency (Barcelo-
    na, 16 Feb. 1976); the Prevention of Pollution of the Mediterranean Sea by Dumping from
    Ships and Aircraft (Barcelona, 16 Feb. 1976); the Protection of the Mediterranean Sea
    Against Pollution from Land-Based Sources (Athens, 7 May 1980); and Mediterranean
    Specially Protected Areas (Geneva, 3 April 1982).

international legislative process is certainly one of the factors that has fostered this development.[34]

i.

The drafting and the adoption of regional conventions following the same pattern makes it easier to adapt generally agreed upon principles and rules to specific conditions. In the field of the international protection of human rights, this is certainly the case and the regional seas programme of UNEP – which combines it with the technique of umbrella conventions completed by protocol – certainly corresponds to the requirements of realism and efficiency.

j.

More and more often, the drafters of a treaty feel it necessary to provide for an easy updating of the instrument. This is due to the rapid progress in knowledge of the biosphere, its deteriorations, the new forms of pollution, and the new harmful substances that are destroying our planet. The most useful technique in this regard is the adoption of technical norms and specifications – e.g. a list of polluting substances or endangered species – in the form of annexes of the main treaty and of special procedures for modifying such annexes without being obliged to resume the traditional, slow procedure for the modification of treaties.[35] This approach shows the intrusion in international law of a new element, the time factor, to which later developments will be devoted.

All these innovations show implications of global change for international law, even if in some cases the use of such new methods and legal techniques started at the end of the 1940s. However, new approaches mostly stem from the necessity to solve international environmental problems. They all seem to be a part of the fundamental changes that international lawyers have to accept. Indeed, they show a trend towards a legal system in which the intricate web of international relations, in a growing number of fields, must be more flexible. The whole evolutionary process shows the need to negotiate in order

34. Conventional systems following the pattern of the Barcelona Convention have been established for the Gulf, western and Central Africa, the south-east Pacific, the Red Sea, and the Gulf of Aden, the Caribbean Region and South Pacific, *see* Kiss, *supra* note 20, at 143–145.
35. *See,* e.g., Article XV(2) of the London Convention on the Prevention of Marine Pollution by Dumping of Wastes and Other Matter, *supra* note 7, adopted on 29 Dec. 1972; and Article 16 of the Bern Convention on the Conservation of European Wildlife and Natural Habitats, *supra* note 9.

to solve problems, rather than to adopt strict rules, understanding that some fundamental principles and rules are to be defined by determining the goals and creating an adequate framework for action. Dynamism, i.e., the adaptability and openness for change, is also a part of the innovations: this might even be one of the major contributions of global change to the evolution of international law, since it places the whole legal system in a new perspective, that of time.

B. Implications of global change for the implementation of international legal rules

Another aspect of the functions of international law, on which global change certainly has an impact, is the implementation and the enforcement of international legal rules. Indeed, the new requirements modify the tasks of states, they make it necessary to use or to create new international mechanisms for the surveillance of the implementation of such rules and they change our approach to international liability.

a.
Quite often, international treaty rules related to environmental protection constitute an intrusion into the traditional sphere of action of states: for example, control of industrial or other activities, surveillance of the state of the environment,[36] control of the exportation and importation of substances such as chemicals, waste,[37] or of parts or derivatives of protected specimens of wild flora and fauna,[38] etc. In all these fields state authorities must intervene in order to implement the treaty obligations and quite often this means the adoption of specific regulations in national legal systems. In a way, one might speak of a non-self-executing provision, which can be implemented only if the national legislation has adopted corresponding measures. In some cases such measures entail the designation of authorities that can deliver permits[39] or ensure the contact with other national authorities.[40] In certain situations penal sanctions are foreseen by treaty provisions:

36. L.R.T.A.P. Convention, *supra* note 8 at Arts. 3–6.
37. Basel Convention, *supra* note 10, UNEP/IG-80/3 at Art. 4.
38. *See,* Washington Convention on International Trade in Endangered Species of Wild Fauna and Flora, 3 Mar. 1973, 27 U.S.T. 1087, T.I.A.S. 8249, 993 U.N.T.S. 243. *See also,* Edmonds, *Guidelines for National Implementation of the Convention on International Trade in Endangered Species of Fauna and Flora* (IUCN, 1981), Art. II(3).
39. Edmonds, *supra* note 38 at Art. IV.
40. Basel Convention, *supra* note 10 at Art. 5.

of course they can only be specified and enforced by corresponding national rules.[41] Such methods justify the theory of one of the greatest international lawyers of the century, the late professor George Scelle, on the "dédoublement fonctionnel."[42] This means that, since there is no central executive power in international law, as a rule states have to ensure this function. However, whenever they act for the implementation of international legal rules, they do it on behalf and in the name of the international community as agents of the latter.

b.

New international mechanisms for the surveillance of the implementation of treaty obligations by states are more and more numerous and more and more used. The term "international" may signify another application of the theory of the "dédoublement fonctionnel": a surveillance exercised by a state in the name of the international community. However, most often this means that an international body ensures this task.

Article 218 of the Law of the Sea Convention is a good illustration of the first method.[43] According to it, when a vessel is voluntarily within a port or at an offshore terminal of a state, that state may undertake investigations, and, where the evidence so warrants, institute proceedings in respect of any discharge from the vessel outside the internal waters, territorial sea, or exclusive economic zone of that state in violation of applicable international rules and standards.[44] Such surveillance thus covers acts that take place either on the high seas or in internal waters, territorial sea, or exclusive economic zone of another state, although in the latter case the port state cannot institute proceedings against the polluter, unless it is requested to do so by the concerned state.

Another method, which is gaining more and more importance, is the use of existing international bodies or the creation of new ones for the surveillance of the implementation of international legal obigations. Initially, such mechanisms were mainly created in the field of the international protection of human rights, with rather encouraging results. Different solutions are used: the international body

41. London International Convention for the Prevention of Pollution from Ships, 2 Nov. 1973, 12 *I.L.M.* 1319 (1973), Art. 4 (hereinafter M.A.R.P.O.L.).
42. G. Scelle, *Droit International Public: Manuel Elémentaire* (1944), pp. 21–22.
43. Law of the Sea Convention, *supra* note 4 at Art. 218, 1312.
44. *Id.*

may be an organ where states are represented, like the UN Commission on Human Rights,[45] an expert group, like its Sub-Commission on the Prevention of Discrimination and Protection of Minorities,[46] a quasi-judiciary organ like the European Commission of Human Rights,[47] or a real tribunal, like the European or the American Court of Human Rights.[48] The procedure depends not only on the nature of such bodies, but also on the progress of international awareness and cooperation in this field. Communications may be addressed in some cases by states,[49] in others by individuals or groups of individuals,[50] or even by both categories[51] to determined bodies. Sometimes these are real applications submitted to strict rules of admissibility.[52] The role of international public opinion is always very important, although the form of its intervention may be different according to the different procedures. Non-governmental organizations participate in the discussions of the UN Commission on Human Rights and are given the floor, but confidentiality is the rule in certain procedures.[53] However, at the end, findings and reports on violations of human rights are generally made public and in some cases this constitutes the main sanction.[54] In other circumstances the procedure ends with a formal decision of an international court of human rights that may condemn the concerned state to reparation.[55]

Such a complete outfit certainly does not exist for the surveillance of the implementation of obligations related to the environment, at least not yet. However, the "reporting system" is more and more often used. One of the models was Article 11 of the 1973 International Convention for the Prevention of Pollution from Ships (MARPOL),[56] according to which the contracting parties undertake

45. Stockholm Declaration, *supra* note 11.
46. *See,* Humphrey, "The United Nations Sub-Commission on the Prevention of Discrimination and the Protection of Minorities," 62 A.J.I.L. 869 (1968).
47. European Convention for the Protection of Human Rights and Fundamental Freedoms, 4 Nov. 1950, Art. 20, Europe. T.S. No. 5, 213 U.N.T.S. 222 (1950).
48. *Id.* at Art. 38: American Convention on Human Rights, 22 Nov. 1969, Art. 52 s. (1969).
49. African Charter on Human and Peoples' Rights, 27 June 1981, O.A.U. Doc. CAB/LEG/67/3 Rev. 5. 21 *I.L.M.* 59 (1982), at Art. 47.
50. American Convention on Human Rights, *supra* note 48 at Art. 44.
51. *See* European Convention for the Protection of Human Rights and Fundamental Freedoms, *supra* note 47 at Arts. 24, 25.
52. *Id.* at Arts. 26–27.
53. T. Buergenthal, *International Human Rights,* 247, 73 (1988).
54. European Convention for the Protection of Human Rights and Fundamental Freedoms, *supra* note 47 at Art. 32(3).
55. American Convention of Human Rights, *supra* note 48 at Art. 63.
56. M.A.R.P.O.L., *supra* note 42.

to communicate to the Intergovernmental Maritime Organization, *inter alia*, the text of laws, orders, decrees, regulations, and other instruments that have been promulgated on the various matters within the scope of the convention, as well as official reports that show the results of the application of the Convention, and also an annual statistical report of penalties imposed for infringement of the Convention. The latter communications are to be circulated to all parties.[57]

The most recent worldwide international convention related to the environment was the Basel Convention on the Control of Transboundary Movements of Hazardous Wastes and Their Disposal, of 22 March 1989,[58] which shows some progress when compared to the 1973 London Convention,[59] but of course, between the two instruments quite a few others have organized reporting systems. According to the Basel Convention, the Parties shall inform each other through the Secretariat – which is at this moment UNEP – of transboundary movements of hazardous wastes in which they were involved, on the measures adopted by them in the implementation of the Convention, as well as of accidents occurring during the transboundary movement and disposal of hazardous wastes and on the measures undertaken to deal with them.[60] The Secretariat then prepares reports based upon such information, as well as upon, as appropriate, information provided by relevant intergovernmental and non-governmental entities.[61] It may be presumed that such reports are to be submitted to the conference of parties, since this body created by the Convention "shall keep under continuous review and evaluation the effective implementation of this Convention."[62] As this had been stressed, the role recognized to non-governmental entities, such as associations, for ensuring the implementation of a treaty related to environmental protection is an important step forward.

Further developments in this direction are to be envisaged: in fact, they are needed more and more. Some proposals have been made tending to the establishment of a real international jurisdiction in this

57. *Id.*
58. Basel Convention, *supra* note 10.
59. *See* M.A.R.P.O.L., *supra* note 42.
60. Basel Convention, *supra* note 10 at Art. 13(2) and (3), 21.
61. *Id.* at Art. 16(1)(b), 26.
62. *Id.* at Art. 15(5), 24.

field.[63] At a first stage, surveillance of the implementation of state obligations should be expanded to all the major treaties and ensured by independent international expert bodies. They should agree to consider communications submitted by non-governmental entities. Final reports on the findings of such bodies should be publicized and submitted to competent UN or other such organs, without excluding the possibility of submitting the case to an international jurisdiction.[64]

c.

An overview of the international practice concerning the place and role of international liability in the field of environmental protection also shows the impact of global change on our traditional conceptions. The liability of states in international law is generally understood as the consequence of damage caused by a state to another and generates the obligation to repair such damage, generally by adequate compensation. The international practice shows that, in spite of a mass of writings, this pattern hardly works when environmental prejudice is at stake. Several reasons can explain this: the causal link between the supposed harmful activity and the damage may be difficult to establish, the identification of the source in the legal sense of the term may be difficult if not impossible to ascertain, and the evaluation of the damage suffered by the environment raises very hard problems.[65] In order to escape these obstacles, states, which never have agreed to draft precise rules on international liability in environmental matters, prefer to transfer the problem of compensation for such damages from the inter-state to the inter-individual level, by providing for procedures that allow the victim of the damage to be compensated by suing the source directly, who is generally a private person.[66] The best description of the present situation is given in Article 235 of the Law of the Sea Convention,[67] if its meaning is expanded to other aspects of the environment: "States shall ensure that recourse is available in accordance with their legal systems for

63. *Per un Tribunale Internazionale dell'Ambiente* (A. Postiglione, ed., 1990).
64. World Commission on Environment and Development, Experts' Group on Environmental Law, *Environmental Protection and Sustainable Development, Legal Principles and Recommendations* (Martinus Nijhoff, 1987).
65. Kiss, *supra* note 20 at 106–110.
66. *Id.* at 118.
67. Law of the Sea Convention, *supra* note 4 at Art. 235, 1315.

prompt and adequate compensation or other relief in respect of damage caused by pollution of the marine environment by natural or juridical persons under their jurisdiction."[68]

As a matter of fact, international conventions provide for procedures ensuring at least partial compensation for the damages that seem to be the most considerable: those caused by nuclear accidents,[69] those resulting from the pollution of the sea by hydrocarbons,[70] and damages to the Antarctic environment by mineral resource activities.[71]

But the same article of the Law of the Sea Convention also opens a door for a larger conception of international liability. According to the first paragraph, "states are responsible for the fulfillment of their international obligations concerning the protection and preservation of the marine environment. They shall be liable in accordance with international law."[72]

This clause makes no distinction between the obligations resulting from a damage caused to another state and the consequences of the breach of a treaty obligation. The preamble of the 1989 Basel Convention on the Control of Transboundary Movements of Hazardous Waste and Their Disposal reproduces this provision as a general principle, adding that, "in the case of a material breach of the provisions of the convention or any protocol thereto, the relevant international law of treaties shall apply."[73]

Most writers in international law are hypnotized by damage as the principal if not the exclusive condition for liability. However, as has been demonstrated, damage is extremely hard to establish in certain fields, while potential violations of the thousands of existing treaty provisions, which tend to protect the environment, become more and more a reality. One of the consequences of global change is the fan-

68. *Id.*
69. Paris Convention on Third Party Liability in the Field of Nuclear Energy, 29 July 1960, U.K.T.S. 69 (1968), 55 A.J.I.L. 1082 (1960); Vienna Convention on Civil Liability for Nuclear Damage, 21 May 1963, 2 *I.L.M.* 727 (1963). *See also* Brussels Supplementary Convention (to the 1960 Convention on Third Party Liability in the Field of Nuclear Energy), 31 Jan. 1963, U.K.T.S. 44 (1975), 2 *I.L.M.* 685 (1963).
70. Brussels International Convention on Civil Liability for Oil Pollution Damage, 29 Nov. 1969, 9 *I.L.M.* 45 (1970); London Convention on Civil Liability for Oil Pollution Damage Resulting from Exploration for and Exploitation of Seabed Mineral Resources, 1 May 1977, 16 *I.L.M.* 1450 (1977).
71. Wellington Convention on the Regulation of Antarctic Mineral Resource Activities, 2 June 1988, 27 *I.L.M.* 868 (1988).
72. Law of the Sea Convention, *supra* note 4 at Art. 235, 1315.
73. Basel Convention, *supra* note 10.

tastic development of international regulations in different fields, and the main task of the international rule concerning liability seems to ensure their respect. In this regard it is irrelevant whether damage has occurred: a state that authorizes or tolerates the dumping of wastes prohibited by the 1972 London Convention[74] is liable whether the existence of damage has been proven or not. It is also irrelevant whether there is another state that pretends to be the victim.

Another consequence of this approach is that international "commons," such as the high seas or outer space, can be better protected. In the present state of international law, no state could file a claim for damage that was suffered not by itself but only by the high seas, or for the pollution of outer space. The recognition of international liability for the violation of a treaty provision allows such an action.

Thus, international liability stresses the public-law character of international law, instead of the still dominating civil-law concepts. Would it be possible to imagine that in the field of the protection of human rights a state would be liable only if there is material damage caused to a person? A parallel evolution of our conceptions in other fields must necessarily follow. This directly leads to the implications of global change for the structures of the international legal order.

The impact of global change on international structures

Traditionally, international law was based upon the vision of an international society composed of sovereign states that had supreme power over their respective territories and that created legal rules applicable to their relations only by their free will. The focal point of the whole international system was thus the concept of the state, the interests of which were the most important factors in its functioning.

This conception was directly inspired by civil law, whereby private interests predominated and the only condition was that they could not be in contradiction with the more or less vague concept of public order. Global change, which must not be represented as a sudden event but as an evolution that started at the end of the Second World War, deeply modifies this perspective. Its main consequence is the awareness that mankind has common interests that are superior to that of individual states and that are not necessarily – at least in the short-term – the sum of individual states' interests. Thus, the focal

---

74. London Convention on the Prevention of Marine Pollution by Dumping of Wastes and Other Matter, *supra* note 7.

point of the whole international system centres more and more on mankind and not individual states. The protection of human rights, the peaceful uses of outer space and the oceans, the development of poor countries, and the conservation of the biosphere, which are considered as major tasks for the international community, cannot be understood if they are not founded on the concept of a common interest for mankind.

One should be reminded of the basic principles of Roman Law, which are at the root of our present legal systems, such as the principle formulated by Ulpianus in the second century: "Publicum ius est, quod as statum rei Romanae spectat, privatum quod ad singulorum utilitatem."

In the present circumstances the same idea would be expressed by saying that public law is concerned with the state of mankind, while private interests are those of the individual state. The emergence of mankind's common interests that is being achieved by global change must be reflected in international legal rules. This necessarily means a shift in the whole approach of international law from the states' central role towards that of the international community as a whole. Some of the consequences of the change could be the following.

A. The place and role of the state in the international community

While the realm of the competence of states has expanded during the last century, incorporating more and more tasks that formerly were left to private initiative (for example, teaching, health care, and guidance of economic life), a parallel evolution resulted in the modification of our conceptions of the place and the role of the state. For several decades, the justification of the power and even of the existence of states was to ensure to their subjects the enjoyment of fundamental rights, personal security, and the highest standard of living. Thus, a utilitarian approach has replaced the sacred character formerly recognized by states. The target of the competition between socialist and liberal countries in the 1960s was the improvement of the quality of life inside the two camps; the recent collapse of the Eastern systems that have lost the competition are to be explained by this utilitarian approach.

This approach naturally limits the genuine tendency of the states to exercise their power for its own sake. Other factors also contribute to such limitations. If throughout history facts could never be ignored by rulers, today they have a much larger impact on the conduct of national policies. Decisions are preempted by facts and situations stated and interpreted not only by members of royal councils or by politicians, but also by experts whose conclusions cannot be ignored: for example, scientists, economists, and sociologists. No government in the world can ignore expert opinions, in spite of their certain proportion of scientific uncertainty. Given the examples of the expansion of AIDS, the problem of the ozone layer, or global warming, no single government could refuse to take action or, at least, to publicly recognize the need of such action. Moreover, such statements and interpretations generally have an international character, based on the findings of scientists of different countries. Thus, sovereign states are more or less bound to their conduct by external factors over which they have no power.

The impact of scientific findings is greatly intensified by the reactions of public opinion. Today, echoes of major events are heard all over the "planetary village." The rapidity of the awareness of the threatening modification of the global climate, in different countries and even in spheres that are usually not receptive to environmental matters, shows that states are not free to ignore such facts. Indeed, they are limited in their freedom to decide whether they will do anything or not. A concrete example will show the limits of their action in this field. Even if nobody would contest the sovereignty of a given African state over its territory and its wild fauna and flora, reactions within the world's opinion would prevent that state from making the decision of exterminating all the rhinoceros inside its boundaries.

It may be added that, as noted earlier, mechanisms guaranteeing the implementation of international obligations more and more incorporate into their procedure the information regarding international public opinion and sometimes even consultation with its representatives, concerned non-governmental organizations.

However, the most important factor that limits state sovereignty is the unavoidable need to cooperate with others in a growing number of fields in order to solve essential problems. If such cooperation was needed in the first centuries of the existence of modern international law for political and military security, for trade and communications, nowadays no major branch of states' activities can escape it. The list of essential problems include the economy, health care, the protection of human rights development, environmental protection emergencies, meteorology, traffic and communications, the control of drugs and of terrorism: and the list gets longer and longer from one

333

decade to another. The principle of cooperation, which was stressed on several occasions by the International Court of Justice, is in fact as much a necessity inspired by realities as a legal rule. Countries that tried to refuse such cooperation under certain regimes – the USSR, China, Iran – had to pay a heavy price later for their attempt to escape the international system. Global change still reinforces this trend and contributes by limiting the freedom of individual states to act.

B. New factors of the international system

The growing role of a new factor of the international system, public opinion, has just been mentioned. The emerging importance of some others can be added.

One of the dominating trends in the two decades following World War II was decolonization. Seen from a legal point of view, this meant in the first place the recognition that certain peoples were able to select from the state to which they belonged. Formally, the concept has been recognized by the two International Covenants on Human Rights that proclaim that all peoples have the right of self-determination and that they may freely dispose of their natural wealth and resources.[75] The African Charter on Human and Peoples' Rights develops different aspects of the concept of people,[76] adding, *inter alia,* that all peoples shall have the rights to a generally satisfactory environment favourable to their development.[77]

Certainly, the new concept can be criticized because of its vagueness, although concepts such as "nation," which is the basis of the existence of most modern states, is not easier to define. Still, it exists and even nowadays, after decolonization, it plays an important role in international politics and in the life of a number of states. Should this amount to a consecration of the concept of "peoples" by international law outside the proclamations in different human rights instruments? Maybe "peoples" are not – or not yet? – subjects of international law, but they are certainly factors of the international system. The recognition of their right to their resources and to a generally satisfactory environment may be an important step towards future legal developments.

75. International Covenant on Economic, Social, and Cultural Rights 6 *I.L.M.* 360 (1967); International Covenant on Civil and Political Rights, Art. 1.
76. The African Charter on Human and Peoples' Rights, *supra* note 49 at Arts. 19–24.
77. *Id.* at Art. 24.

Another concept has appeared as a consequence of global change. The concept is one of mankind as a whole. The first legal instrument that mentions it was the charter of the Nuremberg Tribunal,[78] although one may wonder whether the notion of "crime against humanity" expresses the idea that certain crimes constitute an offence to all mankind as a subject of international law or whether it corresponds to the violation of human feelings, which is a moral concept. Anyway, the idea of mankind appears again with that of "common heritage of mankind" at the end of the 1960s, at the same time as environmental law.[79]

As a rule, the law takes care of a person when its interests are to be recognized and protected. The recognition of common interests of mankind is an ongoing process: more and more legal instruments imply or even proclaim it. Such instruments can be identified by the fact that they do not provide for reciprocity or any immediate advantage for the contracting states, while these accept obligations. In the past, such conventions usually dealt with specific fields, such as the improvement of the condition of victims of war or that of workers. More recently, various conventions with a much wider application have sought to ensure the protection of human rights. While more than 70 conventions exist, both universally and regionally, in this field, all of them were drafted after the Second World War. The evolution was even faster in the realm of environmental protection: since the end of the 1960s hundreds of texts have been drafted. In all these cases the treaties do not offer any direct advantage for the states that are parties to them – only obligations.

The general recognition that there are common interests of mankind and the definition of the most important of them has been reinforced by the idea that such interests may have materialized in specific fields, such as the deep seabed's mineral resources, the moon and other celestial bodies, or the world's cultural and natural heritage. The basic principle is that such elements of the world should be conserved and in order to do so they must be correctly managed, in the interest of present and future generations. This concept is much less focused on the sharing of benefits than on the conservation and, as a consequence, the obligations of the present holders of such

78. The Charter of International Military Tribunal, London, 8 Aug. 1945, 82 U.N.T.S. 284 (1945).
79. A. Kiss, *La notion de patrimoine commun de l'humanité, Académie de droit international, Recueil des cours 1982-II* (Martinus Nijhoff, 1983), pp. 99–256.

goods: they should be considered as trustees acting on behalf of all mankind.[80] The concept of common heritage of mankind could expand in the coming years as we understand more and more that the common interests of mankind include conservation of the ozone layer, of tropical forests, of the global climate, and of genetic diversity – all these elements might, in the future, be considered as belonging to the common heritage of mankind that the present generations must use with wisdom and conserve for future generations. The report of the "Brundtland Commission" on Environment and Development[81] shows a way that must be followed in order to avoid compromising the future of the planet.

The question has been raised as to how mankind, which constitutes the framework of the international legal system, can be a subject of international laws. One should not forget in this regard that in national legal orders, the state itself is a subject of the law that it created and that it enforces: it can defend its interests and other subjects can protect themselves against it by legal means. This is one of the aspects of the "rule of law" that is the aim of present democratic societies.

The very idea of a common heritage for mankind states that all the resources and all the cultural wealth that we have inherited shall be transmitted to future generations. Is the present state of law such that we can speak of a right of future generations to inherit cultural wealth? In-depth studies lead to a positive answer.[82] Anyway, it raises the question of the representation of future generations and it stresses the importance of a factor that is emerging in international law: time. While the first question, which concerns institutional implications of global change, will be treated later on, the new perspective, that of time, is an important factor that has to be discussed as such.

Traditionally the role of law has been considered to be mainly the protection of existing values and interests, without necessarily caring for the impact of present or future evolutions. The necessity to conserve the environment is a dynamic concept, particularly since mankind is transforming the biosphere in an unprecedented way and our

80. A. Kiss, "The Common Heritage of Mankind: Utopia or Reality?" 40 *International Journal,* 423, 439 (1985).
81. The World Commission on Environment and Development, *Our Common Future* (Oxford, 1987).
82. E. Brown Weiss, *In Fairness to Future Generations* (Transnational/United Nations University, 1989).

knowledge of the biosphere and its mechanisms is constantly progressing. The growing scarcity of resources, such as clean water or space, increases their economic and moral value. Hence, natural resources and their continued interrelationships need to be more and more protected, which requires the constant development of legal rules and the updating of existing ones. When examining the implications of global change on the law-making process, different techniques were used, which resulted from the need for developing and adapting international law in this new field. Examples of these new techniques include procedures recognizing and formulating new values, progressive techniques in the international regulatory process, and simplification of the modification of existing rules. Thus, global change introduces a sort of ferment of dynamism into the legal systems that naturally tend to be static. This is another aspect of the functional approach imposed by it.

However, the meaning of the time factor is not only technical: it also has an influence on the very finality of law in general and of the international legal system in particular. The simple idea that our biosphere must be protected includes the perspective of the future, i.e., the objective of legal rules is the preservation not only of existing values and situations but also of those that have yet to come into existence. Indeed, if we do not care for the coming decades and centuries, the entire biosphere can be destroyed for the benefit of the present. Rules that we adopt today in order to preserve the ozone layer will only stop its destruction in several decades. There is thus a close link between environmental protection and fairness to future generations: both are future-oriented.

C. The implications of global change for international institutions

The transformation of the international community, due to the expansion of areas where international cooperation became a necessity, has required since the Second World War the creation of a growing number of international institutions. Indeed, the nineteenth-century pattern, whereby the fate of the world could be settled by periodic international conferences, had to gradually be replaced by permanent cooperation, which is necessarily institutional. Global change enhances this development by adding new fields that must be covered by cooperation and by making the intrusion of the international concern into the life of nations even deeper. Meeting the modification of

337

the global climate means drastic reductions in the use of fossil fuel, i.e., a deep impact on national and even personal activities. The consequence will be the strengthening of international cooperation, which is in most cases necessarily institutional.

Inside and outside international institutions, negotiation between states plays a growing role. It was not too surprising that after the nuclear accident of Chernobyl, negotiations started in a very short time in order to adopt international regulations imposing the duty of early notification on the states where the accident took place.[83] In bilateral relations, the obligation of states that intend to start activities that may damage the environment of foreign states to inform the latter and to consult with them may imply negotiation. The procedures foreseen by framework conventions such as the 1979 Convention on Long-Range Transboundary Air Pollution[84] or the 1985 Convention on the Protection of the Ozone Layer[85] imply that further progress in cooperation will be achieved – which again means negotiation.

The care that must be taken to prevent the depletion of existing natural resources, and at the same time to ensure their continued use, also imposes upon us more and more institutional cooperation and more and more negotiation. Conservation and continued use of resources imply management and eventually such management will become international, unless we are willing to take the risk that conflicts, of a well-known type, for space and resources will prevail. Thus, international regulation will increase and will govern national legislation.

The expansion of fields where the presence of mankind's common interests have been recognized make it necessary to create adequate institutions that can defend such interests. In several fields such as the protection of human rights institutions exist but sometimes need to be improved. In others, such as the protection of the global environment, or the preservation of the rights of future generations, existing organizations should be given the necessary power to represent those interests. Of course, new ones can also be created, although there is a general trend not to establish new international organizations. Anyway, the Intergovernmental Committee for the Protection of the World Cultural and Natural Heritage, established by the Paris

83. I.A.E.A. Convention on Early Notification of a Nuclear Accident, 26 Sept. 1986, 25 *I.L.M.* 1370 (1986).
84. L.R.T.A.P. Convention, *supra* note 8.
85. Vienna Convention, *supra* note 2; *see also* Montreal Protocol, *supra* note 2.

Convention of 23 November 1972, could be considered in this regard as a subject for further reflection.[86]

Therefore, it seems that global change encourages the present trend of the international system to behave like a real system, i.e., a more and more intricate web of dynamic relations. As a consequence, the approach must also be a global one, envisaging the international community as a whole and considering the different functions inside it according to its needs and its aims – and no longer according to the interests of individual states. The distribution of such functions has to be empirical: the principles included in all the programmes of action of the European Economic Community in the field of the environment are good examples of this: "In each different category of pollution it is necessary to establish the level of action (local, regional, national, community, international) that benefits the type of pollution and the geographical zone to be protected should be sought."[87]

The guidance is thus given by way of the level of action that ensures the best solution. In other words, the basic criterion is the common interest of the community, which must be mankind when global change is at stake. However, this needs a fundamental basis, which can be found in the emergence of real world ethics.

86. Unesco Convention for the Protection of the World Cultural and Natural Heritage, *supra* note 15.
87. Declaration of the Council of the European Communities and of the Representatives of the Governments of the Member States, 22 Nov. 1973, 1973 O.J. (C 112).

11

Restructuring the international organizational framework

Paul C. Szasz

A. The current structure

1. Description

Even more rapid than the increase in the real threat of environmental problems has been the exponential growth in the seriousness with which these are taken and in the cost of the solutions that have been or are being contemplated. It is therefore by no means surprising that the rather modestly designed institutional structure installed by the United Nations two decades ago at the dawn of the international environmental age is now no longer fully suitable to operate or even just to steer the massive efforts undertaken and planned to counter both present and especially anticipated dangers to Planet Earth. But before deciding what should and might be changed, it is useful to describe briefly the current structure of environment-related institutions now functioning within the international community.

(a) Within the United Nations proper

The rather slight – though still remarkably effective – centre-piece of the world organization's efforts in this field is of course the United Nations Environment Programme (UNEP), the product of and successor to the 1972 United Nations Conference on the Human Environment in Stockholm. Formally a subsidiary organ of the UN

340

General Assembly,[1] and one of a number of quasi-autonomous subsidiary organs of the United Nations itself,[2] UNEP consists in effect of a political organ, the 58-member Governing Council, and of a "small" Environment Secretariat headed by the UNEP Executive Director (one of some 25 Under-Secretaries-General of the United Nations). Its small administrative budget is part of the Regular Budget of the Organization for which all Member States are assessed, but its operational activities are in large part financed from an Environment Fund fed from unrestricted voluntary contributions and for the rest from dedicated trust funds established for individual projects or programmes.[3] For purely political reasons (an abortive attempt to decentralize the UN system into the developing world) unrelated to UNEP's functions, its headquarters are located in Nairobi,[4] far from the offices of the international institutions whose environ-

1. UNEP was established by General Assembly Resolution 2997 (XXVII) of 15 December 1972, entitled "institutional and financial arrangements for international environmental co-operation," which was reaffirmed by Resolution 31/112 of 16 December 1976. It should, however, be noted that the former resolution does not explicitly establish the Programme – evidently because of the reluctance at that time to create new international institutions – but rather establishes a Governing Council of the United Nations Environment Programme (section I), an Environment Secretariat (section II), an Environment Fund (section III), and an Environment Co-ordination Board (section IV), which, some years later, as a con-sequence of the directive in para. 54 of the Annex to A/RES/32/197 of 20 December 1977 on "restructuring the economic and social sectors of the United Nations system," was in effect replaced by the interagency board of Designated Officials on Environmental Matters (DOEM), a UNEP-created quasi-subsidiary of the Administrative Committee on Co-ordination (*see* the 1982 Annual Report of the UNEP Executive Director, Ch. III, paras. 16–18).
2. This term refers to UN subsidiary organs, for the most part established by the General Assembly, whose executive head is appointed in some collaborative fashion between the Secretary-General and the Assembly (e.g., the UNEP Executive Director is "elected by the General Assembly on the nomination of the Secretary-General for a term of four years," A/RES/2997 [XXVII], para. II.2), has its own political organ (e.g., the UNEP Governing Council), and whose financing is usually provided largely outside of the UN Regular Budget appropriated by the Assembly (for UNEP, see note 3 below).
3. For 1990, UNEP received approximately $4.8 million from the UN Regular Budget, $52.3 million from contributions to the Environment Fund, $18.7 million from 13 general and 26 technical cooperation trust funds, and $5.2 million from counterpart contributions. The Regular Budget funds, which only cover administrative costs, financed 46 of the total of 385 posts, and for many years now have only been adjusted for inflation (pursuant to the UN's zero-growth budgeting). It should also be noted that although the contributions to the En-vironment Fund have increased from year to year over the past decade, if considered in real terms they have decreased in most years and a big jump in 1990 only restored them to their 1980 value. See UNEP 1990 Annual Report of the Executive Director (Nairobi, 1991), Chapter V and Annex III.
4. *See* A/RES/3004(XXVII) of 15 Dec. 1972.

ment-related activities it is charged with guiding and coordinating. It reports to the General Assembly through the Economic and Social Council. With its modest resources, UNEP has over the past two decades operated a remarkably varied and important set of programmes, which include the stimulation of research, the collection and coordination of data, publications, education, the sponsorship of negotiations leading to the adoption of international treaties and the establishment of numerous specialized environmental organs, as well as the issue of guidelines and other types of "soft law."[5] Some of the most important activities, projects, and accomplishments are the following:[6]

1. *Ozone Layer:* UNEP sponsored the negotiations leading first to the 1985 Vienna Convention for the Protection of the Ozone Layer and to its 1987 Montreal Protocol, becoming the interim secretariat for the treaty organs (e.g., the Meetings of the Parties) to both instruments; in the latter capacity it assisted in the Helsinki and London meetings at which important amendments to the Protocol were negotiated and adopted, and in subsequent ones for establishing the Fund called for by the London amendments.

2. *Climate:* UNEP and WMO co-sponsored the Intergovernmental Panel on Climate Change (IPCC) in which the scientific, technical, and political foundations were laid for the negotiation of a regime to protect the global climate from greenhouse warming.

3. *Hazardous Wastes:* In 1987 the UNEP Governing Council adopted the Cairo Guidelines and Principles for the Environmentally Sound Management of Hazardous Wastes, and UNEP sponsored the negotiations that led to the adoption of the 1989 Basel Convention on the Control of Transboundary Movements of Hazardous Wastes and Their Disposal.

---

5. *See* chap. 2, sect. D.
6. Systematic information about UNEP activities can be obtained since 1982 from the *Annual Reports* of the Executive Director, and from the recently introduced and episodically published *UNEP Profiles* (which set out cumulative information). The *Reports* of the UNEP Governing Council to the General Assembly (always published as Supplement No. 25 to the Official Records of the General Assembly) merely report on the Council's biannual (and sometimes special) sessions and are not particularly informative. UNEP also issues a very considerable number of miscellaneous publications reporting on or describing particular programmes, projects, subsidiary or associated organs, or reproducing the texts of various legal instruments or expert committee reports; unfortunately, these papers are rarely numbered and are thus hard to cite and even harder to find; no complete publications catalogue exists. Information about selected technical assistance and other projects can be found in the annual *Evaluation Reports* (e.g., that for 1989 reports on 15 projects).

4. *Marine Environment:* In 1974 UNEP initiated its Regional Seas Programme,[7] which now covers 11 distinct seas, for each of which an Action Plan has been adopted by the states concerned (some 120 in all the programmes), eight of which are being implemented by a respective framework convention supplemented by one or more protocols[8] (by now, 18 in all).

5. *Fresh Water:* Under its Programme for the Environmentally Sound Management of Inland Water (EMINWA), UNEP has sponsored the 1987 Zambezi Action Plan, and is assisting in the negotiation and preparation of such plans for Lake Chad and for the Aral Sea.

6. *Land Degradation:* With the assistance of FAO and Unesco, UNEP prepared and in 1982 the Governing Council adopted a World Soils Policy.

7. *Forests:* UNEP has cooperated with a number of other UN agencies in developing FAO's 1985 Tropical Forest Action Plan, and assisted in formulating the environmental provisions of the 1985 International Tropical Timber Agreement.

8. *Biological Diversity:* In 1987 UNEP initiated the preparation of a framework convention on the protection and preservation of biological diversity. It acts as the secretariat of both the 1973 Washington Convention on International Trade in Endangered Species of Wild Fauna and Flora (CITES) and of the 1979 Bonn Convention on the Conservation of Migratory Species of Wild Animals (CMS).

9. *Monitoring and Information Systems:* Under its Earthwatch Programme, UNEP has established the Global Environment Monitoring System (GEMS), in which four specialized agencies, as well as IUCN and over 140 states participate. It established INFOTERRA, a decentralized international mechanism for the exchange of environmental information, maintains the International Register of Potentially Toxic Chemicals (IRPTC), and with ILO and WHO operates the International Programme on Chemical Safety (IPCS).

7. *See* the series of publications entitled *UNEP Regional Seas Reports and Studies*.
8. For example, the 1976 Barcelona Convention for the Protection of the Mediterranean Sea Against Pollution, supported by two simultaneously adopted Protocols for the Prevention of Pollution of the Mediterranean Sea by Dumping from Ships and Aircraft and concerning Co-operation in Combating Pollution of the Mediterranean Sea by Oil and Other Harmful Substances in Cases of Emergency, the 1980 Athens Protocol for the Protection of the Mediterranean Sea Against Pollution from Land-Based Sources, and the 1982 Geneva Protocol Concerning Mediterranean Specially Protected Areas.

343

In addition, UNEP has taken a number of important initiatives for setting or resetting the UN system's environmental agenda, such as the formulation of the United Nations System-Wide Medium-Term Environment Programmes for 1984–1989[9] and 1990–1995,[10] and the establishment of both the Intergovernmental Inter-sessional Preparatory Committee on the Environmental Perspective to the Year 2000 and Beyond and of the World Commission on Environment and Development (Brundtland Commission), the reports of which were endorsed by the General Assembly.[11] It also provides secretariat services for such inter-agency organs as DOEM and CIDIE (see below).

Aside from UNEP, a number of UN subsidiary organs, such as the five Regional Commissions,[12] the UN Development Programme (UNDP), the UN University (UNU), the UN Institute for Training and Research (UNITAR), and many parts of the central secretariat perform environment-related functions. From time to time other permanent or temporary environmental bodies have been established, such as the UN Scientific Committee on the Effects of Atomic Radiation (UNSCEAR)[13] and, more recently, the Preparatory Commission for the Conference on Environment and Development (UNCED).[14]

Several of the six UN principal organs perform or stand ready to perform miscellaneous functions in this area, though for each of them these are rather minor and peripheral:

9. UNEP/GC/DEC/10/13 of 31 May 1982.
10. UNEP/GC/DEC/SS.I/3 of 18 Mar. 1988. The Plan is reproduced in document UNEP/GCSS.I/7/Add.1, and *inter alia* sets out, in over 400 paragraphs, the "problems addressed," the "general objective," the detailed "specific objectives," the "system-wide strategy," and the "implementation of the strategy" on some 32 programmatic items grouped under 16 headings.
11. A/RES/42/186 and 187 of 11 Dec. 1987.
12. For example, the Economic Commission for Europe (ECE) – for many decades the only body in which east and west European states, as well as Canada and the United States, regularly collaborated – in 1974 established as a subsidiary organ the Senior Advisers to ECE Governments on Environmental Problems (ECE/DEC/8[XXIX] of 29 April 1974). Under the sponsorship of the latter, the Co-operative Programme for Monitoring and Evaluation of the Long-Range Transmission of Air Pollutants (EMEP) was established, followed by the 1979 Geneva Convention on Long-Range Transboundary Air Pollution (LRTAP) and its 1984 Geneva Protocol on the Long-Term Financing of EMEP, the 1985 Helsinki Protocol on the Reduction of Sulphur Emissions, the 1988 Sofia Protocol on the Control of Nitrogen Oxides Emissions, and the 1991 Protocol on Volatile Organic Compounds.
13. A/RES/913(X) of 3 Dec. 1955. At present the Secretary of UNSCEAR functions within the UNEP Secretariat.
14. A/RES/44/228 of 22 Dec. 1989. By para. II.5 of the resolution, a special secretariat was established to service the PrepCom and eventually the Conference; the failure to assign this function to UNEP (the off-spring of the 1972 Conference) was no doubt a major political set-back for that organ.

1. The *Economic and Social Council (ECOSOC)* receives the reports of the UNEP Governing Council on each of its sessions, as well as those of most other quasi-autonomous UN subsidiaries active in areas relevant to the environment, and also those of the specialized and related agencies of the UN system. However, the Council itself has no environment-oriented main or standing committee or functional commission,[15] and consequently has rarely performed any significant work or conducted any decisive debates in this field. Instead, it merely passes the UNEP report, and those of several other of the above-mentioned organs, to the General Assembly.

2. The *General Assembly* considers environmental issues in its already over-burdened Second (Economic and Financial) Committee, for the most part in odd-numbered years; in these, "Environment" constitutes one of several sub-items of a large collective item entitled "Development and International Economic Co-operation,"[16] which from session to session is supplemented by some specifically environmental ones and is debated at a few plenary meetings before private consultations start on the texts of the ever more numerous environmental resolutions that emerge from each regular session of the Assembly – including some resolutions giving specific programmatic guidance and administrative directives to UNEP.[17]

   In spite of the relatively scant attention that the General Assembly has until recently devoted to the environment, it has from time to time issued or endorsed important directives designed to set the environmental agenda of the international community: first the convening of the 1972 Stockholm Conference on the Human Environment and then the endorsement of its Declaration and the implementation of its structural recommendations

---

15. ECOSOC has some subsidiary organs operating in related areas, such as the Population Commission (a "functional commission"), the Committee on Natural Resources, the Commission on Human Settlements, and the Committee of Experts on the Transport of Dangerous Goods, as well as the already mentioned Regional Commissions.

16. *See* sub-item 77(e) of the agenda of the forty-sixth regular session. *See also* the biennial programme of work for the Second Committee for 1992–1993, General Assembly Decision 46/455 of 20 Dec. 1991.

17. *See,* e.g., A/RES/46/150 (study of Chernobyl disaster), /167 (women, environment, population, and sustainable development), /168 (UNCED), /169 (climate), /208 (environment and international trade), /215 (large-scale pelagic drift-net fishing), /216 (environmental consequences of Gulf War), /217 (preparation for environmental emergencies), and decisions 46/460 (environment and agricultural policies), /462 (UNEP Governing Council report), /463 (documents relating to the environment), as well as /417 (environment and armed conflict – adopted on the report of the Sixth Committee).

(the establishment of UNEP); 10 years later, the issue of the World Charter for Nature;[18] in 1987, the approval of Environmental Perspective for the Year 2000 and Beyond (evaluating the outlook and setting detailed goals and recommended actions on 10 key environmental issues)[19] and the endorsement of the report of the UNEP-established World Commission on Environment and Development (the Brundtland Commission);[20] and, most recently, the convening of UNCED.

3. The *Secretary-General* is the nominal supervisor of the UNEP Executive Director, though in effect he can exercise little influence over an official who is responsible to and has the support of his own political body (the Governing Council), the representatives to which are located far from UN Headquarters.[21] The Secretary-General does have more influence over those offices of the central (or headquarters) secretariat that are charged with environment-related tasks, but these are largely peripheral to the main activities in this field.

4. Finally, it should be mentioned that while the *International Court of Justice* (ICJ or World Court) stands ready to decide any environment-related legal disputes that governments may decide to submit to it or to give relevant legal advice to international organs authorized to request advisory opinions, in practice no directly environmental case or request has ever been submitted to the Court.[22]

5. The other two principal organs, the *Security Council* and the *Trusteeship Council*, do not now have any directly relevant func-

18. A/RES/37/7 of 28 Oct. 1982.
19. A/RES/42/186 of 11 Dec. 1987, Annex.
20. A/RES/42/187 of 11 Dec. 1987. The Commission's Report is set out in A/42/427 (also published as *Our Common Future*).
21. Most members of the UNEP Governing Council maintain special representatives in Nairobi to deal with UNEP business, and these naturally establish close relations with its staff and Executive Director. Aside from the few formal meetings of the Governing Council, the Executive Director from time to time convenes the Permanent Representatives to UNEP, which thus constitute an unofficial organ that he advises of new developments and consults on certain matters requiring decisions.
22. It could be argued that the recently filed *Passage through the Great Belt (Finland v. Denmark)* case, which concerns the right of Denmark to build a bridge over an international strait that might block the passage of some Finnish vessels, may be considered to have an environmental aspect. Interestingly enough, the *Corfu Channel, Merits, Judgment,* 1949 I.C.J. 4, which is one of those frequently cited by international environmental lawyers, was not really about the environment at all (unless one considers that placing mines in international straits is an environmental offence), but did express a strong affirmation of the *sic utere* principle, later put into environmental terms as the oft-cited Stockholm Principle 21.

tions – though if any trust territories had remained under significant supervision to the present time the latter organ would presumably have added environmental concerns to the others for which it would hold the administering powers responsible.

As already pointed out, in relation to many of the new or more acute environmental concerns, such as long-range transboundary air pollution, the dangers to the ozone layer, or the need to protect some particularly threatened or fragile environment or species, special treaties have been concluded under the auspices of one or more of the above-mentioned organs. Aside from establishing and defining relevant obligations for the States Parties, some of these treaties have created full-fledged though small international organizations, with their own political organs and secretariats. These political or expert "treaty organs" in effect function within the United Nations and also constitute part of its machinery for dealing with environmental matters. For the most part the secretariat functions to service these organs have been assigned, sometimes on a permanent and sometimes on merely an interim or experimental basis, to some existing subsidiary UN organ, such as UNEP[23] or a UN regional commission.[24]

(b) Otherwise within the UN system

Even before the establishment of UNEP, a number of the specialized and related agencies of the United Nations were assigned or gradually assumed some environment-related functions incidental to carrying out their principal tasks:

1. *Food and Agriculture Organization of the United Nations (FAO):* Some important pre-1972 FAO initiatives in the field of the environment include the 1949 Rome Agreement for the Establishment of a General Fisheries Council for the Mediterranean (GFCM),[25] the 1951 Rome International Plant Protection Convention,[26] the 1956 Rome Plant Protection Agreement for the Asian and Pacific Region,[27] the 1969 Rome Convention on the

---

23. For example, the secretariats of CITES and CMS, as well as of the 1989 Basel Convention on the Control of Transboundary Movements of Hazardous Wastes and Their Disposal, are provided by UNEP on a permanent basis, and that of the 1985 Vienna Ozone Convention and the 1987 Montreal Protocol on an interim basis.
24. For example, ECE provides the secretariat for the Long-Range Transboundary Air Pollution Convention and its Protocols.
25. 126 UNTS 237.
26. 150 UNTS 67.
27. 247 UNTS 400.

Conservation of the Living Resources of the South-East Atlantic,[28] and several agreements for the establishment of various regional Commissions for Controlling the Desert Locust.[29] Later important FAO instruments include the 1981 World Soil Charter,[30] the 1983 International Undertaking on Plant Genetic Resources,[31] the 1985 Tropical Forest Action Plan (TFAP),[32] and the 1985 International Code of Conduct on the Distribution and Use of Pesticides[33] (along with numerous guidelines relating to pesticides).

2. *United Nations Educational, Scientific and Cultural Organization (Unesco):* In 1971 Unesco initiated what may be considered as a precursor of broad-based environmental programmes: Man and the Biosphere (MAB).[34] In November 1972 it promulgated the Convention concerning the Protection of the World Cultural and Natural Heritage,[35] which established the Intergovernmental Committee for the Protection of the Cultural and Natural Heritage of Outstanding Universal Value (the World Heritage Committee) and provides that its secretariat be appointed by the Unesco Director-General, which thus in effect functions as part of the Unesco secretariat.

3. *World Bank:* The World Bank's (IBRD) environmental sensitivity grew with that of the rest of the world community. Though it is difficult to identify any pre-1972 initiatives in this field, in 1980 it joined with numerous other multilateral development institutions in a Declaration of Environmental Policies and Procedures Relating to Economic Development[36] and in founding CIDIE (see below), and in November 1989 it adopted its Operational Directive on Environmental Assessment.[37] In 1991 it joined with UNEP and UNDP in establishing the Global Environment Facility (GEF), which will include contributions to the Montreal Ozone Protocol's

28. 801 UNTS 101.
29. Southwest Asia, 1963, 529 UNTS 217; Near East, 1965, 592 UNTS 215; Northwest Africa, 1970, 797 UNTS 97.
30. 21 FAO Conference Resolution 8/81.
31. 22 FAO Conference Resolution 8/83.
32. FAO Publication M-30.
33. 23 FAO Conference Resolution 10/85.
34. *See Man Belongs to the Earth* (Unesco, 1988).
35. 11 *I.L.M.* 1358 (1972).
36. 19 *I.L.M.* 524 (1980).
37. World Bank Operational Manual, OD 4.00, Annexes A, A1, A2.

Interim Multilateral Fund. Since 1990 the Bank has issued annual Progress Reports on *The World Bank and the Environment*.

4. *World Health Organization (WHO):* Although many of WHO's public health measures evidently have an environmental aspect, its specifically environmental activities are mostly undertaken in collaboration with UNEP, such as the 1981 WHO/FAO/UNEP Memorandum of Understanding Governing Collaboration in the Control of Water-Borne and Associated Diseases in Agricultural Water Development Activities.

5. *World Meteorological Organization (WMO):* Although WMO's monitoring activities were originally simply weather-related, their importance for environmental affairs was soon recognized. It was instrumental in organizing the 1979 and 1990 World Climate Conferences, and in November 1988 co-established, with UNEP, the Intergovernmental Panel on Climate Change (IPCC).

6. *International Maritime Organization (IMO – formerly IMCO):* IMO is responsible for the negotiation and/or the administration of a number of important conventions relating to ocean pollution, including the 1954 International Convention for the Prevention of Pollution of the Sea by Oil[38] (including the 1971 London Amendment concerning the Protection of the Great Barrier Reef),[39] the 1972 Convention on the Prevention of Marine Pollution by Dumping of Wastes and Other Matter (London Ocean Dumping Convention),[40] and the 1990 London International Convention on Oil Pollution Preparedness, Response, and Co-operation.[41] In 1973 the IMCO Assembly established the Marine Environment Protection Committee as a standing organ.

7. *International Atomic Energy Agency (IAEA):* The IAEA's statutory concern for nuclear safety evidently always had an environmental aspect. Of special importance are its 1980 Convention on the Physical Protection of Nuclear Material,[42] the 1983 IAEA Guidelines for Mutual Emergency Assistance Arrangements in Connection with a Nuclear Accident or Radiological Emergency,[43] the 1986 (post-Chernobyl) Conventions on Early Notifica-

38. 327 UNTS 3.
39. IMCO/RESA.232(VII), 1 I.P.E. 378.
40. 1046 UNTS 120, 11 *I.L.M.* 1294 (1972).
41. 30 *I.L.M.* 735 (1990).
42. IAEA INFCIRC/274.
43. IAEA INFCIRC/310.

349

tion of a Nuclear Accident and on Assistance in the Case of a Nuclear Accident or Radiological Emergency,[44] and the 1990 IAEA Code of Practice on the International Transboundary Movement of Radioactive Waste.[45]

As environmental concerns have proliferated, such functions have in many organizations increased in response to the demands of member states or of other intergovernmental and non-governmental international organizations. For the purpose of carrying out such functions, these organizations have from time to time established joint organs or other arrangements, such as the Joint Group of Experts on the Scientific Aspects of Marine Pollution (GESAMP – a joint organ of UN, UNEP, FAO, Unesco, WHO, WMO, IMO, and IAEA), the Committee of International Development Institutions on the Environment (CIDIE – a joint organ of by now 16 multilateral development/finance institutions, including several outside the UN system), the UNEP/WMO-sponsored Intergovernmental Panel on Climate Change (IPCC), and the WMO/Unesco/UNEP work in preparation of the Second World Climate Conference (Geneva, October – November 1990).

Finally, note should be taken of the Administrative Committee for Co-ordination (ACC), the device whereby coordination is sought among all these UN system organs and organizations at the secretariat level – as distinguished from the political one, which is principally the formal responsibility of ECOSOC, operating under the direction of the General Assembly and with the assistance of the Committee for Programme Co-ordination (CPC). ACC consists of the executive heads of the specialized and related agencies and of the quasi-autonomous UN organs (including UNEP), meeting several times a year under the chairmanship of the UN Secretary-General and working with the assistance of an elaborate set of standing and ad hoc organs. With the assistance of the interagency board of Designated Officials for Environmental Matters (DOEM) (in which over a dozen UN organs and some eight agencies participate), ACC considers and makes recommendations as to the coordination of, *inter alia,* all those environment-related programmes and projects that fall within the purview of more than one of the participating entities, and annually

44. Respectively, IAEA INFCIRC/335, 25 *I.L.M.* 1370 (1986), and IAEA INFCIRC/336, 25 *I.L.M.* 1377 (1986).
45. IAEA INFCIRC/386.

makes a report (drafted by the UNEP Executive Director with the help of DOEM) to the UNEP Governing Council.

(c) Other intergovernmental organizations
Of course, not all international environmental work takes place under the auspices of the UN system. It should therefore be briefly mentioned that on the one hand there are a number of independent organizations, with significant or exclusive environmental mandates, that function in effect on a global (though usually substantially non-universal) basis, and on the other a number of regional and sub-regional organizations or organs, generally affiliated with a regional political or economic organization. Examples of the former are the International Union for Conservation of Nature and Natural Resources (IUCN) (now often called the World Conservation Union) and the International Whaling Commission; examples of regional organizations are the International Commission for the Protection of the Mosel Against Pollution and the bilateral Canada-United States Committee on Water Quality in the St. John River and its Tributary Rivers and Streams that cross the Canadian–United States Border; and examples of organs are the OECD's Environment Committee, as well as the European Environment Agency and the European Environment Information and Observation Network, both established by the EEC Council of Ministers. In general, these independent and regional organizations and organs work in reasonably satisfactory cooperation with those of the UN system, though formal coordinating organs are lacking.

2. Problems with the current structure

The principal difficulty with the present institutional structure of the UN system – as described above – in dealing with environmental matters is the insufficient clout of UNEP, both among states and among organizations. Though established consequent on the recommendation of what, in retrospect, has been recognized as the watershed 1972 Stockholm Conference, its creation was at best somewhat half-hearted – reflecting on the one hand a lack of conviction on the part of the most powerful decision makers about the importance and urgency of environmental issues (many of which were recognized only dimly or not at all in those still more innocent times) and on the other the opposition of certain less-developed states that perceived a direct contradiction between the then emerging environmental demands and the requirements of rapid development.[46]

The result was that UNEP was constrained in several significant ways. Its secretariat was explicitly specified as "small." Its budget was, except insofar as it could secure voluntary contributions to its Environment Fund or contracts or grants to carry out certain tasks, left to be proposed by the Secretary-General and submitted to the financial organs of the UN at Headquarters (the Advisory Committee for Administrative and Budgetary Questions [ACABQ] and the Fifth [Administrative and Budgetary] Committee of the General Assembly, and later also CPC), all operating at a great distance from and therefore not susceptible of being effectively influenced by the political and administrative organs of UNEP. And, instead of having its headquarters in Geneva, where it would have been close to most of the European-based agencies whose environment-related programmes and activities it was supposed to coordinate and guide, UNEP was exiled to Nairobi as a political concession to the third world, which wished to have at least one worldwide organ seated in one of its capitals – no matter what the cost in both monetary terms and in reduced effectiveness and influence.[47] At least in part in recognition of these several constraints the preparation of the follow-up conference to Stockholm was not assigned to UNEP.

However, there are also other weaknesses in the UN's institutional structure relating to environmental questions. As a latecomer among the issues on which the General Assembly traditionally concentrates – decolonization (which, though almost completely accomplished, still consumes a disproportionate share of the Assembly's attention and appropriations), disarmament, human rights, and development assistance – the environment has regularly been short-changed in the attention it receives in ECOSOC and especially the General Assembly. While each of the just listed subjects has a plenary Main

46. It is evidently the function of the 1992 follow-up conference on Stockholm, that is the United Nations Conference on Environment and Development (UNCED), to try to achieve a reconciliation of the two concepts; an important measure of its success will be the perception of the extent to which it will have managed to do so. So far the most important statement on this subject is the 1987 Report of the World Commission on Environment and Development, established by the UNEP Governing Council (UNEP/GC.11/3 of 23 May 1983), which Report was endorsed by the General Assembly (A/RES/42/187 of 11 Dec. 1987). For an earlier Assembly statement on this subject, *see* para. 8(a) of A/RES/38/161 of 19 Dec. 1983.

47. *See* note 4 above.

Committee of the General Assembly almost completely assigned to it (respectively the Fourth, First, Third, and Second), environmental matters have – as already pointed out – been confined to a small part of the crowded schedule of the over-burdened Second.

Finally, even on the Secretariat level, the counsels of possible pleaders for the environment are muted. While the UNEP Executive Director has a great deal of freedom to operate his agency as he wishes far from the possibly intrusive supervision and interference of Headquarters, his voice is not included in the Secretary-General's cabinet – nor is there any other suitably high official with an environmental mandate who could speak for these issues in New York or Geneva where most of the Organization's and the System's policy decisions about economic affairs and development are made and where available resources are allocated.

B. Some objectives of and constraints on possible improvements

In deciding on whether and how to improve the present institutional structure of the UN system to make it more responsive to and in particular more effective in addressing environmental concerns, it is first necessary to determine the nature of the roles it is desired for that system to play. For this it may be useful to present a menu of potential environmental functions of intergovernmental organizations:[48]

1. Norm-making;[49]
2. Monitoring (both "macro monitoring" for overall environmental developments, such as the growth of the ozone hole, and "micro monitoring" for compliance by particular states or other entities);
3. Assessing (i.e. performing or evaluating environmental-impact assessments in respect of proposed international projects, whether to be carried out or financed by IGOs or by states, and of national ones likely to have significant international impacts);
4. Licensing (i.e. deciding whether a certain operation or enterprise

---

48. For a brief discussion of the various functions listed here, *see* "Possible Functions of a Global Regime to Mitigate Climatic Change," in P.C. Szasz, "The Role of International Law: Formulating International Legal Instruments and Creating International Institutions," in 15:1 *Evaluation Review*, 7, at 8–18 (Feb. 1991, an issue devoted to "Managing the Global Commons"). *See also* P.H. Sand, *Lessons Learned in Global Environmental Governance* (World Resources Institute, June 1990).
49. *See* chap. 3, A above.

is likely to be in compliance with established international environmental norms and should therefore be authorized to proceed);
5. Provision of technical assistance (technology transfers);
6. Provision of financial assistance (resource transfers);
7. Sanctions (i.e. punishment for violating agreed norms);
8. Adjudication (settlement of environmental disputes among states and other international entities, about compliance with agreed norms, damages, etc.);
9. Coordination (among competent IGOs, NGOs, etc.).

If the objective is primarily to generate new legal norms, whether embodied in treaties or in regulatory instruments or just in guidelines, and perhaps also to mobilize the probably massive resources that will be necessary to implement them, then the competent organization should be located visibly and functionally closer to the centre of power in the UN system. In particular, the arrangements should be such that the representatives on the political organs of the environmental body might overlap with or be able to interact closely with those representing the same states in organs like the General Assembly and the Executive Directors of the World Bank and perhaps also in the institutions of the European Communities. In addition, it would be useful to strengthen the specialized secretariat to enable it to service the enhanced expert and political bodies.

If, instead, the primary objective is to create organs capable of implementing, and of assisting states in implementing, the provisions of existing environmental treaties, then the location of the organization is less important but a massive increase in its budget and staff may be necessary to enable it to become an effective functional body, for example as a serious evaluator of international environmental-impact statements, or as an important executing agency for UNDP projects and a recognized subcontractor on those financed by the World Bank or by other financial institutions that include environment-protective provisions among the requirements for granting credit.

Finally, if it is considered that the time has come (as it eventually surely will) to create a body with legislative and/or enforcement powers that are not dependent on the particular consent of individual states, then it may be necessary to amend the UN Charter to endow an existing principal organ with, or to create a new one capable of exercising, whatever coercive powers the world community is ready to assign in this field to an international institution.

It should in any event be recognized that the objective of any change should not be to centralize in a new or a recast organ or organization *all* environmental functions assigned or to be assigned to the UN system. To do so would, aside from being administratively impractical and bureaucratically disastrously contentious, go counter to the principle that almost all international activities must be recognized as having an environmental dimension that should be taken into account in planning and executing such activity. Thus it is necessary that environmental concerns be taken into account in designing development projects, in performing agricultural research, or in designing new space activities. A specialized environmental organ can provide guidance and assistance to the organizations carrying out these other functions, but it cannot effectively intrude in actually carrying them out.

In this connection consideration need also be given to another question: Is it necessary or desirable to combine in one organization responsibility for all manner of environmental concerns, no matter how diverse these may be and no matter how divergent the requirements for their solution? Thus, should there be one all-encompassing environmental agency, or separate ones for the oceans, for each regional sea or for all of them, and for the atmosphere – and should responsibility for that medium be still further subdivided among different agencies respectively responsible for defending the ozone layer, reducing pollution, and protecting the climate?[50] In deciding on how to unite or subdivide this field among actual and potential organizations, account should be taken of certain very general administrative and organizational considerations: evidently, some duplication could be avoided by reducing the number of competent organizations, as could the danger of establishing conflicting requirements; on the other hand, the larger and more complex an organization, the more difficult it is to manage it effectively.

Finally, in considering what changes should be contemplated in existing systems, it is necessary to examine how difficult it may be to get from here to there. Certain changes are mechanically easy to accomplish, such as in the nature, operations, budget, or location of subsidiary organs of international organizations; all that is required is an amendment of the resolution(s) establishing the organ, to be decided by the organ that originally adopted the resolution or by one senior

50. Indeed, that question was one of the principal ones considered by and reflected in the report of the Meeting of Legal and Policy Experts on the Changing Atmosphere, convened by the Canadian Department of External Affairs in Ottawa, February 1989.

thereto; thus the General Assembly could at any time, by a simple or by a qualified (i.e., two-thirds) majority vote, make any changes it considers desirable in respect of UNEP. If it is decided to create treaty organs to carry out certain functions, then it is necessary to formulate, adopt, and bring into force one or more international agreements – usually a somewhat time-consuming process,[51] and one in which it may be difficult to achieve the full participation usually desirable in respect of environmental matters, except if only a regional regime is contemplated. This is also true if a new specialized agency is to be established, since the constitutional instrument of such an institution is a treaty; in addition, a relationship agreement must be concluded with the United Nations to define the place of the new organization within the UN system. Finally, if the objective is to create a compulsory regime, i.e., one that can be imposed on states, then it will be necessary to contemplate an amendment of the UN Charter – a somewhat daunting enterprise[52] requiring *inter alia* ratification by two-thirds of the membership including the five permanent members of the Security Council (each of which thus has an effective veto power over Charter amendments); however such an amendment, once adopted, is automatically binding on all UN members[53] (i.e. on practically the entire world community) – which is generally not true of most treaty actions.

In designing plans for establishing new international organizations or restructuring existing ones, account should be taken of the capacity of international organizations to learn – from their own experience and from that of others.[54] This is important from two points of view: in the first place, when deciding whether an existing organization needs to be supplanted or reinforced by a new organization, account should be taken of the possibility of improving the existing one by merely stimulating any latent and possible politically long-suppressed abilities to develop, without undertaking major and difficult structural changes; in the second, in creating any new structure, it should be endowed with sufficient flexibility so that it can take advantage of experience and rise to new challenges as these may appear.

51. Described more fully in chap. 2 above.
52. In 45 years, Charter amendments have only been adopted to Articles 23, 27, 61, and 109, in order to increase the size of the Security and the Economic and Social councils to adapt these to the growth in the membership of the Organization.
53. UN Charter, Art. 108.
54. This subject is discussed at greater length in the Annex to this Chapter.

C. Changes to be considered

1. Assignment of new responsibilities and powers to principal UN organs

Various suggestions have recently been made, that because of the importance of environmental concerns these ought to be assigned not merely to one of the numerous subsidiary organs of the United Nations but rather to one of the limited number of its principal organs, either one of those already in existence or to a specially created one. Some of those suggestions are merely aimed at giving greater visibility and weight to environmental issues and debates, while others would be designed to utilize the potentially binding force of the decisions of certain principal organs either to create new international environmental law or to enforce it. These various suggestions will now be examined in respect of each of the principal organs.

(a) The General Assembly

As already mentioned, the General Assembly, whose present workload is both heavy and weighted with items of historical but not necessarily current importance, has found it difficult to concentrate sufficiently on environmental issues and thus to give them the attention that many now believe they deserve. While the question of how the Assembly might shed or redistribute some of its existing load goes generally beyond the bounds of the present study, it should be pointed out that it has been recognized that the Fourth Committee, which deals with questions of decolonization and with the few remaining small non-self-governing territories, has for some time been due for retirement, with its remaining items perhaps assigned to the Special Political Committee. While it might be tempting to consign the Fourth Committee entirely to environmental concerns, to do so would disregard two important points: the fact that, interesting and important as these issues might be, they have not yet attained in the international community the prominence that would justify such an exclusive assignment of some two months debate in a plenary organ of the Assembly; furthermore, it is clear (e.g., from the name assigned to the 1992 Conference) that the General Assembly sees environment and development as inextricably linked. Consequently, a more acceptable proposal would appear to be to redistribute the current load of the Second Committee between that and the Fourth with one of them taking all environment- or development-related issues, while all other economic and financial ones go to the other.

Although the General Assembly is already the most important international legislative body, in terms of the number and variety of the international law-making treaties it has adopted or caused to be adopted through conferences and other devices, not to speak of its numerous formal declarations that catalyse the creation of new customary and conventional law, the chances are minimal that it will soon or even in the foreseeable future be granted genuine legislative powers – i.e. authority to adopt legal rules that thereby become binding on states. Aside from the revolution in international legal thinking that the grant of such power to any global organ would entail, the Assembly notoriously suffers from a fatal flaw that would seem to disable it from such a role: its voting system. Although mistakenly sometimes characterized as "democratic," the assignment of the same voting power to a state of over a thousand million inhabitants as that enjoyed by a state with a population of some twenty thousand,[55] disqualifies the Assembly from consideration as the sole approver of any generally binding norms. While it could of course be argued that the same Charter amendment that would be required to give legislative (rather than mere recommendatory) force to certain Assembly decisions could also change the voting rules for such decisions,[56] it is only realistic to recognize that even if the majority of states might be willing, should they consider it absolutely necessary, to create new organs or organizations with expanded powers and an appropriate decision-making process to match, it is most unlikely that they will permit the voting rules of the General Assembly itself to be altered for such a purpose. What might, however, be considered is to have the Assembly act in tandem with some special environmental (or even broader) body (such as the new principal organ proposed under

55. China, compared to San Marino – a ratio of about 60 thousand to 1!
56. This, in effect, is the objective of the "Binding Triad" proposal of the Center for War/Peace Studies. This proposal would give the General Assembly power to adopt binding international law, but would require that proposed legislation be adopted by: (1) a qualified (probably two-thirds) majority of the Member States; (2) a specified percentage (not necessarily a majority – so as not to give the two or three largest states a collective veto) of the world's population; and (3) a specified percentage of the financial (whether only assessed, or assessed plus voluntary) contributions to the Organization. Such a formula (which would not require the Assembly to split into three chambers, but only that each vote cast in the existing single chamber be counted in three different ways) would ensure that binding decisions could only be adopted if supported by most states, including the large and economically significant ones.

heading (e) below), so that an effective law-making decision would require adoption by both organs: by the Assembly representing classic sovereign equality and by a specially balanced organ whose decisions reflect in some realistic way genuine power and interest relationships; this would in effect be a bicameral (or possibly even a still more complex multicameral) world parliament, a device for which some precedents already exist in international constitutional law[57] and indeed in the UN itself (e.g., the necessary collaboration of the Security Council and the General Assembly in taking decisions about UN membership, in electing the Secretary-General and, in a different way, the Judges of the World Court).[58]

For the same reason, i.e. its skewed voting system, as well as because of its size and consequent procedural awkwardness, the General Assembly cannot be seriously considered as an organ to which to assign enforcement powers relating to environmental rules or violations.

(b) The Security Council

The idea of assigning to the Security Council certain functions related to environmental management, particularly in dealing with emergency or otherwise serious situations, has at least two bases: The first, expressed in chapter 13 of this volume, is that critical environmental problems present, in effect, "security" issues, i.e. they are related to human survival in the same or a sufficiently similar sense as those war/peace questions over which the Council already has explicit competence; the other is that the Council, uniquely among UN or indeed intergovernmental organs, disposes (at least in principle) over powers to compel states to comply with its decrees, or to suffer economic, diplomatic, or even military pressures and penalties that the Council can insist that other states impose on any offender.[59]

As to the first point, while the argument that environmental threats may indeed concern human security may be intellectually convincing, it should be noted that the language of the Charter, not to speak of the clear record of the original meaning, does not easily lend itself to such an interpretation – and that in an area where the classi-

57. For example, in the IAEA certain decisions, such as on membership and the adoption of the annual budget, require the concurrence of the General Conference, in which all members are represented (now around 112), and of the Board of Governors, which consists of just 35 members, weighted towards those with significant nuclear activities.
58. Respectively UN Charter, Arts. 4–6 and 97, and Art. 10(1)–(2) of the ICJ Statute.
59. Arts. 41 and 42 of the UN Charter, read together with Arts. 25 and 48(1).

cal rules of treaty interpretation require that in dealing with duties or burdens imposed on States Parties to a treaty a strict rather than a liberal construction be applied.[60]

Secondly, in trying in effect to hitch a ride on the compulsory powers that are given to the Council by Chapter VII of the UN Charter, it should be noted that these powers were not designed for dealing with environmental rather than military concerns.[61] In effect, it would be a case of using an inappropriate instrument to perform a potentially delicate operation – perhaps it can be pulled off successfully, but it certainly would not be either the surgeon's or the patient's choice. Nevertheless, there is one attractive feature to such proposals: if it should prove (as is not unlikely) that it is too controversial and therefore difficult to negotiate a treaty assigning true legislative powers to the United Nations or to a new international organization (which would require the concurrence of all significant states) or to amend the UN Charter in that sense (which would require only the concurrence of two-thirds of the membership, but these must include all five permanent members of the Security Council), it could be argued that the Council already has, albeit in yet undeveloped form, the necessary legislative powers under Article 25 and Chapter VII of the Charter.[62]

60. It should, however, be noted that the Security Council may be preparing to carve out a role for itself in respect to the environment. At the unique summit (i.e. heads of states and of governments) meeting of the Council on 31 January 1992, it included the following in its final declaration (S/23500, p. 3): "The absence of war and military conflicts amongst States does not in itself ensure international peace and security. The non-military sources of instability in the economic, humanitarian and *ecological* fields may become a threat to peace and security." (emphasis added)

61. It might, however, be noted that while the use of military force under Charter Article 42 to enforce an environmental decree of the Security Council would probably never be called for, the use of collective economic pressures under Article 41 might be more effective in respect of environmental offences than it is in respect of military breaches of the peace, because in respect of the latter domestic political considerations may preclude yielding to merely economic pressures, while ultimately almost any environmental dispute can be reduced to economic terms so that the exercise of sufficient pressure of that nature should accomplish the Council's purpose.

62. The argument would run this way: Under Charter Article 39, the Security Council may determine the existence of any threat to the peace and may also decide what measures are to be taken to restore international peace and security. Although what was evidently foreseen in these provisions is that the Council may, when faced with a particular incident or situation (e.g., the invasion of Kuwait), make the indicated determination and decisions; however, it would not seem entirely precluded that the Council might consider a particular practice (e.g., the testing of nuclear weapons, or their very existence) to constitute a threat to the peace and forbid all states from engaging in that practice – i.e., in effect issue general legislation rather than a mere injunction. If, then, the Council can also decide that cer-

The principal difficulty, however, is that neither the composition nor the voting system of the Security Council appear suitable for assigning environmental tasks to that organ. Even aside from the question whether that composition and that system are still appropriate even for the functions for which the Council was originally designed, it would seem absurd if at this time this completely different function (i.e. environmental protection) would be subjected to a system in which the five states who were the principal victors in the Second World War (but which do not include two of the most powerful economies, those of Germany and Japan) would have a veto power over environmental enforcement actions. It may indeed be sensible and even necessary that any such compulsory powers not be easily exercised and that therefore one or more states or groups of states should be able to prevent such exercise by a veto, but the states and the particular voting powers that one would assign them would presumably be quite different from those specified in Articles 23 and 27 of the Charter.

Consequently, to the extent that a Charter amendment would be required to give the Security Council responsibilities in respect of the enforcement of environmental rules or the prevention of environmental violations, it would seem more sensible, if it is desired to vest such powers in a UN organ, to create a new principal organ for that purpose. This is discussed under heading (e) below.

On these several grounds, there is no reason to try to involve the Security Council either in the process of environmental legislation or even in considering and debating such issues. Although it is true that the Council enjoys possibly the highest visibility among UN organs, it would seem likely that instead of enhancing environmental issues with its prestige it would find its own role diminished by dealing with matters for which it is clearly unsuited.

(c) Trusteeship Council
It has been suggested that with the achievement of independence of practically all trust territories, the Trusteeship Council is now or will soon be without any function, and consequently could assume the task of environmental watchdog for the UN System.

---

tain anti-environmental practices (e.g., emitting gases that destroy a neighbouring state's forests or the earth's ozone layer) threaten peace (either because they are provocative and may invite unilateral military intervention or because they impact on the "security" of other states – see note 60 above), it might then "legislate" against such practices.

While perhaps superficially plausible, this proposal has really nothing to commend it. In the first place, there is no Law of Conservation of UN Principal Organs. If one or more organs lose their functions, they should be abolished or abandoned, whether or not any other tasks remain unassigned in the international constellation; on the other hand, if there are tasks that should be performed by new types of principal organs, these should be established as and when sufficient political agreement as to such a requirement can be achieved.

More importantly, the Trusteeship Council is even more unsuitable, from every point of view, than the Security Council to carry out any meaningful environmental tasks. Its Charter functions are irrelevant for that purpose and it has no powers, such as the Security Council has, that would be even potentially valuable in any other field; the powers it does have: to consider reports, to examine petitions, and to provide for periodic visits, are ones that the General Assembly could assign to a suitable subsidiary organ. Most importantly, its composition: all UN Members administering trust territories plus all other permanent members of the Security Council plus enough members elected by the General Assembly to balance the number of administering and non-administering states, is completely unsuitable and certainly unadaptable to the needs of an environmental organ.

Again, since a Charter amendment would be required to adapt the Trusteeship Council to assume any environmental functions, it would be better to consider the establishment of an entirely new organ.

(d) The Economic and Social Council

Although in a sense ECOSOC would appear predestined to be at least one of the principal UN organs to deal prominently with environmental questions, in fact that organ would, for various reasons, be a very weak reed to lean on for this purpose.

To dispose first of any potential role of this Council as an effective legislative or enforcement body, it should be pointed out that though only a third as large as the General Assembly, with 54 members it is still too large for a body to which a delicate task such as the diplomacy required for effective enforcement actions could be entrusted. Furthermore, even though its smaller size permits a slight mitigation of the one-nation-one-vote defect of the Assembly (in that a smaller proportion of small and weak states are elected to the Council compared to the larger and more significant ones), this is still not sufficient to reassure many crucial states that ECOSOC decisions normally reflect a realistic political base. This is especially so because, under Article 67(2) of the Charter, all Council decisions must be taken by a simple majority – i.e. the specification of any higher majorities is constitutionally precluded.

Turning now to the potentiality of the Council as an important forum for environmental debates, it must be pointed out that the Council has not, particularly in recent years, managed to play such a role either in respect of that subject or any other (such as human rights or development, its principal preoccupations). Why that should be so has been extensively examined, with suspicion concentrating on the fact that, because of two increases in its size to reflect the growth in the Organization's membership, the Council has become too large to be an effective intimate forum and too small to be fully representative. Voices have even been raised to suggest that ECOSOC be entirely abolished, with its tasks being taken over by the present plenary Second and Third Committees of the General Assembly, in which all significant Council debates are in any event rehashed; should ECOSOC disappear, these Committees might be authorized to meet between regular sessions of the Assembly, i.e. during the spring and summer. Given this general mood about the Council, it would not seem wise to plan to make it into a showcase for environmental concerns.

(e) A new principal organ
For the reasons sketched above, none of the four principal UN organs so far considered (i.e. all those having a representative character) would seem suitable to assume important responsibilities for either environmental legislation or enforcement – though the General Assembly itself might become one of the most important public environmental fora. If "governmental" responsibilities are to be exercised within the United Nations – and this itself is not entirely clear, in light of the alternatives discussed in particular under heading 4 below – it would then seem necessary to create one, or possibly two new organs for that purpose; moreover it would seem that because of the importance of the proposed tasks, and the need in any event to amend the Charter to endow the Organization itself with the required powers, such organ(s) should be created as principal one(s).

Faced with the prospect of having, in any event, to amend the Charter to create the proposed principal organ(s), it might in the first place be thought that all things are possible, both in terms of the

363

powers of the new entity and in terms of its composition and decision-making rules. While technically this may be true, some constraints should be kept in mind so as not to appear to be utterly utopian: in the first place, the United Nations is an international and not a supranational organization, and consequently it would not seem appropriate, and especially not timely, to try to endow it with excessive powers over its members; secondly, the Organization is an intergovernmental one, so that the principal actors in any new organ should be governments acting through representatives, rather than other types of entities;[63] lastly, account should be taken of the extensive experience of the international community with a large variety of decision-making devices to find one that would seem appropriate for the purposes designated here.[64]

As to powers, one that should obviously be considered is a legislative or norm-making one. As pointed out in chapter 2 above, the principal weakness of the existing international legislative process is not in the formulating and adoption stages – though these too could be improved – but in the final one, that of bringing new legislation into force, against the suspicion or at least the inertia of the domestic authorities of most states. Indeed, the most important reason for contemplating the creation of a new principal organ within the United Nations is to overcome this handicap by endowing some properly constructed organ with authority to impose environmental rules on the entire UN membership and possibly even, by analogy to Article 2(6) of the Charter, on the few remaining non-members.[65] Obviously, this proposed Charter power will have to be carefully circumscribed to make it at all acceptable to the world community, so that the burdens that may be so imposed not be capable of becoming excessively heavy or intrusive, or liable to distort international power or domestic social relations.

63. It might, however, be noted that in the International Labour Organisation, one of the oldest of the UN's specialized agencies and clearly an intergovernmental organization (IGO), the representative organs (i.e. the International Labour Conference and the Governing Body) are so composed that each state has two governmental representatives, and one each representing the employers and the employees (i.e. the labour unions) of that country – all four representatives having equal votes.
64. For example, even though in the United Nations itself and in most of the specialized and related agencies the one-nation one-vote principle prevails, in the financial institutions (IMF, World Bank, IFAD) votes are weighted by capital investment in these institutions.
65. As pointed out in note 48 above, one might, however, argue that in spite of the several contrary grounds discussed under (b) above, the Security Council already has the bases for the necessary legislative powers in existing Charter provisions, particularly those in Chapter VII.

The other, and perhaps more plausibly acceptable, power that should be considered is that of enforcement of existing rules and responsibilities. As already mentioned in connection with the examination of a possibly expanded role of the Security Council (heading [b] above), it may be hoped that in due course the international community will mature enough to be able to assign serious enforcement functions in relation to environmental protection to an international organ, just as it did, in 1945, in principle assign such functions in relation to preserving international peace and security to the Security Council. By analogy to Article 39 of the Charter, the proposed organ might be empowered to determine the existence of any threat to the environment or any breach of an international environmental regime. By analogy to Article 40 it would first call on the state(s) to take certain provisional measures to avert the threat or the breach. Then, by analogy to Article 41, it might call on other states to take suitable economic, communication-related, or diplomatic measures *vis-à-vis* the offending entities. The articles relating to military measures (42–47) would presumably not be directly relevant but some inspiration might be drawn from them for designing in advance certain sanctions that could be put into place readily as and when required.

Though these two potential functions are evidently not unrelated, they also present sufficient differences that it is not clear that they can and should be assigned to the same organ. In particular, any legislative organ must be large enough to be considered reasonably representative of the world community – even if it is provided (as suggested towards the end of heading [a] above) that any proposed legislation must also be approved by the General Assembly. On the other hand, an organ charged with enforcement should, by analogy with the Security Council, be small enough to be able to act effectively.

What is clear is that any organ to which either of the proposed formidable powers are entrusted would have to be carefully composed – as is the Security Council. Evidently there would have to be a heavy role for the principal economic powers, though that might be achieved through devices other than assured permanent membership, i.e. by relying on certain indices (corresponding to those that determine membership in a number of international organs);[66] naturally,

---

66. For example, the composition of the Maritime Safety Committee of IMO is determined by taking into account the tonnes of registered shipping of each IMO member. The Governing Body of ILO includes states with high industrial output, and the Board of Governors of the IAEA states advanced (in the subjective view of the Board itself) "in the technology of atomic energy including the production of source materials."

there would also have to be appropriate representation of the less-powerful states, using selection formulae similar to those that are already customary in the international community. As to the decision-making process, while consideration might be given to allowing certain members (and not necessarily only any "permanent" ones) to exercise a veto, it would seem better instead to require very high qualified majorities (e.g., 90 per cent) for certain types of decisions.[67] Finally, consideration might also be given, in connection with these features, to some form of weighted voting, to reflect more sensibly – as in most of the international financial institutions – the influence in the real world of each member state.

Evidently, all the above-mentioned aspects will require extensive negotiations, which are not likely to be brought to fruition until the world community realizes the absolute importance of being able to rely on enforceable international regimes to save it from environmental catastrophes.

(f) The Secretariat and the Secretary-General

There can, of course, be no question of assigning any independent legislative or enforcement powers to the UN Secretary-General. However, he would, under Charter Article 98 and in accordance with well-established practices, have important responsibilities in assisting any competent representative organs in formulating proposed environmental norms and in actually carrying out or at least coordinating any enforcement measures decided on. By analogy to Charter Article 99 he might even be given the power to call to the attention of the competent organs the need to initiate norm-making or enforcement actions.

A question that may be asked, however, is how an Environment Secretariat might best be structured to offer the maximum effective support to the responsible representative organs. For this two models present themselves: that of a unit of the central secretariat (such as the Department for Disarmament Affairs or the Human Rights Centre) or that of a quasi-autonomous organ (such as the present UNEP, or UNDP or UNICEF) equipped with its own representative organ and led by an executive head who, though nominally selected by the Secretary-General and answerable to him, is confirmed by the General Assembly and is dependent on the support of his agency's special

---

67. However, a consensus or unanimity requirement should be avoided, because that gives every state, no matter how small or outrageously governed, an absolute veto.

political organ, and also has considerable independence in dealing with his staff. The first model, which is more characteristic of policy-making units, evidently gives the Secretary-General a more important role and also a greater stake in the operation of the entity; the latter, which is used mostly for operational organs, gives greater scope for leadership by a dedicated executive head who has responsibilities for only a single programme – in this instance: environmental protection.

One further point to be considered in this connection is the bureaucratic level of the executive head of the secretariat unit. UN departments are normally headed by under-secretaries-general, as are most of the quasi-autonomous units. However, during the past two decades two still higher posts have been established, whose status is explicitly stated to be equal to that of the "executive head of a major specialized agency": one is the UNDP Administrator, the other the Director-General for Development and International Economic Co-operation, who presides over a cluster of departments and other units.[68] The question is whether the secretariat units charged with environmental protection should, if part of the central secretariat, also be subordinated to the Director-General, into whose ambit they would naturally belong, or whether the environmental executive head, whether or not he leads a quasi-autonomous unit such as the UNDP Administrator, also be appointed at the level of those two officials; such an arrangement would of course enable him to speak on terms of greater authority with the heads of the independent agencies.

Some of the above-explored changes would be a natural consequence of establishing the new environmental organ(s) discussed under (e) above, but any or all of them could also be carried out if there should be no current enhancement of the political organs but merely an increase in the budgetary commitment and thus in the staff of the present UNEP in order to reflect the growth in its tasks and responsibilities.

(g) The International Court of Justice
The principal judicial organ of the United Nations is entirely capable, within the general powers it already has to settle disputes between consenting states and to respond to requests for advisory opinions

---

68. It is not entirely clear whether the General Assembly–created post of Director-General has survived the first reorganization announced by the new Secretary-General in early February 1992.

from duly authorized organs of the UN system, to play a useful role in administering an international environmental regime.

Under Article 26(1) of its Statute, the Court has the power to form chambers "for dealing with particular categories of cases," and it has been pointed out that it could, under this power, create a chamber for dealing with environmental disputes.[69] Whether this would be at all useful would depend on whether there would be a sufficient flow of such cases that the existence of such a chamber (which could consist of any number of judges in excess of two) would on the one hand relieve the full Court of a burden that it could not conveniently carry out by itself, and on the other permit the judges assigned to the chamber to acquire sufficient expertise so that that organ would commend itself to states as a particularly attractive forum to which to submit disputes of this type.

Actually, the second condition mentioned above is one unlikely to be realized: the Court, which is necessarily composed of senior international lawyers, is unlikely, either as a whole or through a dedicated chamber, to acquire a real expertise in the scientific and technical aspects of environmental disputes[70] – though this objection might be met by appointing some expert assessors who could participate in the work of the chamber without a vote.[71] Consequently, a different model commends itself: The international community could, either by treaties[72] or by decisions of the General Assembly, establish one

69. The Court itself has recently considered the establishment of an environmental chamber. It reported to the General Assembly that it had taken the view "that it was not necessary to set up a standing special chamber" as it could always, under Article 26(2) of its Statute, create a special chamber to deal with a particular case (A/41/4, para. 14 [1986]).
70. A particular difficulty is that whatever set of judges is assigned to a special environmental chamber, it is not likely necessarily to commend itself politically to all parties that might bring environmental disputes, and therefore such parties are likely to prefer a politically congenial set of judges to ones that might have acquired some special expertise on the general subject of the case.
71. The possibility of appointing assessors, of which no use has yet been made by the World Court, is provided for in Article 30 of its Statute and in Article 9 of the Rules of Court.
72. These treaties might be substantive ones dealing with particular environmental regimes, so that the provisions in question would merely constitute part of the disputes provisions of these instruments. However, there might also be some treaties that merely deal with the settlement of disputes – like the Optional Protocol on the Compulsory Settlement of Disputes that accompanied the four 1958 conventions relating to various aspects of the law of the sea (450 UNTS 169); such specialized treaties could cover disputes arising out of a particular contemporaneously adopted instrument, or could deal with disputes under specified existing instruments, or even with those that might arise under a certain class of future instruments (e.g., all those formulated by or under the auspices of a specified environmental organ).

or more environmental courts to settle disputes under particular regimes (e.g., all those relating to the atmosphere, or all those relating to IMO-administered ocean-pollution treaties); naturally, in each case the states concerned would have to agree. These courts, staffed with technically expert judges, could then serve as the fora of first instance for these disputes, while any residual questions of international law (e.g., relating to treaty interpretation) could be referred to the ICJ either by the States Parties to the dispute or by use of the advisory proceeding device activated by a suitable organ authorized to address requests to the ICJ (which might be the court of first instance itself, if it is one created as an organ of the United Nations).[73]

The ICJ could also become more readily available to the international environmental community by use of its advisory competence. First of all UNEP, or whatever organ succeeds it as the lead organ within the United Nations for environmental matters, might be authorized by the General Assembly to request advisory opinions of the Court within the scope of the organ's activities. Furthermore, various treaty organs associated with the UN system might be assisted in securing legal advice from the Court by authorizing a suitable UN organ, such as UNEP, to pass on their queries to the Court.[74] Although the Court might well be reluctant to permit such a device to be used to settle disputes between states that could submit them directly to the Court's contentious jurisdiction, it would still be useful both for the settlement of disputes to which an international organization, such as a treaty organ, is a party, and to resolve genuine legal queries that arise in the course of formulating new or administering existing international environmental regimes.

73. Under Charter Article 96(2), the UN General Assembly is empowered to authorize other UN organs or any specialized agency to request advisory opinions "on legal questions arising within the scope of their activities." The Assembly has used this authority, *inter alia,* to establish the Committee on Applications for Review of Administrative Tribunal Judgements, which has as its sole function the evaluation of requests by certain specified entities (including staff members of the United Nations) that an ICJ advisory opinion should be sought in respect of a particular Tribunal judgement (Article 11 of the Statute of the UN Administrative Tribunal); the Court, in its Advisory Opinion on the *Application for Review of Judgement No. 158 of the United Nations Administrative Tribunal,* 1973 I.C.J. 166, specifically upheld the Assembly's power to do so and the Court's authority to respond to questions addressed to it by the Committee. There would therefore appear to be no fundamental obstacle to the Assembly creating other subsidiary organs empowered to address questions to the ICJ in relation to a decision of a specialized environmental court, whether or not the parties to the dispute agree in advance to accept such an advisory opinion as final.
74. *See* the immediately preceding note.

2. Improving and extending subsidiary organs

(a) Upgrading UNEP

If the proposals discussed under heading 1(e) above are carried out to establish one or more new principal UN organs to deal with environmental matters, then these would presumably replace the existing UNEP Governing Council. With respect to the Environment Secretariat, heading 1(f) explored various possible enhancements and transformations, at least some of which might be undertaken even without any change in the political organs.

In any event, if the United Nations does assume, with or without a Charter amendment, greater responsibilities in respect of environmental protection, then a corresponding upgrading and transformation of UNEP will be called for. The principal feature of such enhancement should of course be the provision of greater financial resources, preferably reliably from assessed contributions, but perhaps reinforced with political arrangements for more generous voluntary ones. As to functions, those of the Programme itself (as distinguished from that of its organs: the Council, Environment Secretariat, and Fund) might be defined, though the lack of such specificity has not so far hampered its operations. For example, norm-making, and in particular the progressive development and codification of international environmental law, might be explicitly referred to[75] and perhaps spelled out in terms of specific procedures to be followed;[76] however, while such specificity might to some extent strengthen the treaty-making activities of UNEP (which, as pointed out above, are already quite vigorous), it might also inhibit the fruitful inventiveness with which these activities have so far been pursued.

One other way in which such an enhancement could come about would be through a steady increase in the number of treaty organs that UNEP arranges to service. Presumably each such treaty organ would have its own budget, the financing for which would be provided by those states that are parties to that treaty regime, or possibly

---

75. This is a power specifically assigned to the General Assembly by Charter Article 13(1)(a), and which the latter has often partially delegated to various organs, such as the International Law Commission (ILC).

76. For example, as in the ILC Statute (A/RES/174[III] – as amended); for the latest text of the Statute and an authoritative discussion of the operations of the Commission, *see The Work of the International Law Commission* (United Nations, 1988) UN Sales No. E.88.V.1.

in part by contributions from interested non-parties.[77] The advantages and disadvantages of relying on such treaty regimes are discussed under heading 3 below.

Finally consideration might be given, and this is discussed under heading 4 below, to transforming UNEP into an independent international intergovernmental organization, preferably into a specialized agency.

(b) Organs for coordination and cooperation

The Administrative Committee on Co-ordination (ACC), with the assistance of DOEM (described under heading A1[c] above), apparently carries out its environment-related tasks as well as necessary and feasible, given the difficulty of coordinating a number of international entities that were deliberately created separate for diverse political reasons and that ultimately answer to different constituencies.[78] Evidently, if other parts of the UN system are changed, e.g., if UNEP were to be superseded or supplemented by a new specialized agency, this would have to be reflected in ACC's membership and perhaps in its operations.

Whatever new intergovernmental organizations are created within or at the periphery of the UN system, they would presumably be encouraged to participate in the "common system of personnel administration" and to utilize the several organs established therefor, and also to participate in other joint administrative organs that assist governments in imposing certain common standards on operationally diverse international organizations.

---

77. It should, however, be pointed out that in the human rights field, in which a number of successful and important treaty organs function under UN auspices, the financial discipline of the States Parties to these organs has often left much to be desired (*see* A/44/668, A/45/636, and A/RES/46/111, paras. 7–12).

78. In a sense, the ultimate constituencies, i.e. the states or rather the governments of the world community, are always the same – except insofar as regional organizations represent different selections of these entities. However, in practice, the World Health Assembly, whose representatives are largely appointed by national ministries of health and who are quite likely to be medical doctors, constitutes a quite different body than the Sixth (Legal) Committee of the UN General Assembly, which, while consisting of practically the same states, is composed of lawyers and diplomats appointed from and by foreign ministries. Though in principle national governments are supposed to coordinate their various representatives in different international organizations and organs, such coordination is often at best imperfect, and as a result these organizations may have quite different approaches to the same problem.

3. Treaty organizations and organs

For the most part modern multilateral treaties do not only establish rights and obligations for States Parties, but also create some sort of organs to help to develop and implement the consequent legal regime. This has been particularly true of environmental treaties, which mostly function in rapidly developing fields in respect of which it is recognized that static legal obligations can in no way suffice, and which are complicated enough so that at least some of the parties, and perhaps all of them, require assistance and probably some stimulation in executing the undertakings adopted.

In some cases such a treaty creates what is merely a minimal, though complete, international organization consisting of at least one political representative organ (e.g., periodic meetings of States Parties), an expert organ to carry out further studies, to receive reports from the individual parties, and to make proposals to the meetings of parties, and a secretariat, perhaps consisting of only a few persons, to service the political and any expert organs.[79] Such organizations typically rely for many purposes (e.g., premises, non-specialized secretariat services, etc.) on larger, established international organizations, often the one under whose auspices the founding treaty was negotiated.

In other cases the international organization is not quite complete, typically lacking any independent secretariat. When this is so, the treaty normally foresees that some other organization, again typically the sponsoring one, will provide the secretariat services on a temporary or permanent basis.[80] When such arrangements are instituted, some of the activities of the assisting organization become partially governed by the representative and other organs being serviced, so that these are then referred to as "treaty organs" of the servicing organization.

Evidently, both these types of arrangements are potentially very flexible, and this is one of their attractions to those formulating the

79. For example, the 1946 Washington International Convention for the Regulation of Whaling (161 UNTS 72) provides for an International Whaling Commission (in which each party is represented), which has established a Technical and a Scientific Committee and is serviced by its own secretariat.
80. For example, the 1979 Geneva Convention on Long-Range Transboundary Air Pollution (LRTAP) (18 *I.L.M.* 1442 [1979]), provides for an Executive Body (consisting of the representatives of the contracting parties, meeting within the framework of the Senior Advisers to ECE Governments on Environmental Problems) and that the secretariat functions be provided by the Executive Secretary of ECE.

treaties in question. Often enough the latter are actually fooled into believing that some absolute savings can be achieved by not providing for the establishment of a new secretariat, which are known to be expensive and with a Parkinsonian drive to self-enhancement. What is often forgotten is that the missing secretariat is merely established within the bowels of the sponsoring organization, with all the usual requirements for budgetary support and tendencies to grow.

An excessive proliferation of such mini and incomplete international organizations is, however, undesirable from a different point of view. Evidently, it is more difficult to coordinate and supervise the separate activities, decisions, and staffs of numerous small organizations than to do so in respect of one or two large ones with prominent executive heads who make periodic reports on all the activities of their organizations to well-attended periodic meetings of representative organs. One solution is to combine a number of such organizations and organs operating in related fields into a single one, in effect consisting of a sizeable secretariat simultaneously servicing many different representative and expert organs; this is the design of the World Intellectual Property Organization (WIPO), a UN specialized agency.

4. Specialized or related agencies of the UN

More and more, in arranging for the international governance of some field or activity, the emphasis has shifted from the static to the dynamic, in that the States Parties agree not so much to any specific obligations but rather establish a mechanism for studying the subject in question, for formulating guidelines and rules to be followed by states or other entities, for giving technical or material assistance in complying with such standards, for monitoring compliance, for advising what to do if lack of compliance is detected, and for taking any consequent action decided through an agreed procedure.

The normal instrument of choice to take the actions summarized above is an intergovernmental organization, established at an appropriate level, i.e. universal, regional, subregional, or defined by some other relevant criterion. As is well known, during the past decade some hundreds of such organizations have been created, including many at the worldwide level, to deal with subjects as diverse as labour conditions, public health, maritime affairs, or intellectual property. On the other hand, a few international organizations have a wider mandate, dealing with many different subjects. Whether or not a particular subject, such as environmental protection, should be dealt with in a specialized or in a general organization depends in part on whether the nature of the subject requires a sufficient assignment of material and human resources to justify an independent entity, on how closely that subject is related to others that should be dealt with in a more general context, and on whether political or other factors suggest that the subject requires attention close to the centre or may be assigned to the periphery of the relevant international system. As conditions change, the answer to these questions may also change: thus, in 1950, the International Refugee Organization (IRO), originally established at the conclusion of WWII as a UN specialized agency, was reduced to becoming a quasi-autonomous UN organ, the Office of the High Commissioner for Refugees (UNHCR); on the other hand, in 1975 it was decided that the United Nations Industrial Development Organization (UNIDO), which had originated as a Secretariat unit and had later become a quasi-autonomous UN organ, should be converted into a specialized agency with the same name.

Evidently, not all independent international organizations are UN specialized agencies, which are defined in UN Charter Article 57 as "established by international agreement and having wide international responsibilities... in economic, social, cultural, educational, health and related fields" that are brought into relationship with the United Nations by means of an agreement concluded pursuant to Charter Article 63(1). Thus, to qualify, an organization's tasks cannot be so narrow as to negate the characterization of "wide... responsibilities";[81] it cannot be merely regional, for then it might more appropriately become a specialized agency of one of the regional organizations (such as the Organization of American States – OAS); it has to have a sufficiently large membership so as to associate with the United Nations on a par with the other worldwide organizations whose activities it coordinates through ECOSOC and the ACC;[82] and it has to agree to conclude a relationship agreement that

81. The 1946 Whaling Convention (note 78 above) foresaw the possibility that the Commission would become a UN specialized agency (Article III.6) – a development that was never realized, either because it was considered that the Commission did not really have "wide" enough responsibilities, or because the membership (initially 6, and only 39 in 1990) never became sizeable enough (*see* note 82 below).
82. As of the beginning of 1991, the specialized agencies with the smallest membership were the World Intellectual Property Organization (WIPO) with 124, and the International Maritime Organization (IMO) with 133; the two UN-"related" agencies, the International Atomic Energy Agency (IAEA) and the General Agreement on Tariffs and Trade (ICITO/

implies a certain subordination to the central organizations and a willingness to cooperate with it and the other specialized agencies, in part through common administrative or coordinating organs.[83] If for some reason any of these factors are absent or distorted, then the organization may still become one "related" to the United Nations (such as the IAEA), or merely tied to it by a cooperation agreement (such as the World Tourism Organization – WTO).

The question therefore is whether the field of environmental protection is one suitable for the establishment of an, or perhaps of even more than one, independent international organization, and whether such organization should then aspire to specialized agency status.

First of all, assuming that the function of the proposed organization is to be primarily norm-making, especially in the form of treaties, it should be noted that in different fields this is precisely the function of the International Labour Organisation (ILO) and of the World Intellectual Property Organization (WIPO); on the other hand it might also be argued that since environmental instruments to be effective require a far higher rate of participation than the typical ILO Convention or WIPO treaty receives, it might be preferable to maintain a treaty-generating organization within the United Nations itself where the prestige of the General Assembly can reinforce the specialized political organs of an environmental unit. Furthermore, if what is under consideration is legislation to become automatically binding on all states, this could only be accomplished through an amendment of the UN Charter – for the alternate route, a powerful international organization that all states would voluntarily join within a relatively brief span of time, seems impractical of attainment.

Should the potential enforcement function be in the foreground, it could be pointed out that a similar function, i.e. the implementation of safeguards on peaceful nuclear activities, is one of the primary ones of IAEA, a UN "related agency." On the other hand, if the proposed enforcement would require the imposition of coercive sanctions, it might be considered preferable to concentrate such powers in the United Nations, even if a new principal organ (see 1[e] above) would have to be established for that purpose. Also, if the sanctions

---

GATT), had 112 and 97 members respectively. These numbers are higher than that of the number of participants in all but very few international environmental treaties.

83. It should be noted that this subordination is very slight in respect of the international financial institutions, such as the International Monetary Fund (IMF) and the World Bank and its affiliates, nor do these participate in the "common system" of personnel administration or in organs such as the Joint Inspection Unit (JIU).

are to apply to all states, they would have to be imposed by a UN organ.

This having been said, it should once more be recalled that amendment of the UN Charter is not an easy or well-established route,[84] unlike the frequent resort to the establishment of new organizations to meet particular urgent needs of the world community; as recalled above, there is even a precedent (that of UNIDO) for converting a quasi-autonomous UN organ, such as UNEP now is, into a specialized agency. Moreover, if the primary roles of the new organization are to carry out studies, assist in voluntary monitoring, provide technical assistance, raise consciousness about environmental matters, and to serve as a secretariat and general support for environmental treaty organs and organizations, then an independent organization, but preferably one within the UN system, might provide the best combination of flexibility and coordination.

Instead of or in addition to converting UNEP into an independent agency, it is also possible that one or more international organizations be established to deal with specific important environmental problems or areas, such as the implementation of a regime to deal with climate change or more generally with protecting the atmosphere. Whether such organizations would qualify as, and would wish to become, specialized agencies would depend on their membership and on their perceived role in the world community.

D. Conclusion

The environmental consciousness of the world community is growing at a rate unprecedented for the spread of any intellectual concept or the acceptance of new ways of defining the interaction of humanity and nature. Almost surely the result of this growth will be an early (i.e., at or soon after the 1992 Conference on Environment and Development) need to restructure the current international institutional arrangements for dealing with environmental protection, so as to achieve greater prominence, power, and coherence. As this study seeks to show, there is no lack of institutional models, for most of which there are precedents, though some reflect designs yet to be implemented, for accomplishing whatever the world community is prepared for at this juncture, when outmoded military preoccupations are suddenly though belatedly yielding to more urgent economic and scientific imperatives.

84. *See* note 52 above.

Annex: The learning capacity of international organizations

Whether or not the international community as a whole has a learning capacity is difficult to establish, because of the highly amorphous and unstructured nature of that entity. However, to the extent that community increasingly acts through international organizations, and in particular through intergovernmental organizations (IGOs), such a learning capacity can be both affirmed in general terms and studied in particular instances.

Like all complex but structured entities, human organizations obey many of the same rules that biological ones do – though the regularity of that conformity may be more difficult to establish, in part because the building blocks of organizations (ultimately, human beings) are infinitely more complex than those of biological organisms (such as cells), and largely because there are many orders of magnitude more of the latter so that these can be subjected to statistical and other analyses that are impractical in respect of social organizations. But organizations, like organisms, strive to maintain their existence, seek to perpetuate themselves, are territorial and aggressive when their immediate environment is threatened – in other words, unlike Asimov's idealized mechanical creatures, they obey his Third Law of Robotics without being bound by the First and Second.[1]

One attribute of complex organisms, or of organizations of complex organisms, is the ability to learn – often a necessary device for self-perpetuation. In international organizations this capacity can of course be best observed when dealing with the carrying out of distinct repetitive activities, e.g., a series of technical assistance projects or the negotiation of a series of parallel international agreements. Following are some examples of activities of particular organizations that have been carried out over a sufficient period of time that it should be possible to observe developments attributable to learning. (NB: Not all changes in established programmes are due to learning: some may represent reactions to changed material or political circumstances, or responses to fashions, or random consequences of new leaders or managers.)

A. The negotiations of treaties, e.g., by:
  1. The International Labour Organisation (ILO)
  2. The Council of Europe

---

1. Paraphrased, compliments to Asimov, the three laws are: (1) no robot may harm a human being; (2) subject to the first law, no robot may permit harm to come to a human being; (3) subject to the first and second laws, no robot may permit harm to come to itself.

3. The World Intellectual Property Organization (WIPO)
4. The International Maritime Organization (IMO, formerly IMCO)

B. The granting of assistance to countries, e.g. by:
   1. The International Monetary Fund (IMF)
   2. The World Bank (IBRD and IDA)
   3. The UN Development Programme (UNDP)

C. The granting of assistance to individuals, e.g., by:
   1. The International Committee of the Red Cross (ICRC)
   2. The UN High Commissioner for Refugees (UNHCR, building on the experience of the League of Nations' Commissioner and that of the International Refugee Organization (IRO))
   3. United Nations Children's Fund (UNICEF)

D. Regulatory activities, in the fields of:
   1. Narcotic drugs
   2. Nuclear controls:
      a. Safety
      b. Safeguards against diversion for military purposes
   3. Environment:
      1. Protection of various types of animals
      2. Regional seas agreements

E. Operations:
   1. European Centre for Nuclear Research (CERN) (building successively larger accelerators)
   2. International Satellite Communication Organization (INTELSAT) (securing and operating a series of increasingly complex geostationary satellites)

Most IGO learning is unconscious, unsystematic, and more or less constant. That is, by a series of generally unsolicited negative and positive feedbacks, an organization carrying out a certain type of activity will naturally adjust its procedures to avoid past mistakes and to emulate successes. To what extent it can and does so may depend on the extent rigidities are built into its systems: for example, if the constitutional and other legal instruments governing the IGO are very detailed, or the political controls are very strict because of tensions among leading participants, then even adjustments clearly called for by experience may be slow in coming. Similarly an IGO that has had a recognized record of success may be slow to change in response to altered circumstances, even when signs abound that the old ways no longer correspond to current needs. Thus well-established organizations, frequently led and staffed by older people (unless a conscious effort is made to avoid this danger) may be less able to learn in natural and automatic ways.

However sometimes – and perhaps increasingly so as self-conscious management techniques became more prevalent – learning is becoming more of a conscious, systematic, and often episodic process. That is, from time to time the parent organ (in respect of a subsidiary) or the governing organ or chief administrator decides to take stock and to engage in a process of self-examination (sometimes with the help of outside consultants) with a view to improving future performance by studying past successes and failures. For example, during the past several years the United Nations has been scrutinizing and analysing its past "peace-keeping" ("Blue Helmet") operations, as well as its experiences in supervising or conducting referenda and elections, with a view to extracting patterns of successful approaches and devices from which to create models for future operations. Alternatively, standing organs (such as the UN system's Joint Inspection Unit [JIU], which was in many ways modelled on the US General Accounting Office (GAO), Congress's administrative watchdog) are created for the purpose of carrying out evaluations on an automatic and steady basis; such organs of course have the primary task of grading past activities, but as in other learning situations the purpose of grading is in large part didactic.

Sometimes, of course, wrong lessons are "learned" – such as by the cat that jumps once on a hot stove and thereafter will never jump on any stove again. Just so, an organization once burned by a particular failure (or even an overly costly success) may evermore, or at least for a long time, avoid any similar operations, even if clearly distinguishable, in details or by general circumstances, from the one inducing the bad memories. (No doubt there are examples in many IGOs; in the UN one could mention the Congo operation; the Third UN Conference on the Law of the Sea; and the early acrimonious and fruitless Security Council debates on its procedural rules and its agenda – which have still left the Council with a set of "Provisional Rules of Procedure," with a cumbersome and unrealistic list of over 100 largely completely outdated items of which it is allegedly "seized," and with a needlessly complicated procedure of examining even uncontentious membership applications.)

Incidentally, organizations can learn from one another, and even from one another's mistakes. There are many examples of conscious transfers of experiences and procedures, from a founding organization to a new spin-off (e.g., from the UN to the IAEA and UNIDO)

379

or from an established senior organization to a newcomer in a similar field (e.g., from the World Bank to the Inter-American and the Asian Developments banks, and to some extent also to the International Fund for Agricultural Development [IFAD]). Joint management organs, such as the JIU, or even private management consultants that work successively for several IGOs, can carry warnings of mistakes or news of useful techniques from one client to another.

There are other examples of learning, which perhaps are more analogous to an infant starting to walk or talk, when an IGO tackles an entirely new field of activity, i.e. one not only new to it but one that no IGO, and perhaps no one at all, has undertaken before. For example, when INTELSAT started its operations, it did so largely under the tutelage of its US participant: COMSAT; once it had gained some years of experience with ordering and operating communication satellites, it shed its dependency and started operating on its own.

The IAEA's experience in establishing safeguards to prevent the diversion of nuclear materials from peaceful to military activities is one of a different sort, for prior to the Agency no international or national organization had carried out any nuclear controls, indeed any controls of any sort that offered even a useful analogy. (One that was often referred to in the early days of the IAEA, but that really turned out to be of minimal utility, was the system of drug controls evolved under the League and taken over by the UN.) So, the Agency deliberately started its safeguards activities slowly, with simple facilities, in non-contentious situations. Some of the important stages in this process were:

a. The conclusion of an experimental, initial safeguards agreement for a "project" in which the Agency had been asked to assist in the transfer of three tons of natural uranium from Canada to Japan, which request was explicitly made for the purpose of getting the Agency's project and safeguards machinery going so it could gain some experience.

b. The formulation, very painfully, of a "Safeguards Document," i.e. a set of principles to be observed and to be taken into account in the conclusion of safeguards agreements with member states, covering only nuclear facilities with quite minimal power.

c. The negotiation of a series of safeguards agreements based on the first Safeguards Document, each successive text differing from the previous one as new insights were gained. (Incidentally, the ability to improve successive tests in situations of this kind is limited, because each agreement is known to all states, and each party to such an agreement watches jealously that it is not treated worse than another state. In effect it is recognized that it is most difficult ever to move from lighter to more severe controls and that thus over time, in an entropy-like process, the tendency is steadily towards a less-burdensome regime; consequently an effort is also made to start any new series of agreements with overly severe conditions. All this of course inhibits the "learning" process, for experience gained cannot always be fully utilized.)

d. After some experience had been gained in negotiating real safeguards agreements for small facilities, the USA offered the Agency an opportunity to test its system on some larger reactors, which of course would not be really safeguarded because the USA in any event had a substantial military programme and thus had no need to "divert" materials to it from its nascent nuclear power programme. Thus the conclusion and implementation of this agreement with the USA were explicitly to provide the Agency with a learning experience.

e. At this stage the Agency formulated an extension of its earlier Safeguards Document, based on its experience in implementing the latter, to cover somewhat more powerful facilities. This exercise having gone smoothly, a completely new and improved Safeguards Document was adopted, rather rapidly.

f. Thereafter a comparatively large number of safeguards agreements were formulated, as states gained confidence in the Agency's system. As the latter was by then well-established, successive agreements differed only minimally from each other.

g. Another result of the increasing confidence in the Agency's safeguards was the decision to rely on that system in implementing the Tlatelolco and Non-proliferation treaties. This, in turn, necessitated the Agency formulating yet another Safeguards Document attuned to those two treaties but taking into account all the experience gained in the formulation and implementation of the previous versions.

h. The implementation of the NPT and Tlatelolco treaties required the conclusion of a larger number of safeguards agreements than ever before. By now, however, the system was relatively mature, and successive agreements rarely differed significantly from each other: in this respect, the learning curve had become saturated and thus flat. However, learning continued and continues in respect of the techniques for implementing safeguards.

i. As suggested in (c) above, control standards tend to deteriorate over time because it is practically impossible, without some extraneous impulse, to apply stricter measures in a later agreement than in an earlier one with another state – while there is apt to be a demand for applying any concession made earlier even if the context is different from the one that originally justified it. It is this process of deterioration that led the Agency to give up on carrying out any truly intrusive inspections – the lack of which in Iraq permitted its government to build up a most extensive clandestine nuclear weapons programme, which was only disclosed when the Agency received an extraordinary mandate from the Security Council after Iraq's defeat in the Gulf War. The consequent disclosure of how extensive a military programme had for many years escaped the Agency's limited scrutiny carried out to monitor compliance with the government's obligations under NPT is currently leading to a thorough re-examination of the safeguards system, with a view to tightening it so as to avoid future débâcles. It is thus likely that the Agency, and the world community, will have learned from this experience. Rather similarly, the IAEA and the world community have received some harsh lessons about the downside of the previously relaxed attitude towards national implementation of adequate safety standards in operating nuclear facilities. In the wake of first the near disaster of Three Mile Island, and then the genuine catastrophe of Chernobyl, the Agency is belatedly considering how to make compliance with certain minimum standards compulsory and possibly even subject to its controls. Unfortunately, the initial indications are that the lesson, that this is another area in which unrestricted national sovereignty must yield to transnational concerns, appears not yet to have been adequately learned, for the Agency-convened September 1991 International Conference on Nuclear Safety and the organs following up on its recommendations still take as their starting point a restrictive interpretation of the Conference-enunciated principle that "safety should primarily be enforced at national levels."

There are evidently some less self-conscious examples of learning within and between international organizations. One example is the General Assembly's technique, which it copied repeatedly after the initial success with the Universal Declaration of Human Rights, of preceding many of its major treaty-making projects by a solemn declaration that serves to guide the negotiations while also creating in the meantime a soft-law regime expressing the main principles to be observed – a regime that may even harden into customary law before or soon after the codification process is completed. In the human rights field we have the examples of the several declarations on Racial Discrimination, on Discrimination against Women, on the Elimination of Torture, and on the Rights of the Child, all followed by corresponding conventions; in other areas one could mention the Declarations of Legal Principles Governing the Activities of States in the Exploration and Use of Outer Space and of Principles Governing the Sea-Bed and the Ocean Floor, and the Subsoil Thereof, beyond the Limits of National Jurisdiction. Another successful device that started in the human rights area and is now being examined for wider application, including in respect to environmental regimes, is the reinforcement of the substantive obligations of a treaty by the creation of an expert control organ to which the parties must submit periodic reports on their compliance and that may also be authorized to examine certain accusations against the parties. In the environmental field itself, the technique of starting with a basically procedural framework convention to be complemented by one or more substantive protocols was pioneered in the Geneva Long-Range Transboundary Air Pollution Convention and then followed spectacularly in the Vienna Ozone Protection Convention, which in turn has become the model for the current negotiations of a Climate Protection Convention.

A quite different, and ultimately less successful effort of an IGO attempting consciously to learn from its own experience and from that of other organizations, was the nearly decade-long study carried out in the Legal (Sixth) Committee of the UN General Assembly on the Multilateral Treaty-making Process. The purpose of the exercise was to see whether the UN could improve its very extensive and ever-more significant treaty-making activities, carried out through a multitude of general or specialized organs, by systematically studying the experience gained in the past in these organs as well as in other organizations. Ultimately, even though much valuable data were assembled and analysed,[2] political constraints prevented the drawing of any really useful conclusions.

There can thus be no doubt that IGOs can and do learn. However,

2. Review of the Multilateral Treaty-Making Process, UN Publication ST/LEG/SER.B/21, Sales No. E/F.83.V.8 (New York, 1985). *See* P.C. Szasz, "Reforming the Multilateral Treaty-Making Process: An Opportunity Missed?", *International Law at a Time of Perplexity: Essays in Honour of Shabtai Rosenne* (Y. Dirnstein, ed., Martinus Nijhoff, 1988), 409–441.

there are constraints on that process, and just like other types of entities, some are better students than others, and some are better students at certain stages of their development than at others. IGOs are also becoming more conscious of the need to include systematic learning exercises in their programmes if they are to avoid becoming obsolete or unable to tackle certain new tasks. To learn from one's own experience it is necessary to build into all significant programmes effective feedback cycles. To learn from the experience of others it is necessary to remain alert to what others are doing and to be prepared to change one's own programmes in response to successes and failures experienced by others – something that may require more perspective than many organizations can muster. But, as IGOs become more regular features of the international landscape it may be expected that systematic management techniques, including conscious "learning," will be adopted by more and more of them.

12

Intergenerational equity: A legal framework for global environmental change

Edith Brown Weiss

Sustainable development rests on a commitment to equity with future generations. In 1972 the United Nations Stockholm Conference on the Human Environment recognized that we had a responsibility to "protect and improve" the environment for both present and future generations. In 1992, we are faced with defining and implementing this commitment to future generations in the context of environmentally sustainable development.

Global environmental change affects our capacity to achieve sustainable development; it may help or hinder this process, although the focus is more on the latter. In turn, economic development causes global environmental changes. The implications of global environmental change are inherently long-term and require that we address equity issues that span two or more generations.

We have developed economic instruments to try to satisfy the needs of the present generation efficiently, but these are not adequate for addressing equity issues with future generations. While the incorporation of externalities is intended to ensure that the benefits from a proposed action exceed the costs and that those who bear these costs be adequately compensated, in practice it operates from the perspective of the present generation. Environmental externalities are focused primarily on the costs that the present generation bears in polluted air, water, and soils from industrial development, in

This chapter is adapted from E. Brown Weiss, *In Fairness to Future Generations: International*

385

deforestation, and in other aspects of economic development. The discount rate is used to consider future costs and benefits, again from the perspective of the present generation. Reliance on the discount rate to consider the future means that short-term benefits nearly always outweigh long-term costs, in part because long-term costs to the environment are hard to quantify.

International law has been fundamentally concerned with questions of fairness. It addresses the normative dimension that economic instruments implement. If we are going to achieve intergenerational equity, it is essential to analyse this normative relationship between generations. This chapter sets forth a theory of intergenerational equity in the context of global environmental change.

I. The temporal dimension in international law

International law has always been concerned with justice, but usually between states in their present or past relationships with each other. Concern with intergenerational equity requires attention to the normative relationship between present and future generations.

In the past states have made general claims for intergenerational justice in few areas: the debates over a new international economic order[1] and the negotiations for the Law of the Sea Convention regarding exploitation of seabed minerals.[2] Intergenerational issues have recently surfaced in debates over responsibility for paying for mitigation of anticipated global environmental change, such as climate change or ozone depletion, resulting from countries' past and present industrial activities.

International law to date has addressed intertemporal issues primarily in the context of relating *the present to the past*. In public international law, an intertemporal doctrine applies to territorial claims and to certain other rules of customary international law and to several aspects of treaties. In private international law it is reflected in questions of choice of time, as in conflict-of-law rules.

Law, Common Patrimony, and Intergenerational Equity (Transnational/United Nations University, 1989) and E. Brown Weiss, "Our Rights and Obligations to Future Generations for the Environment," 84 *American Journal of International Law,* 198 (1990). The analysis in this chapter also applies to cultural resources. For details, *see In Fairness to Future Generations*.

  1. Charter of Economic Rights and Duties of States, 12 Dec. 1974, 14 *I.L.M.* 251 (1975); Declaration on the Establishment of a New International Economic Order, 1 May 1974 13 *I.L.M.* 715 (1974).
  2. *See* E.G. Bellow, "International Equity and the Law of the Sea," 13 *Verfassung und Recht in Übersee,* 201–212 (1980); R.J. Dupuy, *L'Océan Partagé* (A. Pedone, 1979).

In public international law, Judge Huber enunciated the intertemporal doctrine in the classic *Island of Palmas Arbitration*,[3] which involved a dispute between the United States and the Netherlands over sovereignty of the small Pacific island. As described by Judge Huber, the doctrine has two elements: that acts should be judged in light of the law at the time of their creation; and that rights acquired in a valid manner may be lost if not maintained in a manner consistent with the changes in international law.[4] The principle has been subsequently applied in a number of cases before the International Court of Justice, including the *Minquiers and Ecrehos Case, The Western Sahara Case, The North Sea Continental Shelf Case,* and the *Aegean Sea Continental Shelf Case*.[5] While the first element of the intertemporal doctrine has been widely accepted as a basic principle, the second has been controversial.[6]

In 1975 the Institut de Droit International adopted an authoritative resolution on intertemporal law that encompasses both elements of the doctrine.[7] The Institute's restatement extended beyond Judge Huber's formulation only in that it encouraged states to develop agreement among themselves on how to handle intertemporal problems that might arise in negotiating treaties and other agreements. It did not, however, extend beyond the classical formulation to include other related intertemporal issues, such as the development of international law by international declarations and resolutions of the United Nations General Assembly.

Although most disputes raising the intertemporal doctrine have involved territorial claims, the doctrine is applicable more broadly to other issues in customary international law and to treaties. For example, in the 1971 *Namibia Advisory Opinion*,[8] when the World Court considered whether South Africa's presence in Namibia by virtue of

3. *Island of Palmas Arbitration*, 2 R. Int'l Arb. Awards 831 (1928).
4. *Id.* at 831.
5. *Minquiers and Ecrehos Case*, 1953 I.C.J. Rep. 47; *The Western Sahara Case*, 1975 I.C.J. Rep. 39; *The North Sea Continental Shelf Case*, 1969 I.C.J. Rep. 3; *Aegean Sea Continental Shelf Case*, 1978 I.C.J. Rep. 1.
6. *See* T.O. Elias, "The Doctrine of Intertemporal Law," 74 A.J.I.L. 285 (1980). The late Judge Jessup criticized the second aspect of the doctrine in the *Palmas* decision as requiring constant vigilance by a state to avoid losing its territory by default. P. Jessup, "The Palmas Island Arbitration," 22 A.J.I.L. 735 (1928). But as Brownlie has noted, intertemporal law is subject to "the effect of recognition, acquiescence, estoppel, prescription, the rule that abandonment is not to be presumed," which counters this possibility. I. Brownlie, *Principles of Public International Law*, 131–132 (Clarendon Press, 3rd ed., 1980).
7. 56 *Annuaire de l'Institut de droit international*, 536–541 (1975).
8. *Namibia Advisory Opinion*, 1971 I.C.J. Rep. 16.

its 1919 League of Nations Mandate continued to be valid, it concluded that the meaning of "sacred trust" had evolved to "self-determination and independence of the people," which did not sustain South Africa's claim. While the Court did not refer to intertemporal law, MacWhinney has correctly characterized it as embracing it.[9] Similarly, Judge Elias notes that the doctrine of intertemporal law has also applied to the customary law of sovereign immunity.[10]

The doctrine of intertemporal law applies to treaties as well as to customary international law, as indicated in *The Grisbadarna Case,* and the *North Atlantic Fisheries Case.*[11] The deliberations of the International Law Commission in drafting the convention on the law of treaties revealed, however, divergent opinions and approaches to the precise formulation of the doctrine.[12] There are several intertemporal issues raised by treaties: the proper interpretation of a treaty over time, the continuing validity of a treaty in the face of changed circumstances, and retroactive application. The Vienna Convention on the Law of Treaties contains specific provisions addressing these issues, although the doctrine of intertemporal law is not explicitly mentioned.[13] Customary international law doctrines, such as *pacta sunt servanda* and *rebus sic stantibus,* respond to the intertemporal question of the continuing validity of treaties.[14]

9. E. MacWhinney, "The Time Dimension in International Law: Historical Relativism and Intertemporal Law," in *Essays in International Law in Honour of Judge Manfred Lachs,* 1979 (J. Makarczyk, ed., Martinus Nijhoff, 1984).
10. *See* Trendtex Trading Corporation v. Central Bank of Nigeria, 2 W.L.R. 356 (1977), reprinted in 16 *I.L.M.* 471 (1977). Elias, *supra* note 6 at 293–296.
11. *The Grisbadarna Case,* 11 R. Int'l Arb. Awards 155 (1909); and the *North Atlantic Coast Fisheries Case,* 11 R. Int'l Arb. Awards 167 (1910).
12. 1 *Y.B. Int'l L. Comm'n,* 199–203 (1964); 2 *Y.B. Int'l L. Comm'n,* 211–222 (1966); Elias, *supra* note 6 at 302–305.
13. *See,* e.g., Art. 28 (non-retroactivity of treaties), Art. 31 (general rule of interpretation), Art. 32 (supplementary means of interpretation), and Art. 62 (fundamental change of circumstance), Vienna Convention on the Law of Treaties, 23 May 1969, 8 *I.L.M.* 679 (1969).
14. The maxim *pacta sunt servanda* ("treaties must be observed") was tempered by the principle of *rebus sic stantibus* ("while things remain as they now stand"), which holds that treaty obligations are terminated in the case of a fundamental change in the circumstances existing at the time the treaty was concluded, as long as the consent of the parties was based on the existence of those circumstances. An excellent study of the doctrine, and summary of state practice, is A. Vamvoukos, *Termination of Treaties in International Law: The Doctrines of Rebus Sic Stantibus and Desuetude* (Oxford, 1985). For the legislative history of Art. 62 of the Vienna Convention on the Law of Treaties, which most writers believe codifies the current practice on the change of circumstances, *see* I. Sinclair, *The Vienna Convention on the Law of Treaties,* 192–196 (2d ed., Manchester, 1984) and the list of references in S. Rosenne, *The Law of Treaties: A Guide to the Legislative History of the Vienna Convention,* 324–327 (Oceana, 1970).

Intertemporal issues also arise in the context of procedural rules set by international tribunals. For example, the rule that local remedies must be exhausted raises issues such as the appropriate time to pursue local remedies, the point at which the pursuit is considered to be exhausted, and the appropriate time for raising objections based on this rule.[15] These issues have been particularly important in human rights cases, particularly those in Europe where the European Convention on Human Rights provides that the European Commission of Human Rights may address the issue of exhaustion of local remedies only within six months from the date of the final domestic decision.[16] While the time frames for these procedural intertemporal issues is relatively brief, the issues nevertheless demonstrate that we are already addressing intertemporal issues routinely in international law in relating the present to the past.

Intertemporal problems also occur in private international law. They arise primarily as conflicts in time of rules of private international law adopted in a particular country, conflicts in time of rules of intertemporal law of the *lex fori* and *lex causae,* and conflicts of time and space caused by changes in the connecting factor.[17] In the late 1970s, the Institut du Droit International undertook a comprehensive study of intertemporal problems in private international law that included both questions of applicable law and of relevant jurisdiction.[18] In 1981 the Institute adopted a resolution setting forth applicable rules to govern intertemporal problems in private international law.[19]

---

15. A.A. Cançado Trindade, *The Application of the Rule of Exhaustion of Local Remedies in International Law,* 213 (1983).
16. *Id.* at 213–249. Cançado Trindade analyses in detail the temporal aspects of the six-month rule of the European Convention on Human Rights.
17. Most expositions on the temporal dimension of private international law have focused on issues raised by changes in a forum's conflicts rule, changes in substantive law, and changes in the connecting factor. *See* J.H.C. Morris, *The Conflict of Laws,* 493–503 (3rd ed., Stevens, 1984); A. Dicey and J.H.C. Morris, *The Conflict of Laws,* 51–63 (10th ed., Stevens, 1980); J. Grodecki, 3 *Int'l Encyclopedia of Comparative Law,* ch. 8 (1975). The Institut de Droit International has considered the issue of changes in rules of private international law over time. 59 *Annuaire de l'Institut de droit international,* 246 (1982, Part II). 58 *Annuaire de l'Institut de droit international,* 77 (1979, Part I).
18. *See* "The Problem of Choice of Time in Private International Law," 58 *Annuaire de l'Institut de droit international,* 1–96 (1979, Part I).
19. "The problem of choice of law in private international law," Resolution adopted 29 Aug. 1981, 59 *Annuaire de l'Institut de droit international,* 246–251 (1982, Part II). The Commission previously held extensive discussions on the problem. 58 *Annuaire de l'Insitut de droit international,* 1–96 (1979, Part I). *See also* the report prepared for the Commission by M.

Intertemporal problems are common in national legal systems. Frequently they appear as conflict-of-law questions. The civil law tradition has a well-developed theory in conflicts-of-law cases of intertemporal law that invokes such distinctions as "intertemporel," "droit transitoire," and "conflit mobile," terms that have no ready equivalence in English or the common law traditions.[20] The common law system addresses the temporal dimension in conflicts of law empirically as it arises in specific cases. Courts have often reached contradictory conclusions on temporal issues in these cases.[21]

Temporal issues also arise in tort liability cases, most notably in compensatory claims by people who were exposed to radiation, harmful drugs, or toxic substances years previously. The numbers of cases have increased, as environmental harms from activities a decade or more ago emerge.

Thus, there is a temporal element in many aspects of public international law, private international law, and national legal traditions. The theory of intergenerational equity proposed in this chapter, which addresses the relationship between present and future generations, as well as past, extends the basic concern we already have with intertemporal problems to a longer time horizon.

Since World War II, states have expressed concern in international legal documents for the welfare of future generations. A growing number of international agreements, declarations, charters, and United Nations General Assembly resolutions reflect such concern and set forth principles or obligations intended to protect and enhance the welfare of both present and future generations. Even the United Nations Charter, drafted in the aftermath of World War II, affirmed the universal concern for the welfare of future generations in its opening paragraph: "We the peoples of the United Nations, determined to save succeeding generations from the scourge of war. . . ."[22]

Concern for justice to future generations regarding the natural environment first emerged as a major concern in the preparatory meetings for the 1972 Stockholm Conference on the Human Environment.

Max Sorensen, "Le problème du droit intertemporel dans l'ordre international," 55 *Annuaire de l'Institut de droit international*, 4 (1973, Part I).

20. For cases in the civil law tradition, *see* J. Grodecki, 3 *Int'l Encyclopedia of Comparative Law*, ch. 8 (1975).

21. For the common law tradition, *see* A. Dicey and J.H.C. Morris, *supra* note 17.

22. United Nations Charter, 26 June 1945, 59 Stat. 1031, T.S. 993.

The preamble to the Stockholm Declaration on the Human Environment expressly refers to the objective of protecting the well-being of future generations, " . . . to defend and improve the environment for present and future generations has become an imperative goal for mankind – a goal to be pursued together with, and in harmony with, the established and fundamental goals of peace and of world-wide economic and social development."[23] The Declaration's first principle provides that "man . . . bears a solemn responsibility to protect and improve the environment for present and future generations," while the second declares that the "natural resources of the earth, including the air, water, land, flora and fauna . . . must be safeguarded for the benefit of present and future generations through careful planning and management."[24] The Stockholm Conference led directly to the creation of the United Nations Environment Programme (UNEP). The explicit concern for future generations and for enhancing the environment were new contributions to the process of developing international law in this area.

The concept of protecting the natural environment for future generations was explicitly incorporated into the language of three treaties negotiated more or less contemporaneously with the Stockholm Declaration: the 1972 London Ocean Dumping Convention, the 1973 Convention on International Trade in Endangered Species, and the 1972 Convention Concerning the Protection of the World Cultural and Natural Heritage.[25] The regional seas conventions that were subsequently negotiated under UNEP carried forward concern for future generations.[26]

There have been other international agreements in the last two decades that have contained language indicating either a concern for

23. Sixth proclamation in the preamble, Stockholm Declaration of the United Nations Conference on the Human Environment, U.N. Doc. A/Conf. 48/14 (1972).
24. *Id.* at preamble.
25. Convention for the Prevention of Marine Pollution by Dumping from Ships and Aircraft, 15 Feb. 1972, 26 U.S.T. 2403, T.I.A.S. No. 8165; Convention on International Trade in Endangered Species of Wild Fauna and Flora, 3 Mar. 1973, 27 U.S.T. 1087, T.I.A.S. No. 8249; Convention Concerning the Protection of the World Cultural and Natural Heritage, 23 Nov. 1972, 27 U.S.T. 37, T.I.A.S. No. 8226.
26. *See,* e.g., the Barcelona Convention, the preamble of which notes that the states are acting because they are "fully aware of their responsibility to preserve this common heritage for the benefit and enjoyment of present and future generations." Convention for the Protection of the Mediterranean Sea Against Pollution, and Protocols, 16 Feb. 1976, 15 *I.L.M.* 290 (1976).

sustainable use of the environment or a concern for future generations, sometimes by reference to the common heritage of mankind.[27] Other legal instruments evidence similar concern. The 1982 World Charter for Nature, not a formal agreement, refers explicitly to a global concern for the heritage we leave to future generations.[28] At the tenth anniversary of the Stockholm Declaration, countries reaffirmed the continuing validity of the Declaration and urged "all Governments and peoples of the world to discharge their historical responsibility, collectively and individually, to ensure that our small planet is passed over to future generations in a condition which guarantees a life in human dignity for all."[29]

The more recent attempts to develop a precautionary principle in international law reflect concern about the effects of our actions today on the environment of future generations. The principle attempts to answer the question of when to constrain activities that risk harming the environment in the future. It was first endorsed in 1987 at the International Conference on the North Sea and has been invoked most extensively in marine instruments. It has been heatedly invoked during the negotiations for a climate change convention.

While there has been considerable debate about the principle and its content, there is no single agreed formulation. The Group of 7 Ministerial Declaration in July 1990 stated (in relation to climate change) that "in the face of threats of irreversible environmental damage, lack of full scientific certainty is no excuse to postpose actions which are justified in their own right."[30] The UN Economic Commission for Europe ministerial meeting in Bergen in May 1990 declared: "Where there are threats of serious or irreversible damage, lack of full scientific certainty should not be used as a reason for postponing measures to prevent environmental degradation."[31] Since

27. For a review of the extent to which international agreements concerned with conservation of natural and cultural resources contribute to the protection of future generations, *see* E. Brown Weiss, "The Planetary Trust: Conservation and Intergenerational Equity," 11 *Ecol. L. Q.*, 495, 540–563 (1984). For analysis of the common heritage of mankind in relation to future generations, *see* B. Nagy, "Common Heritage of Mankind: The Status of Future Generations" (mimeo, Budapest, 1988).
28. The World Charter for Nature, *adopted* by the United Nations General Assembly, 9 Nov. 1982, G.A. Res. 37/7, 37 U.N. GAOR Supp. (No. 51) at 17, U.N. Doc..A/37/51 (1982).
29. The Nairobi Declaration, 18 May 1982, U.N.E.P. Report of the Governing Council, 37 U.N. GAOR Annex 2, Supp. (No. 25) at 49, U.N. Doc. A/37/25 (1982).
30. Ministerial Economic Declaration, Group of Seven, *N.Y. Times,* 12 July 1990, p. A15, cols. 1–5.
31. Bergen Conference, Ministerial Declaration on Sustainable Development, 20 *Envt'l Pol'y & L.,* 100 (1990).

there is never scientific certainty but always some uncertainty, these formulations do not address the difficult issues of whether, when, and how to take action against identifiable risks.[32] The fall 1991 meeting of parties to the London Ocean Dumping Convention adopted text that provides a useful formulation of a precautionary principle in a specific context.[33]

The internationally evolving precautionary principle has deep roots in the domestic environmental statutes and regulations of countries, many of which focus on pollution prevention in water, air, and soils. This approach reflects a growing willingness to relate the present to the future in legal norms.

The concern already expressed in legal instruments with the environment we pass to future generations serves as an important starting point in defining and implementing international legal principles for achieving justice among generations: past, present, and future.

II. Alternative approaches to intergenerational equity

There are several approaches to defining intergenerational equity in the context of the relationship among generations to the planet Earth.

The first is the preservationist model, in which the present generation does not destory or deplete resources or significantly alter anything; rather it saves resources for future generations and preserves the same level of quality in all aspects of the environment. This preservationist model has deep roots in the original natural-flow theory of English water law, in which riparians could use stream water so long as their use did not impair in any way the quantity or quality of water for those downstream. Ultimately this benefits the last riparians before the stream enters the ocean or disappears, because they have no one to whom they owe an obligation.

The preservationist model, if carried to its extreme in saving un-

---

32. For a skeptical analysis of the principle, *see* D. Bodansky, "The Precautionary Principle: Scientific Uncertainty and International Environmental Law," *Proceedings, 1991 Annual Meeting of American Society of International Law* (ASIL, 1992).

33. The parties indicated that in implementing the London Dumping Convention they would be guided by a "precautionary approach," in which preventive measures would be taken when there is reason to believe the dumped material is likely to cause harm even where there is no conclusive evidence to prove a causal link to certain effects and agreed that in implementing this approach they would be guided by certain specific measures. LDC 14/WP.7, Annex (1991).

spoiled ecosystems, would promote the status quo.[34] It is only consistent with a subsistence economy, not with an industrialized world. In a more flexible form, the model supports the socialist model of economic development applied by Stalin, in which citizens were urged to sacrifice today for a better tomorrow.[35] This attitude was common to the Calvinists as well.[36] In both, future generations benefit at the expense of earlier generations.

The other extreme can be termed the opulence model, in which the present generation consumes all that it wants today and generates as much wealth as it can, either because there is no certainty that future generations will exist or because maximizing consumption today is the best way to maximize wealth for future generations.[37] This model overlooks the long-term degradations of the planet that may be generated, such as irreversible losses of species diversity and of renewable resources such as soils and fish, and costly environmental contamination as by insufficiently controlled nuclear or hazardous wastes that make areas unfit for habitation and use. Further under this model, the present generation may trigger irreversible changes in the global climate system that will affect habitability in parts of the world.

Even if we knew that we were the last generation of the human

34. The term "preservation" is traditionally associated with saving nature for its own sake, rather than for its usefulness in fulfilling later human needs, which is associated with "conservation." *See* J. Passmore, *Man's Responsibility to Nature,* 111 (Scribner, 1974). For a critique of "preservation" and "conservation," *see* B. Norton, "Conservation and Preservation: A Conceptual Rehabilitation," 8 *Env. Ethics,* 195 (1986).

35. The Stalinist model of economic development, as epitomized by the Five-Year Plans in the 1930s, required the people to sacrifice the benefits of consumer goods and services in order to further the rapid industrialization of a poor country. The agricultural sector was collectivized and elemental needs of citizens were neglected to achieve the high rate of forced savings and investment necessary to finance heavy industry. *See,* e.g., D. MacKenzie and M.W. Curran, *A History of Russia and the Soviet Union,* ch. 34 (2d ed., rev., Dorsey Press, 1982); for a more detailed account of the period, *see* A. Nove, *An Economic History of the U.S.S.R.* (Allen Lane, 1969).

36. The Calvinist society put a premium on thrift and sobriety, valued effort and diligence, and encouraged the accumulation of the fruits of one's labour instead of the immediate enjoyment of them. *See* J. T. McNeill, *The History and Character of Calvinism* (Oxford, 1954). The theology of Calvin is said to have contributed to the development of Western capitalism. The classic exposition of this idea is Max Weber, *The Protestant Ethic and the Spirit of Capitalism* (originally appeared in German in 1904, rev. in 1920, English trans. 1930, Scribner, 1958); *see also* R.H. Tawney, *Religion and the Rise of Capitalism* (J.M. Murray, 1926). For more current views, *see* G. Poggi, *Calvinism and the Capitalist Spirit* (U. Massachusetts, 1983).

37. *See* H. Barnett and C. Morse, *Scarcity and Growth,* 11–12 (Johns Hopkins, 1963).

community to live on earth, it is still not clear that we would have the right to desecrate it, or to destroy it, since the human community is, in the end, only part of a much larger natural system, which we can use for our own benefit but must also pass on for others.

A variant of the opulence model is the technology model, in which we do not need to be concerned about the environment for future generations, because technological innovation will enable us to introduce infinite resource substitution.[38] While technology will undoubtedly enable us to develop some substitutes for certain resources and to use resources more efficiently, it is by no means assured that it will suffice or will make the robustness of the planet irrelevant.

Finally, we have the environmental economics model, which argues that if were to do proper natural resource accounting, we would fulfil our obligations to future generations. The economic tools that we have developed today – environmental externalities and discounting – are sufficient, were we to apply "green" economics. While proper accounting is essential to implementing intergenerational equity, it arguably is not sufficient as presently conceived.

The proposed theory of intergenerational equity

Sustainability is possible only if we look at the Earth and its resources not only as an investment opportunity but as a trust, passed to us by our ancestors, to be enjoyed and passed on to our descendants for their use. Such a "planetary trust" conveys to us both rights and responsibilities. Most importantly, it implies that future generations too have rights – although to be sure, these rights have meaning only if we the living respect them and if this respect transcends the differences among countries, religions, and cultures.

The theory of intergenerational equity proposed argues that we, the human species, hold the natural environment of our planet in common with all members of our species: past generations, the present generation, and future generations.[39] As members of the present generation, we hold the Earth in trust for future generations. At the same time, we are beneficiaries entitled to use and benefit from it.[40]

---

38. J. Simon, *The Ultimate Resource* (Princeton, 1981).
39. *In Fairness to Future Generations, supra* unnumbered note on p. 385.
40. The theory also applies to cultural resources, since they form an integral part of the legacy we give to future generations and are linked to our role as a member of the natural system. *See id.*

There are two relationships that must shape any theory of intergenerational equity in the context of our natural environment: our relationship to other generations of our own species and our relationship to the natural system of which we are a part. The human species is integrally linked with other parts of the natural system; we affect and are affected by what happens in the system. We alone among all living creatures have the capacity to shape significantly our relationship to the environment. We can use it on a sustainable basis or we can degrade environmental quality and deplete the natural-resource base. As the most sentient of living creatures, we have a special responsibility to care for the planet.

The second fundamental relationship is that between different generations of the human species. All generations are inherently linked to other generations, past and future, in using the common patrimony of earth. The theory of intergenerational equity stipulates that all generations have an equal place in relation to the natural system. There is no basis for preferring the present generation over future generations in their use of the planet.

This premise finds deep roots in international law. The Preamble to the Universal Declaration of Human Rights begins: "Whereas recognition of the inherent dignity and of the equal and inalienable rights of all members of the human family is the foundation of freedom, justice and peace in the world . . . "; the reference to all members of the human family has a temporal dimension, which brings all generations within its scope. The reference to equal and inalienable rights affirms the basic equality of such generations in the human family.

Partnership between generations is the corollary to equality. It is appropriate to view the human community as a partnership among all generations. In describing a state as a partnership, Edmund Burke observed that "as the ends of such a partnership cannot be obtained in many generations, it becomes a partnership not only between those who are living but between those who are living, those who are dead, and those who are to be born."[41] The purpose of human society must be to realize and protect the welfare and well-being of every generation, in relation to the natural system, of which it is a part. This requires sustaining the robustness of the planet: the life-support

41. E. Burke, "Reflections on the Revolution in France," 130–140 (1790), in 2 *Works of Edmund Burke,* 368 (London, 1854; Reprint Services, 1987).

systems and the ecological processes and environmental conditions necessary for a healthy and decent human environment.

In this partnership, no generation knows beforehand when it will be the living generation, how many members it will have, or even how many generations there will ultimately be. If we take the perspective of a generation that is placed somewhere along the spectrum of time but does not know in advance where it will be located,[42] such a generation would want to inherit the Earth in at least as good condition as it has been in for any previous generation and to have as good access to it as previous generations. This requires each generation to pass the planet on in no worse condition than it received it in and to provide equitable access to its resources and benefits. Each generation is thus both a trustee for the planet with obligations to care for it and a beneficiary with rights to use it.

If one generation fails to conserve the planet at the level of quality received, succeeding generations have an obligation to repair this damage, even if costly to do so. However, they can distribute the costs across several generations, by means of revenue bonds and other financial measures, so that the benefits and costs of remediation are distributed together. While the generation that allows environmental quality to deteriorate still benefits at the expense of immediate future generations, more distant future generations are protected. Moreover, the generation inflicting the harm may have passed on a sufficiently higher level of income so that immediate successor generations have sufficient wealth to manage the deterioration effectively.

While intergenerational equity may be viewed as in conflict with achieving intragenerational equity, the two can be consistent and in fact must go together. Members of the present generation have an intergenerational right of equitable access to use and benefit from the planet's resources, which derives from the underlying equality that all generations have with each other in relation to their use of the natural system.

Moreover, even the most selfish members of the present generation who care only about their own descendants must as they extend further into time increasingly care about the general environment that they will inherit. Since no one country or group of countries has the power alone to ensure a healthy environment, all must cooperate

---

42. *See* J. Rawls, *A Theory of Justice* (Belknap Press, Harvard, 1971).

to ensure a robust planet in the future. Since poverty is a major cause of ecological degradation, this means meeting the basic needs of the poor, so that they will have both the desire and ability to fulfil their intergenerational obligations to conserve the planet.

To be sure, there are instances where the actions needed to protect the health of the planet for future generations may conflict with the need to alleviate poverty as quickly as possible. In these instances, we need to develop appropriate mechanisms and allocate sufficient resources to maximize the ability to advance both goals.

The theory of intergenerational equity has a deep basis in international law.[43] The United Nations Charter, the Preamble to the Universal Declaration of Human Rights, the International Covenant on Civil and Political Rights, the Convention on the Prevention and Punishment of the Crime of Genocide, the American Declaration on the Rights and Duties of Man, the Declaration on the Elimination of Discrimination against Women, the Declaration on the Rights of the Child, and many other human rights documents reveal a fundamental belief in the dignity of all members of human society and in an equality of rights that extends in time as well as space. Indeed, if we were to license the present generation to exploit our natural and cultural resources at the expense of the well-being of future generations, we would contradict the purposes of the United Nations Charter and international human rights documents.

The proposed theory of intergenerational equity also finds deep roots in the religious, cultural, and legal tradition of the world. Islamic law regards man as having inherited "all the resources of life and nature" and having certain religious duties to God in using them.[44] Each generation is entitled to use the resources but must care for them and pass them to future generations.

. . . The utilization and sustainable use of these resources, is in Islam, the right and privilege of all people. Hence, man should take every precaution to ensure the interests and rights of all others since they are equal partners on earth. Similarly, he should not regard such ownership and such use as restricted to one generation above all other generations. It is rather a joint ownership in which each generation uses and makes the best use of nature, according to its need, without disrupting or upsetting the interests of future

---

43. *In Fairness to Future Generations, supra* unnumbered note on p. 385, at 25–26.
44. *See Islamic Principles for the Conservation of the Natural Environment*, 13–14 (IUCN and Saudi Arabia, 1983).

generations. Therefore, man should not abuse, misuse or distort the natural resources as each generation is entitled to benefit from them but is not entitled to own them permanently.[45]

Islamic law supports collective restrictions, which are to be observed under a principle of good faith, and collective rights, which are rights of the community of believers as a whole.[46]

In the Judeo-Christian tradition, God gave the earth to his people and their offspring as an everlasting possession, to be cared for and passed on to each generation.[47] This has been carried forward in both the common law and the civil law traditions. The English philosopher John Locke, for example, asserts that whether by the dictates of natural reason or by God's gift "to Adam and his posterity," mankind holds the world in common. Man may only appropriate as much as leaves "enough, and as good" for others. He has an obligation not to take more fruits of nature than he can use, so that they do not spoil and become unavailable to someone else for use – i.e., an obligation not to waste the fruit of nature.[48] To be sure, there are many instances where law has been used to authorize the destruction of our environment, but the basic thesis that we are trustees or stewards of our planet is deeply embedded.

In the civil law tradition, this recognition of the community interest in natural property appears in Germany in the form of social obligations that are inherent in the ownership of private property.[49] Rights of ownership can be limited for the public good, without the necessity to provide compensation to the owners. Thus legislatures can ban the disposal of toxic wastes in ecologically sensitive areas and invoke the social obligation inherent in property to avoid monetary compensation to the owner of the land. In common law countries such as the United States, local governments can do this through the

---

45. *Id.* at 13.
46. *See* M. Khadduri, *The Islamic Conception of Justice*, 137–139, 219–220, 233–239 (Johns Hopkins, 1984).
47. *Genesis* 1:1–31, 17:7–8. "I will maintain my Covenant between Me and you, and your offspring to come, as an everlasting covenant throughout the ages, to be God to you and to your offspring to come. I give the land you sojourn in to you and to your offspring to come, all the land of Canaan, as an everlasting possession. I will be their God." *Genesis* 17:7–8.
48. J. Locke, "An Essay Concerning the True Original, Extent and End of Civil Government," *Second Treatise on Civil Government*, paras. 25, 31, 33, 37, in *Social Contract* (Sir E. Barker, 2nd ed., Oxford, 1979).
49. R. Dolzer, *Property and Environment: The Social Obligation Inherent in Ownership* (IUCN, 1976).

exercise of the police power[50] – the power to protect the health and welfare of its citizens – or the public trust doctrine.

The socialist legal tradition also has roots that recognize that we are only stewards of the earth. Karl Marx, for example, states that all communities, even if taken together, are only possessors or users of the earth, not owners, with obligations to protect the earth for future generations.[51]

African customary law contains deep roots for the principle that we are only tenants on Earth, with obligations to past and future generations. Under the principles of customary land law in Ghana, land is owned by a community, which goes on from one generation to the next. A distinguished Ghanaian chief said, "I conceive that land belongs to a vast family of whom many are dead, a few are living, and countless host are still unborn."[52] Land thus belongs to the community, not to the individual. The chief of the community or head of the family is like a trustee who holds it for the use of the community. Members of the community can use the property, but cannot alienate it. Customary laws and practices of other African communities, and indeed of peoples in other areas of the world, also view natural resources as held in common with the community promoting responsible stewardship and imposing restrictions on rights of use.[53]

The non-theistic traditions of Asia and South Asia, such as Shinto, also provide deep roots for a respect for nature and for our responsibilities to future generations as stewards of this planet. In most instances they call for living in harmony with nature.[54] Moreover, the

50. The U.S. Constitution reserves such powers for the states. "The owners not delegated to the United States by the Constitution, nor prohibited by it to the States, are reserved to the States respectively, or to the people." U.S. Const. Amend. X. *See* Garton, "Ecology and the Police Power," 16 *S.D.L. Rev.* 261 (1971).
51. "Selbst eine ganze Gesellschaft, eine Nation, ja alle gleichzeitigen Gesellschaften zusammengenommen sind nicht Eigentuemer der Erde. Sie sind nur ihre Besitzer, ihre Nutzniesser, und haben sie als *boni patres familias* den nachfolgenden Generationen verbessert zu hinterlassen." Karl Marx, *Collected Works* (1985).
52. Attributed to Nan Sir Ofori Atta. N.A. Ollennu, *Principles of Customary Land Law in Ghana,* 4 (Sweet & Maxwell, 1962). For discussion of relationship between generations, *see* also A. Allott, *Essays in African Law,* 70 (Greenwood Press, 1975).
53. *See,* e.g., I. Schapera, *A Handbook of Tswana Law and Custom* (F. Cass, 1970); X. Vlanc-Jouvan, "Problems of Harmonization of Traditional and Modern Concepts in the Land Law of French-Speaking Africa and Madagascar," *Integration of Customary and Modern Legal Systems in Africa* (Africana, 1971). L. Obeng, "Benevolent Yokes in Different Worlds," in *Global Resources: Perspectives and Alternatives,* 21–32 (C.N. McRostie, ed., University Park Press, 1980). Obeng notes that such observances are found among peoples in Afria, Asia, the Pacific, Papua New Guinea, and the American Indians.
54. J. Stewart-Smith, *In the Shadow of Fujisan* (Viking Penguin, 1987). The reverence for na-

orthodoxy of Hinduism, Buddhism, and Jainism indirectly support the conservation of our diverse cultural resources in their acceptance of the legitimacy of other religious groups.[55]

III. Principles of intergenerational equity

Three principles form the basis of intergenerational equity. First, each generation should be required to conserve the diversity of the natural and cultural resource base, so that it does not unduly restrict the options available to future generations in solving their problems and satisfying their own values, and should also be entitled to diversity comparable to that enjoyed by previous generations. This principle is called "conservation of options." Second, each generation should be required to maintain the quality of the planet so that it is passed on in no worse condition than that in which it was received, and should also be entitled to planetary quality comparable to that enjoyed by previous generations. This is the principle of "conservation of quality." Third, each generation should provide its members with equitable rights of access to the legacy of past generations and should conserve this access for future generations. This is the principle of "conservation of access."

The proposed principles recognize the right of each generation to use the Earth's resources for its own benefit, but constrain the actions of the present generation in doing so. Within these constraints they do not dictate how each generation should manage its resources. They do not require that the present generation predict the preferences of future generations, which would be difficult if not impossible. Rather, they try to ensure a reasonably secure and flexible natural resource base for future generations that they can use to satisfy their own values and preferences. They are generally shared by different cultural traditions and are generally acceptable to different economic and political systems.

While the principle of quality may be viewed as including the principle of diversity, they are separate and complementary. To illustrate this, we can invoke the analogy of a common law trust, whose corpus consists of investments in two different energy companies and a com-

---

ture in Japan, for example, is transformed into important symbolic representations, such as flying cranes on wedding kimonos. *See also* F.S.C. Northrup, *The Meeting of East and West* (Oxford, 1949).

55. *See* F.S.C. Northrup, *id.* at 415–470.

puter company. If the trustee shifts the investments into other energy and computer companies that turn out to be lower in quality as investments, the value of the trust corpus declines, but the diversity of the holdings does not change. By contrast, if the trustee combines all the investments into a single oil company, the value of the holdings may remain the same, but the diversity of the holdings is sharply compromised.[56]

In our planet, environmental quality may decline, but this does not necessarily reduce significantly the diversity of the resource base. Similarly, it may be possible for one generation to sustain the quality of air and water but substantially destroy the diversity of the resource base, as by a significant loss of genetic diversity. Certainly the two principles interact and feed upon each other. It is easier to maintain quality if there are many options available for doing so, and serious water pollution may cause fish to disappear. It is easier to conserve options when there is concern for maintaining quality. Both principles are essential for a robust planet for future generations and must be implemented in tandem.

Conservation of options

Future generations are more likely to survive and attain their goals if they have a variety of options for addressing their problems. Conserving the diversity of the natural and cultural resource bases is designed to give our descendants a robust and flexible heritage with which to try to achieve a decent and healthy life.[57]

The principle of conserving options rests on the premise that diversity, like quality, contributes to robustness. This can be seen in the contribution of biological diversity to the robustness of ecosystems. If diverse strains and species are present in an ecosystem and the system is perturbed, some strains and species will survive and multiply. While the distribution of the biological population may change, the ecosystem remains viable.[58] By contrast, farmers producing monocultures have to work hard to preserve them, for they are

---

56. *See,* A. Scott, 3 *The Law of Trusts,* 228 (3rd ed., 1967, and Supp., Little Brown, 1982).

57. *See* T. Page, "Intergenerational Justice as Opportunity," *Energy and the Future* (D. Mac-Lean and P. Brown eds., Rowman and Littlefield, 1982). Page has independently proposed that intergenerational justice have as its object the preservation of opportunities for future generations, which means preserving the "valuable parts." *See also* T. Page, *Conservation and Economic Efficiency* (Johns Hopkins, 1977).

58. *See,* e.g., *Diversity and Stability in Ecological Systems* (G. Woodwell and H. Smith, eds., Clearinghouse for Federal Scientific and Technical Information, Springfield, Va., 1969).

easily eliminated through the invasion of weeds, insects, and other pests. Some theoretical scientific research suggests, however, that as systems become more complex (more species and a richer structure of interdependence), they may become more dynamically fragile. This suggests that we need to understand the special kinds of complexity that promote stability.[59]

Biological diversity as it relates to robustness encompasses change in the species and strains that make up the ecosystem.[60] This point is essential to intergenerational justice, for it means that change, which is essential for economic development, is an integral part of implementing the principle.

The wisdom of conserving options is reflected more broadly in conventional economic practices, such as maintaining diversity in the corpus of a common law trust, portfolios of investments, and national economies. In these latter examples, diversity is primarily viewed as a means of spreading risks to avoid reliance on only one investment or industry. At the same time it offers an effective strategy for improving economic wealth.

The question arises, however, whether conserving options does not disregard the needs of the present generation. It may be argued that the best way to conserve options is to preserve the status quo, which means that poor people in particular will continue to suffer.[61]

This argument applies the principle incorrectly. Conservation of options can be accomplished by new technological developments that create substitutes for existing resources or processes for exploiting them more efficiently, as well as by conservation of existing resources. Certainly any investment in the development of particular resources forecloses other options for that resource. The decision to convert an area to solar panels will foreclose use of the land for crops, at least for that period of time. But the solar panels may help to conserve more scarce energy supplies, such as helium-rich natural gas reserves, or to avoid fossil-fuel emissions that contribute to climate change. To the extent that a hydroelectric dam or mine will destroy a unique natural resource, however, we must proceed extremely cautiously, if at all, because future generations might be willing to pay us handsomely to conserve it for them.

59. R. May, a Princeton University biologist, questions the generally accepted assertion that complexity always implies stability, a concept that is sometimes used interchangeably with robustness. R. May, *Stability and Complexity in Model Ecosystems* (Princeton, 1975); R. May, *Theoretical Ecology: Principles and Applications* (Blackwell Scientific, 1981).
60. *See* B. Norton, *Why Preserve Natural Variety?*, 73–97 (Princeton, 1987).
61. Conversation with Pablo Guttman, an economist, Buenos Aires, Argentina, 11 June 1986.

The principle of conservation of options requires that on *balance* the diversity of the resource base be maintained. It acts as an important brake on those who would destroy biological diversity by clear-cutting tropical areas, developing crop monocultures to the exclusion of conserving wild cultivars, exhausting all known quantities of essentially non-renewable resources such as oil and helium-bearing natural gas, or discarding the cultural resources of all but a few dominant cultures.

Conservation of quality

The principle of conservation of quality requires that we leave the quality of the natural and cultural environments in no worse condition than we received it. Recent generations have used resources of air, water, and soils as free resources for dumping their wastes, thereby passing on the costs of their activities to future generations in the form of degraded quality of air and water, with accompanying harms to plant and animal life and to human health.

The principle of conserving quality is consistent with environmentally sustainable growth. It does not mean that the environment must remain unchanged, which would be inconsistent in any event with conserving the present generation's access to the benefits of the planet. In determining whether one generation is conserving quality, trade-offs are inevitable. For example, we may exhaust more reserves of a natural resource and cause modest levels of pollution, but pass on a higher level of income, capital, and knowledge sufficient to enable future generations to develop substitutes for the depleted resource and methods for abating or removing pollutants. A framework must be developed in which such balancing can take place. Necessary components will be predictive indices of resource diversity and resource quality, baseline measurements, and an improved capacity to predict technological change.

It is natural to assume that present trends in natural and social systems will continue. However, breaking-points may exist in key variables beyond which these systems will reorganize and substantially change their properties. Predicting these breaking-points is thus of critical importance, probably more important than predicting specific technological changes, since such breaking-points would indicate the need for deliberate human intervention.[62]

62. Discussion with G. Gallopín, President, Fundación Bariloche, June 1986. This is consistent

According to the Gaia hypothesis, the Earth's biosphere is a complex entity that has a homoeostatic feedback system capable of maintaining an optimal physical and chemical environment for life on Earth.[63] Even if this is the case, there is still a question of whether there are limits in critical variables beyond which this homoeostatic quality no longer obtains.

Conservation of access

Conservation of access gives the members of the present generation a reasonable, non-discriminatory right of access to the natural and cultural resources of our planet. This means they are entitled to these resources to improve their own economic and social well-being provided that they respect their equitable duties to future generations and do not unreasonably interfere with the access of other members of their generation to these same resources.

This offers a principle of justice between generations and between members of the same generation. The refinement of what conservation of access means as applied to members of the present generation is extremely complex. It implies both that the patrimony itself to which they have access should be comparable in quality and diversity (or robustness) to previous generations and that they should have a minimum level of resources so that they can in fact have access to such a patrimony. Thus, members of the present generation must not degrade the patrimony available, and to the extent that some members are too impoverished to have effective access, must assist them to gain such access.

IV. Intergenerational rights and obligations

The principles of options (diversity), quality, and access form the basis of a set of intergenerational obligations and rights, or planetary rights and obligations, that are held by each generation. These rights and obligations derive from each generation's position as part of the intertemporal entity of human society. Planetary intergenerational

---

with the theories of catastrophe and of complex systems far from equilibrium. For catastrophe theory, *see* R. Thom, *Mathematical Models of Morphogenesis* (Halsted Press, 1983); for complex systems, *see* I. Prigogine and I. Stengers, *Order Out of Chaos: Man's New Dialogue With Nature* (Bantam, 1984).

63. J. Lovelock, *Gaia, A New Look at Life on Earth* (Oxford, 1979).

rights and obligations are integrally linked; the rights are always associated with obligations. They represent in the first instance a moral protection of interests, which must be transformed into legal rights and obligations.

Planetary rights and obligations coexist in each generation. In the *inter*generational dimension, the generations to which the obligations are owed are future generations, while the generations with which the rights are linked are past generations. Thus the rights of future generations are linked to the obligations of the present generation. In the *intra*generational context, planetary obligations and rights exist between members of the present generation. They derive from the *inter*generational relationship that each generation shares with those who have come before and those yet to come. Thus, intergenerational obligations to conserve the planet flow from the present generation both to future generations as generations and to members of the present generation, who have the right to use and enjoy the planetary legacy.

Intergenerational rights of necessity inhere in all generations, whether these be immediately successive generations or ones more distant. There is no theoretical basis for limiting such rights to immediately successive generations. If we were to do so, we would often provide little or no protection to more distant future generations. Nuclear and hazardous-waste disposal, the loss of biological diversity, and ozone depletion, for example, have significant effects on the natural heritage of more distant generations.

Intergenerational planetary rights may be regarded as group rights, as distinct from individual rights, in the sense that generations hold these rights as groups in relation to other generations – past, present, and future.[64] They exist regardless of the number and identity of individuals making up each generation. When held by members of the present generation, they acquire attributes of individual rights in the sense that there are identifiable interests of individuals that the rights protect. However, those interests derive from the fact that those living now are members of the present generation and have rights in relation to other generations to use and benefit from planet Earth. The remedies for violations of these rights will benefit other members of the generation, not only the individual.

64. For a thoughtful analysis of group rights in relation to goods that are enjoyed together, *see* J. Waldron, "Can Communal Goods Be Human Rights?" (paper delivered at Conference on Development, Environment and Peace as New Human Rights, Oxford University, Oxford, England, 28–31 May 1987).

More broadly, intergenerational rights may provide a theoretically attractive framework for linking a number of disparate rights that have inherently a temporal dimension. These include cultural rights and rights to development, which implicitly assume that there are continuing processes that are to be protected.

It has been argued that future generations cannot have rights, because rights exist only when there are identifiable interests, which can only happen if we can identify the individuals who have interests to protect. Since we cannot know who the individuals in the future will be, it is not possible for future generations to have rights.[65]

This paradox assumes the traditional conceptual framework of rights as rights of identifiable individuals. But planetary intergenerational rights are not in the first instance rights possessed by individuals. They are, instead, *generational* rights, which must be conceived of in the temporal context of generations. Generations hold these rights as groups in relation to other generations – past, present, and future. This is consistent with other approaches to rights, including the Islamic approach, which treats human rights not only as individual rights, but as "rights of the community of believers as a whole."[66] They can be evaluated by objective criteria and indices applied to the planet from one generation to the next. To evaluate whether the interests represented in planetary rights are being adequately protected does not depend upon knowing the number of kinds of individuals that may ultimately exist in any given future generation.

One might still ask whether it is not preferable to speak only of planetary obligations toward future generations without corresponding intergenerational rights. Can intergenerational obligations exist without rights?[67] While rights are always connected to obligations, the reverse is not always true. Theoretically, an obligation need not always entail a right. For example, a moral obligation of charity does not give those who benefit a right to charity.

---

65. This has been referred to as Parfit's paradox and was developed in D. Parfit, "On Doing the Best for Our Children," in *Ethics and Population*, 100 (M. Bayles, ed., Schenkman, 1976) and D. Parfit, "Future Generations, Further Problems," 11 *Phil. & Pub. Aff.*, 113 (1982).

66. M. Khaduri, *supra* note 46 at 233 (1984).

67. It has been argued that if one accepts the model of rights as limited to individual rights, it is preferable to recognize general obligations toward the integrity of environmental systems rather than to discuss environmental protection in the framework of rights, since this framework cannot encompass such categories as future generations, whose individual members are still contingent. B. Norton, "Environmental Ethics and the Rights of Future Generations," 7 *Soc. Theory & Prac.*, 319, 337 (1981).

While this approach may be attractive, it ignores the fundamental temporal relationship that each generation has to all other generations and that gives rise to the rights of each generation to share equitably in the use of the planet and its natural resources. These rights focus discussion on the welfare of generations, what each generation is able to have and to enjoy, in a way that obligations cannot. If obligations of the present generation are not linked with rights, the present generation has a strong incentive to bias the definition of these obligations in favour of itself at the expense of future generations. Intergenerational rights have greater moral force than do obligations. They provide a basis for protecting the interests of all generations in a healthy and robust planet.[68]

The content of intergenerational rights is framed by the principles of intergenerational equity. Within this constraint, each generation has the responsibility to set criteria for defining the actions that infringe upon these rights. Appropriate criteria would be whether activities have a significant impact, either spatially or over time, whether the effects are irreversible or reversible only with unacceptable costs, and whether the effects will be viewed as significant by a substantial number of people.

Certain categories of actions can be identified as likely infringing upon intergenerational rights. They include the following:
- wastes whose impacts cannot be confidently contained either spatially or over time;
- damage to soils such that they are incapable of supporting plant or animal life;
- tropical-forest destruction sufficient to diminish significantly the overall diversity of species in the region and the sustainability of soils;
- air pollution or land transformations that induce significant climate change on a large scale;
- destruction of knowledge essential to understanding natural and social systems, such as residence decay times of nuclear wastes;
- destruction of cultural monuments that countries have acknowledged to be part of the common heritage of mankind;
- destruction of specific endowments established by the present generation for the benefit of future generations, such as libraries and gene banks.

68. The Cousteau Society has drafted a Petition for the Rights of Future Generations, for which it is soliciting signatures around the world. *See* 19 *Calypso Log,* 7 (February 1992) for text of the petition.

Some international agreements already obligate countries to guard against such actions. These include the London Ocean Dumping Convention, which controls dumping of hazardous and nuclear wastes in the marine environment; the Antarctic Treaty and the new Environmental Protocol; the World Soils Charter; the Montreal Protocol on Substances That Deplete the Ozone Layer; and the World Heritage Convention.

Intergenerational planetary rights may also be linked to certain procedural norms, which are important to achieving the substantive norms. For example, access to information, public participation, and long-term impact assessments are emerging as potentially important instruments for achieving intergenerational equity.

Enforcement of intergenerational planetary rights is appropriately done by a guardian or representative of future generations as a *group*, not of future individuals, who are of necessity indeterminate. While the holder of the right may lack the capacity to bring grievances forward and hence depends upon the representative's decision to do so, this inability does not affect the existence of the right or the obligation associated with it.

Developments in international law outside the field of the environment make acceptance of intergenerational rights a natural and desirable evolution. Indeed, international human rights law – the genocide convention, and the prohibition against racial discrimination, to cite two examples – are arguably directed as much to the protection of future as to present generations. The extinction of, for example, an entire people is more odious in law than the murder of an equal number of people constituting a minority of each of several groups. Similarly, discrimination denies an "equal place at the starting gate" not only to the generation of the suppressed group, but (by implication) also to future generations. Provisions in other human rights agreements refer to rights of children and of the elderly, and to education and training, which are implicitly temporally oriented.

Intergenerational rights and obligations may have implications for population policies. While the existence of the rights does not depend upon knowing the composition of the future generation, nevertheless, if the earth's population continues to grow rapidly, the amount of diversity and degree of quality that must be passed on will be higher than if the population in the future were at the same level or less than it is today. Whether a generation chooses to meet its obligations by curtailing exploitation, consumption, and waste or by constraining population growth is a decision it must make. The fact that future generations have a generational right to receive the planet in a certain condition limits the extent to which a present generation can ignore this choice.

Almost every policy decision of government and business affects the composition of future generations, whether or not they are taken to ensure their rights under the guidelines enunciated above. Decisions regarding war and peace, economic policy, the relative prosperity of different regions and social groups, transportation, health, education – all influence the demographics and the composition of future generations by affecting the lives and fortunes of the present generation. This opens the possibility that all decisions deserve to be scrutinized from the point of view of their impact on future generations. The possibility that intergenerational equity may place limits on our actions is an important new area of research on sustainable development. But such constraints must be applied narrowly, however, so that concern for future generations does not become a blunt instrument to thwart proposals for change. The purpose must be only to protect against long-term environment damage, such as toxic groundwater pollution, radiative pollution of the oceans, soil degradation, etc., whose effects are difficult or impossible to reverse – unless there are extremely compelling reasons to do so beyond profitability.

Planetary rights of future generations provide a normative framework for implementing environmentally sustainable development. They mean that we do not have to rely on a sense of patronizing generosity by the present generation, but on a fundamental entitlement of future generations. It is an entitlement that we ourselves, as members of the present generation, held in relation to our ancestors and that we need now to protect for our descendants.

V. Implementation of intergenerational equity

Strategies for implementing intergenerational equity are set forth in detail elsewhere.[69] Several of them merit special attention in this chapter.

Representation to future generations

Future generations are not effectively represented in the decision-making processes today, although the decisions we make today will determine their initial welfare. While future generations may be will-

---

69. *See In Fairness to Future Generations, supra* unnumbered note on p. 385.

ing to pay us handsomely to prevent certain actions or to have us undertake others, they have no way of voicing this preference. Representation must take place in several different fora: in the market place, in legislative and administrative decision-making, and in judicial decision-making.

Future generations are not effectively represented in the market place today; they must be. This requires that we understand the fundamental entitlement among generations correctly, so that we recognize that future generations have an equal claim with the present generation to use and benefit from the natural environment. Once we recognize this entitlement of equality among generations, economic instruments can be developed to achieve intergenerational equity efficiently.[70]

In administrative and judicial decisions, we can appoint and publicly finance an office that has responsibility for ensuring that the interests of future generations are considered and for ensuring that laws regarding our environment and natural resources are observed, for investigating complaints, and for providing warnings of pending problems. States could give standing in their national courts and administrative bodies to a representative of future generations, who might function as a guardian *ad litem*. Another approach is to designate an ombudsman for future generations or to appoint commissioners for future generations. These could operate internationally, nationally, or locally. The World Commission on Environment and Development recommended that countries consider a national ombudsman.[71]

Development in international legal instruments

To encourage cooperation between countries and among communities to fulfil obligations to future generations, it is useful to elaborate and codify the relevant norms of intergenerational equity. Codification reduces the ambiguities about expected behaviour and defines cooperative behaviour from uncooperative behaviour.

Some of these legal instruments will be binding. Others may be non-binding legal instruments, or may become binding over time. To the extent that the norms represent customary international law, they

---

70. *See* R. Norgaard,"Sustainability as Intergenerational Equity: The Challenge to Economic Thought and Practice" (World Bank Report No. IDP 97, 1991) for discussion of methods for accomplishing this.
71. World Commission on Environment and Development, *Our Common Future*, 332 (Oxford, 1987).

will become binding upon all countries, whether or not they are party to the relevant agreement. We need to encourage both general legal instruments articulating intergenerational rights and obligations in relation to our planet, as well as binding agreements directed to conserving specific resources, such as forests and living resources essential to maintaining biological diversity, or to pollution prevention.

International regimes to manage or to coordinate measures for managing particular natural resources or environmental pollutants are important. They facilitate the development and exchange of information, make it more difficult for a party to defect since there are costs involved, and may contribute to the developing of new norms. It is important that relevant states participate in the regime in order to avoid pollution havens or free riders in the international community. This calls for states to provide incentives and disincentives to encourage participation.

Planetary ethos

To implement intergenerational equity, we need an ethos that is planetary in scope and encompasses all generations. This requires that we raise public consciousness and educate people about environmentally sustainable development. Communities have a right to know about the environmental contaminants in their area and about the sustainability of natural-resource consumption patterns. Nongovernmental organizations, whether corporate or environmentally based, have a particularly important role in ensuring this. The information revolution that is upon us should greatly assist in providing the information necessary to do this and in mobilizing public participation in developing and implementing measures to achieve intergenerational equity.

If we review the progress of the international community in addressing intergenerational environmental concerns in the last two decades, we can conclude, on the one hand, that it is highly insufficient to the task. But if we compare where we are today to 1972, we cannot help but be impressed by the rapid learning curve of countries in addressing these issues.

The issue for 1972 was the reconciliation of environment and development. The issue in 1992 is achieving environmentally sustainable development and committing to a new ethos of intergenerational fairness.

13

Ecological security: Response to global challenges

Alexandre S. Timoshenko

The environmental problem has already acquired global parameters. Environmental challenges are on a global scale, have global implications, and are becoming increasingly significant to all nations. Ozone-layer decay, climate change, biological diversity depletion, and chemical pollution are just a few but the most illustrative examples of how badly the international community needs a new global approach to ecological issues.

For decades the world has been living in a paradoxical situation. On the one hand, the activities to protect the environment have been mushrooming locally, nationally, regionally, and internationally. On the other hand, the environment has been deteriorating more and more. In spite of all efforts, this negative process cannot even be stopped. Such a widening gap between scope and result inevitably leads to a conclusion that there is something substantially wrong with the very approach to the ecological problem. A conceptual breakthrough is essential.

I. Conceptual paradigm

Several new concepts have already been introduced by politicians and by scholars: including primacy of international law, common interest, intergenerational equity, common heritage of mankind, common European home, redefined security, and ecological (environmental)

413

security. These are in addition to certain fundamental changes of methodological character that have manifested in recent years. The international legal regulation of environmental protection has been shifting more and more from a traditional "media control approach" (rivers, marine environment, air, and wildlife) to a "problem control approach" (population, desertification, hazardous wastes, and global warming).

The concepts recently introduced are all based on the assumption that the overwhelming importance of protection of the natural environment requires awareness of its global, all-human, long-term dimensions. This means that these conceptions would be complimentary rather than competitive. When thoroughly and evenly elaborated, they could create a new legal regime for truly efficient environmental protection.

The primacy of international law presupposes the supremacy of law over force in international relations. Primacy of international law requires recognizing the supremacy of values common to all mankind over all other values and interests, including giving the highest priority to human survival through the protection of the natural environment.[1] When applied to global environmental challenges, this means that these problems cannot be resolved via the power pressure of several states, however influential they may be. However, through voluntary uniform behaviour by all countries or their overwhelming majority through the exposure of common interest by political methods and its realization through a system of appropriate international legal prescriptions, these problems can be resolved.

The existence of a common interest has long since been recognized as the main driving force in the development of international law. It is precisely the need for its legal manifestation that has given birth to a great deal of multilateral international treaties regulating various spheres of cooperation among states on problems being of common interest to them. Comprehending the existence and importance of vital ecological values expands the concept of common interest. Still today we must state that the world community has not yet come to appreciate the problem of global environmental protection as a concentrated expression of common interest.

The urgency and acuteness of the problem are assessed in various

---

1. V.S. Vereschetin and R.A. Mullerson, "New Thinking and International Law," *Soviet State and Law*, n. 3 at 3–4 (Moscow, 1988).

ways by industrially developed and developing countries. The latter assess global environmental threats as a problem regarding primarily developed countries, though the recent scenarios of ecological catastrophes show how devastating their affects can be on many developing nations.[2]

At the same time, there are realistic political possibilities for bringing the positions of various groups of countries closer together through comprehensive evaluation and understanding of environmental challenges and the vital necessity of global consensus based on common ecological interest. The meeting in Moscow on 15 July 1989 between the former Soviet leader Mikhail Gorbachev and former Indian Prime Minister Rajiv Gandhi may serve as an example of statements regarding such a common interest. Both leaders expressed the conviction that a realistic solution to the problems of worldwide significance can only be found via their internationalization.[3]

Another example could be the attitude toward ecological problems demonstrated by governmental leaders at the Paris "Big Seven" meeting (July 1989).[4] In the declaration on East-West relations adopted by the meeting, one can see favourable prospects for joint pursuits of equitable resolutions in the area of environmental protection. On the other hand, four presidents of top developing countries turned to the "Seven" with a proposal for a North-South meeting, in the near future, on global problems of the economy and the environment.[5]

The concepts of a "common heritage of mankind" and "intergenerational equity" are interconnected. Both concepts aim to endow common human rights and interests within a legal context. The attempts of scholars and politicians to apply both concepts to the global environment are well known.

The concept of a "common heritage" has been widely represented and discussed at various international conventions, thereby manifesting a different and sometimes conflicting understanding of its substance and content. One may even say that the initial scope of the conception has undergone a certain deformation under the influence of the political interests of various groups of countries. Currently

2. *See,* for example, the scenario of possible flooding of part of the territory of Bangladesh resulting from sea-level rise in *World Resources 1988–89*, 173–174 (Basic Books, 1988).
3. *Pravda,* 16 July 1989.
4. *Pravda,* 18 July 1989.
5. *Id.*

there are a variety of legal, political, and doctrinal definitions of this concept. Today the obvious impossibility of establishing a single legal context of the common heritage of mankind makes it tempting to apply this concept to the most varied spaces, resources, and phenomena.

The "intergenerational equity" concept is one of the most recent and it has been courageously elaborated mainly on the level of academic thinking.[6] The noble goal of the conception is to create legitimacy for the ecological rights of future generations, to establish a legal obligation to preserve favourable environmental conditions for future generations, to guarantee them equal access to natural resources and benefits. However, future generations still lack the status of the subject of international law. Some scholars stress the extreme difficulty of achieving an international consensus on the right of intergenerational equity, since countries frequently do not wish to forego immediate benefits for the sake of distant advantages.[7] At the same time, the great potential of intergenerational equity for preserving the global environment must be recognized. This concept deserves thorough discussion and further elaboration.

The most recent concept that is appropriate in this context is the concept of common concern of mankind. It is deeply rooted in such concepts as common interest, global commons, and common heritage of mankind; and it is closely linked to the concept of intergenerational rights. Indeed, the significant controversies and conflicting interpretations that have appeared during application of the "common heritage" approach in different areas (e.g. the law of the sea and space law) inspired governments to choose another derivative, i.e. common concern, to serve concerted actions in equitable sharing of burdens in environmental protection, rather than of benefits from exploitation of environmental wealth.

The "common concern" concept has at least two important facets: spatial and temporal. The spatial aspect means that common concern implies cooperation of all states on matters being similarly important to all nations, to the whole international community. The temporal aspect arises from long-term implications of major environmental

---

6. *See*, e.g., E. Brown Weiss, *In Fairness to Future Generations: International Law, Common Patrimony, and Intergenerational Equity* (Transnational/United Nations University, 1989).
7. L.K. Caldwell, *International Environmental Policy: Emergence and Dimensions* (Duke Univeristy, 1984), pp. 258–259.

challenges, which affect the rights and obligations not only of present but also of future generations. Indeed, a complex interaction of natural environmental factors preconditions a prolonged time-lag between the cause and effect of many human activities. For example, a complete revelation of the causal relationship between chloro-fluoro-carbon emissions and ozone-layer destruction, or between greenhouse-gas emissions and global warming, can take several generations. Both facets of the "common concern" conception can be traced in positive environmental law and various UN General Assembly resolutions and declarations.

One more aspect of the "common concern" is the social dimension. Common concern presumes involvement of all structures and sectors of the society in the process of combating global environmental threats, i.e., legislative, judicial, and governmental bodies together with private business, non-governmental organizations, and citizen groups. This relatively new phenomenon has been manifested via green movements, comprehensive environmental policies introduced by governments and even market forces, but it needs to be supported with stronger legal guarantees.

In December 1988, the UN General Assembly in its resolution 43/53 explicitly stated that climate change was a common concern of mankind. This was partially a way out of the controversies related to the common heritage of mankind concept, which had initially been introduced by Malta as a basis for this resolution. At the same time, the resolution wisely indicated a new path to achieving a consolidated set of legal obligations to protect global climate. A new formula, though well originated in the past, was enthusiastically welcomed in other international fora. In the report of the 1989 Ottawa Meeting of Legal and Policy Experts, it was attempted to reformulate this concept by defining the atmosphere as a "common resource of vital interest to mankind." Meanwhile the 1989 Noordwijk Declaration expressly stated that "climate change is a common concern of mankind." In December 1989, the UN General Assembly recalled that climate change had been recognized as a common concern of mankind (UNGA resolution 44/207). In August 1990, the Fourth Session of the Intergovernmental Panel on Climate Change adopted the IPCC First Assessment Report Overview, which recommended as an urgent international action the elaboration of an international convention on global climate that would serve as a "firm basis for effective co-operation to act on greenhouse gas emissions and adapt to any adverse effects of climate change." The report stressed that "the Convention should recognize climate change as a common concern of mankind." A wider application of such a new notion as "common concern of mankind" by the world community undoubtedly appeals to all international agencies to assist to this growing international consensus, which in the long run might reach an *opinio juris* on the applicability of the concept to a wide range of global environmental matters.

The concepts described above lack one important quality. They are all based on notions that are understood primarily by professionals in international law and politics. Thus, they are neither intelligible nor appealing to ordinary people whose support and personal involvement are crucial for such a wide-scale task as that of global environmental protection. The notion of "security" is universally understood and has served as a basic ingredient in all periods of human history. The conception of ecological security adds a security dimension to the ecological problem and vice versa, thereby putting global ecology into the range of security issues.

Jessica Mathews of the World Resources Institute stresses the necessity to redefine our classical understanding of security: "Global developments now suggest the need for another analogous, and broader definition of national security which will include resource, environmental and demographic issues."[8] One only need add that this assumption is equally valid for international security. Political scientist Grigory Khozin writes that "ecological security is by its content significantly higher than the traditional idea of national security, it speaks to the interests of all humanity and can only be universal, common to all mankind."[9]

The UNEP Executive Director, Dr. M.K. Tolba, recently identified ecological destruction and inequitable development as a global time bomb threatening our future. He further stressed that "the escalating ecological crisis is destabilizing national security interests, and threatening our planetary life-support systems."[10]

---

8. J.T. Mathews, "Redefining Security," 68 *Foreign Affairs*, 162 (1989).
9. G.S. Khozin, "Ecological Security: International Aspects," in *Ecology: Means for the Survival and Development of Humanity: Scholarly Position*, 32 (Association of Ecology and Peace, 1988).
10. "From Common Concern to a Common Future." Statement by Dr. Mostafa K. Tolba, Executive Director, United Nations Environment Programme, to the convocation of Williams College, Williamstown, Massachusetts, 15 Sept. 1990.

The introduction of the concept of ecological security has objective prerequisites of an ecological, economic, political, technological, and socio-psychological nature. The latest Worldwatch Institute report, "State of the World 1990," which is ironically subtitled "Report on Progress Toward a Sustainable Society," gives a number of record figures that reveal the growing ecological instability of the planet.[11] Thus, in 1989 the global annual emissions of carbon dioxide reached a record total of 5.7 billion tons.[12] The annual addition to world population, which reached a record high in 1989 of 88 million people, is likely to average 96 million during the nineties.[13] Subsequently one of the authors of the Report came to the conclusion that environmental security issues now share the stage with more traditional economic and military concerns, inaugurating a new age of environmental diplomacy.[14]

The Report clearly indicates how critical the ecological situation in the world is: " . . . If the world is to achieve sustainability, it will need to do so within the next 40 years. If we have not succeeded by then, environmental deterioration and economic decline are likely to be feeding on each other pulling us into a downward spiral of social disintegration."[15] This short citation contains two important connotations. Firstly, it stresses the interconnection of environmental, economic, and social phenomena. Secondly, it presupposes that if the world community wishes to cope with global environmental threats in such a short time limit, urgent and radical improvements in the approach to the problem are needed.

Another argument is that dealing with the global environment means dealing with global security. This argument is contained in the Hague Declaration, adopted in March 1989 by the representatives of 24 countries, including 17 heads of government.[16] Based on the evaluation of only two global challenges (global warming and ozone depletion), the Declaration nevertheless stressed: "The right to live is the right from which all other rights stem. Guaranteeing this right is the paramount duty of those in charge of all States throughout the

---

11. *State of the World 1990*, 5–16 (Worldwatch and W.W. Norton, 1990).
12. *Id.*
13. *Id.*
14. *Id.*
15. *Id.* at 174.
16. Declaration of the Hague, 19 *Envt'l Pol'y & L.*, 78 (1989).

world. Today, the very conditions of life on our planet are threatened by the severe attacks to which the earth's atmosphere is subjected."[17] It may only be added that there are more ecological threats, which put the future of human civilization at stake: and deforestation, loss of biological diversity, toxic and radioactive pollution are among them.

Having a more modern technological pattern is another threat to ecological security of the planet. The industrial and technological developments are still waste-producing and resource-wasting. They become more and more fraught with accidents that may cause an ecological catastrophe of planetary scale. The Brundtland Commission report stated: "Emerging technologies offer the promise of higher productivity, increased efficiency, and decreased pollution, but many bring risks of new toxic chemicals and wastes and of major accidents of a type and scale beyond present coping mechanisms."[18]

Academician Valery Legasov, who tragically died shortly after the Chernobyl accident, warned in one of his last articles that the devastating effect of large industrial accidents was comparable to a military threat. He also indicated that the growing stationary non-accidental industrial impact on the environment and human health must also be closely monitored. Combining these two factors creates, in his view, a serious threat to security.[19] Professor Vid Vukasovic, in 1978, stressed that science and technology possess the potential to endanger the stability of basic rules of international law and international relations. He wrote: "One should not consider that the development of science and technology is by itself progressive for the future development of international relations. It all depends on which way and for which way and for which goals the results of this development are utilized."[20]

The socio-psychological factors that are pushing the world community towards creating an ecological security regime manifest themselves primarily in the outstanding growth in public awareness in this field. The individual right to have a safe and healthy environment, which could be deduced from a vague formula of Principle One of the

---

17. *Id.*
18. *Our Common Future: The World Commission on Environment and Development*, 16 (Oxford, 1987).
19. V. Legasov, "Iz segodnja v zavtra" (From today to tomorrow), *Pravda*, 5 Oct. 1987.
20. V. Vukasovic, *Razvoj nauke i technologije i medunarodno pravo*, 271–278 (Belgrade, 1978).

1972 Stockholm Declaration on the Human Environment,[21] is now considered ripe for exploitation through inclusion in the relevant internationally legally binding documents on human rights.

The environmental NGOs, whose input during the 1972 Stockholm Conference seemed almost insignificant, have developed into strong opponents of national governments and are close to becoming new actors in the international decision-making process. Various NGOs have recently produced a number of documents on an international scale whereby the concept of a human right to a safe and healthy environment and ecological security have melded to become a key element.[22] The level of public awareness in the environmental field is clearly manifested by the fact that on 22 April 1990 (Earth Day 1990) more than 100 million people all over the world agreed to come to the streets to express their will to liberate the planet Earth from such enemies as deforestation, carbon dioxide, CGSs, wastes, overpopulation, and pollution.[23]

Political factors in favour of an ecological security approach are numerous, though their interplay is often contradictory. Today no national government or administration can risk not including an environmental component in its political platform. In two decades the green movements have developed into an influential political power (the "green" faction in the European Parliament is just one example).

It is important that an ecological security approach be discussed today not only by scholars, but also by practising diplomats. Swedish diplomat Lars Bjorkbom gave an interesting analysis of the weak and strong points of the ecological security concept as applicable to everyday policy-making. With reference to numerous international fora, he pointed out the risks to international security from the ongoing environmental degradation and the non-sustainable use of living

---

21. Stockholm Declaration on the Human Environment of the United Nations Conference on the Human Environment, 16 June 1972 11 *I.L.M.* 1916 (1972), Principle I (hereinafter Stockholm Declaration).
22. *See,* e.g., A Declaration of Interdependence: A New Global Ethics (endorsed by the Tenth World Congress of the International Humanist and Ethical Union, 1988); Earth Covenant – A Citizens' Treaty for Common Ecological Security (Global Education Associate's Publication, undated); American Bar Association Initiative for International Intergenerational Environmental Rights, 413–414 Intern'l Env't Rep., August 1989; Soviet-American Citizens' Treaty on Ecological Security (adopted by the Soviet-American Forum on Life and Human Rights in San Diego, Ca., on 29 Sept. 1989).
23. *La Nazione* 3 Rome, 22 April 1990.

natural resources. He stressed that security is a wider concept than that of military security alone, and that the growing imbalance between man and nature threatens the well-being and thus the security of all nations.[24]

Still, the widened security concept, although it seems to be reasonably clear and relevant to the problems facing mankind, evidently lacks something in quality to make it accepted by experts on international security issues or to function as a basic concept for international crisis management. According to Bjorkbom, better analytical work is needed that would lay bare the crucial links between environmental degradation and social, economic, and political destabilization. It is indispensable that the results of such analytical work be presented in terms familiar to politicians and experts on international security issues.

The interrelatedness of economic and ecological factors in the new concept of security is evident. A degraded environment always offers fewer natural resources for further economic development. The inefficient economies lead to high pollution and rapacious exploitation of natural wealth. In addition ecological security may serve as a tool to solve difficult economic-political problems. The most recent is the problem of reconverting the military sectors of natural economies. This problem promises to promptly become a full-scale task if international disarmament continues. Ecological security offers not only a sphere where huge material and intellectual resources, currently concentrated in the military sector, can be utilized, but by definition would make it easier to shift resources from one security sector to another.

It may be noted that politically, ecological security can be considered in three dimensions. The first derives from the environmental threat to political and economic stability. The second is based on the assumption that the inter-state disputes, arising from transboundary pollution or abuse of one's right to use shared natural resources, may develop into military conflicts. The third originates from the supposition that overreaching ecological imbalances may cause severe disruption of major natural processes that are indispensable to human existence on the planet.

The first two dimensions are primarily of a national and regional

---

24. L. Bjorkbom, "Resolution of Environmental Problems: The Use of Diplomacy," in *International Environmental Diplomacy: The Management and Resolution of Transfrontier Environmental Problems,* 136–137 (J.E. Carroll, ed., Cambridge University, 1988).

scale. The last and the most serious one has global implications. The best available example of the third dimension of ecological security is global climate change.[25]

The ecological security concept was initially introduced as a political idea within a comprehensive paradigm of international security. The first international document to which one may refer was adopted in May 1987 by the Warsaw Treaty Political Consultative Committee, where the Warsaw Treaty member states declared their decisiveness to strive for the creation of the all-embracing system of international security (ASIS), which would include political, economic, humanitarian, and ecological aspects.[26]

Later that year, the former Soviet leader Mikhail Gorbachev discussed the ecological dimension of international security while meeting with the UN Secretary-General.[27] And finally, in his article "Reality and Guarantees for a Secure World," published in September 1987, Mikhail Gorbachev stressed the universal character of ecological security.[28]

At the forty-second session of the UN General Assembly, the former Soviet Union and East European countries attempted to include ecological security into the agenda of urgent matters that the world community faced. A draft resolution called "International Ecological Security" was jointly proposed by the former Ukrainian SSR and Czechoslovakia.[29] The draft noted, *inter alia,* the continuing degradation of the environment and stressed the necessity to study and elaborate on the mutually acceptable conception of international ecological security, and in particular, to define relevant fundamental norms and principles of state behaviour.[30] Regrettably, despite the evident viability of the ecological security approach and the compromise character of the resolution (note "mutually acceptable conception"), this document could not obtain sufficient support at the General

25. For example, one of the most important international conferences dealing with climate change treats it as a threat to global security. *See* Conference Statement, "The Changing Atmosphere: Implications for Global Security," International Conference held in Toronto, 27–30 June 1988. For similar doctrinal positions, *see* A.S. Timoshenko, "Global Climate Change: Implications for International Law and Institutions," in *Addressing Global Climate Change: The Emergence of a New World Order?,* 15–36 (Environmental Law Institute, 1989); A.S. Timoshenko, "Ecological Security: Global Change Paradigm," *Den J. Int'l L. & Pol'y.*

26. *Pravda,* Moscow, 30 May 1987.

27. *Pravda,* Moscow, 30 June 1987.

28. *Pravda,* Moscow, 17 Sept. 1987.

29. UNGA Doc. A/C.2/42/L.34, 30 Oct. 1987.

30. *Id.*

Assembly. This was clear evidence of how the political conservatism that reigned in a limited sphere of East-West relations could easily overweigh the interests of saving the entire world from ecological catastrophe.

At the forty-third session of the UN General Assembly, the Soviet leaders continued to give special attention to ecological security. Speaking at the session, Mikhail Gorbachev called for defining "the world ecological threat."[31] The former Soviet foreign minister, Eduard Shevardnadze, not only proposed the creation of an "international regime of ecological security" but also offered a programme of its implementation.[32] Still, a full-scale discussion of this topic did not occur at the UN General Assembly.

II. Legal regime

The ecological security conception has been gradually moving from a political debate into juridical thinking. The first step is the recognition of the link between the environment and security and of the necessity to make relevant improvements in the legal and institutional order. Lloyd Timberlake, from the International Institute of Environment and Development, claimed that environmental disasters are the real security threats of the next century. He also said that national governments and electorates should change their security priorities and that a series of treaties should be negotiated to protect the world from the new dangers.[33]

A number of known legal scholars and politicians associate the new notion of "security" primarily with an ecological threat.[34] Others use the very notion of "ecological (environmental) security" widely.[35] The president of the World Resources Institute, James Speth, emphasizes that "a new kind of international security is advancing on us. The world's geopolitical systems may be faring better, but its ecological systems are in trouble," and he proposes a programme of poli-

---

31. *Pravda,* Moscow, 8 Dec. 1988.
32. *Pravda,* Moscow, 28 Sept. 1988.
33. L. Timberlake, "The Greatest Threat on Earth," *The Independent,* 19, 12 Sept. 1988.
34. L. Caldwell, *supra* note 7 at 12; T.W. Wilson, "Global Climate, World Politics and National Security," in *World Climate Change: The Role of International Law and Institutions,* 71–77 (Westview, 1983); H. Taubenfeld, "The Atmosphere: Change, Politics, and World Order," in *World Climate Change, supra,* pp. 145–166.
35. A. Westing, "An Expanded Concept of International Security," in *Global Resources and International Conflict: Environmental Factors in Strategic Policy and Action,* 183–200 (Oxford, 1987).

cy and institutional transitions to cope with these new threats.[36] Professor Juraj Cuth from Czechoslovakia analyses the history of the formation of the ecological security system starting from loosening bloc confrontation to recent political and legal factors in international ecological security.[37] Oscar Hugler and Reinhard Müller from the former East Germany, in their article "International Legal Aspects of Ecological Security Conception," reveal correlations between ecological security, common security, and fundamental principles of general international law.[38]

Arthur Westing, from the Stockholm International Peace Research Institute (SIPRI), not only identifies a variety of environmental impacts resulting from military activities,[39] but elaborates on them with four policy directions of "an attack on the problem of safeguarding our civilization from environmental collapse" (population control, pollution abatement, habitat protection, and conflict resolution).[40] Norman Myers suggests that a sizeable national security return can be generated by protecting the global environment.[41]

Robert Boardman of Dalhousie University, retracing the development of ecological security within the context of common security and the law of the sea, came to the conclusion that environmental components formed an essential ingredient of the definitions of security in the late-twentieth-century world society and that in common security, assumptions of the common interests of states in ecological stability are combined with those of security interdependence in more traditional areas.[42] Professor Richard Gardner of Columbia University, analysing qualitative changes in the vulnerability of superpowers in modern times, points out that "the main threat to the future security of the superpowers may be not from each other but from ominous

36. J.G. Speth, "Environmental Security for the 1990's," in *Six Not-So-Easy Steps, WRI Issues and Ideas* (World Resources Institute, January 1990).

37. J. Cuth, *International Legal Aspects of International Ecological Security* (Working paper, submitted to the 32nd plenary assembly of the World Federation of the United Nations Associations), 9–14 Oct. 1989.

38. O. Hugler, R. Müller, "Das Konzept der ökologischen Sicherheit und seine völkerrechtlichen Aspekte," 393–395, no. 10 (1988) *Neue Justiz*.

39. A. H. Westing, "The Military Sector vis-a-vis the Environment," *Journal of Peace Research*, September 1988.

40. A. H. Westing, "Towards Non-Violent Conflict Resolution and Environmental Protection: A Synthesis," in *Cultural Norms, War and the Environment*, 151–157 (Arthur H. Westing, ed., Oxford, 1988).

41. N. Mayers, "Environment and Security," 74 *Foreign Policy*, 41 (Spring 1989).

42. R. Boardman, *Ecological Security, the Oceans, and Common Security* (Paper presented at the Pacem in Maribus XVII International Conference, Moscow, June 1989).

developments in the Third World . . . a multiplication of conflicts fueled by underdevelopment, overpopulation and ecological catastrophe." He continues that ". . . in a time of military, economic and environmental challenges, multilateralism has become realpolitik."[43]

The analysts predict future growing numbers of environmental disputes, some of them potentially leading to military conflicts. The examples of such disputes could be conflicts on distribution of rights over shared natural resources of vital importance to national economies (water, energy resources), or disputes arising from massive or noxious transboundary pollution. The 1990 Iraqi invasion of Kuwait was partially motivated by disputes over distribution of rights over the world's richest oil resources. Thus, it can be considered as an environmental dispute, seriously endangering international security. On the other side, it has been argued that a regional water crisis may trigger the next Middle Eastern war.[44]

Many authors, when writing on issues regarding the global environment, refer implicitly or explicitly to environmental threats and relevant security implications. Maurice Strong, for many years a key figure in international environmental cooperation, discusses a World Federation of United Nations Associations (WFUNA) initiative to establish an international commission on global risk and security, which stressed the interdependence between the world economy, the global environment, and human security. He also indicated the universal significance of this phenomenon: "Our planet and the whole of human society are at risk. The challenge is to all nations, collectively. . . . It is clear that conventional notions of security, perceived in a narrow, nationalistic sense, are becoming outmoded by new global scale threats, for example climate change, nuclear accidents, international terrorism, transboundary pollution, and ozone depletion."[45] Frederick Bernthal, the US Assistant Secretary of State for Oceans and International Environmental and Scientific Affairs, addressing the National Press Club's Conference on Earth Observations and Global Change, stated: "What defense has been to the world's leaders for the past 40 years, the environment will be for the next 40."[46] Some writers go further and emphasize that today's environmental

---

43. R.N. Gardner, "Global Topics on the Superpower Agenda: Not So Utopian After All," *International Herald Tribune*, 8 May 1989.
44. 13 *Int'l Env't Rep.*, 413 (October 1990).
45. Interview with Maurice Strong, *Options*, 12–13 (September 1989).
46. F.M. Bernthal, U.S. Climate Change Policy. Current Policy, n. 1216, United States Department of State, Bureau of Public Affairs, Washington, D.C.

challenges demand from politicians strategic thinking, and that a new era of strategic thinking about the environment is a pillar of national security.[47]

Even usually more abstract philosophical thinking pays great attention to global environmental challenges and possible reflections in a new ideology of different *modus vivendi*. Professor A.R. Drengson from Victoria University in Canada insists that to resolve the crisis of our degrading environment, human society needs a radical ecological transformation toward this way of thinking and acting.[48] This thesis is easily applicable to the shift from the classical security approach to the ecological security approach. American philosopher Jeremy Rifkin also calls for a radical change in existing life-styles. New societal organizations based on the principles of low-entropy paradigms were proposed to save the world from ecological suicide.[49] Thus, it is not peculiar that in 1989 Pope John Paul II devoted his annual message entirely to the environment. Using unusually strong language, John Paul emphasized "the dramatic threat of ecological breakdown."[50]

The evolution of the concept of ecological security, in spite of its controversial character, finds reflection in various international fora, beginning with the UN system down to non-governmental organizations. Back in 1972, the Stockholm Declaration on the Human Environment proclaimed what might be seen as prerequisites for ecological security: " . . . Man has acquired the power to transform his environment in countless ways and on an unprecedented scale. . . . Wrongly or heedlessly applied, the same power can do incalculable harm to human beings and to the human environment. . . . We can do massive and irreversible harm to the earthly environment on which our life and well-being depend."[51]

The Nairobi Declaration, though adopted in 1982, "ten years after Stockholm," did not add much to new environmental conceptualism.[52] The statement that "the human environment would greatly

47. E.D. Junkin, "Environment as National Security – Buzzword." 1 *Envt'l J.*, 38–41 (Summer 1989).
48. A.R. Drengson, *Beyond Environmental Crises: From Technocrat to Planetary Person* (P. Lang, 1989).
49. J. Rifkin, *Entropy: Into a Greenhouse World* (Bantam, 1989).
50. *The Register Guard,* Eugene, Oregon, 6 Dec. 1989.
51. *Report of the United Nations Conference on the Human Environment,* Stockholm, 5–16 June 1972 (United Nations, New York, 1973), p. 3.
52. *Taking a Stand: From Stockholm 1972 to Nairobi 1982: Declarations on the World Environment* (UNEP, 1982).

benefit from an international atmosphere of peace and security"[53] is hardly arguable but has at the same time an overly vague and broad meaning.

The All-European process that began in 1975 at the Helsinki Conference on Security and Co-operation in Europe included the environment as a key element in the security agenda. The Final Act of the Conference contained a special part (part 5) dedicated to environmental protection.[54] Special "ecological" chapters were also included in conclusive documents of follow-up meetings. Some analysts consider these documents as being of special significance to international ecological security.[55]

Several UN General Assembly resolutions are worth mentioning in connection with the evolution of views on ecological security. One resolution is 35/8 (1980), which proclaimed that "the historic responsibility of the States is for the protection of the nature of the Earth for the benefit of present and future generations."[56] The other resolution is 42/93 (1987), by which the United Nations agreed that cooperation in the environmental field was an inalienable element of an all-embracing international security.[57]

Of no less importance are some other documents, recently approved within the United Nations, specifically "Environmental Perspective to the Year 2000 and Beyond," "Disarmament, Environment, and Sustainable Development," "Global Resources and International Conflict: Environmental Factors in Strategic Policy and Action." These documents refer, in a greater or lesser measure, to the concept of international ecological security.[58]

"The U.N. System-wide, Medium-term Environment Programme for the Period 1990–1995," approved at a special session of the United Nations Environment Programme (UNEP), says that one of the primary objectives is to build up the conceptual basis for a coordinated solution of the task of preserving the environment by all the relevant components of the United Nations system with a view to promoting ecological security.[59] In February 1988, an ad hoc ex-

---

53. *Id.*
54. *See,* e.g., Vienna Meeting (1988), Sofia Meeting (1989).
55. J. Cuth, *supra* note 37 at 5.
56. U.N. Resolution 35/8 (1980).
57. U.N. Resolution 42/93 (1987).
58. *Concept of International Ecological Security* (*aide-mémoire,* E/1988/105, reflecting the views of the countries of eastern Europe. Submitted by Ambassador Milos Viejvoda [Czechoslovakia] at ECOSOC, Geneva, 6–29 July 1988), reviewed in 18 *Envt'l Pol'y & L.,* pp. 189–190.
59. U.N. system-wide programme for 1990–1995, p. 17 ad hoc.

pert group meeting on the expanded concept of international security took place within UNEP. The conclusions drawn by the participants included recognition of the need to embody ideas of the concept of ecological security in all UNEP programmes.[60] In line with the above is the research project "Studies in Environmental Security" initiated jointly by UNEP and the Peace Research Institute in Oslo (PRIO).

The Brundtland Commission report, *Our Common Future,* contains a special chapter, number 11, on "Peace, Security, Development, and the Environment" dedicated primarily to the matter of ecological security.[61] The following citation may serve to summarize the report's approach to the problem: "The whole notion of security as traditionally understood – in terms of political and military threats to national sovereignty – must be expanded to include the growing impacts of environmental stress – locally, nationally, regionally, and globally."[62] This is one more argument that such a, or a similar, formula is becoming a universally accepted truism of our time.

The interpretation of ecological security by the Brundtland Commission seems fairly narrow. It concentrates mainly on the interplay between the environment and military activities (environment as a potential source of military conflict, military activity as a source of environmental harm). Nevertheless, the Commission elaborated on several important basic points regarding the development of ecological security.

The first point claims that "threats to environmental security can only be dealt with by joint management and multilateral procedures and mechanisms. . . . Some of the most challenging problems require co-operation among nations enjoying different systems of government, or even subject to antagonistic relations." This is very much in line with the basics of the so-called "new international law," such as principles of "collective responsibility" and "transnational humanitarian solidarity."[63]

The second point states that action to reduce environmental threats to security requires a redefinition of priorities, nationally and globally. This could mean a considerable but still not a dramatic redistribution of material and financial resources. The report illustrates that four of the most urgent environmental requirements – relating to tropical forests, water desertification, and population – could be

---

60. *Id.*
61. *Our Common Future, supra* note 18 at 291–307.
62. *Id.* at 19.
63. For more details, *see,* e.g., A. Cassese, *International Law in a Divided World* (Clarendon, 1988).

funded with the equivalent of less than one month's global military spending.

The whole spectrum of problems connected with the formation of a system of international environmental security have been discussed in the 1988 international conference co-sponsored by the former USSR Academy of Sciences, United Nations Environment Programme, International Peace Research Institute in Oslo, and the Ecoforum for Peace (Sofia).[64] Looking at environmental security as a component of comprehensive international security, the conference discussed regional and global dimensions of environmental security and the strategies for achieving this new level of security. Among the important conclusions of the conference are the following:

1. The present practice of "react-and-correct" is not adequate when applied to such serious problems as burgeoning environmental pollution, losses in biological species diversity, global warming, soil erosion and desertification, stratospheric ozone depletion, and tropical deforestation and must be replaced by a policy of "foresee-and-prevent."

2. Upholding a new kind of security is a shared responsibility of the entire international community (this again is very much in line with the recent ideas of "collective responsibility" and "transnational solidarity").

3. Environmental security requires a strengthening of international environmental law that should crystallize in a universal declaration of principles on environmental security and by developing an international legal action plan.[65]

An example of collective international conceptual thinking was the Twenty-fourth UN Conference on "Environmental Problems: A Global Security Threat," the Next Decade Conference of 1989, sponsored by the Stanley Foundation.[66] The Conference convened to discuss the degree of political acceptance to such recently popular concepts as environmental security and sustainable development. The

---

64. *Environmental Security* (Report from a Conference in Moscow, 28 Nov. – 1 Dec. 1988, co-sponsored by the USSR Academy of Sciences [Moscow], the International Peace Research Institute in Oslo, the United Nations Environment Programme [Nairobi], and the Ecoforum for Peace [Sofia]) (PRIO/UNEP Programme on Military Activities and the Human Environment, 1989).

65. *Id.*

66. *Environmental Problems: A Global Security Threat* (Report of the 24th UN of the Next Decade Conference sponsored by the Stanley Foundation, 18–23 June 1989, convened at Hamilton Parish, Bermuda).

Conference stated that in spite of the general agreement that environmental problems currently pose, or have the potential to pose, severe threats to the general well-being and long-term survival of human life on the planet, characterizing environmental threats as security issues was more controversial. Since security has been, and remains, a national rather than a global concept, implementing a comprehensive security concept will be difficult while nationalism is still very much alive and the global system is not integrated. Thus, what is really needed is for national leaders to see the environmental threat for what it is, a clear and present danger for the continuation of human civilization – a danger that demands action and mobilization of national will and resources.[67]

Another international gathering took place in April 1990 in Siena, Italy, where the Forum on International Law of the Environment was convened by the Italian Government as a follow-up of the Summit of the Seven Most Industrialized Nations, held in Paris on 16 July 1989.[68] The major scope of the Forum was to consider the need for a digest of existing rules and to give in-depth consideration to the legal aspects of the environment at the international level. Though ecological security was neither on the agenda nor in the background document prepared for the Forum,[69] the "Conclusions of the Siena Forum on International Law of the Environment" contains an important statement:

"The sector by sector" approach, adopted in concluding conventions, often dictated by the need to respond to specific incidents, involves the risk of losing sight of the need for an integrated approach to the prevention of pollution and the continued deterioration of the environment. The "react and correct" model should be complemented by a "forecast and prevent" approach: this would enhance security in global environmental matters.[70]

The analysis of doctrinal thinking, discussions in the UN bodies and other international fora show that the ecological security conception, while getting more profound, goes beyond the limits of political aspirations, involves both national and international dimensions, and

67. *Id.* at 67.
68. Introductory Document Prepared by the Italian Government for the Forum on International Law of the Environment, Siena, 17–21 April 1990 (Rome, January 1990) (the document was prepared by the Italian government in collaboration with Professors Giandomenico Caggiano, Francesco Francioni, Riccardo Pisillo Mazzeschi, Mauro Politi, and Tullio Scovazzi).
69. *Id.*
70. *Id.* at para. 4.

acquires universal significance. Initially formulated as one of the elements of an all-embracing (comprehensive) system of international security, ecological security has been getting a multi-aspectal character, acquiring certain autonomy, and turning into the key component of comprehensive security.

The ecological security concept began forming fairly recently. It needs more profound theoretical and practical elaboration. But it is possible already to describe some of its qualitative indications: ecological security is universal, fair and equal; it covers the natural environment, both within and outside national boundaries; ecological security interacts with the other components of the comprehensive system of security; ecological security takes into account the sovereign right of states to exploit their own resources pursuant to their own environmental policies (though it does not exclude mutual and voluntary exceptions from this right or reducing it); international cooperation is an indispensable condition of ecological security implementation; ecological security presupposes the relevant national and international legal regulation with adequate participation of competent intergovernmental and non-governmental organizations.

The concept of ecological security offers the needed methodological breakthrough for environmental protection. Its fundamental conceptual novelty lies in converting an ecological problem into a security issue, which in turn helps to fulfil several important tasks.

Firstly, ecological security makes environmental protection a problem of human survival, reflecting the seriousness of existing and future ecological threats. It gives the problem the highest priority traditionally attributed to security matters. It introduces a new basis for resolving environmental problems – the "forecast-and-prevent" model – instead of the usual "react-and-correct" model. It creates an opportunity to redistribute resources allocated for security in favour of environmental tasks, thus it may help to solve the problem of reconverting the military sector of national economies.

Secondly, ecological security envisages that the obligation to create the relevant legal and managerial regime will be placed upon the international community as a whole, which coincides with such general trends in international law as collective responsibilities and obligations *erga omnes*.

Thirdly, being a component of the comprehensive security system, ecological security functions in conjunction with other elements (military, political, economic, and humanitarian). This not only creates a needed correlation between ecological security and other global problems, but also conditions the achievement of a synergistic effect.

And lastly, the security approach in the environmental field serves to integrate related concerns under a common rubric. Security has often served as a strong motivation for integration. The universal collective security system under the United Nations Charter and regional security systems like NATO or the Warsaw Treaty illustrate this. This integrative force greatly enhances the efficiency of environmental protection. This has been clearly demonstrated by the European Communities.

According to the accepted definition, regime means a totality of rules, measures, and norms aimed at achieving a certain goal. The ecological security regime, like security in general, presupposes a certain state of long-lasting stability with inter-state relations, and a continuing uniform behaviour by states in the environmental sphere. This in turn predetermines the specific role of international legal instruments consisting of juridical norms and principles.

Since the ecological security conception is offered as a new methodology in the environmental field, one may stress that methodology itself is understood to be a system of principles and ways of organizing and structuring theoretical and practical activities, as well as the doctrine concerning this system. This leads to the conclusion that to structure the ecological security regime, a system of relevant principles should be created. These principles should be primarily of an international legal character. The modern world has changed from the Hegelian philosophy of law based on a priority of municipal law in the direction of creating universal world order ensuring the primacy of international law.[71] The indispensability of international legal principles for the ecological security regime was stressed by M. Strong and R. Boardman.[72] It is also worthwhile mentioning the statement, "The Consequences of the Arms Race for the Environment and Other Aspects of Ecological Security," adopted by the member countries of the Warsaw Treaty on 16 July 1988, which pointed out that "the achievement of ecological security requires adoption of the binding norms and principles of State behavior."[73]

Thus, it seems necessary to elaborate on a system of fundamental principles containing basic obligations of states in the field of ecolog-

---

71. "International Law," in *Perestroika and International Law,* 31–40 (W.E. Butler, ed., Kluwer 1990).
72. *See supra* notes 42, 45.
73. *Pravda,* Moscow, 17 July 1988.

ical security. The logic of the discussion leads us to assume that the structuring of the ecological security system should be based on that which has already been achieved by international environmental law, and at the same time demands a considerable acceleration of the law-making and codification processes in this field. On the other side, one must keep in mind that the sphere of ecological security is objectively narrower than the sphere regulated by international environmental law; the former does not cover a significant amount of relations regarding resource utilization. Ecological security is aimed at preventing negative anthropogenic impacts primarily of an extraordinary nature and scale.

Together with the basic principles of international environmental law the ecological security principles must reflect the general regularities common to any system of security. The most elaborate in this sense is the sphere of military security, where one may find a number of models and mechanisms that have already been reflected in adopted or negotiated arms limitation treaties.[74]

Hence, principles of ecological security should be constructed by synthesizing the most progressive fundamental provisions of both military security and international environmental law. A creative utilization of military security models seems expedient not only because this component of the comprehensive security system has been elaborated upon the most, but also because of the specific interrelatedness of military and ecological security. This interrelationship derives from the common character of their tasks: protection of human civilization against threats of destruction, thereby securing the conditions of human. survival.

As a result of the above deliberations, the following system of ecological security principles can be proposed.

III. Principles

The principle of equal ecological security is, to a certain extent, analogous to the principle of equal security that had been formed in the military-political sphere, but the content and prerequisites of the former are different. In the military field, security can be achieved and is often achieved, though temporarily, at the expense of the opponent's

---

74. Among other such treaties are: Moscow Nuclear Test Ban Treaty (1963), Nuclear Non-Proliferation Treaty (1968), Tlatelolco Treaty Banning Nuclear Weapons in Latin America (1967), USSR-USA SALT treaties.

insecurity. This makes equal military security somewhat disputable. Ecological security, especially in its global dimension, can be greatly enhanced through a combination of the ecological security of individual states. Environmental instability in one part of the globe undermines the ecological security on a planetary scale.

This is genetically related to one of the fundamental *(jus cogens)* principles of international law – the principle of sovereign equality, which envisages equal rights and obligations of states. All states have an equal right to ecological well-being. Thus, the principle of equal ecological security bans the achievement of ecological well-being by one state or group of states at the expense or to the harm of the legitimate interests of other states. A similar idea was formulated in the 1972 Stockholm Declaration on the Human Environment (principle 24): "International matters concerning the protection and improvement of the environment should be handled in a cooperative spirit by all countries, big and small, on an equal footing."[75]

Such a view is also shared by legal scholars. O. Hugler and R. Müller write that the first principle that is valid in the system of comprehensive security and can be applied to ecological security is the principle of equality and equal security for all.[76] R. Boardman stresses that "the pursuit of security, if it is not to be self-defeating, is inextricably bound up with the search for conditions assuring the security of adversaries. Security, in other words is interdependent."[77] The *aide-mémoire,* "Concept of International Ecological Security," submitted in July 1988 by the former East European countries to ECOSOC emphasized that " . . . all States, without exception, and concerned international bodies and organizations could and should join in developing the concept and the ensuing system of international ecological security to be built up on the basis of full equality of rights."[78]

Besides not complying with the general principles of international law, the attempts to achieve ecological well-being unilaterally also contradict the objective indivisibility of global natural processes. Of course, unilateral actions of states aimed at betterment of the environment within national boundaries, provided they do not cause negative transfrontier effects, do not break the requirements of the principle of equal ecological security. However, experience has

75. *Report of the United Nations Conference on the Human Environment, supra* note 51 at 5.
76. O. Hugler, R. Müller, *supra* note 38 at 393.
77. R. Boardman, *supra* note 42 at 2.
78. *Concept of International Ecological Security, supra* note 58 at p. 190.

proven that these measures cannot help against global environmental deterioration.

The material content of the principle includes, *inter alia,* a prohibition to transfer polluting or other ecologically harmful industries and technologies to other countries, to dispose of there hazardous and toxic wastes, and to rapaciously exploit natural resources of other states. An example of such a prohibition was experienced by the *Mobro* garbage barge that travelled for 162 days and 6,000 miles looking for a place to dump its 3,100 tons of garbage – it was believed to contain hazardous materials.[79] The garbage was rejected by three developing countries and several states in the United States before returning full circle to New York.[80]

The principle banning ecological aggression was essentially formulated in the 1977 Convention on the Prohibition of Military or Other Hostile Use of Environmental Modification Techniques.[81] Along this line, special attention might be drawn to Article Y of the Convention that entrusts states to complain to the UN Security Council if they believe that the provisions of the Convention have been broken, and to have recourse to joint actions that may be interpreted as mutual assistance according to Article 49 of the UN Charter, or even collective self-defence (Art. 51 of the Charter). To a certain extent, the illegal character of deliberate military damage to the environment was indicated in the UN General Assembly resolution on the "Historic Responsibility of States for the Protection of the Nature of the Earth for the Benefit of Present and Future Generations."[82] Reference to the 1972 Stockholm Declaration on the Human Environment (Principle 26) and the 1982 World Charter for Nature are also appropriate.[83]

In Soviet international law doctrine, a deliberate hostile impact on

---

79. "The End Begins for Trash No One Wanted." *N.Y. Times,* 2 Sept. 1987. When the trash was finally incinerated in New York, officials discovered that the garbage contained no hazardous materials.
80. *Id.*
81. Convention on the Prohibition of Military or Any Other Hostile Use of Environmental Modification Techniques, 18 May 1977, 16 *I.L.M.* 88 (1977).
82. G.A. Res. 35/8 (1980).
83. Stockholm Declaration, *supra* note 21 at Principle 26. "Man and his environment must be spared the effects of nuclear weapons and all other means of mass destruction. States must strive to reach prompt agreement, in the relevant international organs, on the elimination and complete destruction of such weapons." *Id.* World Charter for Nature, 28 Oct. 1982, 22 *I.L.M.* 455 (1983). "Article Y. Nature shall be secured against degradation caused by warfare and other hostile activities. Article XX. Military activities damaging to nature shall be avoided." *Id.*

the environment – ecocide – has for a long time been qualified as an illegal act and even more has been reckoned in the category of international crimes.[84] The principle was endorsed when previous acts of ecocide in Vietnam and other S.E. Asian countries were condemned by world public opinion. It is also essential that the International Law Commission in its Draft Articles on State Responsibility (Art. 19) attributed mass pollution of the biosphere to international crimes.[85]

It is obvious that for practical implementation, the principle needs further elaboration. A better sense of what qualifies as ecological aggression and the juridical consequences for violating the principle must be developed. In particular, the definition of aggression adopted by the UN General Assembly in 1974 is no longer adequate. The existing definition of aggression refers exclusively to the use of armed force in Article 1.[86] In Article 3, the same assumption lies as the basis of the list of acts of aggression.[87] The definition should be expanded to include deliberate environmental modifications for military and other hostile purposes aimed at incurring damage to the environment of other countries.

Control measures, such as monitoring state compliance with treaty provisions, are essential to any security system. The control measures are accepted as fundamental in the military security field. The principle of controlling and monitoring the observance of agreed upon requirements of ecological security is just as important. Only by using a developed system of monitoring and controlling can we guarantee the enforcement of international norms, which are of vital significance. Besides the relevant national instruments, the control system should include international control procedures: international requests on state observance of ecological security obligations, on-site inspections and investigations, consultations, creation of permanent international control institutions, and the participation of competent international organizations.

The current stage of verification of implementation of international obligations shows that predominant is the interaction of states through the ad hoc mechanisms created under individual legal instruments. This form of verification has almost exhausted its potential. The participation of competent international organizations would

84. *See,* e.g., V.A. Vasylenko, *Otvetstvennost' Gosudarstva za Mezhdunarodnve Pravonarusheniia* (State responsibility for international offences) §192 (Vishcha Shkola, 1976).
85. 31 U.N. GAOR Supp. (No. 10), U.N. Doc. A/31/10 (1976).
86. *Id.* at Art. 1.
87. *Id.* at Art. 3.

strengthen further development of control procedures. Some UN agencies participate in verification of selected environmental legal instruments, according to their specific competence. But the only UN body with comprehensive competence and coordinating responsibilities in the environmental field is the United Nations Environment Programme. Thus, strengthening the role of UNEP, utilizing to the fullest extent its potential provided by its constituent act, is a way to develop and strengthen the verification process in the field of ecological security, transforming it into a system of coordinated measures and mechanisms.

Another option might be the creation of a special international body with functions of monitoring, surveying, and controlling compliance with the ecological security regime. It could be analogous to a similar international agency in the disarmament field that was proposed by former Soviet foreign minister Eduard Schevardnadze at the Third Special Session of the UN General Assembly on Disarmament in 1988.[88]

The principle of control is inseparably linked to the principle of the exchange of information on national and regional ecological situations. Such informational feedback would create a minimal material basis of verification of state observance of ecological security requirements. The linkage between informational and control functions is so close that some scholars name informational functions control functions.[89]

The significance of the informational support of environmental protection policies on the national and international levels clearly follows from existing practice. It was reflected in the general definition of the information goal given in the 1972 Stockholm Action Plan: specifically, "to ensure that decision-makers at all levels shall have the benefit of the best knowledge that can be made available."[90] In the field of transboundary natural resources, the exchange of information is regarded as an established principle of international environmental law.[91] The great importance that is given to the infor-

---

88. "Intervention of the U.S.S.R." Foreign Minister E.A. Schevardnadze at the Third Special Session of the UNGA on Disarmament, *Pravda,* Moscow, 9 June 1988.

89. *See,* e.g., W. Morawiecki, *Funkcje Organizacji Miedzynarodowej* (Functions of international organizations), part 3, §§275–292 (Kaiazka i Wiedza, 1971).

90. *Report of the United Nations Conference on the Human Environment, supra* note 51 at 23.

91. Such a view, expressed by the legal experts assigned by the Brundtland Commission, was augmented with numerous examples from international treaty practice. *See, Environmental Protection and Sustainable Development,* Legal Principles and Recommendations Adopted by the Experts' Group on Environmental Law of the World Commission on Environment and Development (Graham & Trotman, 1987), pp. 95–98.

mational support of control functions is clearly identifiable in the European Community environmental protection practice.[92]

The systematic exchange of information was identified as an essential part of international environmental cooperation by the 1990 Siena Forum on International Law of the Environment, which gathered highly qualified legal experts from all over the world.[93] The conclusions of the Siena Forum recommended a "systematic exchange of data and information on the state of the environment and levels of pollution."[94] Moreover, the Forum recommended assistance to developing countries upon their request, and in full respect of their sovereignty, for collecting such data and information required, particularly through environmental-auditing mechanisms. Transmission of data and information to competent international organizations must be performed in order to make the information available to governments, local authorities, and individuals.[95]

In the ecological security field, the permanent availability of environmental information is directed to minimize tension that usually occurs in the security sphere due to the insufficiency of relevant data. This exchange of information would permit an adequate evaluation of the national and regional input into strengthening or weakening global ecological security. Practical implementation of the principle would require legally binding international agreements on the regularity and periodicity of the exchange, on the amount of information provided, and on mechanisms and channels of information transfer. An *aide-mémoire* of the eastern European countries in the "Concept of International Ecological Security," proposed *inter alia* that such forms of information exchange as "annual reporting by Governments on their activity in the field of environmental protection and notification on ecological accidents, including those prevented" should be available.[96]

Certain technical questions should also be settled when organizing a standing system of information exchange. Compatibility and a correlation of the data received from different countries should be provided. In order to attain this goal, a unified methodology is needed for environmental data evaluation, assessment, an inter-calibration of measuring instruments, etc.

92. N. Haigh, *EEC Environmental Policy and Britain*, 5 (Longman, 1987).
93. Conclusions of the Siena Forum on International Law of the Environment, para. 15 (Siena, Italy, 17–21 April 1990).
94. *Id.*
95. *Id.* at para. 15.
96. *Concept of International Ecological Security, supra* note 58 at 190.

Among the ecological security principles recruited from international environmental law, the most important is the principle preventing transboundary environmental harm. The significance of the principle follows from the necessity to change major conceptual orientations, dictated by the security approach: specifically to shift regulating environmental protection from a "react-and-correct" model (the principle way in which international environmental law has been forming) to a "foresee-and-prevent" model.

A prevention policy is fundamental for any branch of security, in particular, military security. The importance of a preventive approach achieves its utmost degree in the ecological security field for two major reasons. First, the damage incurred in natural ecosystems is, in most cases, irreparable. Second, many environmentally harmful processes are irreversible. Once anthropogenically triggered they can be slowed down or more rarely stopped, but never turned back. An excellent example of such an assumption is global climate change.

The principle of prevention of environmental harm has been introduced in a number of international instruments whose juridical nature varies. The major reasons for this are the impossibility of adequately evaluating ecological damage and subsequently providing full compensation, and the even less probability of restoring environmental quality. Back in 1972, the UN General Assembly recognized the importance of having activities within national jurisdiction carried out "with a view to avoiding significant harm that may occur in the environment of the adjacent area."[97] The final act of the 1975 Helsinki Conference on Security and Co-operation in Europe (CSCE) pointed out that damage to the environment was best avoided by using preventive measures.[98] A special section was devoted to preventive measures in the Nairobi Declaration of 1982, which said in particular: "Prevention of damage to the environment is preferable to the burdensome and expensive repair of damage already done."[99] The final document of the 1989 Vienna Follow-up Meeting begins the environmental section with "recognizing the need for preventive

---

97. "Co-operation Between States in the Field of the Environment," UNGA Resolution 2995 (XXVII), 2112th Plenary Meeting, 15 Dec. 1972.
98. Final Act of the Conference on Security and Co-operation in Europe, 1 Aug. 1975, reprinted in 14 *I.L.M.* 1292 (1975).
99. *Taking a Stand, supra* note 52. The Nairobi Declaration was adopted by 105 governments at the UNEP Governing Council Special Session, commemorating the tenth anniversary of the 1972 Stockholm Conference on the Human Environment.

action."[100] The Brundtland Commission, consisting of legal experts, referred to authoritative international judicial decisions, treaty practice, and numerous international recommendations identified in the "prevention principle" as "the well-established basic principle governing transboundary environmental interferences."[101]

Along with recognition that the prevention of environmental harm is a fundamental principle of international environmental law, similar sectoral assumptions can be quoted. The World Climate Conference (Geneva, 1979), defying the traditional approach of reacting to global climate as an already quantifiable problem, emphasized the need "to foresee and prevent" the effects of human activity on the climate. Philippe Sands, a legal scholar from the UK, based on the analysis of international practice, suggested that the obligation to prevent transboundary environmental harm caused by nuclear pollution has emerged as a universally accepted rule.[102]

Regional experience has demonstrated the viability of the preventive approach to environmental protection. The First EEC Action Programme on the Environment of 1972 set out 11 general principles of a community environmental policy,[103] which were applied throughout the Second and Third Programmes and remain valid under the Fourth.[104] The first of the 11 principles reads as follows: "Pollution or nuisances should be prevented at their source, rather than subsequently trying to counteract their effects."[105] The Single European Act[106] introduced three fundamental principles that called for preventive measures against environmental pollution.

One may conclude that an international consensus has been forming on the preferability of preventive measures as the most ecologically expedient method for environmental protection on both the national and international levels. The preventive nature of international environmental law has been thoroughly investigated by Professor Toru Iwama in chapter 4 of this book.

The principle of prevention is of a generalized character. In turn, the principle includes a number of independent elements, such as environmental-impact assessment, notification on any activity that

---

100. 19 *Envt'l Pol'y & L.*, 31–32, (1989).
101. *Environmental Protection and Sustainable Development, supra* note 91 at 75.
102. P. Sands, *Chernobyl: Law and Communication*, 7–15 (Grotius, 1988).
103. First Action Programme on the Environment, OJ EEC, N.C. 112/73, p. 2 and p. 6 et seq.
104. Fourth Action Programme on the Environment, OJ EEC, N.C. 328/87 p. 1, para. 1.1 and Annex 1.
105. *First Action Programme, supra* note 104.
106. Bulletin of the European Communities, Supplement, Feb. 1986.

may cause transboundary environmental harm, providing necessary information on such potentially harmful activities, and relevant international consultations.

Environmental-impact assessment (EIA) should be considered as the most important element within the prevention principle. It is deeply rooted in the national environmental legislation of many countries and forms a part of positive international environmental law.[107] The institution of environmental-impact assessment is mainly aimed at implementation of the first half of the formula, "foresee and prevent." The governing bodies of UNEP and the ECE have both commissioned special expert groups to elaborate on the elements of an international impact-assessment mechanism.[108] Senior advisers to the ECE governments on environmental and water problems have recommended the drafting of a European convention on this matter.[109] The UNEP special expert group has also been researching uniform international procedures for EIA. These procedures are aimed at the assessment of both short- and long-term ecological consequences. Impacts on all categories of natural objects, both within and outside of national jurisdictions, should be assessed.

Preventive policy becomes more and more evident also with regard to national protection of the environment, since corrective measures have proved to be ineffective. "There is a growing recognition," said William K. Reilly, Administrator of the US Environmental Protection Agency, "that traditional approaches, which stress treatment and disposal after pollution has been generated, have not adequately dealt with existing environmental problems."[110] A preventive strategy was the basis for restructuring environmental legislation and management in the former Soviet Union. Examples included the prevention-oriented functions of the former USSR State Committee on Nature Protection, the strong preventive provisions proposed in the former All-Union environmental legislation, and the position of the standing Committee on Ecology in the former USSR Supreme Soviet. A similar approach prevails in Russia today.

Experts all over the world indicate that there is a growing number

107. For details, *see* A.S. Timoshenko, "The Problem of Preventing Damage to the Environment in National and International Law: Impact Assessment and International Consultations," 5 *Pace Envt'l L. Rev.*, 475–486.
108. *See* U.N. Doc. UNEP/WG. 107/2 (1984); ECE Doc. ECE/ENV/52 (1987).
109. ECE Doc. ECE/ENVWA/9 (1988).
110. "With Pollution Control Costs Rising, Many Take a New Tack: Prevention." *N.Y. Times*, 18 Nov. 1989.

of industrial catastrophes that are tending to have serious environmental impacts. On the other side, natural disasters can result in the destruction of industrial and energy installations (chemical, nuclear, or other types of hazardous activities), which could cause significant damage to the environment. The third source of ecological emergencies is certain long-lasting processes of environmental degradation (global climate change, ozone depletion) whose quantitative characteristics may at any moment convert into a sudden qualitative change. Chernobyl in Ukraine, the Sandoz plant in Switzerland, the Exxon Valdez in Alaska are but a few examples – the complete list of environmental emergencies that happened recently could be much longer. All the above conditions lead to the inclusion of the principle of cooperation during environmental emergencies into the ecological security system.

The formation of the principle has been indicated by certain developments in the law of the sea, space law, conventions on notification and assistance in case of a nuclear accident, adopted in 1986 under the aegis of IAEA.[111] When referring to the marine environment, the Siena Forum on International Law of the Environment listed only two treaties[112] – the Convention Relating to Intervention on the High Seas in Cases of Oil Pollution Casualties (Brussels, 1969)[113] and its Protocol Relating to Pollution by Substances Other than Oil (London, 1973)[114] – that allow states injured or threatened by pollution to take emergency measures on the high seas. There is not, however, a universal treaty establishing cooperative measures in drawing up and putting contingency plans into action.

More developments in the practical implementation of the principle of cooperation in environmental emergencies can be expected on global and regional levels of international environmental cooperation. After a number of chemical industry catastrophes,[115] the UNEP Governing Council took initiative to elaborate on two international

111. IAEA Convention on Early Notification in the Case of a Nuclear Accident, 26 Sept. 1986, 25 *I.L.M.* 1370 (1986); IAEA Convention on Assistance in the Case of a Nuclear Accident or Radiological Emergency, 26 Sept. 1986, 25 *I.L.M.* 1377 (1986).
112. Introductory Document for the Siena Forum on International Law of the Environment (Siena, Italy, 17–21 April 1990), p. 15.
113. Brussels International Convention Relating to Intervention on the High Seas in Case of Oil Pollution Casualties, 29 Nov. 1969, 26 U.S.T. 765, T.I.A.S. 8068.
114. Protocol Relating to Pollution by Substances Other Than Oil, London, 2 Nov. 1973, T.I.A.S. 10561, 34 U.S.T. 3407, 13 *I.L.M.* 605 (1974).
115. The best-known cases of massive chemical pollution are Minamata (Japan), Love Canal (USA), Seveso (Italy), Bhopal (India), Sandoz Co. Plant (Switzerland).

conventions, thereby creating a mechanism of international cooperation in case of serious chemical accidents.[116] Using the recent IAEA
conventions as a model, the UNEP conventions on chemical accidents would impose legal obligations of early notification and international assistance in case of chemical catastrophes.

A rather comprehensive approach to emergency situations was
proposed at the 1989 Ottawa Meeting of Legal and Policy Experts on
the Elements of a Global Convention on the Protection of the
Atmosphere.[117] The proposal included obligations "to immediately
take appropriate measures. . . to control the cause of the emergency
situation and immediately notify other states affected or likely to be
affected, . . . to provide those states and organizations with such
pertinent information as will enable them to minimize the harmful
effects and cooperate with them, in order to prevent or minimize the
harmful effects of an emergency situation," and "to develop contingency plans in order to prevent or minimize the harmful effects of
such an emergency situation."[118]

Regionally, the relevant activities of the ECE should be referred
to. Following the recommendations of the CSCE Meeting in Sofia
(1989), the ECE initiated elaboration of elements for an international
convention (code of practice or other appropriate legal instruments)
on the prevention and control of the transboundary effects of industrial accidents.[119] On the basis of the relevant provisions of the ECE
Regional Strategy for Environmental Protection adopted in 1988,[120]
the former Soviet government proposed to establish a Centre for
Emergency Environmental Assistance in Europe.[121]

Similar institutional proposals have been recently placed before
the UN General Assembly by Austria, to create special environmental emergency assistance forces – a sort of "Green Cross" or "U.N.
Green Helmets" – and by the former USSR, to establish a World
Centre for Emergency Environmental Assistance.

---

116. UNEP News 3–4 (1987).
117. 19 *Envt'l Pol'y & L.*, 79/2 (1989).
118. *Id.*
119. *See* ECE Doc. ENVWA/R.26, 22 Dec. 1989.
120. According to para. 112(b) of the *Regional Strategy for Environmental Protection and
    Rational Use of Natural Resources in ECE Member Countries up to the Year 2000 and
    Beyond* (ECE/ENVWA/5), the ECE governments agreed to, *inter alia,* "consider the
    possible role of ECE with regard to . . . possible development of programmes to prevent
    and mitigate chemical accidents which could have transboundary impacts as well as the ex-
    change of information on such accidents. . . . *Id.*
121. ECE Doc. ENVWA/R.34, 24 Jan. 1990.

The political will is sufficient to declare one's devotion to the idea and principles of ecological security.[122] But practical implementation of an ecological security regime requires adequate scientific and technological potential. To introduce a global ecological security regime, it is necessary to apply the latest achievements in the field of environmental control and monitoring, low-waste and resource-saving technology. The results of scientific and technical progress in this field shall be easily and widely accessible. There is also a need to provide optimal conditions for integrating scientific and technological potentials of all members of the world community towards development of ecologically safe technology.

The unevenness of economic and technological development of individual countries is well known. From this unevenness emerges the specific needs and interests of developing countries that were already articulated during the preparation of the 1972 Stockholm Conference as one of the serious obstacles for uniform international environmental behaviour. Certain steps had been taken to harmonize the interests of developed and developing countries both before the Stockholm Conference[123] and at the Conference itself.[124] Scientific and technological cooperation and transfer are crucial for integrating efforts of different countries towards environmental protection. Principle 20 of the 1972 Stockholm Declaration proclaimed that the free flow of up-to-date scientific information and the transfer of experience must be supported and assisted to facilitate the solution of environmental problems: "Environmental technologies should be made available to developing countries on terms which would encourage their wide dissemination without constituting an economic burden on the developing countries."[125]

Regretfully, no acceptable mechanism for implementing the formula of Principle 20 has ever been developed. Instead certain concepts about the "basic needs," "intermediate" or "appropriate technologies" were proposed[126] to single out the developing countries as

---

122. Though the disappointing results of the Bergen Conference (May 1990) demonstrated the current insufficiency of the political will of the international community to radically improve environmental policies.
123. *See* Founeaux Report, U.N. Doc. GE 71-13738 (1971).
124. More than one-third of the Stockholm Declaration, *supra* note 21 (Principles 8–16), were dedicated to specific needs and interests of the developing countries.
125. *Id.* at Principle 20.
126. *See*, e.g., J. McHale, *Basic Human Needs: A Framework for Action: A Report to the U.N. Environment Programme* (New York, 1976); E. Schumacher, *Small is Beautiful* (Harper Collins, 1973).

second-rate partners in world technological development. The problem of full involvement by the developing countries in the concerted efforts to save the natural environment still exists. In order to resolve the problem, radical economic and political measures should be undertaken. It becomes evident that a possibility to stop Brazilians from cutting tropical forests lies in offering them adequate economic or technological substitutes.

The acuteness of the necessity to secure universal environmental protection has been evidenced by the global degradation of the environment. This dictates that the principle of scientific and technological cooperation be incorporated into ecological security principles. The principle acquires a new content under an ecological security regime. Its major element should be the creation of the most favourable conditions for international exchange of ecologically safe technologies, and utilization of the latest means and methods of environmental control and monitoring. This will require substantial change in the system of international technical assistance. Implementation of the principle, given its new understanding, would fully activate the mechanism of an international division of labour for the purposes of ecological security and also involve the developing countries, which possess the largest resource potential of the planet.

Radical improvement in the economic and ecological conditions of developing countries will not be feasible without massive financial or technical assistance from the well-to-do countries. An international consensus has been forming such that developing countries should be assisted in their efforts to redress the conditions of underdevelopment that are causing local environmental disruption. This consensus lends support to claims by developing countries that there is a need for financial or technical assistance in order to protect resources of global significance.[127] A similar position was held by the former East European countries, which proposed that for the achievement of international ecological security, *inter alia,* there must be "intensification of international economic and ecological cooperation, including cooperation in exchange of technology, for purposes of protecting the environment; attention should be given in this area to the specific situations of developing countries."[128]

The UN General Assembly at its forty-third session commented

---

127. G. Handl, "Environmental Protection and Development in Third World Countries: Common Destiny – Common Responsibility," 20 *N.Y.U.J. Int'l L. & Pol'y*, 608 (1988).
128. *Concept of International Ecological Security, supra* note 58 at 190.

more explicitly on the matter. In its resolution, "A United Nations Conference on the Environment and Development," the Assembly recognized "the importance of international co-operation in the research and development of environmentally sound technology and the need for an international exchange of experience and knowledge as well as promoting the transfer of technology for the protection and enhancement of the environment, especially in developing countries."[129] It also reaffirmed "the need for developed countries and the appropriate organs and organizations of the United Nations system to strengthen technical co-operation with developing countries to enable them to develop and strengthen their capacity for identifying, analysing, monitoring, preventing and managing environmental problems."[130] The exchange of science and technology should not be limited to the North-South dimension. An integrated environmental revolution technology is required that would integrate environmental goals into the basic design of transportation, manufacturing, energy, and other systems. Its potential must be fully developed and available from East to West and North to South.[131]

The principle of scientific and technical cooperation has found a certain reflection in treaty law. Comprehensive examples are the provisions of Art. 202 of the 1982 UN Convention on the Law of the Sea, which include such cooperative measures as the training of scientific and technical personnel, facilitating the participation in relevant international programmes, supplying the necessary equipment and facilities, enhancing the capacity to manufacture such equipment, developing facilities for research, monitoring, educational, and other programmes, providing appropriate assistance for the minimization of the effects of major accidents and for the preparation of environmental assessments.

Another scenario of deeper environmental involvement of developing countries is not directly linked to scientific and technological exchange, but if properly realized it could enhance ecological security in the world. The scenario, the so-called "debt-for-nature" exchange, has already proven to be useful in biodiversity conservation and needs a wider application. At the Conference on the Global Environment and Human Response to Sustainable Development (Tokyo, 1989) it was stated that one innovative approach would be the trans-

---

129. *Supra* note 51.
130. 19 *Envt'l Pol'y & L.*, 28 (1989).
131. J.G. Speth, *Environmental Security for the 1990's*, at 2 (mimeo).

formation of debt obligations to support environmental programmes. A similar statement was included in the Declaration of Brasilia on the Environment, adopted in 1989 at the Latin America and Caribbean Summit. James Speth indicates that the global environment would receive triple benefits if the public funds needed to purchase discounted debt from commercial banks were to come from taxes levied by industrialized-country governments on greenhouse gas emissions.[132] This arrangement is but one of many ways that large-scale debt relief can be tied to long-term agreements to conserve forests and other natural resources for sustainable production.[133] A wider view of the North-South "debt-for-nature" bargain might be offered. To complete the "global bargain," which links debt relief to change toward policies encouraging sustainable development, the North would have to agree to put its own house in order regarding pollution, emission of gases, and so on.[134]

Peaceful settlement of international disputes is covered by the provisions of the UN Charter.[135] Meanwhile, conflict resolution in the environmental field is obtaining a certain degree of specificity. This may induce states to attempt to elaborate on their specific mechanisms of environmental-dispute settlement. The growing threat of transboundary damage resulting from violations of international environmental law, caused by regular lawful activities, or ecological accidents may, once again, threaten global ecological security.

The principal aim of ecological security is to prevent hostility between man and the natural environment. Yet another security aspect should be added: that of preventing hostility between men because of environmental disruptions. Experts consider transboundary environmental impacts to be a potential impetus for inter-state conflict, including military retaliation.[136] These conditions point to another principle of ecological security – that of peaceful settlement of international environmental disputes.

An attempt to delineate the basic features of international environmental conflict resolution was undertaken while elaborating

132. J.G. Speth, "Coming to Terms: Toward a North-South Bargain for the Environment," *WRI Issues and Ideas*, World Resources Institute, June 1989, p. 4.
133. *Id.* at 4.
134. "The Debt Crisis and Conservation," *The Leaf*, Newsletter of the IWLF, August 1989, p. 5.
135. U.N. Charter at Art. 33.
136. "Not only is it true that conflicts, be they internal or international, destroy the environment, but it is also true that a ruined environment creates conflicts." Introductory Document for the Siena Forum, *supra* note 112 at 8.

upon the guiding principles of conservation and harmonious utilization under the aegis of UNEP. The code of the guiding principles,[137] adopted in 1979 by the UNEP Governing Council and supported at the UN General Assembly,[138] included provisions on the peaceful settlement of disputes resulting from shared natural resources utilization (Principle 11). Having referred to the relevant provisions of the UN Charter, the principle proposes the adoption and utilization of any other procedure for peaceful settlement that would be mutually agreed upon. The procedure should satisfy at least three requirements: it should be speedy, effective, and compulsory. The parties to the conflict should refrain from any action that would worsen the situation under dispute.

One of the traditional methods of dispute settlement has been judicial proceedings. Experts in international conflict resolutions evaluate highly the role of such international judicial bodies as the International Court of Justice.[139] The ICJ has recently emphasized its suitability for and willingness to deal with disputes related to environmental matters. The idea to establish a special ICJ chamber for environmental disputes was proposed in 1980 by ICJ Judge Manfred Lachs.[140] The statement of the former president of the International Court of Justice, Naghendra Singh, on the occasion of the fortieth anniversary of the Court, in 1986, also confirmed the continued relevance of establishing a special ICJ chamber for considering such disputes.[141] Another argument in favour of such an institutional development would be the growing recognition of the compulsory jurisdiction of the Court.[142] Another model of the mandatory jurisdiction includes the provisions of the 1982 UN Convention on the Law of the Sea.[143] Thus, in the environmental sphere, there would be an autonomous judicial body that is analogous to the judicial mechanism provided by UNCLOS 1982 (Art. 286 et seq.).[144]

137. U.N. Doc. UNEP/GC. 9/2/Add. 5 (1979).
138. UNGA Resolution 34/186, 18 Dec. 1979.
139. A.H. Westing, *Towards Non-Violent Conflict Resolutions and Environmental Protection,* at 155.
140. M. Lachs, *The Revised Procedure of the International Court of Justice – Essays on the Development of the International Legal Order,* 42 (The Hague, 1980).
141. ICJ Communique, N. 86/5, 1 May 1986, p. 8.
142. For example, the former USSR came out in favour of mandatory jurisdiction of the International Court of Justice. *See* Gorbachev, "Realities and Guarantees for a Secure World," *New Times,* Moscow, n. 39, 1987, p. 6.
143. UN Convention on the Law of the Sea, 10 Dec. 1982, 21 *I.L.M.* 1261 (1982).
144. *Id.* at Art. 286.

However, the existing ICJ practice in environmental disputes is still limited and disputable. The 1974 Judgements by the ICJ (Fisheries Jurisdiction Cases and Nuclear Test Cases) gave rise to disappointing commentaries regarding the ability of the Court to handle environmental disputes. It is also noteworthy that the ICJ still has not established a special chamber for environmental disputes, though it has been repeatedly advocated by some members of the Court.

At the same time, international practice indicates that the specificity of certain areas of international cooperation dictates specific institutional arrangements for conflict resolution. Again, one may refer to provisions for the creation of the International Tribunal of the Law of the Sea under the 1982 UN Convocation on the Law of the Sea as to a useful precedent. Analogous is the GATT practice that established special judicial procedures for dispute settlement in the field of international trade law.

These indicate that some innovative approaches to environmental dispute settlement should be looked for. One of the options could be a closer involvement of the United Nations Environment Programme in this process. It should be noted that after almost 20 years of existence, UNEP has acquired a unique and voluminous experience in dealing with a wide variety of environmental problems. The UNEP Executive Director, in accordance with his responsibility pursuant to the UN General Assembly Resolution 2997 (XXVII), "to secure the effective cooperation of, and contributions from, the relevant scientific and other professional communities in all parts of the world," has created an impressive corpus of independent, top-quality experts on all aspects of environmental protection and resource use. It is widely accepted that fact-finding either in the form of inquiry or as an element of conciliation or arbitral or judicial settlement may be expected to play a role of growing importance. According to WCED legal experts, compulsory resort to conciliation involves an impartial investigation of the facts, followed by recommendations for a peaceful settlement of the dispute. This clearly indicates that there are many crucial stages in the environmental dispute settlement process, for which UNEP has obtained the necessary technical means and organizational skills that must be utilized.

A violation of ecological security shall result in legal consequences based on the principle of international responsibility for environmental harm. Strong international sanctions shall provide stability for the ecological security regime. The principle of international responsibility for environmental harm was strongly recommended at the 1972

Stockholm Conference: "States shall cooperate to develop further the international law regarding liability and compensation for the victims of pollution and other environmental damage caused by activities within the jurisdiction or control of such States to areas beyond their jurisdiction."[145]

Despite the recognition that the principle of international responsibility cannot be effectively implemented without a detailed body of eco-norms, the cooperation of states in developing this important area of international environmental law has been minimal. Thus, the International Law Commission tackled this problem only along the lines of the general codification of international responsibility norms. Environmental harm was expressly mentioned only in the context of international crimes.[146] A timid attempt by UNEP to elaborate in 1976–1977 upon certain norms of ecological responsibility failed to work out any substantial recommendation.[147] A similar discussion by OECD experts resulted in an elaboration of definitions of state obligation in the environmental field.[148]

Existing treaty practice does not give ground for optimism. The majority of environmental treaties do not contain provisions regulating responsibility. In rare cases a treaty includes a very general formula, usually referring to future arrangements on responsibility procedures. The 1976 Barcelona Convention for the Protection of the Mediterranean Sea against Pollution might serve as an illustration.[149] Article 13 of the Convention bears the title "Liability and Compensation" but contains only a general obligation "to co-operate in the formulation and adoption of appropriate procedures for the determination of liability and compensation for damage resulting from the pollution of the marine environment deriving from violations of the provisions of this Convention and applicable Protocols."[150] A provision of similar generality can be found in the 1974 Helsinki Convention on the Protection of the Marine Environment of the Baltic Sea Area."[151]

145. Stockholm Declaration, *supra* note 21 at Principle 22.
146. *See* Article 19 of the ILC draft articles on state responsibility, 31 U.N. GAOR Supp. (No. 10), U.N. Doc. A/31/10 (1976).
147. *See* UNEP Governing Council Decision 66 (IV), 13 April 1976; U.N. Doc. UNEP/WG. 8/2 (1977).
148. OECD, *Observations on the Concept of the International Responsibility of States in Relation to the Protection of the Environment* (Note by the OECD Secretariat, 1977).
149. 15 *I.L.M.* 290 (1976).
150. *Id.* at Art. 13.
151. 13 *I.L.M.* 1291 (1973).

Even if the international community acknowledges the existence of a general principle of international responsibility for environmental damage, there are still many uncertainties about the exact content and limits of such a principle. In particular, the most important problems concern the scope of the application of the principle of responsibility, the forms of responsibility, the relationship of the wrongful act, and the subjects who have the standing to bring legal actions.[152]

All that has been said stresses the growing necessity for a precise and explicit formulation of the principle of international responsibility for environmental harm. Firstly, it would provide an additional stimulus for the elaboration of a relevant institution of international environmental law. Secondly, it would strengthen the prevention mechanism by determining the illegality of significant transboundary environmental harm and by providing appropriate sanctions. At a minimum, the principle should require the termination of harmful activities and compensation for their damage.[153]

The principle of sustainable development perfectly fits the ecological security regime, since both concepts have ecologically safe development as their nucleus. Moreover, both demand shifting the resources from the military security section to the ecological and development sectors. *State of the World 1990* points out that "sustainability cannot be achieved without a massive shift of resources from military endeavors to energy efficiency, tree planting, family planning, and other needed development activities."[154]

The roots of the sustainable development conception go down to the "eco-development" doctrine,[155] which calls for the harmonization of socio-economic interests with ecological imperatives. However, if "eco-development" was dictated primarily by the interests and needs of developing countries, the scope of "sustainable development" would be broader, as it seeks to meet the interests of all states. The latter concept requires states to conserve those ecosystems and ecological processes that are critical to the normal functioning of the biosphere. States must also conserve biological diversity and observe

---

152. Introductory Document for the Siena Forum, *supra* note 112 at 50.
153. An analogous interpretation of the principle of state responsibility for environmental harm was given by the WCED legal experts. *See Environmental Protection and Sustainable Development, supra* note 91 at 127–130.
154. *State of the World 1990, supra* note 11 at 189.
155. *See generally* P. Maldoon, *The International Law of Ecodevelopment: Emerging Norms for Developing Assistance Agencies* (1987).

standards of optimal sustainability while using biological resources and living ecosystems.[156]

A major premise of sustainable development is similar to that of ecological security: the prevention of environmental harm is economically more advantageous than *post factum* corrective measures.[157] While being implemented, sustainable development has turned from a mere conceptual idea into multiple programmes and organizational structures and should be reinforced with relevant legal instruments. This was acknowledged at the 1986 Ottawa International Conference on Conservation and Development, which produced a set of principles and measures for promoting sustainable development and, in particular, recommended an elaboration of national and international sustainable development codes.[158] The World Commission on Environment and Development has also commissioned much of its work for elaboration of the whole complex of legal and organizational measures for achievement of environmental protection and sustainable development.[159]

A workable theory of ecological security is not confined to state activity: it begins with the interests and participation of individuals. Indeed, human beings and/or private persons are primary subjects of ecological security. The major form of achieving ecological security is then the preservation of the human environment and not of the environment in general terms. In other words, the fundamental principle of ecological security should be the principle of the human right to a favourable environment. To benefit from that right, however, individuals must recognize the corresponding obligation to observe the requirements of the ecological imperative.

It is well known that the principle in question was not included in

156. The concept was first introduced by the IUCN in the World Conservation Strategy, proclaimed in 1980. The three main objectives of the Strategy as stated in its executive summary are: "(a) to maintain essential ecological processes and life support systems, (b) to preserve genetic diversity and (c) to ensure the sustainable utilization of species and ecosystems." *See World Conservation Strategy: Living Resource Conservation for Sustainable Development* (IUCN, UNEP, WWF, 1980).

157. It is calculated that the pollution damage in the developed countries equals approximately 3–5 per cent of the gross national product (GNP) and the cost of its prevention should be around 1–2 per cent of GNP. In the developing countries, it is sufficient to spend 0.5–1 per cent of the GNP for water-supply and sewage facilities to effectively prevent infectious diseases and raise health and productivity levels. *See* J. Dilloway, *Is World Order Evolving?* 88 (Pergamon, 1987).

158. Conference Recommendations, Conference on Conservation and Development, Ottawa, 31 May – 5 June 1986.

159. *Our Common Future, supra* note 18 at 308–348.

the Universal Declaration on Human Rights and related documents. However, a certain inherent linkage with the provisions of the 1966 UN Covenant on Economic, Social, and Cultural Rights can be revealed.[160] The 1972 Stockholm Declaration (Principle 1) did not explicitly provide for the "right to a favorable environment" but rather described the environmental protection problem in terms of human rights: "Man has the fundamental right to freedom, equality and adequate conditions of life, in an environment of a quality that permits a life of dignity and well-being. . . ."[161]

Such ambiguity can be traced down from the 1966 UN Covenant, which included among the guarantees of the right to physical and mental health "the improvement of all aspects of environmental and industrial hygiene."[162]

One cannot explain why current national legislation and international laws do not handle the problem of one's human right to a favourable environment. Though formulated very differently, the relevant provisions are found in a number of national constitutions and such international acts as the 1981 African Charter for Human Rights and Peoples[163] (Art. 24), the 1988 Protocol to the 1969 American Convention on Human Rights, on Economic, Social, and Cultural Rights[164] (Art. 11), or the Declaration of Fundamental Rights and Freedoms adopted by the European Parliament in April 1989.[165] Despite certain normative acknowledgements, there is not evident *opinio juris* for the right to a favourable environment, neither can it be interpreted as "a general principle of law recognized by civilized nations." In the view of WCED legal experts, it remains "an ideal which must still be realized." But to a certain extent, this definition can equally refer to ecological security itself.

Since the legal formation of the human right to a favourable environment has yet to be concluded, one may question the substantive and procedural categorization of this right.

160. *See,* e.g., P. Kromarek, Le droit à un environnement sain et équilibré. Rapport préparé pour le Colloque sur les nouveaux droits de l'homme: les "droits de solidarité," Mexico, 12–15 Aug. 1980.
161. Stockholm Declaration, *supra* note 21 at Principle 1.
162. 1966 UN Covenant, International Covenant on Economic, Social, and Cultural Rights, 16 Dec. 1966, 993 U.N.T S.3, 6 *I.L.M.* 360 (1967).
163. 1981 African Charter for Human and Peoples' Rights, 27 June 1981, 21 *I.L.M.* 59 (1982), at Art. 24.
164. 1988 Protocol to the 1969 American Convention on Human Rights on Economic, Social, and Cultural Rights, Nov. 1988 25 *I.L.M.* 161 (1989), Art. 11.
165. The Declaration of Fundamental Rights and Freedoms adopted by the European Parliament in April 1989.

The importance of inherent interrelatedness of human rights and environmental protection issues has induced Judge Pathak and Professor Cançado Trindade to dedicate to these problems special chapters in this book (respectively, chapters 8 and 9).

The approach of Cançado Trindade was to transpose the whole or at least a significant part of environmental law to humanitarian law by giving an expanded interpretation to Art. 60(5) of the 1969 Vienna Convention on the Law of Treaties. One may easily subscribe to these arguments since, from the 1972 Stockholm Conference, protection of the environment has been explicitly understood as protection of the *human* environment. Discarding the principle of reciprocity in implementation of environmental treaties has been the result of the deepening understanding that without protecting human rights and preserving a favourable environment, the governmental structures of modern states could hardly survive. The relevance of the right to a favourable environment to the context of ecological security can be further supported by Cançado Trindade's assumptions of a clear correlation between the right to life, the right to a healthy environment, and the right to peace and the right to disarmament.

The majority of scholars relate this point to the category of "solidarity," "collective," or even "peoples'" rights. Like other solidarity rights, the right to a favourable environment has both individual and collective dimensions. An individual right means the right of an individual, being the victim of environmental damage, to file a claim for termination of the harmful activity and relevant compensation. The collective aspect means the obligation of states and other social actors to regard all-human interests as superior to national or individual interests and to participate via international cooperation in resolving global environmental problems.

The substantive content and procedural connotations of the right to a favourable environment include the obligation of the state to (1) provide to individual human beings, groups, and other non-governmental entities free access to veracious and complete environmental information and (2) grant them the right to participate in environmental decision-making and relevant administrative and judicial proceedings. Regrettably, the statement that was made by W.P. Gormley in 1986 is still valid: "international (and regional) law has not yet evolved to the level where injured individuals and environmental associations have the necessary *locus standi* to defend their own legal rights or those rights of the international community."

However, there are persuasive indications that a new actor in legal

455

environmental relations, both national and international, has been born. The *ECE Regional Environmental Strategy* stresses the importance of public participation for its implementation: ". . . The public must understand how and why the decisions are made, and they must have opportunities for meaningful input into the decision-making process. The public should also be properly informed and should have available information about the state of the environment."[166] The CSCE Vienna (Third) follow-up meeting pointed out that "the participating States acknowledge the importance of the contribution of persons and organizations dedicated to the protection and improvement of the environment, and will allow them to express their concerns. They will promote greater public awareness and understanding of environmental issues. . . ."[167] These developments in environmental law correspond with the general trends in international law. The emergence of new subjects of international law, such as international organizations, nations, and national minorities, all include individuals as having been one of the major characteristics of the modern international legal order.

The emerging principle of the human right to a favourable environment must be considered as a poly-system entity. It transpierces environmental law, ecological security, and humanitarian law. This principle can and shall be the key element in the ecological security system, as an inalienable part of basic human rights and freedoms, included in the future Declaration of Peoples' Rights.

166. Economic Commission for Europe, *Regional Strategy for Environmental Protection and Rational Use of Natural Resources,* (United Nations, 1988), para. 126 at 48.
167. Conference on Security and Co-operation in Europe: Concluding Document from the Vienna Meeting, 28 *I.L.M.* 527, 540 (1989).

Appendices

Appendices

A

Global learning: Concept and applications

Edward Ploman

I. Introduction: Antecedents

Global learning represents one response to what appears as a crucial feature of the situation that faces humanity today and that can be summed up as global change. Admittedly, global change is applied specifically to the changing global environment, but it also refers to interlinked changes in the world's situation, for example: unprecedented new demographic configurations, reversals of geo-political and strategic patterns, continuing disorder of the international economy, changes in the nature of technology, and in religious and socio-cultural attitudes. Change is sweeping through all areas of human life. As never before, all regions are being affected simultaneously, and human activities have had long-range and potentially irreversible effects from these sweeping changes.

The expression "global learning" may be of recent origin, but in substance the concept draws upon both proven and emerging ideas and practices, in diverse disciplines and cultures. There are precursors to global learning, discernible strands of influence in this evolving web of ideas and practices. One such strand reflects reactions to current crises of education everywhere. Thus, it is increasingly recognized that conventional systems of education can no longer absorb or disseminate the range of knowledge generated, in the usual educational time span. Nor can conventional systems respond to the demands for equitable, timely, and widespread access to knowledge and information or to the learning needs caused by the rapid outdating of knowledge. New modes for learning and knowledge-sharing, using all available services and techniques, are therefore required at all levels of society.

Another strand of influence draws upon the recognition of learning as a more basic, more inclusive – and to some, more exciting – intellectual discipline than education or training; it even has its own learned name: the science of mathematics. This perspective has provided a new focus on social, political, and cultural implications of learning, as well as on the socio-cultural embodiment of learning.

Certain aspects of these emerging attitudes were granted official expression in the well-known Unesco report on the future of education that was given the revealing title "Learning to Be."[1] It is significant that this report *inter alia* endorsed the idea of education/ learning as a lifelong, permanent process.

In a later development, a report to the Club of Rome entitled "No Limits to Learning" focused on innovative and integrated learning techniques.[2] Set against the background of the "world problematic as a human challenge," this approach to learning is based on two key concepts. *Participatory* learning creates solidarity in space. The aim is to foster participation in the learning and information-sharing processes from people of all ages and at all social levels. *Anticipatory* learning is seen as promoting solidarity in time by anticipating and having the capacity to face new, often unprecedented situations and to create new alternatives where few or none existed. The report also mentions the concept of "societal learning" and warns that the link to individual learning is not well established.

The importance of these new approaches can best be seen against the backdrop of traditional concepts. Traditionally, at least in the West, learning was conceived in narrow, anthropocentric terms as being a characteristic capacity of (1) the human species in contrast to animals and other "lower" life forms; and (2) human individuals. New scientific and cultural approaches have gone beyond these facile and self-serving assumptions. Not only has learning proved to be an inherent characteristic of animal behaviour, but it also provides such

1. International Commission on the Development of Education, *Learning to Be: The World of Education Today and Tomorrow* (Unesco, 1972).
2. J. W. Botkin, *No Limits to Learning* (Pergamon Press, 1979).

concepts as information transfer and learning that are, in advanced scientific theory, applied generally to open systems, ranging from cells to computers. From this perspective, learning emerges in what appears to be a striking feature of evolutionary history. The operation of phylogenesis created improvements in organic adaptability to the point where learning organisms could be generated. Biological organisms function as learning systems and biological evolution serves as a stochastic learning process. In the human species, the learning process has reached another level at which learning largely becomes socialized; therefore, it is no longer a purely stochastic process, but it is also a conscious and goal-oriented process. In this socialized process, learning takes place both at the individual's level and at the level of groups and other social entities. Thus, social learning subsumes both individual socialized learning and social system learning. Social learning is obviously directed towards self-maintenance of the individual and the group. Both foci frequently encounter situations in which predetermined forms of adaptation are inadequate and they then display a unique component of social learning, behaviourally directed at changing behaviour.

Given this perspective, anthropology has always been concerned with a wide approach to learning: since all culture is learned, it must therefore have a learning dimension and can be conceived of as a learning process. The link to cultural and socio-economic development becomes clearer as the goal of development changes attitudes and behaviour. Consequently, development can be fruitfully approached as a learning process. There has, in development thinking, been a change of focus towards a recognition that learning is a fundamental process whereby individuals, as well as groups, institutions, and societies, do – or do not do, whichever the case may be. The Indonesian development thinker Soedjatmoko has analysed the entire development process as primarily a learning process.[3]

This approach to social learning is not an isolated or unique phenomenon. Recent developments in other fields are moving towards similar approaches; even though the terminology and emphasis vary, the approach is essentially the same. Examples include paradigms and approaches in science, history,[4] philosophy (process philosophy and evolutionary epistemology), general systems theory,[5] decision

3. Soedjatmoko, 1985 (citation incomplete). *See* generally Soedjatmoko, *infra* note 12.
4. Kuhn (citation incomplete).
5. Van Bertalanffy, Boulding, et al. (citation incomplete).

and organization theory, sociology, management studies, and cognitive sciences.[6]

The global learning perspective is also related to recent emerging scientific paradigms that in different disciplines concern themselves with the nature and behaviour of complex systems, whether natural, social, or even man-made "artefacts" (e.g. chaos studies). A recurring theme in these new approaches emphasizes the emergence of self-organization, auto-poesies, and autonomy as characteristics of complex systems. All of them are processes that include learning system behaviour and self-generation of meaning.

This approach to learning is holistic and global in that it emphasizes the need for an all-inclusive process. This approach is one dimension of the multidimensional concept known as "global." In addition to the linkage of global to the learning process, global also refers to the world, to the total natural and social environment. Global thus goes beyond traditional concepts such as international, which, strictly speaking, denotes no more than relations between nations, and is generally confined to nation-states. Global as used here comes closer to a worldwide or planetary focus.

As implied in the expression itself, the focus of global learning is on global issues and how they affect all societies and all levels within society. The state of the world is such that lists of global issues are legion and also contradictory in their explanations and solutions – if and when any are proposed. The UNU Charter serves as a good starting point: it speaks of "pressing global problems of human survival, development, and welfare."[7]

The urgency of global learning is caused not only by the obvious dangers to these three basic goals but also by the emerging sense that the world today is facing not only difficult rearrangements of political, economic, and ecological priorities, but also a full-scale civilization change. The challenge to learning is thus the challenge of learning how to cope with a rapidly changing set of circumstances that touches every facet of society.

Pressing global problems also demonstrate the need for global learning. As the search for a common ground and a common under-

---

6. Varela (citation incomplete).
7. Revised draft charter of the United Nations University, reprinted in *United Nations University: Report of the Secretary General*, U.N. GAOR, 28th Sess., Agenda Item 52 at 2, U.N. Doc. A/9149/Add.2 (1973).

standing in a situation of increasing interdependence becomes crucial, the increasing complexity and dangerous paradox of simultaneous cognitive homogenization and fragmentation intensifies. In all countries, the tendency is to tackle each problem in isolation. Analysis of the issues tends to be one-dimensional in spite of the fact that, global issues, by their very nature, are multidimensional and interwoven. The development of the required global-learning strategies therefore faces another and more complicated challenge: that of adopting both a horizontal and vertical approach. The horizontal approach means integrating knowledge across disciplines, ideologies, and cultures, and uniting scientific, professional, and exponential knowledge. The vertical approach requires cutting through and integrating problems at various levels, for example, at the local, national, regional, international, and planetary levels. How, for instance, should we, given this perspective, make local, indigenous views and values compatible with global outlooks and universal values? The well-known admonition, think globally, act locally, is not enough. Thinking, as well as acting, will have to encompass all relevant levels.

II. Approaches to global learning

1. Assumptions about global learning

The introduction has already pointed to a number of assumptions about global learning. In this section, selected assumptions that can contribute to clarifying the characteristics of global learning will be discussed.

A.

In relation to traditional concepts such as education and training, learning is both wider and deeper than ever before, while still providing access to both sets of experience, in addition to many others.

Global learning goes beyond traditional conceived limits. It extends over time, to outer space, and outside of the traditional context. Over time, global learning has not been linked to a specific period in the life of an individual, institution, or society. Learning is a continuous and permanent activity. The idea of anticipatory learning carries an important time element that is focused on the future. Nevertheless, it should be complemented by learning derived from the past, by drawing lessons from past successes and failures. The

463

wealth of a traditional knowledge – be it in medicine, environmental-ly adapted and energy-conserving architecture, or methods of conflict resolution – it is still like the wealth of genetic diversity that exists in our environment. Both form a part of our common heritage and both are necessary in the search for valid solutions to current problems and for keeping options open for future generations. In addition, global learning has to be set in the context of different time frames. Government and television are characterized by short time spans; economic cycles and libraries represent larger ones: while environ-mental and ecological time spans stretch over generations, even cen-turies and millenia.

With regard to outer space, global learning implies a world or planetary perspective beyond the merely international paradigm. The perspective from outer space is relevant in that the concept of the spaceship Earth, which combines the image of the planet Earth as "one world" with the recognition of the need for planetary manage-ment, extends beyond this planet to include all that humankind affects. Since the framework is planetary, the focus is on issues that are global in the sense that they affect all peoples, and communities, also life-forms on this planet, and, ultimately, the life-supporting capacity of this planet.

Thus, global learning implies a holistic approach to learning. The total, natural, and social environment provides both the context and content of global learning. Learning is mediated through the natural and man-made shaping of the world, by way of all socio-cultural pro-cesses and products. For example, languages, tools, cities, individual values, human relations, rites ceremonies, art, war, customs, and laws, all create images of the world and impart their positive and/or negative effects.

Seen in more structured terms, major systems that make up the so-cial environment, for example, religion, the economy, government, the military, and the mass media, serve in addition to their overt primary function also as learning systems. In the present context, the function of law as a learning system is crucial. Generally, law is not discussed in these terms; a traditional manner of approaching this issue is through analysis of the use of law to bring about social change. In fact, however,

law is used as an educator. . . . The success of law depends on the ability of law-making and the law-enforcing agencies to convince the people that the behavior legislated for is right and proper. The more such active laws are dependent upon the sense of obligation and the less they are dependent upon the need for sanctions, the more successful the laws are.[8]

B.
The intellectual and conceptual context for global learning does not depend solely on current pressing issues. The realities of the sudden global economic, demographic, and ecological interdependence represent a new crucial challenge to human development, welfare, and even survival. Global learning must therefore draw upon the most advanced and progressive thinking available.

The most striking feature of the scientific-intellectual context of global learning is the reaction against the traditional models in Western-dominated thinking and the consequent change in the intellectual climate. There is first the emergence of new scientific paradigms, even of a new scientific rationality, or, in the words of Nobel Laureate Ilya Prigogine, "the opening up of a new theoretical space."[9] The new scientific rationality that emerges in a number of disciplines goes beyond the traditional Western linear, deterministic, and, finally, reductionist model of reality. In various disciplines, recent inquiries into the nature and behaviour of complex systems and processes, natural and social, refuse deterministic, static reductionism, and incorporate into scientific models of reality concepts such as randomness, openness, and non-linear and stochastic processes, thus giving surprise, risk, discovery, and creativity new significance and meaning. This evolving new scientific rationality represents in itself a challenge to global learning. In addition, in the cognitive sciences there are emerging new theories about knowledge and learning in self-organizing, auto-poietic systems and theories that go beyond the Western tradition of "understanding as a mirror image of nature" in favour of creative cognition, a concept of cognition as an effective action toward global learning.[10] This approach does not only reaffirm emphasis on the context but also provides guidelines for the develop-

---

8. Freeman, 1974:45 (citation incomplete).
9. (Citation incomplete); *see* generally, Ilya Prigogine, "Irreversibility and Space-Time Structure," in *Physics and the Ultimate Significance of Time* (David Ray Griffin, ed., 1986); Ilya Prigogine and Isabelle Stengers, *Order Out of Chaos* (New Science Library, 1984); Ilya Prigogine, *From Being to Becoming* (W.H. Freeman & Co., 1980); Gregoire Nicolis and Ilya Prigogine, *Exploring Complexity* (W.H. Freeman & Co., 1989).
10. *See* Varela 1988, 1989 (citation incomplete).

ment of conceptual tools required to advance the self-understanding of organizations as complex learning systems.

Whatever else, global learning would imply sensitivity to the different ways in which societies have organized and managed learning, stretching from the intensely personal guru-disciple relationship to the extensively impersonal flow of the mass media.

C.

As any other knowledge activity, global learning is embedded in the complex, rapidly changing, and barely understood context that has been described as the advent of an information-oriented society, of a new dominant economic focus known as the service economy or the technocratic, computerized knowledge society. Whatever expressions are used, they point to a change in the nature of dominant technologies. The new electronically-based technologies differ from traditional industrial technology primarily in that they no longer construct brutal configurations of matter and physical energy but directly draw upon scientific findings. They represent technologies of organization and information. These technologies, including telecommunications, computers, informatics, and audio-visual systems, have rapidly pervaded modern society as a basic infrastructure in manufacturing and services, in public and private administration, in scientific work, and in entertainment. The forms and modes for the generation, processing, presentation, and distribution of information are multiplying, changing, and converging. They affect patterns of perceiving and coding information. Through the new communications and informations systems we are changing both our way of learning and our knowledge of the world.

Thus, global learning has to be set in this new context, not only theoretically, but also practically. It has to be capable of reaching audiences that are, at the same time, increasingly fragmented and increasingly homogeneous. All media and methods must be within reach of global learning. There must also be an appreciation of their strengths, their weaknesses, and their positive and negative effects as they are deployed.

2. Values of global learning

Assumptions about global learning lead directly to questions of values in a double sense: first, the values and ethical judgements that seem implied in or linked to the concept of global learning, and second, the related question of whether global learning is itself a normative concept.

A global approach, as formulated in the UNU Charter,[11] in terms of human survival, development, and welfare, obviously expresses a set of positive values. Thus, what we should be concerned with is a search for an "ethics of human survival," for ethical systems "that are relevant to the crowded, confused, hungry, rapidly-changing, and interdependent world we live in."[12]

The state of the world makes it obvious that we have not yet managed to evolve into a global morality. There is an obvious requirement not to accept poverty and violence as solutions to problems. There is the ethically more difficult question of how to provide a balance between the specific and the universal, or between competing claims and exclusive universal competence (as is clearly shown by the Salman Rushdie case). Should mutual tolerance then be one of the goals as well as one of the outer limits of global learning?

There are additional moral dimensions to global problems and global learning. The time dimension is one concern. Never before have the consequences of human action – or inaction – presented such a heavy weight on future generations and societies. Thus, our responsibility is not only to present but also to future generations. Another moral concern is that of responsibility in spatial terms: decisions reached on one side of the globe very quickly affect, for good or for evil, populations on the other side. Thus, these extended dimensions in space and time carry their own moral imperatives.

The concept of global learning also carries with it ethical imperatives. From an evolutionary perspective, it seems to be an accepted idea that survival and other basic drives towards self-organization are better served by adaptability than by adaptation; that is, by a highly developed learning capacity. The biologically acquired learning faculty, which has developed into the process called social learning, concerns itself not only with maintenance, but also with growth and development.

It can be hypothesized that, in the long run, it is not enough for social systems to amplify man's behavioral capacity. They must take as their proper role the amplification of the individual himself. The higher order goal that is consistent with, and fundamental to, the evolutionary process is the creation

11. *Supra* note 7.
12. (Citation incomplete); *see* generally Soedjatmoko, "Global Issues and Human Choices," 19 *World Futures*, 191 (1984).

of meaning, which provides the framework for the development of human potential.[13]

It must, however, not be overlooked that learning can be "negative" as well as "positive." There are many kinds of negative learning – whether by individuals, groups, institutions, or societies. Examples of past and present negative learning abound. The need for unlearning old behaviour patterns is obvious if we are to ensure both survival and welfare, not only for some members of the human race but for all, and not only for humans, but also for other life-forms with which we share this planet.

3. Global learning: Purposes, intentions, goals

Some of the values linked to global learning do in fact also act as intentions, purposes of global learning. In its most succinct form, the goal of global learning is to facilitate learning about global processes and global issues, learning to understand them, and how to act accordingly. In this perspective, global learning appears as both an individual and societal response to current global issues.

This, though, remains too general. To achieve its overriding goal, global learning would imply enhancement of the capacity for innovation, improvisation, and creativity; preparation to deal with change, risk, complexity, and interdependence, including economic, demographic, and ecological interdependence. This would in most cases imply an upsetting and difficult process of relearning, and even unlearning, reductionist but apparently secure simplicity as a way of avoiding reality's complexity. An example is the need for the rich North to un-learn its refusal to do anything decisive about poverty, hunger, and deprivation in the South within the framework of what the OECD calls the "two-track world economy" and begin to accept and address global interdependence.[14]

Good intentions, although elevated, are obviously not enough. Global learning can also be approached by analysing the failure of global learning, in particular the failure of learning how to manage global issues. From this perspective, global learning will have to be set against not only expectations, but also declared intentions and attendant action, or lack thereof.

It is a basic fact that, all stated intentions to the contrary, we have not learned, either because we have not been able to or have not

13. Citation incomplete.
14. Dunn, 1971, p. 185 (citation incomplete).

wanted to learn how to deal with international poverty. This fact is most intolerably demonstrated in the African crisis. Nor have we learned how to humanely manage a world economy except by the rich cynically accepting a two-track economy, within and between countries. We have not learned how to base economic growth on the safeguard of environmental and social continuity.

And in what capacity have we learned to cope with the situation facing us at the end of this century, with another two billion people crowded into a shrinking global village already beset by social erosion, violence, hunger, poverty, environmental deterioration, ungovernable mega-cities, and threats to our survival not only from earth but also from space?[15]

These failures point to global learning needs. Admittedly, there is a need to learn how to cope with specific issues in their specific contexts. Moreover, there is a need, at a more general level, to learn how to understand and manage complex, interlocking systems and processes that are open to change and thus marked by instability, risk, and unpredictability – and freedom. We need to learn how to manage situations in which facts are often uncertain, opinions divided, values in dispute, decisions urgent, and where action – or inaction – might result in long-term or even irreversible effects.

Approaches to knowledge and learning now vary not only between disciplines and in time but also by and within cultures. There is a growing recognition of the interaction between the questions produced by a culture and the range of solutions that can be offered in that culture. This new openness, the still modest but promising renunciation of claims for a particular rationality, provide an opening; specifically, the recognition that learning how to cope with global issues cannot be sought in any single language, rationality, or culture. A single-culture approach will not be adequate for solving global issues, just as a single-issue or single-discipline approach would be insufficient. We need to learn how to accept and use multiple perceptions and polyvalent perspectives. Different rationalities and cultures are valuable resources in the search for solutions or for methods of coping with global issues. There is thus a need to go beyond the traditional Western "either-or" to encompass the kind of "both-and" that is so strongly expressed in the yin-yang symbolism.

This approach is also valid for the future development of international law. Since international environmental law, as a tool to cope with global change, will require not only adherence but also under-

---

15. Citation incomplete.

standing and implementation in all countries and cultures, there is a need to broaden the philosophical and conceptual bases of international law. Major legal systems of the world should be seen as resources for this development since none of the existing systems by themselves will be capable of achieving the required results. For example, there is a need to find a means of overcoming the profound differences between legal systems focused on the adversary trial system and those that have developed otherwise sophisticated methods for resolving conflicts, which include many traditional legal systems such as the "Confucian-based" legal systems common in China, Korea, and Japan.[16] It has equally been noted that both common law and civil law express an exploitative and reductionist attitude toward nature and the environment. In contrast, other systems such as African customary law generally draw upon the opposite approach.

III. Global learning: Facilitation and obstacles

Essential for global learning is the impact in different situations and different cultures of factors such as permission to learn, encouragement to learn, direction and mode of learning, preventing or forbidding certain learning, and learning outcomes. Relevant questions include: who is learning what, under what conditions, towards what objectives, and at what and whose expense?

We have already mentioned some of the current learning needs, with explicit and implicit reference to the societal requirement to facilitate such learning in support of *inter alia* environmental policies and practices designed to introduce adoptive and preventive measures in response to global change. This perspective opens a series of difficult and controversial questions.

It would go beyond the scope of these reflections even to attempt a comprehensive analysis. The selection has therefore focused on certain issues that have a clear legal dimension, nationally and internationally, and that require consideration from a different perspective than has been used in the past.

1. New media

Given this perspective, a set of socio-cultural activities becomes crucial: those that concern themselves with the means, methods, and

16. Soedjatmoko, 1984 (citation incomplete); *see* generally Soedjatmoko, *supra* note 12.

modes of handling, generating, processing, storing, transferring, accessing, and disseminating information. While there exists a certain societal competence in dealing with traditional media such as the written and printed word, and traditional performance of dramatic or musical works, confusion abounds about how to deal with new media such as television, video, high-speed data systems, and new technologies such as microwave, cable, satellites, and computers – which tend toward technical convergence of different forms of expression and transmission. Proof of the current confusion is the constant change of national legislation everywhere, which often appears to be a desperate attempt to catch up with technical novelties and cultural changes. The result, at both the national and international levels, is legislation that risks being "incompetent, inconsistent, incompatible, and inefficient."[17] The competition between political, economic, and cultural considerations largely remains unsolved. An example, in light of the recognized need for changing practices that satisfy environmental requirements, is that the required learning or relearning at all levels of society makes it necessary to use all available means for getting the information, training, and learning required. A basic question is: can society afford not to use a medium like television for this purpose? There are splendid but isolated examples of the use of television for global learning, ranging from documentaries on global issues to Live Band Aid as a showing of global solidarity. With the trend of reducing television to no more than a commodity-producing industry, there are urgent questions about the emphasis in much of the television programming, and on the behaviour patterns that go directly against the need for new conduct, particularly with respect to such global issues as environmental protection, energy conservation, and developmental needs. The question, therefore, is whether society can avoid grappling with the problem of priorities between claims for the "free flow" of entertainment and advertising, and environmental requirements.

2. The "public" and the "private"

In recent years, confusing changes have occurred in the conception and practice of what properly belongs to the public sphere and what belongs to the private sphere, thus changing the relationships between the public and the private domains. Activities that traditionally

---

17. Chief Justice Michael Kirby (citation incomplete).

were assigned to the private sphere have become issues in the public domain. Striking examples include reproductive behaviour and associated family and personal relationships. These have traditionally been anchored in the private sphere. A series of profound and simultaneous socio-economic and cultural changes have catapulted the processes of biological reproduction into the public sphere. A similar development has taken place with respect to economic and social behaviour, thereby having major environmental effects. The need for increasing environmental legislation is proof that certain activities, previously managed in the private sphere through decision by individuals and enterprises, can no longer be left to private initiative except under public scrutiny and accountability.

There has also been a movement in the opposite direction for which the expression "privatization" is often used as a shorthand to indicate a range of phenomena, including denationalization, deregulation, commercialization, and commodification. The current trend of privatization based on ideology or economic pragmatism has, in theory and practice, also hit areas of immediate concern to global-learning ventures. A basic issue would be: what are the effects either facilitating or hindering the movement of technology and information? How do they access both the public sphere and the private sphere?

It is clear that global learning requires wide and open means and access to information and knowledge. While there has always existed an unresolved tension between the "free flow of information" and intellectual-property rights, the situation has changed radically under the influence of both new technologies and wide claims for different kinds of proprietary rights. Thus, difficult issues have arisen in the scientific field that have succinctly been described in the title of a recent book, *Science as a Commodity: Threats to the Open Community of Scholars*.[18] Thus, in the context of global learning, there is a need to consider questions such as: will an increase in the private funding of research lead to a decrease in the volume and type of knowledge that reaches scientists, policy makers, and the public? If indeed whole sectors of education and training are to be removed from the public domain into private operation, how will intellectual exchanges and academic development take place?[19] Another similar trend that has not been given sufficient attention is the increasing commercialization

18. (Michael Gibbons, Bjorn Wittrock, eds., Longman, 1985).
19. Sargent, 1989 (citation incomplete).

472

of publicly-produced information, paid for by public means, that was previously made available on an open and non-discriminatory basis.

These trends must be set in the context of controlling information and knowledge; it does not matter whether this control is exercised by public authorities or private enterprises. It is a tricky field because it is ideologically loaded. It has, however, taken on a new sense of urgency through the advent of new communication and information systems. Particularly through the convergence of computer and tele-communication systems, these problems have become pervasive and awkward, evolving mainly outside of the scope of public accountability.

Thus, a basic question about privatization is whether or not it will represent an obstacle to global learning. Privatization would, from one perspective, be a factor in a series of potential obstacles to global learning. These obstacles may arise from a range of situations and conditions, including the cultural area, via institutional-legal rules, and socio-economic trends, to psychological factors.

There exists abundant information on various aspects of this complex problem. Some of the problems include obstacles to innovation, the dissemination of innovation, the transfer and acceptance of information, and the simultaneous phenomena of information overload and information under-use. However, as far as is known, these findings have never been analysed in a coherent fashion from a global-learning perspective.

In addition to phenomena that appear obvious and relatively easy to understand, there are other, more subtle practices that might constitute obstacles to global learning. One such practice is the ancient phenomenon of the "professionalization" of knowledge, which nowadays has degenerated into the reign of the expert, and the descent of instant experts from the North upon developing countries.

IV. Content of global learning

To many observers, global learning seems to remain vague, somewhat unclear, when discussed in the abstract. In real life, global learning not only represents an intellectual framework or perspective, it is linked to concrete purposes and is embedded in a specific context. Thus, global learning also entails learning about something. We will now turn to the content of global learning.

First, some remarks on the specific content that are represented by different social levels and needs. Although it seems obvious, there is a constant need to repeat the fact that the same phenomenon will not have the same impact in different socio-cultural settings. It is one thing to add still another television channel in an already TV-saturated environment and quite another to introduce television in a setting where there is little, if any, access to modern media. In the UNU context, global-learning activities have been concerned at one end of the scale with participatory learning at the most urgent and most neglected level. How can scientific information, relevant to the survival and basic quality of life of unfavoured groups in developing countries, be in a timely fashion, in a manner and form that makes sense to them and, most importantly, on subjects of their choice? At the other end of the scale, studies have concerned themselves with the manner in which learning about global issues can contribute to ameliorate a situation in which higher education is often seen as inadequate for addressing "current human problems."

The basic thrust is that global learning concerns itself with global issues as they are worked out at different levels of society, in terms of both needs and opportunities. The following discussion of possible issue areas that would be the content of global-learning activities is based on the consideration of proposals for projects and action in this field.

1. Development

The perhaps most obvious and one of the most urgent global-learning concerns is development. As mentioned earlier, development has a clear learning dimension that has often been perceived as no more than the education and training of people to become fit for service as producers and consumers to conform to the image of what has happened in the industrialized world. It is in this context that the concept of "human resource development" becomes problematic: resources are means to an end, while the basic current concept is that human beings should be the subjects of development, not the objects of development.

The form of learning that lies at the heart of development is the "rather elusive process" of social learning, in the global sense used here. As to what needs to be learned, the content of this learning process, Soedjatmoko has indicated various sets of goals, each one by implication pointing to failures in development thinking and development practice. These sets of goals include:
– individual and collective enhancement of a society's ability to adjust to change and to direct change even in the face of such phe-

nomena as new demographic patterns, new technologies, new modes of production, and new stages of political consciousness;

- capacity to develop policies and attitudes that can come to grips with the common structural impediments to change;
- the need, morally and politically, to deal effectively with poverty as symptomatic of a process of economic and environmental decay, often compounded by social and political instability;
- the willingness to socialize and bring into the national mainstream hitherto marginalized groups without raising unacceptable levels of social tension. This implies learning how to motivate and release the energies of those whom Gandhi called "the last, the least, the lowest, and the lost";
- organizing for new purposes, the adjustment of traditional institutions to serve these needs;
- new lessons in the management of development activities. Government bureaucracies and institutions must learn how to adjust to the required systems of self-management and self-reliance, as well as to cope with economic interdependence. In addition, they must also learn how to develop the skill of consensus-making, in the context of pluralism, and to deal with the violence of emerging groups that perceive that their aspirations are not being accommodated;
- ability to live together in increasingly higher population densities, finding new ways to make urban communities function, concerning ourselves not only with how these mega-cities can be assured of their food, energy, and housing needs, but also with the ways in which communities of such size and density can function effectively, with civility, thereby avoiding violent conflict and retaining their creativity;
- capacity to meet the learning needs, brought on by development, through an unprecedented flow of information into the villages and urban neighborhoods. This also implies developing individuals and communities, a capacity for continuous learning, creative impulses, and critical assessment.[20]

These points have been mentioned in some detail because in many respects they are applicable to several subject-matters such as global change.

It is clear that this kind of required learning involves not only individuals at all social levels over their life-span, but also all major institutions in society, be they governmental or non-governmental, in-

---

20. Soedjatmoko (citation incomplete); *see* generally Soedjatmoko, *supra* note 12.

cluding business enterprises, labour unions, the military, professional associations, women's movements, grass-roots and environmental groups. Learning for the purposes of development implies learning by individuals, by communities, by societies, and in the final count, by the human species.

2. Environment

Concerns about the environment are not new. Yet only in recent years have ecological crises reached such pervasive, disruptive, and potentially disastrous levels that "suddenly the world itself has become a world issue."[21] Thus, today's environmental problems are closely interlinked, planetary in scale, and, literally, deadly serious.

However, more important than another list of issues is the interlinkage of environmental problems, particularly what they all amount to in the aggregate. The Brundtland Commission has aptly used the image of our earth seen from space as an entry point when it said, "From space we see a small and fragile ball, dominated not by human activity and edifices, but by a pattern of clouds, oceans, greenery, and soil. Humanity's inability to fit its doings into that pattern is fundamentally changing planetary systems. Many such changes are accompanied by life-threatening hazards. This new reality, from which there is no escape, must be recognized – and managed."[22]

A complement from the national level arrived in a recent study of resources, population, and the future of the Philippines. The study came to the conclusion that, "the grim prospect of a deepening subsistence crisis throws a long shadow over Philippine socio-economic and political development extending into the next century. . . . Without effective policies to slow population growth, broaden access to land and other natural resources, and stem environmental degradation, these problems could contribute to increased social unrest, and possibly political violence.[23]

Social unrest due to environmental degradation, resource depletion, and social injustice have already occurred in various countries. Analysts also foresee that if present trends continue unchecked, environmental problems might well become major reasons for interna-

21. Shabecoff, "Suddenly the World Itself is a World Issue," *New York Times*, 25 Dec. 1988 at A4.
22. World Commission on Environment and Development, *Our Common Future*, 1 (Oxford University, 1987).
23. G. Porter, with D. J. Ganapin, Jr., *Resources, Population, and the Philippines' Future: A Case Study* (World Resources Institute, Washington, D.C., 1988).

tional conflict, and even war. In the coming decades such problems will range from squabbles over mineral deposits and other natural resources to controversies over unilateral decisions in one country that will affect situations in other countries (transborder pollution, downstream effects of effluents, deforestation, over-fishing, and destruction of habitat).

In fact, analysts have pointed out that comparisons to the environmental changes now under way can only be found by going back millions of years in earth's history; the situation is thus totally outside of any human experience. As a result, learning how to cope with these changes is, and will continue to be, a new and difficult experience.

The reluctant and/or partial recognition of this new reality has already led to some action. Despite often bitter scientific and sociopolitical controversy in this area, the ecological crises have reached such a level that the scientific community has merged and agreed on a number of scientific projects on a global scale.

There have also been some surprisingly rapid intergovernmental agreements on specific problems such as the Vienna Ozone Treaty[24] and its Montreal Protocol,[25] as a well as a series of high-level meetings. However, in addition to the difficulties in getting even limited agreements accepted and implemented, voices are already raised in concern that what has been done is not enough and often too late. In general, the agreements are attacking symptoms rather than causes.

Even though the reality of the situation is only partly perceived and accepted even less so, it has led to a new look at the causes, trends, and phenomena that make current measures appear inadequate, insufficient, and sometimes frivolous. It would be easy to find some examples of these newly perceived issues that hint at the kind of changes that are required. However, it is more important to recognize the interlinkage between development, population, and environment. Far from being antagonistic to development, environmental protection is an irreplaceable partner to development. Environment and development are now seen as opposite sides of the same coin.

Today's challenges require that ecological principles and environmental understanding permeate economic activity. In the future, environmental protection must become a process of designing environmentally sustainable patterns of providing an environmentally non-destructive livelihood. In both

24. Vienna Convention for the Protection of the Ozone Layer, 22 Mar. 1985, 26 *I.L.M.* 1529 (1987).
25. Montreal Protocol on Substances That Deplete the Ozone Layer, 16 Sept. 1987, 26 *I.L.M.* 1550 (1987).

rich and poor countries, economic and environmental goals must be integrated in powerful new ways. . . ."[26]

In summary, what is required is a change in thinking, and changes
in the way things are done and organized. While little has so far been
said about the global learning that is required, it is obvious that the
learning dimension will be crucial if we are to achieve:
- the necessary integration of population, environment, and development policies;
- growth beyond such immature attitudes as growth for growth's
  sake or hiding behind "technological fixes";
- economic stability by rethinking our economies;
- a change in attitudes towards nature and the interrelationship between man and nature.

Take the following two examples. One, there seems to be increasing agreement that there is a need for a complete transformation of
technologies, production, and consumption, but very little debate on
what this actually might mean. If environmental factors must be integrated into the design of our energy, transportation, and other systems, it might well mean extensive changes in the provision for private and public transport. Energy might have to be provided at its
real price. The inevitable industrialization for the third world will
take place, bringing with it the polluting technology invented in and
disseminated by the industrialized North.

The other example concerns itself with international cooperation,
which will have to take place at hitherto unknown levels. Unilateral
decisions by countries on any matter that might affect the environment will probably have to be subjected to negotiations and agreements. This means that there is a need to upgrade international environmental agencies so that they can work out new international
treaties and integrate environmental concerns into trade and other
rules governing international economic relations.

And, finally, there is a moral and ethical dimension, a need to
rethink humanity's global obligations, but even more:

to act without rapacity, to use knowledge with wisdom, to respect interdependence, to operate without hubris and greed – these are not simply
moral imperatives. They are an accurate scientific description of the means
of survival. It is this compelling force of fact that may, I think, control our
separatist ambitions before we overturn our planetary life.[27]

26. Speth, 1989 (citation incomplete).
27. This was said by Barbara Ward shortly before her untimely death (citation incomplete).

478

B

Chronological index of selected international environmental legal instruments

Pre-1900

Baden (Federal Republic of Germany)-Switzerland: Berne Convention Establishing Uniform Regulations Concerning Fishing in the Rhine between Constance and Basle, 9 December 1869, 149 CTS 137.

Baden (Federal Republic of Germany)-France-Switzerland: Basle Convention Establishing Uniform Regulations Concerning Fishing in the Rhine and its Tributaries, Including Lake Constance, 25 March 1875, 149 CTS 139.

1900–1924

London Convention for the Protection of Wild Animals, Birds and Fish in Africa, 19 May 1900, 94 BFSP 715.

Convention for the Protection of Birds Useful to Agriculture, 19 March 1902, 102 BFSP 969, 191 CTS 91.

Canada-United States of America: Washington Treaty Relating to Boundary Waters and Questions Arising Along the Boundary Between the United States and Canada, 11 January 1909, 12 Bevans 319, 36 Stat. 2488, TS 548, 102 BFSP 137.

Treaty for the Preservation and Protection of Fur Seals, 7 July 1911, 37 Stat. 1542, TS 564, 104 BFSP 175.

Convention for the Preservation of the Halibut Fishery of the Northern Pacific Ocean, 2 March 1923, 32 LNTS 93.

1925–1949

Convention for the Regulation of Whaling, 24 September 1931, 155 LNTS 349, 49 Stat. 3079, TS 880.

London Convention relative to the Preservation of Fauna and Flora in Their Natural State, 8 November 1933, UKTS No. 27 (1930), 172 LNTS 241.

Washington Convention on Nature Protection and Wild Life Preservation in the Western Hemisphere, 12 October 1940, 161 UNTS 193, 3 Bevans 630, 56 Stat 1354, TS 981.

London Convention for the Regulation of the Meshes of Fishing Nets and Size Limits of Fish, 5 April 1946, 231 UNTS 199.

Washington International Convention for the North-West Atlantic Fisheries (Preamble, Art. VI[1]), 8 February 1949, 157 UNTS 157, 1 UST 477, TIAS 2089.

1950s

Paris International Convention for the Protection of Birds, 18 October 1950, 638 UNTS 185.

Paris Convention for the Establishment of the European and Mediterranean Plant Protection Organization, 18 April 1951, UKTS No. 44 (1956).

FAO International Plant Protection Convention, Rome (amended 1979), 6 December 1951, 150 UNTS 67.

International Convention for the Prevention of Pollution of the Sea by Oil, London (and 1962, 1969, 1971, (2x) Protocols), 12 May 1954, 327 UNTS 3, 12 UST 2989, TIAS 4900.

FAO Plant Protection Agreement for [South-East] Asia and the Pacific Region, Rome (amended 1967, 1979, 1983), 27 February 1956, 247 UNTS 400.

Convention on Fishing and Conservation of the Living Resources of the High Seas, 29 April 1958, 559 UNTS 285, 17 UST 138, TIAS 5969.

Antarctic Treaty, Washington (Arts V[l], IX[f]), 1 December 1959, 12 UST 794, TIAS 4780, UKTS No. 97 (1982) 402 UNTS 71.

1960s

1960–1964

Steckborn Convention on the Protection of Lake Constance against Pollution, 27 October 1960, UNLegSer No. 12, p. 438.

European Social Charter (Arts, 3[1], [3], 11), 18 October 1961, 529 UNTS 89, ETS No. 35.

Paris International Convention on the Protection of New Varieties of Plants, 2 December 1961, 815 UNTS 89.

Protocol Concerning the Constitution of an International Commission for the Protection of the Mosel Against Pollution, 20 December 1961, 940 UNTS 211.

Berne Convention on the International Commission for the Protection of the Rhine against Pollution, 29 April 1963, 994 UNTS 3.

Treaty Banning Nuclear Weapons Tests in the Atmosphere, in Outer Space and Under Water, 5 August 1963, 480 UNTS 43, 14 UST 1313, TIAS 5433.

Nordic Mutual Emergency Assistance Agreement in Connection with Radiation Accidents, 17 October 1963, 525 UNTS 75.

1965–1969

International Convention for the Conservation of Atlantic Tunas, 14 May 1966, 673 UNTS 63.

International Covenant on Economic, Social and Cultural Rights (Arts. 12[2][b], 25. *See also* Arts. 7, 11, 12[1], [2][c]), 16 December 1966, 993 UNTS 3, 6 ILM 360 (1967).

Treaty on Principles Governing the Activities or States in the Exploration and Use of Outer Space, Including the Moon and Other Celestial Bodies (Art. IX), 27 January 1967, 610 UNTS 205, 18 UST 2410, TIAS 6347.

Phyto-sanitary Convention for Africa South of the Sahara, 13 September 1968, UNEP3 No. 12.

African Convention on the Conservation of Nature and Natural Resources, 15 September 1968, 1001 UNTS 3.

Tanker Owners Voluntary Agreement Concerning Liability for Oil Pollution, "TOVALOP," 7 January 1969, 8 ILM 497 (1969).

Bonn Agreement for Co-operation in Dealing with Pollution of the North Sea by Oil, 9 June 1969, 704 UNTS 3, 9 ILM 359 (1970).

La Paz Convention for the Conservation of the Vicuña, 16 August 1969, 969 IELMT 61.

FAO Convention on the Conservation of the Living Resources of the South-East Atlantic, Rome, 23 October 1969, 801 UNTS 101.

Brussels International Convention on Civil Liability for Oil Pollution Damage, 29 November 1969, 973 UNTS 3, UKTS No. 106 (1975), 9 ILM 45 (1970).

Brussels International Convention Relating to Intervention on the High Seas in Cases of Oil Pollution Casualties, 29 November 1969, 970 UNTS 211, 26 UST 765, TIAS 8068.

1970s

1971

Oil Companies: Contract Regarding an Interim Supplement to Tanker Liability for Oil Pollution, "CRISTAL," 14 January 1971, 10 ILM 137 (1971).

Ramsar Convention on Wetlands of International Importance, Especially as Waterfowl Habitat, 2 February 1971, 11 ILM 963 (1972), UKTS No. 34 (1976), 996 UNTS 245.

Brussels International Convention on the Establishment of an International Fund for Compensation for Oil Pollution Damage (amending Protocols 1976, 1984), 18 December 1971, 1110 UNTS 57, UKTS No. 95, 11 ILM 284 (1972).

1972

Oslo Convention for the Prevention of Marine Pollution by Dumping from Ships and Aircraft (1978 Protocol), 15 February 1972, 932 UNTS 3, UKTS No. 119 (1975), 11 ILM 262 (1972).

Convention on International Liability for Damage Caused by Space Objects, 29 March 1972, 961 UNTS 187, 24 UST 2389, TIAS 7762.

Stockholm Declaration on the Human Environment of the United Nations Conference on the Human Environment, 16 June 1972, A/CONF.48/14, 1972 UNYB 319, 11 ILM 1416 (1972).

UNESCO Convention Concerning the Protection of the World Cultural and Natural Heritage, 16 November 1972, 27 UST 37, TIAS 8226, 11 ILM 1358 (1972).

UNGA Resolution: Institutional and Financial Arrangements for International Environmental Co-operation (UNEP Statute), 15 December 1972, A/RES/299(XXVII).

IMO Convention on the Prevention of Marine Pollution by Dumping of Wastes and Other Matter (London Ocean Dumping Convention – LDC) (amended 1978 (2x), 1980, 1989), 29 December 1972, 1046 UNTS 120, 26 UST 2403, TIAS 8165, 11 ILM 1294 (1972).

1973

Washington Convention on International Trade in Endangered Species of Wild Fauna and Flora (CITES), 3 March 1973, 993 UNTS 243, 27 UST 1087, TIAS 8249, UKTS No. 101 (1976), 12 ILM 1085 (1973).

London International Convention for the Prevention of Pollution from Ships (MARPOL), 2 November 1973, IMO: MP/CONF/WP.35, 12 ILM 1319 (1973).

Oslo Agreement on the Conservation of Polar Bears, 15 November 1973, 27 UST 3918, TIAS 8409, 13 ILM 13 (1973).

1974

Nordic Convention on the Protection of the Environment, 19 February 1974, 1092 UNTS 279, 13 ILM 591 (1974).

Helsinki Convention for the Protection of the Marine Environment of the Baltic Sea Area, 22 March 1974, 13 ILM 546 (1974).

OECD Council Recommendation on Principles Concerning Transfrontier Pollution (with annexed "Some Principles"), 14 November 1974, OECD C(74) 224.

OECD Council Recommendation on the Implementation of the Polluter Pays Principle, 14 November 1974, OECD C(74) 223, 14 ILM 234 (1975).

OECD Council Recommendation: Analysis of the Environmental Consequences of Significant Public and Private Projects, 14 November 1974, OECD C(74) 216, OECD p. 28.

1975

Helsinki Final Act of the Conference on Security and Co-operation in Europe (Basket Two: "Co-operation in the Fields of Economics, of Science and Technology and of the Environment," Sec. 5: "Environment"), 1 August 1975, 14 ILM 1307 (1975).

1976

Barcelona Convention for the Protection of the Mediterranean Sea against Pollution, 16 February 1976, 15 ILM 290 (1976).

Barcelona Protocol for the Prevention of Pollution of the Mediterranean Sea by Dumping from Ships and Aircraft, 16 February 1976, 15 ILM 300 (1976).

Barcelona Protocol Concerning Co-operation in Combating Pollution of the Mediterranean Sea by Oil and Other Harmful Substances in Cases of Emergency, 2 April 1976, 15 ILM 306 (1976).

Convention on the Conservation of Nature in the South Pacific, 12 June 1976, UNEP3 No. 68.

OECD Council Recommendation: A Comprehensive Waste Management Policy (with annexed Principles), 28 September 1976, OECD C(76)155 Final.

Bonn Convention for the Protection of the Rhine against Chemical Pollution, 3 December 1976, 1124 UNTS 375, 16 ILM 242 (1977).

Bonn Convention for the Protection of the Rhine against Pollution by Chlorides, 3 December 1976, 16 ILM 265 (1977).

Convention on the Prohibition of Military or Any Other Hostile Use of Environmental Modification Techniques, 10 December 1976, 1108 UNTS 151, 31 UST 333, TIAS 9614, 16 ILM 88 (1977).

1977

London Convention on Civil Liability for Oil Pollution Damage from Offshore Operations [Resulting from Exploration for and Exploitation of Sea Bed Mineral Resources], 1 May 1977, 16 ILM 1450 (1977).

OECD Council Recommendation: Implementation of a Regime of Equal Right of Access and Non-Discrimination in Relation to Transfrontier Pollution (with annexed Principles), 17 May 1977, OECD C(77)28 Final, 16 ILM 977 (1977).

Additional Protocol I to the 1949 Geneva Conventions Relating to the Protection of Victims of International Armed Conflict (Arts. 35[3], 53, 55, 56), 8 June 1977, 16 ILM 1391 (1977)

Additional Protocol II to the 1949 Geneva Conventions Relating to the Protection of Victims of International Armed Conflict (Arts. 14–16), 8 June 1977, 16 ILM 1442 (1977).

ILO Convention Concerning the Protection of Workers Against Occupational Hazards in the Working Environment Due to Air Pollution, Noise and Vibration, Geneva, 20 June 1977, UNEP3 No. 73.

1978

UNEP Government Council Decision: Principles of Conduct in the Field of Environment for Guidance of States in Conservation and

Harmonious Utility of Natural Resources Shared by Two or More States, 19 May 1978, A/RES/(XXVIII), 17 ILM 1091 (1978).

Brasilia Treaty for Amazonian Co-operation, 3 July 1978, UNEP Reg. p.164, 17 ILM 1045 (1978).

OECD Council Recommendation on Strengthening International Co-operation on Environmental Protection in Transfrontier Regions (with annexed guidelines), 21 September 1978, OECD C(78)77 Final.

Canada–United States of America: Great Lakes Water Quality Agreement (amending Protocol 1987), 22 November 1978, 30 UST 1383, TIAS 9257.

1979

Bonn Convention on the Conservation of Migratory Species of Wild Animals, 1979, 19 ILM 15 (1980).

Council of Europe Convention on the Conservation of European Wildlife and Natural Habitats, 19 September 1979, ETS No. 104, UKTS No. 56 (1982).

ECE Convention on Long-Range Transboundary Air Pollution, 13 November 1979, TIAS 10541, 18 ILM 1442 (1979).

1980s

1980

IUCN World Conservation Strategy, Living Resources Conservation for Sustainable Development (in cooperation with UNEP, WWF, FAO, and Unesco), 1980, UNEP/GC/DEC/8/11.

Multilateral Development Institutions: Declaration of Environmental Policies and Procedures Relating to Economic Development, adopted by ADB, Arab Bank for Economic Development in Africa, AFDB, World Bank, EEC (Commission), OAS, UNDP, and UNEP, 1 February 1980, 19 ILM 524 (1980).

IAEA Convention on the Physical Protection of Nuclear Material, 3 March 1980, UNTS Reg. No. 24631, IAEA INFCIRC/274.

UNEP Governing Council Decision: Provisions for Co-operation between States in Weather Modification Activities, 29 April 1980, UNEP GC/DEC/8/7/A.

Athens Protocol for the Protection of the Mediterranean Sea against Pollution from Land-Based Sources, 17 May 1980, Doc. No. 79, UNTS Reg. No. 22281, 19 ILM 869 (1980).

Convention on the Conservation of Antarctic Marine Living Re-

sources (CCAMLR), 20 May 1980, 33 UST 3476, TIAS 10240, UKTS No. 48 (1982), 19 ILM 841 (1980).
UNGA Resolution: On the Historical Responsibility of States for the Protection of Nature for the Benefit of Present and Future Generations, 30 October 1980, A/RES/35/8.

1981

FAO: World Soil Charter, 1981, 21 FAO Conf. Res. 8/81.
Abidjan Protocol Concerning Co-operation in Combating Pollution in Cases of Emergency, 23 March 1981, 20 ILM 756 (1981).
Abidjan Convention for Co-operation in the Protection and Development of the Marine and Coastal Environment of the West and Central African Region, 23 March 1981, 20 ILM 746 (1981).
African Charter on Human and Peoples' Rights (Art. 24), 27 June 1981, 21 ILM 59 (1982).
Lima Convention for the Protection of the Marine Environment and Coastal Area of the South-East Pacific, 12 November 1981, UNEP/CPPS/IG/32/4.
Lima Agreement on Regional Co-operation in Combating Pollution of the South-East Pacific by Oil and Other Harmful Substances in Cases of Emergency, 12 November 1981, UNEP Reg. p. 197.

1982

Jeddah Regional Convention for the Conservation of the Red Sea and Gulf of Aden Environment, 14 February 1982, UNEP Reg. p. 201.
Jeddah Protocol Concerning Regional Co-operation in Combating Pollution by Oil and Other Harmful Substances in Cases of Emergency, 14 February 1982, UNEP Sales No: GE.83-IX-02934.
Geneva Protocol Concerning Mediterranean Specially Protected Areas, 3 April 1982, UNTS Reg. No. 24079.
Benelux Convention on Nature Conservation and Landscape Protection, 8 June 1982, UNEP Reg. p. 207.
ILA Montreal Rules of International Law Applicable to Transfrontier Pollution, 4 September 1982, 60 ILA 158 (1983).
World Charter for Nature, 28 October 1982, A/RES/37/7, 22 ILM 455 (1983).
UN Convention on the Law of the Sea, Montego Bay (Arts. 43, 64–67, 116–120, 145, 192–237, Annex I), 10 December 1982, A/CONF.62/122, 21 ILM 1261 (1982).

1983

Cartagena Convention for the Protection and Development of the Marine Environment of the Wider Caribbean Region, 24 March 1983, 22 ILM 221 (1983).

Quito Protocol for the Protection of the South-East Pacific Against Pollution from Land-Based Sources, 23 July 1983 UNEP Reg. p. 199.

FAO International Undertaking on Plant Genetic Resources, 23 November 1983, 22 FAO Conf. Res. 8/83.

1984

Geneva Protocol on Long-Term Financing of Co-operative Programme for Monitoring and Evaluation of the Long-Range Transmission of Air Pollutants in Europe (EMEP), 28 September 1984, EB.AIR/AC.1/4.

1985

Vienna Convention for the Protection of the Ozone Layer, 22 March 1985, 26 ILM 1516 (1987).

Nairobi Convention for Eastern African Region, 1985, Nairobi Protocol Concerning Protected Areas and Wild Fauna and Flora in the Eastern African Region, 21 June 1985, UNEP Reg. p. 228.

Helsinki Protocol on the Reduction of Sulphur Emissions or Their Transboundary Fluxes by at Least 30 Per Cent, 8 July 1985, 27 ILM 707 (1988).

ASEAN Agreement on the Conservation of Nature and Natural Resources, 9 July 1985, 15 EPL 64 (1985).

1986

EEC Single European Act (Art. 18 – adding Art. 100a to the EEC Treaty, Art. 25 – adding Title VII [Arts. 130 R-T]: Environment, to the EEC Treaty), 17 February 1986, OJEC 1987 L 169/1, 25 ILM 506 (1986).

IAEA Convention on Early Notification of a Nuclear Accident, 26 September 1986, IAEA INFCIRC/335, 25 ILM 1370 (1986).

IAEA Convention on Assistance in the Case of a Nuclear Accident or Radiological Emergency, 26 September 1986, IAEA INFCIRC/ 336, 25 ILM 1377 (1986).

EEC Commission Regulation: Protection of Forests against Atmospheric Pollution, 17 November 1986, OJEC 1986 L 326/2, Reg. No. 3528/86.

Protocol for the Prevention of Pollution of the South Pacific Region by Dumping, 25 November 1986, UNEP Reg. p. 243.

Convention for the Protection of the Natural Resources and Environment of the South Pacific Region, 25 November 1986, UNEP Reg. p. 241.

Protocol Concerning Co-operation in Combating Pollution Emergencies in the South Pacific Region. 25 November 1986, UNEP Reg. p. 245.

1987

Agreement on the Action Plan for the Environmentally Sound Management of the Common Zambezi River System, 28 May 1987, 27 ILM 1109 (1988).

UNEP Governing Council Decision: Goals and Principles of Environmental Impact Assessment 17 June 1987, 17 EPL 36 (1987), UNEP GC/DEC/14/25.

Montreal Protocol on Substances That Deplete the Ozone Layer, 16 September 1987, 26 ILM 1550 (1987).

Amending Protocol to the Great Lakes Water Quality Agreement (1978), 18 November 1987, TIAS 10798.

1988

Convention on the Regulation of Antarctic Mineral Resources Activities (Preamble, Arts. 1[4], [15], 2[1][a], 4[2–4], 8, 10, 13[2], [6], 15, 21[1], [9][c]), 2 June 1988, 21 ILM 859 (1988).

Sofia Protocol Concerning the Control of Emissions of Nitrogen Oxides or Their Transboundary Fluxes, 31 October 1988, 28 ILM 212 (1989).

UNGA Resolution: Protection of Global Climate for Present and Future Generations of Mankind, 6 December 1988, A/RES/43/53, 28 ILM 1326 (1989).

1989

UNEP London Guidelines on the Exchange of Information on Chemicals in International Trade, 17 February 1989, UNEP/PIC/WG.2/2 p. 9.

Hague Declaration, 11 March 1989, A/44/340, 28 ILM 1308 (1989).

Basel Convention on the Control of Transboundary Movements of Hazardous Wastes and Their Disposal, 22 March 1989, UNEP/WG.190/4, 28 ILM 657 (1989).

Brasilia Declaration on the Environment, by the Sixth Ministerial Meeting on the Environment in Latin America and the Caribbean, 31 March 1989, A/44/683, Annex, 28 ILM 1311 (1989).

OECD Council Recommendation on the Application of the Polluter-Pays Principle to Accidental Pollution, 7 July 1989, OECD: Doc. C(89)88, 28 ILM 1320 (1989).

1990s

1990

Convention on the Marine Environment of the Wider Caribbean Region, 1983, Protocol Concerning Specially Protected Areas and Wildlife, 16 January 1990.

Decisions of the Second Meeting of Parties to the Montreal Protocol (MP) (Nos. II/1-20 and Annexes I [Adjustments to MP], II [Amendments to MP], III [Non-Compliance Procedure]), 29 June 1990, UNEP/OzL.Pro.2/3.

IAEA General Conference Resolution on Code of Practice in the International Transboundary Movement of Radioactive Waste, 21 September 1990, 30 ILM 556 (1991).

Accord of Cooperation for the Protection of the Coasts and Waters of the Northeast Atlantic Against Pollution Due to Hydrocarbons or Other Harmful Substances, 17 October 1990, 30 ILM 1227 (1991).

International Convention on Oil Pollution Preparedness, Response and Co-operation, 30 November 1990, 30 ILM 733 (1990).

1991

Bamako Convention on the Ban of the Import into Africa and the Control of Transboundary Movement and Management of Hazardous Wastes Within Africa, 29 January 1991, 30 ILM 773 (1991), with annexes I–V, 31 ILM 163 (1992).

United Nations Convention on Environmental Impact Assessment in a Transboundary Context, 25 February 1991, 30 ILM 800 (1991).

Canada–United States Agreement on Air Quality, 13 March 1991, 30 ILM 676 (1991).

Arctic Environmental Protection Strategy, 14 June 1991, 30 ILM 1624 (1991).

Protocol on Environmental Protection to the Antarctic Treaty (with Schedule on Arbitration and four Annexes – Environmental Im-

pact Assessment, Conservation of Antarctic Fauna and Flora,
Waste Disposal and Waste Management, and Prevention of Marine
Pollution), 21 June 1991.

Protocol to the 1979 Convention on Long-Range Transboundary Air
Pollution Concerning the Control of Emissions of Volatile Organic
Compounds or Their Transboundary Fluxes, 18 November 1991.

C
Contributors

EDITH BROWN WEISS, Professor of International and Environmental Law at Georgetown University Law Center and former Associate General Counsel for International Law, U.S. Environmental Protection Agency. Member of Board of Editors of the *American Journal of International Law* and Chair of the Social Science Research Council's Committee on Research in Global Environmental Change. Elected to the American Law Institute and the Council on Foreign Relations. Recipient in April 1990 of the Certificate of Merit Award of the American Society of International Law for her book *In Fairness to Future Generations* (Transnational/United Nations University, 1989).

ANTÔNIO AUGUSTO CANÇADO TRINDADE, Ph.D. (Cambridge), Professor of International Law at the University of Brasilia and the Rio Branco Diplomatic Institute, Judge *Ad Hoc* of the Inter-American Court of Human Rights, former Legal Adviser to Brazil's Ministry of External Relations, and member of the Board of Directors of the Inter-American Institute of Human Rights.

TORU IWAMA, Professor of Law at Fukuoka University, Faculty of Law, Japan. Visiting Research Scholar at Australian National University, Faculty of Law, 1981, and Georgetown University Law Center, 1988–1989. B.A., International Christian University; M.A., University of Hawaii; Master in Law, Hitotsubashi University.

ALEXANDRE KISS, Director of Research at the Centre National de la Recherche Scientifique, Paris, Director of the Centre for Environmental Law of the Robert Schuman University at Strasbourg, President of the European Council for Environmental Law, and Vice-President of the International Institute of Human Rights. Consultant to many international organizations involved in legal aspects of environmental problems.

PEIDER KÖNZ, lawyer, the United Nations University Representative in Europe. Previously served as the Legal Adviser to the OECD, Resident Representative/UN Coordinator in Brazil, senior legal consultant to the IAEA, and Research Associate at Harvard Law School. Holder of *licence en droit* from Geneva and LLB/SA from George Washington University.

LAI PENG CHENG, Professor of Law and Vice-Dean at the Law Department of Fudan University. General Editor of "Contemporary Law Studies," as well as author of numerous books and articles in the field of international law, environmental law, and international relations. Member of the international advisory board of the "International Encyclopedia of Law," published by Kluwer.

FRANCISCO ORREGO VICUÑA, Professor of International Law at the Institute of International Studies and the Law School of the University of Chile. President of the Chilean Council on Foreign Relations. Ph.D. in international law, London School of Economics and Political Science, University of London.

RAGHUNANDAN SWARUP PATHAK, Judge on the Supreme Court of India 1978–1986, Chief Justice of India 1986–1989, Judge on the International Court of Justice at the Hague 1989–1991. Currently President of the Indian Society of International Law and member of the Executive Committee of the International Law Association. Recipient of numerous honorary degrees, former professor at the Institute of Advanced Studies in the Humanities at Edinburgh University.

PAUL C. SZASZ, Legal Officer since 1958 of, successively, the International Atomic Agency, the World Bank and the International Centre for Settlement of Investment Disputes, and the United Nations. Served as Deputy to the Legal Counsel and Director of the General

Legal Division, United Nations. Teacher at Pace, Berkeley, and New York University law schools.

Peter S. Thacher, United Nations appointment in 1971 as Programme Director of the staff preparing 1972 UN Environment Conference in Stockholm, served thereafter as Director of UNEP European Office and Deputy Executive Director of UNEP, with rank of UN Assistant Secretary-General. Since retiring in 1983, associated with the World Resources Institute and consultant/adviser to a number of organizations. Senior Adviser to the Secretary-General for the 1992 UN Conference on Environment and Development.

Alexandre S. Timoshenko, leading scholar in international environmental law at the former USSR Academy of Sciences. Formerly chairman of the Sector on Ecological Law at the Academy's Institute of State and Law. Served as consultant to the United Nations Environment Programme, UN Economic Commission for Europe, Brundtland Commission, International Union for Conservation of Nature and Natural Resources, and other international bodies.